Everyday State and Democracy in Africa

Everyday State and Democracy in Africa

Ethnographic Encounters

Edited by Wale Adebanwi

Foreword by Jean and John L. Comaroff

Ohio University Press • *Athens*

Ohio University Press, Athens, Ohio 45701
ohioswallow.com
© 2022 by Ohio University Press
All rights reserved

Printed in the United States of America
Ohio University Press books are printed on acid-free paper ∞ ™

31 30 29 28 27 26 25 24 23 22 21 5 4 3 2 1

Library of Congress Cataloging-in-Publication Data
Names: Adebanwi, Wale, editor. | Comaroff, Jean, writer of foreword. | Co-
maroff, John L., 1945–writer of foreword.
Title: Everyday state and democracy in Africa : ethnographic encounters /
edited by Wale Adebanwi ; foreword by Jean Comaroff and John L. Comaroff.
Other titles: Cambridge Centre of African Studies series.
Description: Athens : Ohio University Press, 2022. | Series: Cambridge Cen-
tre of African Studies series | Includes bibliographical references and index.
Identifiers: LCCN 2021050767 (print) | LCCN 2021050768 (ebook) | ISBN
9780821424902 (paperback) | ISBN 9780821424872 (hardcover) | ISBN
9780821447796 (pdf)
Subjects: LCSH: Public administration—Social aspects—Africa. |
Bureaucracy—Social aspects—Africa. | Africa—Politics and government.
Classification: LCC JQ1875 .E94 2022 (print) | LCC JQ1875 (ebook) | DDC
320.96—dc23/eng/20211014
LC record available at https://lccn.loc.gov/2021050767
LC ebook record available at https://lccn.loc.gov/2021050768

In fond memory of J. D. Y. Peel (1941–2015):

teacher, mentor, friend.

[Williams James took the stand that] any
philosophical system which does not answer the
questions of life—of real, grimy, everyday life—can
be called to account as not fulfilling its vocation.

> —"Dr. James Lectures," *Wellesley College News,*
> 15 March 1904, in William James, *Pragmatism*
> (1975, 275)

It is important to clarify that the critique of life
is not carried out in the abstract but is rather
a meditation on the conditions that make
the struggle to live, to stay alive, to survive, in
sum, to live a human life, the most important
aesthetic—and therefore *political*—question.

> —Achille Mbembe, *Critique of Black Reason*
> (2017, 174)

And what does this prove? That everyday life
should be put to the question as a whole. *Homo
sapiens, homo faber* and *homo ludens* end up as *homo
quotidianus,* but on the way they have lost the very
quality of *homo;* can the *quotidianus* properly be
called a [wo]man? It is virtually an automaton,
and to recover the quality and the properties of a
human being it must outstrip the quotidian in the
quotidian and in quotidian terms.

> —Henri Lefebvre, *Everyday Life in the Modern
> World* (2000, 164)

In understanding what it means to be well, we must
therefore take into account not only what we need
as a bare minimum to survive but what we need for
our lives to be worthwhile.

> —Michael Jackson, "Smoke and Mirrors," in *Life
> within Limits: Well-Being in a World of Want*
> (2011, 60)

Contents

Foreword

JEAN AND JOHN L. COMAROFF

This volume, notable for both its timeliness and breadth of vision, mobilizes the distinctive, decentering perspectives of ethnography to capture the living practices, the everyday vernaculars, of the state and democracy in contemporary Africa. The essays in it exemplify the turn in African studies—perhaps, more accurately, return—to treating these phenomena, in the first instance, as ordinary activities of world-making rather than as formal institutions or enshrined sovereignties; although, to be sure, those ordinary activities animate the manifest architectures of governance, the concrete abstractions, that bear down on the human beings who create and inhabit them.

Everyday State and Democracy in Africa: Ethnographic Encounters finds uncanny resonance in what, on the face of it, is a starkly different take on the enigmas of African politics today, politics at once mundane, material, mythic: William Kentridge's haunting *Shadow Procession* (1999) and its sequel, *More Sweetly Play the Dance* (2015). These animated films depict a recurring progression of moving images, the relentless march of history across the African continent—embodied here in anonymous human forms tramping en masse across the dystopic landscape of Johannesburg, amid the detritus of abandoned mines, industrial ventures, im/possible futures (Maltz-Leca 2018, 178). Some figures stumble or limp on prosthetic limbs. Some drag their possessions or tote the master's burden. Some wear robes, bearing aloft palm fronds. Others march in coordinated defiance, striving, it seems, to interrupt the inexorable flow. A jubilant female soldier, up high on a platform, pans the horizon with an oversized gun as an associate waves a mammoth flag. A third holds aloft what looks like an iron cage in which he appears entrapped. Max Weber's modernity on the move—economy, society, state, democracy?—going who-knows-where. Then a giant megaphone strides by on legs of human scale, as if broadcasting in the "language of stateness" (Hansen and Stepputat 2001, 5).

These visual metaphors trace the predatory, performative, self-inflating logics of power, the ostensibly immaculate authority of ruling hegemonies; what Kentridge, artfully, calls "concepts on legs."[1] But they also make poignantly plain that it is ordinary walkers—and how better to capture the distinctive, self-mobilizing quality of the human?—who, in their joy, inspiration, or vengeance, breathe life into the larger visions and vehicles, the ways and means, of political society. We have no idea where the interminable stream, a regiment of load-bearing walkers, comes from or where it is headed. But it presses ever onward, flowing over barriers and around obstacles, thus to trouble the integrity and fixity of established forms (Fischer 2018). All this renders manifest a democracy in, and of, practice: it enacts, for whoever may be watching or listening, the endless mystery of what it takes to make and unmake a *conscience collective,* to produce society, to conjure into being that other fetish-on-the-hoof, the state.

William Kentridge's relentless walkers reiterate what he terms the "fugitive nature of anything you might be tempted to think of as an essence."[2] All social forms, in sum, are artifacts, structures of longer or shorter duration, constructed by people on the move, migrants of one sort or another, as they traipse across time and space. This, he insists, is a general truth that is less escapable in Africa than elsewhere; in places, that is, where normative fictions appear more sustainable, more resolutely "factual."[3] Similarly, we suggest, with ethnographically grounded social analysis. The point of the ethnographic gaze, not least when it is directed toward settled concepts like democracy and the state, is to look *behind* surface forms, elective affinities, and narrated certainties in real time, on the ground. By these means may everyday social and cultural practices be made to reveal "how realities become real, how essences become essential, how materialities materialize." And how they persist, or melt into air (Comaroff and Comaroff 1992, 20).

The turn to the everyday, the handmade, the unfinished, the transient might seem especially apposite to the experience of our precarious, deregulated times; times in which performativity, impermanence, self-making, and "responsibilization" are leitmotifs of public discourse. But it also speaks to a more enduring truth about the variable, evanescent life span of *all* social forms and conventions, past and present. And to their rootedness, however stable and structured they may appear, in the practical activity of sentient agents, existing in labile symbiosis with wider human and nonhuman worlds. While early functionalist anthropologists might have fashioned timeless, ideal-typical models of "traditional" African societies, these were self-consciously systematized renderings of colonized communities whose internal political arrangements were no less under constant construction, no less pragmatically constituted, than those of liberal-modernist, putatively democratic postcolonies; after all, over the centuries, Africa witnessed the birth, rise, fall, and demise of precolonial states, including empires and kingdoms.

Of course, Africanist political anthropology has, from the first, challenged many of the Euro-normative axioms of political science—and done so in a manner directly relevant to the perspectives and objectives of the present volume. Recall that, in his preface to *African Political Systems*, Radcliffe-Brown (1940, xiii, xxiii) famously asserted that the empirical observation of "simpler societies" could not be accommodated by the received paradigms of Western political philosophers or economists. Scholars of comparative institutions, he observed, were wont to depict the state as "an entity over and above the human individuals who make up a society," attributing to it "something called 'sovereignty,' and 'will,'" But states do not "exist in the phenomenal world" in this form. What *do* exist are a "collection of [individuals] . . . connected by a complex system of relations," who together seek to control and regulate the use of brute force.

Radcliffe-Brown, it scarcely needs saying, was proudly structural-functionalist. Yet he was quite nuanced in his denunciation of naked positivism: without "new and fruitful ideas," he wrote, "method in itself gives birth to nothing" (1940, xiii), a point well taken in the era of big data and neo-empiricism. In his insistence on deflating the phantasmic supremacy of the state as a "fiction" obscuring the actually existing substance of political life, he anticipated one of the genealogies to which this collection is heir: a rich seam of grounded theoretical writing in anthropology and beyond that has shown, in fastidious detail, how dispersed practices of governance and sovereignty generate the effects of the state as a reified, hegemonic form of "politically organized subjection" (Abrams 1988, 63; see also Sharma and Gupta 2006). Also, how rites of conviviality, consumption, even terror crank the handle that inflates images of stateness (Mbembe 1992)—much like the magic through which ritual and mimesis generate "society" as something sui generis, something metaphysical (Foucault 1991; Taussig 1997; Hansen and Stepputat 2005; Mazzarella 2017).

But the charmed life of reified abstractions like the state or democracy—and the aspirations they inspire—are never above the socio-material forces of history. However much energy is given to the work of their everyday production, they remain vulnerable to discrepancies between the vision they articulate and the realities of life-as-lived: between, on one hand, the idyll of equality, rights, inclusion, security, well-being—the elemental components, these, of consociality—and, on the other, the disruption, disempowerment, immiseration, and necropolitics that render tenuous the legitimacy of their claim to be anything other than the self-serving rhetoric of plutocratic elites (Ake 2000, 7).

The slippage between promise and realization has been all too evident since the end of the Cold War, a period, as we all know well, that has seen dramatic shifts in the global political-economic order; specifically, in the triangulation of state, democracy, and market, exacerbated by the planetary consolidation of financially founded corporate power. The implications of these transformations have been particularly acute in Africa. The impact here of liberalization, deregulation, and the outsourcing of the operations of state—ostensibly to decentralize authoritarian rule and to free economic enterprise from predatory accumulation—have opened up new modalities of "private indirect government" (Mbembe 1999), rogue accumulation, and the expropriation by capital of communal assets (Peters 2018). All of which has driven ever larger numbers of unwaged people into what Kentridge has called the recurring "procession of the dispossessed" (Maltz-Leca 2018, 176).

Again, that *Shadow Procession*. Again, *More Sweetly Play the Dance*—an allusion to Paul Celan's "Todesfuge" ("Death Fugue"), a poem from 1940s Germany—which speaks of "a way of living through violence and a way of dying by it."[4] The questions raised by the current moment, questions arising out of the rearticulation of state, democracy, and market, questions about whether the procession leads to new ways of living or hitherto unimaginable ways of dying, are these: With the state itself becoming ever more the institutional instrumentation of the market, ever more "captured" by capital, ever less bound by any sort of social contract, wherein lies the place of a politics of ordinary life? How, under these conditions, might everyday practices engage in making a democratic politics, and, even more, sustainable sociality? What sorts of *state*ments might they, do they, make about the predicament of the present, a present in which the state and liberal-modernist democracy, far from having entered a new symbiosis at fin de siècle, may be caught up in their own *danse macabre,* a *negative* dialectic? Given that *African Political Systems,* the founding text of political anthropology, began by problematizing the state and the fictions hidden by its reification—given, also, that several studies contained in that volume addressed the richness of indigenous democratic practices—what does revisiting the nature of both, of both the state and democracy, eighty years on tell us about them? And about the kinds of quotidian activity that seek to address them, animate them, live them in the here-and-now? This is the clutch of questions toward which *Everyday State and Democracy in Africa: Ethnographic Encounters* leads us. It is an intellectual procession *out* of the shadows, less a *danse macabre* than a lively scholarly tournament of ideas, ethnographically choreographed, about the present and future of political life in Africa, and in the world in which it is situated.

Notes

1. The phrase comes from a text by Kentridge accompanying an installation in his retrospective exhibition at the Zeitz Museum of Contemporary Art Africa (MOCAA), Cape Town, South Africa, January 2020.
2. William Kentridge, "SA's Most Acclaimed Artist William Kentridge on his Retrospective Exhibitions Covering 40 Years," interview by Graham Wood, *Wanted,* 9 September 2019, https://www.wantedonline.co.za/voices /interviews/2019-09-09-sas-most-acclaimed-artist-william-kentridge-on-his -retrospective-exhibitions-covering-40-years/.
3. Nicholas Wroe, "Out of South Africa: How Politics Animated the Art of William Kentridge," *Guardian,* 10 September 2016, https://www.theguardian .com/books/2016/sep/10/out-of-south-africa-how-politics-animated-the-art -of-william-kentridge.
4. Anna Heyward, "More Sweetly Play the Dance," *Paris Review,* 6 October 2015, https://www.theparisreview.org/blog/2015/10/06/more-sweetly-play-the -dance/.

References

Abrams, Philip. 1988. "Notes on the Difficulty of Studying the State (1977)." *Journal of Historical Sociology* 1 (1): 58–89.

Ake, Claude. 2000. *The Feasibility of Democracy in Africa.* Dakar: Council for the Development of Social Science Research in Africa.

Comaroff, John L., and Jean Comaroff. 1992. *Ethnography and the Historical Imagination.* Boulder, CO: Westview Press.

Comaroff, John L., and Jean Comaroff. 2018. "Chiefs, Capital, and the State in Contemporary Africa: An Introduction." In *The Politics of Custom: Chiefship, Capital, and the State in Contemporary Africa,* edited by John L. Comaroff and Jean Comaroff, 1–48. Chicago: University of Chicago Press.

Fischer, Michael M. J. 2018. *Anthropology in the Meantime: Experimental Ethnography, Theory, and Method for the Twenty-First Century.* Durham, NC: Duke University Press.

Foucault, Michel. 1991. "Governmentality." In *The Foucault Effect: Studies in Governmentality,* edited by Graham Burchell, Colin Gordon, and Peter Miller, 87–104. Chicago: University of Chicago Press.

Hansen, Thomas Blom, and Finn Stepputat. 2001. "Introduction: States of Imagination." In *States of Imagination: Ethnographic Explorations of the Postcolonial State,* edited by Thomas Blom Hansen and Finn Stepputat, 1–38. Durham, NC: Duke University Press.

Hansen, Thomas Blom, and Finn Stepputat. 2005. "Introduction." In *Sovereign Bodies: Citizens, Migrants, and States in the Postcolonial World,* edited by Thomas Blom Hansen and Finn Stepputat, 1–36. Princeton, NJ: Princeton University Press.

Maltz-Leca, Leora. 2018. *William Kentridge: Process as Metaphor and Other Doubtful Enterprises.* Berkeley: University of California Press.

Mazzarella, William. 2017. *The Mana of Mass Society.* Chicago: University of Chicago Press.

Mbembe, Achille. 1992. "The Banality of Power and the Aesthetics of Vulgarity in the Postcolony." *Public Culture* 4 (2): 1–30.

Mbembe, Achille. 1999. "On Private Indirect Government." *Politique Africaine* 73 (1): 103–21.

Peters, Pauline. 2018. "Land Grabs: The Politics of the Land Rush across Africa." *Oxford Research Encyclopedias: Politics.* https://doi.org/10.1093/acrefore /9780190228637.013.825.

Radcliffe-Brown, Alfred R. 1940. "Preface." In *African Political Systems,* edited by Meyer Fortes and E. E. Evans-Pritchard, xi–xxiii. London: Oxford University Press for the International African Institute.

Sharma, Aradhana, and Akhil Gupta. 2006. "Introduction: Rethinking Theories of the State in an Age of Globalization." In *The Anthropology of the State: A Reader,* edited by Aradhana Sharma and Akhil Gupta, 1–41. Oxford: Blackwell.

Taussig, Michael. 1997. *The Magic of the State.* New York: Routledge.

Preface

The ideas crystalized in this volume were long in gestation. They started with a course I developed and taught for many years at the University of California, Davis, and later at the University of Oxford: the Politics of Life in Africa. I thank the students in the classes who raised the questions that forced me to think further about some of the issues of quotidian life in Africa.

My first attempt to engage with some of these questions in a book eventuated in the edited volume *The Political Economy of Everyday Life in Africa: Beyond the Margins* (James Currey, 2017). After that book was published, I realized that there are still other questions about everyday life in Africa—particularly in relation to the state and democracy—that I wanted to invite scholars working in different parts of the continent to engage with. When I decided to pursue this a year after *The Political Economy* was published, I found it a bit daunting because of the pressures of the administrative duties I had taken on at Oxford. As the Director of the African Studies Centre at Oxford, I kept postponing developing a concept paper for the book. This went on for about two years. In the end, between "hiding" in my office at St. Antony's College and coffee stores in the city, I was able to write the initial concept paper in 2019. After contemplating hosting a conference around the central theme of this book and inviting potential contributors, I abandoned the idea of holding one.

I am delighted, though, that many of the contributors were eventually able to present their chapters during the annual conferences of two professional organizations. I co-organized a panel with Katrien Pype at the African Studies Association (US) annual conference (online) in November 2020, where some of the chapters were presented. I thank all those who presented their chapters at the conference, including Pype, Nicholas Rush Smith, Lori Leonard, and Ebenezer Obadare, and the discussant, Victoria Bernal. I thank Bernal for the excellent critique she offered. It was because of this that I invited her to revise and expand her comments as the afterword to the volume. I also co-organized two other panels with Pype during the Association of Social Anthropologists (UK) annual conference (online) in April 2021. I am grateful to all those who presented their chapters at the conference, including, again, Pype, Eric Trovalla (on behalf of himself and his coauthor, Ulrika Trovalla), Rose Løvgren, Helle Samuelsen, and Rogers Orock. Loes Oudenhuijsen of Leiden University, although not a contributor to this volume, also presented a paper during the first panel. I thank all the presenters and our discussant, Richard Werbner, who gave a magisterial response to the papers and raised critical questions for future research.

I thank all the contributors to the volume for their patience and perseverance. They understood my occasional "gentle reminders" as not particularly gentle but still responded gracefully and always with timeliness. I hope the final product is worthy of their individual and collective efforts. Jean and John L. Comaroff are as supportive as ever. I am grateful to them for the preface—written in their trademark ornate prose.

My gratitude also goes to the series editors and our editor at Ohio University Press (OUP), Ricky Huard. Huard is not only very professional but also prompt and courteous in responding to queries. I have never experienced a smoother process of working with an editor at any of the presses I have had the opportunity to engage with in my life in the academy. I am grateful to the others at OUP, Tyler Balli, Beth Pratt, Sally Welch, and Anna Garnai. The copyeditors—Ed Vesneske, Jr., and Kristin Harpster—did an excellent job, for which I am thankful.

Much of the work on this book was completed before I moved from Oxford to the University of Pennsylvania. The Oxford School of Global and Area Studies provided financial support for the book through the Higher Studies Fund. I thank Head of the Oxford School of Global and Area Studies, Tim Power, and Head of Administration and Finance, Erin Gordon. I thank my colleagues at the Oxford African Studies Centre, particularly David Pratten and Miles Larmer, and my predecessor as Rhodes Chair, William Beinart. Final editorial work was done in my first few months at UPenn. For their support, I thank my colleagues, particularly Michael Hanchard, Camille Z. Charles, and Department Administrator Carol L. Davis.

I have dedicated this book to my former supervisor, mentor, and friend, John David Yeadon Peel, who passed away on 2 November 2015. I have no doubt that, if he were still here with us, he would—in his inimitable way—have much to say about the various chapters in the book. JDYP was a consummate ethnographer who combined penetrating sociological insight with theoretical sophistication. I hope his spirit is pleased with this *memorial*.

The revised version of this volume was submitted to our editor as the world was getting some relief from the COVID-19 pandemic in mid-2021. Among the many issues raised by the pandemic, there are two that are relevant to the theme of the book. The first is that, as a species, we do not have another instrument with the inherent and massive capacity for the protection and preservation of our individual and collective lives other than what we call "the state." The second is the value (and the limits) of *transparency* central to democratic governance. It was the absence of transparency—especially *ethical or radical transparency*—that, more than any other factor, made it impossible to quickly respond, globally, to the spread of the virus. As to the first factor, it was the nature of the vision, capacity, and sincerity (or otherwise) of those in charge of the state in different parts of the world, particularly in countries with the most advanced scientific capacity, that determined the different kinds of responses that either exposed millions of people to sudden death or saved millions of lives at the earliest possible juncture. For now, and in the foreseeable future, as a species we still *need* and *depend* on the capacity of the state to protect and preserve our individual and collective lives. We also need and depend on the capacity of democratic life to promote and support human flourishing.

WA

Philadelphia, December 2021

Introduction

The Everyday State and Democracy in Africa

WALE ADEBANWI

.

THIS BOOK IS ABOUT ETHNOGRAPHIC APPROACHES TO everyday encounters with and experiences of "the state" and democracy in contemporary Africa. It examines how an ethnographic approach to the quotidian experiences of the state and democracy in African can advance our understanding of the social, political, and economic dynamics that define everyday life in the continent. It also examines how the daily struggles for life and the potential for a rich fulfillment of life for most people in Africa are enabled and/or constrained, and also complicated by, the state and the democratic process.

Anthropology's elaborate *reengagement* with "the state" and embrace of civil society as useful perspectives for the analysis of social formation in Africa (see Mafeje 1986; Ensminger 1990; John L. Comaroff and Jean Comaroff 1999; Hann 1996)—and elsewhere—occurred roughly around the period that Africanist political science was becoming pessimistic about the African state (see Bayart 1993; Bayart, Ellis, and Hibou 1999; Chabal and Daloz 1999), while also interrogating the value of civil society (Bayart 1986; Allen 1997).[1] About two decades before most African states gained independence from colonial rule, Alfred Radcliffe-Brown concluded that "the factual material available for a comparative study of the political institutions of the *simpler societies* is inadequate both in quantity and quality" (1940, xiii, emphasis added). This was in his preface to the classic work of political anthropology, *African Political Systems,* edited by Meyer Fortes and Edward E. Evans-Pritchard—which the authors hoped would be "of interest and of use to *those who have the task of administering African peoples*" (Fortes and Evans-Pritchard 1940, vii, emphasis added).[2] Before and for a few decades after this period, Africanist anthropology was dominated by the study of kinship, family structure, customs, culture, myths, symbols, social organization, religion, ritual, exchange, consumption, socialization, urbanization, law, conflict, festivals, and the like—which is to say, not of the political per se.[3]

African Political Systems became recognized as the precursor to anthropological studies of political institutions and the political process in Africa—and elsewhere in the global south—though many Africanist scholars avoided studying what was then the colonial state. In his preface, Radcliffe-Brown, prefiguring Philip Abrams (1988) and others, suggested that anthropologists should abandon the idea of the state "represented as being an entity over and above the human individuals who make up a society, having as one of its attributes something called 'sovereignty,' and sometimes spoken of as having a will (law being often defined as the will of the State) or as issuing commands." Such a phenomenon, he argued, is "a fiction of the philosophers." What *exists,* he advanced, "is an organization, i.e. a collection of individual human beings connected by a complex system of relations. Within that organization different individuals have different roles, and some are in possession of special power or authority. . . . There is no such thing as the power of the State; there are only, in reality, powers of individuals—kings, prime ministers, magistrates, policemen, party bosses, and voters." This *reality,* he concluded—that is, of political organization—qualified for "an objective study" (1940, xxiii).

This objection to the study of the state evidently influenced many Africanist anthropologists for a considerable period. As Jack Goody (1971, 17) acknowledges, in the decades prior to the 1970s, "the comparative study of centralized institutions in Africa has not been great."[4] In the 1940s and 1950s, a few significant ethnographers examined the genealogy and forces at work within and/or among what Goody (1971, 73) describes as the "traditional state in [precolonial] Africa"—what Max Gluckman (1965) terms "tribal states." It can be argued that the origins of anthropology as a study of "primitive" peoples and "tribes" and the objection to the study of the state by anthropologists, as articulated by Radcliffe-Brown, resulted in the avoidance of the study of *modern* political institutions and processes, particularly the *ur*-political institution—the State.[5] Therefore, for a long time, anthropology had not "acknowledged the state as a proper subject for ethnographic inspection" (Das and Poole 2004b, 4). The focus was on "nonstate" societies—which Radcliffe-Brown described as "simpler societies." Even as late as the last decade of the twentieth century, as Joan Vincent (1990) notes, most anthropologists still did not take the state seriously as an object of study (see also Fuller and Harriss 2000, 1–2).[6] And when they did, it was always the "traditional" chiefly states that were studied, because the modern, rational-legal state was initially assumed to be unamenable to the ethnographic method of inquiry (Gupta 1995, 375; Fuller and Harriss 2000, 1).

Nonetheless, it must be noted that, even by the 1960s, some ethnographers did not heed Radcliffe-Brown's *injunction* regarding the African state, given that ethnographic studies, as Aidan Southall argues, "put the institution of the state itself in a much clearer empirical perspective" (1974, 153). Though some of these scholars writing between the 1960s and 1980s did not study the *state qua state* in Africa, they more usefully paid "careful attention to the cultural constitution of the state—that is, how people perceive the state, how their understandings are shaped by their particular locations and intimate and embodied encounters with state processes and officials, and how the state manifests itself in their lives" (Sharma and Gupta 2006b, 11).[7] They explored the ("tribal") state and civil strife (Gluckman 1965),[8] "different aspects of the structure of the political arena" (Swartz 1968, 49), "the political life of local communities, or ethnic groups in and of themselves and as parts of larger wholes" (Cohen 1969, 590), state formation (Southall 1974), interactions among local organizations in which the impact of the state was central (Geschiere 1982), and the consequences of state socialism.[9] However, since the 1990s, anthropologists have paid greater attention to the state in Africa, not only the contemporary state, but also the implications of the encounters of African people with the colonial and postcolonial state in the *longue durée*—and the implications of past encounters for the present constitution of the state. To draw two examples of these approaches—starting with the latter—John and Jean Comaroff in their two-volume magnum opus, *Of Revelation and Revolution*, volume 1, *Christianity, Colonialism, and Consciousness in South Africa* (1991) and volume 2, *The Dialectics of Modernity on a South African Frontier* (1997), examine the incorporation of the Tswana into a colonial, and later a postcolonial, state (Jean Comaroff and John L. Comaroff 1991, 4).[10] This produced what they describe as a complex system of "reciprocal determinations" (John L. Comaroff and Jean Comaroff 1997b, 28).[11] Since Joan Vincent's *Anthropology and Politics* (1990), the rapidly evolving nature of the postcolonial state has required new perspectives on the local role of the state and the ways politics around and about access to the state have redefined everyday encounters with the state.[12] The second example is Jonathan Spencer (1997; see Fuller and Harriss 2000, 2), who was one of the first scholars to take up the challenge of anthropological analysis of politics and the postcolonial state in late twentieth century, even as Africanist political scientists were exhausting the process of inventing different terms for discussing (and deriding) the African state. Recently, ethnography—as "a mode of knowing that privileges experience," focusing on "realms of the social that are not easily discernible within the more formal protocols used by many other disciplines" (Das and Poole 2004b, 4)—has provided a more useful method for studying, understanding, explaining, and theorizing the African state.

Ethnographic studies of the African state in the last three decades have provided more nuanced and insightful ways of accounting for the everyday processes in which the state and democracy are experienced or encountered by most people in contemporary times in the continent.

A similar aversion to studying democracy was dominant in anthropology for a long time. In fact, as recently as 2007, Spencer declared that "anthropological contribution to the analysis of democracy has been rather disappointing" (2007, 74). Mikael Karlström, surveying the Africanist literature about a decade earlier, concluded that "despite the resurgence of interest in democratisation in Africa, the systematic [anthropological] study of local understandings of democracy on the continent has barely begun" (1996, 485). The disappointing contributions of anthropology to the analysis of democracy even in the first decade of the twenty-first century, Spencer (2007, 74) argues, could be due to the fact that anthropologists regarded democracy as "an ideological chimera—an imaginary *telos*," and/or because democracy's ubiquity had rendered it banal as an object of anthropological analysis. However, since Karlström and Spencer rendered their observations, anthropological study of democracy has blossomed (for a few examples, see Paley 2002, 2004, 2008b; Goldman 2013; von Schnitzler 2016) as anthropologists have embraced the fact that "through the dialogical methods of extended fieldwork and ethnographic writing [they] potentially have much to contribute to facilitating and strengthening democracy as variably defined by people in diverse locales around the globe" (West 2008, 119).

The foundational notion of state sovereignty as inhering in the people, particularly in a democracy—which is the form of government in which the notion of the sovereignty of the people is (expected to be) most evident—often comes into great relief and/or tension in the everyday life of the people. This is particularly so in most African states, where, on the one hand, democratic revival has, since the end of the Cold War, renewed the questions of the reason of the state,[13] the nature of the state, the ownership of the state, as well as the uses of the state, and, on the other hand, neoliberal policies/governance have thrown into crisis the possibilities for human thriving raised by democratic rule. Thus, democratic renewal along with the challenges of neoliberal governance have triggered (re)new(ed) forms of organizing within and beyond civil spaces in the everyday life of people in the continent. As neoliberal policies and programs succeed and/or fail in the *destatization* of governance (see Ismail 2006, xx), the implications are most evident in the quotidian life of the citizens in contemporary African polities.

Against this backdrop, in the last few decades, ethnographic studies of democratic political institutions and democratic political processes in Africa have sprouted. Everyday formal and informal encounters of ordinary people with, and the simultaneous reproduction of, the institutions, agencies, and processes that constitute the state and/or (de)regulate democratic life in Africa have consequently gained greater attention in the literature.[14] This includes (re)considering how "ordinary forms of sociability" (Blundo et al. 2006, 8) and the "ordinary texture of existence" (Fassin 2018, 109) determine and are determined by the ways in which people experience and reproduce the state and its institutions in their concrete and fluid practices while also participating in democratic life.

Encountering the State and Democracy: Emergent Questions

This book expands on extant studies of such encounters and experiences. In this volume, we hope to (a) build on the extant literature on everyday formal and informal experiences of ordinary people with the state and the democratic process in Africa, (b) extend the emerging insight by probing the intricate and complex ways in which the state and democracy are (re) produced and (re)constituted by everyday encounters, and (c) respond to de Certeau's (1984, xi) famous demand that scholars use theoretical questions, methods, categories, and perspectives to *penetrate* the obscurity—and, we dare add, interrogate the mundanity—of everyday practices that constitute and are constituted by the representations as well as the practices of the state and democracy.

The central questions that we seek to answer are these: In the context of democratic life, how does the state, in both its illusory and concrete manifestations (Hansen and Stepputat 2001, 5)—through its institutions, agencies, agents, processes, (il)logics, etc.—determine and regulate, and/ or are determined and regulated by, the socially constitutive processes in which people participate in everyday life? How does everydayness provoke meaning and significance regarding the state and democratic life? How do the everyday experiences of ordinary people, in both their symbolic and material dimensions, give particular meanings to the state and democracy and thus (re)constitute the state and democratic life in Africa?

We assume that the momentary or episodic, short- and long-term, experiences of people who *inhabit* the state (Friedman 2011, 3) through their everyday transactions involving the state and its institutions and agencies (such as the bureaucracy, police, courts, tax office, housing agency, licensing office, immigration service, refuse collection service, etc.) are important not only in addressing "the question of what states do when they are working" (Bierschenk and Olivier de Sardan 2014, 5), but also in defining the meanings, discourses, practices, and significance of democratic life as well as its simultaneously enabling and distressing realities. In seeking to understand, through critical/ethnographic perspectives, how the state and democracy manifest in what Patrick Chabal (2009, x) describes as "key areas of human existence," we hope to account, in fresh ways, for *everyday grammars of the state and democratic life in contemporary Africa,* including how these *grammars* are determined by local, regional, and global processes and are re-determined by the actions, conceptions, and agencies of manifold actors along different forms of temporalities and spatialities.[15] The centrality of temporality and spatiality in experiencing and encountering the state and democratic processes underlines the concomitant need to account for the "socio-historical genesis of the state" (Dubois 2018, 39) in every context.

In addition to sociohistorical contexts, the "concentric rings of connection, between the material culture of [individual] everyday life, larger communities, and worldwide patterns of consumption and production" (Ginsborg 2005, 5), we suggest, are not only templates for constituting democratic life, they also represent grounds for critical reflections on democratic practices within particular social formations.[16] Furthermore, we assume that everyday life alerts us to the state (in its materiality, disciplinarity, biopolitical manifestations, etc.) as a "zone of different and differing encounters" (Obadare and Adebanwi 2010, 21) determined simultaneously by *ideas* of the state (Migdal and Schlichte 2005, 15), particular cultural constructions of the state in different contexts (Jessop 1982, 1990; Abrams 1988; Mitchell 1991, 1999; Herzfeld 1992; Gupta 1995; Taussig 1997; Sharma and Gupta 2006a), as well as state practices.[17]

Since the vision of liberal democracy became dominant in the analysis of the African state in the post–Cold War era, scholars have faced the critical challenge of accounting for the significant improvement in state-society and state-citizen interactions that followed decades of tyranny and arbitrariness by one-party states, military regimes and presidents-for-life, while also ensuring that the "routinized practices of state [and democratizing] institutions" (Gupta 2012, 5), which cause great damage and violence to the lives of millions of Africans, do not "disappear from view" (ibid.). They try to do so even in light of the "vernacular cultures of participatory politics" (John L. Comaroff and Jean Comaroff 1997a, 123) and "local understandings of democracy and its assimilation to existing political cosmology and practices" (Karlström 1996, 485) that have become dominant in the post-1989 African state and society.

In the post-1989 era, anthropologists have emphasized their recognition of "a place for an ethnographic project at the heart of [the] democratic [process]" (Greenhouse and Greenwood 1998, 1; cf. Michelutti 2007, 639–40; Tanabe 2007, 558) because ethnography can help us in linking the state—as a form of "politically organized subjection" (Abrams 1988, 63), as a "relay or point of coordination and multiplication of power relations" (Ferguson 2006, 281), and as "a relational setting that . . . exists within the relations between actors who have unequal access to material, social, regulatory, and symbolic resources and who negotiate over ideas of legitimate power" (Thelen, Vetters, and von Benda-Beckmann 2018b, 7)—and the democratic process in Africa with "the richly varied and flexible imagination for collective life among ordinary people in society at large" (Greenhouse and Greenwood, 1998, 2). Thus, greater attention should be paid to "the local meanings, circulating discourses, multiple contestations, and changing forms of power accompanying the installation of new [democratic] political regimes" (Paley 2002, 469–70) and the "culturally meaningful and politicoeconomically functional [ways in which ordinary people secure] their legitimate and dignified position in participatory politics" (Tanade 2007, 558), and "how people act, think, and feel about power on a daily basis" (Paller 2019, 4) in Africa, including the "context of daily life . . . where leaders legitimate their authority, as well as make decisions about how to distribute resources" (ibid.); to how these are implicated in the *vernaculars* of daily life such as sorcery and ritual practice; and to the different argots of democracy—including the "assimilation" of democracy to "existing political cosmologies and practices" (Karlström 1996, 486; see also Apter 1987; Geschiere 1997; Schaffer 1997; West 1998) and "how ideas and practices of democracy have been internalized in the popular consciousness" (Michelutti 2007, 633). Consequently, beyond the macroanalysis of democratic "transition" and "consolidation" (e.g., O'Donnell and Schmitter 1986; Bratton and van de Walle 1997; Diamond et al. 1997; Diamond 1999; Lindberg 2001) by political scientists, it is in the everyday, routinized encounters with, or experiences of, the state that ethnographers can help to account for what *is,* as well as the *nature* of, the state and its (in)efficacies, including "the paradoxical relation of different groups of . . . people to the state, which simultaneously articulates inclusion and care with arbitrariness and structural violence" (Gupta 2012, 41).

Michel-Rolph Trouillot (2001, 126) has suggested that we "focus on the multiple sites in which state processes and practices are recognizable through their effects." Therefore, in this volume we are interested in multiple sites in which ethnographic insights, based on theoretical reflections, can help in explaining what happens when people come "face to face" with the (democratic) state and its agencies—sometimes as [a] "metaphorical person[s]" (see Oldenburg 2006). Even though the state is not "a visible or tangible body" (Kelsen 1945, 191), it has *faces*—in the senses of both aspect and facade—including even an assumed "ideal face" that people search for (Obeid 2010, 330, 332); at the same time, the state manifests "through institutions which are empirical and visible" (ibid., 332), which can *see* (Blundo 2014). Against this backdrop, the Austrian jurist, Hans Kelsen (1945, 191), alerted us to "our tendency to personify [the state] and then to hypostatize our personifications"—thus imputing "a human action to the State"—partly because the invisible and intangible state must manifest itself in social life (ibid.) and as individual agents.

In this volume, we do not assume the democratic nature of the state; rather, we are interested in what the *democratic state* means and/or how it is interpreted through experiential deductions, inferences, or conclusions.

Following Mbembe, we would like "to throw intelligible light on fundamental problems touching on the nature of social reality in Africa" by examining "the effects of the *longue durée* [on] the paths taken by different societies and to account for contradictory contemporary phenomena" manifesting in daily life (2001, 6). We want to take up Mbembe's challenge to students of Africa to engage in critical ethnographic descriptions "distinguishing between causes and effects, asking the subjective meaning of actions, determining the genesis of practices and their interconnections" (9). In addition, we also would like to question the abstractions of the state and democracy based on assumptions of a universal understanding of what both mean and entail. In this context, Claude Ake has famously argued that democracy has been globalized only "because it has been trivialized to the point at which it is no longer threatening to political elites" (2000, 7). Is this trivialization enabling or disenabling of social action, does it provoke further engagement or encourage disengagement by the people in their everyday life?

Additionally, we are interested in an exploration of the temporal and spatial experiences of, or encounters with, the state and democracy and how these experiences and encounters produce meanings, discourses, and representations which have their own materiality (Mbembe 2001, 5). What do the different experiences and practices of democracy mean for the people in Africa? For instance, does democracy mean the same in Togo and Gabon (where inherited power masquerades as democratic succession) as in Botswana and South Africa (where the possibility of democratic change is more evident and far less rigged)? How do the meanings of democracy and the state emerge from everyday local encounters and practices in such different African social formations?

While this volume is devoted to exploring the ethnographic experiences of the state, it is not limited to strictly anthropological perspectives. The contributors, including anthropologists, political scientists, sociologists, political economists, and historians, engage in fruitful conversations on the state and democracy produced by the embrace of ethnographic methods in the different disciplines.

In our efforts to "rethink the state [and democracy] as an object of ethnographic inquiry," we depart slightly from Das and Poole's argument in that the contributors are not only looking "for signs of administrative and hierarchical rationalities that provide seemingly ordered links with the political and regulatory apparatus of a central bureaucratic state" (2004b, 5). We are also interested in how the people who live under the strictures of the state—and engage with or disengage from it, encounter and experience it, legitimize or subvert it—are often convinced about the state's irrationalities. Thus, in interpreting and appropriating, in "culturally [and experientially] informed" ways, the ideas, practices, and manifestations of the state, citizens do not often take the rationality of the state for granted. In so doing, they further reconstitute the state as a terrain of (ir)rational processes but with its own understandable and relatable logics. The contributors also reflect (on) how and why "forms of illegibility, partial belonging, and disorder" (ibid., 6) are not exclusively inhabited in the "margins of the state," as examined by the contributions to the important volume, *Anthropology and the Margins of the State* (2004). We follow Das and Poole and their contributors in examining "sites of practice on which law and other state practices are colonized by other forms of regulation that emanate from the pressing needs of populations to secure political and economic survival" (ibid., 8). Some of the contributors to this volume also show that such sites are not necessarily "on the margins of what is accepted as the territory of unquestioned state control (and legitimacy)" (ibid.). They can be in the very terrain of, in the (hidden) purview of, or sometimes just across the street (literally and metaphorically) from, core state institutions, agencies, or agents. In fact, in some cases, such "other forms of regulations" emanating from pressing needs for survival are perpetrated by agents of the state who subvert the rules of engagement imposed by the abstraction called the state.

Everyday Life in Africa

Everyday life is the secret yeast of history.

—Agnes Heller (1978, 25)[18]

In the last few decades, the literature on socioeconomic and political processes and relations around the world has experienced what can be described as the "quotidian turn"—or "everyday turn." Between the 1950s and 1970s, sociologists and later "new social" historians started embracing everyday life as "an important—perhaps the most important—place people find meaning, develop habits, and acquire a sense of themselves and their world" (Trentmann 2012, 522). The leading scholars in this moment in the trajectory of the study of everyday life were Henri Lefebvre and Michel de Certeau. In the postwar era in Western Europe, specifically in France, Lefebvre's three-volume *Critique of Everyday Life* (*Critique de la vie quotidienne*, 1947, 1961, and 1981) began a new era of rigorous academic analysis of quotidian life, which was subsequently taken up in another landmark work, Michel de Certeau's *The Practice of Everyday Life* (*L'invention du quotidien*, vol. 1, *Arts de faire*, 1980). In *Everyday Life in the Modern World* (*La vie quotidienne dans le monde moderne*, 1968), Lefebvre raises fundamental questions about the state and society in modernity in relation to accelerating change by analyzing the "dull routine . . . of daily existence" in the context of "a sense of being in the world beyond philosophy . . . the grey reality enveloping all we do" (Wander 1984, vi–viii). Lefebvre argues that "everyday life is non-philosophical in relation to philosophy and represents reality in relation to ideality"; it consists of, among other things, "a moment made of moments" and "the dialectical interaction that is the inevitable starting point for the realization of the possible" (Lefebvre 2016, 10, 12). In his own work, which seeks to "indicate pathways for further research," de Certeau advances that we should no longer approach "everyday practices, 'ways of operating'" as mere "obscure background of social activity." He is less concerned directly with "subjects" (or persons) than with "modes of operation or schemata of action" and "operational logic"—involving disguises and transformations for the purpose of survival—which have "been concealed by the form of rationality currently dominant in Western culture" (1984, xi). Approaching the dominated in society—who, he argues, should not be assumed to be passive or docile—through the *euphemistic term* of "consumer," de Certeau concludes that "everyday life invents itself by *poaching* in countless ways on the property of others" (xii, emphasis in original). In his reading of the everyday life of the masses (*consumers*), de Certeau argues that the masses experience or encounter the *products* "imposed by the dominant economic order" by inventing their own "*ways of using* the products" (xiii, emphasis in original).[19] While his argument that "users" always retain the capacity to manipulate the "products" of "makers"—that is, the dominant socio-economic and political order—is now prevalent and useful,[20] de Certeau's assumption that such *use* is always already in the service of resistance seem too deterministic.[21] While this is what happens in most cases, this process is also open to collaborative or *nonresistant* uses of the *products*—of the state and of democratic processes. As Fernand Braudel has argued, "the everyday . . . *pulls us along*, not necessarily because of agency and politics" (Trentmann 2012, 529, emphasis added)—and not only because of the possibility and actuality of resistance.

Yet what seems like a "momentous eruption of everyday life into literature" (Lefebvre 2016, 2) from the second half of the twentieth century—when postwar Western Europe "was coming to terms with the American empire of goods" (Trentmann 2012, 524)—has a longer history.[22] To draw two examples: Liberal pragmatists in the early twentieth century, represented by William James, insisted that philosophical ideas had to be brought into a practical, concrete level (ibid., 534). James implied in his 1904 lecture that "any philosophical system which does not answer the questions of life—of real, grimy, everyday life—can be called to account as not fulfilling its vocation" (James 1975, 275). And Georg Lukacs, in his *History and Class Consciousness* (*Geschichte und Klassenbewußtsein*, 1923), "saw the everyday as a hybrid of alienation and emancipation" (ibid., 533). Therefore, the postwar era that produced a focus on everyday life, argues Trentmann, constitutes "one chapter in a longer story. . . . It was in the decades on either side of 1900 that we can discern a growing fascination with the quotidian, in terms of cultural praxis and intellectual reflection as well as political ambition" (ibid., 524).

The early twentieth-century approach to the question of the quotidian was different from previous eras in that it was infused with an energetic agenda of the transformation of everyday life (ibid., 536). Against this background, different societies and different social formations determined what mattered in everyday life in their social formation. For instance, while in the United States the everyday was approached largely from the point of its democratic potentials, for Trotsky, as reflected in his 1923 *Pravda* article, "How to Begin" (Trotsky 1973), the focus was on how the Russian Revolution had to be followed by *the revolution of the everyday* in which people replaced the cultures and practices of the past with those appropriate for socialism (see Trentmann 2012, 537).[23] The approach is also different in postcolonial Africa, with her formidable socioeconomic, political, and environmental/climatic challenges in confronting the possibilities of a good life for the majority of the people.

Generally, in contemporary liberal democratic contexts, the everyday is regarded as the terrain of democratic life (Trentmann 2012, 522)—which, despite its "openness," still "presents us with a recalcitrant object that does not give up its secrets too readily" (Highmore 2002b, 1). However, the legacy of the multiple meanings of the everyday remains with us in the literature. Thus, the everyday has been approached in different ways, some of which are not only incompatible but also contradictory (Trentmann 2012, 522–33). However, what is included in everydayness is largely determined by the spatiotemporal context in relation to a manifold of factors.

Ben Highmore (2002b, 15) asks, "What happens when everyday life is viewed from 'elsewhere'? How might we imagine globalising the study of everyday life?" Addressing these questions would mean that we need to not only "globalize" the study of the everyday, as Highmore has requested, it would also mean, *pace* Trentmann, that we broaden the time frame of contemporary perspectives on the history of modern politics of everyday life beyond its geographical center (the West), so as to be able to account not merely for its longer history, but also to explain its value for other areas of the world outside of this *center* and the related time frame (see Trentmann

2012, 524). In the light of this, two important points raised by Trentmann are very useful for our intellectual agenda in this volume. One is that contemporary "interest in the everyday grew out of a suspicion of big structures and determinist accounts of capitalism and class" (ibid., 525). The second is that, in the postwar era, building on the younger Marx, contemporary scholarship on the everyday centers on how people *appropriate* their world. This has produced "significant differences about the nature of the everyday, its political content and, for intellectual praxis" (ibid., where Trentmann provides examples of the differences).

In this volume, we approach everyday life as involving the ordinary, recurring, trivial, and/or crucial actions, struggles, engagements, interactions, enactments, performances, exchanges, needs, communications, and other manifold forms of deeds or acts that define and condition human existence. These deeds or acts involving ordinary people are often geared toward attempts to manage, cope with, suffer through, struggle with, and/or improve the terms of human existence and human viability in relation to, or in the context of, various agencies, structures, institutions, processes, and rules and regulations that enable or circumscribe living and *living well*. Thus, everyday life is the terrain where people (a) make sense of the modes, practices and systems that define or determine existence in (un)certain contexts, particularly the state and the democratic process, (b) develop, through their micro experiences and encounters, their understanding of the state and its agencies and the democratic process, and (c) respond to, confront and/or navigate, or even transcend the conditions of marginality, uncertainty, precarity (and death), and the challenges that these pose to the possibility of *living* and *living well*.[24] Everyday life creates and constricts opportunities for the expression of feelings, fears, hopes, ambitions, etc. in the effort to compose a decent and livable life, especially in the contexts in which, as Joe Moran hints, "the quotidian coalesces with the political in unnoticed but pervasive ways" (2005, 9). Therefore, in the context of everyday life, people do not merely make (non)sense of the state and democracy, they mobilize this in finding meaning for themselves and constructing a pathway in the moment as well as in the short and long terms. Given the critical role of the state, even when it is *absent in its presence* or *present in its absence*—as some of the chapters in this volume show—it is useful to examine how ordinary people maintain and/or challenge their *(in)dependence* vis-à-vis the state (Hyden 1980).

The Africanist literature is slowly developing a "quotidian turn." There is increasing awareness in the last few decades among Africanist scholars, particularly ethnographers, that the dominant Weberian approach to politics—with an emphasis on states, classes, and modernization (see Trentmann 2012, 524)—is inadequate in accounting for contemporary life in Africa, where, in many ways, regular people "have to possess [an] arcane, yet . . . self-evident, knowledge to be able to safely navigate the politics of everyday life" (Schubert 2017, 2).[25] However, given that everydayness is a phenomenon of modernity, Africa's history of colonial subjection and the complicated history of the development and spread of modern concepts and practices of autonomy and subjectivity form an important backdrop for understanding of contemporary everyday life in Africa.[26]

Since the last two decades of the twentieth century, everydayness has, for most Africans, ironically presented (an awareness of) limitless opportunities for self-actualization or self-realization while at the same time circumscribing their capacity for participating in these opportunities in meaningful ways—or in maximizing their potentials. For instance, while new means of communication present endless opportunities, capacities, and possibilities (see Wasserman 2011; Pype 2020) for African youth in their everyday life (including mobile telephony, social media, transnational online communities, cash transfer, etc.), access to and the use of these means of communication for personal, social, economic, and political interactions and advancement are sometimes limited by other factors, including limited access to resources, poor infrastructure, poor services, limited access to the internet or Wi-Fi, restrictive laws, and the like.

In this volume, we examine some of the dimensions of these possibilities and capacities as well as the constraints of everyday life in Africa. Following Trentmann (2012, 524), we do not approach everyday life as a separate realm. Rather, we approach it as a realm that not only connects the local and the national, the national and the global, but also puts the opportunities and challenges of the local, the national, and the global in bold relief at the micro level, and thus refracts the micro back to the macro. While some scholars have approached quotidian life as "a world apart from politics and markets" (Trentmann 2012, 525), as the chapters in this volume show, the everyday is a world that not only reflects and mirrors politics and markets, but also contests the logic of politics and the market and sometimes bends the logic in particular instances—and for particular purposes. The contributors to this volume analyze the contours of existence of those whose agential powers and potentials have been circumscribed—if not stolen, if only episodically—by different systems, institutions, and local, national, and global processes, but who, on a daily basis, re(dis)cover and/or enact new forms of agency to make life and living possible.

The State and Democracy in Everyday Life

For much of the twentieth century, state theory did not question the *actual* existence of the state (Jessop 1990, 7; Bratsis 2006, 4). However, there are a few notable exceptions, including Kelsen (1945), Abrams (1988), Jessop

(1990), and Mitchell (1991, 1999). These scholars have raised interesting questions about the *reality* and *rationality* of the state, while pointing to the illusory nature—*the fetish*—of the *idea* of the state, and to how, through our beliefs, actions, and practices, we engage in the *reification* and *entification* of the state. Against the background of the illumination provided by these scholars, ethnographic interrogations of the state entered a new era after the seminal studies by Michael Herzfeld (1992) and Michael Taussig (1997). Taussig asks why is it that we invent so much materiality into a "woeful insufficiency of being" (1997, 3) that we call the state, while Herzfeld asks if "the state" is "a construct deployed by certain manipulative individuals to legitimize their authority" (1992, 1).

In this book, we explore the manifestations and effects of the *woeful insufficiency* and the *manipulative* agents and agencies and their implications for everyday life. We assume that one of the most productive ways of understanding everyday life is to study "the relationships through which the state and its citizens [within a democratic context] are mutually constituted in [locally] and historically specific ways" (Mosse 2000, 164). The everyday life of ordinary people is connected to the state, state agencies, and democratic institutions and practices through the power invested in, or appropriated by, the state and its institutions to intervene in the life of the population—to authorize, validate, endorse, protect, preserve, correct, deter, constrain, prohibit, compel, coerce, promote, support, and/or instruct, etc. Therefore, analyzing both the institutional (such as schools, hospitals, camps, bureaucracies, electoral bodies, consulates, etc.) and noninstitutional (access to energy, the road/street, scarcity, etc.) arrangements, measures, or engagements that organize and dominate everyday life (see Highmore 2002a, 14), as well as understanding the quotidian ways in which or through which "the state and its citizens are mutually constituted" (Mosse 2000, 164) can illuminate the conditions of people's lives—and the nature and character of the state. In this volume, in explicating state-citizen interactions, Riggan and Quaretta locate the everyday in the school, Ikanda locates it in a refugee camp, Løvgren in a "rehabilitation centre," the Trovallas in the struggle for access to and the quality of infrastructures, Samuelsen in health services, Adebanwi and Obadare in the alternative economy of visas, Orock at checkpoints, Smith in the streets, Leonard in shortages, Fouksman in local and international NGOs, Markó in the citizens' office, Agbiboa in "war" and vigilantism, Pype in voters' cards and CCTV, and Pearce in "democracy."

Yet the contributors make no assumptions about *stateness*—as manifested in the "state idea" (Abrams 1988) and "state effects" (Jessop 1977)—nor about the state's singularity and its unitary sovereignty. Perhaps more than any other scholar in the second half of the twentieth century, Michel

Foucault (1991) has alerted us to the dispersed nature of (governmental) power. Thus, we recognize the "complex and conflictual character of state apparatuses and institutions" (Jessop 1990, 8). Indeed, what the contributors to this volume attempt to accomplish is to show the various ways in which that which is called the state is experienced in its various (*real* and illusory) manifestations and (dis)guises. Contingency is, therefore, central to ordinary people's—and our—approach to the state. By not essentializing the state, the contributors are able to account for what happens when ordinary people believe that, or act *as if,* they are encountering the state, given that the state is encountered or experienced differently by people based on several factors—political, economic, social, spatial, temporal, etc. Thus, when they experience or encounter the state, or what acts as/for/on behalf of the state, do everyday people regard the particular state as familiar, supportive, empowering, or impartial, or alien, negligent, hostile, or prejudiced (see Rudolph and Jacobsen 2006b, xi)—and do such experiences or encounters bewilder or give pleasure, delight or depress (see Highmore 2002a, 1)?

Some scholars have argued that, in postcolonial contexts, the "'state-idea' . . . is not part of ordinary [people's] understanding" (Fuller and Harriss 2000, 9), with Satish Saberwal asserting that "state institutions such as the courts and bureaucracies have not had the 'normative support necessary for their reliable, effective functioning' because their western logic 'does not command much of either understanding or respect on the ground'" (ibid., quoting Saberwal 1996, 150). However, it can be argued that these scholars confuse two issues. The superficiality of the idea of the modern state should not be confused with its everyday effects on the people—which themselves produce certain understandings of the "state-idea." The fact that modern state institutions were imported and imposed in postcolonial contexts does not necessarily mean that the people still do not have an understanding of the "state-idea" in the twenty-first century. The people's *idea of the state* may not conform to (neo-)Weberian ideas of the modern state, but people have their own *experientially conditioned ideas* of the particular state with which they have everyday interactions. Thus, they create their own *state-idea* from the reality of their experiences, even though they also have, particularly in democratic contexts, some notions of what a *proper, good,* or *ideal*—that is, a well-functioning and responsible—state should *be* or *do.*[27] Thus, over time, regular people develop a *practical* awareness of the state and the democratic process.

At any rate, historically, given the nature of the colonial experience in Africa, ordinary people have always (re)produced their own notions of the modern state—which largely dictated their attitude to the state (see Ekeh 1975). For instance, as Peter Geschiere (1982) shows in his study of the interactions between village communities and the state in the context of the Maka in southeastern Cameroon, ordinary people often express their conceptions of the state through their everyday interactions with agencies and agents of the state. And as Bratsis argues, "from the point of view of the colonized, the state has often been experienced as a contingent product of a political project and not as some essential and natural thing" (2006, 5n8). It is therefore not surprising, Bratsis adds, that postcolonial theory has been critical of the state while examining the modes of "producing" the state. Thus, in the postcolonial context, the ordinary people's sense of the state is constructed from, and verified by, their long-term experiences of the state in relation to several other factors—as evident, for instance, in what Juan Obarrio describes in the Mozambican case as "everyday material entanglements between the temporalities of the state and the customary" (2014, 2). Therefore, a critical departure point for the ethnographic study of the "current predicament and potential of the state in Africa," Obarrio argues, is "the ways in which concurrent regimes of subjectification and subjecthood shape the democratic monad, the postcolonial citizen" (ibid., 10). In examining the case of Kaokoland in northwestern Namibia, John T. Friedman analyzes how "individuals and communities engage the new State in their everyday lives," and concludes that, for these people and communities, "the Namibian State is encountered as an educational system, a development project, a bureaucrat, a memory, a war wound and/or a patrilineal ancestor" (2011, 4).

Against the backdrop of the late Zairian state (now *reborn* as the Democratic Republic of Congo [DRC]), Filip De Boeck contends that "the concept of the state should . . . be problematised and redefined in terms of *a great number of political strategies* which cannot simply be described as forms of political 'decay' or pathological dysfunctioning, but which *aim at the creation of networks and spaces of contact, palaver, (asymmetric) exchange, solidarity and complicity, enabling the circulation of commodities, money and wealth in people*" (1996, 98, emphasis added). The different forms of political as well as social and economic "strategies" that ordinary people employ in their interactions with the state in the creation of—to summarize the different actions and processes described above by De Boeck—(everyday) life often mean that they have to *personify* the state to make sense of the state's (and its agents') actions.

The personification of the state has interesting implications in African democratic contexts. In such contexts, local conceptions and practices of democracy produce specific interpretations of democracy reflecting the realities of everyday life. Therefore, as Mikael Karlström has argued, we need to pay attention to "the complexity and dynamism of the process of articulation whereby elements of Western and global democratic discourse and practice have been selectively assimilated to an existing political cosmology, while also transforming that cosmology in important respects" (1996, 485). Using both discourse (local language) and practice in examining the Ugandan case, Karlström alerts us to the local meanings, metaphors, and translations of "democracy" and their implications for the practices of democracy in the Ugandan context. For instance, among the Baganda of Uganda, "democracy" (from the Greek *demos* and *kratia*) translates in Luganda (the local language) to *eddembe ery'obuntu*, a composite term, with *eddembe* being closer to "liberty" than to "rule" or "power" (*kratia*). There-fore, democracy "is generally used in the sense of having the freedom or liberty to carry out some particular activity without constraints imposed from above"—including freedom of speech (*eddembe ery'okwogera*) and free/leisure time (*ebiseera eby'eddembe*). But the term also includes the connota-tion of "peace." Other terms, such as *eddembe ery'obuntu*, which can be taken to mean "civil liberty" (including establishing limits both to authority and to liberties themselves) can also be used as translations for "democracy" and "human rights" (ibid., 485–86). Karlström's Ugandan examples and analysis are critical in that they point to how the practice of *translation* not only contextualizes democracy and its meaning and practices, but also how translation can also *improve* or *diminish* democracy's value and rel-evance in the cultural context—depending on how "democratic reforms" are reconciled with "existing political cultures" (ibid., 500). As Karlström states, within certain sociopolitical cosmologies, "translation both effects and reflects the assimilation of the imported notion of 'democracy' to an historically anchored local constellation of conceptions of authority and the proper relationship between rulers and subjects" (ibid., 486).

Building on De Boeck's insight on the meaning and practice of de-mocracy in the DRC, Katrien Pype argues that "at the end of Mobutu's regime . . . democratisation meant the creation of a new model of inter-action 'between multiple, dialectically interdependent, socio-political and cultural spaces and groups'" (Pype 2011, 626–27, quoting De Boeck 1996, 97). Pype points to the different meaning of "democracy" in different con-texts (see also Pearce, in this volume). In light of this, Pype states that a "Zaïrean/Congolese understanding of *démocratie* could be cast in terms of 'personalised, "feudal" structures of decision-making, deliberation, sharing of power and distributing of wealth'" (Pype 2011, 627, quoting De Boeck 1996, 99).

The everyday grammars of democracy include ways, means, and meth-ods of *democratic* claim-making by regular people, particularly *against* elites, leaders, and "big men" (see Nilsen 2018, xv) who, whether they are operators/agents of the state or not, are all assumed to be *state's (wo)men* (Obadare and Adebanwi 2010, 3). Within the different democratic states in Africa, regular people have their own idioms or vocabularies for understanding democracy and the democratic process in order to make claims—including claims about their rights as citizens, their dignity, their livelihood, freedom of speech, etc. Some of the specific claims could include, in the case of postapartheid Namibia, the "negotiation of democracy" and contestation of the state at various levels (Friedman 2011, 4), in the case Malawi, claims against "those who have caused [the people] injury" (Englund 2011, 4), or, in the case of the Zaire/DRC, claims "about urban misery, often resulting from a malfunctioning state, in which Kinshasa's inhabitants testify about their difficulties and press fellow citizens, as well as local and national leaders, to bring about change" (Pype 2011, 625). Such "vernacular understandings of 'democracy'" in Zaire/DRC are pressed daily by the people into the service of a "new kind of interaction between political leaders and citizens to [ensure] the transformation of the late Zaïrian 'state'" (ibid.)—as "the state and the president himself are called upon to intervene immediately, to render life not only more bearable but also safer" (ibid., 628) in light of failing public utilities, such as water and electricity.

Everyday Grammars of the State and Democracy in Contemporary Africa

The contributors to this volume examine contemporary everyday grammars of the state and democratic life in contemporary Africa. Through nuanced ethnographic details, they analyze what the state and democracy *are, mean,* and/or *do* in particular contexts and instances in Africa. They explore how imaginations, metaphors, literality, and materiality mesh and clash in the experiences and/or articulations of the state and democracy in contemporary Africa. Based on this volume's approach to everyday life as described above, we selected five themes as windows through which to capture aspects of everyday deeds and actions of ordinary people by means of which they attempt to manage, cope with, suffer through, struggle with, and/or improve the terms of their existence and viability, particularly in relation to, or in the context of, various agencies (the bureaucracy—local, national, transnational, and global), structures (democratic formations), institutions (hospitals, schools, law enforcement—both legal and para-legal, *reform* centers), processes (electoral procedures and contestations), and socioeconomic rules and regulations (particularly those governing access to and the provision of social services and amenities, including electricity and gas) that enable and/or circumscribe living and living well.

Understandably, these issues—which define the "intense involvement of the state in so many of the most ordinary aspects of social life [that constitute] the *prosaic* aspect of the state" (Painter 2006, 753, emphasis in original)—are connected. Thus, dividing up the sections presented a challenge as to what to put together and what to separate out in the linked processes of experiencing the state and the democratic process. Yet some of the chapters contain central issues that lend them to certain themes in particular sections, even when they are relevant to some of the issues in other sections. Indeed, this explains why all the chapters belong together in the book. The five themes include: experiencing the bureaucratic machine; the social economy of infrastructures and shortages; disciplinarity, subjectivity, and violence; the social life of democracy; and everyday politics of rights and responsibility. Each of the chapters, written by senior, midcareer, and junior scholars based in three continents (Africa, Europe, and North America), examines everyday life and the formal and informal experiences of ordinary people with the state and democratic processes in five of the regions of the continent: Central Africa, East Africa, North-East (Horn of) Africa, Southern Africa, and West Africa. The authors probe the intricate and complex ways in which the state and democracy are (re)produced and (re)constituted by everyday encounters. Collectively, the contributors use ethnography, which "provides invaluable elements of intelligibility" (Fassin 2018, 111) on the social process, to address the general questions that the experiencing of the state and democracy by ordinary people raise by focusing on the particular.

Experiencing the Bureaucratic Machine

One of the most crucial ways of understanding the state is through a focus on the machine that keeps the state running; that is, the bureaucracy. As Bernstein and Mertz have argued, "scholars interested in the workings and the effects of the state should look, at the very least, to the bureaucracies that keep it running" (2011, 6). In neo-Weberian conceptualization, as Paul Bratsis argues, the state is approached as "a distinct actor by virtue of the bureaucratic rationality that unites its members and that provides a socially autonomous set of interests such members act to maximize" (2006, 11). This institutionalist approach implies that a form of subjectivity is invested in the state, such that it becomes *state-as-actor*. Therefore, the institutions of the state act "as if" they are "thinking, calculating agents," thus reifying the state (ibid., 11–12). Therefore, the isolated actions of these agents have far-reaching implications for the everyday well-being of many people. In light of this, Michael Herzfeld alerts us to the experiences of "the pettiest forms of bureaucratic indifference to human needs and sufferings" within "democratic polities designed to benefit all citizens" (1992, 1). It is therefore useful to examine how "people navigate the inexplicable and sometimes horrific experiences of the everyday" bureaucracy (Newell and Okome 2014b, 3). Consequently, ethnographers of bureaucracy have offered some of the most fascinating accounts of ordinary people's experiences of the *(non-) acting* state, particularly in the global south. In offering "rich fieldwork-based information on the workings of actual bureaucracies, the lives and thoughts of bureaucrats, and their public counterparts [I would add, as well as on how ordinary people encounter these bureaucracies and bureaucrats], material often missing from the more formal work done in other fields" (Heyman 2012, 1269), ethnographers such as Ferguson (1900), Blundo, Olivier de Sardan, Arifari, and Alou (2006), Gupta (2012), Hetherington (2011), Hull (2012), Bierschenk and Olivier de Sardan (2014), Blundo (2014), Eckert (2014), Hamani (2014), and Mathur (2015) take us into the interstices of this awesome—and sometimes awful—machine for governing society.

The four chapters in the first section, focusing on South Sudan, Nigeria, and Kenya, examine how the (il)logic of bureaucracies determine and are (re)determined at the confluence of the encounters between the bureaucratic state and regular people. In examining the "important connection between documented citizenry and sociopolitical class in South Sudan," Ferenc Dávid Markó analyses the nature of the troubled South Sudanese state, which had been forced by circumstances to develop "a bifurcated bureaucracy." "This Janus-faced structure," argues Markó, "is growing out of colonial and postcolonial forms and methods of government, further intensified by the inheritance of the civil war, and pressurized by the peace-time *nation-building* narrative." The result of these combination of factors is that "every state office developed separable 'civilian' and 'military clusters,' and the two clusters live in an unequal but symbiotic relationship." Given that the bureaucracy needs to serve everyday needs of people, including filling customs declarations, issuing passports, updating land registry files, and recording court cases, South Sudanese state offices often "find themselves grinding between the contradictions of the need for efficiency and the will to serve the rent-seeking patronage networks." The citizenship office, the focus of this chapter, brings this contradiction into bold relief. For the world's newest "sovereign" state, recently forged out of a long period of war (only to collapse into another civil war), documenting its citizens (and therefore governing its population) is a daunting task. As Markó notes, most of the estimated twelve million citizens possess "no material evidence of their legal belonging to the new state." The complicated and nightmarish process of *proving* belongingness to the South Sudanese state through a unique form of *evidence,* that is, by bringing the applicant's traditional leader and a next-of-kin relative, presents a peculiar form of experience of bureaucratic (ir)rationality. Thus, the proof of citizenship is not only *evidenced* by birth, but through everyday negotiations with various "military clusters" of the state.

Wale Adebanwi and Ebenezer Obadare take up the theme of experiences of the bureaucratic machine by using the concept of "consularity" in reference to "the whole panoply of official and unofficial, bureaucratic and pseudo-bureaucratic practices and processes . . . that the regimes of seeking and applying for visas impose and/or provoke, particularly among those who are least favored in the process of procuring exit visas by the existing circumstances, rules, and requirements imposed by the state." They provide an interesting but troubling account of how young people who are faced with daunting odds in their everyday struggle for survival turn to the subversion of the bureaucratic process of documentation demanded by local and foreign states for granting of visas to travel abroad. For these young people—who invest themselves with the juridical capacity of the local and foreign state to issue, authenticate, and/or legitimize documents—and for their customers, the challenges of making or building decent lives under the harsh conditions of post–Cold War/poststructural adjustment in Nigeria provide powerful excuses for their undertaking. Focusing on Oluwole (faking of documents), which they approach as both locale and practice of a "parallel economy" (of falsification), the authors examine everyday practices in which ordinary people succeed or fail in beating the state in its "game of papers." They conclude that, "fundamentally, this specific practice of forgery is an everyday direct challenge to the state's right to authenticate, to adjudicate between the true and the false, and to determine and delimit the spatial mobility of the 'undesirables' from the margins." Thus, this account provides examples of everyday ruses of powerlessness in response to the everyday (ruses of) power.

Though *formal* bureaucracies are the regular instruments of the modern state for governing populations, where such formal bureaucracies are absent, people have to invent their own informal bureaucratic machines for "self-regulation." Such experiences challenge our understanding of social regulation, particularly in the margins of the state. The challenge is further complicated and made more insightful for our understanding of encounters with the state where such self-regulating groups of people are noncitizens of the state, for example, Somali refugees in Kenya. Fred Ikanda examines such self-regulating in the context of a refugee camp. He analyses how kinship "became an important terrain for realizing bureaucratic aims inside the camps by bringing into dialogue the ethnography of bureaucracy with the literature on humanitarian regimes and Africanist conversations about the relationship between pastoralist peoples and the state." The reproduction of kinship as well as the transformation of kin-based networks of access to resources among the Somali refugees in Kenya, which Ikanda examines, are partly a response to the deliberate *distancing* of the refugees in Dadaab, and, by that token, the distancing of the Kenyan state from them. The chapter shows how kinship contextualizes the work of bureaucracy inside the camp and exposes the inadequacies of the state and humanitarian governance. The everyday experiences of the Somali refugees in the camp in their relationship with the local state and the "international state"—represented and reproduced by international humanitarian organizations—again raises the critical point made by Adorno in *Minima Moralia: Reflections from Damaged Life*, which Judith Butler reformulates as a question: "Can one lead a good life in a bad life?"[28] How do people find purpose for themselves in such "zones of abandonment" (Biehl 2005) where "the good life is structurally or systematically foreclosed for so many" (Butler 2012, 9), such as the Dagahaley camp? And what are the implications of such processes of finding a purpose in life for people's understanding of the state and humanitarian intervention? Ikanda provides some useful answers.

E. Fouksman shows how a development-focused civil society, acting as a "subcontractor of the state," works to transform the ordinarily adversarial relationship between local civil spaces/citizens and the state into a collaborative relationship, thus robbing civil society and citizen groups of their potentially transformational capacity. Thus, international NGOs ensure that, rather than transforming the local state, the local NGOs are deployed to manage and improve aspects of the state's duties—therefore shielding the state from the needed transformation that might make the work of the international NGOs less crucial or even necessary. They also manage the state and its agencies to ensure that they are not encountered in adversarial terms. Therefore, these development-focused NGOs not only depoliticize civil society, they depoliticize the state as well. Using an ethnography of Kenyan citizens' everyday encounters with the state via civil society organizations, Fouksman examines how these NGOs, the international foundations that fund them, and the local groups they collaborate with circulate and filter "certain facts about state mechanisms, legal instruments, and ways of accessing state resources" in facilitating citizens' engagement with the state, while also shaping such engagements and delimiting their form. This is an example of the ways in which the state disguises itself (in this case, as development-focused NGOs) in the process of an assumed positive intervention in the everyday life of regular people, while undermining citizens' capacity to reflect back their critical responses to such interventions.

(Un)Making Lives: The Social Economy of Infrastructure and Shortages

Two of the most expressive means by which the everyday lives of people intersect with the state, thus exposing the (in)capacities of the state and the (ine)quality of generalized care for citizens, are (the availability/quality/cost of) infrastructures and energy. The social economy of everyday life is largely determined by the quality of, as well as access to, infrastructures and services. Against this backdrop, Frank Trentmann has argued that "one way forward for research [on everyday life] is to use moments of disruption such as water scarcity, electric blackouts, and traffic jams as historical passageways into the creation of normality. The normal," he adds, "does not just happen.

Breakdowns reveal the effort needed to integrate technology, meaning, and competence to keep a practice going" (2012, 544; see also Trentmann 2009). In the second section, Ulrika Trovalla and Eric Trovalla as well as Lori Leonard take up this challenge in analyzing how everyday life is permeated by the state in a democratic context through the availability of and access to energy, water, electricity, telephone services, etc.

In examining the everyday experiencing of the Nigerian state as an "infrastructural enigma," the Trovallas depict life in the Nigerian city of Jos as "inextricably nestled into webs of wires, roads, and pipes." Thus, "through the materiality of infrastructure, the state surrounds its citizens, invades their homes, and structures life to such an extent that it becomes part and parcel of nearly any mundane undertaking, aspiration for the future, and memory of the past." For these citizens, the state manifests itself most palpably, the Trovallas argue, "in the riddles and enigmas posed by the severe unpredictability of these grids." In such contexts as this, ordinary people need to acquire *knowledge* about these grids of wires, roads, and pipes and what they *convey* in order to be able to access and/or sustain the services that are central to their lives. However, because of the confusion, inadequacy, and scarcity that attend these services, the process of acquiring critical knowledge about them is akin to one of divination, argue the authors. Thus, everyday life translates to a ritual of gaining *rational* insight into the irrational and erratic nature of infrastructures that are the means of a decent life, not only today, but *tomorrow*. And because, as the authors brilliantly articulate it, "suspicion is deeply engrained in these divination acts, as they almost always deal with possibilities that are imaginable and even plausible but hardly ever resolve into facts," the unreliability and erratic nature of infrastructures "emerge as clues in an ongoing investigation into what the state is, what it used to be, and what it may turn into."

The centrality of the "comings and goings" of socioeconomic *amenities* which, as the Trovallas note, ordinarily should be in the background of people's lives but have been forced to the front and center by inadequacy, inefficiency, and shortages is taken up in Lori Leonard's chapter on Chad. She argues, based on the Chadian context—but this is true of all African contexts—that "shortages are events that contribute to discursive representations of the state as corrupt, inept, punitive, and callous, and shortages also mobilize and assemble consumers, who form queues on major roads and thoroughfares in front of gas stations and other businesses." Following Gupta (1995, 377) and others who have argued that "representations of the state emerge from 'multiply mediated' contexts," Leonard's chapter examines how periodic shortage of cooking gas disturb or disconcert residents and unsettle everyday life in the capital city, N'Djamena. While the shortages localize the state and make it visible, the chapter shows how they also produce certain constructions and representations of the state in public discourse (cf. Gupta 2012, 82), including in terms of the local state's history of entanglements with transnational oil companies.

In important ways, the two chapters in this section point to how the postcolonial state can be represented as well as experienced in terms of its responsibilities—that is, to ensure the conditions for living a good life—as an assemblage of *shortages*.

Disciplinarity, Subjectivity, and Violence

In its *legitimate* use of violence, the everyday state ought to be experienced by a law-abiding citizen only in terms of its positive capacities—that is, the capacity to protect and preserve life. However, in many contexts, to avoid experiencing state violence and other disciplinary regimes of the state that violate or challenge the subjectivity of ordinary people, it is not sufficient that the citizen be law-abiding. Disciplinary power is often not guided by law. This is particularly so in post–Cold War African democracies—in light of the emphasis on the "deregulation of monopolies over the means of legitimate force, of moral orders, of the protection of persons and property" (John L. Comaroff and Jean Comaroff 2006, 2) and despite the high rhetoric of respect for human rights and the personal freedoms of citizens. Though the African state's everyday capacity for efficient and effective *supervision* and *control* of *the population* is challenged, in both senses of being limited and being contested, this does not preclude its general attitude of regarding the people as largely *delinquents* in need of *discipline,* including constant patrol and control as well as punishment. In this context, ordinary people are treated as *objects* of power—and therefore often exposed to both latent and manifest violence. However, in claiming and enacting their subjectivity, ordinary people respond in different ways to the regimes and institutions of discipline and the specific challenges to human possibilities, sometimes through violence.

The three chapters in the third section, by Rose Løvgren, Nicholas Rush Smith, and Daniel Agbiboa, address how everyday life is shaped and reshaped by the experiences of disciplinary regimes and/or violence within specific contexts of social life in Rwanda, South Africa, and Nigeria. Approaching subjectivity as "both a strategy of existence and a material and means of governance" within what João Biehl, Byron Good, and Arthur Kleinman describe as "concrete constellations in which people forge and foreclose their lives around what is most at stake" (2007, 5), Løvgren, Smith, and Agbiboa focus on particular contexts in which certain disciplinary regimes and/or violence provoke and/or contend with particular forms of "strategies of existence."

Rose Løvgren examines how certain regimes of disciplinarity and forms of political subjectivity, that is, "how people relate to power and authority, as well as the role played by structures of power in forming subjective experiences," are informed by the potential of loss of life—as one of her respondents hinted ("It is very easy to lose your life in Rwanda"). Focusing on a country that has experienced the most recent African example of the extreme, devastating consequences of the combination of life-and-death struggle for power and identity politics, Løvgren studies how postgenocide Rwandan forms of governmentality, with its emphasis on, and practices of, compliance, have forced its subjects to accept these practices, thus investing themselves in "patience." "The incessant conflict between repression and evasion, compulsion and adaptation *is the history of everyday life,*" argues Henri Lefebvre (2016, 125, emphasis in original). However, Løvgren counters the tendency to approach the experiencing of the state through polarities. Opening up "a space for questions related to political subjectivity that are currently undertheorized" in the binary analysis of everyday encounters with the state, particularly the special attention paid to resistance, Løvgren shows how an examination of "political subjectivity expressed in patience, acceptance, and compliance, as well as the agency enacted in these attitudes" in the Iwawa Rehabilitation Centre, where the Rwandan state detains male youth termed "delinquent" for one to three years for the purposes of "moral rehabilitation and vocational skills training," can enrich our understanding of everyday experiences of the state under the oxymoronic democratic-authoritarian ruler of Rwanda, Paul Kagame. In the context of *the camp,* Rwandan young men embrace self-regulation, both in order to snatch from the state its power of forced regulation and as a condition of survival under the everyday threat of state violence and even death.

In an examination of the underlying logics of the postapartheid democratic state, using the metaphor of the Golem (which speaks to "the ambivalent nature of the state"), Nicholas Rush Smith places the much-analyzed killings at Marikana in South Africa in relief against the quotidian policing of South Africa's townships as experienced by young township men. The chapter, based on ethnographic research conducted in the townships outside of Durban and Johannesburg in an era when the state decided on the remilitarization of the South African Police Service, provides a poignant example of contexts where, to use Fiona C. Ross's words, "violence—both interpersonal and structural—and forms of what might be characterised as 'uncare' puncture everyday life" (2010, 5). Given the spate of (and rumors of) extrajudicial killings of young Black men by the police, and the pervasive quotidian fears that the actual and rumored killings generated, young men experienced the state as "potentially protective but always at threat of becoming [a danger to its] ostensible citizen-masters." Smith confronts the question of why a postapartheid state that was eager to project and defend the image of a democratic state with one of the world's most progressive rights regimes could also be so eager and willing to emphasize its violent capacity in its everyday relations with its citizens. Yet both the power and the limits of everyday policing are revealed in the episodic nature of police capacity, as evident in the case of the killing, night vigil, and funeral of Juba—one of KwaMashu's best-known gangsters.

In Daniel Agbiboa's chapter, the case of a loosely knit vigilante group of youth in northeast Nigeria organized against the Boko Haram insurgency, the Civilian Joint Task Force (CJTF), complicates the phenomenon of citizens' agency and usurpation of the protective role of the state in response to state delinquency. Agbiboa interrogates "how non/state terror, victimization, and fear shape the everyday survival of civilian communities, and how these communities create a sense of order within an otherwise insecure environment" by "deploying their very insecurity as a resource for collective organizing." He shows that when citizens' groups *play the state* they can complicate the original problem that they seek to (re)solve. The CJTF, by seeking to protect the lives and livelihood of regular people in the absence of, or because of the inadequacy of, state responses, has transformed Boko Haram's "antistate insurgency" into a "messy civil war." Thus, the terrain of everyday life violated and disrupted by the insurgency transforms into a generalized Hobbesian state of nature—a sad but poignant reminder of why we need the state.

The Social Life of Democracy

If we approach democracy and ethnography "as corollary forms of social knowledge and political agency" (Greenhouse and Greenwood 1998, 3), what new directions or attentions might ethnography provide in our study of democratic practices, processes, and institutions? How does ethnography help us in answering the question of what democracy *actually* means—especially in terms of how "it engage[s] with vernacular cultures of participatory politics" (John L. Comaroff and Jean Comaroff 1997a, 123)? Going beyond—or, in fact, *underneath*—"the parochialism and formalism that has so disfigured the academic understanding of [democracy]" (Spencer 2007, 5) would require, among other things, that we (a) pay attention to the everyday grammars of democratic life, including the *vernaculars* or *dialects* of democracy that ordinary people use and act upon in their engagements with democracy and its institutions, as well as in their participation in the democratic process (Banerjee 2008; Nugent 2008, 22; Paley 2008, 7), given that democracy always happens in culturally inflected ways (Spencer 2007, 6); (b) identify phenomena, uncover "hidden transcripts" (Scott 1992), discern irregular (in)actions, and discover the "imaginative potency" (Khilnani 1997, 16, cited in Spencer 2007, 72) unleashed in the *performance* of democracy in specific contexts (Spencer 2007; see also von Schnitzler 2016, esp. chap. 6), which standard modes of studying the democratic process in other disciplines are unable to account for (Paley 2008, 9); (c) examine objects, symbols, and signs that constitute or articulate relationships between the rulers and the ruled and among both categories (see Pype in this volume); (d) reflect on "the technology of democracy—the rituals, procedures, and material culture of the ballot" (Spencer 2007, 75) that, despite and given their mundanity, provide the most ordinary opportunities for most people to connect with the *soul of democracy*—that is, popular participation; and (e) analyze how the ethnographer's own experiences of democracy (either as citizen or foreigner—or even *citizen/foreigner*) and encounters with state and democratic institutions, agencies, personnel, and processes can *regulate* his/her understanding of these institutions, agencies, personnel, and processes (see Orock's chapter in this volume).

The contributors to the fourth section do not address all of these five points. Thus, they represent grounds for further research. Indeed, as Claude Lefort has argued, a spirit of "ubiquitous contingency" (cited in Spencer 2007, 74; see also Hansen 1999, 57) as well as the "radical indeterminacy" inherent in and "engendered by democracy [provide a] compelling . . . object for anthropological enquiry"—though the "empirical evidence for everyday engagement with democratic institutions in all parts of the world is quite simply overwhelming" (Spencer 2007, 74–75).

In her chapter, Katrien Pype provides a refreshing account of everyday engagements with ubiquitous contingencies of democracy and its institutions and processes in the DRC. In providing an account of state-citizen relations in Kinshasa during the final eight years of Joseph Kabila's regime, she articulates regular citizens' everyday enactments of autonomy and critique of the state in their responses to the state as well as their discourse of the Congolese stateness. Focusing on the kind of political subjectivities that "emerge in a Central African city in and through political objects" such as the voter's card (*carte d'élécteur*) and *caméra de surveillance* (surveillance camera), both regarded as "objects [that] constituted building blocks of new relationships between Kabila and Kinois (inhabitants of Kinshasa)," Pype points to citizens' understandings of the state as a trap—therefore provoking acts of camouflage as the best "strategy to engage with the Kabila state."

This chapter reflects on how technology can be used by the "democratic" state to governmentalize its rule, as well as on how the population can, through various kinds of everyday conduct and "misconduct" (including counterfeiting the voter's card), respond to the governmental process. The voter's cards (which also alternate as ID cards) make voters of citizens, though without the rights and privileges of being a citizen. Thus, Kinois have "added new meanings and significance to the document in their everyday lives that [escape] the Kabila state"—including mobilizing the document in the display of "multiple identities, multiple realms of sense-making, and of future-making." The *caméras de surveillance* is "embedded in a *relationship of mutual entrapment.*" Yet there were different interpretations of the meaning and purpose of these objects. Among the many interpretations of the surveillance camera, two can serve as significant examples of how regular people experience the state. The first is that, for many people, the cameras were interpreted not merely as surveillance but as a *reflection* of the Kabila state's fear of regular citizens' mobility and collective power in mobilizing against the state. The second is that people also interpreted the cameras as an *expression* of the fear of potential revolt of elements of the state's own exclusive apparatus of violence, the military. Many of the cameras were assumed to be nonoperational, with the exception of the ones at the entries to the military camps around the city. Thus, the surveillance practices of the state were interpreted as a ruse in a double sense: as a *disguise* of the state's nervousness concerning people's power, and as the state's *pretension* to possessing the power of extraordinary monitoring of potential threats. Yet in a state under the perpetual threat of armed insurrection, mutiny, and civil war—and where, to paraphrase Mbembe (2009a), political time is war time (and vice versa)—life has to go on. In the end, everyday life in the Congo is for those who "*ne craignent pas l'affrontement*" (who don't fear a fight).

Rogers Orock reflects on a similar but different trajectory of documents—that is, national identity cards in Cameroon, "crucial material objects that mediate everyday life"—in what we might call a pseudo-biometric state (Breckenridge 2014) that Rogers describes as a "garrison state." While reflecting on some of the contributions to their edited volume, *Anthropology in the Margins of the State,* Veena Das and Deborah Poole emphasize the "pedagogic aspects of the state [that] are manifested . . . through the practices by which subjects are made to learn the gap between membership and belonging" (2004b, 17). Orock encounters this specific *pedagogy* being produced by one of the most interesting anthropological objects of the contemporary era: the checkpoint (see Jeganathan 2004). Even in a pseudo-biometric state such as Cameroon, what Keith Breckenridge describes as "technologies of identification [that lie] at the heart of the work that the state arrogates to itself" become an "infrastructure of citizenship," critical for identity as well as mobility (2014, 8). Thus, in his analysis of everyday experiences—focused on military/police checkpoints in the context of democracy and the Anglophone revolt in Cameroon—Orock, himself an Anglophone Cameroonian living abroad, finds that the threats, felt by the dominant population, of violence and the potential dissolution of the Cameroonian state dominated by President Paul Biya (seemingly *on behalf* of the

Francophonie), could be a lesson in the differential exposure to arbitrariness which the Anglophone Cameroonians, as well foreign-based Cameroonians, have to contend with. Orock argues that identification documents such as national identity cards can be significant forms of mediation in the relationship between the citizen/subject and the state.

"Do not annoy me this early morning. We are here breaking our sweat for your safety and comfort while you guys are enjoying yourselves abroad. Give me five thousand francs, I say!," a policeman yells at Orock at a security checkpoint, while clutching his gun tightly and pointing it at him. He had just told the policeman he was traveling between Cameroon and Nigeria to attend to a family emergency concerning his mother and brother, and that he did not have any money on him to give to the policeman. "The temporal configuration and experience of such encounters with the arbitrary power of the state," argue Das and Poole, "can also be thought of as . . . highly mobile spaces. . . . These are spaces where the pedagogic claims and assurances of law and the nation become unsettled by state practices" (2004b, 17). Thus, just as Orock's experience shows in his chapter on the everyday challenges of mobility within another of Africa's democratic-authoritarian states, "the military or police checkpoint emerges as a site from which this troubling of expectations and legibilities [of the 'claims and assurances of law and the nation'] rubs up against the [ab]normalcy of the everyday" (ibid., bracketed interpolations mine). Orock's chapter again demonstrates Das and Poole's conclusion that "as a site where assumptions about the security of identity and rights can become suddenly and sometimes violently unsettled, the checkpoint [leads] us to think also about the distinct temporal dynamics surrounding people's interactions with the state and state documents" (ibid., 10).

In his chapter, Justin Pearce also takes up the theme of people's interactions with the state in a democratic context in Mozambique, particularly through the turn and tide of popular (electoral) support for Renamo (Resistência Nacional de Moçambique). Pearce raises a question about how to understand people's everyday engagement with a political party (Renamo) "that simultaneously played a constitutional role in formal politics and violently challenged the state." In much of central and northern Mozambique, "democracy" is not only a formal procedural system and substantive political participation, it also constituted a discourse for the popular evaluation of the actions of the opposition, Renamo, and the state-party, Frelimo (Frente da Libertação de Moçambique). This chapter again illustrates the emphasis in recent literature that, in its practices in specific contexts, democracy has connotations that vary from those associated with Western-style liberal, multiparty democracy (see De Boeck 1996; Englund 2011; Pype 2011). For instance, for the regular people supporting Renamo, the party's antistate violence is "democracy." However, Pearce departs from extant literature in that, rather than analyze democracy as a legitimating concept and practice, he argues that those opposed to the state-party and party-state in Mozambique use democracy as a delegitimizing concept and practice (see Worby 1998 for a contrasting case in Zimbabwe, where the postcolonial regime "claimed the state as an act of redemption" [56]).

Contextualization is important here, though. This is especially so, given that Pearce not only provides the historical backdrop for understanding contemporary experiences of the state under the formalism of *democracy* in Mozambique, but also accounts for regional dimensions of experiences of a state where democratic "goods and rights" are widely regarded as unequally distributed. As Harry G. West similarly observes, through their own experiences the Muedans of Northern Mozambique have concluded that the state devalues its citizens (2008, 111). Against this backdrop, Pearce alerts us to the fact that "democracy," as appropriated in state as well as antistate discourses, has a specific Mozambican history, distinct from other postliberation contexts in Southern Africa. This chapter therefore demonstrates how regular people's discourses of democracy, in the context of the historical evolution of a specific postcolonial state, can illuminate the forms of everyday life assumed to be possible both in their imagination and in *reality*. Thus, the discourses in this chapter "emerge from the daily life of the people [and] address everyday fears and nightmares" (Geschiere 1997, 7).

Everyday Politics of Rights and Responsibility: Education, Welfare, and Health

The simultaneous mutuality and hostility between rights and responsibilities of the state and citizens experienced in different African contexts took a new turn as most of the states in the continent returned to plural democratic rule in the last decade of the twentieth century. However, the literature on democracy focusing on this era has paid more attention to *rights claims* by regular citizens than *responsibility claims*. Yet one of the core practical manifestations of the regime of rights enjoyed by citizens in the democratic states is based on the politics of responsibility—of the state as well as of the citizens. The manifold changes witnessed in Africa since the end of the Cold War, as Rubbers and Jedlowski argue, "have transformed the way in which [responsibility] is imagined, discussed and organized in African societies" (2019, 1). Among the very interesting perspectives for understanding emergent regimes of responsibility, therefore, is the examination of "the mechanisms through which responsibility is generated, imputed or claimed by institutional and non-institutional actors" (ibid., 2). However, Barry D. Adam reminds us that "everyday life often presents competing and inconsistent emotions and rationalities that make the execution of a singular ethic hard to realize even with the best of intentions" (2017, 187).

Leading off the fourth section with a very nuanced and stimulating analysis of the confluence of the (enactment of the) *idea of the state* and *state effects,* Jennifer Riggan throws into sharp relief the challenges of the everyday politics of rights and responsibility by examining Ethiopia's Civic and Ethical Education (CEE), a program designed by the "democratic" Ethiopian state to teach young people about liberal, democratic, constitutional governance in the post-1991 era. She argues that, as agents of the state with their own autonomy, "teachers give us a particular insight into the everyday state because they are not only charged with navigating the shifting fault line between state repression and revolutionary change but *constitute* that fault line." She argues further that, though the ruling EPRDF has failed to practice liberal democracy, it "has done a very good job of educating the population about liberal, constitutional, democratic ideas"—thus, even if not deliberately, creating "a desire for democracy that is asynchronous with everyday encounters and experiences with the authoritarian state."

Riggan's account returns us to the crucial nature of pedagogy in state-citizen relations. Indeed, civics, as a subject of study, is the pedagogic embodiment of the everydayness of ethical state-citizen relationship—encompassing (the projections and/or reality of) both rights and duties. Thus, when political intentions are challenged by everyday experience, as Riggan found in the Ethiopian case, a paradox arises at the heart of the state project. The experience of the teacher who was detained by security forces for answering a question posed by her student about the arrest of protesters—given that she had taught them about the right to protest—reflects, for the author, the simultaneously politicizing and de-politicizing dimensions of the CEE, as pedagogy and as everyday political practice. Overall, Riggan uses this chapter to raise critical questions central to the ethnography of the state and democracy in Africa, particularly in contexts in which "the promotion of the idea of [a particular state] as a liberal democracy [creates] a desire for democracy that is asynchronous with everyday encounters and experiences."

Edoardo Quaretta also addresses the question of responsibility, this time at the level of the state, but still within the ambit of education. However, in contrast to the Ethiopian case examined by Riggan, in which education and pedagogy were central to the state project, Quaretta studies the case of the abandonment of state responsibilities in the area of education. This abandonment is one fact of the general experience of the Congolese, because "the Congolese state is not a welfare state able to provide public services to its citizens." Focusing on two schools in Lubumbashi, a high school in the suburbs and a Catholic school complex in the city center, Quaretta shows that schools are (adopting Anselm Strauss's term) a "negotiated order" through which ordinary people and institutional actors (state and nonstate agents) not only "enable the educational sector to survive," but "shape ideas about the postcolonial state." This, the author reminds us, is evident in the popular Congolese painting, the *Parlements Debout* (standup parliament), in which groups of parents are seen discussing school fees, the quality of education, politics, and state institutions. This chapter points strongly to the fact that these "standup parliaments" are not mere reflections of *discourses* about education, public life, and the state; they capture the *concrete* experiences of Lushois (inhabitants of Lubumbashi) regarding the consequences of the presence/absence of the state in their everyday life. A complex of consequences results from this reality. While the absence of public school is, for people, the clearest sign of the state's lack of interest in the well-being of the population, interpersonal relationships in the community fill the space that should have been occupied by the state—with the Catholic parish becoming the institutional agent regulating the governance of the school. A form of "bureaucracy" is then invented to take charge, and this involves "a process of depersonalization and mechanization of relationships and social practices." The decrease in social negotiation, increase in school effectiveness, individualization of school costs, and limitations to school access that result from this (un)usual situation are part of the complicated results of *replacing* the "sorcerer" state—one which, like the witch, not only disregards the welfare and well-being of others, but *eats* others to nourish itself.

The "absent-present" state is neither limited to the education sector, nor is it an exclusive phenomenon of the Congolese state. Apart from education, another critical area of public life where the politics of rights and responsibility—in their "absence-presence"—is contentious is that of health services. In the final chapter of this book, Helle Samuelsen examines the "often shambolic relationship between rural citizens and the public health care system" in Burkina Faso, as well as the consequences for these citizens and their mistrust of the democratic state. Significantly, Samuelsen notes that in their everyday life, next to the school, the local dispensary is the most important institution of the state and the one with which citizens in Keru have the most contact. She provides a challenging account of the relationship between citizens and the public health *care* system in rural Burkina Faso that points to the fragility of the system from the point of view of both patients and health care workers. The question of *knowledge* again surfaces here. There is mutual awareness on the part of the people and health care workers of the everyday and long-term "diagnostic limitations at the dispensary." Therefore, the people turn to traditional healers, a practice which the health care workers are not only aware of but to which they seem to reconcile themselves.

One of the reviewers of this volume alerted us to questions of state violence and state failure that might arise in reaction to some of the chapters in this volume by asking, "Is there another way of conceptualizing the African state outside violence?" The answer is a definite yes. Indeed, this is central to our goals in this volume. In providing an account of views "from below" on the state and democracy, unlike prevailing views on the state and democracy in Africa, the contributors refrain from deciding *what either the state or democracy is* in each of the African states in focus. Rather, they let everyday people *speak* about their quotidian experiences or encounters with the state. Again, we do not assume state failure. On the contrary, we let everyday people reflect (on) how the state and democracy *perform* in every context. In fact, with the exception of four chapters—those by Smith, Agbiboa, Orock, and Pearce—(threats of or actual) physical violence is not central to how most of the authors approach their subjects. Where their subjects experienced the state and its institutions as doing violence (manifest or latent) to them, the authors explore such experiences or encounters. The core project, however, is to examine what constitutes the state and democracy for everyday people in their quotidian lives. If direct or indirect (manifest or latent, physical or nonphysical) violence is a major part of this, we do not ignore it.

Reflecting on our subjects' critique of the everyday life that they are involved in does not constitute "Afro-pessimism." Indeed, through these ethnographies, we are suggesting that the exploration of how people negotiate their everyday life is an *Afro-optimist* endeavor, in that this approach gives attention to people's everyday resourcefulness, creativity, ingenuity, and cheerfulness in the face of daunting odds. The general statistics about the quality of life in Africa already point to the devastating odds that many Africans are compelled to live with.[29] Rather than regurgitating such statistics and presenting the mass of Africans who face these challenges as lacking agency, we explore the ways in which, to paraphrase Judith Butler (2012), people try to make a "good life" out of a "bad life"—by sidestepping or going past, ignoring, cheating, duping, conning, collaborating with, or pooling resources with others, state agencies, or agents, and nurturing, cultivating, or fostering some positive aspects of the state institutions (even when, sometimes, any one of these means of maneuvering could invite regime violence in the immediate), all in order to expand the possibilities of everyday life. Thus, what many of the chapters that highlight some measure of potential or actual state violence show is how people *keep keeping on*, sometimes through "inventive practices" (Hamani 2014), living their lives, or *making* their lives, despite the odds. The "detailed, vivid, and richly textured ethnography and historiography of life-forms" (as Mbembe would describe them) contained in this book offer, we believe, "powerful examples of how we should think and write about human agency, as well as what analytical strategies we should deploy in order to describe and interpret specific forms of social life in particular settings" (Mbembe 2021, 26).

The "*effectivity* of the mundane and the ordinary" (Painter 2006, 761, emphasis in original), as evident in the chapters of this book, is connected to, contends with, makes manifest, contests, and/or extends "the myriad mundane actions of officials, clerks, police officers, inspectors, teachers, social workers, doctors, and so on" (ibid.). Perhaps the most striking attribute that runs through the lives of the everyday people readers will encounter in this book is their capacity for endurance in the face of great hardships, including their "capacity to make the best of very little" (Mbembe 2009b, 155): "the extraordinary strength of familial forms of solidarity; the virtues of openness and hospitality; all those small acts of everyday life . . . ; the vitality of intellectual reflection, and that kind of pride and natural self-respect that [reflect] a self-presence that colonialism was not able to destroy" (ibid.).[30] The chapters in this volume not only contribute to a localized and more nuanced understanding of the everyday state and democracy in Africa, they also provide the basis for comparative ethnographic analysis of the state and democracy in Africa and beyond. Additionally, the book offers a pathway for further ethnographic analysis of the state and democracy in the global south. Perhaps the most critical significance of the volume, however, is that it illuminates, in a *decentered* way, the living practices of people in different parts of Africa as they experience the state and the democratic process.[31]

Notes

I thank the Oxford School of Global and Area Studies for its grant from the Higher Studies Trust Fund in support of my research. I am also grateful to Katrien Pype and Rogers Orock, who read and commented on the draft of this introduction, and the publishers' anonymous reviewers for their insightful comments. I am grateful to Richard Werbner for our conversation on the work of the Manchester School.

1. In 1997, Rosemary Coombe declared "civil society" as "ripe for anthropological debate and ethnographic consideration," even while admitting that "political anthropologists have come rather lately to debates about civil society," although "not because it is peripheral to the issues they address" (Coombe 1997, 1). Different emphases on the "pathologies" of the state in Africa have provoked interesting descriptions, such as "swollen state" (Diamond 1987), "rentier state" (Yates 1996), "over-developed state" (Leys 1976), "weak state" (Jackson and Rosberg 1982), and "rhizome state" (Bayart 1993). For two examples of critical perspectives on the state in Africa, see Ake (1985), and Saul (1979).

2. The latter phrase, which I am emphasizing, constitutes Fortes and Evans-Pritchard's euphemistic description of colonialists.

3. For a discussion of the mission of the Rhodes-Livingstone Institute, "from which the Manchester School arose," see Werbner, *Anthropology after Gluckman,* 2020. Werbner raises critical questions about the focus and contributions of the Manchester School—reflecting the heritage of the RLI—which are relevant to my argument here.

4. Goody came to this conclusion even while noting the extant work in this area, including that of Fortes and Evans-Pritchard (1940), Schapera (1956), Southall (1956), Colson (1958), and Mair (1962) (see Goody 1971, 99, 10, and 17). In email exchanges, Richard Werbner, who is not only a product but a historian of the Manchester School of Anthropology, agreed that "more attention to the State came for [the] Manchester [School] in the [19]70s and after with [the] generation after the greats in the [Rhodes-Livingstone Institute]" (email to author, 12 May 2021).

5. On "primitive" peoples and tribes, see Archie Mafeje's critique of "anthropological misdirection" in the study of Africa in "The Ideology of 'Tribalism'" (1971).

6. Aidan Southall argues that, as African countries approached or achieved independence in the 1950s and 1960s, "the dominant interests of social anthropology no longer focused on political structure or the state" as anthropologists instead concentrated "on intensive microstudies of political behavior and processes" (1974, 154).

7. Two of the most important volumes published in this era include Marc J. Swartz, Victor W. Turner, and Arthur Tuden, eds., *Political Anthropology* (1966) and Marc J. Swartz, ed., *Local-Level Politics* (1968). Such had been the dominance of *African Political Systems* that Chandra Jayawardena celebrated the publication of *Political Anthropology* on behalf of "teachers who have long felt the need to replace" the 1940 volume, though seven of the seventeen essays in it are on African communities. Seven of the seventeen cases in *Local-Level Politics* are also on Africa. See Jayawardena's (1968) review of *Political Anthropology* in *American Anthropologist;* and Ronald Cohen's (1969, 590) review of *Local-Level Politics.*

8. Earlier in chapter 2 of *Order and Rebellion in Tribal Africa,* Gluckman also examines similar issues about a "relatively stable political system" (84).

9. I thank one of the anonymous reviewers for alerting me to aspects of the more complicated genealogy of the study of the political and the state in anthropology.

10. It is significant that, in the two volumes, the Comaroffs are emphatic about the value of everyday life in understanding the transformative possibilities in the Tswana's encounter with Missionary Christianity and the colonial state.

11. Such is the complexity of these "reciprocal determinations" that, in the case of the pastoral Orma of Northeastern Kenya, as Jean Ensminger finds, "the shift away from local autonomy is not merely an exogenous change forced upon the Orma by the state, but reflects a perceived need (at least by some segment of the population) for change in local institutions" (Ensminger 1990, 663).

12. Vincent has explained that part of what led to her important book was her "anti-structuralist, or anti-the Africa that I was taught, with its emphasis on kinship, community, social order, and stability. I see far more need for recognition of

'men in motion,' social fields, power, violence, and global relations" (Nugent 1999, 539). As a reflection of the significance of *Anthropology and Politics* at the time it was published, in his review, John Middleton stated that the book was "especially welcome in light of the recent proliferation of course offerings *at the margins of the discipline, blurring social anthropology around the edges*" (1996, 121, emphasis added).

13. Not in the sense in which Giovanni Botero used this phrase in his *Della ragion di stato* (*The Reason of State*)—a sixteenth-century work of political philosophy which examines how to acquire, preserve, and augment the dominion of the state. Here it means the fundamental purposes of the state.

14. See Worby 1998; Frederiksen 2000; Chabedi 2003; Buur and Jensen 2004; Blundo et al. 2006; Ismail 2006; Smith 2007; Blundo and Le Meur 2008; Lockhart 2008; Rodgers 2008; Burchardt 2009; Engelke 2010; Adebanwi and Obadare 2010; Ross 2010; Friedman 2011; Grunebaum 2011; Ibrahim and Shepler 2011; Wasserman 2011; Enwezor and Bester 2013; Ferme 2013; Bierschenk and Olivier de Sardan 2014; Newell and Okome 2014a; Obarrio 2014; Fourchard and Segatti 2015; Salomon 2016; Adebanwi 2017; Schubert 2017; Newcomb 2017; Di Nunzio 2019; and Paller 2019. For the literature beyond Africa, see de Certeau 1984; Cohen 1962; Scott 1998; Hansen and Stepputat 2001; Highmore 2002a, 2002b; De Genova 2002; Lefebvre 2016; Bernstein and Mertz 2011; Rudolph and Jacobsen 2006a; Ginsborg 2005; and Thelen, Vetters, and von Benda-Beckmann 2018b.

15. By "grammars" we do not mean merely the languages/symbols/discourses of the state, but also how languages/symbols/discourses figure in, shape, and are shaped by practical experiences and the concreteness that the state assumes or achieves in the everyday lives of people—including how they are able to *speak* to, about, and with the state and thus enfold themselves in the processes that continue to authorize the state. While Hansen and Stepputat (2001) use the apt term "languages of stateness" to describe both representations of the state and state practices (cf. Thelen, Vetters, and Benda-Beckmann 2018b, 3), we prefer "grammars," because grammars point more specifically to the *systems, structures,* and *rules* that govern a set of practices or the particular social uses to which something is deployed.

16. Ginsborg's "concentric rings of connection" seem to mirror Henri Lefebvre's (2016, 5) philosophical conclusion that "everyday life is composed of cycles within wider cycles."

17. Though Migdal and Schlichte (2005) and others emphasize the "idea" (singular) of the state, I argue that in their encounters with the state and in the daily practices of the state, people derive different and not always coherent *ideas* of the state.

18. Translation of quote by Frank Trentmann, 2012.

19. It is instructive that Lefebvre also describes everyday life as "products," in terms of how this is produced in particular social contexts by the total organization of power. He states that, "as a compendium of seemingly unimportant activities and of *products* and exhibits other than natural, everyday life is more than something that eludes natural, divine and human myths" (2016, 12, emphasis added).

20. As Trentmann reminds us, "in [its] earlier gestation . . . everyday life was a utopia of modernization, directed by states, experts, and social movements" (2012, 524).

21. For instance, de Certeau notes that, "If it is true that the grid of [Foucauldian] 'discipline' is everywhere becoming clearer and more extensive, it is all the more urgent to discover how an entire society resists being reduced to it, what popular procedures (also 'miniscule' and quotidian) manipulate the mechanisms of discipline and conform to them only in order to evade them, and finally, what 'ways of operating' form the counterpart, on the consumer's (or 'dominee's'?) side, of the mute processes that organize the establishment of socioeconomic order" (1984, xiv).

22. For a proficient review of this history, see Trentmann 2012.

23. Trotsky even urged the speeding up of the education of "agitators against custom," among others, leading to the possibility that in the near future "we may have to institute a course of lectures on questions relating to the customs of everyday life" (1973, 89).

24. Di Nunzio has argued correctly, based on his ethnography of street life in Ethiopia, that "living contained the seeds of open-endedness, possibility, and reversibility" (2019, 4). See also Lockhart 2008.

25. Richard Werbner describes what Schubert calls "arcane, yet . . . self-evident, knowledge" as "the practical wisdom of everyday life" (2002, 2).

26. See Olufemi Taiwo (2010) for a brilliant take on the domestication of the Enlightenment in Africa.

27. For an example of the search for the "ideal face of the state," see Obeid 2010.

28. Butler 2012. Adorno's assertion that "wrong life cannot be lived rightly" (originally, "Es gibt kein richtiges Leben im falschen") is found in Theodor Adorno, *Minima Moralia,* trans. E. F. N. Jephcott (London: Verso, 1974), 39.

29. Though Mbembe (2021) admits that, in Africa, "a huge amount of labor is still put into eliminating want, repairing that which has been broken, making life possible, or simply maintaining it" (12), he highlights "a way of defining and reading African life-forms that . . . turns to statistical indices to measure the gap between what Africa is and what we are told it ought to be," describing this as a "way of reading [that] always ends up constructing Africa as a pathological case, as a figure of lack. It is a set of statements that tell us what Africa *is not.* It never tells us what it *actually is*" (26, emphasis in original).

30. In a different context, this "vitality of intellectual reflection" displayed by regular people has been described by Mbembe as their ability to "build up a system of intelligibility to which they can refer in order to explain the causes and effects of various phenomena . . . in order to determine the domains of what is possible and feasible" (Mbembe 2000, 272).

31. I thank one of the reviewers for the reminder about the important point regarding our "decentered" approach, as reflected in the preface by the Comaroffs.

References

Abrams, Philip. 1988. "Notes on the Difficulty of Studying the State (1977)." *Journal of Historical Sociology* 1 (1): 58–89.

Adam, Barry D. 2017. "The Politics of Responsibility in HIV." In *Competing Responsibilities: The Ethics and Politics of Contemporary Life*, edited by Susanna Trnka and Catherine Trundle, 181–92. Durham, NC: Duke University Press.

Adebanwi, Wale, ed. 2017. *The Political Economy of Everyday Life in Africa: Beyond the Margins*. Woodbridge, Suffolk, UK: James Currey.

Adebanwi, Wale, and Ebenezer Obadare, eds. 2010. *Encountering the Nigerian State*. New York: Palgrave Macmillan.

Ake, Claude. 1985. "The Future of the State in Africa." *International Political Science Review/Revue internationale de science politique* 6 (1): 105–14.

———. 2000. *The Feasibility of Democracy in Africa*. Dakar: Council for the Development of Social Science Research in Africa.

Allen, Chris. 1997. "Who Needs Civil Society?" *Review of African Political Economy* 24 (73): 329–37.

Apter, Andrew. 1987. "Things Fell Apart? Yoruba Responses to the 1983 Elections in Ondo State, Nigeria." *Journal of Modern African Studies* 25 (3): 489–503.

Banerjee, Mukulika. 2008. "Democracy, Sacred and Everyday: An Ethnographic Case from India." In Paley 2008a, 63–95.

Bayart, Jean François. 1986. "Civil Society in Africa." In *Political Domination in Africa: Reflections on the Limits of Power*, edited by Patrick Chabal, 109–25. Cambridge: Cambridge University Press.

———. 1993. *The State in Africa: The Politics of the Belly*. New York: Longman.

Bayart, Jean-François, Stephen Ellis, and Béatrice Hibou. 1999. *The Criminalization of the State in Africa*. Oxford: James Currey.

Bernstein, Anya, and Elizabeth Mertz. 2011. "Introduction: Bureaucracy: Ethnography of the State in Everyday Life." *PoLAR: Political and Legal Anthropology Review* 34 (1): 6–10.

Biehl, João. 2005. *Vita: Life in a Zone of Social Abandonment*. Berkeley: University of California Press.

Biehl, João, Byron Good, and Arthur Kleinman. 2007. "Introduction: Rethinking Subjectivity." In *Subjectivity: Ethnographic Investigations*, edited by João Biehl, Byron Good, and Arthur Kleinman, 1–23. Berkeley: University of California Press.

Bierschenk, Thomas, and Jean-Pierre Olivier de Sardan. 2014. *States at Work: Dynamics of African Bureaucracies*. Leiden: Brill.

Blundo, Giorgio. 2014. "Seeing Like a State Agent: The Ethnography of Reform in Senegal's Forestry Services." In Bierschenk and Olivier de Sardan 2014, 69–89.

Blundo, Giorgio, and Pierre-Yves Le Meur, eds. 2008. *The Governance of Daily Life in Africa: Ethnographic Explorations of Public and Collective Services*. Leiden: Brill.

Blundo, Giorgio, and Jean-Pierre Olivier de Sardan. 2006. "Why Should We Study Everyday Corruption and How Should We Go About It?" In Blundo et al. 2006, 3–14.

Blundo, Giorgio, Jean-Pierre Olivier de Sardan, Nassirou Bako Arifari, and Mahaman Tidjani Alou, eds. 2006. *Everyday Corruption and the State: Citizens and Public Officials in Africa*. London: Zed Books.

Bratsis, Peter. 2006. *Everyday Life and the State*. Boulder, CO: Paradigm.

Bratton, Michael, and Nicholas van de Walle. 1997. *Democratic Experiments in Africa: Regime Transitions in Comparative Perspective*. Cambridge: Cambridge University Press.

Breckenridge, Keith. 2014. *Biometric State: The Global Politics of Identification and Surveillance in South Africa, 1850 to the Present.* Cambridge: Cambridge University Press.

Burchardt, Marian. 2009. "Subjects of Counselling: Religion, HIV/AIDS and the Management of Everyday Life in South Africa." In *Aids and Religious Practice in Africa,* edited by Felicitas Becker and P. Wenzel Geissler, 333–58. Leiden: Brill.

Butler, Judith. 2012. "Can One Lead a Good Life in a Bad Life?" *Radical Philosophy,* no. 176 (November–December): 9–18.

Butler, Judith, and Athena Athanasiou. 2013. *Dispossession: The Performative in the Political.* Cambridge: Polity.

Buur, Lars, and Steffen Jensen. 2004. "Introduction: Vigilantism and the Policing of Everyday Life in South Africa." *African Studies* 63 (2): 139–52.

Chabal, Patrick. 2009. *Africa: The Politics of Suffering and Smiling.* London: Zed Books.

Chabal, Patrick, and Jean-Pascal Daloz. 1999. *Africa Works: Disorder as Political Instrument.* Oxford: James Currey.

Chabedi, Marks. 2003. "State Power, Violence, Crime and Everyday Life: A Case Study of Soweto in Post-apartheid South Africa." *Social Identities: Journal for the Study of Race, Nation and Culture* 9 (3): 357–71.

Cohen, Ronald. 1962. "Everyday Life in Africa." *International Journal* 17 (1): 34–39.

———. 1969. Review of *Local Level Politics: Social and Cultural Perspectives,* edited by Marc J. Swartz. *American Political Science Review* 63 (2): 590–91.

Colson, Elizabeth. 1958. "The Role of Bureaucratic Norms in African Political Structures." In *Systems of Political Control and Bureaucracy in Human Societies,* edited by Verne F. Ray, 42–49. Seattle: University of Washington Press for the American Ethnological Society.

Comaroff, Jean, and John L. Comaroff. 1991. *Of Revelation and Revolution.* Vol. 1, *Christianity, Colonialism, and Consciousness in South Africa.* Chicago: University of Chicago Press.

———, eds. 2006. *Law and Disorder in the Postcolony.* Chicago: University of Chicago Press.

Comaroff, John L., and Jean Comaroff. 1997a. "Postcolonial Politics and Discourses of Democracy in Southern Africa: An Anthropological Reflection on African Political Modernities." *Journal of Anthropological Research* 53 (2): 123–46.

———. 1997b. *Of Revelation and Revolution.* Vol. 2, *The Dialectics of Modernity on a South African Frontier.* Chicago: University of Chicago Press.

———. 1999. "Introduction." In *Civil Society and the Political Imagination in Africa: Critical Perspectives,* edited by John L. Comaroff and Jean Comaroff, 1–43. Chicago: University of Chicago Press.

———. 2006. "Law and Disorder in the Postcolony: An Introduction." In Jean Comaroff and John L. Comaroff 2006, 1–56.

Coombe, Rosemary J. 1997. "Identifying and Engendering the Forms of Emergent Civil Societies: New Directions in Political Anthropology." *PoLAR: Political and Legal Anthropology Review* 20 (1): 1–12.

Das, Veena, and Deborah Poole, eds. 2004a. *Anthropology in the Margins of the State.* Sante Fe, NM: School of American Research Press.

Das, Veena, and Deborah Poole. 2004b. "State and Its Margins: Comparative Ethnographies." In Das and Poole 2004a, 3–33.

De Boeck, Filip. 1996. "Postcolonialism, Power and Identity: Local and Global Perspectives from Zaire." In *Postcolonial Identities in Africa,* edited by Richard Werbner and Terence Ranger, 76–106. London: Zed Books.

de Certeau, Michel. 1984. *The Practice of Everyday Life.* Translated by Steven F. Rendall. Berkeley: University of California Press. Originally published as *L'invention du quotidien.* Vol. 1, *Arts de faire* (Paris: Union générale d'éditions, 1980).

De Genova, Nicholas P. 2002. "Migrant 'Illegality' and Deportability in Everyday Life." *Annual Review of Anthropology* 31:419–47.

Diamond, Larry. 1987. "Class Formation in the Swollen African State." *Journal of Modern African Studies* 25 (4): 567–96.

———. 1999. *Developing Democracy: Toward Consolidation.* Baltimore: Johns Hopkins University Press.

Diamond, Larry, Marc F. Plattner, Yun-han Chu, and Hung-mao Tien. 1997. *Consolidating the Third Wave Democracies: Themes and Perspectives.* Baltimore: Johns Hopkins University Press.

Di Nunzio, Marco. 2019. *The Act of Living: Street Life, Marginality, and Development in Urban Ethiopia.* Ithaca, NY: Cornell University Press.

Dubois, Vincent. 2018. "The State, Legal Rigor, and the Poor: The Daily Practice of Welfare Control." In Thelen, Vetters, and von Benda-Beckmann 2018a, 38–55.

Eckert, Andreas. 2014. "'We Must Run While Others Walk': African Civil Servants, State Ideologies and Bureaucratic Practices in Tanzania, from the 1950s to the 1970s." In Bierschenk and Olivier de Sardan 2014, 205–19.

Ekeh, Peter P. 1975. "Colonialism and the Two Publics in Africa: A Theoretical Statement." *Comparative Studies in Society and History* 17 (1): 91–112.

Engelke, Matthew. 2010. "Past Pentecostalism: Notes on Rupture, Realignment, and Everyday Life in Pentecostal and African Independent Churches." *Africa* 80 (2): 177–99.

Englund, Harri. 2011. *Human Rights and African Airwaves: Mediating Equality on the Chichewa Radio.* Bloomington: Indiana University Press.

Ensminger, Jean. 1990. "Co-opting the Elders: The Political Economy of State Incorporation in Africa." *American Anthropologist,* n.s., 92 (3): 662–75.

Enwezor, Okwui, and Rory Bester. 2013. *Rise and Fall of Apartheid: Photography and the Bureaucracy of Everyday Life.* New York: International Center of Photography.

Fassin, Didier. 2018. *Life: A Critical User's Manual.* Medford, MA: Polity.

Ferguson, James. 1990. *The Anti-Politics Machine: "Development," Depoliticization, and Bureaucratic Power in Lesotho.* Cambridge: Cambridge University Press.

———. 1999. *Expectations of Modernity: Myths and Meanings of Urban Life on the Zambian Copperbelt.* Berkeley: University of California Press.

———. 2006. "The Anti-Politics Machine." In Sharma and Gupta 2006a, 270–86.

Ferme, Mariane C. 2004. "Deterritorialized Citizenship and the Resonances of the Sierra Leonean State." In Das and Poole 2004a, 81–115.

———. 2013. "Introduction: Localizing the State." *Anthropological Quarterly* 86 (4): 957–63.

Fortes, Meyer, and E. E. Evans-Pritchard, eds. 1940. *African Political Systems.* Oxford: Oxford University Press.

Foucault, Michel. 1991. *The Foucault Effect: Studies in Governmentality*. Edited by Graham Burchell, Colin Gordon, and Peter Miller. London: Harvester, Wheatsheaf.

Fourchard, Laurent, and Aurelia Segatti. 2015. "Introduction of Xenophobia and Citizenship: The Everyday Politics of Exclusion and Inclusion in Africa." *Africa* 85 (1): 2–12.

Frederiksen, Bodil Folke. 2000. "Popular Culture, Gender Relations and the Democratization of Everyday Life in Kenya." *Journal of Southern African Studies* 26 (2): 209–22.

Friedman, John T. 2011. *Imagining the Post-apartheid State: An Ethnographic Account of Namibia*. New York: Berghahn Books.

Fuller, C. J., and Véronique Benei, eds. 2000. *The Everyday State and Society in Modern India*. New Delhi: Esha Béteille Social Science Press.

Fuller, C. J., and John Harriss. 2000. "For an Anthropology of the Modern Indian State." In Fuller and Benei 2000, 2–30.

Geschiere, Peter. 1982. *Village Communities and the State: Changing Relations among the Maka of Southeastern Cameroon since the Colonial Conquest*. London: Kegan Paul.

———. Peter. 1997. *The Modernity of Witchcraft: Politics and the Occult in Postcolonial Africa*. Charlottesville: University Press of Virginia.

Ginsborg, Paul. 2005. *The Politics of Everyday Life: Making Choices, Changing Lives*. New Haven, CT: Yale University Press.

Gluckman, Max. 1963. *Order and Rebellion in Tribal Africa*. London: Cohen and West.

———. 1965. *Politics, Law and Ritual in Tribal Society*. Oxford: Basil Blackwell.

Goldman, Marcio. 2013. *How Democracy Works: An Ethnographic Theory of Politics*. Herefordshire, UK: Sean Kingston.

Goody, Jack. 1971. *Technology, Tradition and the State in Africa*. Oxford: Oxford University Press.

Greenhouse, Carol J., and Davydd J. Greenwood. 1998. "Introduction: The Ethnography of Democracy and Difference." In *Democracy and Ethnography: Constructing Identities in Multicultural Liberal States*, edited by Carol J. Greenhouse with Roshanak Kheshti, 1–24. Albany: State University of New York Press.

Grunebaum, Heidi Peta. 2011. *Memorializing the Past: Everyday Life in South Africa after the Truth and Reconciliation Commission*. New Brunswick, NJ: Transaction.

Gupta, Akhil. 1995. "Blurred Boundaries: The Discourse of Corruption, the Culture of Politics, and the Imagined State." *American Ethnologist* 22 (2): 375–402.

———. 2012. *Red Tape: Bureaucracy, Structural Violence, and Poverty in India*. Durham, NC: Duke University Press.

Hamani, Oumarou. 2014. "'We Make Do and Keep Going!' Inventive Practices and Ordered Informality in the Functioning of the District Courts in Niamey and Zinder (Niger)." In Bierschenk and Olivier de Sardan 2014, 145–73.

Hann, Chris. 1996. "Introduction: Political Society and Civil Anthropology." In *Civil Society: Challenging Western Models*, edited by Chris Hann and Elizabeth Dunn. EASA Monographs series. London: Routledge.

Hansen, Thomas Blom. 1999. *The Saffron Wave: Democracy and Hindu Nationalism in Modern India*. Princeton, NJ: Princeton University Press.

Hansen, Thomas Blom, and Finn Stepputat. 2001. "Introduction: States of Imagination." In *States of Imagination: Ethnographic Explorations of the Postcolonial*

State, edited by Thomas Blom Hansen and Finn Stepputat, 1–38. Durham, NC: Duke University Press.

Heller, Agnes. 1978. *Das Alltagsleben: Versuch einer Erklärung der individuellen Reproduktion.* Translated by Peter Kain. Frankfurt: Suhrkamp. Originally published as *A mindennapi élet* (Budapest: Akadémiai Kiadó, 1970).

Herzfeld, Michael. 1992. *The Social Production of Indifference: Exploring the Symbolic Roots of Western Bureaucracy.* Chicago: University of Chicago Press.

Hetherington, Kregg. 2011. *Guerrilla Auditors: The Politics of Transparency in Neoliberal Paraguay.* Durham, NC: Duke University Press.

Heyman, Josiah. 2012. "Deepening the Anthropology of Bureaucracy." Review of *Red Tape: Bureaucracy, Structural Violence, and Poverty in India,* by Akhil Gupta; *Guerrilla Auditors: The Politics of Transparency in Neoliberal Paraguay,* by Kregg Hetherington; and *Government of Paper: The Materiality of Bureaucracy in Urban Pakistan,* by Matthew S. Hull. *Anthropological Quarterly* 85 (4): 1269–77.

Highmore, Ben. 2002a. *Everyday Life and Cultural Theory: An Introduction.* New York: Routledge.

———. 2002b. "Introduction: Questioning Everyday Life." In *The Everyday Life Reader,* edited by Ben Highmore, 1–34. New York: Routledge.

Hull, Mathew S. 2012. *Government of Paper: The Materiality of Bureaucracy in Urban Pakistan.* Berkeley: University of California Press.

Hyden, Goran. 1980. *Beyond Ujamaa in Tanzania: Underdevelopment and an Uncaptured Peasantry.* Berkeley: University of California Press.

Ibrahim, Aisha Fofana, and Susan Shepler. 2011. "Introduction," in "Everyday Life in Postwar Sierra Leone." Special issue, *Africa Today* 58 (2): v–xii.

Ismail, Salwa. 2006. *Political Life in Cairo's New Quarters: Encountering the Everyday State.* Minneapolis: University of Minnesota Press.

Jackson, Robert H., and Carl G. Rosberg. 1982. "Why Africa's Weak States Persist: The Empirical and the Juridical in Statehood." *World Politics* 35 (1): 1–24.

James, William. 1975. *Pragmatism.* Cambridge, MA: Harvard University Press.

Jayawardena, Chandra. 1968. Review of *Political Anthropology,* edited by Marc J. Swartz, Victor W. Turner, and Arthur Tuden. *American Anthropologist* 70 (4): 764–66.

Jeganathan, Pradeep. 2004. "Checkpoint: Anthropology, Identity, and the State." In Das and Poole 2004a, 67–80.

Jessop, Bob. 1977. "Recent Theories of the Capitalist State." *Cambridge Journal of Economics* 1 (4): 353–73.

———. 1982. *The Capitalist State; Marxist Theories and Methods.* New York: New York University Press.

———. 1990. *State Theory: Putting the Capitalist State in Its Place.* Cambridge: Polity.

Karlström, Mikael. 1996. "Imagining Democracy: Political Culture and Democratisation in Buganda." *Africa* 66 (4): 485–505.

Kelsen, Hans. 1945. *General Theory of Law and State.* Translated by Anders Wedberg. Cambridge, MA: Harvard University Press.

Khilnani, Sunil. 1997. *The Idea of India.* London: Hamish Hamilton.

Lefebvre, Henri. 2016, *Everyday Life in the Modern World.* New ed. Translated by Sacha Rabinovitch. London: Bloomsbury Academic. Originally published as *La vie quotidienne dans le monde moderne* (Paris: Gallimard, 1968).

Leys, Colin. 1976. "The 'Overdeveloped' Post Colonial State: A Re-evaluation." *Review of African Political Economy,* no. 5:39–48.

Lindberg, Staffan I. 2001. "Forms of States, Governance, and Regimes: Reconceptualizing the Prospects for Democratic Consolidation in Africa." *International Political Science Review* 22 (2): 173–99.

Lockhart, Chris. 2008. "The Life and Death of a Street Boy in East Africa: Everyday Violence in the Time of AIDS." *Medical Anthropology Quarterly,* n.s., 22 (1): 94–115.

Mafeje, Archie. 1971. "The Ideology of 'Tribalism.'" *Journal of Modern African Studies* 9 (2): 253–61.

———. 1986. "South Africa: The Dynamics of a Beleaguered State." *African Journal of Political Economy/Revue africaine d'économie politique* 1 (1): 95–119.

Mair, Lucy P. 1962. *Primitive Government.* London: Penguin Books.

Mathur, Nayanika. 2015. *Paper Tiger: Law, Bureaucracy and the Developmental State in Himalayan India.* Cambridge: Cambridge University Press.

Mbembe, Achille. 2000. "Everything Can Be Negotiated: Ambiguities and Challenges in a Time of Uncertainty." In *Manoeuvring in an Environment of Uncertainty: Structural Change and Social Action in Sub-Saharan Africa,* edited by Boel Berner and Per Trulsson, 265–76. Aldershot, Hampshire: Ashgate.

———. 2001. *On the Postcolony.* Berkeley: University of California Press.

———. 2009a. "On Politics as a Form of Expenditure." In Jean Comaroff and John L. Comaroff 2006, 299–335.

———. 2009b. "Why Am I Here?" Translated by Maureen Anderson. In *At Risk: Writing on and over the Edge of South Africa,* edited by Liz McGregor and Sarah Nuttall, 144–70. Johannesburg: Jonathan Ball Publishers.

———. 2021. *Out of the Dark Night: Essays on Decolonization.* New York: Columbia University Press.

Middleton, John. 1996. Review of *Anthropology and Politics: Visions, Traditions, and Trends,* by Joan Vincent. *PoLAR: Political and Legal Anthropology Review* 19 (2): 121–26.

Migdal, Joel S., and Klaus Schlichte. 2005. "Rethinking the State." In *The Dynamics of States: The Formation and Crises of State Domination,* edited by Klaus Schlichte, 1–40. Aldershot, Hampshire: Ashgate.

Mitchell, Timothy. 1991. "The Limits of the State: Beyond Statist Approaches and Their Critics." *American Political Science Review* 85 (1): 77–96.

———. 1999. "Society, Economy, and the State Effect." In *State/Culture: State Formation after the Cultural Turn,* edited by George Steinmetz, 76–97. Ithaca, NY: Cornell University Press.

Michelutti, Lucia. 2007. "The Vernacularization of Democracy: Political Participation and Popular Politics in North India." *Journal of Royal Anthropological Institute* 13 (3): 639–56.

Moran, Joe. 2005. *Reading the Everyday.* Abingdon, Oxon: Routledge.

Mosse, David. 2000. "Irrigation and Statecraft in Zamindari South India." In Fuller and Benei 2000, 163–93.

Newcomb, Rachel. 2017. *Everyday Life in Global Morocco.* Bloomington: Indiana University Press.

Newell, Stephanie, and Onookome Okome. 2014a. *Popular Culture in Africa: The Episteme of the Everyday.* New York: Routledge.

———. 2014b. "Introduction." In Newell and Okome 2014a, 1–23.

Nilsen, Alf Gunvald. 2018. *Adivasis and the State: Subalternity and Citizenship in India's Bhil Heartland.* Cambridge: Cambridge University Press.

Nugent, David. 1999. "A Conversation with Joan Vincent." *Current Anthropology* 40 (4): 531–41.

———. 2008. "Democracy Otherwise: Struggles over Popular Rule in the Northern Peruvian Andes." In Paley 2008a, 21–62.

Obadare, Ebenezer, and Wale Adebanwi. 2010. "Introduction: Excess and Abjection in the Study of the African State." In Adebanwi and Obadare 2010, 1–28.

Obarrio, Juan. 2014. *The Spirit of the Laws in Mozambique.* Chicago: Chicago University Press.

Obeid, Michelle. 2010. "Searching for the 'Ideal Face of the State' in a Lebanese Border Town." *Journal of the Royal Anthropological Institute* 16 (2): 330–46.

O'Donnell, Guillermo, and Philippe C. Schmitter. 1986. *Transition from Authoritarian Rule: Tentative Conclusion about Uncertain Democracies.* Baltimore: Johns Hopkins Press.

Oldenburg, Philip. 2006. "Face to Face with the Indian State: A Grass Roots View." In Rudolph and Jacobsen 2006a, 184–211.

Painter, Joe. 2006. "Prosaic Geographies of Stateness." *Political Geography* 25 (7): 752–74.

Paley, Julia. 2002. "Toward an Anthropology of Democracy." *Annual Review of Anthropology* 31:469–96.

———. 2004. "Accountable Democracy: Citizens' Impact on Public Decision Making in Postdictatorship Chile." *American Ethnologist* 31 (4): 497–513.

———, ed. 2008a. *Democracy: Anthropological Approaches.* Santa Fe: School for Advanced Research Press.

———. 2008b. "Introduction." In Paley 2008a, 3–20.

Paller, Jeffrey W. 2019. *Democracy in Ghana: Everyday Politics in Urban Africa.* Cambridge: Cambridge University Press.

Pype, Katrien. 2011. "Visual Media and Political Communication: Reporting about Suffering in Kinshasha." *Journal of Modern African Studies* 49 (4): 625–45.

———. 2020. "Stones Thrown Online: The Politics of Insults, Distance and Impunity in Congolese Polémique." In *Theorising Media and Conflict,* edited by Philipp Budka and Birgit Bräuchler, 237–54. New York: Berghahn Books.

Radcliffe-Brown, Alfred R. 1940. "Preface." In Fortes and Evans-Pritchard 1940, xi–xxiii.

Rodgers, Graeme. 2008. "Everyday Life and the Political Economy of Displacement on the Mozambique–South Africa Borderland." *Journal of Contemporary African Studies* 26 (4): 385–99.

Ross, Fiona C. 2010. *Raw Life, New Hope: Decency, Housing and Everyday Life in a Post-apartheid Community.* Claremont, Cape Town: UCT Press.

Rubbers, Benjamin, and Alessandro Jedlowski. 2019. "Introduction: Regimes of Responsibility in Africa: Towards a New Theoretical Approach." In *Regimes of Responsibility in Africa: Genealogies, Rationalities and Conflicts,* edited by Benjamin Rubbers and Alessandro Jedlowski, 1–19. New York: Berghahn Books.

Rudolph, Lloyd I., and John Kurt Jacobsen, eds. 2006a. *Experiencing the State.* New Delhi: Oxford University Press.

———. 2006b. "Introduction: Framing the Inquiry: Historicizing the Modern State." In Rudolph and Jacobsen 2006a, vii–xxix.

Saberwal, Satish. 1996. *Roots of Crisis: Interpreting Contemporary Indian Society.* Thousand Oaks, CA: Sage.

Salomon, Noah. 2016. *For Love of the Prophet: An Ethnography of Sudan's Islamic State.* Princeton, NJ: Princeton University Press.

Saul, John S. 1979. *The State and Revolution in Eastern Africa.* New York: Monthly Review.

Schaffer F. C. 1997. "Political Concepts and the Study of Democracy: The Case of *Demokaraasi* in Senegal." *PoLAR: Political and Legal Anthropology Review* 20 (1): 40–49.

Schapera, Isaac. 1956. *Government and Politics in Tribal Societies.* London: C. A. Watts.

Schubert, Jon. 2017. *Working the System: A Political Ethnography of the New Angola.* Ithaca, NY: Cornell University Press.

Scott, James C. 1992. *Domination and the Arts of Resistance: Hidden Transcripts.* New Haven, CT: Yale University Press.

———. 1998. *Seeing Like a State: How Certain Schemes to Improve the Human Condition Have Failed.* New Haven, CT: Yale University Press.

Sharma, Aradhana, and Akhil Gupta, eds. 2006a. *The Anthropology of the State: A Reader.* Malden, MA: Blackwell.

———. 2006b. "Introduction: Rethinking Theories of the State in an Age of Globalization." In Sharma and Gupta 2006a, 1–41.

Smith, Daniel Jordan. 2007. *A Culture of Corruption: Everyday Deception and Popular Discontent in Nigeria.* Princeton, NJ: Princeton University Press.

Southall, Aidan. 1956. *Alur Society: A Study in Processes and Types of Domination.* Cambridge: W. Heffer.

———. 1974. "State Formation in Africa." *Annual Review of Anthropology* 3:153–65.

Spencer, Jonathan. 1997. "Post-colonialism and the Political Imagination." *Journal of the Royal Anthropological Institute* 3 (1): 1–19.

———. 2007. *Anthropology, Politics and the State: Democracy and Violence in South Asia.* Cambridge: Cambridge University Press.

Swartz, Marc J., ed. 1968. *Local-Level Politics: Social and Cultural Perspectives.* Chicago: Aldine.

Swartz, Marc J., Victor W. Turner, and Arthur Tuden, eds. 1966. *Political Anthropology.* Chicago: Aldine.

Taiwo, Olufemi. 2010. *How Colonialism Preempted Modernity in Africa.* Bloomington: Indiana University Press.

Tanabe, Akio. 2007. "Towards Vernacular Democracy: Moral Society and Post-postcolonial Transformation in Rural Orissa, India." *American Ethnologist* 34 (3): 558–74.

Taussig, Michael T. 1997. *The Magic of the State.* New York: Routledge.

Thelen, Tatjana, Larissa Vetters, and Keebet von Benda-Beckmann, eds. 2018a. *Statography: Toward a Relational Anthropology of the State.* New York: Berghahn Books.

Thelen, Tatjana, Larissa Vetters, and Keebet von Benda-Beckmann. 2018b. "Introduction: Statography: Relational Modes, Boundary Work, and Embeddedness." In Thelen, Vetters, and von Benda-Beckmann 2018a, 1–19.

Trentmann, Frank. 2009. "Disruption is Normal: Blackouts, Breakdowns and the Elasticity of Everyday Life." In *Time, Consumption, and Everyday Life: Practice, Materiality and Culture,* edited by Elizabeth Shove, Frank Trentmann, and Richard Wilk, 67–84. Oxford: Berg.

———. 2012. "The Politics of Everyday Life." In *The Oxford Handbook of the History of Consumption,* edited by Frank Trentmann, 521–47. Oxford: Oxford University Press.

Trotsky, Leon. 1973. *Problems of Everyday Life.* New York: Pathfinder. Originally published as *Problems of Life* (London: Methuen, 1924).

Trouillot, Michel-Rolph. 2001. "The Anthropology of the State in the Age of Globalization: Close Encounters of the Deceptive Kind." *Current Anthropology* 42 (1): 125–38.

Vincent, Joan. 1990. *Anthropology and Politics: Visions, Traditions, and Trends.* Tucson: University of Arizona Press.

von Schnitzler, Antina. 2016. *Democracy's Infrastructure: Techno-Politics and Protest after Apartheid.* Princeton, NJ: Princeton University Press.

Wander, Philip. 1984. Introduction to *Everyday Life in the Modern World,* by Henri Lefebvre, vii–xvii. Translated by Sacha Rabinovitch. New Brunswick, NJ: Transaction. Reprinted as "Introduction to the Transaction Edition," in Lefebvre 2016, vii–xvii.

Wasserman, Herman. 2011. "Mobile Phones, Popular Media, and Everyday African Democracy: Transmissions and Transgressions." *Popular Communication* 9 (2): 146–58.

Werbner, Richard. 2002. "Introduction: Postcolonial Subjectivities: The Personal, the Political and the Moral." In *Postcolonial Subjectivities in Africa,* edited by Richard Werbner, 1–21. London: Zed Books.

———. 2020. *Anthropology after Gluckman: The Manchester School, Colonial and Postcolonial Transformations.* Manchester, UK: Manchester University Press.

West, Harry G. 1998. "Traditional Authorities and the Mozambican Transition to Democratic Governance." In *Africa's Second Wave of Freedom: Development, Democracy, and Rights,* edited by Lyn Graybill and Kenneth W. Thompson, 65–80. Lanham, MD: University Press of America.

———. 2008. "'Govern Yourselves!' Democracy and Carnage in Northern Mozambique." In *Democracy: Anthropological Approaches,* edited by Julia Paley, 97–121. Santa Fe: School for Advanced Research Press.

Worby, Eric. 1998. "Inscribing the State at the 'Edge of Beyond': Danger and Development in Northwestern Zimbabwe." *PoLAR: Political and Legal Anthropology Review* 21 (2): 55–70.

Yates, Douglas A. 1996. *The Rentier State in Africa: Oil Rent Dependency and Neocolonialism in the Republic of Gabon.* Trenton, NJ: Africa World.

PART ONE

Experiencing the Bureaucratic Machine

ONE

ID Cards and Social Class

The Intensification of the Bifurcated State in South Sudan

FERENC DÁVID MARKÓ

"WE KNEW THERE WERE GOVERNMENT SOLDIERS AMONG the raiders, we found lots of identity cards with the bodies after the fighting." The young national security officer of the SPLA-IO (Sudan People's Liberation Army in Opposition), the largest rebel movement in South Sudan, was reflecting on the 2018 dry-season attack by the neighboring Murle ethnic group in Akobo town. "Only [those] people have IDs who need them, regular people don't have IDs. Our cattle-boys are without IDs. These Murle [who had ID cards], they were not NGO workers, they were not administrators, so they must have been government soldiers." Possession or lack of an ID card was a clear indication of someone's class, and the security sector officer was arguing that local Nuer youth, who often engaged in cattle-raiding, did not belong to the same social class as some of the Murle attackers. If the fighting had been between ID-less, uneducated Nuer youth and their Murle counterparts, it would not have been of any political significance. However, the participation of Murle members of the "salaried class" signified to him that higher political levels were involved.

Regarded as mere "local intercommunal violence," cattle-raiding usually escapes the interest of scholars and practitioners of peace-building. However, political "leaders have strategically manipulated these local conflicts in order to mobilize armed herders for their political movements" (Wild, Jok, and Patel 2018, n.p.; see also Pendle 2015, 2017). In this case, the young rebel security officer pinpointed the evidence that proved the political embeddedness of the Murle youth during the 2018 dry-season attack: their

ID cards. This ethnographic encounter illustrates the important connection between documented citizenship and sociopolitical class in South Sudan.

The connection between ID cards and social class is obvious for South Sudanese in other contexts as well. "We had forty-eight revenge killings just last season," a tired old chief explained to me at a tea stall. He had been deliberating and judging court cases for several days under a mango tree. "The peace commissioner called us, all chiefs, and we called all sections involved, all the families, and told them to reconcile, and now the families pay compensation. Usual compensation [for a revenge killing] is fifty cows, but you see, the main problem is that they started killing intellectuals. . . . Intellectuals are people with NGO jobs, or chiefs, commissioners, soldiers, teachers, educated people, traders, *everyone with an ID,* from the town. In the cases of intellectuals, the compensation is two hundred cows" (emphasis added). Unlike in some Dinka-populated areas of Bahr el Ghazal, where a marriage might cost between fifty and two hundred cattle (Pendle 2018), in this part of Nuerland bridewealth prices had plummeted to twenty-five to forty heads of cattle, a clear sign of the area's impoverishment under the war economy. In this context, killing someone from the "salaried class" is an immoral and dangerous act against the community, as it results in more killings of "intellectuals," potential breadwinners for entire families. Everyone who has even the very distant potential of access to money is part of the valuable salaried class. Government employees, teachers, chiefs, and even soldiers have been largely without salaries since the outbreak of the civil war in 2013: basically, everyone outside the political elites and the NGO world. However, as my informants explained, the salaried class will have a chance to earn again if peace returns to the country and the economy improves. The potential of belonging to the salaried class sometimes plays in favor of women as well. Bridewealth increases if the girl is educated and has a chance of future employment by an NGO. Both Dinka and Nuer call the practice *hok galam* (cattle of the pen), adding another twenty to thirty heads of cattle to the equation.

This chapter analyzes the nature of the South Sudanese state, building on several years of fieldwork in the country, including a yearlong ethnographic observation within the citizenship office in 2013 in Juba, the capital of South Sudan. It argues that the independent nation has developed a bifurcated bureaucracy. This Janus-faced structure is growing out of colonial and postcolonial forms and methods of government, further intensified by the inheritance of the civil war and pressurized by the peacetime *nation-building* narrative. Every state office has developed distinct civilian and military clusters, which live in an unequal but symbiotic relationship. The chapter is limited in scope and ambition, however, as it only focuses on South Sudanese who are applying for ID documents. This section of

FIGURE 1. Policewoman checks the documents of a southern Sudanese woman prior to issuing a Sudanese citizenship identity card at the Ministry of Internal Affairs South Sudan Police, 6 October 2010. Photo by Mohamed Nureldin Abdallah/Reuters.

society—the "salaried class"—amounts to a mere fraction of the general population, and their experiences cannot be seen as representative of an entire country.

The Second Sudanese Civil War (1983–2005) ended with the signing of the Comprehensive Peace Agreement (CPA) between the government of Sudan and the rebel Sudan People's Liberation Movement (SPLM). The CPA became the basis of all future power-sharing peace agreements and was heralded as a success story. Billions of dollars of oil money started to flow to the accounts of the SPLM, and a fragile societal equilibrium was maintained by the nominally high salaries and incentives given state employees. However, the improvident decision by South Sudan in early 2012 to shut down oil production to coerce Sudan into a better deal on payments dried up its foreign currency reserves. The worsening economic situation of the new country, combined with rampant corruption and political struggle among the top echelons of the governing SPLM, led to the outbreak of the civil war.

The gravest crisis for South Sudan erupted in December 2013, just two and a half years after the pompous celebration of independence. The disagreement started as a political struggle for leadership of the party, and thus the nomination for the presidency. After the possibility of a political loss became evident, President Salva Kiir suspended the highest decision-making organs of the party, ordered the arrest of thirteen influential politicians, and accused them of plotting a coup against him, under the leadership of estranged Vice President Riek Machar. The political struggle quickly took a deadly turn as fighting broke out in the capital between Nuer and Dinka members of the Tiger Division, the country's elite military force protecting the president.

Ethnically motivated killings of Nuer civilians in Juba started almost immediately, carried out by poorly trained Mathiang Anyoor militia members recruited in the president's ethnic homeland, sometimes supported by Sudan People's Liberation Army (SPLA) soldiers (Boswell 2019; Pinaud 2014; African Union Commission of Inquiry on South Sudan 2015). Riek Machar escaped Juba and quickly took over the leadership of the forming rebellion, which gained sizable military strength as more and more Nuer commanders of the SPLA announced their defections, joined by their soldiers. Machar's movement became known as the Sudan People's Liberation Army/Movement in Opposition (SPLA/M-IO) (Young 2015, 2016, 2017; Craze, Tubiana, and Gramizzi 2016). Rebel forces supported by quickly assembled Nuer youth militias took revenge on Dinka civilians in Bor and Bentiu.

The opposing factions signed an internationally brokered elite-level power-sharing agreement (Agreement on the Resolution of the Conflict in South Sudan, or ARCSS) in July 2016. The terms offered a return to the prewar status quo, with Riek Machar reinstated with the new title of first vice president and the possibility of an open contest for the party leadership, future free and fair elections, accountability for war crimes, the promise of a federal state, and a fair distribution of resources. Both sides broke the agreement in a flamboyant fashion and fighting between the thirteen hundred bodyguards of Riek Machar and the elite troops and helicopter gunships of the government again quaked Juba. The country slid back into civil war as Machar escaped Juba once again, this time on foot, toward the Democratic Republic of Congo (Small Arms Survey 2017). Previously peaceful territories and ethnic groups had been brought into the civil war, most notably Equatoria, the southern region of the country (Kindersley and Rolandsen 2017). The opposition further fragmented itself, with Riek Machar maintaining overall command of his SPLA-IO troops from house arrest in South Africa while new, smaller rebel forces emerged and alliances quickly shifted.

The international community tried again, under the leadership of the Intergovernmental Authority on Development, an eight-country trade bloc in East Africa, and brokered the Revitalised Agreement on the Resolution of the Conflict in the Republic of South Sudan (R-ARCSS). The two main parties, alongside some members of the extremely fractured smaller opposition groups, signed the new agreement in September 2018. The peace deal stipulated a six-month pre-transitional period in which to unify the various forces into a national army and demarcate the boundaries for the future administrative division of the country. Once again, accountability for war crimes, future free and fair elections, and the development of a democratic state were the fig leaves for what was really an elite power-sharing agreement. By March 2021, the peace deal was crumbling and South Sudanese communities throughout the country were experiencing an increase in violence (Human Rights Division of the United Nations Mission in South Sudan 2021).

Necropolitical Terrain

Current scholarship on Africa identifies gray zones, abandoned places beyond state control that are "no longer regulated but poached . . . by states" (Piot 2010, 11; see also Agamben 1998, 2000; Roitman 2005; Mbembe 2006; Behrends 2011; Friedman 2011; Reyna 2011). South Sudan—along with Somalia, Chad, the Central African Republic, Eastern Congo, and parts of the West African Sahel—is usually depicted as one of the prime examples of "necropolitical" places (Mbembe 2003), abandoned by states and preyed upon by a network of NGOs, Pentecostal churches, witchcraft accusations, visa and green card lotteries, and sanguinary warlords. Most scholars analyze such cases from the perspective of the "lack of the state": it is the state that is missing, withdrawing and evaporating into a shadow of its former being to become a mere "simulacral regime" (Mbembe 1992), surviving on empty performances and meticulously planned, often dramatic events.

The case of South Sudan is somewhat different from others, even though no less tragic. The state—and the way of governance—was always based on two fundamental principles: external rents, and exploitation of human and financial resources. In the nineteenth century, exploitation took the form of slave and cattle raids (Jok 2001). The twentieth century, under both the Anglo-Egyptian Condominium and independent Sudan, brought a combination of subventions from Cairo and Khartoum and the exploitation of free labor, mostly through the system of traditional authority (Leonardi 2013, 56–86). During the course of two civil wars (1955–72 and 1983–2005), the government held major garrison towns and survived on subsidies from Khartoum, while the rebel movements coerced and exploited the rural populations under their control and lived off external rents through the diversion of humanitarian aid and funding from neighboring governments that supported the struggle (de Waal 1997; Johnson 2003). Since the 2005 signing of the CPA, the rents come from oil and humanitarian aid, while both the government and various rebel groups forcibly conscript the civilian population in times of crisis (Thomas 2015).

Income apart from oil revenue and humanitarian aid revenue provides a mere fraction of the national budget. Governance through rents has led to the complete detachment of elites from society and the burgeoning development of extended kinship-based patronage networks (Pinaud 2014). As historian Edward Thomas asserts, "rents mean that the elites share no economic interests with ordinary people: the government is economically autonomous from society. Elite factions fight hard for a share of the rents because they cannot build up economic interests elsewhere" (2016, 40). This chapter argues that this detachment and "rent-seeking" attitude affected the solidifying bureaucracy of the new nation and the ways of governance in all state offices (see de Waal 2015, 23). However, this process did not happen in a straightforward and unostentatious way. Visual symbols and real effects of "officialdom" are utterly important in all social situations, throughout the country, among all social groups. For instance, the young, inspiring research assistant in a rebel-held town, who is talking about his idea of opening a restaurant, and who before anything else proudly shows me the official stamp of his future company. The teenagers in the fields near Yambio, asking for money for a ball, who produce a letter from the local ministry of sports acknowledging their existence as a football team, thus validating their request. The headman of a few families in a suburb of Juba who, for no reason of the moment, quickly searches for a piece of paper to display, signed and stamped by all his chiefly superiors, four levels above him, all the way to the paramount chief of his community. These seemingly empty gestures and invocations of state authority signify a deeply embedded idea of and craving for an imagined statehood and the social order that is associated with it.

South Sudan experienced a brutal civil war from December 2013 to September 2018, as a result of which millions are traumatized and have been forced into displacement. Approximately four hundred thousand people were killed (Checchi et al. 2018), mostly along ethnic lines. In a war that was waged not for territory but population control, entire ethnic communities were immiserated and forced to leave their homelands (Craze 2019). There has been a magnitude of death and deliberate displacement that some scholars argue reached the levels of genocide (Pinaud 2021).

Peace can only be sustainable if the bifurcated nature of the state is taken into account. The observations below seek to demonstrate how this bifurcation comes into play in the everyday working of the state in South Sudan.

The Bifurcated Nature of State Offices in South Sudan

Every state office in South Sudan is permeated with nepotism and patronage. However, several of the offices have genuinely engaged in the creation of "projects of legibility" and fulfill basic state functions (Scott

1998). Customs declaration forms need to be filled out, passports issued, land registry files updated, court cases recorded. All South Sudanese state offices find themselves grinding between the contradictions of the need for efficiency and the will to serve the rent-seeking patronage networks. Therefore, this chapter argues, all offices develop dual, parallel, but sometimes not easily separable sections. The nominal head of the office is usually a political appointee from the "gun class," a war veteran in most cases (Pinaud 2014). He staffs the office partially with members of his own patronage network—usually consisting of both former military comrades and ethnic kinsmen—and partially from the patronage networks of his superiors. On the other hand, the office needs to fulfill its state function effectively, therefore there is the need to hire a whole range of trained personnel, frequently younger, based on qualifications and experience. In the case of the citizenship office—as I have done elsewhere (Markó 2016b)—I call these two sides of the office the "military" and the "civilian" clusters. All South Sudanese state offices develop this bifurcated nature, and the offices with an important and visible state function tend to develop bigger and more powerful civilian clusters.

The military cluster is responsible for top-level decision-making and for representing the office within the government and the office of the president. Internal policy, appointments and dismissals, management of regional offices, and distributions of income are all decided within the military cluster. On the other hand, the civilian cluster has several different functions. First, it is responsible for the smooth running of the basic functions of the office and ensures that it is regarded as "effective and well-organized, both for the average citizens and for the political leadership."[1] Second, the civilian cluster needs to generate revenue for the entire office. Since the outbreak of the civil war, ministries and their offices have generally received only a small fraction of funds necessary to cover their expenses through allocations in the national budget. In fact, one of the main attributes of a good military leader of a state office is his ability to procure a large chunk of the tabulated budget for his office from the Ministry of Finances. The civilian cluster has several means of generating revenue, which vary among the assorted offices. For most capacity-building projects, UN agencies or the plethora of NGOs, operating under the broad themes of "transparency," "good governance," "security sector reform," or "human rights," work with the civilian clusters. The civilian cluster can bring in UN- or NGO-related projects, and members of the civilian cluster—in consultation with the military cluster—can attend international workshops in various regional capitals or in hotels in Juba. Following the devaluation or nonpayment of their salaries, the per diems granted for these events have become the basic source of income for state administrators employed in civilian clusters. According to one midlevel bureaucrat interviewed in late 2019, the per diems can constitute as much as 80 percent of someone's annual income. The civilian cluster can also collect fees and fines from citizens, thus generating income that remains within the office. A third function of the civilian clusters is to convey the image of a nonfailed state to the international community (see Markó 2016b).

Case Study: The Citizenship Office

Two days prior to the declaration of independence, South Sudan set up its Directorate of Nationality, Passports and Immigration (DNPI) within the structure of the Ministry of Interior.[2] The DNPI is responsible for overseeing the international borders, issuing visas, and vetting all citizenship applications, and issuing identity cards and passports for the citizens of the new country. The task is daunting. The overwhelming majority of the estimated twelve million citizens have no material evidence of their legal belonging to the new state, so each and every applicant has to personally appear in front of the military officers of the DNPI to prove their right to citizenship. The applicant's traditional leader and a next-of-kin relative, preferably from the patrilineal ancestry line, should also accompany her (Markó 2016a).

South Sudan signed up for the most state-of-the-art biometric technology to produce ID cards and passports. The result, on the one hand, is one of the most expensive application fees in Africa (US$20 for an ID card), a sum out of range for ordinary South Sudanese. On the other hand, the result is an overly complex system that, due to its complexity, cannot fulfill the promises of modernity. However, these disadvantages are not unintended consequences of some "failed state" operations, or of mere recklessness, but calculated collateral phenomena. The high cost serves to enforce that only those apply who need an ID for their work or travel. ID cards, as signifiers of belonging to the "salaried class," are intended to not come cheap, as implied by the security officer in his remarks about the documented attackers from Akobo at the beginning of this chapter. The failure of biometric modernity serves another purpose. As I argue elsewhere, the main reason "the South Sudanese state decided to apply the high-modernist vision and introduced the biometric identity management system was not the belief in enhanced state surveillance capacity or the goal of achieving a better grasp on its citizens, but the possibility of creating an image of a modern, efficient, depoliticized, and professionally bureaucratized state—in other words, a non-failed state. Instead of the will to improve, the ideology was reduced to the will to impress" (Markó 2016b, 115).

FIGURE 2. Southern Sudanese show their documents in order to receive their Sudanese citizenship identity cards at the Ministry of Internal Affairs South Sudan Police, 6 October 2010. Photo by Mohamed Nureldin Abdallah/Reuters.

The military cluster in the citizenship office, headed by the director, a military general, represents the office on a political level. This cluster is responsible for the hiring, promotion, and dismissal of all staff within the office. It also decides about the distribution of incoming funds, both from diminishing core funding from the Ministry of Finances and from revenue generated by the office via application fees. Most importantly, the military cluster carries out all the interviews with citizenship applicants and evaluates all evidence before a formal decision.

According to the Nationality Act of 2011, applicants have to prove that they "belong to one of the indigenous ethnic communities of South Sudan" (Markó 2015). The applicant, accompanied by his or her next-of-kin and in certain cases by a traditional chief, must convince a mid-ranking police officer within the military cluster during a formal interview. Following the first interview, the applicant has to appear again, this time alone, before a high-ranking officer. The officers are usually war veterans, and the overwhelming majority of them are Dinka or Nuer, belonging to the two main ethnic groups of Southern Sudan, which also made up the majority of the SPLM.

The civilian cluster only becomes involved if the applicant passes the first two interviews. The applicant's data, fingerprints, and full biometric profile are recorded in the computerized system operated by the civilian cluster. Low-ranking officers—some of them not even employees of the directorate, but of the private company running the ID-producing machinery—take a digital identification photo. In sharp contrast to the military cluster, this side of the office is bright and electrified, much of the communication is in English, and the civilian employees are generally friendly and effective. However, they are entirely powerless, as those in the civilian cluster cannot make decisions by themselves; in doubtful cases they must refer the applicant back to the military cluster. Employees themselves recognize the clustering of offices. "We don't hang with the veterans," one young female bureaucrat explained when I asked if civilian employees would participate in the retirement ceremony for a colonel from the verification offices. One of the most contentious issues during the period of my fieldwork was the ordering of new uniforms and military training for junior civilian bureaucrats. Most young bureaucrats were against the idea of both uniforms and the monthlong training. "You can get malaria five times in the six months while you are out there in the swamp," one urbanite officer said in describing his horror of the proposed training. For their part, veterans from the military cluster assert the rightness of such decisions, as they feel that the methods they developed throughout the civil war apply to times of peace as well. Lt. Colonel Light—who got his name at infancy because of his extremely light skin color and who, ironically, was the recognized master of ethnic profiling in the office—explained, "I served in every corner of South Sudan [during the civil war]. I know who is lying, and who belongs where. I can tell or learn it very quickly, just a few questions."

The treatment of doubts over someone's legal status further demonstrates the power imbalance between the military and civilian clusters. Both the police (the infamous Criminal Investigation Department) and the National Security Services routinely question the citizenship of criminal suspects and others. In these cases, the biometric records in the system are useless, as the burden of proof is on those being questioned, who have to prove again that they belong to the South Sudanese state.

However, there is something very fundamental about the nature of the South Sudanese state in this duality—or, more precisely, about how citizens imagine the state. South Sudanese patiently queue for citizenship interviews and playfully enter into negotiations over their status during the application procedure. Sometimes officers question their positions, their witnesses, or individual stories, and they are sent away for further evidence; in other cases, they successfully convince the officers about their case. Throughout these democratic negotiations, they shape the way the state is working, and also solidify their understanding of the South Sudanese state.

In this scenario, unlike most traditional Western understandings of the issue, citizenship is not a birthright, not a constant, but a questionable position, one that may have to be renegotiated from time to time with various "military clusters" of the state. For ordinary South Sudanese, this constant negotiation with military figures in various social situations is part and parcel of everyday life. As a result, there is no contradiction, from their point of view, between the operations of the military and the civilian clusters. Two ethnographic stories about ID cards, life, death, negotiations, and the constant limbo of belonging illustrate this point.

Street Corner Killings

"Did I tell you my story of December, when they almost killed me at a checkpoint here?"

Black smoke was puffing from under the hood of our white Toyota Land Cruiser as David and I drove through the deserted streets of Juba on a hot afternoon in July 2016, just a few days before the elite-level power-sharing peace agreement collapsed and the capital again became a major battlefront of the South Sudanese civil war. The streets were empty due to the stratospheric price of fuel, the growing political instability, and the militarization of street corners. A liter of diluted petrol cost the equivalent of three US dollars on the black market. Apart from international organizations, NGOs, and the military, very few people could afford to drive around. The irony that this was happening in East Africa's major oil-producing country remained unremarked in the moment.

David was referring to the dramatic events following 15 December 2013, when the coalition embodied in the National Liberation Council broke down, leading to catastrophic civil war. He smiled at me, holding the wheel with one hand while pointing at his scarification marks with his other. I recalled Evans-Pritchard's description of "six long cuts from ear to ear," horizontal lines unmistakably signifying David's apparent ethnic identity—his belonging—and thus his presumed position in the civil war.[3]

"This got me into trouble. Nuer marks. They were nicknamed the 'Death Certificate' after the killings. They came to you in the dark, put their fingers on your forehead, and counted the lines. If it is six, you are done. Shot."

David is a middle-aged, mid-ranking, poor bureaucrat at one of the legally independent check-and-balance institutions of the state. He was helping me in the organization of a high-level workshop. Although David is not a person from the "gun class" with a high political position, his intimate knowledge of South Sudanese government elites and his friendships with countless important figures open all doors for him, and thus he became indispensable to me. David had not received his salary for eight months by now, not that it really mattered for his survival, as the South Sudanese pound had lost most of its real value during the three years of civil war. David's SS£2,000 monthly salary was worth US$630 at the time of the outbreak of the war in 2013, while three years later it equaled less than twenty dollars. However, he was still very proud to be working for the government of independent South Sudan.

"I am a mix, you know?" David continues. "Half Dinka, half Nuer. My mother is Nuer, I am a mix. As a small kid, I was raised by my mother's family, so I got these Nuer marks. I speak Nuer and Dinka. I can be both, but sometimes it is not you who choose. You know, *they* select, and *bang*, there you go! It almost happened to me. Here. At this corner, near my house."

David keeps smiling. Still, I see his eyes cloud over as he recounts the traumatic events welling up from his memories.

> This was a Nuer neighborhood [at] that time, mostly Nuer, and they rounded up the men. They started at eight p.m., after sunset. Mathiang Anyoor.[4] Dinka cattle-boys. Very young. *Very* young. All with AKs [AK-47 Kalashnikov rifles]. This group had a few boys, no commanders, just the boys. They rounded up us, eight from the neighborhood and started asking questions. "We are defending the president! We are defending the president!" they shouted. They went one by one, a few quick questions in Dinka, and [then] they grabbed the [man they were questioning] and took him behind the house. You just heard a single shot. They shot everyone in the head. One by one. I was the last in the queue. I tell you, Feri, my mouth was so dry, I had it in my mind that I will not be able to speak. Seven shots, I counted, seven. But I swear you, once it was my turn, something changed. They tossed me to the ground, in this very suit you see on me. I was coming home from office. So I was on the ground, got up, and I started shouting in Dinka. Shouting into their faces: "I could be your father! I am Dinka, like you, and I can be your father, I work for the government, I represent the government, I *work* for the president!" They became concerned. So, I reached my pocket and looked for my ID. My work ID. They could not read at all, but I have seen they are worried to kill me. What if they make a mistake? So, they called for an older soldier. An SPLA officer, a sergeant, arrived, and checked my ID, and told me that I can call someone to explain me. I called General Kuch. I never prayed that hard for a call to go through. He cleared me, and sent a car, and I spent the next two weeks in the general's house. But Feri, this experience still lives in me. I'm in cold sweat now, as I tell you.

David's story is a very typical narrative of struggle and survival in South Sudan. Almost everyone has a similar, even though sometimes less dramatic, account of life-changing events. According to a methodologically sophisticated study, 383,000 people died as a direct consequence of warfare between 2013 and 2018 (Checchi et al. 2018). As of December 2018, seven million people from the estimated entire population of twelve million had been affected by conflict, hunger, and displacement, and were in dire need of humanitarian assistance. According to a 2017 UN report, more than 4.2 million people had fled their homes, with nearly two million finding shelter inside the country in UN Protection of Civilians (PoC) camps and 2.2 million living outside the country in refugee camps. These ramshackle camps, both within and outside the country, have solidified into over-crowded peri-urban settlements and remain a sad symbol of how the war urbanized the once largely rural population of South Sudan. Almost half of South Sudanese households experienced or witnessed violence in the year 2015 alone (United Nations Development Programme 2017, 48–50).

Dual Citizenship, Single Loyalty

The second story is, sadly, no less horrendous. Matthew is an educated and exceptionally smart South Sudanese. He was born in Juba but attended high school in Nairobi, and would go on to earn a PhD in the Netherlands, where he also received Dutch citizenship. Since South Sudan's independence, he has been working on and off in the country, consulting for international NGOs and research institutions, but lives with his family in Amsterdam. Shortly following independence, he proudly surrendered his Sudanese passport and claimed South Sudanese citizenship. Each time he has traveled to South Sudan, he has left Europe under the Dutch passport but used the South Sudanese one to enter the country, as it saved him an expensive visa and the mandatory alien registration—a daylong process at the immigration office in downtown Juba. As mentioned above, the fragile peace deal between the opposition and the government collapsed in July 2016, and Juba once again became a battlefield. A few days into the fighting, as he stayed locked inside his house, Matthew got a call from the Dutch embassy, which told him that a military plane would be landing soon to evacuate German and Dutch citizens and advised him to leave. As he is not a Nuer but an Equatorian Bari, he felt that it would be fairly safe to leave his house. However, at the airport, he was treated differently than he had expected.

> So they, the Dinka soldiers, picked me from the line. I am the
> only Black person there, you know. They check my Dutch passport
> and ask, "But, my friend, where is your stamp into the country?"
> They go through all my pockets and they find the South Sudan
> passport. "Tsch! You! Come with us." And they bring me behind
> a house and they beat me with the butt of the rifle. Viciously.

And this soldier, takes my [South Sudanese] passport and tears it into pieces and shouts at me, "Traitor! Coward! Fight is coming against the Nuer, the country needs you and you just run away!" But they let me go. I can barely walk, but try to get back into the line. The soldiers [were] still there, so even if it's an evacuation, you have to go through all the passport control and you have to get a stamp. So, I tried to leave the country, covered in blood, when the immigration officer just got angry with me. "Where is your visa?" I don't have my South Sudan passport anymore, I realize that I am in the country illegally. The immigration officer tells me that I have to buy a visa, so I have to get to the other side of the airport, to arrivals. It's crazy, as no plane landed since the war broke out again, you know, but they opened the counter for me. I had to pay one hundred dollars, even got a receipt of it, stamped *into* the country, just to be evacuated ten minutes later.

The radical and brutal stories of David and Matthew encapsulate several layers of contradictions, but also allow their unpacking. Academic literature tends to make a clear distinction between African elites and the poor (see Bayart 1993). However, the borderline here is much more porous and complex. David has an unpaid salaried job, works in the civilian cluster of an important state office, has access to international and local workshops and conferences, lives off his per diems, and has a very wide social network. Matthew is a regular consultant for research projects and international NGOs at a high daily rate, albeit in the precarious position of a freelance researcher. Neither of them is part of either the manipulative elite or the exploited poor. David is proud to be working for the very same state that sought to annihilate him, while Matthew is still optimistic about the future possibilities of the country, despite his personal humiliation. They both acknowledge the supremacy of the military cluster but imagine the future of the country positively, including through their own contributions to the civilian cluster.

Sharon Hutchinson has demonstrated that, in the 1980s, western Nuer already differentiated between two sides of the government.

Interestingly, many Nuer men and women drew a marked distinction during the early 1980s between what they called "the government of the left" (*kume in caam*) and "the government of the right" (*kume in cuec*). The "government of the left"—being identified with regional administrative networks of government chiefs, courts, police, district officers, and the like—was said to *nhɔk tëŋ naadh* ("agree/want people to live"). It was defined as a positive, peacekeeping force in that it was capable of containing and defusing outbreaks of intercommunity violence. The "government of the right" or "the army," in contrast, was said to bring only death: *E liaah*. This dualist image of the contradictory impulses of "the government" reveals the extent to which many contemporary Nuer had come to accept the idea of a national state government while simultaneously rejecting current limitations on their abilities to influence its powers in ways that would promote both their immediate well-being and their political objectives in the longer term. (Hutchinson 1996, 110)

While South Sudanese experienced the bifurcated nature of government offices, the logics of postindependence state-building both intensified the process and made it even more complex. Due to both internal and external pressures, after the Comprehensive Peace Agreement the two sides of the government amalgamated down to the level of single offices. One of the main driving forces behind that process was the will to impress upon the international community that South Sudan was not a failed state. Naturally, some parts of the government remained mostly "military"—places like the National Security Services had to issue travel permits and paperwork for sensitive issues, like satellite phones. Nevertheless, most South Sudanese state offices experienced the development of a bifurcated bureaucracy, a Janus-faced administration with separated responsibilities, roles, and operative logics. Both David's and Matthew's story are clear indications that in times of war and crisis, the two clusters of the state may behave unexpectedly and formerly familiar distinctions may not be applicable to new situations. Threatened by militia youth, David used an ID card, a product of the civilian cluster, to validate his claim that he was not an enemy, and his life was saved not through a patronage or kinship network, but by a friend, a Dinka general, who took a risk by his action. At the airport, Matthew was further humiliated through the meticulous application of rules and regulations by the civilian cluster at the airport after a physical assault by the military cluster and the revocation of his South Sudanese nationality in the most brutal way.

I have argued that, due to the inherent logic of two centuries of governance and amid extreme internal and external pressure, all South Sudanese state offices developed a bifurcated modus operandi. The dual nature of state offices and the imbalance between the two clusters intensified in the period after the Comprehensive Peace Agreement (2005–13). However, while the military cluster retained its power and decision-making authority over the civilian cluster, there were substantial counterbalancing factors and leverage in the hands of the civilian side. On the one hand, salaries kept the equilibrium. While the employees of the military cluster—due to their senior military ranks—were on a higher pay scale, the civilians also received fair pay for their work. In early 2013, the average monthly salary in the civilian cluster of the citizenship office was US$550. Another point of leverage for the civilian cluster was its access to UN and NGO nation-building projects and workshops. These projects usually targeted existing state institutions with the objective of reforming them from within, often with a foreign adviser embedded in the office. The projects brought technical help, donations of equipment and vehicles, and workshops and retreats that provided employees with a hefty per diem, enough to at least partially cover the salaries of a handful of the bureaucrats within the civilian cluster. These exercises were essential in income-generating and allowed the offices to carry out their mandated tasks more effectively.

However, these counterbalancing factors dried up after the outbreak of conflict in late 2013. Due to the economic collapse and the hyperinflation of the local currency, salaries lost 95 percent of their real value in a mere six years. The devaluation of salaries affected every state employee, but the consequences were more severe for the civilian cluster. Even the younger officers of the military cluster were part of patronage systems that provide for bare survival in times of extreme crisis, while the older generation of military officers learned how to navigate their way through this crisis situation. As one high-ranking officer told me in 2016, reflecting on the unpaid salaries, "This is not my time to eat well." Meanwhile, as salaries continued to lose value, the nation-building projects evaporated as well. Due to growing evidence of grave human rights violations and war crimes committed by the government forces, previously generous donors became reluctant to support any office associated with the national government. Some of the funding allocated to civil society organizations could still be channeled to certain state functions, but most opportunities to access UN or NGO funding disappeared for the state offices.

As a consequence of the evaporation of salaries and donor funds, there has been an exodus of civilian bureaucrats. Various UN agencies and NGOs hired some of these qualified personnel—especially due to the aforementioned concerns, as former members of the civilian cluster were considered less likely to cooperate too closely with state offices. The positions that the fleeing officers of the civilian cluster left behind did not offer any immediate benefit, so instead of new, trained civilians occupying these jobs, they were filled through the patronage network of the military cluster. As a result, state services rapidly deteriorated. Furthermore, due to the militarization of society during the war, the logic of the military cluster, and the lost influence of the civilian cluster, the state offices became even more politicized and divisive. The professional pushback effect from the civilian cluster, which usually tried to avoid getting involved in direct politics, almost completely disappeared.

The citizenship application process for immiserated populations provides a case in point. Several Shilluk residents of the Malakal Protection of Civilians Camp complained to me in late 2019 that they could not access the citizenship office at Malakal, the capital of Upper Nile state. "We cannot get through even the gate," one of them said. "They tell us, you are Shilluk, now you have your own state, go to Fashoda and do it there. There are no services in Fashoda, we cannot go there." In late 2015, President Salva Kiir had issued a decree that reorganized the country from ten into twenty-eight states. Malakal was suddenly part of the newly created, Dinka-majority Central Upper Nile state, while Fashoda state was created on the western banks of the Nile. Another decree in January 2017 further divided the country into thirty-two states. Over the course of this period, Malakal, a formerly multicultural town populated by both Padang Dinka and Shilluk, was ransacked several times, and the Shilluk population mostly escaped to the UN-administered and protected PoC camp on the outskirts of the town. Although the country reverted to ten states under the R-ARCSS in December 2018, the earlier administrative divisions had done their damage: the new boundaries between communities intensified interethnic conflict, which remains a major obstacle to lasting peace agreements (Craze 2019, 58–74). Nor did the R-ARCSS bring any relief to the Shilluk residents of the PoC camp, who still cannot acquire ID cards.

For state offices, the effect of all this administrative gerrymandering, coupled with that of years of military campaigns, was further intensified as various populations pushed for access to government services in "their" respective states. In Malakal as elsewhere, the entire citizenship office was brought into the conflict. This became possible, I argue, and was in fact reinforced, because of the above-described bifurcated nature of everyday governmentality in South Sudan.

Why did the grand nation-building projects of the UN and NGOs fail after the Comprehensive Peace Agreement of 2005? Many of the promises of development of South Sudan's civil society—toward "democracy," "good governance," "transparency," and an "active citizenry"—were vague, but they did offer the prospect of a shift to efficiency and professionalism in the delivery of government services. However, the projects only affected the civilian cluster, and never the decision-making authority of the military cluster. Donors either turned a blind eye to the political realities of state offices or claimed neutrality and sought to answer what were essentially political questions with technical solutions. In a glaring example, one of the UN agencies helped the DNPI set up the system of citizenship registration. When I asked if they were concerned about the underlying ethnic nature of the vetting of applicants and the growing influence of traditional authorities, I was told that this question was not even open for discussion.

"South Sudan is a sovereign state that decides these things alone," a young UN employee angrily argued—turning a conveniently blind eye to realities on the ground, technicalizing political questions out of the way, and exemplifying James Ferguson's (1990) infamous "anti-politics machine."

With the elite in government imagining the new nation of South Sudan as an interconnected texture of ethnic groups, the basis of identification became the "tribe." However, what seemed to be a logical administrative and organizational practice only contributed to the instrumentalization and "militarization" of ethnicity (Jok and Hutchinson 1999; Hutchinson 2000). The international community, while offering billions of dollars through nation-building projects, never questioned this basis of the new nation they were helping to build. For the donors, the question of *how South Sudan decides who is South Sudanese* remained a merely technical and not a fundamentally political question, which it clearly is. "South Sudan is a sovereign nation. I just have to provide technical assistance," was a typical answer given by a Japanese employee of the International Organization for Migration (IOM) when I asked if she found the methods used in assigning or refusing to assign citizenship problematic.

With the signing of the R-ARCSS, not only "peace" has returned to Juba, but the nation-building projects as well. Seemingly untouched by the failed attempts of the previous round a mere decade before, the donors again speak of national sovereignty while distilling political questions into mere technical problems. In early 2021, during a background call on the oncoming census—stipulated by the peace agreement—I asked the UN employee tasked with implementing technical assistance throughout the process about the possibility of sample selection being influenced and who would decide whether certain territories were deemed too insecure for a count to take place. These are fundamentally political questions: everything from elections to political representation to the distribution of the nation's wealth in the form of government resources will be decided based on the results of the census. The UN agency employee was baffled that I thought it should be their role to get involved in "technical issues" that "[needed] to be sorted out by the local Bureau of Statistics."

The people of South Sudan have learned how to navigate between rent-seeking military rulers and weak civilian clusters over the course of the last two hundred years. During citizenship applications and in other situations where they have to deal with state authorities, people regularly demonstrate exceptional skills and a very democratic and brave understanding of speaking to power. The quest to acquire identity cards—and thus to belong to a certain social class—is pursued in frequently contradictory but still effective ways. Confronted by reduced state capacity and deteriorating state services, the people of South Sudan still hold and express very clear and strong ideas about the imagined state and how it should function. In future, the conception of South Sudanese statehood and governmentality, and the policies that are put in place as a result of that conception, must build upon these experiences and ideas of the South Sudanese citizens themselves.

Notes

1. Interview with the director general of the citizenship office, March 2013.
2. I have published extensively on the citizenship office of South Sudan. Some of the following argument is set forth in greater detail in Markó 2015, 2016a, and 2016b.
3. On Nuer scarification and age-sets, see Evans-Pritchard 1940, 249–66. About the role of scarification in identifying individuals, Garve at al. write, "In the ongoing civil war in South Sudan, members of the conflicting ethnic groups and clanships are easily recognisable" (2017, 710).
4. On the unofficially trained Dinka ethnic militia, see Boswell 2019.

References

African Union Commission of Inquiry on South Sudan. 2015. *Final Report of the African Union Commission of Inquiry on South Sudan.* Addis Ababa: African Union.

Agamben, Giorgo. 1998. *Homo Sacer: Sovereign Power and Bare Life.* Stanford, CA: Stanford University Press.

———. 2000. *Means without End: Notes on Politics.* Minneapolis: University of Minnesota Press.

Bayart, Jean-François. 1993. *The State in Africa: The Politics of the Belly.* London: Longman.

Behrends, Andrea. 2011. "Fighting for Oil When There Is No Oil Yet: The Darfur–Chad Border." In Behrends, Reyna, and Schlee 2011, 81–106.

Behrends, Andrea, Stephen P. Reyna, and Günther Schlee, eds. 2011. *Crude Domination: An Anthropology of Oil.* London: Berghahn Books.

Boswell, Alan. 2019. *Insecure Power and Violence: The Rise and Fall of Paul Malong and the Mathiang Anyoor.* Geneva, Switzerland: Small Arms Survey.

Checchi, F., A. Testa, A. Warsame, L. Quach, and R. Burns. 2018. "Estimates of Crisis-Attributable Mortality in South Sudan, December 2013–April 2018: A Statistical Analysis." London: London School of Hygiene and Tropical Medicine. https://www.lshtm.ac.uk/research/centres/health-humanitarian-crises -centre/south-sudan-report-2018.

Craze, Joshua. 2019. *Displaced and Immiserated: The Shilluk of Upper Nile in South Sudan's Civil War, 2014–19.* Geneva, Switzerland: Small Arms Survey.

Craze, Joshua, Jérôme Tubiana, and Claudio Gramizzi. 2016. *A State of Disunity: Conflict Dynamics in Unity State, South Sudan, 2013–15.* Geneva, Switzerland: Small Arms Survey.

de Waal, Alex, ed. 1997. *Food and Power in Sudan: A Critique of Humanitarianism.* London: African Rights, 1997.

———. 2015. *The Real Politics of the Horn of Africa: Money, War and the Business of Power.* Cambridge: Polity.

Evans-Pritchard, Edward Evan. 1940. *The Nuer: A Description of the Modes of Livelihood and Political Institutions of a Nilotic People.* Oxford: Oxford University Press.

Ferguson, James. 1990. *The Anti-Politics Machine: "Development," Depoliticization, and Bureaucratic Power in Lesotho.* Cambridge: Cambridge University Press.

Friedman, Kajsa Ekholm. 2011. "Elves and Witches: Oil Kleptocrats and the Destruction of Social Order in Congo-Brazzaville." In Behrends, Reyna, and Schlee 2011, 107–31.

Garve, Roland, Miriam Garve, Jens C. Türp, Julius N. Fobil, and Christian G. Meyer. 2017. "Scarification in Sub-Saharan Africa: Social Skin, Remedy and Medical Import." *Tropical Medicine & International Health* 22 (6): 708–15. https://doi.org/10.1111/tmi.12878.

Human Rights Division of the United Nations Mission in South Sudan. 2021. *Annual Brief on Violence Affecting Civilians.* Geneva, Switzerland: Office of the High Commissioner for Human Rights. https://unmiss.unmissions.org/sites /default/files/unmiss_annual_brief_violence_against_civilians_2020_final_for _publication.pdf.

Hutchinson, Sharon Elaine. 1996. *Nuer Dilemmas: Coping with Money, War, and the State.* Berkeley: University of California Press.

———. 2000. "Nuer Ethnicity Militarized." *Anthropology Today* 16 (3): 6–13. https:// doi.org/10.1111/1467-8322.00024.

Johnson, Douglas H. 2003. *The Root Causes of Sudan's Civil Wars.* Bloomington: Indiana University Press.

Jok, Jok Madut. 2001. *War and Slavery in Sudan.* Philadelphia: University of Pennsylvania Press.

Jok, Jok Madut, and Sharon Elaine Hutchinson. 1999. "Sudan's Prolonged Second Civil War and the Militarization of Nuer and Dinka Ethnic Identities." *African Studies Review* 42 (2): 125–45. https://doi.org/10.2307/525368.

Kindersley, Nicki, and Øystein H. Rolandsen. 2017. "Civil War on a Shoestring: Rebellion in South Sudan's Equatoria Region." *Civil Wars* 19 (3): 308–24. https:// doi.org/10.1080/13698249.2017.1417073.

Leonardi, Cherry. 2013. *Dealing with Government in South Sudan: Histories of Chiefship, Community and State.* London: James Currey.

Markó, Ferenc Dávid. 2015. "Negotiations and Morality: The Ethnicization of Citizenship in Post-secession South Sudan." *Journal of Eastern African Studies* 9 (4): 669–84. https://doi.org/10.1080/17531055.2015.1105441.

———. 2016a. "Thoughts on Kinship at the Citizenship Office in South Sudan." *Acta Ethnographica Hungarica* 61 (1): 213–26. https://doi.org/10.1556/022.2016 .61.1.10.

———. 2016b. "'We Are Not a Failed State, We Make the Best Passports': South Sudan and Biometric Modernity." *African Studies Review* 59 (2): 113–32. https:// doi.org/10.1017/asr.2016.39.

Mbembe, Achille. 1992. "Provisional Notes on the Postcolony." *Africa: Journal of the International African Institute* 62 (1): 3–37. https://doi-org.brkproxy.minlib.net /10.2307/1160062.

———. 2003. "Necropolitics." *Public Culture* 15 (1): 11–40. https://doi.org/10.1215 /08992363-15-1-11.

———. 2006. "On Politics as a Form of Expenditure." In *Law and Disorder in the Postcolony,* edited by Jean Comaroff and John L. Comaroff, 299–335. Chicago: University of Chicago Press.

Pendle, Naomi R. 2015. "'They Are Now Community Police': Negotiating the Boundaries and Nature of the Government in South Sudan through the Identity of Militarised Cattle-Keepers." *International Journal on Minority and Group Rights* 22 (3): 410–34. https://doi.org/10.1163/15718115-02203006.

———. 2017. "Contesting the Militarization of the Places Where They Met: The Landscapes of the Western Nuer and Dinka (South Sudan)." *Journal of Eastern African Studies* 11 (1): 64–85. https://doi.org/10.1080/17531055.2017.1288408.

———. 2018. "'The Dead Are Just to Drink From': Recycling Ideas of Revenge among the Western Dinka, South Sudan." *Africa: Journal of the International African Institute* 88 (1): 99–121. https://doi.org/10.1017/S0001972017000584.

Pinaud, Clémence. 2014. "South Sudan: Civil War, Predation and the Making of a Military Aristocracy." *African Affairs* 113 (451): 192–211. https://doi.org/10.1093/afraf/adu019.

———. 2021. *War and Genocide in South Sudan.* Ithaca, NY: Cornell University Press.

Piot, Charles. 2010. *Nostalgia for the Future: West Africa after the Cold War.* Chicago: University of Chicago Press.

Reyna, Stephen P. 2011. "Constituting Domination/Constructing Monsters: Imperialism, Cultural Desire and Anti-Beowulfs in the Chadian Petro-state." In Behrends, Reyna, and Schlee 2011, 132–64.

Roitman, Janet. 2005. *Fiscal Disobedience: An Anthropology of Economic Regulation in Central Africa.* Princeton, NJ: Princeton University Press.

Scott, James C. 1998. *Seeing Like a State: How Certain Schemes to Improve the Human Condition Have Failed.* New Haven, CT: Yale University Press.

Small Arms Survey. 2017. "Spreading Fallout: The Collapse of the ARCSS and New Conflict along the Equatorias-DRC Border." Geneva, Switzerland: Small Arms Survey.

Thomas, Edward. 2015. *South Sudan: A Slow Liberation.* London: Zed Books.

———. 2016. "Visiting Akobo." *Sudan Studies* 54:34–40.

United Nations Development Programme. 2017. "National Small Arms Assessment in South Sudan." http://www.ss.undp.org/content/south_sudan/en/home/library/democratic_governance/national-small-arms-assessment-in-south-sudan.html.

Wild, Hannah, Jok Madut Jok, and Ronak Patel. 2018. "The Militarization of Cattle Raiding in South Sudan: How a Traditional Practice Became a Tool for Political Violence." *Journal of International Humanitarian Action* 3 (art. 2). https://doi.org/10.1186/s41018-018-0030-y.

Young, John. 2015. *A Fractious Rebellion: Inside the SPLM-IO.* Geneva, Switzerland: Small Arms Survey.

———. 2016. *Popular Struggles and Elite Co-optation: The Nuer White Army in South Sudan's Civil War.* Geneva, Switzerland: Small Arms Survey.

———. 2017. *Isolation and Endurance: Riek Machar and the SPLM-IO in 2016–17.* Geneva, Switzerland: Small Arms Survey.

TWO

Paper Games

Consularity and Ersatz Lives in Urban Lagos

WALE ADEBANWI AND EBENEZER OBADARE

> But what does one do if the road is
> blocked, one's movement impeded, no
> means at hand to attain one's goal, no
> opportunities forthcoming?
>
> —Michael Jackson, "The Road to Kabala"
> (2011, 113)

> If we want to understand the principles of
> how people act in a state of uncertainty in
> order to achieve certain goals, we have to
> start from the premise that everything is
> subject to re-negotiation.
>
> —Achille Mbembe, "Everything Can Be
> Negotiated" (2000, 274)

An Intercessor's Prayer

"*Come-today, come-tomorrow* will not be your portion in Jesus's name."
Small bowl in hand in hope of some alms, the disheveled man still manages
to project a subdued aura of dignity in his singular prayer, even as he seems
to alternate between a sincere concern—for those on the queue waiting to
know their fate inside the American consulate in Lagos, Nigeria—and a
desperate need for pecuniary support to survive. If you visited Eleke Crescent (later Walter Carrington Crescent), where the United States Consulate (as well as other major consulates) was based, to apply for a visa in the
late 1990s and early 2000s, you could not miss the man—and his distinctive

prayer.[1] At the US consulate, considered the ultimate bureaucratic *border* between real or assumed *bad* life (in Nigeria) and *good* life elsewhere (in the United States, for instance), the man was a haunting presence outside its well-guarded gates, where many aspiring migrants go to perform one of the most crucial parts of the rituals of migration—which is also a critical ritual of *stateness*.[2] Slight in stature, with a world-weary look, he had seen thousands come and go in practical supplication to the "visa god(s)" (see Obadare and Adebanwi 2010b) at Eleke/Carrington Crescent—in their quest to leave a country that one victim of fake-visa merchants described as "this land of frustration" (Okolie 2010).[3]

The visa applicants and would-be migrants are technically on foreign soil in the frontage and premises of the American consulate. Thus, while in a sense they may be psychologically *halfway* between Nigeria and the United States, the physical space of the consulate is, *juridically* speaking, outside the purview of the local state—unless the consulate requires and requests the agencies or agents of the Nigerian state to provide one form of assistance or the other. Thus, even though they might be able to seek redress in the aftermath of any experience that they regarded as "unfair" or even "unlawful" while at the consulate, the visa applicants were completely at the mercy of the foreign state and its agents even while in their own country. They needed all the prayers they could get.

Although we are unsure of the beggar's native tongue (he refused to say), being a Lagosian, he seemed to understand the Yoruba language well enough. "Come-today, come-tomorrow" is a literal translation of the Yoruba expression *wa l'oni, wa l'ola*, used in everyday conversation to express endless goings and comings, repetitive appointments or visits, anxious waiting, vexing repetition, apprehension, uncertainty, and precarity.[4] Sociologically, the expression often captures the unreliability, capriciousness, unpredictability, and/or duplicity of those in positions of authority, especially bureaucratic authority, from whom regular people may desire one thing or the other, including service or support. It is an acknowledgment of the capriciousness and perfidy of bureaucracy, and the assumed inherent contingency of the outcome of one's dealings with it. Thus, when regular people encounter (agents of) officialdom or the privileged who tell them to "come back," as often happens, they pray against *ogun wa l'oni, wa l'ola*—literally "war of come-today, come-tomorrow," but meaning the experience or phenomenon of repeated visits.[5]

In a sense, none of those who seek visas, though not all "regular" people, are immune from this experience of repeated visits, as expressed by the beggar, in their encounters with the local bureaucracy. Thus, when the beggar transposed the experience with local bureaucracy to the consular (foreign) bureaucracy, emphasizing that both bureaucracies are unreliable, unpredictable, capricious, and/or duplicitous, he was not only confirming the intuition of many visa applicants, he was also expressing the way in which aspiring migrants *saw,* and *still see,* the local or foreign state (see Kyle and Siracusa 2005). This attitude toward consular bureaucracy and consular bureaucrats is not limited to Nigeria. As Maybritt Jill Alpes (2013) shows in the case of Cameroon, consular bureaucrats who collect fees but refuse to grant visas are regarded as "thieves," because their *rationale* for refusing to grant visas after taking fees from applicants is regarded as *irrational* and even *illicit.* Thus, as David Kyle and Christina A. Siracusa argue regarding such "competing ways of moral reasoning," "state discourses of licitness are challenged by multiple coherent discourses of justice within sending and destination countries" (2005, 26).

The daily prayer intercessions of the man at the consulate for the visa *supplicants*—or those he regarded as such (most of whom also so regarded themselves)—can be read as a form of propositional hinge that on the one hand connects the need for divine intervention (elicited through prayer) with a pragmatic recognition of the *nonrationality,* if not *irrationality,* of the visa-granting process, and, on the other, connects the unpredictability, capriciousness, even callousness of the consular officials with an understanding of the socioeconomic and political conditions that predispose people to want to migrate (escape) to the West (in this case the United States) in the assumption that such an escape would lead to a good life elsewhere. That is, the beggar at the US consulate is not merely praying for supplicants (visa applicants) but also making a commentary on the visa process as one that does not consistently derive from bureaucratic rationality, while acknowledging the disciplinary techniques that the visa-granting process, by way of the consulate officers, imposes on would-be migrants. As we have argued elsewhere, this poverty of rationality and predictability is the immediate trigger for various acts of desperate subversion, whether spiritual (Obadare and Adebanwi 2010b), quasi-legal, or involving outright illegal procurement of required documentation. Thus, the beggar's invocation can be read as a commentary not only on the visa process itself but on a social phenomenon.

The phrase "propositional hinge" is borrowed from Ludwig Wittgenstein via Elizabeth Povinelli. In his reflections in *On Certainty* (1972, passages 341–43), Wittgenstein argues, in Povinelli's words, that "propositional hinges function as axles around which an entire apparatus of practical and propositional knowledge about the world turns rather than a set of propositions about the state of the world" (Povinelli 2016, 37). We are specifically interested in the way in which Povinelli has articulated this perspective based on her reflections on Wittgenstein's assertion in stating that "one either remains within the axial environment of a hinged world or one converts to another" (ibid., 38). The propositional hinge regarding the apparatus of "practical and propositional knowledge" about visas has led many to believe not only that the process functions in ways that collapse both the *rational* and the *irrational,* but also, as noted above, that this *collapse* necessitates, if not in fact legitimizes, all sorts of responses: spiritual, legal, para-legal, or even outright illegal, including the resort to fake documents. Thus, through their bureaucratic regimes of documentality—the *juridical* power and process of investing "an inscription with institutional value" (Ferraris 2013, 249) and the associated disciplinary techniques—that govern life in the local state as well as the processes of exit from the local to the foreign state, both the local and the foreign state *constitute* or *form* certain kinds of subjectivity in those wishing to procure the "necessary" documents and structure "the very conditions of [their] existence . . . and the trajectories of their desires and aspirations" (Obadare and Adebanwi 2010a, 2) regarding what it takes to *achieve* a *good life*—through what Cameroonians call "bushfalling"; that is, going abroad against all odds to make money (see Nyamnjoh 2011; Alpes 2013, 2017).

Documental regimes have been described by some as "government *of* paper" (Hull 2012, emphasis added), or as popularly described in India, *Kaghazi Raj,* "government *by* paper" (see Mathur 2015, 3, emphasis added). Veena Das and Deborah Poole argue that "the documentary . . . practices of the state are all intended, in some sense, to consolidate state control over subjects, populations, territories, and lives" (2004b, 9). This is partly what Das and Poole speak to regarding how "life" is put in question (2004b, 9). The struggle to achieve a good life, for many young people in Nigeria and elsewhere in Africa, involves encounters and negotiations with what we describe as *consularity.*

By "consularity" we do not mean merely the office of a consul or the (experience of the) acts and practices of consulship. Beyond that, consularity, for us, refers to the whole panoply of official and unofficial, bureaucratic and pseudo-bureaucratic practices and processes—including the legal, the para-legal and the illegal, as defined by the state's laws and rules—that the regimes of seeking and applying for visas impose and/or provoke, particularly among those who are least favored in the process of procuring exit visas by the existing circumstances, rules, and requirements imposed by the state. In this context, both the local and foreign (target) state merge into a "translocal entity, which localizes itself in particular sites, and at particular times" (Ferme 2013, 958, following Gupta 1995, 376). Therefore, consularity in this context involves alternatively, or where necessary, simultaneously, mastering and/or subverting the rules of engagement, including the *disciplinary* rules for the production and reproduction of documents and the associated processes of affirming, confirming, or gaining documentary authenticity. And because, prior to the consummation of the *thirst for else-where* prevalent among potential migrants in Africa, the thirst must first be "consularized," the process of acquiring what is demanded by *the consul,* for those that we studied, necessarily involves investing themselves, or others on their behalf, with the *pretend* juridical capacity to produce or procure the necessary papers—through fakery or counterfeiting. This process, to use Das and Poole's words, involves "tactics that are parasitical on law even as they draw repertoires of action from it" (2004, 10).

It is obvious that the beggar at the consulate *believed* that some of the ways, means, or reasons why people are granted visas are not necessarily rational—or legal. For many years, as we traveled in and out of Nigeria, both authors encountered this beggar—and his prayers—at the consulate. He was a fixed presence, first as we sought US visas to attend international conferences or participate in fellowship programs in the United States and elsewhere, later when on our way to the United Kingdom to study for our doctorates, and eventually as we headed for the United States to work and eventually made the country our second home. While we were both not particularly prayerful about visas, we could not but grasp the logic of the man's prayer and would experience its import in the course of our applications for visas.

In this chapter, we explore how marginalized agents (would-be migrants) respond to this seemingly endless demand for "proper" documentation by setting up and becoming key participants in the Nigerian transnational visa economy—an ensemble of practices, private and institutional actors, institutions, and state and para-state agents involved in the facilitation of the complicated process of emigration, including the production of official as well as alternative travel documentation for clients who hail from Nigeria and, increasingly, other parts of the West African subregion (see Pype's and Orock's chapters in this volume on ID cards and passports in the DRC and Cameroon, respectively). In the quote that opened this chapter, anthropologist Michael Jackson (2011, 113) raises a set of critical questions that mirror the conditions that predispose our subjects to contest both the local and foreign states' exclusive right and capacity to determine the authenticity and legitimacy of documents needed for traveling to the West: "What does one do if the road is blocked, one's movement impeded, no means at hand to attain one's goal, no opportunities forthcoming?"

Wale Ismail, in a critical essay on the phenomenon of fake documents in Nigeria, called "Oluwole" (both as *practice* and as *site*), raises a question as to why there is "an embarrassing silence" about Oluwole in extant scholarly literature, despite "occasional media sensationalism." He suggests that perhaps this is because even members of the intelligentsia in Nigeria are "caught in the web of the Oluwole phenomenon" (2010: 29). While we do not make any assumptions about the reasons for the dearth of scholarly examination of the phenomenon, in this chapter we aspire to fill a small, though critical, niche in the scholarly discourse on "globalization (or counter-globalization) from below" in the context of the much-debated new challenges to the sovereignty of the state in the global age. We seek to demonstrate how those who work within the Oluwole economy not only experience and encounter the state and define it for themselves and others, but also *facilitate* globalization and become participants in the transnational process by producing agents who, in a significant number of cases, eventually become transnational migrants.[6] Further, we situate the workings of the parallel visa economy within a larger economy of falsification. We argue that the parallel visa economy is a fallout of a combination of factors: the arbitrariness of visa regimes set up by the consular offices and officials of key Western states, the aggravating and complicated slowness of the bureaucratic process in the local state, the thirst or appetite for elsewhere fostered by the scarcity of opportunities for material gain and professional enhancement in post–Cold War (West) Africa, and the related freeze in social mobility as a result of endemic unemployment and the vicious dis-embedding of the state from ordinary people's lives.

We draw motivation from the following critical questions: Who are the key participants in this economy? What are its mechanisms, logics, and procedures? Who are its clientele and why do they patronize it? What is the significance of this economy in the context of everyday life in the contemporary postcolony, and why has it endured, even prospered, despite the state's apparent commitment to its eradication? The question regarding the state becomes crucial given how the state often emerges as a zone of forgery and falsification, as many of its apparatuses and agents have also been master forgers.[7] Thus, in this zone of *mutual forgery,* many young people regard themselves as (a) "mediating evidential authority" (Yeh 2012, 713) of both the municipal and metropolitan state in helping themselves and others to survive or escape the agonizing conditions of life imposed by the irresponsibility of the municipal state; and (b) approaching the postcolonial states, in which they have been forced to live and are "contained," as an *original* colonial forgery by the same master forgers (former colonial masters—and, by extension, the United States, though not an original colonial power in Africa) which now impose boundaries and limits on their capacity to thrive—or live well. These young people are often in what Judith Butler describes as "a difficult bind, if not an impossible one," in that they are desiring to "to live, even to live well, within social organizations of life, biopolitical regimes, that sometimes establish [their] very lives as disposable or negligible or, worse, seek to negate [their] lives" (2015, 210).

Therefore, if the postcolonial state was *forged* by metropolitan powers, for these young people, ipso facto, both the local and the foreign state must be forced to recognize that the forgery perpetrated to escape the *initial* forgery (the post/colonial state and its boundaries) cannot be worse, or more morally repugnant, than the original forgery. In a sense, these young people seem to provide quotidian evidence for Philip Abrams's argument that the state is a massive fakery behind which different forces hide. Thus, the *pretension* that is the state can be unveiled or uncovered in everyday practices (see Navaro-Yashin 2002).

Accordingly, the thrust of this chapter is these young agents' efforts to beat consularity at its own "game of papers," through the performance (as *rule-based* and as a form of *play*) of a key ritual of (e)migration. In order to understand these efforts, in 2005 and 2006 and afterwards intermittently until 2016, we conducted ethnographic research at Oluwole, the notorious headquarters of the "alternative documentation" market based in the Central Business District of Lagos Island and in full view of the major Western consulates on Walter Carrington Crescent, Victoria Island. Oluwole is the perfect double entendre. While it is the name of a particular location on Lagos Island, at the same time it denotes a congeries of practices and/or processes of document forgery or counterfeiting, and serves as the name of the *kind* of products associated with that location. Hence, to be in possession of an *Oluwole passport* is to carry a fake passport that may or may not have been sourced from the site Oluwole, which was notorious as the "best" place to get whatever kind of counterfeit documents or any form of documentary *evidence* required—including the associated symbols of *authenticity:* stamps, signatures, seal, etc. (see Ismail 2010). Ismail has described Oluwole as being "at the interstices between the real and abstract, official and unofficial, local and international, and the legal and illegal identity and manifestation of the Nigerian state," while it also "poignantly defines the complex channel of encountering, accessing, (mis)appropriating, and interaction between the dysfunctional Nigerian state and the agency (and artistry) of its citizenry" (ibid., 30).

In the main, we seek to understand the workings and mechanisms of Oluwole as a parallel economy, the protocols of its "underground" operation, its connections to the official documentation regime (of the state and of consularity), its relationship with law and law enforcement, and the ways in which it challenges both the local and the foreign states' "monopoly position over the legitimate means of mobility control" (Alpes 2013, 146, following Torpey 1998). Before narrating the techniques and mechanics of Oluwole, however, it is important to understand what Oluwole responds to. That imperative, we argue, is the regime of consularity and the arbitrariness that seems to be its chief characteristic, as demonstrated by the experience of the average person seeking to procure a travel visa at any of the Western embassies. As the stories below demonstrate, not only is the process of attempting to procure a travel visa marked by a high degree of arbitrariness, interactions within the physical space of the embassy are frequently punctuated by violence to the persons of visa applicants.[8] Hence, apart from being an attempt to subvert consularity by beating it at its own game of documentation, Oluwole, to stay close to the logic that we encountered during fieldwork, is also approached by its operatives and their clients as uniquely "ethical."[9] It is driven by an understandable imperative to either avoid or "retaliate" against the random physical, verbal, and psychic violence meted out to visa applicants.[10] If our inference about *retaliation* is accepted, the operators of Oluwole are, therefore, not involved in the production of "mere" documentation. They also see themselves as *moral* agents motivated by a concern for social dignity in the practice of snatching from the state (both local and foreign) its power and capacity to *authenticate* and *validate* words, actions, requests, dreams, and aspirations through documents. In imitating the state's production, authentication, and validation of documents, these agents are also challenging and contesting the state's right, power, and capacity to produce, authenticate, and validate documents, thereby establishing what is *true* and *valid* about papers.

A Day at the Consulate

> Visit any of the foreign embassies in Nigeria today especially British or US embassies to see the way they treat Nigerians like animals irrespective of whether you are a Professor, Engineer, Doctor, Chief, Pastor, Evangelist it does not make much difference to them. They will stand everybody outside from around 3am in the morning till when they will stop receiving Visa applications, and interviews. Whether it is raining, drizzling, sun shine [*sic*], cold weather, windy or dusty it does not matter to them.
>
> —Okafor (2014, 74)

We are arguing that the process of applying for a travel visa to Western destinations is arbitrary, often humiliating, and carries a threat of casual violence to applicants, and that the parallel economy in documentation symbolized by Oluwole is best understood as partly a direct response to this mix of arbitrariness and random violence—physical and/or psychic. This understanding of the visa application process as inherently arbitrary and often violent came through clearly in our conversations both with visa applicants at various Western embassies and with prospective applicants who had yet to visit the embassies of the countries they intended to travel to, but who viewed their upcoming encounters with trepidation.

There is an encyclopedia's worth of reports across the Nigerian media that speak to these elements of unpredictability, humiliation, and assault on the bodies of applicants.[11] The above lament by a Nigerian public commentator is representative of the despair of many Nigerians at the belittling treatment of Nigerian visa applicants at various Western consulates. Yet rather than recapitulate these reports, we wish to mention here our own unpalatable experience, which in some sense triggered our determination to undertake the research on which this chapter partly draws. It is important to note, however, that our experience and the experiences of several people who have gone through a similar process should be understood against the backdrop of the fundamental attitude of the officials of the (mostly) Western consulates toward most visa applicants in many countries in Africa. As Alpes notes, against the backdrop of the experience in Cameroon, "as always potentially implicated in fraud, *all* visa applications were a priori criminalised and suspicious as potential threats to national security. . . . *[All]* aspiring visa applicants were considered to be potentially illegal immigrants, [but] the discourse . . . also allowed [that] aspiring migrants [could be] potential victims of migration brokers" (2013, 154, emphasis added).[12]

When, in July 2001, Obadare applied for a British visa, he did so full of confidence. He had a letter of admission into a PhD program at the London School of Economics and evidence of financial support from the Ford Foundation. He had to run the gauntlet that was the process of applying for a visa, including being threatened with expulsion from the premises of the British High Commission by a consular officer for expressing shock that the officer didn't know of the Ford Foundation, his sponsors. "What is Ford Foundation?" she had asked. Yet that bewildered question was hardly the worst of Obadare's experience as, on a different visit (he, too, having had to "come-today-come-tomorrow"), he was hit on the chest with the butt of a gun by one of the soldiers stationed outside the High Commission for, as the irritated soldier saw it, not staying on the queue.

For his part, in October 2001 Adebanwi was insulted by a consular officer at the US consulate in Lagos when he returned to collect his visa/passport because he forgot to drop off the Form IAP-66 sent by his host institution in the United States. This form, issued by the United States Citizenship and Immigration Service, is sent to a J-1 visa applicant by his or her US host institution. As he stepped out of the consulate after submitting his application, Adebanwi realized that he had forgotten to submit the Form IAP-66 along with the application. When he requested to go back inside the consulate to submit the form, the security guards refused to let him back in, despite his plea that the form was needed by the consular officials to determine the kind of visa he had applied for. He returned two days later and tried to explain to an official that he had forgotten to submit the Form IAP-66 and had not been let back into the premises by the security guards, but the official shouted at him and threatened to expose his "attempted fraud"—though it was obvious that he would not attempt any deceit in order to get a restrictive (J-1) visa for the specific purpose of his travel (a fellowship) when he already possessed a two-year nonrestrictive (B1/B2) visitor visa in the same passport that he submitted. When this particularly rude officer saw that Adebanwi was unfazed as he talked back at him, the officer threw Adebanwi's passport through the hole and told him to leave. Adebanwi later approached his contacts (who he had met when he was a journalist) at the United States Information Service in Lagos for intervention. One of them collected his documents and passport and submitted them to the consulate for the J-1 visa.[13]

One of our respondents, Sola John,[14] an employee of a major transnational corporation, incidentally with its Nigerian headquarters on the same street as the US consulate in Lagos—explained how he felt humiliated at the US consulate when he applied for a visa in 2008. He had traveled to the United Kingdom and Ireland (his adoptive mother was Irish) many times and a couple of times to the United States. In 2008, he applied for a visa to spend his holiday in the States. After his application was denied, he was so shocked that he asked the interviewing officer, "Why? I have all the necessary documents." The officer responded, "My concern is security." He was not allowed to ask further questions, as the officer called on the next person on the queue. All those waiting in line heard the exchange, which further worsened our respondent's humiliation. The decision didn't make sense to him. He was left wondering what "security" threat he constituted as a professional working for a blue-chip company who had traveled to various Western cities multiple times. He felt that if he were carrying an Irish passport, he would not have been so humiliated—or needed a visa to travel to the United States in the first place. Indeed, it is to avoid such humiliation for the rest of their lives that many young people seek to emigrate to countries in the West where they can eventually gain citizenship or at least right of residence, so they no longer have to face the constant humiliation entailed in the process of procuring visas.

To further illustrate the fact that this *irrationality* is not experienced only by the subaltern, our last example is the experience of one of Nigeria's most prominent poets, Odia Ofeimun. Next to luminaries of the generation of Chinua Achebe and Wole Soyinka, Ofeimun is one of the most respected members of the literati in the country. Between the 1980s and early 1990s, he lived in Oxford as a visiting scholar at the university, after serving on the editorial board of Nigeria's flagship newspaper, the *Guardian,* and, before that, as the private secretary to one of Nigeria's founding fathers, Chief Obafemi Awolowo. Since returning to Nigeria from the United Kingdom in 1993, Ofeimun had visited the country a few times—and elsewhere around the world. In 2006, as he explains in a preface to a poem he wrote in reaction to his experience, "exactly ten years after the British High Commission denied me a visa to enjoy a facility provided by the British Council to see the London Book Fair, and then relented, . . . my visa application was rejected again, this time, with a sticker on my passport, which says 'he *claims* to be a writer'" (emphasis added).[15]

How does one make sense of the British Consulate denying a visa to someone who had been invited by the British Council? And can the original decision be regarded as "rational" when, upon intervention, the consulate "relented"? What is interesting is that, after the rejection was reported in *TheNEWS* magazine, the consulate contacted Ofeimun and granted him a ten-year visa (he had applied originally for only four years).[16] While this was a commendable reversal upon recognition of their error in refusing Ofeimun a visa, many who heard about this encounter were further convinced that the decision-making process for granting visas was not entirely rational. It further cemented the view of many aspiring migrants that the foreign state, or at least the officials of the foreign state in the consulates, do not reach decisions on the basis of rationality.[17] In his poetic denunciation of the British High Commission for regarding his claim of being a writer as either a lie or an indication that he had no *valuable* job, Ofeimun writes, "I do not claim to be, I am a writer . . . / though the syllabus of errors / at the British High Commission / may set no column for my stripe."[18]

Collectively, these experiences (ours and those of the average Nigerian applicant) substantiate the general idea that the visa application process is far from rational and is designed to humiliate, sometimes violently, visa applicants at Western consulates. While the "social discipline" at the consulates has hardly tempered the flow of visa applicants (such is the dreariness of their economic prospects in Nigeria that, for our respondents, mostly young people, humiliation at the consulate was a price they would rather pay for a chance to "get out"), it has created a situation in which the visa interview itself becomes a "performance" in the sense established by Erving Goffman. The manifest irrationality of the visa application process produces an aesthetic in which visa applicants are forced to construct a "self" that is "assembled" for the visa process, even if that "self" is radically different from the "self" that they "present" on a normal day. This "staging of identity" includes but is not limited to the choice of dress, shoes, and other sartorial accompaniments that enhance one's "presentability" for the all-important visa interview.[19] For women in particular, "appropriate dressing" is essential

FIGURE 1. A view of the Oluwole Urban Market in the central business district, near Marina, Lagos, December 2016. Photo by Akintunde Akinleye/Reuters.

given their quite legitimate apprehension at being miscategorized as prospective prostitutes.[20] The crystallization of this relationship of simulacra between the consulate and applicants, we argue, is the "arrangement" of documentation meant to, as it were, thwart the latter. This is where Oluwole, home of imitation, comes in.

"Oluwole"

Mechanics and Protocols

We have established in the foregoing that the recourse to Oluwole by visa applicants is partly a function of the arbitrariness and opacity of the visa application process and the rough treatment that applicants are constantly subjected to.[21] Arbitrariness here is understood in two senses. First is the perceived dissociation between the quality or volume of the documentation supplied by the visa applicant and the outcome of his or her application, leading to the paradoxical situation wherein "legitimate" applicants are denied visas while those who play the "game of papers" are successful. Thus, contrary to its own intentions, the visa application system not only incentivizes its own subversion, it often ends up rewarding the very category of visa applicant that the system was presumably designed to eliminate.

Second, we refer to arbitrariness in the kind of documentation required of visa applicants, and the use made of such documentation by consular officials once the applicant has managed to produce it. Several of our respondents (both successful and unsuccessful applicants) expressed their amusement or frustration, as the case may be, that there seems to have been no real interest in scrutinizing the documents they had put so much effort into gathering, giving rise to the impression that their fates were determined on a whim and leading to the conclusion that the outcome of a visa application was not correlated to the quality or volume of the documentation provided in support—as the experience of Sola John shows. As a result, and as we discovered in our research, it is not only the visa applicant aiming to manufacture a new identity who goes to Oluwole, it is also the visa applicant whose bona fides are otherwise "real" but who is apprehensive of falling short in the not unlikely event that a consular official demands a piece of documentation that he or she should have brought along. Such examples are an apt reminder of the intriguing layering of the "authentic" and the "fake" and the ceaseless intermeshing of both in the everyday drama of postcolonial subjectivity. Further examples of this dynamic are provided below.

In its overall logic, Oluwole (also fondly called the "Territory" by those who work there), epitomizes this amalgam of the "real" and the "inauthentic." For instance, although it exists, properly speaking, outside the law, that in no way makes it alien to the law and its theoretical enforcers. As a matter of fact, not only is the law (from police through immigration to customs officials) integral to its operations, Oluwole could neither exist nor be successful without it, as, for the most part, its existence depends on the willingness of law enforcement and other officials of the state to either look the other way or render covert cooperation, depending on the needs of Oluwole. As we learned, Oluwole relies on a network of officials of the state, such as those who work in the passport offices of the Nigeria Immigration Service (NIS), and police officers. The former provide the Oluwole operatives with original copies of the Nigerian passport immediately after a new version is released by the NIS. The latter give tip-offs about impending police activity and, at calculated intervals, carry out fake arrests (also known as "PR [public relations] arrests") designed to convey the impression to the general public that the law is doing its best to clamp down on Oluwole's operations. Such "straddling" police officers are remunerated either on a weekly or monthly basis. From what we gathered, these law enforcement agents do not work in isolation, but form an effective quasi-criminal network with embassy investigation officers, immigration/customs officials, and bank staff—the latter supplying the necessary bank statements to be presented at the consulate by the visa applicant. The role of the officials of the passport office is critical, particularly when a new version of the Nigerian passport with improved security features is released by the NIS. The officials not only provide a copy of the latest version of the passport to the Oluwole operatives; they will also explain the new security features. Ahmed Ilori,[22] who claimed to be one of the top Oluwole operators in the 1980s and early 1990s—before he moved on to more legitimate businesses—revealed that they adapted their methods of faking the Nigerian passport and visas in response to new passport and visa technologies and the nature of the demands. The operators, who called themselves *arrangees* (those who *arrange* things), worked constantly with the NIS officials. He explained that in the 1980s, because the pages of the Nigerian passport were stitched together by a machine, if a client needed to use someone else's passport, they would remove the plastic covering the headshot of the original passport owner and change the headshot to that of the person who would be using the passport, and then return the plastic before sewing the page back into the passport. The code for this is *ori olori*—literally, "someone else's head." He explained that there were some arrangees who specialized in removing and returning the plastic covering on the relevant page of the passport and others whose expertise was in sewing back the page of the passport into the passport booklet. They sought out these specialists if they needed to ensure the substitution of the headshot was "smooth." Ilori disclosed that when the NIS later added a seal to the photo page, he and the other operators would remove the entire page when changing the headshot and then add a fake seal exactly like the original. The NIS changed the passport again at some point in the early 1990s, adding a new plastic covering to the pages of the passport booklet. After receiving a copy of this new edition from their colluders in the passport office, the operators realized that the only way to fake the relevant pages of the passport was to "laminate" the pages. After removing the plastic in order to add "ori olori," they would then place a cloth on the page and use a clothes iron to glue the plastic to the page. When the NIS later released digital passports, the arrangees still found a more complex way around it, though, as he said, this was more challenging. But they succeeded because some NIS officials constantly colluded with them.

The role of embassy investigation officers is also crucial given the reliance of various embassies on the "knowledge" that they produce based on their investigations of individual visa applications. Other than that, Oluwole operates more or less like a "real" or regular place of employment, complete with its norms and protocols.

First, it operates on the basis of a clear division of labor, with tasks allocated in line with the skills of respective workers. For instance, in the alteration of a passport, those who remove the stamp are different from those who produce the passport information page. There are calligraphers who are in charge of signatures, while others attend to statements of accounts to be presented to Western embassies, or certificates and other documents to support applications.

Second, different forms of "alteration" exist, depending on the specific needs of individual clients. The two basic ones are "boosting" and "transplanting." "Boosting" arose in response to the requirement by Western embassies that visa applicants show proof of financial stability. The whole point of "boosting" is to augment a bank balance with a record of transactions that never happened in the first place. This is typically done with the cooperation of liaisons or contacts within the banking industry. Such contacts either supply otherwise legitimate documents or stand by to provide validation for claims made by visa applicants if or when contacted by specific embassies. As a rule, there are "sleepers" within the banks (and the embassies, we were told) who act as the eyes of Oluwole within the banking industry. A second method of "alteration" is known as "transplanting." Transplanting is what happens when an entirely new information page is superimposed on an existing passport with a valid visa to a Western destination. As part of this process, sometimes the visas of other countries are transplanted into a passport in order to give the impression that the owner of the passport has traveled before and is therefore not saddled with the dreaded "virgin passport"—that is, a previously unstamped passport, denoting that the owner has never traveled outside the country and thus inviting greater scrutiny. To bypass this problem, Oluwole generates imitation stamps (certain African and East Europeans countries, one of the operators said, are easiest to imitate) that are then embossed on scattered pages of a given passport to give the impression that the holder is a frequent traveler, thus *boosting* their chances of getting a visa into one of the choice European or North American destinations. In this example, a collection of fake visas improves one's chances of getting the real one, demonstrating yet again the intriguing coexistence of the inauthentic and the authentic.

Travel visas are not the only documents for which Oluwole produces imitations on demand. A partial list would include college and university diplomas (all levels of tertiary education, including PhD), bank account statements, travel stamps (in and out), college entrance examination (e.g., Joint Admissions and Matriculation Board and West African Examinations Council results, university and polytechnic admission letters, National Youth Service Corps discharge certificates, business registration certificates, tax clearance certificates, and even death certificates). Finally, Oluwole also offers "predeparture coaching" for patrons adjudged to be in need of such. Typically, these are individuals who are planning to travel with "transplanted" passports to destinations they have supposedly visited before. As such, predeparture coaching can involve educating the prospective traveler in the geography of a chosen urban center, for instance, London. For this, Oluwole would typically draw on the knowledge of people who have actually visited or lived in London (some of the respondents who agreed to speak to us were deportees from the UK).[23] At Oluwole, it was not unusual to meet a prospective traveler to London who, having never seen the inside of an airplane, yet is able to recite the different stops on the entire London Underground without the briefest glance at a map. In market terms, Oluwole represents the classic meeting of need and product—that is, between the desire to travel (to escape harsh material conditions) and the need to survive on the part of the operators of the "Territory." Fundamentally, both operators and clientele are responding to not-too-dissimilar socioeconomic stimuli. In fact, we suggest, following Karin Barber's (1987) insightful analysis of popular arts in Africa, that Oluwole's fakeries can be approached as *popular*—though, in this context, illegal—*art forms* "situated in 'unofficial' spaces of cultural production" and circulating "around the everyday worlds of people on the streets and outside the limits and hierarchies of officialdom" (Newell and Okome 2014, 3).

Yet there is deception even within this system of deceptive documentality. Ilori revealed that arrangees are constantly attempting to deceive their clients, either by swindling them of their money or forcing them to pay much more than required for their services. There were arrangees in the outer part of Oluwole, when it still existed as a territorial location, whose only purpose was to take money off clients without even offering any service. There were others who tricked clients into parting with more money than the real (inside) operators would charge. In this context, Oluwole has its lingo for clients and victims. Generally, those who are cheated of their money are called *mungunu*, a corruption of *mugun*—a popular word for a dupe in urban southwestern Nigeria—or specifically, *Ajao* (an otherwise regular Yoruba name), a code reserved for those who have been swindled while seeking a fake passport or a fake visa.

Extrapolations

On the basis of the analysis and data presented on Oluwole in the foregoing, we are led to a few tentative extrapolations. First, and consistent with the argument we have been advancing, the market in travel documentation seems to have grown out of and continues to be nourished by a widespread belief among both "producers" and their clientele that "the whole documentation thing" is an innately amoral game that is won or lost, not necessarily because of the basic authenticity or validity of one's papers, but based on how well one is able to "arrange one's papers." This is the essence of the idea of "the paper games." In this sense, procuring relevant travel documentation is about "generating" the necessary papers in order to satisfy a bureaucracy, rather than actually producing "authentic papers." Here, it is productive to think about the discordance between what is "true" versus what is true "on paper."

A second extrapolation relating specifically to Oluwole is that, as a strategy of survival by people on the margins, it is ultimately inseparable from the phenomenon of hustling. Hustling is a way "out" (materially and symbolically) for the excluded or marginalized, those anthropologist Janet Roitman (2006) describes as "economic refugees." Forging alternatives (both life alternatives and documentary alternatives) is one dimension of hustling that needs to be placed in the global context of the politics of survival (see Chabal 2009, esp. chap. 6) among those shunted to the margins of society by local and transnational socioeconomic forces. In this sense, those whose technical labor makes Oluwole possible (many are young graduates who cannot seem to find regular employment) are, vicariously or not, participants in a cosmopolitan conversation.

Third, and to revisit a theme previously flagged, it is interesting to consider the ethics of Oluwole's existence and operations. There are at least five key observations here. First, most of those who work in the industry are convinced that if they are committing a crime at all, it is a victimless one. In fact, many of them think they are doing something charitable, to the extent that what they do will ultimately help other people actualize their dream of getting out of Nigeria. Second, many see no moral content in the local state and its institutions and apparatuses of governance and, therefore, in their instruments of document production and validation. In light of this, they conclude that a state that is unable to provide the opportunities for making a good life does not deserve any respect for its protocols regarding governing documents. Third, there is a notion of doing anything to "get one over on" a "West" that some hold responsible for the country's woes, even as they continue to see Western countries as the ultimate El Dorado. Fourth, and related to the last point, some see getting one over on the West (especially the United States and United Kingdom) as part of a moral debt that these countries owe African countries—based on past colonial domination and present global inequalities. Fifth, there is an ambivalent attitude in the general society toward Oluwole's operations, with some refusing to blame young people who are merely trying to make the best of the hand they have been dealt by the local state, if not by fate.

Under-Writing the State?

> The variety and variability of the realm of documentality can be grasped by thinking of the various *grades of inscription,* which is to say the hierarchy that turns a mere trace into a document, and of the different *levels of validity* of documents, which may be underwritten by the intervention of a figure like a notary public or an attorney.
>
> —Maurizio Ferraris, *Documentality*
> (2013, 251)

Global mobility is the essential backdrop to the analysis presented in this chapter. As acknowledged by a vast literature and as reiterated earlier, the African dimension to this is the continued emigration of hundreds of thousands of young men and women (via regular and not so regular means) to various global destinations in their search to consummate their lives and gain "existential potency" (Jackson 2011, 99). In this chapter, we have followed the relevant literature in locating this seemingly ceaseless flow in the conjoined failure of governance at various national levels, and the unsettling consequences of global economic and political forces. But the word "flow," while understandable, is often misapplied to this process. For, while it may capture something of the urgent appetite for travel, it fails to apprehend the various impediments and blockages that are part and parcel of global mobility. We have attempted here to focus on one such blockage—that is, the production of an arbitrary visa application and processing regime as a way to frustrate potential travelers (hence, we suggest, drastically limiting the numbers of emigrants to Western countries) and, consequently, the attempt to undermine and undo this regime through the setting up of a parallel infrastructure for the systematic generation of alternative documentation.

In setting up this parallel infrastructure, young people, we argue, appear to contest if not directly challenge the authority of local and foreign states to shape and limit mobility. Indeed, unlike the Kuranko people of Sierra Leone studied by Michael Jackson, while these young people in Lagos have learned to "negotiate the obstacles and uncertainties of everyday life," they do not believe that this knowledge "is more worthy than the search for transcendence or escape" (2011, 62). For them, this *knowledge* is the condition of their *transcendence* or *escape* from the harsh conditions of quotidian life in Nigeria. Document forgery, as symbolized by Oluwole, we propose, is one such instrument of contesting both local and foreign states' exclusive rights to determine who leaves and who is welcome, respectively. Fundamentally, this specific practice of forgery is an everyday direct challenge to the state's right to authenticate, to adjudicate between the true and the false, and to determine and delimit the spatial mobility of the "undesirables" from the margins. Document forgery can therefore be approached as a subaltern strategy to undermine the authority of *state writing*—a way of *under-writing* the state, that is, *writing* the state under the table—which determines the forms of transnational mobilities. Following Ferraris's (2013) insight in the above quote, we argue that the documents emerging from Oluwole achieve a dubious *level of validity* underwritten by the intervention of those we would describe as *"notaries private"*—who appropriate or pretend to the authority of notaries public and attorneys.

In closing, therefore, we wish to emphasize two key points. The first is that the industry in alternative travel documentation is itself only a slice of a wider economy of imitation, one in which the existence of an original (a passport, a certificate, a travel visa, a CD, a DVD, Nigeria's currency, or any currency for that matter) is almost invariably seen as an invitation or a challenge to produce its "authentic" double.[24] In this economy of imitation, people generally take for granted the existence of fake banks, fake academic conferences, forged electoral victories, fake soldiers, fake policemen, ghost workers, fake pastors, and, last but not least, a pretend state. Instructively, the first great scandal of the Nigerian Fourth Republic was the revelation in July 1999 by a national newsmagazine, *TheNEWS*, that the then newly elected speaker of the Federal House of Representatives, Salisu Buhari, had lied about his age (he was twenty-nine, not thirty-six as claimed) and tendered a fake University of Toronto diploma.

Now, we are by no means suggesting that every Nigerian is involved in counterfeiting, or, crucially, that the very existence of the parallel economy creates no moral tension. On the contrary, the point we are making here is similar to the one that anthropologist Daniel Jordan Smith makes concerning the moral struggles of agents who are "participants in perpetuating corruption in their society, [but] do so in circumstances that are partly beyond their control." Smith goes on to propose that "the explanation for corruption in Nigeria requires understanding the intersection of local culture and larger systems of inequality, and in ways that refute a simplistic scenario that blames the victims" (2007, 6).

Along the same line, we want to suggest that the explanation for the imitation economy, specifically the existence and flourishing of the economy in alternative travel documentation, requires an understanding of the intersection of youth angst, social alienation, general destitution, technological knowledge, and an ambivalent attitude toward both the "local" and the "global" state that involves a mix of adoration, repulsion, humiliation, and retaliation. Further, insofar as the travel visa and other such official permits and documents consecrate and sanctify the state as the exclusive space, zone, and instrument of, and for the determination of, the genuine, the imitation economy is a symbolic challenge to this exclusivity. In this manner, the historical conceit of the state, particularly in its postcolonial manifestation, is challenged by the subaltern, the young underprivileged, who have been cast out or cast off by the state. "Genuineness," therefore, becomes, in the zone of forgery and falsification, a play on the access (and also excess) and authority that the state backs up by its capacity to mobilize exclusive violence and compel and command obedience. Inside the "Territory," the state's sovereignty is mimicked by those with the capacity to make the "doubles" of official authorization through (access to) practical ingenuity (in relation to the *genuine*) and the mobilization of both legal and illegal resources that invest them with counterfeit, or what we call ersatz, "authority."[25]

As a matter of fact, what the Salisu Buhari scandal mentioned above underscores is that textual deception/imitation in Nigeria is hardly the preserve of any particular social class, let alone the underclass. On the contrary, the alternative economy is seen as a resource (often, but not always, a last a resort) by both the political and business elite and subalterns. Some may see the issue here as that of a straightforward contest between legality and illegality. While it is at a certain level, one thing that a student of postcolonial Nigerian or African politics must contend with is the ethical conundrum of an action that can be morally justified even though the law may have declared it illegal. In her essay on "The Ethics of Illegality in the Chad Basin," Janet Roitman (2006) speaks to this uneasy commingling of legality and ethically defensible lawlessness whereby what is "legal" is often a function of the social contexts of relationships, as state officials charged with upholding the law exhibit as much duplicity as those intent on subverting it.

The recourse to alternatives is not just a reflection of this interface. Fundamentally, it is a symbol of a particular attitude to political modernity itself, this time modernity as constituted in the postcolonial state and its system of law. Historical sociological scholarship in Africa, drawing on Peter Ekeh's (1975) pathbreaking study on the "two publics," has described how the same social actors within an African community relate to the "primordial" and "civic" publics on the basis of ostensibly contradictory moral principles. The connection here is that an important part of the reason people feel little or no compunction about paper simulation, especially when it comes to state regulation, is that for most people the state has always been something that exists "out there" (in the amoral civic public) as opposed to "in here" (in the moral primordial public). As such, even among so-called state functionaries, there is usually no serious guilt attached to deceiving or getting something at the expense of the local state, the ethical mooring and bona fides of which are seen as questionable at best, let alone a foreign state to which they owe no allegiance.

Postscript: Deterritorialization

Sunday, 31 July 2011. Business as usual in Oluwole, followed by sudden pandemonium as agents from the Nigeria Police Force, the Nigeria Immigration Service, and the State Security Service swoop down on the site. Oluwole operators and their customers scatter in different directions. Some are arrested. At the end of the raid, security men display electronic systems used for forgery, copies of fake international passports, fake visas, fake certificates, fake government documents, etc. (Usman 2011; Sunday 2011).

Such raids were not new to Oluwole. In fact, as mentioned earlier, most had been staged assaults, agreed to in advance between Oluwole operators and law enforcement, aimed at giving the public the impression that the state was "doing something." But the raid of July 2011 was different, and what shocked the Immigration Service was the discovery of fake copies of electronic passports. Partly due to the continued faking of the Nigerian passport, and to conform with emergent global practices, the Nigeria Immigration Service had introduced e-passports in 2007. In theory, electronic passports are inimitable.

At the time, those who had the old pre-digital passports were still able to use them until they expired. Thus, the service had assumed that Oluwole faked only the old passports. They did not reckon with the ingenuity of Oluwole, which had somehow figured out how to fake e-passports as soon as the Immigration Service started issuing them. A newspaper reported that "displaying the exhibits which included electronics systems used for forgery . . . the Comptroller of Immigration, Lagos State Command, Mr Sule Abass Ahmed, *marveled at the sophistication with which the fraudsters operated.* For instance, he pointed out that they were well informed about any change either in signature or documents of any country at their disposal" (Usman 2011, emphasis added). Desperate, perhaps, to emphasize that the service, as an agency of the Nigerian state, exclusively authorized *genuine* Nigerian passports, the comptroller assured "Nigerians as well as the international community that the *credibility* of the e-passport was still intact" (ibid., emphasis added).

The July 2011 raid may have been an indication of the state's resolve to efface Oluwole once and for all. Currently, a Lagos state government-backed retail and commercial complex named Oluwole Urban Mall stands on the site of the old Oluwole. However, while the 2011 raid disrupted Oluwole's operations and scattered its operatives, it wasn't long before they regrouped. An earlier raid had led some of the operators to move to Ajisomo Street and Ita Alagbaa. After the 2011 raid, some of the operators moved to Lewis Street, others to different locations in the city. In fact, in 2016, Lagos police discovered a replica of Oluwole in the Oyingbo area of the city, which they promptly sacked (Sunday 2016). While the old Oluwole has been superseded by a shopping mall, its disembodied spirit lives on in other parts of the city, a reminder that, as far as the documents needed for getting visas are concerned, unless there is a radical change in the socioeconomic conditions that provide a warrant for out-migration, the law of supply and demand will continue to operate in the Nigerian parallel economy for travel documentation.[26]

Notes

1. Under General Sani Abacha (1993–98), the street was temporarily renamed Louis Farrakhan Crescent in retaliation for the 1998 renaming of the street

corner where the Nigerian Mission to the United Nations was based after Kudirat Abiola, the activist wife of Moshood Abiola, the winner of the 12 June 1993, presidential election. She was assassinated on 9 June 1996.

2. We thank Victoria Bernal for bringing this point to our attention.

3. This particular victim paid N450,000 (circa US$2,800) to some visa racketeers for what he assumed to be a *real* UK visa. He got through the checks in the Lagos airport but was arrested at Heathrow Airport, London, where the immigration officers discovered that his visa was fake. He was deported. He had avoided Oluwole because of its reputation and went to Lewis Street for the visa, only to discover that it was the same process in the old and new Oluwole sites. He said that, upon returning to Nigeria, he had "to start over again" (Okolie 2010).

4. Nayanika Mathur has described similar displeasure in people's experiences with bureaucracy in India, a bureaucracy noted for "its staggering slowness and propensity for making people wait endlessly even when swift, decisive action is desperately required" (2015, 2).

5. This attitude of every social experience as a potential basis for "war" has taken on a different tone and intensity as Pentecostalism has become a dominant force in everyday understanding of socioeconomic and political life in Nigeria—and many parts of Africa—in the last two decades. The process of seeking and getting visas has therefore been transformed by some people into a way of *levying prayerful war* against the (in)visible force(s), the visa god(s) (see Obadare and Adebanwi 2010b). For an account of the wide-ranging impact of Pentecostalism on sociopolitical life in Nigeria, see Obadare (2018).

6. For further discussion, see Obadare and Adebanwi (2009).

7. Hibou (1997) alerts us to the idea of *l'état falsificateur,* the state as agent of deception, in people's understanding of the postcolonial state. See also Ferme (2004, 81).

8. In the wake of recent protests, attacks, and terrorist actions against major Western embassies around the world, particularly in countries with majority or significant Muslim populations—the latter including Nigeria—Walter Carrington Crescent (Victoria Island, Lagos), where the American, British, Dutch, German, and other embassies are based, is now effectively a high-security zone spatially organized to prevent random or calculated violence.

9. This discourse of what is ethical in the context of migration is a global one. Though Itty Abraham and Willem van Schendel argue that "students of illicit practices need to begin by discarding the assumption that there is a clear line between illicitness and the laws of states" (Abraham and van Schendel 2005, 7), Kyle and Siracusa contend, in the context of Ecuadorian migrants in Spain, that "where the *socially licit* dominates the *formally illegal,* . . . the public spheres . . . [including the state and relations with state agencies] become the site for a visible flouting of the letter of the law" (Kyle and Siracusa 2005, 22, emphasis added).

10. Nor is violence as part of the visa application process limited to the space of the embassy. Often, frustration at not getting one's application approved, or failure to raise the funds needed to have the necessary documents processed, can be

a trigger for violence. For instance, see Ben Duru, "Son Kills 71-Year-Old Father," *Daily Independent* (Lagos), 6 August 2004.

11. Including such totally unwarranted and indefensible lines of investigation as asking applicant couples how, and how often, they slept with each other. For a glimpse of the humiliation typically involved in applying for a travel visa, see the opinion article by Nigerian writer Chimamanda Ngozi Adichie, "The Line of No Return," *New York Times,* 29 November 2004, https://www.nytimes.com /2004/11/29/opinion/the-line-of-no-return.html.

12. After the experience recounted below regarding Adebanwi, someone volunteered to him at the United States Information Service that the man who insulted him, an African member of the consulate staff, was encouraged to "vigorously challenge" visa applicants when processing their documents and their entry into the premises so as "destabilize" those who might be bearing false papers or lying. The man, who always wore a frown, obviously understood the job to include raising his voice at applicants and casually insulting them.

13. This was a courtesy service that USIA officials occasionally offered to their contacts in Nigeria, such as journalists, academics, and NGO officials.

14. To hide his identity, he prefers a pseudonym.

15. See Ofeimun's poem, "I Am a Writer," Poetry International website, https:// www.poetryinternational.org/pi/poem/27224/auto/0/0/Odia-Ofeimun/I-AM -A-WRITER/en/tile.

16. Adefayi Martins, "Rebutting the British . . . and Their Visas, in Verse," *The-NEWS* (Lagos), n.d., quoted in "He Claims to Be a Writer," *Wordsbody* (blog), 30 October 2006, http://wordsbody.blogspot.com/2006/10/he-claims-to-be -writer.html.

17. For examples of how some of the consular officers explain the bases of their decision-making, see Alpes (2013, 149–54). Two visa-granting officers at the American consulate in Cameroon observed by Alpes "would joke that they felt as if they were working at McDonalds. Instead of handing out burgers, they were deciding whether or not to hand out visas" (ibid., 151). It can be argued that, though they were joking, the attitude of these officers confirms some of the suspicions of the visa applicants. However, the analogy they drew is paradoxical. In one sense, it cheapened their "customers"—because they were seeking "junk food" and were, therefore, not deserving of *bespoke* service. Yet both the officers and their "customers" recognized that what the applicants were seeking was highly valuable to the latter. The analogy may also be approached as a way not only of *depersonalizing* the process of decision-making regarding visas, but also of *depersonalizing* the "customers," even while attempting to present the officials' actions as *technicist* and therefore "disinterested" and merely "bureaucratic."

18. To further demonstrate his accomplishments, which were ignored or diminished, if not dismissed, in the statement by the officer at the British High Commission that "he claims to be a writer," in stanzas 2 and 5 of the poem, Ofeimun states:

> my waify poems at eighteen
> elevate siblings at the WAEC
> stocking ten-legged thesis

on muses who bring the unborn
to quaking life before stamps
hit the pad at the Passport Office.

. . . .

I do not claim to be, I am a writer
beyond the prisonhouse of English
in which I wrest my djinns

. . . .

wherever my English envy
denies a tongue its entry,
I'm happy, beyond mere fashion
for trips that visas can't deny

19. Alpes, observing the visa-granting process from inside the American consulate in Cameroon, confirms that "interpretations of [an] applicant's physical posture" (2013, 152) are part of what determines the decision to grant visas to the applicants.

20. Due to the well-documented activities of Nigerian prostitutes in Italy (see Achebe 2004), a degree of opprobrium attaches to female visa applicants, especially those planning to travel to continental Europe. A professor of microbiology at the University of Ibadan told us how she got "the look" and received excessive scrutiny when she applied for a travel visa to attend an international conference in Rome.

21. There is no suggestion here that Oluwole arose solely on account of the transnational visa economy, or that the market attends only to those aiming to satisfy the demands of the visa application process. On the contrary, Oluwole is firmly inserted in and caters to the wider Nigerian market in parallel documentation, as Obadare (alive at the time of writing) was able to confirm by procuring a death certificate for himself and, being generous, diplomas for degrees from prestigious international universities for many of his friends.

22. Not real name.

23. Invariably, these deportees see themselves as "victims" who are using their knowledge gained from travel to and temporary stay in Western countries to "retaliate" against the respective consulate.

24. Here, Achille Mbembe's insight on the "simultaneous multiplicities" that are a key feature of everyday life in postcolonial Cameroon looms large (see Mbembe 2001, 146).

25. Even a state that has genuine authority may also produce fakes of its and other state's documents. An example that immediately comes to mind is the fake documents, including travel documents such as passports, produced by the world's leading intelligence agencies. A couple of years ago, it was discovered that Israel's Mossad agents used fake or fraudulently obtained passports and travel documents of European (British, Irish, French, and German) countries and Australia to travel to Dubai to assassinate Mahmoud al-Mabhouh, a co-founder of the Izz ad-Din al-Qassam Brigades, the military wing of Hamas. Though twenty-six suspects and their aliases were subsequently placed on Interpol's most-wanted list, it is clear that the Israeli state will neither admit that

these people were its agents nor ever surrender them for prosecution—thus placing them beyond, if not also outside, the reach of the law.

26. This chapter is part of a larger project on "Migration, Transnational Resource Flow and the Paradoxes of Citizenship in Nigeria." The authors gratefully acknowledge funding support from the MacArthur Foundation (2005). We thank Bolaji Moyosore, Sola Asa, and Surajudeen Mudasiru for their assistance with data collection. We dedicate this chapter to the sweet memory of Raimi Oladunjoye, one of our most able guide into the Oluwole underworld.

References

Abraham, Itty, and Willem van Schendel. 2005. "Introduction: The Making of Illicitness." In van Schendel and Abraham 2005, 1–37.

Abrams, Philip. 1988. "Notes on the Difficulty of Studying the State (1977)." *Journal of Historical Sociology* 1 (1): 58–89.

Achebe, Nwando. 2004. "The Road to Italy: Nigerian Sex Workers at Home and Abroad." *Journal of Women's History* 15 (4): 178–85.

Adebanwi, Wale. 2012. "Glocal Naming and Shaming: Toponymic (Inter) National Relations on Lagos and New York's Streets." *African Affairs* 111 (445): 640–61.

Adebanwi, Wale, and Ebenezer Obadare, eds. 2010. *Encountering the Nigerian State.* New York: Palgrave Macmillan.

Alpes, Maybritt Jill. 2013. "'Why Do They Take the Money and Not Give Visas?' The Governmentality of Consulate Offices in Cameroon." In *Disciplining the Transnational Mobility of People,* edited by Martin Geiger and Antoine Pécoud, 145–61. New York: Palgrave Macmillan.

———. 2017. *Brokering High-Risk Migration and Illegality in West Africa: Abroad at Any Cost.* New York: Routledge.

Barber, Karin. 1987. "Popular Arts in Africa." *African Studies Review* 30 (3): 1–78.

Butler, Judith. 2015. *Notes Toward a Performative Theory of Assembly.* Cambridge, MA: Harvard University Press.

Chabal, Patrick. 2009. *Africa: The Politics of Suffering and Smiling.* London: Zed Books.

Dare, Olatunji. 2018. "'Oluwole' Revisited." *Nation* (Lagos), 9 January. https://olatunji4.rssing.com/chan-10734337/article260.html.

Das, Veena, and Deborah Poole, eds. 2004a. *Anthropology in the Margins of the State.* Sante Fe, NM: School of American Research Press.

———. 2004b. "State and Its Margins: Comparative Ethnographies." In Das and Poole 2004a, 3–33.

Ekeh, Peter P. 1975. "Colonialism and the Two Publics in Africa: A Theoretical Statement." *Comparative Studies in Society and History* 17 (1): 91–112.

Ferme, Mariane C. 2004. "Deterritorialized Citizenship and the Resonances of the Sierra Leonean State." In Das and Poole 2004a, 81–115.

———. 2013. "Introduction: Localizing the State." *Anthropological Quarterly* 86 (4): 957–63.

Ferraris, Maurizio. 2013. *Documentality: Why It Is Necessary to Leave Traces.* Translated by Richard Davies. New York: Fordham University Press.

Gupta, Akhil. 1995. "Blurred Boundaries: The Discourse of Corruption, the Culture of Politics, and the Imagined State." *American Ethnologist* 22 (2): 375–402.

Hibou, Béatrice. 1997. "Le 'capital social' de l'état falsificateur, ou les ruses de l'intel-ligence économique." In *La criminalization de l' état en Afrique,* edited by Jean-François Bayart, Stephen Ellis, and Béatrice Hibou, 105–58. Paris: Éditions Complexes.

Hull, Matthew S. 2012. *Government of Paper: The Materiality of Bureaucracy in Urban Pakistan.* Berkeley: University of California Press.

Ismail, Wale. 2010. "Deconstructing 'Oluwole': Political Economy at the Margins of the State." In Adebanwi and Obadare 2010, 29–53.

Jackson, Michael. 2011. "The Road to Kabala." In *Life within Limits: Well-Being in A World of Want.* Durham, NC: Duke University Press.

Kyle, David, and Christina A. Siracusa. 2005. "Seeing the State Like a Migrant: Why So Many Non-criminals Break Immigration Laws." In van Schendel and Abraham 2005, 153–76.

Mathur, Nayanika. 2015. *Paper Tiger: Law, Bureaucracy and the Developmental State in Himalayan India.* Cambridge: Cambridge University Press.

Mbembe, Achille. 2000. "Everything Can Be Negotiated: Ambiguities and Challenges in a Time of Uncertainty." In *Manoeuvring in an Environment of Uncertainty: Structural Change and Social Action in Sub-Saharan Africa,* edited by Boel Berner and Per Trulsson, 265–76. Aldershot, Hampshire: Ashgate.

———. 2001. *On the Postcolony.* Berkeley: University of California Press.

Navaro-Yashin, Yael. 2002. *Faces of the State: Secularism and Public Life in Turkey.* Princeton, NJ: Princeton University Press.

Newell, Stephanie, and Onookome Okome. 2014. "Introduction." In *Popular Culture in Africa: The Episteme of the Everyday,* edited by Stephanie Newell and Onookome Okome, 1–23. New York: Routledge.

Nyamnjoh, Francis. 2011. "Cameroonian Bushfalling: Negotiation of Identity and Belonging in Fiction and Ethnography." *American Ethnologist* 38 (4): 701–13.

Obadare, Ebenezer. 2018. *Pentecostal Republic: Religion and the Struggle for State Power in Nigeria.* London: Zed Books.

Obadare, Ebenezer, and Wale Adebanwi. 2009. "Transnational Resource Flow and the Paradoxes of Belonging: Redirecting the Debate on Transnationalism, Remittances, State and Citizenship in Africa." *Review of African Political Economy* 36 (122): 499–517.

———. 2010a. "Introduction: Excess and Abjection in the Study of the African State." In Adebanwi and Obadare 2010, 1–28.

———. 2010b. "The Visa God: Would-Be Migrants and the Instrumentalization of Religion." In *Religion Crossing Boundaries: Transnational Religious and Social Dynamics in Africa and the New African Diaspora,* edited by Afe Adogame and James V. Spickard, 31–48. Leiden: Brill.

Okafor, Samuel Chuks. 2014. *Africa's Backwardness, Misfortunes, and the Word of God.* Johannesburg: Partridge Publishing Africa.

Okolie, Ifeanyi. 2010. "Police Swoop on Visa Racketeers, Arrest Suspect with 120 Passports." *Vanguard* (Lagos), 14 May. https://www.vanguardngr.com/2010/05/police-swoop-on-visa-racketeers-arrest-suspect-with-120-passports/.

Piot, Charles. 2010. *Nostalgia for the Future: West Africa after the Cold War.* Chicago: University of Chicago Press.

Piot, Charles, with Kodjo Nicolas Batema. 2019. *The Fixer: Visa Lottery Chronicles.* Durham, NC: Duke University Press.

Povinelli, Elizabeth A. 2016. *Geontologies: A Requiem to Late Liberalism.* Durham, NC: Duke University Press.

Roitman, Janet. 2006. "The Ethics of Illegality in the Chad Basin." In *Law and Disorder in the Postcolony,* edited by Jean Comaroff and John L. Comaroff, 247–72. Chicago: University of Chicago Press.

Smith, Daniel Jordan. 2007. *A Culture of Corruption: Everyday Deception and Popular Discontent in Nigeria.* Princeton, NJ: Princeton University Press.

Sunday, Odita. 2011. "Immigration, SSS Raid Oluwole Market, Smash Forgery Syndicate." *Guardian* (Lagos), 23 August.

———. 2016. "Police Uncover Another 'Oluwole' in Lagos." *Guardian* (Lagos), 14 March. https://guardian.ng/news/police-uncover-another-oluwole-in-lagos/.

Usman, Evelyn. 2011. "Day of Reckoning for Oluwole Fraudsters as Security Agents Raid Hideout." *Vanguard* (Lagos), 2 August. https://www.vanguardngr.com /2011/08/day-of-reckoning-for-oluwole-fraudsters-%E2%80%A2as-security -agents-raid-hideout/.

van Schendel, Willem, and Itty Abraham. 2005. *Illicit Flows and Criminal Things: States, Borders, and the Other Side of Globalization.* Bloomington: Indiana University Press.

Wittgenstein, Ludwig. 1972. *On Certainty.* Bilingual edition. Edited by G. E. M. Anscombe and G. H. von Wright. Translated by Denis Paul and G. E. M. Anscombe. New York: Harper and Row.

Yeh, Rihan. 2012. "Two Publics in a Mexican Border City." *Cultural Anthropology* 27 (4): 713–34.

THREE

Somali Kinship and Bureaucratic Governance at a Refugee Camp in Kenya

FRED NYONGESA IKANDA

THE DIFFICULTY OF POLICING THE DADAAB REFUGEE camps in Kenya was highlighted by the abduction of two Spanish agency workers in October 2011. In response, the Kenyan military went to Somalia to fight the Al-Shabaab militia, which the government had blamed for the incident. The government also embarked on a series of what it called "peace meetings," which turned into avenues for brazen threats that refugees would be expelled or services withheld if they did not reveal Al-Shabaab militants within their "midst." In one of these meetings, the district peace chairman (DPC) addressed the gathering of refugees and locals, saying, "The DC [district commissioner] is here because of the seriousness of security issues. We should respect him and feel honored because he is the president's representative. . . . We have accommodated you here because of the troubles caused by those terrorists in your country. If you don't help us to identify them, we shall ask you to go. Mister DC, I request you to concentrate your security efforts on this recently created Ifo 2 camp with new refugees, where Al-Shabaab are residing. We have to stop their nonsense."

The "new refugees" the DPC was referring to had been arriving throughout the year in a massive influx due to a ravaging drought across the Horn of Africa. The Ifo 2 camp the DPC mentioned in his speech had, in fact, been set up only recently to accommodate these people. Blaming these people for the abduction seemed odd, given the area's palpable sense of insecurity, which has led to a system where police regularly escort humanitarian convoys. But this rhetoric would hardly be surprising for those familiar with how clan and interclan rivalries have often elevated the importance of kinship among Somalis (see Lewis 1999). The DPC's remarks therefore make sense when viewed within a wider context of kinship alliances and oppositions. By referring to these residents as "new" refugees, he tried to portray them as being different from "old" Somali refugees and locals in a context where shared Somaliness between refugees and locals often blurred these distinctions. Indeed, the old-new divide referenced lineage and clan dynamics, considering that many of the earliest arrivals shared kinship ties with locals because of the clan-inspired war in Somalia. They had specifically chosen to flee to Dadaab because it was inhabited by members of their Ogaden subclan, unlike later arrivals who largely belong to other clans.

After completing his address, the DPC invited the DC to speak, which gave the impression that he was the second-highest-ranking official in the district. This was despite his holding an informal position that wasn't recognized in government circles. As I discuss below, the measure of how kinship had emerged as a dominant governing structure in the Dadaab camps' setup was often reflected in the immense power that was wielded by local elites. It was remarkable, for example, that the DPC's eerie warning was followed by a "security operation" inside the new camp that resulted in reported cases of police brutality, including rape, looting, and other forms of human rights abuses (Ikanda 2014). The Dadaab camps are also located in a vast, remote, semidesert area that remains inaccessible due to a long-standing history of marginalization. This contributed to a lack of encounters between Somalis and the state, which weakened the influence of government in people's lives. As I discuss below, the setting up of camps increased the government's presence in the area. Still, it relied on local mechanisms to manage the camps.

FIGURE 1. A Somali refugee stands with her children outside their makeshift shelter at the Dagahaley camp in Dadaab, near the Kenya-Somalia border. Photo from Reuters.

The importance of kinship in administering the Dadaab camps questions accounts that portray state and humanitarian bureaucracies as powerful entities with near-total control over refugee lives in camp settings (e.g., Agamben 1998; Duffield 2001; Agier 2011; Rozakou 2012). The apparent runaway lawlessness across Africa's refugee settings, moreover, implies that loose state control over the working of camps is more the rule than the exception. The Goma refugee camp in the Democratic Republic of Congo was, for example, infamous for harboring Interahamwe militia activities following the Rwandan genocide of 1994 (Polman 2011). Cases of armed incursions inside refugee camps have, moreover, been reported in countries such as Guinea, Zambia, Tanzania, and Uganda, while incidents of petty and organized crime, political radicalism, and recruitment of refugees in military units are a common occurrence in wide-ranging camp settings, including those in Kenya, Mauritania, and Algeria (Jacobsen 2002). These camps are also widely believed to be sites of human trafficking as well as smuggling of illicit goods.

Based on twelve months of ethnographic fieldwork at Dagahaley refugee camp in northeastern Kenya (from August 2011 to August 2012), this chapter highlights the complex leadership structures that emerged inside the camp when kinship was allowed to provide the context for the working of government. This often exposed inadequacies of bureaucracy in effectively managing the camp, which were highlighted by the standard litany of many Kenyans' complaints that the camps were terrorist breeding grounds and centers of unregulated, untaxed consignments of goods and capital from lawless Somalia (Ikanda 2014). The camp's existence has also been characterized by cases of banditry, rape, kidnappings, bombings, murder, and intercommunal strife (CASA Consulting 2001). Dagahaley camp is part of the Dadaab Refugee Complex, which also includes Ifo, Hagadera, and the recently closed Kambioos and Ifo 2 camps. They are typically regarded as one facility because they are located in close proximity to each other in Garissa County in Kenya's northeastern region. These camps mostly host Somali refugees. They have been in existence since 1991, when the Somalia became stateless following the overthrow of then-president Siad Barre. The large refugee numbers, coupled with the protracted hosting situation had transformed the camps into self-contained "cities" with schools, shops, restaurants, lodgings, hospitals, and other social amenities (de Montclos and Kangwanja 2000). But as mentioned above, these camps were governed by a combination of kinship and formal mechanisms, unlike other cities that are under municipal or state control.

The Somali locals and refugees who mainly inhabit the Dadaab camps are a patrilineal, nomadic, and predominantly Muslim people who are divided into clans, subclans, and lineages. According to Lewis (1999), kinship has always reigned supreme among Somalis because of the segmentary and exclusive nature of their political system, which leads people to only trust their kinsmen. Somali segmentary support systems are even said to operate across several continents, such that relatives in different places are typically bound in strong reciprocal relationships (Goldsmith 1997). The camps are located about seventy-five kilometers from the Kenya-Somalia border, which has historically been ignored by Somali nomads on either side of it. The siting of the camps in close proximity to the border therefore seems to have merely intensified previous relationships: there are Somalis living both inside and outside the camp walls. However, new arrivals were vulnerable because they could neither use kinship connections to defend themselves against unfounded accusations about criminal culpability nor mobilize kin-based networks to access resources.

Here, I examine how kinship became an important terrain for realizing bureaucratic aims inside the camps, by bringing into dialogue the ethnography of bureaucracy with the literature on humanitarian regimes and Africanist conversations about the relationship between pastoralist peoples and the state. The chapter is divided into four sections. The first section situates the chapter in the literature on bureaucracy and humanitarian governance. I then analyze Somali kinship dynamics that served to limit bureaucratic power, before showing how kinship and bureaucracy worked as hybrid systems in managing camps. This is followed by a highlight of humanitarian camp procedures. Finally, I discuss Somali responses to bureaucratic governance with regard to how refugees perceived humanitarianism as their right.

Working of Bureaucracy within Humanitarian Setups

Bureaucracy in its Weberian sense is said to be supreme because of how formalism, neutrality, documentation, record keeping, and "rationality" enable bureaucrats to disguise subjective, irrational goals as logical, universalized policies (McGoey 2007; Hoag 2011). Modern state bureaucracies, moreover, wield unparalleled power in the way they regulate the conduct of their respective populations through legitimate force as well as rewards and sanctions. It is not just sovereignty that gives states unparalleled and monopolistic power in a territorially defined political space. As Peter Nyers (2006) and other authors observe, states also have an observer status that allows them to deploy the concept of a "state of exception" to preserve their sovereign power. This entails preserving states by using legal means to suspend law if the state is threatened by serious danger from within or without. Commentators even suggest that state law has achieved unprecedented importance in the present era of declining religious influence (Tamanaha 1993). The Kenyan state has had a troubled history with its nomadic populations in general and Somali citizens in particular that has led it to deploy drastic measures that fit in the "state of exception" framework (see Hyndman 1996; Lochery 2012). Commentators have even pointed out that the Kenyan government deliberately located the Dadaab camps in a remote semiarid area to isolate and monitor Somalis, who it often blames for the proliferation of firearms (de Montclos and Kangwanja 2000; CASA Consulting 2001; Ohta 2005). As I discuss below, however, the government largely relied on local institutions not only because it lacked a considerable physical presence in the area, but also because of how shared Somaliness had rendered problematic the local-refugee categorizations that bureaucratic actors sought to impose.

The power of humanitarian organizations in camp contexts is equally great. As a body legally mandated to provide international protection for refugees, the UNHCR and its humanitarian partners have the responsibility of establishing policing and justice mechanisms that provide refugees with basic elements of what might be considered as the rule of law. The importance of the UNHCR in providing basic needs and services to refugees in camp settings has indeed imbued it with state-like qualities (Slaughter and Crisp, 2009). Meanwhile, UNHCR has been accused of becoming increasingly bureaucratized (Barnett 2010). Such charges insinuate that UNHCR has come to resemble a state bureaucracy, one that is often characterized by irrationality, inefficiency, and opaqueness. These attributes empower its officials to have unlimited monopoly over livelihood resources. The power inequalities that exist between these officials and their refugee clients has led several scholars to follow Giorgio Agamben (1998) in concluding that humanitarianism can only conceive refugee lives as "bare life" (e.g., Duffield 2001; Rozakou 2012). This view is apparently informed by grim camp conditions that are characterized by a lack of political rights, restricted mobility, waste of human potential, and few economic opportunities, all of which fuel perceptions that camps are spaces of exception that seek to depoliticize occupants (Harrell-Bond 1986; Finnström 2008; Agier 2011).

If state and humanitarian bureaucracies are monolithic entities with near-total control over people's lives, as they are commonly portrayed in the literature, it is apposite to ask why a lack of enforcement of basic rules and regulations is the dominant trope of camp dynamics at Dadaab and in other camp contexts. It also prompts us to ask what keeps these camps going for so long in the face of weak institutional control. I suggest that bureaucracies are not the all-powerful, abstract entities they are often portrayed to be, and that bureaucratic action often depends on the realities on the ground. This is in line with what ethnographic literature on bureaucracy, the state, and development schemes in non-Western contexts has shown us: bureaucratic governance is dialogic and less rigid than we might think, as its success commonly depends on collaboration (Mathews 2005; Mosse 2005; Ikanda 2020). In what follows, I describe how kinship realities and ambiguous security measures tended to render ineffective government and humanitarian agencies' efforts in managing the camps.

Kinship Realities That Rendered Bureaucracy Ineffective

The enormity of the task facing the Kenyan state in effectively governing this vast area became evident to me when I first conducted fieldwork at Dadaab from November 2002 to March 2003. Government presence in the area at that time was thin—with chiefs, a few police officers, a district officer, and a liaison officer usually the only representatives of its existence. Humanitarian agencies had virtually taken over the functions that would otherwise have been performed by government, and many locals had moved into the camps to benefit from the services that were being offered to refugees. The government had even abdicated its role in registering refugees, until 2006, when the Refugee Bill was passed. Prior to this period, the UNHCR was registering refugees as the Kenyan state preoccupied itself with issuing threats to close down the camps for what it termed security reasons. The passage of the Refugee Bill appears to have been a spark for more government involvement in the management of camp affairs. When I returned for my second period of fieldwork in 2011, Dadaab had been upgraded from a division to a district and was now headed by a district commissioner, assisted by several district officers. There was a heavy police presence and there were functional government departments, including the Department of Refugee Affairs (DRA), which now registered refugees and issued them travel documents whenever they left the camps. Still, there was loose state control, as officials largely operated outside the camps.

These realities exposed the limits of bureaucratic power, in that the government was generally depending on local kinship mechanisms in its administrative duties. The dependence on local institutions tended to collapse the roles of state and aid agencies—mirroring the blurriness of local-refugee distinctions. This indistinctness was most visibly demonstrated by the blame games that often ensued between government and UNHCR officials whenever a bombing or bandit attack occurred around the camps. Government officials would typically accuse UNHCR for harboring criminals in the course of enforcing refugee protection principles. Following the abduction incident mentioned in the opening of this chapter, for example, the DC told me in an informal conversation that he had repeatedly warned the UNHCR that "so-called refugees are former warlords who should be facing charges of crimes against humanity, yet people bearing guns protect them here." He then reiterated the government's resolve to close the

Dadaab camps in the following terms: "I don't consider them to be camps at all. What is the difference between the camps and the local settlements? Why do UN people insist on calling them camps as if refugees are confined, when we all know they are establishing themselves in every part of this country?" There was indeed an entrenched feeling among government officials that refugees were "overprotected." A police officer once told me about the case of his colleague, who had been suspended for impregnating a refugee woman. According to the officer I was speaking with, the fear of being accused of harassing or sexually exploiting refugees informed police reluctance to interfere in refugee affairs. For many agency officials I interacted with, however, allegations that refugee "overprotection" fueled insecurity lacked merit, because refugees were expected to operate under the laws of the host country—which was, in any case, responsible for maintaining security.

What emerged from these exchanges was a sense that the state did not see itself as being responsible for maintaining law and order inside the camps unless there were exceptional circumstances. The security operation mentioned above was the only police operation inside any camp that I was made aware of during my yearlong fieldwork, which underscored the rarity of state interference in camp affairs. That said, the role of state and international agencies in administering the camps also converged on a number of issues relating to the common security and administrative challenges they faced. Apart from investing heavily in expanding the area's road network, UNHCR had partnered with the government to fund an increase of police posts around the camp. UNHCR also partnered with the government to provide water, education facilities, and other social services to local and refugee populations, which seems to have improved the government's standing in the eyes of locals.

It was not just government officials who were averse to visiting the camps. Agency workers lived in fortified compounds, traveled only under heavy police escort, and avoided venturing inside the camps due to the prevailing insecurity (see Ikanda 2018). In light of this arrangement, the Dadaab camps were largely self-administered units where refugees had taken a leading role in steering camp operations. This long-standing agency practice has been popularized over the years with reference to UNHCR's stated objective of considering refugees as partners in the community's decision-making process (Hyndman 1996). The effectiveness of Somali kinship units was what largely gave camps a semblance of functionality, which in turn provided the bureaucracy with the necessary traction for actualizing its governance role. The significance of kinship had, however, also entrenched clan rivalries that largely benefited "old" refugees, who came to exile already enmeshed in relationships with their hosts because of the centuries-old interactions across the Kenya-Somalia border.

To appreciate the saliency of kinship in structuring camp affairs, one might consider the case of my host father. Like many other "old" refugees and locals, my host father only started to identify himself as a local in the late 1990s, following the move by humanitarian agencies to include locals in their assistance programs. In 2007, he moved out of Dagahaley camp to a neighboring village inhabited by his Aulian sub-subclan (which is part of the larger Ogaden subclan) and became its chairman in 2010. He used his old Kenyan identity card and kinship claims to assert local status based on the fact that he had been born in Kenya in 1955 but later moved to Somalia in search of better economic opportunities. Finally, he returned as a refugee in 1992. Many "old" arrivals who had taken similar trajectories deployed a shared sense of Somaliness as a means of accessing resources, but relied on "old-new" distinctions to exclude nonrelatives from the camp's sociopolitical processes. This strategic fluidity explains the relative advantage that was conferred on "old refugees" by virtue of having arrived earlier. The influence of the DPC in government circles was similarly informed by his standing as a revered elder of the local Aulian subclan, which also incorporated mostly "old" refugees. As I show below, he relied on kinship connections inside and outside the camp to shape the bureaucratic functioning by lobbying successfully for the postponement of refugee elections. He also influenced how development and security-related issues were coordinated in the area.

Working of Kinship and Bureaucracy in Camp Administration

From the foregoing, it is evident that the political power of Somali kinship played an important role in shaping bureaucratic camp practices. Kinship networks and the bureaucracy worked together to create hybrid formations in regard to governance and resource access, despite the rhetoric about international standards that ostensibly shaped and determined these functions. The Lutheran World Federation (LWF), for instance, was in charge of administering the Dadaab camps. However, it did not have a physical presence inside the camp, but instead collaborated with refugee leaders in running the camps. The LWF worked through the Community Peace and Security Teams, which consisted of elected refugees who coordinated security issues in and around the camps. The teams were trained by LWF to perform the role of community policing through camp patrols and were often called upon to solve various problems, including queue jumping, theft, plot disputes, and providing protection for women and other vulnerable groups. The camp also had a hierarchical system of administration, with a chairman and chairwoman at the top, followed by section leaders in charge of the various camp sections, and block leaders in charge of individual blocks within a section. At the time of my fieldwork, there were ten sections in Dagahaley camp. Each section comprised about ten blocks, with each block having an average of fifty households.

The model of camp administration through self-governance had put a premium on leadership positions and the numerical strength of kinship units. Leadership positions were highly coveted. Although refugee leaders were not salaried, they drew allowances for attending agency meetings. In addition, they often used their positions as leverage to get and to bestow numerous benefits. Section leaders were, for example, expected to forward names of people to be employed on an "incentive" basis as food distribution clerks. These were refugee community members who were paid "incentives"—usually $50 per month—to work for agencies. Block leaders were charged with identifying people in need of housing and latrines. The distribution clerk position offered the opportunity to steal food. A refugee friend once recounted to me his unsuccessful attempt to bribe his section leader to be considered for the position. He was not considered, despite promising to give the section leader all the incentive pay he would receive during the entire six-month period of the contract position, and cited his lack of kinship connection to the section leader as a reason for this failure. Many of those who served as distribution clerks were either locals posing as refugees or "old" refugees who were members of the hosting community's subclan (see Ikanda 2019).

FIGURE 2. Newly arrived refugees wait to receive their rations at a food distribution center at the Dagahaley refugee camp in Dadaab. Photo by Thomas Mukoya/Reuters.

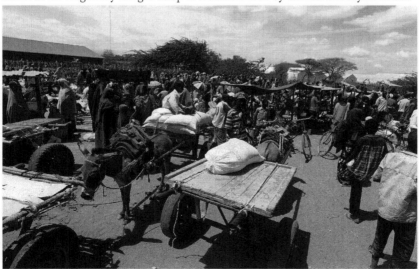

According to my informants, many people tried to bribe sectional leaders to be employed as distribution clerks because of the lucrative nature of *baramuda* (the practice of clerks taking part of every refugee's food ration during distribution). The widespread nature of baramuda is captured in an incident that dominated discussions during my fieldwork. In 2010, the local member of Parliament disguised himself as a refugee and joined those waiting to get food rations to investigate the widespread complaints of people getting less than they were entitled to. However, everyone got proper shares on that occasion because word had leaked out. Refugees often questioned the government's and the agencies' commitment to eradicating baramuda, especially given that the stolen food was always on public display in the numerous food stores that were situated directly opposite the distribution center.

This incident should not be read as a case where the MP was acting as an elected representative and state agent coming to supervise or facilitate humanitarian practices for the benefit of his political constituency. Rather, he was responding to complaints from his kinsmen. Similarly, it is inaccurate to attribute all refugee complaints concerning baramuda to being about corruption of an ostensibly rational bureaucracy. As the experience of the man who tried to bribe his section leader has shown, it was not obvious that having money to bribe officials was all it took for one to be appointed as a distribution clerk. Indeed, many of those who failed to secure these positions attributed their failure to lacking relatives in high places to facilitate the process, not to lacking money for bribes. Those who received inadequate rations or missed out on obtaining positions found it easier to frame baramuda as a form of corruption, but in reality those making the complaints consistently tended to highlight their vulnerability as people without influential kinsmen. This illustrates the need for scholars who write against tribalism, corruption, and other common vices to take into account the critical role that kinship plays in ordering social relations in African societies.

The value of kinship in gaining access to camp resources was well illustrated by the campaigns for electing refugee leaders that coincided with my fieldwork. The Community Peace and Security Team (CPST) positions did not attract much interest from the government, locals, or the refugee community because they were deemed to be nonlucrative. Apart from an occasional meeting allowance and the highly efficacious badges that officials were provided, there was little else to inspire one to participate in the election—especially because of the risky camp environment, illustrated by the killing of two CPST officials by suspected Al-Shabaab militants during my fieldwork. Thus, CPST elections remained largely peaceful. However, the campaigns for camp chairman, chairwoman, and section and block leaders assumed a kinship dimension. The DC set the electioneering tone by directing the Department of Refugee Affairs to liaise with the UNHCR in organizing the long-overdue exercise (elections had initially been sched-uled for 2010 before being postponed). After the DRA announced the 30 June 2012 election date, campaigns kicked off in earnest as candidates started pouring money into printing campaign materials and hiring ve-hicles in what was increasingly turning into a show of might. Incumbent leaders seemed to have more campaign resources, as exemplified by their long campaign convoys. However, their challengers' campaign promises to root out baramuda strongly resonated with "new" refugees. Meanwhile, claims of intimidation and bribery surfaced as locals injected themselves into the affair as a means of keeping off "outsiders."

A group of aspirants comprising five men and one woman approached a team of DRA officials at Dagahaley, alleging that their competitors had told them they would not be shortlisted because they were strangers in the area. Eventually, the DRA shortlisted almost everybody who had applied to run for office, but in public meetings and informal discussions locals continued to express their preference for having earlier arrivals serve in these positions "for security reasons," which greatly sharpened the new-old divide. In response, many non-Ogaden refugees dismissed this argument as a ploy for maintaining the status quo, seeing that those currently occupy-ing these positions belonged to the subclan of local inhabitants. The locals' stance was particularly represented by the DPC, who lobbied in public meetings for the postponement of the election.

The intensity of the rivalry between candidates in the run-up to the elections reached its high point with a bomb attack on the convoy of the sitting chairwoman of Ifo camp that left her with critical injuries. As it had been widely feared in non-Ogaden refugee circles, the wishes of "locals" carried the day when the elections were postponed indefinitely a week be-fore they were to be held. The concerns about "outsiders" leading "insiders" could simply not be overcome. I learned of the cancellation from a group of aspirants who had assembled outside the UNHCR compound to seek clarification on the way forward. After failing to get an audience with ei-ther government or agency officials, a refugee aspirant in his midthirties ex-plained to me why humanitarian organizations had canceled the elections: they feared that young, "learned" refugees like him would topple the mostly elderly and illiterate crop of Aulian leaders the agencies preferred. Agencies were more interested in pleasing locals through maintaining the status quo than tackling refugee issues, he said, adding that the current leaders were only motivated by advancing the locals' agenda and "the envelopes [money] they get when meetings come to an end."

Pronouncements about refugee leaders representing local interests as opposed to refugee interests had become a popular campaign theme in light of a previous incident involving the chairman of a neighboring village. He turned up with his family for a refugee verification exercise after having recently led a violent protest against the expansion of refugee shelters. A UNHCR officer raised the alarm when he saw him posing as a refugee, but when the Aulian refugee chairman was called to verify his identity, he declared that the chairman's family could not be classified as locals because both of his wives were refugees. This became a well-known incident and was, for many, an eloquent illustration that the agencies were in charge of the distribution of food and other resources only in theory. In practice, refugee leaders actually selected "scoopers" (a term that referenced the work of these clerks at the camps) who distributed food aid, identified prospective recipients of housing and sanitary materials, and consistently supported the claims of their kinsmen.

What emerged in this case was a sense that locals would only tolerate the refugee presence if those unrelated to them shelved their political ambitions. But as I show in the next section, the influence of kinship in the camp setup—which largely disadvantaged "new" refugees—was also strengthened by endless bureaucratic procedures that made it difficult for humanitarian officials to assist their refugee clients.

Elusiveness of Bureaucratic Assistance

At Dadaab, the UNHCR's state-like governance structure was illustrated by the more than thirty agencies it had contracted with to provide specialized services. CARE International ran various programs that provided a host of services ranging from education to water, campaigning against gender-based violence, and other initiatives. The LWF was in charge of camp security and administration while Médecins Sans Frontiers (MSF, also known as Doctors Without Borders) provided medical services. The International Organization for Migration (IOM) offered transport services from border areas to the camps to refugees fleeing famine or violence, as well as conducting camp-based relocations. The World Food Programme's task was to source and supply food to refugees. The Norwegian Refugee Council (NRC) and Danish Refugee Council (DRC) were in charge of constructing shelters and pit latrines. Other organizations working at the camps included Handicap International (now called Humanity & Inclusion), which provided material support to refugees with disabilities; the Red Cross, which provided various emergency services including reunification of family members separated during war; and a host of other organizations including the International Rescue Committee (IRC), the National Council of Churches in Kenya (NCCK), Oxfam International, Terre des Hommes, FilmAid International, Save the Children UK (SCUK), and the German Corporation for International Cooperation (Deutsche Gesellschaft für Internationale Zusammenarbeit, or GIZ). Most of these organizations were based at Dadaab but had offices at the Dagahaley camp from which officials could operate whenever they visited the "field." Only CARE, LWF, and MSF agency workers resided at their respective Dagahaley compounds because they offered essential services that were required on a continuous basis.

The extent to which the UNHCR bureaucracy has come to resemble state bureaucracy is evidenced by the irrationality, inefficiency, and opaqueness that dominate its practices (Hoag 2011; Sandvik 2011; Thomson 2012). Many organizations at Dadaab performed overlapping roles and tended to place proper procedure at the forefront of their operations. One example was the value they assigned to badges. It often seemed that having a badge was a prerequisite to working in the camp areas. Without an official badge, one could neither use agency vehicles nor gain access to their compounds. Badges were, therefore, an important bureaucratic practice that imbued one with what Pandolfi calls accreditation: "To be accredited means that in addition to rights claimed through citizenship—the right to cross a border with your passport, for example—an additional right has been granted to you by the badge of the international organization. . . . The badge . . . becomes your new identity . . . [and] serves as the key for opening the doors to your involvement in places where war, conflict, soldiers of peace, barbed wire, and checkpoints profoundly modify and regulate people caught within these clearly delimited spaces" (2010, 232–33). At Dadaab, agency staff who misplaced their badges had to get authorization from their seniors before they were allowed access to vehicles or compounds, even if the G4S security guards who manned the agency compounds knew them.

Another bureaucratic preoccupation that outshone other agendas was attending meetings. A friend working for CARE International once told me that he had not been to the camp for close to six months even though his job entailed identifying and dealing with gender-based violence cases. Like the other agency workers who provided outreach services to refugees, his daily routine now chiefly involved attending meetings and writing reports. He expressed frustration at the lack of rhythm in his daily activities, which made planning for his work difficult: "Attending meetings is not my main job description and, to be honest, I cannot explain what I am doing here." Ironically, as he pointed out, it was not unusual to hear complaints about inadequate staffing in the very meetings where participants felt a sense of being underutilized. He compared life inside the agency compound to being in a prison cell, in light of the many restrictions due to then-prevailing insecurity.

The preoccupation with procedure meant that less emphasis was put on achieving results (see Gupta 2012). The experiences of a thirty-eight-year-old refugee woman illustrate the frustrations of negotiating the several bureaucratic layers in seeking agency services. Habibo's sixteen-month-old child had a physical disability and had been diagnosed with a heart problem soon after birth, but the mother was no longer willing to take her to the nearby MSF clinic. Although she had visited the clinic three times every week for the past year, the child's condition had gradually been deteriorating, and she saw no need to continue with the medical regime. She had initially hoped she would secure a referral to Nairobi to enable the child to receive specialized treatment, but the doctor at MSF had informed her that he had more serious cases to consider for the limited opportunities. Her decision to abandon the many hospital visits was also informed by her other family obligations: she was raising eight other children as well as nursing her mentally unstable husband.

Habibo's was a typical case of giving up after knocking on every agency door. She had approached SCUK, which directed her to Handicap International due to the child's physical disability. She thought Handicap International would write to MSF to support her medical referral request, but all they offered was a promise to provide crutches to help the child's mobility at her walking stage. She had also been advised by her neighbors to visit CARE's gender division and the NCCK, which they claimed assisted women like her. CARE officials referred her back to SCUK after informing her that they only handled "domestic issues." After listening to her narrative, I convinced the district children officer to assist Habibo's child through his working relationship with agency officials. Together, we visited the SCUK manager at Dagahaley, who at first declined to venture into the camp, citing agency prohibitions, but later reluctantly agreed to accompany us to see Habibo's family in an unmarked hired vehicle.

When we arrived at Habibo's house, the manager asked her whether she had ever approached Handicap International, which elicited her earlier narrative. He then explained that he would need a recommendation from Handicap International before initiating any assistance, considering that her child had a physical disability. He nevertheless took down the family's details and promised to "remind" Handicap International about their duty. On our way back, he emphasized to us that his organization could not be expected to deal with all cases in the sprawling camp because it was overwhelmed. He then offered me some "friendly" advice: I should not be distracted from my work by refugee stories that I would have done well to take with a pinch of salt. When I called on him a month later to find out about the case's progress, he reminded me how he had illegally gone to the camp on our previous visit before explaining that it was hard for him to pursue the matter further without Handicap International's assistance.

Thomson (2012) notes in relation to a Tanzanian refugee camp that compartmentalization serves to facilitate bureaucrats' continued dispersal or deflection of individual agency through apportioning responsibility to others. This mirrors Habibo's experiences. The existence of numerous agencies at Dadaab had made it easier for bureaucrats to shirk responsibility by shifting blame to others. Knowing who to approach was, therefore, one of the biggest challenges that refugees faced. The SCUK manager's case shows how bureaucrats' role as gatekeepers for information and resources and their ability to deploy opacity and procedural tactics as means of denying claims has endowed them with immense power over their clients.

None of these bureaucratic constraints justify apprehending humanitarianism through the lens of "bare life." Doing so leaves little room for understanding how vulnerable people might respond to these power inequalities. Somalis—as I show in the following section—often framed humanitarian relief as a right they were entitled to.

Charity as a Right

Humanitarianism is often perceived as a form of exception (Fassin and Vasquez 2005) that is linked to compassion (Ticktin 2006). As I show in this section, however, Somalis (refugees and locals) were always quick to perceive the implications of particular measures and often considered humanitarianism as their "refugee right." Jennifer Hyndman (1996) has remarked that expatriate relief workers and administrators generally perceive Somali refugees as a difficult group to work with due to their reputation of "talking back" to relief workers, which is construed as unsettling the charitable, hierarchical power relationship. At the Dagahaley camp, the refugee relationship with bureaucratic officials was often characterized by ambivalent feelings. While refugees recognized and acknowledged that the agencies were indispensable in their lives, they also exhibited antagonistic tendencies. My informants often remarked that agency workers would not be at Dadaab if Somali refugees were not there. As such, they deserved to be accorded their refugee *rights*. In contrast, agency workers often emphasized the ethical and moral imperatives of humanitarianism.

These conflicting interpretations were vividly highlighted by the events that followed the abduction of two agency officials mentioned above. Humanitarian operations were suspended immediately after the incident as agency workers declined to travel around the camps due to security concerns. During the "peace meetings" described in the opening vignette, refugees were asked to reveal Al-Shabaab militants within their "midst" as a condition for resumption of aid. Refugees were initially defiant. Through local radio talk shows, many refugees condemned the suspension of relief operations, pointing out that they could not be denied their rights because of the activities of a few terrorists. After four weeks without basic provisions, however, signs of the indispensable role of agencies emerged, most notably when refugees organized a peaceful demonstration displaying posters lauding government and agency "peace" efforts. This was shortly after Kenya had sent its troops into Somalia.

At the Dagahaley "peace meeting," the DC threatened that the government was going to close down the camps if refugees did not reveal criminals who were operating in their midst. The LWF manager also warned refugees against demanding food and services "as if it your right." The four weeks they had endured without food and services was a clear demonstration that agencies were merely assisting refugees out of compassion, and they could as well withdraw completely if the continued insecurity made their compassion untenable, she added. In the end, agencies resumed services after these peaceful demonstrations, followed by assurances from camp leaders that refugees would fully cooperate with security agents in curbing insecurity.

Non-Somali government and agency workers seemed to hold stereotyped perceptions about Somalis in general, because of the refugees' perception of humanitarianism as a right and also as a result of the marginal position that Kenyan Somalis occupy in Kenya's sociopolitical circles. Views touching on "Somali rudeness" recurred in many interactions involving refugees and non-Somali Kenyans. What was surprising was that most of those holding these views justified their own harshness on the basis of the refugees' supposed rudeness. I witnessed many incidents when refugees were shouted at for not being able to communicate in English or Swahili. Many of my Somali interlocutors, including the aspirants mentioned above, claimed that government and agency workers disliked being told the truth, and that was why they held negative perceptions of Somalis who were merely demanding their rights. One clan elder told me that agency workers had an obligation to serve refugees well because they owed their jobs to the refugee presence: "Would they be driving those big vehicles if Somali refugees were not here? They are thriving on our miseries!" On another occasion, during an informal chat with a group of elders in the camp, a man in his late forties jokingly pointed out that everybody, including researchers like myself, were just benefiting from "Somali miseries." Local leaders like the DPC offered similar arguments. They commonly accused the UNHCR of seeking to selfishly benefit from Somali miseries by inflating refugee numbers. These perceptions imbued the tensions in social relations between bureaucrats and Somalis in general. Many Somali refugees, for example, did not perceive themselves simply as humanitarian victims needing assistance or as mere visitors, but as important agents whose presence provided justification for having agencies at Dagahaley. As such, it was their right to demand services and other humanitarian benefits.

Apart from challenging humanitarian charitable assumptions through envisioning charity as a right, refugees also knew that humanitarianism was not always guided by benign intentions. A refugee youth leader once pointed out in an informal discussion that the "survival" of agencies depended on an endless cycle of crises. "They were overwhelmed by high numbers of refugee arrivals before the border was closed, and before that, the drought. They are now highlighting the floods and malaria to appeal for even more funding, and one wonders what they really wish for, if they portray rain and drought as being bad in the same breath."

Nell Gabiam (2012) and Ilana Feldman (2012) make similar observations concerning Palestinian refugees who conceive humanitarianism as a right and contextualize their suffering as an arena for making political claims. Unlike the Somali case, however, the Palestinians' sense of entitlement is perceived as "a question of historical and political responsibility, the price the United Nations must pay for its failure to find a solution to the Palestinian refugee issue" (Gabiam 2012, 101). But like the Palestinians, Somalis use their suffering as a channel for making rights-based claims to humanitarian aid. It is not uncommon for humanitarianism to be internalized as a natural refugee right, especially in protracted refugee contexts such as the Somali refugee situation. As I show in the case of Nur below, notions about rights can be extended to include agency property as well. Where this is the case, it can lead to a sense that agency workers are "stealing" from refugees if they are suspected of misappropriation.

Nur came into exile in 1992 with his parents and six siblings when he was only eight years old. He worked for CARE International from 2002 until November 2011, when he was arrested on suspicion that he was a member of Al-Shabaab. His case was popularized by the nature of his work—as a driver in the water and sanitation sector, his job was to distribute fuel for water generators. Thus, the entire camp faced a water shortage that lasted two weeks following his arrest, during which many refugees were forced to fetch water from village boreholes. When he was released on bail in February 2012, he approached me through my research assistant in the hope that I could assist him with legal advice concerning his case. Despite explaining to him that law was not my forte, he insisted on telling me the circumstances surrounding his case, pointing out that he trusted me because he had heard that I was "learned" and friendly to refugees. As far as he was concerned, the genesis of his problem was an earlier disagreement with his supervisor, who was a non-Somali Kenyan. He stated that he once confronted his supervisor in 2010 about suspect fuel authorization. The supervisor was signing for fuel that was not being delivered, which amounted to theft of "refugee property." The supervisor warned Nur to keep out of his affairs or risk losing his job if he persisted with questioning his actions. Nur decided to expose his boss and chose the CARE country director's Dagahaley visit as a good occasion for doing so. He revealed the supervisor's fuel theft in a meeting that the director was chairing. The supervisor vowed to sack him for the embarrassment he had endured and started using proxies to fight him. One of the supervisor's collaborators threatened Nur with death in the presence of police officers, but when he was arrested, Nur's supervisor bribed the police to have him released. Later, the same person was arrested for being in possession of an illegal firearm, which he claimed belonged to Nur. Consequently, Nur was arrested and tortured to reveal other suspects, but the search for firearms in his house yielded nothing. The police therefore substituted their earlier terrorism charges with robbery charges, due to lack of evidence. Nur concluded his story by expressing his determination to "say the truth" in ensuring that refugee property and rights were protected.

An important lesson from Nur's encounter with the state is that the supremacy of kinship did not turn bureaucratic structures into mere bystanders. Kinship helped locals and "old" refugees to influence bureaucratic action as well as exclude their "new" refugee counterparts from senior leadership positions in the camp. However, it could not resolve issues that pitted individuals against powerful bureaucrats—echoing the relative power inequalities between refugees and humanitarian officials at a personal level. That said, kinship and bureaucracy often worked side by side in governing camps.

This chapter has shown that the line between locals and "old" refugees was blurry. For example, locals vigorously influenced the camps' political process by lobbying for their relatives to occupy refugee positions that would enable them to control camp resources. However, the bureaucracy also played an important role in structuring camp dynamics. For example, it encouraged people to elect leaders of their choice—at least in CPST elections—and ensured that the camp's leadership structure conformed to the hierarchical setup that would be expected from bureaucratic systems. Thus, kinship and bureaucracy worked hand in hand to shape human relationships. However, kinship tended to overshadow bureaucracy in the camps' internal working. This meant that those without strong kinship networks were less likely to get leadership positions and some camp resources. As the precarious position of "new" refugees has shown, less-connected refugees were also more likely to be exposed to violence while being simultaneously blamed for it. These internal dynamics, coupled with the lack of economic opportunities for most refugees, seem to explain the high insecurity rates in African refugee camps.

Studies that apprehend humanitarianism through "bare life" conceptions tend to portray refugees and local groups as being completely helpless.

This chapter has demonstrated that the power of bureaucratic actors to manipulate socioeconomic relations was not without constraints. Refugees challenged humanitarian assumptions by framing charity as a right. They also recognized the self-interest of humanitarianism. Using bare life as a lens for viewing camp dynamics might, therefore, give an inaccurate picture of refugee dynamics at Dadaab. Gupta (2012) questions the adequacy of bureaucratic theory in contextualizing the lived realities of people in Third World countries who seldom draw a line between actors' roles as public servants and private citizens. A similar charge can be made in relation to Somalis. Thus, for example, agencies were directly in charge of distributing relief aid in the camp, yet the noise about unfairness in food allocation kept increasing each passing day. This was because they relied on incentive workers, whose appointment was governed by the rules of kinship disguised as fair selection.

Discussions of how the Kenyan state unfairly treats its Somali citizens and refugees rarely put into perspective what's at stake, what shapes state officials' conception of refugees, and how this is reflected in the larger Kenyan population. As shown by the DC's platitudes about the difficulties of governing Somalis, suspicions about refugees causing insecurity through entrenching themselves in Kenya speak to how the refugees' presence is seen as threatening sovereignty. These fears shape the difficult encounters that African states often have with refugee populations within their borders.

References

Agamben, Giorgio. 1998. *Homo Sacer: Sovereign Power and Bare Life.* Stanford, CA: Stanford University Press.

Agier, Michel. 2011. *Managing the Undesirables: Refugee Camps and Humanitarian Government.* Cambridge: Polity.

Barnett, Michael N. 2010. *The International Humanitarian Order.* New York: Routledge.

CASA Consulting. 2001. *Evaluation of the Dadaab Firewood Project, Kenya.* Geneva, Switzerland: Evaluation and Policy Analysis Unit, United Nations High Commissioner for Refugees.

de Montclos, Marc-Antoine Pérouse, and Peter Mwangi Kangwanja. 2000. "Refugee Camps or Cities? The Socio-economic Dynamics of the Dadaab and Kakuma Camps in Northern Kenya." *Journal of Refugee Studies* 13 (2): 205–22.

Duffield, Mark R. 2001. *Global Governance and the New Wars: The Merging of Development and Security.* London: Zed Books.

Fassin, Didier, and Paula Vasquez. 2005. "Humanitarian Exception as the Rule: The Political Theology of the 1999 'Tragedia' in Venezuela." *American Ethnologist* 32 (3): 389–405.

Feldman, Ilana. 2012. "The Humanitarian Condition: Palestinian Refugees and the Politics of Living." *Humanity: An International Journal of Human Rights, Humanitarianism, and Development* 3 (2): 155–72.

Finnström, Sverker. 2008. *Living with Bad Surroundings: War, History, and Everyday Moments in Northern Uganda.* Durham, NC: Duke University Press.

Gabiam, Nell. 2012. "When 'Humanitarianism' Becomes 'Development': The Politics of International Aid in Syria's Palestinian Refugee Camps." *American Anthropologist* 114 (1): 95–107.

Goldsmith, Paul. 1997. "The Somali Impact on Kenya, 1990–1993: The View from Outside the Camps." In *Mending Rips in the Sky: Options for Somali Communities in the 21st Century,* edited by Hussein M. Adam and Richard Ford, 461–83. Lawrenceville, NJ: Red Sea.

Gupta, Akhil. 2012. *Red Tape: Bureaucracy, Structural Violence, and Poverty in India.* Durham, NC: Duke University Press.

Harrell-Bond, Barbara E. 1986. *Imposing Aid: Emergency Assistance to Refugees.* New York: Oxford University Press.

Hoag, Colin. 2011. "Assembling Partial Perspectives: Thoughts on the Anthropology of Bureaucracy." *PoLAR: Political and Legal Anthropology Review* 34 (1): 81–94.

Hyndman, M. Jennifer. 1996. "Geographies of Displacement: Gender, Culture and Power in UNHCR Refugee Camps, Kenya." PhD diss., University of British Columbia.

Ikanda, Fred Nyongesa. 2014. "Kinship, Hospitality and Humanitarianism: Locals and Refugees in Northeastern Kenya." PhD diss., University of Cambridge.

———. 2018. "Good and Bad Muslims: Conflict, Justice, and Religion among Somalis at Dagahaley Refugee Camp in Kenya." In *Pursuing Justice in Africa: Competing Imaginaries and Contested Practices,* edited by Jessica Johnson and George Hamandishe Karekwaivanane, 222–42. Athens: Ohio University Press.

———. 2019. "Forging Associations across Multiple Spaces: How Somali Kinship Practices Sustain the Existence of the Dadaab Camps in Kenya." In *Refugees and Forced Migration in the Horn and Eastern Africa: Trends, Challenges and Opportunities,* edited by Johannes Dragsbaek Schmidt, Leah Kimathi, and Michael Omondi Owiso, 287–304. Cham, Switzerland: Springer International.

———. 2020. "The Role of Somali Kinship in Sustaining Bureaucratic Governance around Dagahaley Camp in Kenya." *Ethnos.* https://doi.org/10.1080/00141844.2020.1773894.

Jacobsen, Karen. 2002. "Can Refugees Benefit the State? Refugee Resources and African Statebuilding." *Journal of Modern African Studies* 40 (4): 577–96.

Lewis, I. M. 1999. *A Pastoral Democracy: A Study of Pastoralism and Politics among the Northern Somali of the Horn of Africa.* Hamburg: Lit Verlag. First published 1961.

Lochery, Emma. 2012 "Rendering Difference Visible: The Kenyan State and Its Somali Citizens." *African Affairs* 111 (445): 615–39.

Mathews, Andrew S. 2005. "Power/Knowledge, Power/Ignorance: Forest Fires and the State in Mexico." *Human Ecology* 33 (6): 795–820.

McGoey, Linsey. 2007. "On the Will to Ignorance in Bureaucracy." *Economy and Society* 36 (2): 212–35.

Mosse, David. 2005. *Cultivating Development: An Ethnography of Aid Policy and Practice.* London: Pluto.

Nyers, Peter. 2006. *Rethinking Refugees: Beyond States of Emergency.* New York: Routledge.

Ohta, Itaru. 2005. "Multiple Socio-economic Relationships Improvised between the Turkana and Refugees in Kakuma Area, Northwestern Kenya." In *Displacement Risks in Africa: Refugees, Resettlers and Their Host Population,* edited by Itaru Ohta and Yntiso D. Gebre, 315–37. Kyoto: Kyoto University Press.

Pandolfi, M. 2010. "Humanitarianism and Its Discontents." In *Forces of Compassion: Humanitarianism between Ethics and Politics,* edited by Erica Bornstein and Peter Redfield, 227–48. Santa Fe, NM: School for Advanced Research Press.

Polman, Linda. 2011. *The Crisis Caravan: What's Wrong with Humanitarian Aid?* New York: Picador.

Rozakou, Katerina. 2012. "The Biopolitics of Hospitality in Greece: Humanitarianism and the Management of Refugees." *American Ethnologist* 39 (3): 562–77.

Sandvik, Kristin Bergtora. 2011. "Blurring Boundaries: Refugee Resettlement in Kampala—between the Formal, the Informal, and the Illegal." *PoLAR: Political and Legal Anthropology Review* 34 (1): 11–32.

Slaughter, Amy, and Jeff Crisp. 2009. *A Surrogate State? The Role of UNHCR in Protracted Refugee Situations.* New Issues in Refugee Research, research paper no. 168. Geneva, Switzerland: United Nations High Commissioner for Refugees.

Tamanaha, Brian Z. 1993. "The Folly of the 'Social Scientific' Concept of Legal Pluralism." *Journal of Law and Society* 20 (2): 192–217.

Thomson, Marnie Jane. 2012. "Black Boxes of Bureaucracy: Transparency and Opacity in the Resettlement Process of Congolese Refugees." *PoLAR: Political and Legal Anthropology Review* 35 (2): 186–205.

Ticktin, Miriam. 2006. "Where Ethics and Politics Meet: The Violence of Humanitarianism in France." *American Ethnologist* 33 (1): 33–49.

FOUR

Inside the Anti-Politics Machine

Civil Society Mediation of Everyday Encounters with the State

E. FOUKSMAN

DOES DEVELOPMENT-FOCUSED CIVIL SOCIETY DEMOCRATIZE or depoliticize? Do development projects run by nongovernmental organizations (NGOs), facilitated by aid professionals and funded by global foundations and intergovernmental organizations, facilitate and enable encounters with the state, or rather divert citizens' energy and attention away from the state and toward "aidland" (Mosse 2011)? The debate was sparked in the early 1990s by two nearly simultaneous publications. First came the World Bank's report *Governance and Development* (1992), which promoted what became known as the "good-governance agenda." The good-governance agenda posits that civil society institutions play a key role in ensuring a society with well-functioning markets, wide-reaching social services, and a responsive state (Lewis 2002). Looking to the role of associations and grassroots movements in the collapse of the Soviet empire, proponents of good governance argue that the state is just one entity among many that fulfill particular roles or needs (be they provisioning schools or building infrastructure), and that citizens (like consumers) can put pressure on the state by exercising choice via civil society organizations. In this view, civil society writ large is a key counterbalance to the power of the state, helping with both accountability and wide-ranging democratic participation.

This vision of the state as tamed and made accessible and accountable via associational life and civil society dates back to de Tocqueville's *Democracy in America* (1835). Expressions of the neo-Tocquevillian view that the associational nature of civil society can act to mediate the power of the state range from James C. Scott's (1998) assertion that a weak civil society enables the rise of authoritarian state power to Mary Kaldor's (2003) argument that global civil society can defuse and counter conflict and war. Thanks to the good-governance agenda, international institutions and development projects in Africa and beyond see building local civil society as the necessary (and conveniently practicable) first step to encouraging democracy.

Yet alongside this surge of interest in the links between civil society and democracy in the global south came its critique. This has been most famously voiced by James Ferguson in *The Anti-Politics Machine* (1994). Ferguson argues that development-focused civil society does not ensure a responsive state, but rather "is an 'anti-politics machine,' depoliticizing everything it touches, everywhere whisking political realities out of sight, all the while performing, almost unnoticed, its own pre-eminently political operation of expanding bureaucratic state power" (1994, xv). In this view, civil society in Africa thus does not politicize, but rather politically disempowers the communities and citizens it works with.

A host of critical scholarship has followed in Ferguson's footsteps (e.g., Grindle 2004; Lewis and Mosse 2006; Matanga 2010). This chapter will draw in particular on Neera Chandhoke's critique of the good-governance agenda via the concept of the network state. Like Ferguson, Chandhoke maintains that development-focused civil society depoliticizes. Yet Chandhoke argues that it does so by becoming a subcontractor of the state, fulfilling the state's promises and responsibilities without giving its citizens the opportunity to protest or make demands on the state. Thus "state institutions network with other organisations that were formerly contained within the non-state sphere of civil society" (Chandhoke 2003, 2960; see also Jayal 1997). State responsibilities are subcontracted to civil society organizations until the state becomes a pluralized networking polity. And as subcontractors of the state, civil society organizations can no longer be oppositional or mediating actors, but rather become co-opted into the state's agenda.

But how do ordinary people themselves experience good governance—or the anti-politics machine and the network state? This chapter will use an ethnography of Kenyan citizens' everyday encounters with the state via or through civil society organizations to look closely at the lived realities behind these debates. By focusing on the way activists and residents of a small town and a village in northern Kenya engage with the state through a network of internationally funded civil society institutions involved in a forest conservation project, I will unravel the interweave of global, national, reginal, and local civil society actors that connect, mediate, and shape state-citizen encounters in Isiolo town and Beliqo village. In doing so, this chapter argues that development-focused civil society *can* in fact facilitate citizen-state encounters, but that in order to do so, it filters and shapes the scope and the formulations of such engagements.

In particular, this chapter will make the case that development-focused NGOs, the international foundations that fund them, and the local groups they work with utilize a key mechanism to mediate citizen-state encounters: knowledge. By both circulating and filtering certain facts about state mechanisms, legal instruments, and ways of accessing state resources, development-focused civil society organizations facilitate citizens' engagement with the state. Yet they also shape such engagement and delimit its form. While it can be political and demanding, it cannot be confrontational. Such "civil society knowledge networks" (Fouksman 2017) thus defuse the conflictual and activist content of citizen concerns, yet in so doing they make engagement possible. At the same time, because they are part of transnational networks of development institutions, these organizations bring international expectations and norms to the way state actors encounter citizens. Thus, by acting as both *knowledge circulators* and *knowledge filters*, development NGOs can be both *anti-* and *pro*-politics (of a certain kind) by simultaneously promoting and delimiting the contents and form of state-citizen encounters.

The Case Study: Civil Society and the State in Northern Kenya

I will argue here that focusing on the epistemic content of networks of development-focused civil society organizations allows us to subvert and nuance the democratizing/depoliticizing debate. By examining the way activists and citizens talk about and engage with the state throughout a network of different but connected organizations, we are able to complicate the network state, to open up and look more closely inside the anti-politics machine. This argument is based on a multi-sited ethnography (Marcus 1995), conducted in 2011, of one such network. The global node of this network is the Christensen Fund (TCF), a grant-making foundation based in San Francisco that supports work on issues of biocultural diversity (the intersection of cultural diversity and biodiversity) (Loh and Harmon 2005). In Kenya, TCF's key partner is the Nairobi-based Kivulini Trust. Kivulini partners in turn with a variety of ecological and cultural NGOs and movements in the north of Kenya. It is the key connector of TCF to a small but very active grassroots NGO called Waso Trustland Project (WTL), based in the north Kenyan town of Isiolo. The Waso Trustland Project works with a constellation of villages around Isiolo. This case study focuses on the village of Beliqo (also spelled Biliqo) in Isiolo County, where WTL, Kivulini, and TCF together are supporting a forest conservation project run by the village's Community Forest Association (CFA).

While multi-sited and multi-spatial (Burawoy 2001), the ethnography itself is focused largely on northern Kenya, in particular Isiolo County, its capital Isiolo town, and the village of Beliqo. The ethnic group dominant in Beliqo is the Borana, a Muslim pastoralist people (Isack 1986). In many ways, the Borana are a particularly evocative group to be asking about their everyday encounters with the state, as they feel themselves to have been long marginalized and ignored by Kenya's government. This marginalization emerged first out of a purposeful policy of the British, and then out of the 1963–68 Shifta War between secessionists of the north (largely the Somali population and some, though not all, of the Borana) and the Kenyan state led by Jomo Kenyatta (Dahl 1979). In response, the government used measures including forced sedentarization into villages that functioned as concentration camps and confiscation or slaughter of herds of cattle (Whittaker 2008). The Borana see this as the first and most brutal step in a long history of political and economic exclusion and marginalization, crediting their current impoverishment to these policies and to continued neglect by the state (Arero 2007). The village of Beliqo, a six-hour bus ride over a rutted road running northeast from Isiolo town, is a living example of still-simmering resentment over this history and its legacy. Though the community of Beliqo receives a number of state benefits, many of the Borana feel marginalized by the Kenyan state, exemplified by a lack of infrastructure and social services (in 2011 there were no paved roads, electricity, cell phone signal, clinic, or easily accessible secondary school in the village). However, this is changing, with much talk and some action from the national government around economic and infrastructural development, though this rhetoric also inspired fears of land-grabbing and exclusion of local communities from newfound wealth.

The landscape around Beliqo is a wide, unfolding flatland of scrubby bush and acacia trees swept by hot, dry winds. The flatness is broken by a series of hills on one horizon and the shock of the rising bulk of a plateau in the north; when I was there in 2011, the plateau blocked any hope of a cell phone signal. A river winds east to west in this landscape, sometimes vast and swollen, sometimes down to a trickle or disappearing entirely, the only flash of green a strip of forest on either side. No electricity lines interrupt the view. This is a small corner of northern Kenya, a part of the country that used to be the Northern Frontier District. People in Kenya's metropolises speak of it as "upcountry," a word synonymous with remoteness. While members of the Borana ethnic group once lived in small, mobile villages of woven huts that followed the animals, more and more stay in permanent villages of mud-walled houses. Beliqo is tucked around a curve of the Ewaso Niro, a three-kilometer walk from the river.

The two thousand or so residents of Beliqo subsist largely from semi-nomadic pastoralism, and struggle under the pressure of these worsening annual droughts (2011, the year that this research was conducted, saw a particularly bad drought affect northern Kenya). Animals are herded over communally held "trust lands," though Beliqo's residents are increasingly adopting a more sedentary lifestyle in order to give children a primary education, to have access to medicine and, crucially, access to food aid during times of drought. About two-thirds of the families in Beliqo subsist for half of each year on food aid provided by the World Food Programme. The rights to the land are vested in the communities that reside on them and are held in trust by the elected county council. Community members speak of the councillors with a mixture of respect (most are community elders) and exasperation at the corruption that seems to plague the council, which has been accused of controlling access and ownership of the land for personal gain (more on this below).

Despite its geographic remoteness and isolation, Beliqo hosts a kaleidoscope of formally registered and community-based organizations addressing a variety of social causes. During my time in the village there were about twenty active civil society groups, most with between ten and twenty members, varying in scope, membership, and levels of activity, ranging from youth and women's groups to herders' organizations, savings groups, and groups focusing on the use of natural resources. Fourteen of these civil society groups had been since 2009 members of the Beliqo CFA, which is structured as an umbrella group, with a handful of decision-making posts and a representative of each member group on the CFA committee.

The CFA was set up with the impetus and guidance of Hassan Shano, a local activist based in Isiolo, the main regional town of eighty thousand, a busy and dusty tangle of traders, lorries loaded with cattle and people, and concrete and brick government buildings tucked away from the main road. Shano runs the two-man NGO Waso Trustland Project (WTL), itself supported by the Nairobi-based Kivulini Trust (run by Dr. Hussein, who is originally from Beliqo village), and funded by the Christensen Fund (which also funds the Beliqo CFA via Waso Trustland). Waso Trustland built on the 2005 Kenya Forests Act, which shifted management of Kenya's forests away from the government to communities, legally enabling them to both make use of and be responsible for the forests. When Waso Trustland suggested that the village form a CFA of its own with a biocultural diversity bent and Christensen Fund funding, there was already an active grassroots resource-use and conservation group called REAR-Charri in the village. The Community Forest Association grew out of REAR-Charri, with the organizational and legislative knowledge—as well as the continued involvement—of Waso Trustland. The Beliqo CFA's mandate is to protect the riverine forest around the village from logging and burning, which they are able to do by hiring a few local guards to patrol the forest under the

Forests Act's authority. They also started a tree nursery, built a community meeting hall, and helped Waso Trustland collect stories about the river—all tie-ins to the Christensen Fund's emphasis on biocultural diversity.

Civil Society Views on the State

The Kenyans involved in the civil society organizations in this study were explicit about attempting to engage with, influence, and connect citizens with the state. As will be shown in detail below, Hassan Shano, the head of the Waso Trustland Project in Isiolo, makes influencing the state one of his key goals. He seeks to supplement the functioning of the state and utilize state power and resources. Yet there is a level of distrust and ambivalence toward the state in both Isiolo town and Beliqo village, discussed more in the sections to come. While NGOs in the case study network fail to dispel this distrust, they do manage to teach the citizens they work with how to tap into the resources and promises of the state. Indeed, Waso Trustland itself is highly suspicious and disdainful of the state, while WTL's adviser, Dr. Hussein of the Kivulini Trust in Nairobi, makes state inclusion an overt goal. In both cases, the engagement of development NGOs with the state shows that while the state is becoming networked and pluralized through its reliance on civil society actors, this is not the only outcome of the development apparatus. The organizations examined here themselves exert pressure on the state, engage with the state directly through local government institutions, and teach citizens how to access state resources.

Waso Trustland is devoted to land rights and natural resource management in the village communities in Kenya's remote, pastoralist north. Its director, the middle-aged and charismatic Hassan Shano, has a history as a human rights activist and has been jailed on charges of "incitement" during a protest. This background means he has a critical perspective on the role of the state in social projects, including conservation. The north of Kenya was experiencing a particularly severe drought during my fieldwork there in the summer of 2011, and Shano often expressed anger at the way the Kenyan government was handling it, claiming that the ministers were "missing in action" and "ignoring the issue." WTL also criticized the local council's management of the district's game reserves, claiming that there was mismanagement and corruption. Shano argued that if the community had direct control of the reserves, the benefits would be better managed and equitably distributed. Shano was unafraid of conflict with the state, and has not hesitated to take government ministries to court over perceived corruption or mismanagement. This stance toward the state was not simply voiced by Hassan Shano: the chairman of WTL's board saw the Kenyan state as unable to stop illegal logging and other ecological problems "due to corruption," and because the government was "never serious about the environment."

Waso Trustland has expanded its attention from land-rights advocacy to resource rights, ecological activism, and grassroots conservation efforts. Yet the way that WTL talks about environmentalism is still centered on the language of rights, access, and struggle against the state. In explaining that WTL is willing to work with any pastoralist group in the north, its administrative assistant (and jack-of-all-trades) Liban Golicha declared that "the environment doesn't have *boundaries*." Yet WTL *is* focused on the state's recognition of boundaries and land tenure. Liban went on to explain that many of the issues and conflicts that WTL deals with are a result of differences in land tenure between different districts and ethnic groups. In neighboring Meru district, land is privately owned, and both Shano and Liban brought up the Meru ethnic group repeatedly as the perpetrators who hoped to log and sell off the riverine forest around Beliqo. Thus, ideas and rhetoric around ownership, access, and state recognition form the backbone of WTL's approach to environmentalism.

Indeed, WTL's involvement with conservation around Beliqo originated in its concern with water rights and the use and misuse of the Waso River. WTL became involved in the emerging conflict between the farmers of central Kenya, who were diverting the water upriver for agriculture, and the pastoralists downstream in northern Kenya, who rely on the river to water their livestock. From this concern with the misuse of water, WTL became aware of similar concerns regarding the riverine forest in the vicinity of Beliqo village. Indeed, the ecologically focused conversations I had at WTL were almost always related either to access rights or to conflict. As Shano described it, much conflict in the region comes from tensions over land access and the use of natural resources. In recounting the way that WTL became interested in the conservation of the Ewaso Niro River and the forest around it, conflict was a prominent theme—not only conflict between the farmers upstream and the pastoralists downstream, but also competition with other river users and with ethnic outsiders who were accused of trying to destroy the forest around the river for personal gain. Like Shano and Liban, the chairman of WTL's board blamed the Meru ethnic group as the source of ecological problems in Beliqo, describing them as "outsiders with power saws" who cannot be held accountable to Borana law. In his words, formal state mechanisms to stop these outsiders were not working "due to corruption," and because the government was "never serious about the environment."

WTL's view of the connections between state neglect, ethnic conflict, and ecological ownership became clear in a discussion between Shano, Liban, and Maulit, a WTL legal intern provided by the Kenya Land Alliance, one of Waso Trustland's partner NGOs. They discussed Maulit's discovery of ecological degradation caused by deforestation and the diversion of rivers and springs for farming in a neighboring district. In this conversation, all three were incensed at the state's apathy and neglect and planned to lobby various local government offices. They also associated the drying up of the river with deforestation and blamed Meru farmers for cutting down trees, diverting the river, and encouraging herders in the area to start doing the same, thus endangering the ecology of the region and the future of the herders themselves, who need these water sources for their livestock. This conversation highlighted a number of themes: WTL's tense relationship with the state, which is both an important actor and a negative, corrupt, and neglectful one; the ethnic tensions that emerge out of different modes of resource use; the tension over who has legitimate access to these resources; and the central importance of herding for the pastoralist community.

Thus, in WTL's lexicon, resource rights and access are intertwined with interethnic conflict and the ecological is linked with political and economic issues, particularly land rights and state corruption. Throughout my time with WTL, this remained the organization's focus, even when engaged with the biocultural diversity rhetoric of their funders and the conservation work in Beliqo with CFA. Yet for WTL, conservation is not mission drift: as will be outlined in more detail below, WTL is able to forge a viable connection between its emphasis on land rights, government accountability, and conflict on the one hand, and a broader focus on biocultural diversity and conservation on the other.

At the same time, while frequently critical of and adversarial toward the state, Hassan Shano did acknowledge the role and usefulness, both potential and realized, of state actors, especially when it came to conservation and environmental issues. In particular, one of the key mechanisms enabling the existence of the donor-funded forest conservation movement in the village of Beliqo is the 2005 Kenya Forests Act. The act grants communities legal control of local forests through the creation of Community Forest Associations. Shano noted that this was a government policy that legitimized and gave structure to the local forest conservation movement. Hassan Shano was also willing to concede that there were some government agencies that were doing good work—one of them being the Ministry of State for Development of Northern Kenya and Other Arid Lands (Arid Lands for short), which Shano said was "a small office, but it has done a lot." In short, although WTL's relationship with the state seemed both fraught and adversarial, Hassan Shano acknowledged the power and influence of state actors, from the local to the national level.

A particularly telling anecdote arose from my own participation in the evolution of the relationship between Hassan Shano and Councillor Golicha, the elected county councillor for the Beliqo area. Shano had campaigned hard against the establishment of the community nature conservancy that Golicha had supported, and sharply criticized the councillor, accusing him of being a puppet, fooled, or out for personal gain. Every time the councillor came up in our conversations, Shano spoke with great bitterness. Golicha had never visited the WTL office, and Shano claimed that he avoided WTL staff in order to avoid confrontation. At the same time, Shano acknowledged that he would prefer to have the councillor working with WTL, and that though they differed on the conservancy question, they might in fact share similar views and be able to work together on other issues. During my time at the WTL office, I set up an interview with the councillor, and he came to WTL for the first time. Shano joined us at the end of the interview and began a conversation about my research and presence in the organization. By the end of the conversation, Councillor Golicha and Hassan Shano were shaking hands, smiling, and asking me to take photographs of the two of them together. Hassan Shano proclaimed that they should be working together and that they shared the same concerns. After the councillor left, Shano thanked me for being the mechanism via which the rift between the councillor and WTL was healed, and continued to mention the incident with great satisfaction for several weeks afterward. Despite its pointedly adversarial position, WTL clearly saw the advantages of cooperation with local state actors.

This attitude was encouraged by Hassan Shano's connections to national and international civil society organizations and funders, which have tried to soften his relationship with the state. A native of Isiolo County and well acquainted with Shano, Dr. Hussein ran the Kivulini Trust in Nairobi. Kivulini is the Christensen Fund's key partner organization in Kenya and the Waso Trustland Project's connection to TCF funding. Dr. Hussein is upfront that he wants to connect citizens and the state. In his words, Kivulini's broader aim is to "solve big problems through the right routes." One begins with "empowering the communities themselves, giving them voice," which would enable them to engage with institutions bigger than themselves, be they state-based or transnational organizations. In Dr. Hussein's view, this is done by making sure that communities are "proud, both of their culture and themselves." Thus, Dr. Hussein's view of the state is largely instrumental, and, like the Christensen Fund, he is focused on ways to get the state to engage with citizens.

As WTL's main funder, TCF has used this pragmatism to mediate and redirect the often conflictual or adversarial relationship between Waso Trustland and the Kenyan state. TCF seems to view the purpose of on-the-ground civil society organizations to be project implementers, in contrast to Shano's interest in advocacy and activism. Indeed, while facets of the state and state-citizen relations came up spontaneously and repeatedly in my conversations and observations among Kenyan NGOs and in the villages where these NGOs supported activists or ran their programs, staff members at the San Francisco head office of the Christensen Fund seemed hesitant to broach the subject. They did not have much to say about their relationship with or views toward the governments of the countries where they funded civil society organizations. What they did say broadly supports the arguments developed in more detail below—that civil society and the state are not in stark opposition, nor is civil society taking over the functions of the state or entirely depoliticizing people's engagement with it.

Ken Wilson, then-director of the Christensen Fund, saw the foundation's role as partly building trust between the state and local communities. For him, this trust largely had to be built within the state—in his words, TCF "encouraged [governments] to be less frightened of people gaining rights and autonomy." To do this, TCF had to engage the state, but "carefully," with an "informed relationship" that was not oppositional. TCF's strategy to achieve this is to build the *legitimacy* of their grantees in the state's eyes. The fund is perhaps understandably wary of governments seeing it as interfering or adversarial—this can and has led to foreign funding being effectively banned in places like Russia.

Rather than focusing on issues that could be contentious or confrontational, TCF sees itself as building engagement between citizens and the state by "transforming social capital." For instance, Ken told me that many minority ethnic groups in northern Kenya that were previously not recognized by the local and national governments now are, as a result of TCF and TCF's grantees' efforts "on the ground," which enabled local organizations and empowered communities. Thus, Ken sees TCF's work as potentially transforming the state both by engaging with it and by supporting grassroots empowerment (as long as it is not too confrontational). Indeed, for Ken the long-term goal of TCF is to enable its grantees to play a leading role in their nations and communities, to "change the mentality" of local institutions toward biological and cultural diversity, including the mentality of the state. Yet the state is worth directly aiding as well. Ken pointed out that "governments are transforming" due to the "penetration of socioeconomic forces" such as massive energy development. TCF does not aim to stop these processes, but rather to help local communities and national governments engage with these "global processes . . . on their own terms."

TCF thus also sees its role as being an *educator* of the state, as passing the knowledge necessary to guide the state toward greater engagement with both local communities and broader development processes, without alienating it. TCF acknowledges that it cannot operate without state acquiescence, which makes it shy away from contentious politics—and try to keep its grantees from being too contentious as well. Yet it does not shun the political entirely, as it does want to have some engagement with the power of the state. This reflects the complicated and at times ambivalent knowledge relationships between NGOs, communities, and governments, a complex relationship wherein knowledge and power are not all top-down phenomena, and often can be mediated by citizen activists involved in local civil society projects.

This can be seen in the give-and-take surrounding the protection of the Ewaso Niro River (the river which runs through the village of Beliqo) when WTL was originally seeking funding from TCF. WTL wanted TCF to assist with advocacy and awareness about river use and the diversion of river water by big farms upstream, in an attempt to "get people to stand and fight for their rights from the government." According to Hassan Shano, TCF demurred from taking such a contentious and adversarial stance and refused to fund advocacy work. Shano noted with regret that both Kivulini and TCF told him that the river must be dealt with by the government, not by civil society, and that the issue of resource rights was too broad to be dealt with by a regional NGO. But Shano kept on insisting, arguing that the river was so central to the livelihood of the Borana people that the issue could not be ignored, that "there must be people on the ground talking about this." Shano and TCF finally agreed that an appropriate way of using TCF funds to forward WTL interests would be for WTL to work on protecting the forest on the banks of the river, rather than the river itself, changing the focus not only from the river to the forest, but from advocacy to conservation.

Thus, TCF does manage to depoliticize the agenda of activists such as Hassan Shano to some extent, in this case turning Shano away from being an activist and toward being a program implementor or manager. As a result, Shano has shifted from running an organization originally explicitly positioned against and in criticism of the state toward an engagement with natural resource management in a way that is far less politically contentious, and indeed works within the provisions of the state (including the 2005 Kenya Forests Act). Much as Ferguson (1994) argues, here global development institutions are influencing citizens in the direction of ideological and political moderation.

Yet at the same time, while switching his focus to ecological concerns, Shano held on to his activist approach. During the time I spent with him, Shano agitated repeatedly for a government response to Kenya's drought. He repeatedly called local media, including a TV station, and argued passionately about the lack of appropriate state action. He also told me that "everyone must stand and fight [climate change], climate must be protected at any expense." Even with a change in focus, Shano did not become entirely depoliticized. Thus, in Waso Trustland's case, TCF was unable to fully succeed in "rendering contentious issues technical" (Li 2007, 10). Instead, the relationship between TCF and WTL has reformulated expectations and relationships with the state: from contentious advocacy, WTL has in its practices moved to teaching citizens who are neglected by the state to make small-scale demands and access state resources. As we shall see below, development-focused civil society networks in this case have shifted the scope of citizen demands on the state from the macro to the micro, from full inclusion and the rights of citizenship to access to a small slice of state resources. Nevertheless, this has not been a simple process of depoliticization, but a shift in the scope and nature of political engagement.

Forging State Engagement, Mediating State Demands: Development, Citizens, and the State

The people of Beliqo understand themselves to be isolated from broader national and transnational communities not only technologically and geographically, but also politically and historically. As discussed above, shortly after independence the Borana were involved in the Shifta War between the Kenyan state and secessionist movements in the north of the country (Whittaker 2008). Many of those I spoke with remembered parents or grandparents being interned in the camps set up by the Kenyan government during the war, and having cattle, a major source of Borana wealth, confiscated or slaughtered by the state. Ibrahim Boru, a man in his thirties who was the organizing secretary for the Community Forest Association, argued that the Borana people who live in the north are not recognized by the government as Kenyan—that the government "doesn't bother with us." He told me that the government was to blame for Borana impoverishment—that the Borana once had "plenty" of animals that were either killed by the government during the Shifta War or died for lack of good grazing land, which Ibrahim also attributed to the government. Ibrahim's grievance with the state was both historical and contemporary, encompassing both the larger Kenyan state and the local county council, which he saw as complicit with the national government. His sense that northern Kenya was not simply neglected but actually robbed by the Kenyan state was echoed repeatedly in my conversations in Beliqo.

Indeed, this sense of political marginalization could be understood as a struggle for citizenship. Manby (2009) refers to the treatment of pastoralists and residents of the northeast in her depiction of the Kenyan state's uneven apportioning of ID cards. The same people who fought for autonomy now fight for inclusion. Yet it was not primarily ID cards, but rather the lack of resources from the state, together with a history of conflict and deprivation, that I heard about repeatedly in Beliqo, echoed by everyone from the village chief to its water pump attendant. Guracha Sirman, a young livestock owner and youth activist, stated that the Borana of the region have been "marginalized, left behind since the 1960s," when people were put in camps and their livestock taken. In his view, since then "we have been neglected, and schools have passed us by," and it is due to state marginalization that the community does not have money to collect rainwater in a cistern. Abdi Abkula, a middle-aged herder whose livestock had been wiped out by the 2011 drought, stated that for the past five decades the people of the region had been forgotten and that the poverty of the region was brought about by the government. This is a powerful collective narrative of victimhood, one that emerges out of real historical grievances (Dahl 1979; Arero 2007) but also presents the Borana as people in present need, perhaps aiding in conveying these grievances and attracting attention from civil society institutions.

Coupled with this perceived marginalization is a feeling that the state is failing at any attempt to rectify the situation, or indeed to control what happens in the north. This was evident when I asked people in Beliqo their opinion of the role and work of the Kenya Forest Service (KFS) and the Kenya Wildlife Service (KWS). What I heard was largely derision. An elder named Galgalo Jarso said that KFS and KWS cannot reach a remote area like Beliqo, and thus need the help of the community to do their job. Dabaso Godo, another elder, stated more strongly that "KFS and KWS are never seen in the region, and don't seem to exist in the area." Others were more embittered, telling me that KFS "doesn't care about us" and "abandoned the area." Beliqo's grievances with the Kenyan state fit into broader themes around governance and state capture by particular groups, questions that are outside of the scope of this work. What is essential here is that the perceived neglect by KFS and KWS is not only a reflection of the general perception of neglect of the region and the Borana people by the state, but also demonstrates the community's response to such state neglect: the ever more prevalent role of civil society organizations, both local and external. Indeed, I would argue that while Beliqo residents see themselves on the political periphery, Beliqo is connected to the Kenyan state in a very substantial way through networks of development-focused civil society organizations.

The longer I stayed in Beliqo, the more I came to realize that despite the almost universal feelings of abandonment and marginalization by the state, civil society organizations wove mechanisms and institutions of the state into the landscape of the village. Perhaps the most obvious example is the use of the 2005 Kenya Forests Act by CFA. The Forests Act devolves the protection of Kenya's forests to local communities and gives them the legal mandate to set up local organizations to protect forests from unsustainable exploitation by both outsiders and community members. Without WTL being aware of changes in national laws and the opportunities afforded by such legislation, and without Hassan Shano and Liban Golicha integrating this awareness into their work with Beliqo's civil society groups, Beliqo residents would not have known about the legal mandate provided by the state to protect the local forest from logging. Once more, we see the centrality of development institutions in creating networks that connect different geographies of knowledge. It is outside development organizations like WTL that bring in the savvy needed to work with state mechanisms—despite Hassan Shano's overt distrust of and antagonistic position toward the state. It is Shano who told Beliqo residents about the Forest Act and facilitated visits to other Community Forest Associations to observe the way they were taking advantage of the act's provisions.

Thus, the state is still essential to Beliqo residents. Indeed, the fact that the state retained a central role, even if in a negative sense, in the conversations I had in Beliqo points to the limits of the role of civil society and to citizens' continued reliance on and expectations of the state. This echoes one of Chandhoke's (2003) criticisms of the good-governance model, one which points out that civil society cannot fulfill all of the mechanisms of the nation-state. Yet while knowledge of the 2005 Kenya Forests Act is the basis for the founding of Community Forest Associations, it is also this kind of knowledge that allows the residents of Beliqo—with WTL encouragement and TCF support—to circumvent the state, to bypass the neglect of the KWS and the KFS, in a contradictory relationship of criticism and reliance.

Besides the village school and the two chiefs, it is the civil society organizations in the village that utilize the state most heavily. This includes not only drawing on legal mechanisms of the state but also having the know-how to tap various state agencies for resources. For instance, the chairman of CFA was away most of the month I spent in the village, trying to obtain funds for CFA from regional government offices. The Ewaso Niro Development Authority gave CFA roots and seedlings for its tree nursery and has given a farming group in the village tools. Arid Lands, another government agency, gave a water pump. The pump broke and was never repaired or replaced, perhaps indicating the fragility of government support. Yet what is most important to note is that this sort of government aid came not to individuals or even the local government of the village. Instead, it went to formalized, registered, civil society groups, often through the help of other civil society intermediaries like WTL.

In Chandhoke's words, where the state has "subcontracted" services to NGOs and other voluntary groups, "state structures have been loosened, they have been disaggregated, and they have been spanned out" (2003, 2960). This is precisely what is happening in Beliqo: residents feel neglected and isolated by the state and turn to civil society instead, while the state itself willingly utilizes civil society groups to replace or augment its role. Civil society cannot do so entirely, and its "emancipatory potential" (Rieff 1999) is curtailed both by its continued reliance on some state mechanisms and by the limits of its inclusiveness. Yet civil society and its development interventions amount to more than a depoliticizing anti-politics machine. In the case of Waso Trustland and Beliqo, civil society becomes a way to prod the state and gain access to its resources.

When I talked to people in the village about why it was that Beliqo had so many community-based organizations (CBOs) (more than twenty in a village of less than two thousand people) and why people chose to join them (the majority, through certainly not all, of my interviewees were members of two or more CBOs), I was told that outside assistance, whether from the government or NGOs, was always aimed at recognized groups, not individuals. This was widely understood in the village. For instance, Malicha, a herder who lived in a neighboring hut to me in the village and was himself not a member of any group because he had no time to spare from herding, stated that Beliqo had so many groups as a way to seek outside aid. Thus, civil society is a way for inhabitants of Beliqo to attempt to overcome their experience of state marginalization, by providing at least one avenue (though in practice often a difficult or unsuccessful one) by which village residents can access state or NGO resources. As a young man who worked as a forest scout for the CFA told me, "We have no access to internet, but via WTL we can be heard elsewhere."

Shaping State Engagement

The state might sit outside the civil society knowledge networks discussed here, but it emerged again and again as a key concern for both civil society organizations and the people they work with. The state rarely directly interfered or involved itself in the projects examined here, yet its laws, bureaucracy, and resources play a key role in the way the networks function. For instance, laws about the sort of organizational forms recognized as civil society groups give such groups legitimacy and the ability to accept funds. Legislation about access and resource rights, such as the Kenya Forests Act, gave the Community Forest Association of Beliqo the necessary legal power to claim control over the nearby forest. And when solicited, local government officials provided resources such as the seeds to CFA for its nursery.

Much of the knowledge and ideas shared by the development apparatus in this case study concerns how legal frameworks and resources of the state can be accessed and put to use by citizens. However, while NGOs in the networks do create knowledge and relationships with the state, they are able to do so in part by taking a less contentious political stance. Kivulini and the Christensen Fund turned Waso Trustland away—at least in part—from campaigning for land and water rights. Instead, Hassan Shano was convinced to focus on the far less contentious issue of community forestry, even if these partners were themselves slightly influenced by Waso Trustland's political stance.

At the same time, the state is not a passive agent in this process. State organizations and agencies in this case welcomed the opportunity to reassign some responsibilities to local populations and various civil society organizations. Kenya did this very consciously by creating the 2005 Kenya Forest Act, transferring primary responsibility for forests from the KFS to local communities. The act includes means for communities to gain access to state resources while doing so, but these opportunities are not common knowledge—and it is organizations such as Waso Trustland that are able to bring knowledge and expertise about how to make use of these resources.

The development organizations that make up this network not only make use of the state for resources in exchange for services rendered but also wield considerable bargaining power through their privileged access to and knowledge both of local views and of international "expert" development ideas. Indeed, John Meyer (1999; 2010) argues for a similar understanding of the role of civil society as a set of institutions that create systems of actors (particularly including the state), and that maintain and stabilize these systems by embedding them through cultural content and normative material. Meyer argues that civil society organizations, by serving as advisers to actors such as states, spread norms, knowledge, and expectations that influence the way that states take action, simultaneously constraining and empowering them. The civil society institutions in these two case studies certainly do so; indeed, they wield power through the very fact that the state turns to them rather than to individual citizens to engage with issues and problems at the grassroots level, as well as to learn about development "expertise." Yet these institutions are themselves also composed of citizens, who have their own agency and purpose. They do not simply advise, normalize, or goad the state into action, but enact their own agendas, often making use of state resources in the process, while passing knowledge and information between themselves, the state, and the grassroots.

Thus, the interaction between development organizations and the state does not result in a simple anti-politics machine that is "depoliticizing everything it touches, everywhere whisking political realities out of sight" (Ferguson 1994, xv; see also Li 2007); nor is the result simply a network state (Chandhoke 2003). While the civil society knowledge networks do at times take on the role of the state, and at times do promote a depoliticizing agenda, they also facilitate links to and knowledge about the resources and workings of the state for its citizens. The relationships between local communities, NGOs, and the state thus become pluralized and heterogeneous. To create these links, development NGOs must satisfy their funders and the state itself by adopting less contentious agendas, but in return they can both influence the state and forge connections between the state and its citizens.

References

Arero, Hassan Wario. 2007. "Coming to Kenya: Imagining and Perceiving a Nation among the Borana of Kenya." *Journal of Eastern African Studies* 1 (2): 292–304.

Burawoy, Michael. 2001. "Manufacturing the Global." *Ethnography* 2 (2): 147–59.

Chandhoke, Neera. 2003. "Governance and the Pluralisation of the State: Implications for Democratic Citizenship." *Economic and Political Weekly* 38 (28): 2957–68.

Dahl, Gudrun. 1979. *Suffering Grass: Subsistence and Society of Waso Borana*. Stockholm: Department of Social Anthropology, University of Stockholm.

Ferguson, James. 1994. *The Anti-Politics Machine: "Development," Depoliticization, and Bureaucratic Power in Lesotho*. Minneapolis: University of Minnesota Press.

Fouksman, E. 2017. "Civil Society Knowledge Networks: How International Development Institutions Reshape the Geography of Knowledge." *Third World Quarterly* 38 (8): 1847–72.

Grindle, Merilee S. 2004. "Good Enough Governance: Poverty Reduction and Reform in Developing Countries." *Governance: An International Journal of Policy, Administration, and Institutions* 17 (4): 525–48.

Isack, Hussein Adan. 1986. *People of the North: Boran*. Nairobi: Evans.

Jayal, Niraja Gopal. 1997. "The Governance Agenda: Making Democratic Development Dispensable." *Economic and Political Weekly* 32 (8): 407–12.

Kaldor, Mary. 2003. *Global Civil Society: An Answer to War*. Cambridge: Polity.

Lewis, David. 2002. "Civil Society in African Contexts: Reflections on the Usefulness of a Concept." *Development and Change* 33 (4): 569–86.

Lewis, David, and David Mosse. 2006. "Encountering Order and Disjuncture: Contemporary Anthropological Perspectives on the Organization of Development." *Oxford Development Studies* 34 (1): 1–13.

Li, Tania Murray. 2007. *The Will to Improve: Governmentality, Development, and the Practice of Politics*. Durham, NC: Duke University Press.

Loh, Jonathan, and David Harmon. 2005. "A Global Index of Biocultural Diversity." *Ecological Indicators* 5 (3): 231–41.

Manby, Bronwen. 2009. *Struggles for Citizenship in Africa*. London: Zed Books.

Marcus, George E. 1995. "Ethnography in/of the World System: The Emergence of Multi-sited Ethnography." *Annual Review of Anthropology* 24:95–117.

Matanga, Frank Khachina. 2010. "NGOs and the Politics of Development in Africa." *Development* 53 (1): 114–19.

Meyer, John W. 1999. "The Changing Cultural Content of the Nation-State: A World Society Perspective." In *State/Culture: State-Formation after the Cultural Turn,* edited by George Steinmetz, 123–44. Ithaca: Cornell University Press.

———. 2010. "World Society, Institutional Theories, and the Actor." *Annual Review of Sociology* 36:1–20.

Mosse, David. 2011. "Introduction: The Anthropology of Expertise and Professionals in International Development." In *Adventures in Aidland: The Anthropology of Professionals in International Development,* edited by David Mosse, 1–32. New York: Berghahn Books.

Rieff, David. 1999. "The False Dawn of Civil Society." *Nation,* 4 February. https://www.thenation.com/article/archive/false-dawn-civil-society/.

Scott, James C. 1998. *Seeing Like a State: How Certain Schemes to Improve the Human Condition Have Failed.* New Haven, CT: Yale University Press.

Whittaker, Hannah. 2008. "Pursuing Pastoralists: The Stigma of *Shifta* during the '*Shifta* War' in Kenya, 1963–68." *Eras* [Monash University, Melbourne, Victoria, Australia] 10. https://arts.monash.edu/data/assets/pdf_file/0006/1671045/whittaker-article.pdf.

World Bank. 1992. *Governance and Development.* Washington, DC: World Bank.

PART TWO

(Un)Making Lives

The Social Economy of Infrastructure and Shortages

FIVE

Lateral Futurity

The Nigerian State as Infrastructural Enigma

ERIC TROVALLA AND ULRIKA TROVALLA

IN THE NIGERIAN CITY OF JOS, LIFE IS INEXTRICABLY nestled into webs of wires, roads, and pipes, and through the materiality of infrastructure the state surrounds its citizens, invades their homes, and structures life to such an extent that it becomes part and parcel of nearly any mundane undertaking, aspiration for the future, or memory of the past. From the perspective of lived experience in Jos, there is arguably no context in which the state manifests itself more palpably than in the riddles and enigmas posed by the severe unpredictability of these grids. The supply of electricity, communal water, fuel, and so on, is highly intermittent and people incessantly try to predict their arrival and disappearance. They are also constantly raising concerns about the integrity of what is actually being provided. Nothing can be counted on to be what it seems, neither the petrol nor the GSM signals, neither the voltage delivered from the transformer nor the credibility of the utility bill, neither the scrupulousness of the civil servants administering the infrastructures nor, ultimately, the sum of all the parts that make up the state.

Infrastructure has for long been tightly linked to images of modernity and technological as well as social advancement, and has often become "inexorably woven into notions of the modern state and modern identities associated with nationhood" (Graham 2011, 66). When, for instance, Giles Omezi describes a six-lane expressway in Lagos, he calls it "a fragment of an 'imagined modernity'" that has been "inscribed onto the urban fabric" (2014, 278). Brian Larkin notes how states rely on the power of infrastructure to express their commitment to progress and ask citizens "to take those representations as social facts" (2013, 335). Taking as a starting point the city of Jos, the capital of Plateau State, one of the Nigerian federation's thirty-six states, we try to unravel the ways in which the state is called into presence in everyday encounters with the materiality of infrastructure.[1] Wale Adebanwi notes how, in postcolonial Africa, the conception of *the nation* as a unified imagined community is elusive and spectral, whereas *the state* is densely corporeal (2016, 8). However, the densely material nature of the state does not mean that it is easily graspable. Instead, as in the case of Jos, when the state appears in the form of unpredictable infrastructures, a multitude of enigmas materialize as inextricable components of the state.

In this infrastructural landscape of inconsistent coverage where one can count on nothing to be what it seems, knowledge is scarce but at the same time crucially important to obtain. People read the minuscule bits of information that can be gleaned from the vague rhythms of the grids, and the methods with which people put information together into working knowledge assume the structure of divination (E. Trovalla and U. Trovalla 2015, 341; see also De Boeck and Baloji 2016, 127). In a way similar to how diviners search for patterns among seemingly random distributions of matter, people study the fragmented and erratic infrastructure, arriving at interpretations that are tentative, open-ended, and often contradictory. Suspicion is deeply engrained in these divination acts, as they almost always deal with possibilities that are imaginable and even plausible but hardly ever resolve into facts. Here, one should not confuse suspicion with superstition; suspicion is not inherently irrational, misguided, nor a sign of ignorance. As Misty Bastian reminds us, there is no natural connection between conspiracy theories and unreason (2003, 69); however, they do "suggest that there is more to power than meets the eye" (Sanders and West 2003, 7). Through these acts of infrastructural divination, the state comes out as a highly elusive and mutable affair, and questions about what underlying driving forces and intents animate it from the shadows seem to persist beyond any attempts to find firm answers.

The infrastructural flows and nonflows—the comings and goings of water, electricity, petrol, road traffic, telephone signal, etc.—all emerge as clues in an ongoing investigation into what the state is, what it used to be, and what it may turn into. The immediacy and necessity of infrastructural services to everyday life insert these questions into the most mundane of situations. Cooking, taking one's children to school, going to work, tugging on the cord in order to start the generator, or watching the power company's repair truck pass by the neighborhood's broken transformer without stopping—all materialize the conundrums of the state at the level of life-as-lived. Stephen Graham and Nigel Thrift emphasize how moments of infrastructural malfunction make visible tensions between infrastructures, users, and the "complex politics surrounding interruption, regulation, repair and maintenance" (2007, 13). In Jos, the infrastructure, rather than being invisible and moved to the background, is brought to the forefront of everyday encounters. "The need to constantly engage with the unpredictable infrastructure puts the prefix *infra* (below) in brackets" (U. Trovalla and E. Trovalla 2015, 44). As the *infrastructure* moves to the foreground of experience, it turns into an ever-present *suprastructure,* saturated with meanings and replete with clues about the forces that govern and administer the Nigerian state (see ibid.).

Never Expect . . . Always!

Due to this tendency to turn expectations on their heads, infrastructure is the topic of many jokes. The National Electric Power Authority changed its name in 2005, but "nepa" remains the common nickname for grid-based electricity. NEPA as acronym has inspired many humorous interpretations, perhaps the most widespread being "Never Expect Power Always" (see Obadare 2009, 249; Olukoju 2004; U. Trovalla and E. Trovalla 2015). "Ridicule," to quote Ebenezer Obadare, "has emerged as a means through which people attempt to deconstruct and construct meaning out of a reality that is decidedly surreal" (2009, 245). In a video by the Nigerian YouTube comedian Mark Angel (Mark Angel Comedy 2017), motorcycle taxi patrons who disembark in front of a flooded stretch of road are met by an enthusiastic group of young men. One of them excitedly explains how the roads and drainages that the government built were unable to evacuate the rainwater, so now the only option for travelers was to let the young men carry them on their backs across the flooded area, for a fee of fifty naira. "That is good!" replies one of the customers. "Oga [Sir], this is youth empowerment!" says the young man. "Now we have jobs," says another. "Na wah-oo!" exclaims the customer. "This government is trying! They have provided jobs for the youth!" This joke highlights how powerfully the presence of the state is called forth through the nation's infrastructures—as much in their voids, glitches, and cracks as when they work as intended.

The thousands upon thousands of small generators that have come to line markets and residential areas everywhere in Jos have in a similar manner come to embody the state, as their omnipresent and ear-piercing noise has turned the lack of reliable electricity into an integral part of the city's soundscape. The reverse is also true; when the noise dies down, the silence enters one's awareness. When the noise dies down, eyes trained to regularly wander to the main switchboard in the house immediately seek the naked bulb that is typically mounted there to indicate when there is electricity on the grid, while ears scan for the sound of the sirens that some have installed to signal when electricity comes back. When it does, feet rush

ERIC TROVALLA AND ULRIKA TROVALLA

to collect phones and other things that need charging and hurried hands pluck among already crowded extension blocks in an attempt to accommodate all the plugs at once. Outside, one hears pumps starting up and, from the small industries down the street, angle grinders roaring and welding machines crackling again. Through such mundane bodily experiences, the transitions among different intensities that are introduced by the comings and goings of infrastructural services call the state into presence in the very rhythms of everyday life.

In Jos, the Water Board counts only thirty thousand connections in a city of over one million inhabitants—but even for the small fraction of citizens who have access to municipal water, water provisioning is mostly up to the individual's aptitude for improvisation. Water vendors push their carts around even in neighborhoods where Water Board customers' numbers mark most houses. And as people send their children before the crack of dawn to beg their neighbors for water, here as all over the city, as they drill private boreholes in their compounds, as they collect rainwater—a state materializes that appears to be as empty, unpredictable, or absent as the pipes. Another pertinent example of how the absence of the state is dressed in materiality is how the black-market petrol industry booms when the recurring fuel shortages plague Jos. When stacks of yellow jerry cans so emblematic of the black market appear everywhere along extensive stretches of road, little doubt remains that other logics have superseded the official chains of fuel supply. Likewise, in petrol queues that span kilometer after kilometer of vehicles, the massive heft of hundreds of tons of metal in a state of inertia inscribes the vacuity of the state in the tarmac of streets and roads.

As the state materializes in a complex interplay of absence and presence, a highly enigmatic landscape emerges in which profound randomness envelopes some of the most essential necessities of life, compelling people to devise specialized skills of interpretation and prognostication. In Jos, on a good day, you might get eight hours of uninterrupted power; another day, you only get five minutes; and when the power lines are down, they might stay idle for an hour or for several days or weeks. There are no load-shedding schedules or public announcements that could give people an indication of how long the power will stay off or on. As for water, even if you receive it just three to four times per month, the Water Board in Jos expects you to pay the full bill. Like electricity, water might come at any time or not at all, so people hone their skills at reading elusive signs and sensing rhythms to try to anticipate the next delivery. Likewise, they invest a lot of effort in trying to divine the reasons behind the latest fuel shortage, to predict when fuel will be back so as to decide whether they should approach the black market or join one of the many queues steadily growing at petrol stations rumor has it are going to receive a delivery.

Despite all the effort that residents spend trying to predict the flows, uncertainty about access to these most crucial necessities is an inescapable fact of life. A form of infrastructural "hypervigilance" (Cooper and Pratten 2015, 10) has emerged, and people spend an immense amount of everyday effort on trying to divine the elusive movements of presence, scarcity, and absence and to decode any possible patterns and logics that might be behind them—ultimately, trying to grasp what entity is governing these flows. This is how the infrastructure in the city of Jos, instead of residing in the background of people's everyday lives, takes center stage, and how the state, as an infrastructural conundrum of presence, absence, and fluctuation, in a very palpable way comes to enter their lives.

Out of its infrastructural rhythms of presence and absence, a deep-seated notion toward the state emerges among the citizens that may be summarized by paraphrasing the humorous interpretation of the abbreviation NEPA: *Never Expect . . . Always.* In a way that invokes Abdoumaliq Simone's concept of "a politics of anticipation" (2010, 96), people have learned never to assume anything, but instead be prepared to react and adapt swiftly to changing circumstances. In order to endure, one has to stay open to a wide range of alternative outcomes. This requires both a constant readiness to act in relation to the multitude of possible futures that emerge from the divinations of infrastructural flows, as well as continual attempts to interpret what might emanate from the highly elusive state.

FIGURE 1. Failing infrastructure sets the rhythms of life. One of those typical, slow Sunday afternoons, "the pastor" studied his Bible app. Long shadows crept across the room as the fading light mixed with the pale gleam of rechargeable lamps and cell phone screens, while he waited for electricity that may or may not return. Photo by E. and U. Trovalla.

Once Upon a Nation

You Know You Are Flying Nigeria Airways: Part II

Good morning, Ladies and Gentlemen. This is your captain (Boniface) welcoming you on board of Nigeria Airways.

We apologize for the four-day delay in taking off, it was due to bad weather and some overtime I had to put in at the bakery.

This is flight 126 to Lagos. Landing in Lagos is not guaranteed, but we will end up somewhere in the South. If luck is in our favour, we may even be landing on your village!

Nigeria Airways has an excellent safety-record. In fact, our safety standards are so high that even terrorists are afraid to fly with us!

[. . .]

Kindly be seated, keep your seat in an upright position for take-off and fasten your seat-belt. For those of you who can't find a seat-belt, kindly fasten your own belt to the arm of your seat . . . and for those of you who can't find a seat, do not hesitate to get in touch with a stewardess who will explain how to fasten yourself to your suitcase.

YOU ARE WELCOME ON BOARD!

(Nnamdi [2002])

The target of mockery here was once a source of national pride. Nigeria Airways was created in 1958 in anticipation of Nigerian independence, with the Nigerian state holding a 51 percent share. Not six months after independence in October 1960, the Nigerian government bought out its two partners. In the spirit of newly won independence, the government declared it a flag carrier, and all aircraft, vehicles, and equipment showed its logo: the Nigerian flag with its green and white bars. Nigeria Airways developed an excellent international record. In its heyday in the 1980s, the company had thirty-four aircraft, but like so many other examples of Nigerian infrastructure, this peak was followed by an arc of decline, and toward the end of the 1990s, only three aircraft remained. Finally, Nigeria Airways was liquidated in 2003 (Akpoghomeh 1999, 135–38; Ogbeidi 2006, 136–39). Almost two decades after it ended operations, Nigeria Airways is still the topic of many jokes. Its memory lives on in that realm of bitter humor where the daily experience of so many other public infrastructures has found its most pertinent expression.

When Nigeria won its independence, the young nation entered into what for many would be remembered as a golden age of rapid progress during which infrastructures rarely betrayed their roles. A power line was a power line, in the sense that electricity was running through it. A water pipe was a water pipe and could be counted on to produce water anytime somebody turned the tap. A bus stop would be where buses stopped and departed in reasonable accordance with their schedule. Many people recounting their memories of this time say they saw the solid and expanding infrastructure as evidence of inherent qualities of the newly independent state, part of what would carry Nigeria into the highest ranks of countries in the world. Throughout the modern era, infrastructures have been tightly linked to ideas of inherent progress and evolution, and have often been the focal points of the "collective fantasy of society" (Larkin 2013, 329–334, invoking Walter Benjamin).

During the oil boom of the 1970s, the Nigerian government made massive investments in the country's infrastructure. It built new roads and old dirt roads were tarred to accommodate a growing number of vehicles of all kinds—particularly after a salary hike proposed by the Udoji Commission, the mandate of which was to restructure the Nigerian civil service, came into effect in 1974. Seaports and airports brimmed with imported consumer goods en route to the homes of a growing middle class (Freund 1978, 94–95). The naira was worth US$1.60 at its peak, and a sense of national confidence reigned. "In the new object-world of imported commodities and rapid growth," writes Andrew Apter of the time, "seeing was believing" (1999, 269). The many manifestations of national development, ranging from business contracts to museums, monuments, bridges, highways, and traffic jams, were backed by petrodollars. Petroleum revenues passed through the hands of the state, and so, Apter continues, "the state emerged as the locus of truth, not because it wielded arbitrary power but because it was the locus of distribution" (ibid.; see also Akpoghomeh 1999, 135).

But the oil bust of the 1980s initiated a new era of crumbling infrastructure, systemic failure, and shattered dreams (Apter 1999, 268–69). From the economic peak of the oil boom, Nigeria plunged into an age marked by military dictatorships and an economy distinguished by high inflation, devaluation of the naira, rampant poverty, and ever-growing unemployment (Smith 2008, 19). In 1986, to make matters worse, head of state Ibrahim Badamasi Babangida initiated the Structural Adjustment Programme. Emphasizing privatization and deregulation of the Nigerian economy, it threw the state's institutions further into disarray (see Akpoghomeh 1999, 135; Jega 2000). In the words of Claude Aké, the state, while still remaining a powerful force, was no longer a "public force"; it had, in essence, been privatized. Instead of guaranteeing the rule of law, the state had become, as Aké puts it, "a formidable threat to all except the few who control it" (1995, 73).

In the midst of a high rate of inflation combined with a fall in wages, infrastructures such as water supply, electricity, and transportation collapsed (Aké 1996, 87). If, in those years of apparently succeeding development, seeing had been believing, Nigeria now entered an era of "visual deceptions," a world of "smoke and mirrors" (Apter 2005, 235). Nigerians grew increasingly disillusioned with a state that, no longer abounding with oil money, instead "relied on the politics of illusion to maintain its eroding legitimacy" (Smith 2008, 20). From the confusion of an oil state in disarray arose the "419s"— that is, the advance-fee scams for which Nigeria was to become so infamous. The term, which refers to the article in the Nigerian Criminal Code that deals with fraud, emerged in the 1980s during the country's drastic economic decline. Often baiting victims with stories of large sums of stolen oil money that needed safe passage to bank accounts overseas, letters and faxes sent to foreign individuals and companies carried letterheads and insignia "borrowed" from various branches of the Nigerian state. Instead of lending a sense of legitimacy, these symbols only added to a growing perception of the Nigerian state as corrupt (see Apter 2005, 226–36; Smith 2008, 19–20).

With mounting doubts and disappointments that have come to attach to infrastructure in actual life, the collectively imagined teleological trajectories toward the future that the infrastructures once inspired have been eroded. In relation to Zambia, James Ferguson describes how dreams of material comforts no longer represent something one looks forward to in the future, but, instead, what one remembers from a prosperous past that is now forever gone (1999, 13). For many Nigerians, the notion of a functional railway system has come to embody this kind of reversal of an imagined trajectory of time and the loss of a "nobler past" that was once theirs (Ochereome 2013). During the early years of independence in the 1960s and early 1970s, the government-owned railway had a key role in the development of the emergent nation (Agbaeze and Onwuka 2014, 184). However, since 1979, when the government handed over the already dysfunctional Nigerian Railway Corporation to the Rail India Technical and Economic Service (Omoniwa 2012, 3), which was followed by a continuous series of attempts at resuscitation, "moribund" has become a common term to describe the once-proud rail carrier (Akwara, Udaw, and Ezirim 2014, 465, 469; see also Odeleye 2000, 45). After decades of continuous decline, dependable railway traffic has come to seem profoundly incompatible with the way most people perceive the nature of the Nigerian state.

In 2013, newspapers wrote about the reopening of the old railway line between Lagos in the south and Kano in the north (Agabi 2013; BBC 2013; Olukoya 2013), stirring both enthusiasm and skepticism. One commentator wrote, "When next you hear the sound of train horns, smile. It is the sound of promise" (Ochereome 2013). On the other hand, the people we spoke with were not so sure. "There are so many stories," said Umar, a used-car dealer in his forties who had recently moved from the Jos area to Abuja. "I have crossed the line going to Kano several times and it is completely overgrown. It is just lies." Recalling the maiden journey, when the train left Lagos packed with politicians and local and international journalists reporting on the marvels of the train ride, Jethro, a Jos-based engineer who traveled extensively all over the country, smirked. The train, he declared, consisted of only the locomotive and a single wagon, and had been leased from abroad for this one-time appearance. Ever since the train left the country, as hurriedly as it was brought in, nothing had moved on the rails. It had all been for show, he concluded. In 2014, the train station in Jos—which street hawkers had used as storage space since the mid-1990s, when the last train departed from the platform—was cleared out and repainted in anticipation that the crew overhauling the rails some hundred kilometers southwest of Jos would soon reach the city. However, when we raised the subject, the most common response was, "I will believe it when I see it!" When we asked what it was about railways that made these promises so difficult to believe, people replied with stories that echoed nostalgia not only for the affordable, comfortable, and sophisticated mode of travel that rail traffic used to offer, but also for a period irrecoverably lost. Nigeria, it seemed to most people, just was not that kind of country anymore. Recently, railway traffic has been resumed between Abuja and Kaduna and between Lagos and Ibadan, but even with this tangible evidence, there is still a widespread suspicion that these developments, too, will either prove to be a sham or quickly succumb to whatever makes the environment so hostile to railway traffic. In 2021, when we asked Jethro if the trains were running yet, he answered, "Naah, like we have coined the word now, we have an *audio railway*." You hear a lot about it, but it is something you rarely see.

"I am glad I got to experience at least the very end of this time," said Dora, a university student and mother, "because it would have been difficult to believe it now." She remembered how, during the 1980s, she and her sister used to ride the Plateau State–owned Tin City Transportation Service buses from their home in nearby Bukuru to school in Jos, pretending they were in London. When we mentioned the sturdy brick-built bus shelter, which was still there in front of her present house, she was surprised. The notion of a regular bus service seemed so distant that she had not even noticed the shelter. In a way, it had been subtracted from her mental landscape, together with the era during which the bus stops made any sense. In 2000, John, who was in his sixties, lived in the area in Jos called Civil Servants' Quarters, once erected to provide the state's administrative class with well-functioning living conditions, but which now embodied a long history of gradual disconnectedness. The pipes that once fed water to bathrooms and kitchen had been dry for many years. The house was connected to the electricity grid, but the power lines were inactive most of the time. John kept returning to what the city used to be like in the 1970s, when the supply of water and electricity was constant, the roads were not full of potholes, motorcycle drivers wore helmets, and public transport cars in good repair took four passengers instead of the six that now cram into ramshackle vehicles. He preferred to use his own car, but since petrol was so scarce and he avoided the black market for fear of diluted fuel that might ruin the engine, he mostly remained in his dark house.

In a landscape littered with remnants of memories and promises—and, as such, "pregnant with the past" (Ingold 1993, 152)—people struggle to piece together a workable understanding of an infrastructure and a state in constant transformation. John's and Dora's accounts echo the discrepancy between the future that seemed to be inscribed in the infrastructural landscapes of the past, and the realities of the present situation. The dwindling flows and physical deterioration of grids have eroded previously held assumptions of a steady development toward a better future. Instead, silent railway tracks, abandoned bus shelters, and glitching electricity lines give rise to a sense that the linear continuation between past and future is dissolving (De Boeck and Baloji 2016, 23). "In Nigeria," Brian Larkin writes, "the grand modernist project of infrastructure, manifest in the robust presence of a state whose involvement in everyday life was to be present in the turning of a switch or the flushing of a toilet, has broken down" (2008, 243).

The infrastructure that once conveyed promises of a new world has instead come to display echoes, or signs, of a modernity that no longer carries "the content that originally went with it" (De Boeck and Plissart 2004, 228). As long as infrastructures remained faithful to their functions, and *seeing*, as such, was *believing*, they conferred a sense of "transparency" often imagined as part of a rationality inherent in the image of a modern nation in the making (Bastian 2003, 69; Sanders and West 2003, 7). However, as infrastructures have come to constantly betray their roles—through empty water pipes, dead electricity lines, dried-up fuel stations, and vanished buses, railways, and airplanes—in a language that traces back to "the perceived failures of the state" during the turbulent 1980s (Smith 2008, 223–24), they instead project the state itself as another case of "419" and capture the profound notion that nothing Nigerian can be trusted to be what it appears to be. When a friend published a Facebook post consisting solely of the words "Once Upon a Nation" in bold letters, the laconic phrase was immediately intelligible to anyone versed in the discourses of Nigeria's recent history; the four words were sufficient to suggest an abbreviated narrative of Nigeria as a nation that had somehow warped into something else.

Surge Protectors

Toward the end of the 1990s, in the midst of a growing sense that the country was no longer what it once was, the return to democracy brought hopes and dreams that the new democratic government would eliminate whatever was corrupting the Nigerian state. In 1999, ending sixteen years of military rule, Olusegun Obasanjo was elected president of Nigeria. In 2001, as part of the promises of the Obasanjo presidency to finally deliver electricity in a way that could match Nigeria's needs and visions for the future, the government initiated a profound restructuring of the electricity sector, and in 2005 the Power Holding Company of Nigeria (PHCN) was formed as a transitional corporation. The reform aimed to purge the electricity sector of the dysfunctions that were assumed to emanate from NEPA's long history as a deeply corrupt limb of a likewise corrupt state (Nwokoye et al. 2017). The neoliberal reforms that were introduced in many African countries as a response to perceived "failing" states must, Hibou, Samuel, and Fourchard and others (2017) argue, be understood as more complex and ambiguous processes than the clear-cut transfer from a public to a private domain that is often imagined. Rather, postcolonial African states were already characterized by complex and ongoing negotiations between private and public, licit and illicit interests and power relations. Often, state operations could be described in terms of what Hibou calls "discharge," in which the state tasked public offices to carry out their respective responsibilities, but without providing the financial means to do so, and instead gave them free rein to collect money from their customers, often in improvised and irregular ways (Hibou 2017; Mbembe 2017). Consequently, many people initially did not perceive privatization of the electricity sector or other infrastructures as a withdrawal of the state. Rather, in their experience, public offices were profoundly corrupt entities whose duties to the people were already entirely overshadowed by the desire of individuals to line their own pockets. Therefore, to them, privatizing the services instead represented the opportunity to put the leash back on those "rogue" public servants and bring things back to a situation where the state had more, not less, control. However, in the streets of Jos and the rest of Nigeria, it did not take long before the acronym PHCN was mockingly sounded out as "Problem Has Changed Name" or "Please Hold Candle Now" (see Obadare 2009, 249; U. Trovalla and E. Trovalla 2015). The jokes indicated a crushed hope that democracy would cure the infrastructural ailments of the past and that the nation would finally resume its linear development toward a future among the highly ranked "modern" countries that was meant to be hers all along.

Despite all the great hopes attached to the transition to civil rule, the democratic honeymoon was already over in December 1999, when the promise to amend the power situation within six months had been revealed to be just another of many mirages. While the country generally experienced a deteriorating electricity supply and the sales of generators boomed, the situation in 2004 was described as remaining "as dismal as ever" (Olukoju 2004, 61–62, 70). In a bitter online essay ending with a description of how the country was turning into "a dangerous gas chamber" because of fumes from the rapid spread of various kinds of generators filling the atmosphere, the author wrote, "It is, no doubt, a prominent evidence of the abysmal failure of the Obasanjo Administration. After nearly eight years of loud promises and dubious claims, I still cannot write this column without fueling my Chinese toy-generator." He concluded that as long as this "reign of darkness persists," he would be inseparable from his "Chinese toy" (Ejinkeonye 2007). In 2007, a battery-operated lamp made from thin slices of wood and LEDs mounted on a used CD became a nationwide hit that could be found at any street market. Popularly called *"Obasanjo ya kasa"* ("Obasanjo failed" or "Obasanjo was not able to"), the lamp offered an alternative solution to the president's shortcomings in the electricity sector.

After just over a decade of democracy, when the "NEPA switch" became a must-have item in homes in Nigeria, generators were already ubiquitous even in households of modest means. Up until then, the generator had been an improvisation that was brought out when needed from whichever available space it was tucked into. The wall-mounted changeover between the positions typically marked "NEPA" (mainline electricity) and "GEN" (generator) removed its makeshift character. Now the generator had its own dedicated place, often in a little doghouse-like shelter, and was permanently connected to the house through wires generally laid underground. With the NEPA switch, an increasing reliance on individual solutions was permanently wired into matters of everyday life, and the public grid was stripped of its primacy as a provider of electricity. In a way similar to how Larkin, above, describes how the state used to be present in the turning of a switch or flushing of a toilet, the act of physically moving the lever of the NEPA switch away from a dead electricity grid was a bodily experience of the reality that an elusive *something* had been subtracted from the state, and, regardless of all the promises, democracy was not going to bring it back. In 2019, an article in the Nigerian newspaper *Daily Trust* called the power sector a "graveyard of presidential promises." After listing the broken vows of former presidents Umaru Musa Yar'Adua, Goodluck Ebele Jonathan, Obasanjo, and, finally, of current president Muhammadu Buhari, the author concluded, "We just know that the promise made by every Nigerian president since 1999 to rescue the country from the clutches of darkness has seen the mindless influx of imported generators into the country" (Agbese 2019).

The coming of democracy raised hopes of improvements of the infrastructure that the previous military governments had not been able to deliver. "Obasanjo was the one that brought GSM to Nigeria," Joseph, a polytechnic student in Jos, explained, in a statement that mirrored a common reading of the Global System for Mobile Communications (GSM) as one of the fruits of democracy. Until 2001, NITEL, the Nigerian national phone company, had a firm grip on telecommunications in Nigeria, and, for many, its "invariably abysmal" services paired it with NEPA as representative of a "spineless" state bureaucracy (Obadare 2006, 97; see also Smith 2006, 516). In 2001, when GSM was introduced in Nigeria, the telephone industry was extremely stagnant. With a population of over a hundred million, there were around half a million landlines in use and over ten million Nigerians queuing for an installation—with an average wait time ranging from eight to ten years (Onwumechili 2001, 223–24; Obadare 2004, 10; Onwumechili 2005, 24–34).

Promising to revolutionize the telephone industry in Nigeria, one of Obasanjo's first actions as president was to suspend the telecommunications licenses that the previous regimes had issued. In January 2001, the government opened the auctioning process for four mobile licenses. Within two years of the introduction of GSM, Nigeria's telecommunication sector was rated as the fastest growing in Africa (Obadare 2006, 98, 100). The introduction of GSM meant an enormous leap: in 2012, around one hundred million active lines were in use (Nigerian Communications Commission 2012). People attached great hopes for the future to the wireless network that was extended over the Nigerian nation—it was seen as a sign of all the boons democracy was going to bring. "At the very least, mobile telecommunication was expected to accomplish some of the 'miracles' associated with its introduction in other parts of the world, for instance, 'abolishing' distance by facilitating the conduct of business and interpersonal relations" (Obadare 2006, 101).

However, the initial euphoria connected to the introduction of the GSM system was, just like the hopes for improvement of the electricity situation, soon replaced by disenchantment over poor reception and general inadequacy of services. There emerged a widespread sense that the mobile licenses that the Nigerian state had auctioned out were not what they were supposed to be, and a mounting suspicion that the state either was too weak to call the telephone companies into order or was even in cahoots with them (ibid., 101). As these feelings manifested in the Nigerian landscape, mobile phone users en masse switched off their phones in protest on 19 September 2003 (see Obadare 2004; Onwumechili 2005, 32; Obadare 2006, 93, 101; Smith 2006, 518). The deeply felt disillusionment with the mobile phone network was connected to the betrayed hopes of infrastructural "dividends of democracy" that people expected to spring from the return to civil rule (Obadare 2006, 101). Citizens all over the nation-state started to question whether their still young democracy carried any of the content other democracies elsewhere did. As one commentator concluded, "It is true that what works elsewhere doesn't necessarily work in Nigeria. Elsewhere in the world, GSM services are not burdened by the kind of poor quality that afflicts Nigerian subscribers" (Osadolor 2003).

Through people's infrastructural readings, the content of the new democracy and the flows it made possible appeared as not only questionable but also potentially harmful. In July 2004, sitting on a bench at the university grounds in Jos, a woman working at the university started to talk about a dangerous phone number; if you answered when the number called, you would die immediately. The suspicion, transmitted through text messages over the newly introduced lines, spread like wildfire across Jos and the rest of Nigeria (Andersson Trovalla 2011, 99–102). Television broadcast growing lists of "killer numbers," and people tried to memorize them or stored them among their contacts under the name "Evil." Many refused to answer calls from unknown numbers and some even stopped using phones entirely. Voices were raised for the ban of GSM (Adam 2004). Some went to hospitals for checkups after receiving calls (Agbu 2004, 16). These "killer calls," "satanic calls," or "doomsday calls" aggravated millennialist notions that the "end times" were approaching (Agbu 2004, 18–19; see Hackett 1998, 260; Last 2008, 58).

Being connected to the Nigerian public electricity grid gives rise to a similar sense of ambivalence, in that electricity emerges as one of the dubious flows that are felt to emanate from the state. While eagerly awaited to disperse the darkness, it allows a formidable and wayward force to be visited upon homes and families, exposing them not only to the inconveniences brought about by unpredictable rhythms, but also to the realistic fear of shock or fire (see Olukoju 2004, 29). When the lightbulb next to the NEPA switch comes on to signal that the common grid is live again, gazes therefore linger for a second or two. Yes, we got power, but what kind? Is the bulb shining steadily, is it pulsating slowly, is it flickering or shining too strongly? The excitement people feel is mixed with apprehension as, in the volatile landscape of infrastructure, electricity has qualities. It can be rough or smooth, calm or temperamental, benign or dangerous—there could be a high-power surge at any time.

Coming and going according to its own obscure patterns and fluctuating widely in frequency and voltage, Nigerian electricity has a vernacular quality that defies standardization (U. Trovalla and E. Trovalla 2017). Similar to how the GSM technology that seemed to work elsewhere in the world ran into unexpected problems in Nigeria, people talk about the unusual stress the volatile Nigerian electricity puts on appliances. Power inverter systems, which store electricity from the grid or from solar panels in battery cells for later use, have become increasingly popular, but the varieties from China or India, while technologically sophisticated, have proven too dainty for the blustery Nigerian grid. Nigerian artisans produce their own inverters with hand-soldered circuit boards and robust components. In the words of Nigerian engineers, imported products often have to be "modified" or "localized" to be able to survive the harsh climate of the Nigerian public grids.

As a way of monitoring the temperamental flows of the state, extension blocks—readily available in shops, market stalls, and street corners—often have a small voltage meter. As the little needle sways restlessly like a reed in the wind, it makes palpable some of the precariousness inherent in the public infrastructural flows. Similarly, as protection from the state's emanations, people fortify their homes by putting stabilizers and surge protectors between the wall outlet and the household's most valuable appliances.

In the midst of the ambiguities of the young democratic state, a gnawing question lurks in the back of people's minds: Could the all-embracing decline of the state and the nation since the 1970s have been more than a series of accidents? As the nation's unfathomable oil wealth is translated into a chronic energy crisis and cities are turned into landscapes of labyrinthine petrol queues, and as airplanes, trains, and buses have vanished one by one from the transportation infrastructure, people wonder what forces and underlying intents are behind this "reign of darkness" (Ejinkeonye 2007). Indeed, every glitch in the electricity supply, every gurgle in the water pipes, and every pothole in the road seems to be part of a larger narrative of a society undermined by clandestine structures hidden deep within the state.

"Reign of Darkness"

In a comedy video by Splendid Cartoon, a man gets so worried after having three days of uninterrupted power supply that he feels compelled to phone PHCN's customer support line: "Hello, is this PHCN office? There is a problem, o! For good three days now, we have been having uninterrupted power supply! Me I am scared, o! All the drinks in the fridge have turned into ice blocks! Hope there is no problem!" An automated reply follows: "Thank you for calling PHCN customer center! We are experiencing problems switching off the power supply. Our technicians are trying to fix the problem. Once that is done, you can be sure we will take the light!" (Splendid Cartoon 2018).

The protagonist of the joke has grown so accustomed to frequent power outages that he interprets PHCN's "failure" to switch off electricity as a critical disturbance in their normal operations. PHCN's automated reply assures him that service will soon return to normal—that is, it will disappear. To an audience familiar with the electricity situation in Nigeria, it is not exaggeration that makes the joke funny. Instead, it is the absurdity in the fact that, in real life, having more electricity than usual sometimes generates more negative emotions than the opposite situation. What if the power company forgot to switch over to another neighborhood, and, when they realize their mistake, what if they decide that the area has already received its share for the whole week or even longer? Or is the power company trying to groom their customers by granting them a couple of days of good service, before a couple of corrupt PHCN officials come visiting with an outrageous and fraudulent bill?

As people try to predict and decipher the infrastructural flows that emanate from the state, in the very same movement they try to figure out what the underlying driving forces and intents are behind these patterns of presence and absence. At the beginning of June 2015, during the first weeks after Buhari assumed the presidency, social media in Nigeria were abuzz with surprise, skepticism, and misgivings. The reason was that, in several cities all over the country, electricity had been constant for almost four days straight. What was going on? people asked. Some believed that Buhari's enemies had seized control of the electricity sector and were determined to deplete the country's resources in order to make the new president look bad. Others claimed that Buhari was trying to buy the affections of the masses in preparation for some unwelcome political reform. In either case, somebody was up to something, and one way or the other, ordinary people would pay the price. Similarly to how people acquire stabilizers and surge protectors to install a layer of protection between themselves and the state, the way in which an electricity supply that is "too good" conjures images of hidden plans being concocted behind the scenes also highlights the vulnerability citizens experience at the receiving end of public infrastructures.

In the first half of 2017, some months into a massive campaign by the Jos Electricity Distribution Company (JED) to provide their customers with prepaid meters, increasing discontent started to brew. In 2013, the Nigerian government had granted JED the rights to distribute electricity in Plateau, Gombe, Bauchi, and Benue States. This was part of an "unbundling" of PHCN and the profound restructuring of the Nigerian electricity sector that the Obasanjo administration initiated back in 2001 as part of fulfilling its promise to improve the supply of electricity. In 2005, PHCN was formed as a transitional corporation that would divide the functions and assets that NEPA managed into three distinct subsectors in a self-regulating electricity market: private generation companies to produce electricity, private distribution companies to deliver electricity to end-users, and a state-owned transmission company to run the high-voltage network that facilitates long-distance transportation of electricity from the power plants to the distribution companies (Nwokoye et al. 2017).

In Jos, JED not only installed meters among the thousands of customers who were on estimated billing, thereby ensuring a reliable avenue for collecting revenue; according to popular perception, they were even more eager to bring the new meters to customers who already had prepaid meters. Since 2007, when a smaller-scale initiative was initiated to offer prepaid electricity, the limited number of meters on offer had been in high demand. As a way to control the cost, and more importantly as a protective measure against fraudulent and unreasonable billing by PHCN employees, people in Jos were prepared to pay bribes as high as sixty thousand naira to get a meter installed. This time around, however, the new meters were free (although in some areas people had to pay a four-thousand-naira "programming fee"). Why, hard-earned experience had taught people to ask themselves, would anything come for free that used to cost a lot of money? And why was JED so adamant about taking the old meters with them? Not long after, people started to notice that the new meters seemed to run much faster than the old ones. The same number of electricity tokens that used to last for weeks were now used up within a few days. Rumors started to spread that the meters had been tampered with. Some even maintained that the meters were completely fake and the numbers they showed were entirely random. "Some of them are hollow," said Gabriel, an electrical engineer working in Jos, referring to rumors about meters that had fallen down and were taken for repair. "There are no components inside them."

As suspicions and protests grew, things were about to take a turn. After having participated in a radio phone-in show on the topic, David Jafaru Wuyep, state commissioner for water resources and energy, wrote an official letter to the Nigerian Electricity Management Services Agency (NEMSA), the agency responsible for calibrating and certifying this kind of equipment before it was installed. NEMSA wrote in response that they had no records that the meters had been brought to them. NEMSA undertook a formal visit to areas where the new meters had been mounted and discovered that, among many other discrepancies, the meters indeed lacked the seal to prove that they were properly calibrated. In this case, the usually vaporous nature of whatever is suspected to be going on behind the scenes gave way to some almost tangible indices of a conspiracy—one that most people thought must have existed—to deliberately divert the meters from the appropriate procedures of testing and certification in order to launch a mass scam on the public. Together with the experience that the electricity problems had not improved, the above events were a major blow to the hope that the combination of democracy and economic liberalization would amend the situation. It was replaced by the deep-seated feeling that nothing had changed—the forces that governed the emerging state/private power landscape were the same as before.

In order to make predictions about the availability and quality of infrastructural services, people are compelled to try to divine what forces are, in the end, controlling them. The clues derived from divining infrastructure always remain indistinct and seem to multiply and metamorphose at the same speed as the infrastructure landscape itself, producing fewer unambiguous and straightforward answers than it does suspicions. When a certain road receives maintenance while another is left to degrade, who stands to gain? When the scarcity of electricity drives people to buy generators, who benefits? Whose interests are swaying the priorities of the local, state, or federal government? Very often, explanations grow thick and layered, as if small-scale, more limited narratives do not suffice. As citizens observe and engage with the nation's infrastructure, an uneasy feeling arises that malevolent forces with murky motives are directing the state's actions from behind the scenes.

People see how generators are flooding the nation, to the extent that their noise and fumes saturate the urban landscape and it is impossible to imagine life without them. Joseph described how generators had come to completely take over Jos since the return to democracy: the way he saw it, the change was too profound to have occurred naturally. As long as the powerful had their high-capacity generators, he thought, they had no incentive to work toward a better electricity supply. He suspected that many of them were involved in the importation of generators and as such had vested interests in a poorly working public electricity supply. In an essay in the Nigerian newspaper *Vanguard* titled "Power, Generator Mafia and Political Will," the author concluded, "It is my firm belief that the introduction of the generator culture as a relief worsened our case. What was supposed to be a temporary relief became a permanent solution. Generators were a mere placebo that gave us phony relief. And because we did not fight the scourge, we created a monster that is preying on the present valiant effort to give Nigeria steady power. That monster is the generator mafia" (Jason 2012).

The abundance of generators has, for many, become a sign of a conspiracy at work in the form of just such a "generator mafia," which infiltrates the power companies as well as the government. Many believe that these companies, to protect their huge earnings, actively make sure that the national grid keeps deteriorating. Julie, a pharmacist in Jos, added that this was the same reason why the Nigerian trains did not run. There was a "lorry mafia" that made a lot of money from road transportation, and they made sure that the trains would not work. For her, it all connected to the idea that the national government had been corrupted. A news article in *Vanguard* attributed Nigeria's status as "one of the most railway-backward countries of the world" to the way the "haulage mafia," in conjunction with the Nigerian government, had "killed" the railway (Ochereome 2013). Another Nigerian reporter described how Yar'adua's government, despite promises that it had "declared war against the fuel mafia, the power mafia, generator mafia, crude oil mafia, and all other mafia," had failed. All in all, it proved that the administration was "beholden to entrenched interests" (Abami 2009).

Through their many acts of divination, residents imbue infrastructure with a superabundance of meaning and ideas of powerful actors operating behind the scene, while the state appears as a nebulous force field in which dark and destructive schemes flourish. If the term "value chain" captures how value is added to goods and services in the rest of the world, argued Jos-based entrepreneur and social commentator Kiyitwe Gotom as we huddled around the rechargeable lamp in our parlor, this is not necessarily the way things work in Nigeria.[2] To understand the logic behind how things unravel in Nigeria, he instead used the term "negative value chain." In a negative value chain, he explained, value is created when things do *not* work. As long as railway traffic remains inactive, haulage companies, fuel companies, and road construction contractors profit greatly. Similarly, other sectors of the economy thrive on underdeveloped public electricity. Gotom's description of the negative value chain—as a societal logic engrained with destructive forces—reminds one of a sinister version of the invisible hand imagined by Adam Smith.

When disenchantment replaced the euphoria connected to the introduction of the GSM system, there was a general suspicion that the omnipresent "Nigerian factor" was making itself known (Obadare 2006, 101). The Nigerian factor, sometimes also captured in phrases such as "this Nigeria" or "the Nigerian character," is an expression of a "national pessimism" brought about by a downward spiral of trust in the infrastructure and Nigeria's public institutions (see Bastian 1998, 114, 118; Diamond 2001, xiii; Obadare 2006, 101; Smith 2008, 7–8; Obadare 2009, 294, 255). In 2016, Reuben Abati, former spokesperson for President Jonathan, published an essay in which he described how his time in the inner circles of the government convinced him very literally that "there is an evil spell enveloping this country" and that Nigeria needed to be rescued "from the forces of darkness" (Abati 2016).

In a pervasive form of "socio-political demonology" (Obadare 2018, 19), the Nigerian factor has been viewed as a haunting presence that for decades has shaped the way the nation has been governed, derailing it in its pursuit of progress (Obadare 2018, 13–19). With the thwarting of their initial euphoric sentiments—that "true development" had reached the Nigerian nation—citizens were left with profound feelings of loss over a future that was once theirs to have. In his book *The Nigerian Factor: The Unseen Force in Action*, Emmanuel Udoh writes, "It was touted that we were on our way to true development, but alas, the light went off; the monster called the Nigerian factor set in" (2013, 5–6). For Udoh, the Nigerian factor is a force that slows down the actions that were going to shape the nation and, as such, "decelerates" what should have been "accelerated" (2013, 7).

In many people's view, the Nigerian factor "bears the brunt of blame for almost everything that goes wrong in the country" (Aghatise 2015). This idea is tied to the experience that, whatever effort is invested, in Nigeria nothing works (see Obadare 2009, 255), and to a strong notion of a Nigerian exceptionalism according to which things do not work the same way on Nigerian soil as elsewhere (Akpome 2015, 70). John Pepper Clark-Bekederemo's poem "Here Nothing Works" brings out these notions in a very heartfelt way. Like many others, he returns to those matters of everyday life in which the state is most prominently embodied.

> Here nothing works. Services taken
> For granted elsewhere either break down
> Or do not get started at all
> When introduced here. So supply of water
> That is basic to life after air
> Recreates for the people
> Desert conditions even by the sea,
> As every day darkness increases
> Over the land just as more dams go up
> And rivers reach levels approved by experts.
> What is it in ourselves or in our soil
> That things which connect so well elsewhere,
> Like the telephone, the motorway, the airways,
> Dislocate our lives so much that we all
> Begin to doubt our own intelligence?
> . . .
>
> (Clark-Bekederemo 1986, 3)

As in the excerpt above, the notion of an elusive negative power that influences the dealings of the state is often expressed through the mundane encounters with an infrastructure that, by its presences and absences, connects and disconnects the citizens to and from each other as well as from the state. A poem by John "The Beloved" Ajewole titled "The Nigerian Factor" paints a similar picture.

> Our airplanes, flying coffins,
> The highways are filled with potholes of death,
> If you can't swim, don't bother about sea-travel.
> The only hope is in God Almighty
> It's because of the Nigerian Factor.
> [. . .]
> Fluctuating electricity—either half current or overload,

The Light bulb just exploded,
Electronic gadgets destroyed plenty plenty
at least I can see enough to finish my poem
It's because of the Nigerian Factor.

(Ajewole 2003)

In an article on how to overcome the Nigerian factor in doing business in Nigeria, the author keeps returning to the importance of always having "a backup plan" (Business Mopol 2016). As layers upon layers of suspicions encrust the infrastructure and people construe the state as being animated by an evil essence, it has become essential not to rely on assumptions of what is going on, but instead to *never expect . . . always,* and to never fail to keep alternative avenues for action open. In his book *Everything in Nigeria Is Going to Kill You,* Nigerian author, essayist, and lawyer Ayo Sogunro tries to understand the conditions for survival in a system that has become dysfunctional. While arguing that Nigeria has progressed from "not taking care of you" to "actively trying to kill you" (Sogunro 2014, 124), he writes, "But unless you already have an exit plan for when things go to hell, then you might as well go to an undertaker and book your coffin today. Because: everything in Nigeria is going to kill you" (ibid., 127).

Lateral Futurity

A joke that has been popular since the 1980s states that the generator has ceased to be a backup to the grid; instead, the generator has become the main source of electricity and NEPA is the standby (Olukoju 2004, 55–56; U. Trovalla and E. Trovalla 2015, 45). Over time, the hyperbolic effect of the joke has diminished as small generators, mostly owned by private individuals, now appear to produce significantly more electricity than the country's generation plants (Presidential Action Committee on Power 2010, 17), or at least may have greater installed capacity (GOPA-International Energy Consultants GmbH et al. 2015, 33, 120). However, the joke does not rely so much on exaggeration as on a reversal of expectations and a deeply felt sense of the absurdity of life. How can a state, and a petroleum giant at that, allow a swarm of tiny 0.9 KVA Tiger generators to surpass it? There is, however, another truth to the joke: the hierarchy between main and standby source, or, if you will, between plan A and plan B, is becoming increasingly blurred.

The decades that have passed since infrastructures peaked in the 1970s have seen a decline in the coverage and integrity of public grids, but also a diminishing faith in a grand narrative of national progress that used to be backed by the formidable materiality of the state. Riding buses, trains, and cars, reliably en route to one's destination, and being able to flip a switch or turn a tap with confidence that electricity or water would flow, offered citizens a sense that Nigeria was heading somewhere. Now, however, as the deterioration of infrastructures has subtracted considerable materiality from the state, the solidity of this sense of trajectory is disintegrating.

In Jos, James, a retired schoolteacher and philosopher known for his tenacious faithfulness to his vision of what the Nigerian nation should be like, experienced a long string of disturbances to his electricity and water supply. Moreover, despite the fact that his water pipes were completely dried up and he had only a few minutes of electricity per day, exorbitant bills kept being delivered with a diligence—he said jokingly—that he wished had been afforded to the delivery of services as well. When his son, born in the 1970s and fostered in an era of infrastructural disillusionment, tried to acquire a water pump and a generator that could power it, and negotiated with the community by the lake to run a pipe up to the house, James would not hear of it. Instead, he sat down at his old typewriter and started to compose a series of complaint letters to the respective agencies. Knowing full well that it would not happen, but acting *as if* the concerned representatives of the state would respond the way they might have done once upon a time, he engaged in a manner of retrofuturistic (Wilson 2019, 140) intervention that conjured the ghost of a future that the nation once possessed, but now had lost.

Abdoumaliq Simone speaks of a "double time": the sense in many African urban contexts that the memories of practices and dreams that used to shape the city are still there, simultaneous with the present moment (Simone 2010, 8–9). Sometimes, these parallel perceptions of time introduce a sense of disconnection, as they point to very different futures. As Achille Mbembe points out, in a way that is particularly relevant in relation to the heterogeneous ways that the state and infrastructure in Nigeria come to articulate each other through people's endeavors to go about their everyday life, "African social formations are not necessarily converging toward a single point, trend, or cycle. They harbor the possibility of a variety of trajectories neither convergent nor divergent but interlocked, paradoxical." Rather than linear, he continues, time must be understood as entangled (Mbembe 2001, 16–17).

James Ferguson writes about the nonlinear loops that characterize life in Zambia after the demise of the teleological development narrative. Now, outmoded ways of life seem better suited to current conditions than the life-forms that aligned to the modern era. Practices that a linear and progressive narrative declared as "dead ends" "keep coming back, just as the 'main lines' that are supposed to lead to the future continually seem to disappoint" (Ferguson 1999, 250). The nostalgic accounts of the time prior to the infrastructural breakdowns of the oil bust and onward lament the loss of an imagined future of progress and prosperity. However, the way people speak of the past in relation to the future also reveals a loss of a sense of temporal coherence. If the Nigerian factor, as in Udoh's interpretation, is a force of deceleration (2013, 7–9), one can see it as an expression of a lack of forward momentum that adds to the loss of a specific utopian dream. People go about their everyday lives in relation to a timeline that appears less and less linear, in which the present connects to the past and the future in less and less convincing ways.

People's daily divination acts that aim to predict when, where, and how services will be available or unavailable are attempts to discern the reasons behind the infrastructural fluctuations as well as to identify the major players inside and outside the state with the power to connect, disconnect, and redirect infrastructural flows. These divinations often assume a narrative form in which the lack of electricity or fuel, for instance, are the result of actions by corrupt individuals in pursuit of selfish goals. As such, the divinations invoke a temporal order of cause and effect. However, they have nothing to offer to replace the loss of a cohesive and linear grand narrative. Instead, alternative timelines multiply as each divination act suggests its own account of how past events translate into present conditions and expectations for the future. Rather than singular visions of the future, the divination acts prompt citizens' simultaneous accommodation of several parallel scenarios, which all tend to be open-ended and reside in the realm of the suspected but unverifiable.

The multitude of unknown factors that intervene as people make their prognostications, and the experience that they can expect nothing to be what it seems to be, give rise to a *never expect . . . always* attitude toward infrastructure. However, the necessities of life charge people to engage in everyday acts *as if* they could make prognostications with a modicum of certainty. In order to get access to electricity, petrol, water, transportation, etc., one must act, place one's bets, and invest money, time, and hope in solutions and avenues that seem plausible, at least for the time being. But rather than being based on a vision of a future that evolves in a linear and comprehensible way, these are means to "minimize disappointment when preferred ways of doing things do not work out" (Simone 2010, 98). The result has been an increasing reliance on solutions that, similar to the generator, citizens would have seen until recently as secondary to the communal grids. Besides generators, homes and small businesses are brimming with backup solutions that people have promoted to a status equal to the main source: inverter systems, rechargeable lights and candles, and private wells and rainwater buckets. Rather than being standby and second to something higher up in a defined hierarchy of sources, one can better describe these utilities as parallel solutions.

Reflecting this increasing emphasis on parallelism, the NEPA switch has evolved to include several additional slots for different power sources.

Besides the customary "NEPA" and "GEN" positions, it may include a third slot for the inverter and yet another for a second generator of higher capacity that can support heavily power-consuming appliances but is too expensive to run more than occasionally. It has also become common to outfit the house with secondary or even tertiary circuits tailored to the output of the generator or inverter, which only include the appliances the particular source of electricity can support. In houses of some age, cables of various dimensions crisscross the walls, tracing a succession of attempts to answer the question of how to secure access to electricity. Telling stories of a state that, kilowatt by kilowatt, gradually detaches itself from a linear narrative of national progress, the added contraptions and electrical circuits belong to different temporal registers—each articulating a certain past, since they step in to replace something that used to be there, and each with their own interpretations of what the future will require. As such, one can see the NEPA switch as a narrative device that allows the owner to make lateral moves between alternate timelines and visions of the future.

Usually, even if a certain implement falls out of use, it is not physically removed, as current developments may well be reversed in the future and bring old systems back into relevance. It is very common to see energy-saving bulbs that householders have mounted in ceilings in order to slow down the incessant ticking away of prepaid electricity tokens—while next to them, the fluorescent tubes once used are left in place, since nobody can say for sure how long the prepaid regime will last and what will come after it. In kitchens outfitted before the current "reign of darkness," residents still keep electric stoves in place, regardless of the fact that they are nowadays hopelessly impractical. Similarly, in homes that were privileged enough to have a NITEL line before the GSM revolution, you may still find an old landline telephone sitting on a side table. In the abodes of those electricity subscribers who fought so fiercely when JED tried to take away their old meters, the decommissioned devices rest on a shelf somewhere, ready to function again in a configuration yet to be conceived. Like other things in various states of ruination, they are not merely material debris of defunct regimes but "unfinished histories" that still may possess the power to determine future avenues (Stoler 2013, 11).

"Buy new, buy second!" is an idiom that captures another loop on the timeline of everyday experience. If one needs an engine part, bicycle, generator, or whatever one might require to navigate the landscapes of infrastructural services, buying a brand-new one will only mean you have to replace it very soon, since the quality of newly produced items is often poor. Wisdom instead recommends buying "Belgium"; that is, secondhand items imported from Europe, which people perceive to be untouched by the general breakdown that reigns in Nigeria. Belgium items, according to popular narrative, got their name in the 1980s, when the economic hardships during Babangida's regime inspired a couple of Nigerian footballers who played professionally in Belgium to invest their earnings in secondhand cars (and, later on, other commodities), which they imported to Nigeria. As the state and the infrastructure crumbled during the momentous 1980s and 1990s, so did the material trappings of life, as the currency exchange rate left people with consumer goods that seemed to fall apart in their hands and were scornfully labeled "Nigerian quality"—and later on, as commodity flows changed, "China quality" (E. Trovalla and U. Trovalla 2015, 339–40). In this context, the term "Belgium" carries connotations of "the good old" in contrast to highly unreliable newly manufactured products, and represents a reversal of the value of "new and improved": it places good quality in the past, rather than in the future. However, when deployed side by side with the other materialities of everyday life, the Belgium items instead bring the past into simultaneous existence with the present, and represent another example of the lateral moves between many different imaginations of the past and the future.

Returning to the joke above, that NEPA—and, by extension, infrastructure as a whole and even the state itself—has become a standby in relation to what used to be fallback plans, the premise requires some modification. In truth, because of the nature of the state and (its) infrastructures, it is *people* who are standing by, always ready to switch over to something else as infrastructures, utilities, social imaginaries, and narratives fail. And in the waning flows of infrastructure, with collective imaginations fading in regard to the future of the nation, state, and individuals, switching between ways of accessing the necessities that allow the continuation of life is a process in which a forward momentum is translated into a movement sideways—that is, into a lateral futurity.

Notes

This work is part of the FORMAS-funded research project "Suspicious Materialities: Egyptian and Nigerian Cityscapes" (grant number 2016–00345), run by Mark Levine, Maria Frederika Malmström, and the authors.

1. This chapter builds on fieldwork conducted in the Nigerian city of Jos between 2000 and 2017. Unless otherwise noted, the interlocutors quoted here are identified by pseudonyms, in order to ensure their integrity and security.
2. Kiyitwe Gotom is identified by his real name.

References

Abami. 2009. "30 Reasons Why Nigeria Should Get Rid of Yar'adua." *Sahara Reporters,* 2 August. http://saharareporters.com/2009/08/02/30-reasons-why -nigeria-should-get-rid-yar'adua.

Abati, Reuben. 2016. "The Spiritual Side of Aso Villa." *Guardian* (Lagos), 14 October. https://guardian.ng/opinion/the-spiritual-side-of-aso-villa/.

Adam, Sagai John. 2004. "Do You Want To Die? (All the GSM Killer Numbers)." *GSMToday*, 31 March. http://www.mail-archive.com/gsmtoday@freelists.org /msg00140.html.

Adebanwi, Wale. 2016. *Nation as Grand Narrative: The Nigerian Press and the Politics of Meaning*. Rochester, NY: University of Rochester Press.

Agabi, Chris. 2013. "30 Hours inside a Lagos-Kano–Bound Train." *Weekly Trust*, 16 February. https://dailytrust.com/30-hours-inside-a-lagos-kano-bound-train.

Agbaeze, E. K., and I. O. Onwuka. 2014. "Boosting Railway System Infrastructure in Nigeria: The Public-Private Partnership Option." *Journal of Business Administration and Management Sciences Research* 3 (9): 184–93.

Agbese, Dan. 2019. "The Graveyard of Presidential Promises." *Daily Trust* (Abuja), 7 July. https://www.dailytrust.com.ng/the-graveyard-of-presidential-promises .html.

Agbu, Jane-Frances. 2004. "From 'Koro' to GSM 'Killer Calls' Scare in Nigeria: A Psychological View." *CODESRIA Bulletin* 3 (4): 16–19.

Aghatise, Mitchell. 2015. "Democracy and the Nigerian Factor: The Problem with the Nigerian People." *Africa at LSE* (blog), London School of Economics and Political Science, 23 January. https://blogs.lse.ac.uk/africaatlse/2015/01 /23/democracy-and-the-nigerian-factor-the-problem-with-the-nigerian -people/.

Ajewole, John. 2003. "The Nigerian Factor." NigeriaVillageSquare, 12 January. http://www.nigeriavillagesquare.com/articles/the-nigerian-factor.html.

Aké, Claude. 1995. "The Democratisation of Disempowerment in Africa." In *The Democratisation of Disempowerment: The Problem of Democracy in the Third World*, edited by Jochen Hippler, 70–108. London: Pluto.

———. 1996. *Democracy and Development in Africa*. Washington, DC: Brookings Institution.

Akpoghomeh, Osi S. 1999. "The Development of Air Transportation in Nigeria." *Journal of Transport Geography* 7 (2): 135–46.

Akpome, Aghogho. 2015. "What Is Nigeria? Unsettling the Myth of Exceptionalism." *Africa Spectrum* 50 (1): 65–78.

Akwara, Azalahu Francis, Joseph Effiong Udaw, and Gerald E. Ezirim. 2014. "Adapting Colonial Legacy to Modernism: A Focus on Rail Transport Development in Nigeria." *Mediterranean Journal of Social Sciences* 5 (6): 465–75.

Andersson Trovalla, Ulrika. 2011. "Medicine for Uncertain Futures: A Nigerian City in the Wake of a Crisis." PhD diss., Uppsala University.

Apter, Andrew. 1999. "IBB = 419: Nigerian Democracy and the Politics of Illusion." In *Civil Society and the Political Imagination in Africa: Critical Perspectives*, edited by John L. Comaroff and Jean Comaroff, 267–307. Chicago: University of Chicago Press.

———. 2005. *The Pan-African Nation: Oil and the Spectacle of Culture in Nigeria*. Chicago: University of Chicago Press.

Bastian, Misty L. 1998. "Fires, Tricksters and Poisoned Medicines: Popular Cultures of Rumor in Onitsha, Nigeria and Its Markets." *Etnofoor* 11 (2): 111–32.

———. 2003. "'Diabolic Realities': Narratives of Conspiracy, Transparency, and 'Ritual Murder' in the Nigerian Popular Print and Electronic Media." In West and Sanders 2003, 65–91.

BBC. 2013. "Can Nigeria's Renovated Railway Unite North and South?" *BBC News*, 13 February. http://www.bbc.co.uk/news/world-africa-21364541.

Business Mopol. 2016. "Overcoming the Nigerian Factor in Your Business." *Business Mopol*, 3 June. https://www.businessmopol.com/overcoming-the-nigerian -factor-in-your-business/.

Clark-Bekederemo, John Pepper. 1986. *State of the Union*. London: Longman.

Cooper, Elizabeth, and David Pratten. 2015. "Ethnographies of Uncertainty in Africa: An Introduction." In *Ethnographies of Uncertainty in Africa*, edited by Elizabeth Cooper and David Pratten, 1–16. London: Palgrave Macmillan.

De Boeck, Filip, and Sammy Baloji. 2016. *Suturing the City: Living Together in Congo's Urban Worlds*. London: Autograph ABP.

De Boeck, Filip, and Marie-Françoise Plissart. 2004. *Kinshasa: Tales of the Invisible City*. Ghent, Belgium: Ludion.

Diamond, Larry. 2001. "Foreword." In *Federalism and Ethnic Conflict in Nigeria*, edited by Rotimi T. Suberu, xi–xviii. Washington, DC: United States Institute of Peace.

Ejinkeonye, Ugochukwu. 2007. "Problem Has Changed Name (PHCN)." NigeriaVillageSquare, 7 February. http://www.nigeriavillagesquare.com/articles /ugochukwu-ejinkeonye/problem-has-changed-name-phcn.html.

Ferguson, James. 1999. *Expectations of Modernity: Myths and Meanings of Urban Life on the Zambian Copperbelt*. Berkeley: University of California Press.

Freund, Bill. 1978. "Oil Boom and Crisis in Contemporary Nigeria." *Review of African Political Economy* 5 (13): 91–100.

Graham, Stephen. 2011. "Disruptions." In *Urban Constellations*, edited by Matthew Gandy, 65–70. Berlin: Jovis.

Graham, Stephen, and Nigel Thrift. 2007. "Out of Order: Understanding Repair and Maintenance." *Theory, Culture & Society* 24 (3): 1–25.

Hackett, Rosalind I. J. 1998. "Charismatic/Pentecostal Appropriation of Media Technologies in Nigeria and Ghana." *Journal of Religion in Africa* 28 (3): 258–77.

Hibou, Béatrice. 2017. "'Discharge,' the New Interventionism." In Hibou, Samuel, and Fourchard 2017, 149–59.

Béatrice Hibou, Boris Samuel, and Laurent Fourchard, eds. 2017. *The Spirits of Neoliberal Reforms and Everyday Politics of the State in Africa*. Dakar: Amalion.

Ingold, Tim. 1993. "The Temporality of the Landscape." In "Conceptions of Time and Ancient Society," special issue, *World Archaeology* 25 (2): 152–74.

GOPA-International Energy Consultants GmbH, Karsten Ley, Jeremy Gaines, and Anil Ghatikar. 2015. *The Nigerian Energy Sector: An Overview with a Special Emphasis on Renewable Energy, Energy Efficiency and Rural Electrification*. 2nd ed. Abuja, Nigeria: Deutsche Gesellschaft für Internationale Zusammenarbeit; Nigerian Energy Support Programme; and Federal Ministry of Power. https://www.giz.de/en/downloads/giz2015-en-nigerian-energy-sector.pdf.

Jason, Pini. 2012. "Power, Generator Mafia and Political Will." *Vanguard* (Lagos), 29 May. https://www.vanguardngr.com/2012/05/power-generator-mafia-and -political-will/.

Jega, Attahiru. 2000. "The State and Identity Transformation under Structural Adjustment in Nigeria." In *Identity Transformations and Identity Politics under Structural Adjustment in Nigeria*, edited by Attahiru Jega, 41–61. Uppsala,

Sweden: Nordiska Afrikainstitutet; Kano, Nigeria: Centre for Research and Documentation.

Larkin, Brian. 2008. *Signal and Noise: Media, Infrastructure, and Urban Culture in Nigeria.* Durham, NC: Duke University Press.

———. 2013. "The Politics and Poetics of Infrastructure." *Annual Review of Anthropology* 42:327–43.

Last, Murray. 2008. "The Search for Security in Muslim Northern Nigeria." *Africa: Journal of the International African Institute* 78 (1): 41–63.

Mark Angel Comedy. 2017. "Youth Empowerment." Posted 8 September on YouTube by user MarkAngelComedy. Video, 3:43. https://www.youtube.com/watch?v=5h42DE83IlE.

Mbembe, Achille. 2001. *On the Postcolony.* Berkeley: University of California Press.

———. 2017. "On Private Indirect Government." In Hibou, Samuel, and Fourchard 2017, 171–91.

Nnamdi. [2002]. "You Know You Are Flying Nigeria Airways: Part II." NgEx! NigeriaExchange. Accessed 3 December 2019. http://www.ngex.com/lifestyles/jokes/flynigeriaairways2.htm.

Nigerian Communications Commission. 2012. "Subscriber Data." Accessed 17 October 2012. http://www.ncc.gov.ng/index.php?option=com_content&view=article&id=125:art-statistics-subscriber-data&catid=65:cat-web-statistics&Itemid=73.

Nwokoye, Ebele S., Stephen K. Dimnwobi, Chukwunonso S. Ekesiobi, and Casmir C. Obegolu. 2017. "Power Infrastructure and Electricity in Nigeria: Policy Considerations for Economic Welfare." *KIU Journal of Humanities* 2 (1): 5–17.

Obadare, Ebenezer. 2004. "The Great GSM (Cell Phone) Boycott: Civil Society, Big Business and the State in Nigeria." *Dark Roast Occasional Paper Series,* no. 18. Cape Town: Isandla Institute.

———. 2006. "Playing Politics with the Mobile Phone in Nigeria: Civil Society, Big Business & the State." *Review of African Political Economy* 33 (107): 93–111.

———. 2009. "The Uses of Ridicule: Humour, 'Infrapolitics' and Civil Society in Nigeria." *African Affairs* 108 (431): 241–61.

———. 2018. *Pentecostal Republic: Religion and the Struggle for State Power in Nigeria.* London: Zed Books.

Ochereome, Nnanna. 2013. "Return of the Trains." *Vanguard* (Lagos), 26 August. https://www.vanguardngr.com/2013/08/return-of-the-trains/.

Odeleye, Joshua Adetunji. 2000. "Public-Private Participation to Rescue Railway Development in Nigeria." *Japan Railway & Transport Review* 23:42–49.

Ogbeidi, Michael M. 2006. "The Aviation Industry in Nigeria: A Historical Overview." *Lagos Historical Review* 6:133–47.

Olukoju, Ayodeji. 2004. "'Never Expect Power Always': Electricity Consumers' Response to Monopoly, Corruption and Inefficient Services in Nigeria." *African Affairs* 103 (410): 51–71.

Olukoya, Sam. 2013. "Lagos-Kano Rail Link Keeps Death off the Roads." *Radio France Internationale,* 28 August. http://www.english.rfi.fr/africa/20130828-nigeria-lagos-kano-rail-line-keeps-death-off-roads.

Omezi, Giles. 2014. "Nigerian Modernity and the City: Lagos 1960–1980." In *The Arts of Citizenship in African Cities: Infrastructures and Spaces of Belonging,* edited by Mamadou Diouf and Rosalind Fredericks, 277–95. New York: Palgrave Macmillan.

Omoniwa, Moses. 2012. *Nigerian Railway Corporation: An Assessment of Performances and Managements.* Saarbrücken, Germany: Lambert Academic.

Onwumechili, Chuka. 2001. "Dream or Reality: Providing Universal Access to Basic Telecommunications in Nigeria?" *Telecommunications Policy* 25 (4): 219–31.

———. 2005. "Reaching Critical Mass in Nigeria's Telephone Industry." *Africa Media Review* 13 (1): 23–40.

Osadolor, Kingsley. 2003. "The GSM Boycott." *Guardian* (Lagos), 23 September. Copied text available at http://news.biafranigeriaworld.com/archive/2003/sep /24/060.html.

Presidential Action Committee on Power. 2010. *Roadmap for Power Sector Reform: A Customer-Driven Sector-Wide Plan to Achieve Stable Power Supply.* Lagos: Presidency, Federal Republic of Nigeria. http://www.ecowrex.org/system/files /repository/roadmap_for_power_sector_reform_full_version.pdf.

Sanders, Todd, and Harry G. West. 2003. "Power Revealed and Concealed in the New World Order." In West and Sanders 2003, 1–37.

Simone, Abdoumaliq. 2010. *City Life from Jakarta to Dakar: Movements at the Crossroads.* New York: Routledge.

Smith, Daniel Jordan. 2006. "Cell Phones, Social Inequality, and Contemporary Culture in Nigeria." *Canadian Journal of African Studies* 40 (3): 496–523.

———. 2008. *A Culture of Corruption: Everyday Deception and Popular Discontent in Nigeria.* Princeton, NJ: Princeton University Press.

Sogunro, Ayo. 2014. *Everything in Nigeria Is Going to Kill You: Selected Essays.* [Lagos]: Shecrownlita Scribbles.

Splendid Cartoon. 2018. "NEPA Don Bring Light." Posted 10 January on YouTube by user Splendid TV. https://www.youtube.com/watch?v=DrshJFlOL6I.

Stoler, Ann Laura. 2013. "Introduction: 'The Rot Remains': From Ruins to Ruination." In *Imperial Debris: On Ruins and Ruination,* edited by Ann Laura Stoler, 1–35. Durham, NC: Duke University Press.

Trovalla, Eric, and Ulrika Trovalla. 2015. "Infrastructure as a Divination Tool: Whispers from the Grids in a Nigerian City." In "You are Surrounded," special issue, *City* 19 (2): 332–43.

Trovalla, Ulrika, and Eric Trovalla. 2015. "Infrastructure Turned Suprastructure: Unpredictable Materialities and Visions of a Nigerian Nation." *Journal of Material Culture* 20 (1): 43–57.

———. 2017. "Inverter, or, Vernacular Electricity and the Localized Inverter." Cultural Anthropology website, 19 December. https://culanth.org/fieldsights/our -electro-homes.

Udoh, Emmanuel. 2013. *The Nigerian Factor: The Unseen Force in Action.* Self-published, Trafford.

West, Harry G., and Todd Sanders, eds. 2003. *Transparency and Conspiracy: Ethnographies of Suspicion in the New World Order.* Durham, NC: Duke University Press.

Wilson, Paul. 2019. "The Afronaut and Retrofuturism in Africa." *ASAP/Journal* 4 (1): 139–66.

SIX

Gazomania!

Shortage and the State in Chad

LORI LEONARD

WITH MUCH FANFARE, CHAD OPENED ITS FIRST OIL refinery on 29 June 2011. The refinery is a joint venture between Chad, represented by the Société des Hydrocarbures du Tchad (SHT), and China, via its state-owned oil company, the China National Petroleum Corporation, or CNPC. It is located near the village of Djermaya, just thirty-six kilometers north of the capital city of N'Djamena, the main market for its products. The construction of the refinery was a bid to make Chad energy independent.

When the refinery opened, Chad had already been an oil-producing country for nearly a decade. However, the oil produced from the oil fields in the south of the country, as part of an export project financed by ExxonMobil and the World Bank, had not reduced Chad's dependence on imported energy sources (Leonard 2016). The development of new oil fields in the Bongor Basin and the linkage of those fields to the refinery was supposed to resolve the paradox of an oil-producing country dependent on imported oil and put an end to ruptures in the energy supply and the frequent power outages that beset the city. The refinery was designed to process twenty thousand barrels of oil daily and supply the country with diesel, gas, kerosene, A1 jet fuel, and liquid propane gas (or LPG) for cooking fuel and other domestic needs. It was even supposed to transform Chad into a regional supplier of petroleum products.

In the years since the refinery opened, the state—a term I use to refer to an eclectic set of governmental actors and institutions (Gupta 1995;

Gupta 2012)—has moved aggressively to convert households across the country from charcoal and wood to locally produced LPG. State agents have taken coercive measures to bring about this transition, but they have also provided incentives to families to propel the conversion. Government agencies fix the price of petroleum products coming from the refinery and subsidize the cost of purchasing LPG gas canisters and cooking equipment and of refilling or exchanging the canisters. Various governmental bodies have also engaged in what Veena Das and Deborah Poole call a "pedagogy of conversion" (2004, 9). State agents have tried to educate the public about the environmental and economic benefits of adopting cleaner and especially domestic sources of energy and persuade people of the benefits to the nation of a certain kind of environmental citizenship, which includes a reliance on gas produced at the refinery for cooking and other domestic needs. In his annual Address to the Nation, President Idriss Deby told Chadians that protecting the environment was a *"combat commun"* and not something the government could do alone (Adoum 2009).

Yet Chad's push for energy independence and cleaner cooking fuel has not been smooth. Periodic shortages of LPG, as well as other petroleum products, upend daily life in the city and complicate such everyday activities as getting to work, bathing, and feeding the family. In the post-refinery era, these shortages have localized the state in new ways. Shortages contribute to discursive representations of the state as corrupt, inept, punitive, and callous. They also mobilize and assemble consumers, who form queues on major roads and thoroughfares in front of gas stations and other businesses that serve as distribution outlets for the refinery's products, including LPG. The assemblies of people and their brightly colored gas canisters, arrayed in long, wending lines under the heat of the midday sun, are visual reminders of the failure of the state to produce a reliable supply of energy, despite its promises to do so. The danger of this failure is neatly symbolized in the explosive potential of the gas canisters and the crowds.

In this chapter, I look, through a recent shortage of cooking gas that spanned the period from February through April 2019, at how shortages and the collective assemblies of energy consumers that follow are shifting energy politics in Chad. The gas lines are not organized protests, yet they can be read as efforts to be seen and heard by governmental authorities or, in Lisa Mitchell's lexicon, to "hail the state" (Mitchell 2018). These appeals to the state to alleviate suffering by providing access to reliable sources of energy are part of a decades-long conversation about energy in Chad. These ongoing conversations, and Chad's history as a crude oil exporter, dependent on rents and royalties to purchase energy for its own citizens, structure the experience of shortage and shape representations of the state in the post-refinery era. So, too, does the country's recent emergence as a regional supplier of refined petroleum products and junior partner in a business venture with China. In times of shortage, the media focus is on state coercion and the suppression of marches and demonstrations, yet what is missed in these accounts is how the gas lines and citizens' efforts to hail the state have propelled action and even reform.

This chapter is based on firsthand experience of the 2019 shortage. I was in N'Djamena in March and April 2019 and both witnessed and participated in the struggles of families to find domestic gas. I also followed accounts about the shortage through local media, which continued to cover the shortage long after the crisis had subsided. This chapter is also informed by research I conducted between 2000 and 2012 on the oil and pipeline project in the south of Chad that was a precursor to the refinery project and an important touchstone for contemporary energy politics in Chad.

La Gazomania!

From February through April 2019, the nationwide shortage of cooking gas was at the forefront of everyday life in N'Djamena. The press corps dubbed the frenzied efforts of city dwellers to find domestic gas "*la gazomania*" (Editorial Board of *L'observateur* 2019). All over the city, people formed queues with their canisters, emptied of cooking gas, as they waited to exchange them at gas stations and other distribution outlets. The queues began forming before dawn and stretched as far as the eye could see. Family members took turns guarding the canisters and their places in the lines. Journalists photographed children sleeping on the canisters as people waited late into the night, hoping for the arrival of a supply of cooking gas. Throughout the period of the shortage, it was common to see gas canisters strapped to the backs of bicycles and motorcycles, taking up the place typically reserved for passengers, and to see swarms of motorcycles following pickup trucks loaded down with gas canisters to what the motorcyclists thought—or hoped—might be a distribution site (Ibedou 2019). People brought the canisters with them everywhere—including to work, church, and funeral ceremonies, places where they would normally be incongruous—to take advantage of any opportunity for an exchange that might present itself (Editorial Board of *L'observateur* 2019). Occasionally, trucks carrying gas came across the border from Cameroon or Nigeria, but these transborder shipments could meet only a fraction of the demand for LPG in the city. Most of the time, family members returned home empty-handed and rejoined the queue the following day.

The turmoil created by the rupture in the production of LPG is, by one measure, evidence of the success of the government's efforts to convert city dwellers to cleaner energy. Yet the government's efforts also had the effect of aggravating the crisis by dismantling or disrupting supply chains

FIGURE 1. A queue of gas canisters in N'Djamena, 2019. Photo by Lori Leonard.

for alternative sources of fuel, thus leaving city residents with few options in times of shortage. As part of the campaign to promote cleaner domestic energy, government actors and agencies banned the production, transport, and commercialization of charcoal and wood, which were the main sources of cooking fuel in the vast majority of households before the ban took effect (Bambé 2018). A national survey of household energy use in 2003 and 2004 showed that only 2 percent of Chadian households used gas for cooking fuel, while 73 percent used wood and 16 percent used charcoal (Ministère des Finances, de l'Économie et du Plan 2006). The government ministry responsible for enforcing the ban on charcoal and wood, the Ministry of the Environment, Water, and Fisheries, gave residents of N'Djamena one month to wean themselves off traditional energy sources, while rural residents were given three months to make the transition. The ministry also banned the felling of trees anywhere in the country and barred all but rural residents from collecting wood to use as cooking fuel.

Government agents engineered a multitude of responses to the ban. The national defense minister announced that anyone in the army caught cutting down a tree would be immediately discharged (Ali 2018). The minister of the environment ordered mayors to enforce the ban on selling wood in their towns (T. K. and Djimrangar 2018). Forest guards stationed on the outskirts of N'Djamena monitored wooded areas and imposed heavy fines on people caught taking deadwood from the forest floor (Ibedou 2019). Police and customs agents monitored cross-border traffic from Cameroon and Nigeria and confiscated charcoal and wood along with other contraband. When the prohibition on charcoal and wood first took effect, the police set minivans loaded with charcoal aflame to demonstrate the consequences of engaging in the charcoal trade and to underscore the government's commitment to promoting cleaner energy sources. Given the number of people involved in enforcing the ban and the variety of ways they disrupted supply chains, charcoal and wood were hard to find in February 2019 when the crisis hit.

It was not until mid-March, more than three weeks after the shortage began, that the government made any public pronouncements about it. The Société de Raffinage de N'Djamena (SRN), an entity created by the Chadian and Chinese partners in which the CNPC retains a majority share, acknowledged that it had taken the production of LPG off-line to carry out general maintenance at the refinery (A. N. T. 2018a). The SRN spokesperson said that suspending the production of domestic gas was necessary for the safety of factory workers and the efficiency of the refinery. In fact, maintenance on the LPG production line was critically overdue; the equipment was scheduled to be overhauled every three years and the refinery had already been in continuous operation for more than four years. The spokesperson assured the public that the shutdown would have no impact on the production of liquid products—gas, A1 jet fuel, or diesel. However, the refinery would not be able to produce domestic gas for fifty-two days, or would produce minimal quantities of LPG during this time. The public would need to be patient.

The daily lines of people and empty gas canisters that ensued were visual reminders of the state's newfound entanglement in the most mundane aspects of people's day-to-day lives. They were also reminders of the state's incapacity to deliver on its promise of providing clean, affordable, and reliable domestic energy. As construction on the refinery was getting underway, then-president Deby had promised the public that the refinery would end the ruptures in the supplies of gas and electricity. The political dangers of the shortage were therefore not difficult to see. In a city divided along ethnic and religious lines, the gatherings around gas distribution centers and the shared struggle to eat brought people together in denouncing the rupture and the government's failure to anticipate the consequences of the scheduled factory maintenance or to devise a backup plan to ensure that customers had access to gas while production was off-line. In contrast to the "heterogeneous social" that Partha Chatterjee (2004, 136) describes as the outcome of government welfare and development programs to alleviate the suffering of particular populations, everyone in N'Djamena had become dependent on the state for energy and cooking gas; the gas lines united Chadians, blurring the usual divisions of ethnicity, religion, and class.

While waiting in line for gas and in other venues, too, residents of the city swapped stories about how they were making do. They talked about burning old furniture or using animal dung, dried fruit from the *palmier doum,* or discarded rubber to cook their meals (see also Ibedou 2019). Yet, in the midst of the crisis, even these sources of energy were becoming expensive and difficult to find (A. N. T. and T. K. 2018). The gas shortage deepened the ongoing struggles of families to make it in a period of prolonged, government-inflicted austerity measures. Three years earlier, the government had cut the salaries and benefits of civil servants. It had also levied new taxes on goods and services and lowered government subsidies on the refinery's products—subsidies designed to palliate the fiscal crisis. These and other cost-cutting measures had strained household budgets to the breaking point, and now families faced a shortage of cooking gas and were struggling to feed themselves. In this context, the gas canisters themselves were symbolically resonant, spawning media reports about "explosive" publics and "social bombs" that might detonate at any moment (Editorial Board of *L'observateur* 2019).

The allusions to explosive publics were doubly significant given that the shortage of LPG was happening against the backdrop of popular protests over inflation and spiking food prices in neighboring Sudan. The protests, seen by many as an extension of the Arab Spring, led to the ouster of the Sudanese president, Omar al-Bashir, in April 2019. At the time of the rupture in Chad, the latest round of protests in Sudan had been ongoing for several months and had swept the country, prompting al-Bashir to declare a national state of emergency. In Sudan as in Chad, the loss of oil revenue was at the root of a broad and deep fiscal crisis, and in both countries citizens were disenchanted with leaders who had been in power for three decades and were viewed as responsible for the ongoing fiscal crises.

The government response to popular protests was similar in both countries. In Chad, while the government did not declare a state of emergency, it used force to curb dissent. The Ministry of Security (Ministère de l'Administration du Territoire, de la Sécurité Publique et de la Gouvernance Locale) banned protests, including those by groups like the Collectif Tchadien Contre la Vie Chère, a group of unemployed youth who organized marches and demonstrations to draw attention to the crisis and protest the high cost of living in the city. Even press briefings about planned marches and demonstrations were banned. Against this backdrop, the crowds assembled on city streets with gas canisters in tow could be read as an appeal to the state, or as a (still peaceful) demand to be heard and recognized by government officials.

Mitchell notes that not all efforts to hail the state are equally successful, in part because they are not equally visible (Mitchell 2014, 520). The gas lines formed in public places. Most of the gas stations and distribution outlets in N'Djamena are located along the main thoroughfares, and the lines were unavoidable to anyone circulating in the city. Reporters covered the gas lines and the images were diffused to nationwide audiences via television, local newspapers, and social media. The concentrated physical presence of energy consumers along city streets could not be coded as a protest, and therefore government officials could not disband the assemblies. Yet, because the gatherings were so visible and accessible, and generated images that were compelling and widely shared, they were effective at mobilizing public opinion and eliciting a response from officials who had previously been silent about the reasons for the shortage of cooking gas (see Parkinson 2012).

Government officials responded by trying to bring people into alignment with the state's project of energy sovereignty. Ministers and others pleaded with the public to be "calm" and to accept temporary hardship in exchange for the benefits of cleaner and, especially, domestic energy. At a gathering for International Women's Day, President Idriss Deby assured women that they need not worry about the supply of cooking gas. Shortly, he said, gas would be "permanently available," and at a lower price than what they were currently paying (Ngarndinon 2019). Government officials, with camera crews in tow, visited the refinery to check on the progress of repairs and report on this progress to the public. Following a visit in mid-March, an official from the Ministry of Oil and Energy declared that maintenance was already "48 percent complete" (ibid.). He also noted, while pleading for calm and patience, that it would be two more weeks before the refinery could produce domestic gas. This was the price of energy independence.

Government agencies also relaxed enforcement of the bans on charcoal and wood. Even before the crisis hit, state agents differentiated between *fraudeurs,* or those seeking to profit by smuggling large quantities of charcoal and wood into the city, and residents who bought, sold, and used illegal products in small quantities to survive. While many residents have made the conversion to gas, as the lines of people with gas canisters affirm, others cannot afford the initial outlay of cash required for the canisters and cooking equipment, despite government subsidies. While police and customs agents routinely stop and search vehicles crossing the border, enforcement efforts in the city itself are uneven and black markets for charcoal, wood, and petroleum products provide relief to the urban poor. Informal vendors, who are mostly women, sell small quantities of charcoal and wood in open-air markets and hawk water bottles filled with gasoline on city streets. In fact, despite the crackdowns at the border, the black market for all types of petroleum products has at times been large enough to influence government pricing and state subsidies for the refinery's products. During the shortage of LPG, street vendors sold charcoal and wood throughout the city, including at busy intersections in full view of enforcement agents.

Citizen responses to shortage have also renewed government interest in infrastructure projects, especially the construction of storage depots, which government agencies did not always treat as a high priority. The refinery in Djermaya has limited storage capacity for its products, as do the roughly 150 service stations scattered throughout the city (A. N. T. 2015). In 2014, President Deby scuttled plans to build oil and gas storage depots, announcing that his government would use the $100 million set aside for that purpose for other "more pressing" projects (Mitta 2018, 5). Yet, in the wake of the 2019 shortage, government agencies are once again pressing ahead with projects to build the depots. In addition to depots in the capital city, the government has announced plans for a network of regional depots with the capacity to store a two-month supply of critical products. Thus, despite bans on marches and demonstrations and the repression of media references to mass mobilizations, the gas lines, the symbolically resonant images of those lines, and citizens' efforts to hail the state as consumers of domestic gas have pushed the government to take action to ensure a reliable energy supply.

Shortage and the State

The crisis spurred by the shortage of domestic gas in the early months of 2019 was not the first time since the refinery opened that there had been a shortage of one or another of its products. Periodic ruptures in energy supply chains have wracked N'Djamena, despite the proximity of the refinery. Residents of the city complain that they almost instantaneously feel any slowdown or stoppage in production, and they recognize that their energy needs are now tightly dependent on the smooth operation of the refinery and the supply chains that link it to the city.

Periodic problems with the supply of energy lead to accusations of corruption and mismanagement. These accusations are sometimes leveled at intermediaries, such as marketers and distributors, who bypass the city to transport fuel from the refinery to the Central African Republic or other destinations where they can sell it for many times the legal price in Chad. Yet government officials are the most common targets of the accusations, especially given their role in aggressively steering the shift from charcoal and wood to gas. During the crisis in early 2019, when the SRN announced, tardily, that the refinery was undergoing general maintenance, city dwellers were particularly outraged that no steps had been taken to prepare for the shutdown and that the SRN had not anticipated the effects of taking the production of domestic gas off-line. They accused the government of mismanagement and a failure to communicate and of having a callous disregard for the challenges families faced in trying to meet their most basic needs (Absala 2019). Yet citizens' protests were not ultimately explosive.

Explanations for why this was the case have to contend with the fact that experiences of shortage are filtered through and complicated by the entanglement of transnational oil giants, whether private or state-owned, in energy production in Chad. Chad became an oil producer in 2003, when a major oil field development and pipeline project sponsored by ExxonMobil began exporting Chadian crude oil. The World Bank described the project as a model for development projects in the twenty-first century: it was expected to produce jobs and generate revenue for the country that could be invested in health, education, and infrastructure projects. For many people, the promise attached to this experimental project never materialized (Editorial Board of *Le potentiel* 2019). Most conspicuously, Chadians continued to depend on imported energy and be plagued by energy shortages and blackouts. The crude oil that came out of the fields in the south of the country was low quality; it was heavy and viscous and had high levels of calcium and acids, which meant that it had to be processed in specially equipped refineries (Leonard 2016). It also meant that Chadians lived for nearly a decade with the paradox of being among the largest oil-producing countries in Africa while remaining completely dependent on imported oil.

The construction of a refinery that would process domestic oil was therefore welcome news. Newspaper headlines such as "The refinery at Djermaya: A dream become a reality" (Takadji 2011) and "The refinery at Djermaya: For energy sovereignty" (Dokalyo 2012, 14) (my translations) reflected the nationalist sentiment that attached to the project. One editorial writer described the refinery project as "incontestably the most beautiful fruit of the cooperation between China and Chad" (Dokalyo 2012, 14, my translation); others also welcomed it as an opportunity for Chadians to finally benefit directly from their own natural resources. The refinery would allow Chad to reduce imports and even export its own petroleum products to neighboring countries. It was expected to create jobs and secondary industries that would employ even more people. There were plans for the development of an industrial corridor, with factories devoted to the production of plastic sacks, water bottles, and PVC (Kodé 2009). The refinery was also supposed to produce as much as twenty megawatts of electricity for N'Djamena, reducing the cost to consumers and relieving pressure on the national electricity company, which was unable to keep up with demand.

Yet, as the majority shareholder, the CNPC controlled the refinery and its operations, and this complicated the government's claims about energy sovereignty. Periodic disputes over the pricing of products and the management of the refinery shut down operations, creating new sources of instability in supply. In fact, in the fall of 2018, about five months before the refinery's operators halted the production of domestic gas to perform routine maintenance on the LPG production line, the city had been paralyzed by another energy crisis. Unlike most ruptures in supply, this one encompassed nearly all of the refinery's products. For ten days, operations at the refinery ground to a halt, plunging the capital into a full-scale energy crisis. While some of the details of the crisis and the events that precipitated it remain murky, the outlines of the dispute between officials at the SHT and the CNPC that led to the shutdown have since emerged in a series of investigative reports.

The problem began when the assistant director of the plant, the son of President Deby, made a number of high-level appointments at the refinery without the consent of the director, who was in China when they were announced. This included the appointment of executives to oversee the finances of the refinery and external affairs. Senior executives representing the CNPC pointed out that the appointments violated the terms of their contract with the Chadian government, and they sought to mediate the dispute with their Chadian counterparts. In the interim, however, CNPC officials withheld the salaries of Chadian workers at the refinery while continuing to pay expatriate employees, most of whom were Chinese (Mallam 2018). In response, a group of Chadian workers held the CNPC officials hostage, refusing to let them return to their residential quarters, located not far from the plant, until they reinstated workers' salaries.

From public accounts of the incident, it is unclear when or how the workers eventually freed their Chinese counterparts, but before CNPC staff would return to the refinery, they demanded additional security and the right to file legal claims against their captors. During the standoff, the automated systems used to charge finished products into tanker trucks remained locked, halting the delivery of all refined petroleum products to the city. The Chadian minister of oil and energy and the Chinese ambassador to Chad negotiated an end to the standoff, but not before the price of gasoline rose to more than three times the legal price in some parts of the city.

Despite the difficulties caused by the shutdown, residents of the city were sympathetic to workers at the refinery, including those who contributed to the shutdown by holding their Chinese counterparts hostage (Mallam 2018) and employees of the publicly funded SHT, who residents also described as corrupt and incompetent. Local media accounts highlighted the grit and resourcefulness of workers who eventually found ways to bypass the locked charging systems for regular and premium gasoline. The workers were able to supply some gasoline to the city by manually pumping those products into tanker trucks, even if they could not find workarounds for domestic gas or jet fuel (*Le progrès* 2018). People even expressed support for employees of the SHT, including members of the president's family, who generated the crisis by making the appointments. Newspapers, including those typically critical of the regime, described the appointments as "bring[ing] balance" to the joint venture with the Chinese, who sought to exert "total control" over the refinery and whose perceived advantage in the partnership, prior to the appointments, was described as "prejudicial" to the interests of Chadians (A. B. 2018). Triumphant headlines, such as "Chad expels Xu Zhihong" (Mallam 2018) and "Boukar Michel faces the Chinese" (A. B. 2018) (my translations), celebrated the concessions exacted by the Chadian minister of oil and energy. According to media reports, in the wake of the crisis all machines at the refinery would be "co-piloted" by Chinese and Chadian workers, and the officials nominated by the president's son would remain in their posts. Meanwhile, Chinese officials had to stand by "impotently" and watch as their director, Xu Zhihong, was expelled from the country.

Shortage generates anger and frustration as well as accusations about government corruption and incompetence. But shortage is also viewed through the prism of foreign and corporate domination of oil and gas production, under which Chadians remain dependent on others to pay taxes and royalties, unlock charging systems, or supply secret codes. Energy consumers historicize government actions, seeing those actions as evidence of a repressive and callous regime, but at the same time as a manifestation of the continued dependence of the country on exploitative relations with private capital or emerging superpowers. These dual sources of friction may be one reason why the crisis brought about by the shortage of domestic gas in the early months of 2019 was not, ultimately, "explosive" and government pleas for "patience" prevailed. Shortage and energy independence emerge in a context mediated by greedy government officials who make life difficult and threaten poor people with jail time and fines, but also by the actions of those attached to ExxonMobil, the World Bank, and the Chinese state, who can stop production lines, cut workers' salaries, lock charging systems, and thwart dreams of energy sovereignty.

The opening of the refinery at Djermaya heralded a long-awaited era of energy sovereignty in Chad. Yet nearly a decade later, shortage and instability in the energy supply persist. In an era of domestic energy production, shortage localizes the state and makes it visible and vulnerable in new ways.

In this chapter I have shown how people were able to "hail the state," not through protests and demonstrations, but by standing in gas lines throughout the city during a recent shortage of LPG. Public assemblies and the circulated images of energy consumers drew responses from the state. Government officials visited the refineries and provided citizens with progress updates. They took a nuanced approach to the enforcement of clean energy policies by focusing on large-scale importers of banned products while allowing the urban poor to continue buying and selling illicit products in small quantities. They also revived plans to build storage depots in anticipation of future crises. This latter strategy, in particular, is an admission that shortage will be an ongoing problem, and that the era of energy sovereignty will entail managing the crises caused by ruptures in supply, but not eliminating them.

Ruptures in the supply of gas beget discursive constructions of state agents as corrupt, inept, disorganized, indifferent, and even callous. This is a powerful and dangerous narrative and one that demonstrates how the regime has become newly vulnerable in an era of nationalized energy provision. The rupture in the supply of LPG in early 2019 was dangerous, but it was not, ultimately, explosive. This is, at least in part, because the explosive potential of shortage is tempered by Chad's history with transnational oil and gas companies that threaten energy sovereignty by controlling access to revenue streams, employment, technical knowledge about how to operate pumps, gauges, and charging systems, and energy itself.

References

A. N. T. 2015. "Des inquiétudes sur la livraison des produits pétroliers de Djermaya: La raffinerie a un trop-plein de gasoil." *Le progrès* (N'Djamena), 4 December, 1, 3.

———. 2018a. "L'offre d'un produit pétrolier devient insuffisante alors que la raffinerie est en marche: Le gaz domestique se raréfie à N'Djamena." *Le progrès* (N'Djamena), 4 February, 1, 3.

———. 2018b. "Le pétrole offre de nouvelles opportunités: Un parc industriel a Djermaya et une autre raffinerie a Sedigui." *Le progrès* (N'Djamena), 11 September, 1, 3.

A. N. T. and T. K. 2018. "Faute de fagot, le fruit du doum renchérit: Des ménages préparent avec des excréments de bovins." *Le progrès* (N'Djamena), 30 April, 1, 6.

Absala, Adoum. 2019. "Facebook, Twitter, WhatsApp." *Le visionnaire* (N'Djamena), 21–27 March, 7.

Adoum, A. 2009. "La crise énergétique défie les efforts." *Le progrès* (N'Djamena), special edition, 13.

Ali, H. M. 2018. "1 et 3 mois pour abandonner les énergies domestiques traditionnelles: L'interdiction du bois et du charbon se durcit, les habitants de grandes villes devront utiliser le gaz, le réchaud Toumaï. . . ." *Le progrès* (N'Djamena), 16 April, 1, 3.

Bambé, Naygotimti. 2018. "Interdiction de bois-énergie: Une décision préjudiciable pour les populations." *Tchad et culture* no. 366 (N'Djamena), April, 2–3.

Chatterjee, Partha. 2004. *The Politics of the Governed: Reflections on Popular Politics in Most of the World.* New York: Columbia University Press.

Das, Veena, and Deborah Poole. 2004. "State and Its Margins: Comparative Ethnographies." In *Anthropology in the Margins of the State,* edited by Veena Das and Deborah Poole, 3–33. Sante Fe, NM: School of American Research Press.

Dokalyo, Alphonse. 2012. "La raffinerie de Djermaya: Pour la souveraineté énergétique." *Tchad et culture,* no. 312 (N'Djamena), December, 14–15.

Editorial Board of *Le temps.* 2009. "Bluffs et saupoudrages." *Le temps* (N'Djamena), 8–14 July, 4.

Editorial Board of *L'observateur.* 2019. "La gazomania." *L'observateur* (N'Djamena), 20–27 March, 1, 3.

Editorial Board of *Le potentiel.* 2019. "Les séquelles du pétrole!" *Le potentiel* (N'Djamena), 28 March–7 April, 2.

Gupta, Akhil. 1995. "Blurred Boundaries: The Discourse of Corruption, the Culture of Politics, and the Imagined State." *American Ethnologist* 22 (2): 375–402.

———. 2012. *Red Tape: Bureaucracy, Structural Violence, and Poverty in India.* Durham, NC: Duke University Press.

Ibedou, M. N. A. 2019. "Facebook, Twitter, WhatsApp: Le spectacle est insoutenable." *Le visionnaire* (N'Djamena), 21–27 March, 7.

Jonnalagadda, Indivar. 2018. "Citizenship as a Communicative Effect." *Signs and Society* 6 (3): 531–57.

Kodé, K. G. 2009. "C'est parti pour le pétrole du Chari Baguirmi." *Le temps* (N'Djamena), 8–14 July, 3.

Leonard, Lori. 2016. *Life in the Time of Oil: A Pipeline and Poverty in Chad.* Bloomington: Indiana University Press.

Leonard, Lori, and Siba N. Grovogui, eds. 2017. *Governance in the Extractive Industries: Power, Cultural Politics, and Regulation.* London: Routledge.

Le progrès. 2018. "La raffinerie livre à nouveau du gaz: Un accord est trouvé entre Tchadiens et Chinois." *Le progrès* (N'Djamena), 24 September, 1, 5.

Mallam, J. 2018. "Le Tchad expulse Xu Zhihong." *La voix* (N'Djamena), 25 September–2 October, 5–6.

———. 2019. "Raffinerie de Djarmaya: Voici comment la pénurie du gaz est arrivée." *La voix* (N'Djamena), 9 April, 1, 6.

Mitchell, Lisa. 2014. "The Visual Turn in Political Anthropology and the Mediation of Political Practice in Contemporary India." *South Asia: Journal of South Asian Studies* 37 (3): 515–40.

———. 2018. "Civility and Collective Action: Soft Speech, Loud Roars, and the Politics of Recognition." *Anthropological Theory* 18 (2–3): 217–47.

Ministère des Finances, de l'Économie et du Plan. 2006. *Tchad, profil de pauvreté: Deuxième enquête sur la consommation et le secteur informel au Tchad–ECOSIT2.* N'Djamena, Chad: Ministère des Finances, de l'Économie et du Plan.

Mitta, D. 2018. "Garantie de disponibilité et d'unicité des prix du carburant: Le Tchad construit son 1er dépôt pétrolier." *Le progrès* (N'Djamena), 5 April, 1, 5.

Ngarndinon, Madjissembaye. 2019. "Pénurie du gaz butane: La souffrance pour au moins deux semaines encore." *Abba Garde* (N'Djamena), 20–30 March, 5.

Parkinson, John. 2012. *Democracy and Public Space: The Physical Sites of Democratic Performance.* Oxford: Oxford University Press.

T. K. and A. Djimrangar. 2018. "Prévention collective de la dégradation de la nature: Un nouveau dispositif pour protéger l'environnement." *Le progrès* (N'Djamena), 18 July, 3.

Takadji, Edouard. 2011. "Un rêve devenu réalité." *L'observateur* (N'Djamena), 18 July, 4–5.

PART THREE

Disciplinarity, Subjectivity, and Violence

SEVEN

Politics of Patience

Acceptance, Agency, and Compliance in Rwanda

ROSE LØVGREN

DURING MY ATTEMPTED FIELDWORK IN 2016, I HAD A conversation with a middle-aged man, living in a rural area in Rwanda, who was talking about his fear of arrest and death from representatives of the local military chapter. He did not talk about a specific crime he had committed, but about his view that they could always find motivation for an arrest. "It is very easy to lose your life in Rwanda," he told me. When he saw that I furrowed my brows with worry, he gave me a big smile and said, "But don't be afraid!" He had been talking for some time about his view of the many reasons to be afraid, and I found it hard to think that he saw no basis for fear. Rather, I interpreted his instruction as motivated by a concern that he had told me more than I, as a delicate European, could handle. Moreover, we were preparing to walk out into the public sphere, and I also understood his instruction as an encouragement for me to bring my emotions under control, so we would not attract undesired attention.

This chapter sets out to characterize certain forms of political sub-jectivity in Rwanda. By political subjectivity, I mean how people relate to power and authority, as well as the role played by structures of power in forming subjective experiences (Krause and Schramm 2011). I term the practices relating to these expressions of subjectivity "politics of patience" because my analysis centers on compliance and the role played by patience and acceptance in these practices. Political subjectivity in Rwanda is a highly disputed topic because it relates to the operations of the country's current government, which are a source of great conflict among scholars, international development institutions, and the government itself (Pottier 2002; Beswick 2010; Straus and Waldorf 2011; Booth and Golooba-Mutebi 2012). The current government in Rwanda is led by the Rwanda Patriotic Front (RPF), which has been in power since its military branch overthrew the previous government in 1994, following several years of armed conflict and a devastating genocide. This makes it the longest-sitting government since the country's independence in 1962. The RPF government has been characterized as highly effective in enforcing its policies and "determined to the point of ruthlessness" (Booth and Golooba-Mutebi 2012, 15). In this context of coercive governance, some observers have commented on what they perceive to be "the extremely low level of resistance or challenge that he [President Paul Kagame] faces from the Rwandan population" (Marriage 2016, 46). Political culture in Rwanda has been analyzed with an emphasis on "lack of agency" (Stys 2012, 717), "self-policing" (Goodfellow 2013, 436), "uncritical obedience" (Nzahabwanayo, Horsthemke, and Mathebula 2017, 242), and an ancient Rwandan tradition of "*irivuze umwami*" ("what[ever] the king said"; see Mulindahabi 2015, 172).

These characterizations have not sat well with a number of ethnographers, who in response have highlighted the subtleties of resistance, especially among Rwanda's rural population (Huggins 2009; Thomson 2013; Ingelaere 2014; Van Damme, Ansoms, and Baret 2014; Breed 2015; Ansoms and Cioffo 2016; Jessee 2017; Berry 2017). James Scott's (1990, 2000) concepts of "weapons of the weak" and discreet resistance in the space between the public and the hidden transcripts have been especially popular. Scott's "public transcript" is defined as "the *self*-portrait of dominant elites as they would have themselves seen" (2007, 200, emphasis in original). The "hidden transcript" is then understood as an offstage situation "where subordinates may gather outside the intimidating gaze of power [and] a sharply dissonant political culture is possible" (Scott 2007, 201). Scott's ideas have provided a useful point of departure for analyzing the delicate balance undertaken by those who oppose, for example, Rwanda's reconciliation policies, as they seek out ways to express their dissent without suffering arrest, imprisonment, or death (Thomson 2013).

However, this chapter is inspired by critiques of analytical lenses that "romanticize resistance" (Abu-Lughod 1990, 42). Both those who lament the lack of resistance and those who argue that it is present in the hidden transcript seem to be working within a binary understanding of how subjects relate to power (Mahmood 2011): that is, characterizing subjects as either resisting or being passively subjected to power. In paying special attention to practices of compliance, I do not deny the existence in Rwanda of subtle expressions of resistance or more explicitly expressed acts of resistance. Indeed, acts of covert and overt resistance are carried out by a variety of actors in Rwanda (see Uvin 1998; Pells 2011; Purdeková 2015; Shearer 2015).

While I understand the motivation of wanting to honor brave resisters who, for example, speak openly on the radio about the injustices of agricultural policies (Sundaram 2016), and of pointing out the whispers of dissent expressed through the clever use of double connotations (de Lame 2004; Ingelaere 2010a; Thomson 2013; Purdeková 2016), I argue that we should be more wary of prioritizing these expressions of political subjectivity. There is, I argue, an implicit hierarchical ranking of subject performance entailed in our special attention to resistance. By ignoring practices of compliance or insisting that they secretly reflect resistance, our analyses risk foreclosing "certain questions about the workings of power" (Abu-Lughod 1990, 42). The aim of this chapter is to open up a space for questions related to political subjectivity that are currently undertheorized—specifically, political subjectivity expressed in patience, acceptance, and compliance, as well as the agency enacted in these attitudes.

The chapter proceeds by first describing my methodological approach and presenting contextual information about the following discussions. Afterward, I analyze a story where one of my respondents, whom I will refer to as Gilles, argued for the value of acceptance and patience.[1] The rest of the chapter explores the themes the story engages. I relate Gilles's view of acceptance as a matter of life and death to the perspectives of some of my other respondents who have described being calm as a method to survive extreme hardships. To analyze the agency expressed in these attitudes, I use Seyla Benhabib's "narrative model" (1999, 337) and argue in favor of understanding acceptance as one way to express agency. Moreover, Gilles describes a tense form of patience that responds to real or imagined provocations from others in authority positions, which I relate to cultural practices of testing. Tying these different threads together at the end of the chapter, I draw on Ashis Nandy's theorizing of fragmented and shifting selves with "a certain permeability of boundaries" (1983, 107) to characterize the forms of political subjectivity involved in politics of patience.

Methodology and Background

The approach of this chapter is to analyze a set of different situations in which I, in a research capacity, have encountered practices of patience, acceptance, and compliance in Rwanda. These situations arose during my three months of research about the Iwawa Rehabilitation Center for my master's degree in 2013–14 and my ten months of attempted continuation of this research for my PhD in 2015–16, which ended in deportation. While these situations stand alone, I argue that they are telling in regard to larger stories of politics of patience. That is, I analyze these singular instances

FIGURE 1. Rwandan youth at a center on Iwawa Island, west of Rwanda's capital
capital, Kigali. Photo by James Akena/Reuters.

with a view to "extract the general from the unique" (Burawoy 1998, 5).
The methodological approach is not to move from empirical material to
theory by way of generalization. Rather, I approach my empirical material
with an explicit theoretical intention of highlighting different expressions
of political subjectivity than the ones captured in frameworks emphasizing
resistance. In this way, when I claim to be telling a larger story about politics of patience, the intention is not to portray political culture in Rwanda
as such. The larger story coexists with multiple other ways in which people
relate to power and authority in Rwanda.

I contextualize these singular situations using statistics, media reports,
and ethnographic arguments based on the fieldwork of other researchers
working in Rwanda. The chapter does not attempt to present a full picture
of life in the contexts encountered, nor to argue that patience and acceptance mean the same things to these differently situated people. It focuses
on analyzing the themes of patience and acceptance as I encountered them
in these situations and on exploring their uses, meanings, and nuances.
People who are patient and accepting in one context may be carrying out
overt resistance in another. What this chapter intends is to characterize the
political work of patience without claiming to represent the relations of my
respondents to power overall.

For the discussions that follow, two sets of background information
are relevant. The first is about the Iwawa Rehabilitation Center, which is

located on Iwawa Island in Lake Kivu. It holds male youth termed "delin-quent" (National Rehabilitation Service 2018) who are detained for periods of one to three years and focuses on "moral rehabilitation" and vocational skills training. Moral rehabilitation consists of military training without weapons and civic education about Rwanda's history and the societal values promoted by the RPF. Many state officials emphasize the center's role in combating drug abuse, but arrests largely target young men "loitering" on the streets. In my interviews with graduates from the center, the island fea-tures as a place strongly associated with death (Løvgren and Turner 2019): death from beatings by the military commanders or other trainees, death from starvation or untreated diseases, and death from suicide.

The second set of background information concerns ethnicity in Rwanda. There have historically been three ethnic groups in Rwanda: Hutu, Tutsi, and Twa. No reliable statistics on the size of each group exist (Uvin 2002), but Hutu make up the majority, followed by a smaller group of Tutsi, and finally Twa, who are estimated to make up around 1 percent of the population (Des Forges 1999, 37). Extremist Hutu held power in Rwanda from the late 1950s to 1994, when the Hutu-led government organized the genocide in which an estimated five to eight hundred thousand Tutsi, as well as Hutu and Twa opposing the killing campaigns, were murdered (Des Forges 1999; Straus 2008). The genocide ended when the government was overthrown by the RPF, mainly comprised of Tutsi from the Ugandan diaspora (Purdeková, Reyntjens, and Wilén 2018), in July 1994. On their way to seizing power and in the years following the genocide, RPF troops are estimated to have killed three to four hundred thousand Hutu as part of military battles and in revenge missions (Davenport and Stam 2009). In today's Rwanda, it is officially illegal to refer to ethnic identities, but ethnic tensions are rife, especially because a number of RPF policies discriminate against Hutu or complicate life in rural areas, where Hutu make up the majority of the population (Hilker 2009; Ingelaere 2010b; Ansoms 2013; Chakravarty 2016).

Encouraging Acceptance

In early 2016, a young man in his twenties, Gilles, was trying to explain a Kinyarwanda concept of gratitude and debt to me, and the conversation turned to intergenerational conflicts over what a son owes his father or his guardians. He was currently worried about the safety of one of his friends, Damian, because of an inheritance dispute. As the story was related to me, Damian had lost his parents in the 1994 genocide and had been brought up by his uncle. According to Gilles, the uncle had been complaining about the expenses of raising Damian all through his childhood and constantly reminded the child that he was going out of his way to raise him although he was not his son. But as Damian was now growing older, he began to discover that his parents had owned many acres of land before their death, which, according to Rwandan inheritance laws and traditions, would mean that the land belonged to him (Musahara and Huggins 2005). He began to make trips out to the rural area where this land was supposedly located to make inquiries among the local population about which acreage belonged to his parents. Every time he came home from such a trip, however, he became violently ill, with a high fever and convulsive vomiting. Damian was being poisoned by someone working with his uncle, Gilles told me.

Intergenerational conflicts over land and resources are not infrequently sources of violence in Rwanda. Rwanda is densely populated and has seen several mass migrations, first out of and subsequently into the country, in relation to the violent conflicts and the genocide taking place since 1959. Significantly, in recent years Rwanda has undergone extensive political land reform, effectively redistributing land from smallholders to large-scale farmers, following the logic that the latter can better utilize and invest in the land (Newbury 2011; Huggins 2014). Given that an estimated 90 percent of the population rely on agriculture for survival (Ingelaere 2014), land disputes can easily turn into life-and-death conflicts and poisonings are often suspected to be the cause of death (Shyaka Mugabe 2007).[2]

Gilles now repeated to me the advice he had given Damian: he had told him to let the issue be. There was no reason to risk his life over something that might not amount to anything, given that many people in the family—not just his uncle—might try to obstruct him from getting the land. "You are not the only orphan who suffered from this genocide, and you are definitely not the one who suffered the most," he told me, to illustrate how the conversation had gone.[3] "You still have a chance to build something from scratch, but if you lose your life, you have nothing." I nodded in agreement. The story reminded me of many other situations and stories I have encountered as part of my research and my personal life in Rwanda, where people in precarious negotiations assess the different threats to their life. I felt in the situation that Gilles was right to caution his friend to accept the situation and I interjected that the friend should also be careful that his uncle did not have him arrested by the police in an effort to get rid of him. To this, Gilles responded enthusiastically, "Yes! And you know, they [elder relatives] like to provoke us to do something that gives them a reason to have us arrested. They may keep insulting you, hoping that you will finally explode."

In analyzing the story related by Gilles and our discussion of it, I follow Saba Mahmood in emphasizing how "agentival capacity is entailed not only in those acts that resist norms but also in the multiple ways in which one inhabits norms" (Mahmood 2011, 15). By the time Gilles told me this story, I had come to share his perspective that it was likely life-threatening for a young man to be in a conflict over land with his uncle, and his normative assessment that continuing the conflict was not worth such a risk. By adding my own fear that the uncle might work with the police to have him arrested for a made-up offense, he added his understanding of what was at stake when he and other young men like him were in conflict with older authority figures: that "the authorities" like to test them. Bert Ingelaere (2014), Molly Sundberg (2016), and Andrea Purdeková (2016) have in different ways analyzed how, in Rwanda, the concept of "authorities" (Ingelaere 2014, 215) is used to cover a range of different representatives of state power. In these analyses, due to the pervasive presence of state infrastructure in almost all aspects of life, authority figures appear as a diffuse group of people officially or unofficially connected to or collaborating with the state (Purdeková 2016; Sundberg 2016). This understanding of authority resembles the usages of my respondents, and I will continue to use it this way throughout the chapter.

When Gilles advised Damian to accept his loss of inheritance and let the issue be, he first emphasized that the likely alternative was losing his life. In this case, the loss of life was related to a concrete physical threat from poisoning. But in many of my other research encounters with acceptance, it has been described with an emphasis on how people's mental and emotional state can determine their survival. My conversation partners in Rwanda have often told me that they cannot "afford" an emotional reaction.

FIGURE 2. Rwandan youth attend a class at Iwawa Island, west of Rwanda's capital Kigali. Photo by James Akena/Reuters.

In my research concerning life on Iwawa Island, not accepting the situation of living under a constant threat of death by bringing one's emotions fully under control was described as making a person prone to disease and starvation (Løvgren 2018).

In these narratives, accepting your proximity to death, not delving into the wrongness of your arrest and your current mistreatment, secures your survival by giving you the mental peace and energy to keep overcoming threats to your life. Within the social norms that frame this form of acceptance, emotions are seen as having powerful and potentially dangerous effects on the subject. In her analysis of "truth telling" as a reconciliation policy in Rwanda, Karen Brounéus (2010) argues that such an approach to emotions is a common part of posttraumatic stress disorder (PTSD).[4] Her argument, linking PTSD to the perception of strong emotions as dangerous, seems highly relevant to analyses of how power and violence shape how we experience the world. My respondents have often cautioned me against reacting to injustice with strong negative emotions, arguing exactly that it is a dangerous mental state to be in. Among other reasons, I was advised that it would make me lose weight and might cause me to go fully crazy. In some ethnographic analyses, full compliance has been described as effacing a person's "subjectivity and opinions" (Thomson 2011, 453). I propose instead to relocate the understanding of both subjectivity and agency as capacities that can also be expressed through composure and self-control. In the coming section, I turn my attention to the agency expressed in what may be termed "radical acceptance"—acceptance that entails not only obeying orders, but also feeling calm in doing so.

Narrative Agency

To analyze the agency in radical acceptance, I engage Benhabib's concept of "narrative agency." Narrative agency is expressed in the ability to narrate, but not through a commitment to the same specific story over time. As Benhabib puts it, "it is not what the story is about that matters but, rather, one's ability to keep telling a story about who one is" (1999, 347). In the narratives of my respondents from Iwawa, one of the attitudes reflected was that when there is nothing more to do to influence a life-threatening situation, the only remaining course of action is to control how you react to it emotionally. Acceptance, in this light, can be read as a narrative maneuver, a way to take control of how you narrate your situation to yourself. Benhabib's insistence that the content of the story is not central opens up space for contradictions in the narrative. Young men who had been sent to Iwawa and who explained to me that they had been wrongfully arrested, but chose to accept their situation, may be seen as having conflicting narrative elements in their story: How can one think one has been wrongfully arrested and still accept it? Here, I follow Benhabib in arguing that even if the content of the story is full of contradictions and/or illustrates a commitment to the subject's subordination, the capacity to tell a story remains. The continued capacity for storytelling also opens up for the possibility of changing that story when one's situation changes (Benhabib 1999).

Here again, I want to contrast this argument with how compliance has been understood in other ethnographic characterizations of political culture in Rwanda. Analyzing the policy of national unity in Rwanda, Susan Thomson writes, "Obedience to the dictates of the policy . . . is frequently tactical, rather than sincere" (Thomson 2011, 439). Similar characterizations include "surface-level consent" (Purdeková 2015, 127) and a view of practices of compliance in Rwanda as defined by "resentment toward the RPF state" (Chakravarty 2016, 262).

Patience in Testing

Understanding the political meanings of patience and acceptance requires paying attention to the cultural and political practices of *testing* in Rwanda. Testing is a widespread practice in Rwandan culture, and how a person responds to testing is commonly used to determine her or his dignity, command of respect, and social status. Kinyarwanda, with its many ambiguities and double meanings, is used both socially and politically as a test of a person's intelligence, cunning, and composure. Testing by way of the language usually forms part of the negotiation of dowry at wedding ceremonies, and is a common form of entertainment in daily conversations between Rwandans (Adekunle 2007, 97–114; Rusagara 2009, 112–77; Uwanziga 2015).

Discussing the political meaning of this sort of testing, Bert Ingelaere suggests that "an understanding of the cultural conception of *ubwenge* is necessary to fully appreciate the nature of [Rwandans'] interactions and communication. This complex notion incorporates a range of elements, though in the broadest sense, it refers to *a valorization of the kind of intelligence that results in public self-control*" (Ingelaere 2010a, 53–54, emphasis added). Ingelaere ties this cultural conception to the observation (also expressed in de Lame 2004, 303) that what may appear to be moments or points of consensus among "ordinary Rwandans" (Ingelaere 2010a, 50) should not necessarily be taken as actual consensus in a straightforward sense. Arguing from the perspective of those *subjected to* state power, Ingelaere states that "the Rwandan system of communication was (and is) esoteric: statements reveal and conceal at the same time" (ibid., 54). While I agree with these analyses, I would maintain that they generally pay too little attention to the use of ubwenge by those who *yield* power. Analyses that are based on Scott's division between the elite's public transcripts and the subtle weapons of the weak have a tendency to focus on the cunning of those who are subject to power while ignoring the deceitful actions taken by people in power. In the Rwandan context, this results in a failure to pay attention to how those in positions of authority use, or are imagined to use, ubwenge. In my own analysis of such practices, I follow Andrea Grant's focus on the RPF state's "indirect, coded, disingenuous, and cryptic means to police its citizens" (2015, 30). In Gilles's story about Damien and especially in his comments, those with authority work to reveal and conceal the "real" meaning of what is going on. As he described it, older relatives in conflict with younger men deliberately try to provoke them into reacting with aggression in order to use their aggression as an excuse to have them arrested. In this context, a response of vigilant patience, expressed through acceptance and compliance, is framed as a refusal to be arrested, punished, and/or killed with impunity.

In 2013, Bosco, an older man living in a rural area of Rwanda, explained his understanding of Rwanda's politics in a way that shares Gilles's valorization of patience. Bosco is Hutu, and he was telling me about one of his friends, also Hutu, who had gone to prison for promoting "genocide ideology." Genocide ideology, a criminal concept invented by the RPF, refers to ideas that resemble those of the 1994 genocidal regime and thus might provide breeding ground for a new genocide (Republic of Rwanda 2006; Waldorf 2011; Thomson 2011). His friend had been sent to prison, Bosco claimed, for what he had said during that year's public commemoration of the genocide, when the crowd had been forced by local officials to hold a debate about the dangers of genocide. Upon being encouraged to speak, the friend had said that in 1994 there were already existing hostilities in Rwandan society between Tutsi and Hutu, and that the genocide was a result not only of the former government's actions, but also of these hostile sentiments. This statement was taken as an expression of genocidal ideology and the friend was arrested and ended up prison. Bosco, however, explained to me that this statement, considered a crime in 2013, had actually been fed to the people by local officials in the commemoration events held in 2012. That is, this view of the genocide had changed from being mandatory to being a crime. In Bosco's understanding, local officials had done this deliberately. The explanation's changing status was an act of cunning on the part of the authorities, as part of a strategy to increase the number of Hutu arrested for genocide ideology. Viewed in this way, the authorities, too, use ubwenge—but to trick people into making themselves vulnerable to arrest. The best thing for Hutu to do, Bosco argued, was to try to remain silent about these issues in public, and not be tempted by the local officials' sneaky encouragements to speak.

This framing of silence, I argue, is different from Scott's view of "silences" as "disguise" (Scott 1990, 138). Bosco was not describing his own silence as a means to disguise his true beliefs. His silence was a tactical response to his sense of the impossibility of knowing what the mandatory explanation of the genocide was going to be this year. Even if he had wanted to give an acceptable answer to questions about the genocide asked during the commemoration, he felt that he could not possibly succeed in answering them "correctly." That is, his silence was a means to avoid putting himself in a situation in which there would, in fact, be no way for him to actually choose and adopt a disguise. This is not to say that silence is never disguise, but to call attention to other forms of political subjectivity and of situated response expressed through silence.

RPF has often been accused of only accepting its one truth about the genocide in 1994 and punishing every expression of dissent from this story (Davenport and Stam 2009; Ingelaere 2010a; Waldorf 2011; Reyntjens 2015; Jessee 2017; Benda 2018). But while there are many stories about the genocide that are indisputably forbidden to mention in Rwanda—for instance, although RPF accounts of the genocide vary, the high number of Hutu killed by RPF troops is always denied—what is allowed is less clear. Written and verbal statements about the genocide by members of the RPF often carry contradictions and incoherencies.[5] With respect to the issue in dispute in Bosco's story, the RPF has via many outlets argued that the genocide was orchestrated by the former government and that Rwandans as a people naturally love each other—they just needed the right government (Ingelaere 2010a; Mulindahabi 2015; Sundberg 2016). But RPF has also undertaken a range of political initiatives based on the premise that Hutu need to be reeducated because they have genocidal sentiments, including Hutu born after 1994 (Mgbako 2005; Thomson 2011; Blackie and Hitchcott 2018), a viewpoint that seems to be in line with what allegedly sent Bosco's friend to prison.[6] Lars Waldorf has noted in regard to this tension that RPF's campaigns against genocide ideology illustrate the conflict between its reconciliation policies (which deny the role of ethnicity) and its battle against genocide negationism (which emphasize ethnicity) (Waldorf 2011; see also Stys 2012; Purdeková 2015). The impossibility of being secure against accusations of genocide ideology, which is related to the crime of "ethnic divisionism" (Thomson 2013, 13), is highlighted in a report by the organization Human Rights Watch: "When asked to define 'divisionism,' not one judge interviewed by Human Rights Watch researchers was able to do so, despite each having adjudicated and convicted defendants on divisionism charges. Judicial decisions have thus far failed to settle the meaning and scope of this crime." (Human Rights Watch 2008, 34). These practices by state representatives amount to a blurring of illegality. It is in effect impossible to know in advance whether a given statement will cross the lines for what is sayable about Rwanda's history of violence.

Where Bosco read the change in acceptable explanations by local officials as their deliberate use of ubwenge, my thoughts go to the insecurity over and constantly changing demands of their jobs. It is not unthinkable to me that local authorities in areas with many Hutu would, as Bosco suggested, be required to arrest a certain number of Hutus for whatever offense they could come up with. The same topic came up in my research concerning Iwawa, where there seemed to be geographical differences with respect to what caused young men to be arrested. That is, in districts with big Hutu populations, some of the graduates from Iwawa described having been arrested while carrying their identity card on their way to work or church and not in the process of committing any illegal offense. Such respondents repeatedly said that, in their understanding, you could be arrested without matching the description of "delinquency" because the police were operating with a quota system that pressured them into maintaining high numbers of arrests in these areas.

Police officers and other local authorities may also be overzealous in arresting people as a response to their own sense of ubiquitous threat. Being a public servant in Rwanda is a very vulnerable position, and from village level to government ministers, "the authorities" regularly lose their jobs, are imprisoned, or killed. At times, public servants may lose their jobs because they fail to deliver on various development or security objectives, but other firings or arrests receive vague public justifications (Times Reporter 2011; Rwembeho 2012; Ingelaere 2014; Kwibuka 2016; Times Reporter 2016), especially when it comes to prominent members of the cabinet (Himbara 2018; Newz Post 2018; Verhoeven 2012).

The Always Wrong Body

In analyzing a political situation with unclear and constantly changing rules, a parallel may be drawn to the production of bodies taking place in military camps. In my research on military training in civic education, young men have given examples of military commanders punishing trainees for being too short, for being too tall, for not being strong, and for being strong. In the initial phases of military training, one young man was said to have been beaten with a stick by a commander asking him why he was so short. Upon seeing a very tall man, the same commander was said to have told this man to stoop. The commander reportedly held his hand by the top of his own head, telling the tall man that he did not want to see one centimeter stick above his height. As a group, the trainees were punished for being too weak and were made to do drills to get stronger. One trainee was stronger than the rest, which also seemed to provoke the commander. A young man laughingly quoted the commander as saying, "So you like doing push-ups? You can do push-ups for the rest of the day!"

This aspect of military training is not unique to Rwanda (Eisenhart 1975, 13; Samimian-Darash 2013, 47). Military training commonly consists of routinized and highly structured activities (Purdeková 2015, 197; Sundberg 2016, 52), but there is also an element of unpredictability in the military experience during the establishment of authority. Wayne Eisenhart describes how efforts to secure obedience in the military camp entailed that a recruit who performed "to the best of his ability and kept his mouth shut [was still] beaten and terrorized" and told by the commander, "You can't hack it" (1975, 15).

Descriptions of the state as hard to decipher feature in many ethnographic accounts, wherein people describe the Rwandan state as "unpredictable" (Sundberg 2016, 211) and their relationship with it as marked by "extreme uncertainty" (Chakravarty 2016, 182). Grant analyzes contrasting stories of being incapable of having the correct body, examining two different arrests of young men from Kigali. One explains his arrest as related to being "too Hutu" (Grant 2015, 27), meaning that he was suspected of having ties to opposition forces out of loyalty to the old regime. The other explained his arrest as related to being "too Tutsi" (ibid., 28), meaning that his physical features made him look too much like an RPF soldier, which caused him to be accused of desertion. The RPF's ethnic discrimination does not work along a uniform line solely directed at Hutu. Rather, the tension around ethnicity causes a multiplication of violence, where all ethnic groups are discriminated against in different ways (see also Burnet 2012; Thomson 2013).

People who can't hack it, who can't crack the code, who don't have any way of knowing what the authorities want from them or any opportunity of giving it to them, face "infinitely ramifying possible futures" (Carey 2017, 6). Niklas Luhmann's characterization of the dizzying complexity of reality, when actors cannot trust each other and are overwhelmed by the sheer possibilities of a given situation, is relevant for this type of situation. Luhmann proposes that trust is what makes the world bearable and what allows people to take action in the world (1979). In the situations I have analyzed, I propose that patience, acceptance, and a general attitude of openness to the drastic changes that can occur in any situation is another way to navigate this form of complex reality.

Shifting Subjectivities

In his analysis of the self and state violence in colonial India, Ashis Nandy argues that, in situations of severe violence and oppression, survival may require "a certain permeability of boundaries" (Nandy 1983, 107). Responding to the charge that such practices of giving in to power represent an "effeminate" attitude of compromise, he argues that "these 'personality failures' of the Indian could be another form of developed vigilance, or sharpened instinct or faster reaction to man-made suffering" (ibid., 110).

Nandy's own characterization of this form of subjectivity follows Scott's approach to subordination: he argues that these tactics allow the Indian to never be truly penetrated by power. For the purposes of this chapter's argument, I instead return to Benhabib's narrative agency. Rather than finding coherence in the uncontaminated subject who maintains her true beliefs secretly, I propose to use Benhabib's insight about narration: coherence is produced by the subject's capacity to keep narrating. The drastically changing demands from authorities, as well as the general situation of "radical, routinized uncertainty" (Cooper and Pratten 2015, 1) about what may constitute a threat in the everyday lives of Rwandans, produce shifting expressions of subjectivity. Following Nandy, I venture that a certain openness in terms of how subjects define their personal boundaries may at times be necessary to survive these conditions. And the examples I have analyzed in this chapter illustrate, if anything, a high valorization of survival.

In our capacity as social analysts, we are not obliged to consider negatively those who focus on surviving the effects of violence. Earlier drafts of this chapter have been met with the question, "But what would you then say *isn't* an expression of agency?" I don't think social analysis has to give examples of this. Why would this be an important academic task? Rather than working with hierarchical rankings of subject performance in which certain persons are considered "pathetic objects" and "reified purely as object" (Alcoff and Gray 1993, 277, 278) because of a perceived "deplorable passivity" (Mahmood 2011, 15), we can do the interpretive work of exploring political subjectivities, including among those who do not carry out overt or covert resistance. This chapter has sought to illustrate a variety of ways in which agency is expressed in practices of compliance and efforts that center on survival. It calls for more analytical attention to such practices. In analyzing these practices, I argue that the analytical preference for agency in resistance communicates the message that, "when I am passive, incapable, constrained, dependent, I am less a person, I count less" (Reader 2007, 580). Being thoroughly affected by violence, I argue, does not make a person count less, and our analyses can do more to reflect this.

Under the title "Politics of Patience," this chapter has discussed the political meanings and effects of practices of compliance in Rwanda. The politics of patience occur in reference to the precarious political, social, and economic situation in Rwanda, which takes part in producing patient political subjectivities and, in turn, the politics effected by those subjectivities. This chapter has focused on the lived experiences of ubiquitous threat in Rwanda and argued that practices of acceptance and compliance reflect agency and political subjectivity expressed through self-control—a self-control expressed, for example, in the control young men on Iwawa take over the way they narrate their situation to themselves by accepting their condition in order to survive. Self-control is also expressed in the form of a mistrusting patience, one that responds to real and imagined tests from "authorities," be they relatives, police offers, or other government figures, whose actions have been framed as deliberate attempts to provoke aggression and arrest. Describing patience in the face of devious attempts by the powerful to produce arrestable bodies, my respondents depict compliance as the refusal to be conned in this manner. Young men subjected to violence for being too short, too tall, too weak, too strong, too Hutu, or too Tutsi are describing a situation where "you can't hack it." These bodies, which are always "wrong" and always subject to punishment, illustrate the difficulty of knowing what the state wants from them or how to provide it.

As a matter of theory and practice, I am arguing for an analytical move toward engaging with a broader range of aspects of political subjectivity. Analyses of the work of violence need to be able to include narratives that do not center on dignity or alternative signs of strength. It constitutes both moral and analytical wrongdoing not to. Moral wrongdoing because, by centering on the clever ways in which the subordinated push back, we exclude certain modes of being and certain lives from our analyses, as if these don't count as much as others. Analytical wrongdoing because these lenses do not allow us to see the many ways in which agency is enacted in compliance. Capturing the agency of compliant acts in this chapter, I have read Benhabib and Nandy together to characterize shifting and fragmented selves whose agencies are not latched to an uncontaminated core, free from domination. Rather, their agency is enacted in their narration, an ability they retain through a high degree of adaptability in order to accommodate the changing and unclear requirements from authorities.

Notes

1. All names of persons are changed for this chapter.
2. Susanne Buckley-Zistel has proposed interpreting poisonings as a continuation of genocidal violence: "the perception of deaths by poisoning is high, yet impossible to certify" (Buckley-Zistel 2006, 145).
3. The quotes from conversations outside of interviews are from my field notes, usually made a few hours after a conversation.
4. Brounéus draws on this perspective to argue that many aspects of the RPF's reconciliation initiatives have a re-traumatizing effect on the participants, as they are forced to talk in public settings about intimate and highly emotional subjects (see also Nyirubugara 2013).
5. Thus, RPF members will maintain that, prior to colonialism, Rwanda was a harmonious society with no ethnic divisions (see Thomson 2013; Mulindahabi

2015). Others have made the slightly different claim that there were ethnic differences between Tutsis and Hutus prior to colonialism, but that they were limited to things like different nutrition (see Musahara and Huggins 2005). One time, knowing that I was there in a research capacity, members of RPF working in a ministry had a discussion about the ancient precolonial ethnic hostilities in Rwanda with me present in their office.

6. As a methodological comment, let me note that I am not treating either Bosco's or Gilles's stories in terms of whether or not they are factual reports about how these two situations played out. What is interesting to me, and what this chapter analyzes, is how these two men interpreted the situations. That being said, the existing literature is full of documentation of similar examples, and in both situations, I did believe that the story I was hearing could easily be true.

References

Abu-Lughod, Lila. 1990. "The Romance of Resistance: Tracing Transformations of Power through Bedouin Women." *American Ethnologist* 17 (1): 41–55. https://doi.org/10.1525/ae.1990.17.1.02a00030.

Adekunle, Julius O. 2007. *Culture and Customs of Rwanda.* Westport, CT: Greenwood.

Alcoff, Linda, and Laura Gray. 1993. "Survivor Discourse: Transgression or Recuperation?" *Signs: Journal of Women in Culture and Society* 18 (2): 260–90. https://doi.org/10.1086/494793.

Ansoms, An. 2013. "Large-Scale Land Deals and Local Livelihoods in Rwanda: The Bitter Fruit of a New Agrarian Model." *African Studies Review* 56 (3): 1–23. https://doi.org/10.1017/asr.2013.77.

Ansoms, An, and Giuseppe D. Cioffo. 2016. "The Exemplary Citizen on the Exemplary Hill: The Production of Political Subjects in Contemporary Rural Rwanda." *Development and Change* 47 (6): 1247–68. https://doi.org/10.1111/dech.12271.

Benda, Richard. 2018. "Time to Hear the Other Side: Transitional Temporalities and Transgenerational Narratives in Post-genocide Rwanda." In *Time and Temporality in Transitional and Post-conflict Societies,* edited by Natascha Mueller-Hirth and Sandra Rios Oyola, 122–42. New York: Routledge.

Benhabib, Seyla. 1999. "Sexual Difference and Collective Identities: The New Global Constellation." *Signs: Journal of Women in Culture and Society* 24 (2): 335–61. https://doi.org/10.1086/495343.

Berry, Marie E. 2017. *War, Women, and Power: From Violence to Mobilization in Rwanda and Bosnia-Herzegovina.* New York: Cambridge University Press.

Beswick, Danielle. 2010. "Managing Dissent in a Post-genocide Environment: The Challenge of Political Space in Rwanda." *Development and Change* 41 (2): 225–51. https://doi.org/10.1111/j.1467-7660.2010.01640.x.

Blackie, Laura E. R., and Nicki Hitchcott. 2018. "'I Am Rwandan': Unity and Reconciliation in Post-genocide Rwanda." *Genocide Studies and Prevention* 12 (1): 24–37. https://doi.org/10.5038/1911-9933.12.1.1480.

Bognitz, Stefanie. 2018. "Mistrusting as a Mode of Engagement in Mediation: Insights from Socio-legal Practice in Rwanda." In *Mistrust: Ethnographic Approximations,* edited by Florian Mühlfried, 147–67. Bielefeld, Germany: Transcript.

Booth, David, and Frederick Golooba-Mutebi. 2012. "Developmental Patrimonialism? The Case of Rwanda." *African Affairs* 111 (444): 379–403. https://doi.org/10.1093/afraf/ads026.

Breed, Ananda. 2015. "Resistant Acts in Post-genocide Rwanda." In *Anthropology, Theatre, and Development: The Transformative Potential of Performance,* edited by Alex Flynn and Jonas Tinius, 127–46. London: Palgrave Macmillan.

Brounéus, Karen. 2010. "The Trauma of Truth Telling: Effects of Witnessing in the Rwandan Gacaca Courts on Psychological Health." *Journal of Conflict Resolution* 54 (3): 408–37. https://doi.org/10.1177/0022002709360322.

Buckley-Zistel, Susanne. 2006. "Remembering to Forget: Chosen Amnesia as a Strategy for Local Coexistence in Post-genocide Rwanda." *Africa* 76 (2): 131–50. https://doi.org/10.3366/afr.2006.76.2.131.

Burawoy, Michael. 1998. "The Extended Case Method." *Sociological Theory* 16 (1): 4–33. https://doi.org/10.1111/0735-2751.00040.

Burnet, Jennie E. 2012. *Genocide Lives in Us: Women, Memory, and Silence in Rwanda.* Madison: University of Wisconsin Press.

Butler, Judith. 1997. *The Psychic Life of Power: Theories in Subjection.* Stanford, CA: Stanford University Press.

Carey, Matthew. 2017. *Mistrust: An Ethnographic Theory.* Chicago: Hau Books.

Certeau, Michel de. 1997. *The Practice of Everyday Life.* Translated by Steven F. Rendall. Berkeley: University of California Press.

———. 2016. *Investing in Authoritarian Rule: Punishment and Patronage in Rwanda's Gacaca Courts for Genocide Crimes.* New York: Cambridge University Press.

Cooper, Elizabeth, and David Pratten. 2015. *Ethnographies of Uncertainty in Africa.* London: Palgrave Macmillan.

Crépeau, Pierre. 1985. *Parole et sagesse: Valeurs sociales dans les proverbes du Rwanda.* Tervuren, Belgium: Museé Royal de l'Afrique Centrale.

Davenport, Christian, and Allan C. Stam. 2009. "What Really Happened in Rwanda?" *Pacific Standard,* 7 October. Last updated 14 June 2017. https://psmag.com/social-justice/what-really-happened-in-rwanda-3432.

de Lame, Danielle. 2004. "Mighty Secrets, Public Commensality, and the Crisis of Transparency: Rwanda through the Looking Glass." *Canadian Journal of African Studies / Revue canadienne des études africaines* 38 (2): 279–317. https://doi.org/10.1080/00083968.2004.10751287.

Des Forges, Alison Liebhafsky. 1999. *"Leave None to Tell the Story": Genocide in Rwanda.* New York: Human Rights Watch.

———. 2011. *Defeat Is the Only Bad News: Rwanda under Musinga, 1896–1931.* Edited by David Newbury. Madison: University of Wisconsin Press.

Eisenhart, R. Wayne. 1975. "You Can't Hack It Little Girl: A Discussion of the Covert Psychological Agenda of Modern Combat Training." *Journal of Social Issues* 31 (4): 13–23. https://doi.org/10.1111/j.1540-4560.1975.tb01008.x.

———. 1995. *Discipline and Punish: The Birth of the Prison.* Translated by Alan Sheridan. 2nd Vintage Books ed. New York: Vintage Books.

Fujii, Lee Ann. 2009. *Killing Neighbors: Webs of Violence in Rwanda.* Ithaca, NY: Cornell University Press.

Girman, Chris. 2004. *Mucho Macho: Seduction, Desire, and the Homoerotic Lives of Latin Men.* New York: Harrington Park.

Goodfellow, Tom. 2013. "The Institutionalisation of 'Noise' and 'Silence' in Urban Politics: Riots and Compliance in Uganda and Rwanda." *Oxford Development Studies* 41 (4): 436–54. https://doi.org/10.1080/13600818.2013.807334.

Grant, Andrea Mariko. 2015. "Quiet Insecurity and Quiet Agency in Post-genocide Rwanda." *Etnofoor* 27 (2): 15–36.

Hilker, Lyndsay McLean. 2009. "Everyday Ethnicities: Identity and Reconciliation among Rwandan Youth." *Journal of Genocide Research* 11 (1): 81–100. https://doi.org/10.1080/14623520802703640.

Himbara, David. 2018. "Kagame's Stooge James Musoni Is Gone—His Life Is in Great Danger." 18 March. https://medium.com/@david.himbara_27884/kagames-stooge-and-infrastructure-minister-james-musoni-is-in-deep-trouble-45c611d9345e.

Huggins, Chris. 2009. "Agricultural Policies and Local Grievances in Rural Rwanda." *Peace Review* 21 (3): 296–303. https://doi.org/10.1080/10402650903099351.

———. 2011. "The Presidential Land Commission: Undermining Land Law Reform." In Straus and Waldorf 2011, 252–65.

———. 2014. "'Control Grabbing' and Small-Scale Agricultural Intensification: Emerging Patterns of State-Facilitated 'Agricultural Investment' in Rwanda." *Journal of Peasant Studies* 41 (3): 365–84. https://doi.org/10.1080/03066150.2014.910765.

Human Rights Watch. 2008. *Law and Reality Progress in Judicial Reform in Rwanda.* New York: Human Rights Watch.

Ingelaere, Bert. 2010a. "Do We Understand Life after Genocide? Center and Periphery in the Construction of Knowledge in Postgenocide Rwanda." *African Studies Review* 53 (1): 41–59. https://doi.org/10.1353/arw.0.0307.

———. 2010b. "Peasants, Power and Ethnicity: A Bottom-up Perspective on Rwanda's Political Transition." *African Affairs* 109 (435): 273–92. https://doi.org/10.1093/afraf/adp090.

———. 2014. "What's on a Peasant's Mind? Experiencing RPF State Reach and Overreach in Post-genocide Rwanda (2000–10)." *Journal of Eastern African Studies* 8 (2): 214–30. https://doi.org/10.1080/17531055.2014.891783.

Jessee, Erin. 2017. *Negotiating Genocide in Rwanda: The Politics of History.* Cham, Switzerland: Palgrave Macmillan.

Johnson, Barbara. 1994. *A World of Difference.* Baltimore: Johns Hopkins University Press.

Krause, Kristine, and Katharina Schramm. 2011. "Thinking through Political Subjectivity." *African Diaspora* 4 (2): 115–34. https://doi.org/10.1163/187254611X607741.

Kwibuka, Eugène. 2016. "What Should Rwandans Expect from Incoming District Mayors?" *New Times* (Kigali, Rwanda), 11 January. http://www.newtimes.co.rw/section/article/2016-01-11/195993/.

Lemarchand, René. 2018. "Reconsidering France's Role in the Rwandan Genocide." Africa Is a Country, 13 June. https://africasacountry.com/2018/06/reconsidering-frances-role-in-the-rwandan-genocide.

Lestrade, Arthur. 1972. *Notes d'ethnographie du Rwanda.* Tervuren, Belgium: Museé Royal de l'Afrique Centrale.

Løvgren, Rose. 2014. "Governing Young Masculinity in Rwanda: The Intimate Production of Political Subjectivities at Iwawa Island." Master's thesis, University of Copenhagen.

————. 2018. "Conducting Unleashing Interviews Where Control Means Life or Death." In *Experiences in Researching Conflict and Violence: Fieldwork Interrupted,* edited by Althea-Maria Rivas and Brendan Ciarán Browne, 15–30. Chicago: Policy Press.

Løvgren, Rose, and Simon Turner. 2019. "'Winning Life' and the Discipline of Death at Iwawa Island." *Ethnos* 84 (1): 27–40. https://doi.org/10.1080/00141844.2017.1373687.

Lucas, Sarah Drews. 2017. "The Primacy of Narrative Agency: Re-reading Seyla Benhabib on Narrativity." *Feminist Theory* 19 (2): 123–43. https://doi.org/10.1177/1464700117723591.

Luhmann, Niklas. 1979. *Trust and Power.* New York: John Wiley & Sons.

MacLure, Maggie, Rachel Holmes, Liz Jones, and Christina MacRae. 2010. "Silence as Resistance to Analysis: Or, on Not Opening One's Mouth Properly." *Qualitative Inquiry* 16 (6): 492–500. https://doi.org/10.1177/1077800410364349.

Mahmood, Saba. 2011. *Politics of Piety: The Islamic Revival and the Feminist Subject.* Princeton, NJ: Princeton University Press.

Marriage, Zoë. 2016. "Aid to Rwanda: Unstoppable Rock, Immovable Post." In *Aid and Authoritarianism in Africa: Development without Democracy,* edited by Tobias Hagmann and Filip Reyntjens, 44–66. London: Zed Books.

Mbembe, Achille. 1992. "Provisional Notes on the Postcolony." *Africa: Journal of the International African Institute* 62 (1): 3–37. https://doi.org/10.2307/1160062.

Mgbako, Chi. 2005. "Ingando Solidarity Camps: Reconciliation and Political Indoctrination in Post-genocide Rwanda." *Harvard Human Rights Journal* 18:201–24.

Mulindahabi, Charline. 2015. "Obedience Troubled? Exploring Meanings of Obedience in the Post-genocide Rwanda." PhD diss., University of Gothenburg.

Musahara, Herman, and Chris Huggins. 2005. "Land Reform, Land Scarcity and Post-conflict Reconstruction: A Case Study of Rwanda." In *From the Ground up: Land Rights, Conflict and Peace in Sub-Saharan Africa,* edited by Chris Huggins and Jenny Clover, 269–346. Pretoria: Institute for Security Studies.

Nandy, Ashis. 1983. *The Intimate Enemy: Loss and Recovery of Self under Colonialism.* New Delhi: Oxford University Press.

National Rehabilitation Service. 2018. "Iwawa Rehabilitation Center (IRC)." National Rehabilitation Service, Republic of Rwanda. https://www.nrs.gov.rw/index.php?id=138.

Newbury, Catherine. 2011. "High Modernism at the Ground Level: The *Imidugudu* Policy in Rwanda." In Straus and Waldorf 2011, 223–39.

Newz Post. 2018. "Kagame Reshuffles Cabinet, Longest Serving Minister Musoni Fired after Sex Scandal." 7 April. http://newz.ug/kagame-reshuffles-cabinet-longest-serving-minister-musoni-fired-after-sex-scandal/.

Nietzsche, Friedrich Wilhelm. 2008. *On the Genealogy of Morals: A Polemic; By Way of Clarification and Supplement to My Last Book, Beyond Good and Evil.* Translated and edited by Douglas Smith. Oxford: Oxford University Press.

Nikuze, Donatien. 2014. "The Genocide against the Tutsi in Rwanda: Origins, Causes, Implementation, Consequences, and the Post-genocide Era." *International Journal of Development and Sustainability* 3 (5): 1086–98.

Ntampaka, Charles. 1999. "Vérité et opinion dans la société rwandaise traditio-nelle." *Dialogue* 221:3–24.

Nyirubugara, Olivier. 2013. *Memory Traps.* Vol. 1, *Complexities and Dangers of Re-membering and Forgetting in Rwanda.* Leiden, Netherlands: Sidestone.

Nzahabwanayo, Sylvestre, Kai Horsthemke, and Thokozani P. Mathebula. 2017. "Identification and Critique of the Citizenship Notion Informing the Itorero Training Scheme for High School Leavers in Post-genocide Rwanda." *South African Journal of Higher Education* 31 (2): 226–50. https://doi.org/10.20853/31 -2-1047.

Ortner, Sherry B. 1995. "Resistance and the Problem of Ethnographic Refusal." *Comparative Studies in Society and History* 37 (1): 173–93. https://doi.org/10.1017 /S0010417500019587.

Overdulve, Cornelis M. 1997. "Fonction de la langue et de la communication au Rwanda." *Neue Zeitschrift für Missionswissenschaft* 53 (4): 271–83.

Pells, Kirrily. 2011. "Building a Rwanda 'Fit for Children.'" In Straus and Waldorf 2011, 79–86.

Pottier, Johan. 2002. *Re-imagining Rwanda: Conflict, Survival and Disinformation in the Late Twentieth Century.* Cambridge: Cambridge University Press.

Purdeková, Andrea. 2011. "'Even If I Am Not Here, There Are So Many Eyes': Surveillance and State Reach in Rwanda." *Journal of Modern African Studies* 49 (3): 475–97. https://doi.org/10.1017/S0022278X11000292.

———. 2015. *Making Ubumwe: Power, State and Camps in Rwanda's Unity-Building Project.* New York: Berghahn Books.

———. 2016. "'Mundane Sights' of Power: The History of Social Monitoring and Its Subversion in Rwanda." *African Studies Review* 59 (2): 59–86. https://doi .org/10.1017/asr.2016.32.

Purdeková, Andrea, Filip Reyntjens, and Nina Wilén. 2018. "Militarisation of Governance after Conflict: Beyond the Rebel-to-Ruler Frame—the Case of Rwanda." *Third World Quarterly* 39 (1): 158–74. https://doi.org/10.1080/01436597 .2017.1369036.

Reader, Soran. 2007. "The Other Side of Agency." *Philosophy* 82 (4): 579–604. https:// doi.org/10.1017/S0031819107000162.

Republic of Rwanda. 2006. "Rwanda: Genocide Ideology and Strategies for Its Eradication." Kigali: Republic of Rwanda.

Reyntjens, Filip. 2015. "Rwanda: Progress or Powder Keg?" *Journal of Democracy* 26 (3): 19–33.

Rollason, Will. 2017. "'Buying a Path': Rethinking Resistance in Rwanda." *Journal of Eastern African Studies* 11 (1): 46–63. https://doi.org/10.1080/17531055.2017.1287235.

Rukebesha, Aloys. 1985. *Esotérisme et communication sociale.* Kigali, Rwanda: Printer Set.

Rusagara, Frank K. 2009. *Resilience of a Nation: A History of the Military in Rwanda.* Kigali, Rwanda: Fountain Publishers Rwanda.

Rwembeho, Stephen. 2012. "Five Local Leaders Suspended over Nyakatsi." *New Times* (Kigali, Rwanda), 23 July. https://www.newtimes.co.rw/section/read /55381.

Samimian-Darash, Limor. 2013. "Rebuilding the Body through Violence and Con-trol." *Ethnography* 14 (1): 46–63. https://doi.org/10.1177/1466138112448026.

Scheper-Hughes, Nancy. 2008. "A Talent for Life: Reflections on Human Vulnerability and Resilience." *Ethnos* 73 (1): 25–56. https://doi.org/10.1080/00141840801927525.

Scott, James C. 1990. *Domination and the Arts of Resistance: Hidden Transcripts.* New Haven, CT: Yale University Press.

———. 2000. *Weapons of the Weak: Everyday Forms of Peasant Resistance.* New Haven, CT: Yale University Press.

———. 2007. "Domination and the Arts of Resistance." In *On Violence: A Reader,* edited by Bruce B. Lawrence and Aisha Karim, 199–213. Durham, NC: Duke University Press.

Shearer, Samuel. 2015. "Producing Sustainable Futures in Post-genocide Kigali, Rwanda." In *Sustainability in the Global City: Myth and Practice,* edited by Cindy Isenhour, Gary McDonogh, and Melissa Checker, 180–84. New York: Cambridge University Press.

Shyaka Mugabe, Aggée. 2007. "Community Conflicts in Rwanda: Major Causes and Ways to Solutions." Kigali, Rwanda: National Unity and Reconciliation Commission. Available at http://www.genocideresearchhub.org.rw/document/community-conflicts-rwanda-major-causes-ways-solutions/.

Sommers, Marc. 2012. *Stuck: Rwandan Youth and the Struggle for Adulthood.* Athens: University of Georgia Press.

Stearns, Jason K. 2011. *Dancing in the Glory of Monsters: The Collapse of the Congo and the Great War of Africa.* New York: PublicAffairs.

Straus, Scott. 2008. "The Historiography of the Rwandan Genocide." In *The History of Genocide,* edited by Dan Stone, 517–42. New York: Palgrave Macmillan.

Straus, Scott, and Lars Waldorf, eds. 2011. *Remaking Rwanda: State Building and Human Rights after Mass Violence.* Madison: University of Wisconsin Press.

Stys, Patrycja. 2012. "Revisiting Rwanda." Review of *After Genocide,* edited by Phil Clark and Zachary D. Kaufman; *Defeat Is the Only Bad News,* by Alison Liebhafsky Des Forges; *Remaking Rwanda,* edited by Scott Straus and Lars Waldorf; and *Resilience of a Nation,* by F. K. Rusagara. *Journal of Modern African Studies* 50 (4): 707–20. https://doi.org/10.1017/S0022278X12000390.

Sundaram, Anjan. 2016. *Bad News: Last Journalists in a Dictatorship.* New York: Doubleday.

Sundberg, Molly. 2016. *Training for Model Citizenship: An Ethnography of Civic Education and State-Making in Rwanda.* London: Palgrave Macmillan.

Thomson, Susan M. 2011. "Whispering Truth to Power: The Everyday Resistance of Rwandan Peasants to Post-genocide Reconciliation." *African Affairs* 110 (440): 439–56. https://doi.org/10.1093/afraf/adr021.

———. 2013. *Whispering Truth to Power: Everyday Resistance to Reconciliation in Postgenocide Rwanda.* Madison: University of Wisconsin Press.

Times Reporter. 2011. "Local Leaders Resign over Nyakatsi." *New Times* (Kigali, Rwanda), 26 April. https://www.newtimes.co.rw/section/read/30567.

———. 2016. "Local Leaders Told to Tighten Grip on Crimes." *New Times* (Kigali, Rwanda), 15 March. http://www.newtimes.co.rw/section/article/2016-03-15/198000/.

Uvin, Peter. 1998. *Aiding Violence: The Development Enterprise in Rwanda.* West Hartford, CT: Kumarian.

————. 2002. "On Counting, Categorizing, and Violence in Burundi and Rwanda." In *Census and Identity: The Politics of Race, Ethnicity, and Language in National Censuses,* edited by David I. Kertzer and Dominique Arel, 148–75. Cambridge: Cambridge University Press.

Uwanziga, Joy Nzamwita. 2015. *Manners in Rwanda: Basic Knowledge on Rwandan Culture, Customs, and Kinyarwanda Language.* Portland, OR: Inkwater.

Uwiringiyimana, Alexandre. 2014. "Kamaliza Humura Rwanda." Posted 5 June on YouTube by user Uwiringiyimana Alexandre. Video, 5:59. https://www.youtube .com/watch?v=4HODeJjYbVU.

Van Damme, Julie, An Ansoms, and Philippe V. Baret. 2014. "Agricultural Innovation from Above and from Below: Confrontation and Integration on Rwanda's Hills." *African Affairs* 113 (450): 108–27. https://doi.org/10.1093/afraf/adt067.

Verhoeven, Harry. 2012. "Nurturing Democracy or into the Danger Zone? The Rwandan Patriotic Front, Elite Fragmentation and Post-liberation Politics." In *Rwanda Fast Forward: Social, Economic, Military and Reconciliation Prospects,* edited by Maddalena Campioni and Patrick Noack, 265–80. New York: Palgrave Macmillan.

Verpoorten, Marijke. 2010. "Detecting Hidden Violence: The Spatial Distribution of Excess Mortality in Rwanda." *SSRN Electronic Journal.* https://doi.org/10 .2139/ssrn.1551207.

Waldorf, Lars. 2011. "Instrumentalizing Genocide: The RPF's Campaign against 'Genocide Ideology.'" In Straus and Waldorf 2011, 48–66.

EIGHT

The State as Golem

Police Violence in Democratic South Africa

NICHOLAS RUSH SMITH

IN THE WAKE OF APARTHEID'S COLLAPSE, SOUTH AFRICA pursued one of the world's most ambitious police reform projects. The goal was to tame the apartheid police force so that it could be turned into a service for the emerging democracy's newly enfranchised citizenry. To accomplish these goals, police officials set into motion a variety of reforms. These included a demographic transformation so that the police force would look like the citizenry it was charged with protecting (Newham, Masuku, and Dlamini 2006). They included the democratization of the police force via the creation of community policing institutions to allow residents to cooperate with local police stations (Marks, Shearing, and Wood 2009). They also involved a cultural shift in which a police force that was notorious for committing human rights violations would be retrained to protect citizens' rights instead (Hornberger 2011).

Researchers working with the police during this period praised these transformations. Of the police's operational transformation, one well-known policing researcher wrote that the organization's leaders "have affected a hugely impressive turnaround at strategic, organizational and operational levels. They have gotten more resources, and they are deploying them wisely. More, I think, could not really be asked of management" (Altbeker 2005, 263). Regarding the racial transformation of the force, prominent policing experts argued that the South African reform process was "a model of success" and that "there is little doubt" that "the SAPS [South African Police Service] is a fundamentally different organisation from its predecessor, the SAP [South African Police]" (Newham, Masuku, and Dlamini 2006, 8, 9). The changes also seemed to be paying off in slow improvements in the quality of life for average South Africans given that the country's notoriously high violent-crime rates were steadily falling, even as they remained very high by international standards (Kriegler and Shaw 2016).[1] Indeed, the transformation was considered so successful (despite the high crime rates) that it has been the basis for police reform efforts in other transitional regimes (Rauch 2009).

Yet by the time South Africa's democracy celebrated its fifteenth year, things had changed. In early 2010, for instance, the police announced to the nation that the SAPS would return to its apartheid-era military rank structure and become a "force" to be reckoned with once again (South African Police Service 2010). To highlight the difference, the police commissioner at the time, Bheki Cele, became General Cele and started wearing military-styled uniforms. These performances weren't merely playacting but were also reflected in changing policies around the use of force. A year before the remilitarization of the police, the minister of safety and security approached Parliament with a request to free the police from restrictions on their use of force so officers could "fight fire with fire" (quoted in de Lange 2008), arguing that it was absurd that when officers confront "criminals armed with sophisticated weaponry, the police's task would be to take out some human rights charter" (quoted in de Vos 2013).

This chapter considers what this shift reveals about processes of institutional transformation and their contradictions. It focuses particularly on the transformation of the state's violent institutions, given that theorists of the state going back to Thomas Hobbes have argued that the state's ability to wield violence in the service of social peace is the sine qua non of statehood. And, in modern democracies, the violent institution most likely to be charged with regulating social relations is the police.

To understand how institutional transformations are experienced on the ground, the paper draws on approximately twenty-two months of ethnographic and archival research conducted primarily in townships outside of Durban and Johannesburg between 2008 and 2019. The longest stretch of this fieldwork was conducted in 2009 and 2010, which turned out to be the moment when commanders reversed course on nearly fifteen years of (frequently contradictory) human-rights-based reform efforts and began to remilitarize the police (Bruce 2012; Hornberger 2013). This chapter focuses particularly on ethnographic research among young men involved in crime and reflects on what their daily experience of the police reveals about the nature and contradictions of institutional transformation.

Specifically, it draws from events following the death of Juba—a locally notorious young man from KwaMashu, Durban—shortly after the South

African police were remilitarized in early 2010.[2] Although I never conclusively determined how Juba died, rumors circulated that he was killed by
police while "on the round" (stealing) in a nearby neighborhood. Such stories, I have shown elsewhere (Smith 2019, chap. 9), were common among
young Durban men involved in crime during this period and have remained
so since. While these rumors were typically impossible to substantiate, they
nevertheless revealed the ways in which many young men understood the
state to be dangerous and even predatory. The question is what these fears
of predation suggest about the nature of the postapartheid state and about
the democratic state form generally—questions to which I turn in the next
section before considering events in the wake of Juba's death.

The State as Golem

Why would the postapartheid state, which had been trying to project the
image of a democratic state governed by one of the world's most progressive rights regimes, begin to emphasize its violent capacity fifteen years
after a celebrated democratic transition? According to the announcement
by the SAPS explaining the remilitarization, the shift was "part of our new
approach of being fierce towards criminals, while lenient to citizens' safety
and maintaining good discipline within the Force," a shift that would be
reflected in a "change in attitude, thinking and operational duties" among
officers (South African Police Service 2010).[3] Put differently, the SAPS
seemed to suggest that the human rights reforms left them unable to fulfill
their most basic task: producing social order. It was also a task that many
South Africans believed the state had manifestly failed to achieve (Comaroff and Comaroff 2016), despite large declines in the murder rate over the
first decade and a half of democracy (Kriegler and Shaw 2016). In this light,
dramatizing the violent capabilities of the police by remilitarizing them
appears as an attempt to conjure an image of a state capable of producing
the order citizens demanded and that the state had difficulty providing.

Put metaphorically, the SAPS language suggests an image of the state
akin to Hobbes's Leviathan—a fantastical creature that remains among the
world's most influential metaphors for the state because of its ability to
speak to enduring fantasies of an ordered polity and a secure world. Understanding such metaphors is important because the metaphors through
which we see politics help us make "sense of ourselves, our experiences, and
our world" (Schaffer 2018, 17). Even more, if such metaphors help establish
the reality we experience, then fresh metaphors "can establish a different
reality" and "inaugurate new ways to understand the world" (ibid., 18). In
considering the experiences of young men and police in South Africa, this
chapter is a modest attempt to see such metaphors anew by using these
men's experiences to speak back to concepts that dominate our visions of

the state—what Comaroff and Comaroff (2015) refer to as doing "theory from the South." In so doing, we may see something new about how democratic states work generally.

To be sure, there are metaphors other than that of the Leviathan that have shaped how citizens understand their states. John Locke's liberal followers, for instance, would like to see a state act as a restrained "night watchman" that provides light social regulation (see esp. Nozick 1974). On the African continent, people have understood colonial and postcolonial states through various monstrous idioms, including vampires (White 2000), zombies (Comaroff and Comaroff 2002), and witchcraft (Ashforth 2005). But the desires the Leviathan metaphor speaks to—of an independent force capable of producing an ordered people and a secure polity—remain strong, perhaps because there are few symbols that more effectively capture this fantasy than the Leviathan.

But what was the Leviathan, exactly, that it could become such a potent symbol for these collective desires? Carl Schmitt, in an extended study of the Leviathan's symbolism, shows that the Leviathan originally came from the Hebrew bible, where it was depicted as a powerful sea creature locked in battle with a powerful land creature, the Behemoth (2008, 6–8).[4] In Hobbes's hands, the idea of a creature with overwhelming power remains, but it is transformed from a fish into (variously) a mortal god, an artificial man, and an automaton. In the original frontispiece of the book, for example, the Leviathan is famously depicted as a superhuman king whose single body unifies hundreds of smaller bodies, suggesting that the authority and supremacy of the Leviathan comes from its unification of these myriad individuals. The size of the king-like creature also suggests it overwhelms them.[5]

It is in Hobbes's use of these human images, though, that the metaphor may run into trouble as a political symbol. Hobbes depicts the Leviathan as unifying and, indeed, unified, but in so doing, he occludes the state's dual nature; that is, the fact that the state's power to protect some citizens depends on its power to threaten others, two fundamental qualities that sit in tension with one another. In this way, as with all metaphors, the Leviathan shifts our attention to some of the state's qualities and away from others. For instance, as Frederic Schaffer suggests of the common game-like metaphors used to describe warfare, "To point out the chessness of battle is to both focus on the move-countermove strategy of battle and take no note of its horror" (Schaffer 2018, 17). In the case of the Leviathan image, the metaphor highlights the force of the state even as it hides *who* that force is used against.

I would suggest we need new metaphors that bring this ambivalence to the center of our thinking about the state in order to fully apprehend how the state works.[6] If mythological creatures—as with the Leviathan, vampire, or zombie—are useful metaphors through which to think, I propose one useful creature through which to think about the state might be the Golem.[7] Like Hobbes's Leviathan, the Golem is first mentioned in the Hebrew bible. In the Golem's case, as it developed in Jewish folklore, it came to represent a type of artificial man, typically created out of dirt or clay, whose purpose is to serve his creator or protect him from his enemies (Scholem 1965, chap. 5). Unlike the Leviathan, though, whose power Hobbes depicts as broadly predictable and positive, the protective power of the Golem is uncertain and ambiguous, as the Golem may become dangerous if it slips out of the control of its creator (Scholem 1965, 200–203; Scholem 1966, 63; Cohen 2015, 4).

For example, in one version of the legend, a rabbi creates a Golem to help with chores, but it ultimately grows so big that it topples over, crushing its creator (Scholem 1965, 159). In another version, a powerful rabbi has created a Golem to protect his city's Jewish community. The Golem has been given life by the rabbi putting "a slip of paper into its mouth with the mystical and ineffable Name of God written on it," which the rabbi would remove on the sabbath, the day of rest. However, one sabbath, the rabbi forgot to remove the paper. Consequently, the Golem grew massively and, "like one mad, began tearing about in the Ghetto, threatening to destroy everything" (Scholem 1966, 63).

Thus, according to the eminent Kabbalah scholar Gershom Scholem, the Golem myth depicts "a creature created by human intelligence and concentration, which is controlled by its creator and performs tasks set by him, but which at the same time may have a dangerous tendency to outgrow that control and develop destructive potentialities" (ibid.). In each version, the story of the Golem is a parable of the ways in which man plays God, imbuing a clay creature with life, much like God's creation of Adam. Unlike God, though, who was able to give his creation creative potential, man is unable to do the same with the Golem. Instead, the Golem's agency is attenuated, which causes it to lash out when it is finally free, harming those it is meant to serve. The lesson of the parable is, therefore, that a creature we make to serve us always threatens to outgrow our control and become "a destructive power on its own" (ibid.).

The Golem has many analogues in secular thought and literature—Mary Shelley's Frankenstein's monster is perhaps the most familiar example (Cohen 2015, 4). As with such other creatures, the Golem serves as a metaphor for the inability of humans to fully control the consequences of their creative actions. Indeed, the Golem has served as a well-known metaphor for the potentially destructive powers of human forays into artificial intelligence (Wiener 1964; Scholem 1966;). It has been rarely considered as a metaphor for politics, though.[8] If we were to think of the state as Golem-like, we might think of the state as being protective and yet always threatening to perform dangerously erratic actions that can harm its ostensible masters—in the case of democratic South Africa, those ostensible masters being the country's citizens. In this sense, the Golem metaphor is helpful because it captures so much about the ambivalent nature of the state. That is, even as the state may be protective in some instances, we might think of it—like the Golem—as always being at risk of slipping beyond our control and acting unpredictably, erratically, and therefore dangerously toward its creators and supposed beneficiaries: citizens.

This ambivalence is particularly important to recognize in a place like postapartheid South Africa, where the state invested enormous resources in creating a tamed Leviathan by reforming the apartheid policing apparatus to make it serve its new democratic masters (Hornberger 2011), and yet where many officers remain both skeptical of these reforms (Brooks 2020) and capable of extraordinary violence (Bruce 2012). And in considering this violence through the experiences of young township men, we may see something new about the metaphors (like the Leviathan) that we use to apprehend and legitimate the state. In the remainder of the chapter, we will approach this task through an account of events in the wake of the death of Juba, a locally notorious young man in the Durban township, KwaMashu.

Burying a Young Man

So far as I can recall, I only met Juba once before he died and even then it was a brief encounter. He made an impression, though, because even as he had a heavy reputation in KwaMashu, he was an adherent to the teachings of the Zulu prophet Isaiah Shembe, founder of the Nazareth Baptist Church, which was apparent in the large beard I recall him wearing in the style of some of the sect's male adherents. Yet despite his heavy reputation, I never expected to attend his funeral. But that's where I found myself after attending his night vigil—typically, an all-night ceremony of singing and mourning at the deceased's family home, but in this case also a street party—in the late hours of a Saturday night in early 2010.

The crew with whom I attended the night vigil weren't particularly enthusiastic about the event, as Juba hadn't gotten on well with many of them. As one of the guys said while we lounged around a cooler of Heineken and hard ciders in front of Life's house before the night vigil, "I'm not going to give him any salutes. Nothing. I'm just going to go to be seen and to drink." Still, given Juba's reputation and the likelihood of a party, it was an important event at which to socialize. I knew from stories I had been told and cell phone videos that I had been shown that such sendoffs were often raucous affairs with large crowds of young people watching allegedly stolen cars being spun in circles and hearing gun shots fired in salute to celebrate what were often too-short lives (see Altbeker 2001). So despite their ambivalent feelings about Juba, the promise of a party led the guys to pile into cars and drive in a speeding caravan over to his family home a few sections away.

As we entered Juba's section, we slowed, gliding past the dark and quiet houses until we arrived at a noisy and boozy crowd gathered under streetlights near his home, local house music pumping out of cars. A cheer went up as we drove through, by now having picked up speed again to fly down the crowded two-lane road. Teenage girls whistled at our arrival, while teenage boys postured as we went past. We slowed at the end of the strip and parked on the pavement, careful to inch the cars as far onto the sidewalk as possible, as there would likely be people spinning cars as part of the celebration. Due caution had to be taken so that our cars wouldn't be hit by an unskilled or errant driver.

We exited our vehicles and the guys looked around, evidently to see who was there and who was watching. Some of their friends came up and joined our group, greeting us and puffing out their chests. Amid the greeting, one of our crew, David, went off to urinate on the wall of a nearby house. As he finished, he pulled a gun, which I didn't realize he had, from underneath his shirt and fired three rounds into the air in quick succession: pop-pop-pop. The shots sounded like cheap firecrackers. It wasn't intimidating, but I felt a rush of adrenaline surge through me. I tried to keep my face expressionless, as it was clear from the casualness with which he fired the gun and tucked it back into his pants that this was nothing at which to marvel, but a routine and expected act. Although teenage girls on the other side of the road squealed with delight and younger boys jumped with joy, for the men with whom I was standing, the gunfire wasn't even a reason to interrupt conversation. No mention was made of it, although a couple of the guys looked at me with wry smiles, searching for my reaction.

We settled into the scene and chatted about various bits of local gossip. Despite the comradery, the guys seemed almost bored with the event. And, in many ways, it was boring. Occasionally, people leaving the memorial roared Citi Golfs down the street, hit the brakes, and spun their cars around (a maneuver known as *ukushaya isidudla*—literally, "hit the fat one").[9] To the delight of the girls and boys on the other side of the road, one driver took a minute to spin his back tires, creating a thick cloud of white smoke, before roaring down the other way through the crowd and around the bend. But despite these momentary fits of action, the overall scene was rather subdued, in contrast to the raucous party we had expected to join.

"Tamed" might be a more apt description, as the police were apparently surveilling the event. According to the men who had joined us, the police had come through earlier in the night and searched people for weapons.

FIGURE 1. A mother with her baby walks past police vehicles in KwaMashu. Photo by Rogan Ward/Reuters.

The rumor was that they were still patrolling nearby to keep the crowd at bay. Indeed, two cop cars drove through the middle of the party while we were there. The effect, as one of the guys put it, was that "everyone is too afraid of the police to do any shit." I asked my friend, Bhuti, about the supposed tradition of stealing a car and spinning it to honor a thief like Juba—something that had occurred in a few brief stunts, but far from the ongoing show I had expected. He replied, "Who is going to steal a car and bring it here with all of these police? Juba is going to be angry wherever he is because he is not getting the right memorial service. Fucking police."

The two comments have much meaning in them, but I would like to focus on what they suggest about the nature of the would-be South African Leviathan, its agents, and its subjects. Contrary to much of the public's dim view of the police, the comment suggests that the police *do* have some capacity to control a crowd, albeit in a circumscribed way. The young people at the night vigil feared the police—to an extent. The threat of search and arrest was enough to stop some, but not all, of the illegal activities associated with the memorial service, as there was seemingly little appetite for a direct confrontation with the police.

Crucially, though, the cops' interventions were also episodic. The youngsters were still gathered late at night in a noisy crowd on a residential street, making for (at best) a partially legal gathering. People still occasionally fired guns and young men still periodically roared cars up and down the road. Given that several of the men at the gathering made a living through car theft, some of the cars were likely stolen. If the police were to arrive and check engine numbers, they would probably find several that had been changed illegally. Thus, the police were able to produce partial, but not total, quiescence and partial, but not total, order. And the partial nature of their authority and the continuation of some of the illegal activities—spinning cars, shooting haphazardly into the air, ample public alcohol consumption—were conditions that could create very real violence and injury.

To put it analytically, the force of the would-be South African Leviathan was both episodic and negotiated. The Leviathan's force was episodic in that the police only arrived periodically to monitor the crowd (even as there were rumors they were in the general area monitoring the event). And because the police only arrived episodically, the power of the Leviathan was negotiated, not totalizing. As Jonny Steinberg (2008) has written in an important ethnography of South African policing, officers often avoid crowds like the one at Juba's night vigil, finding ways to circle away from them while on patrol. The reason, Steinberg suggests, is that police are likely to be met with hostility—a problem police deal with by avoiding it. This dynamic may have been at work in this case, to the degree that the police did not attempt to break up the illegally gathered crowd. They did not totally avoid it, though, as the reports of searches and the periodic patrols suggest. So the police were neither completely feckless, nor were they particularly dominating. They operated in some gray zone in between, using their power periodically to create partial order.

I would see these dynamics at work again the next morning at Juba's funeral. The event turned out to be a challenge to find. My friend Bhuti and I arrived at Juba's house after the procession departed, leaving us in a quandary about how to find the cemetery, which we knew was likely in nearby Inanda, but not where exactly. We eventually ended up at a nearby garage, thinking that someone might be there filling up who would know the way. The plan worked. As we arrived, a black Citi Golf carrying several of Bhuti's friends was pulling out. Just as I drove up alongside them on the road and Bhuti started to ask about the funeral's location, a car full of police pulled them over and ordered the men to get out of the car. The cops furiously searched the car, seemingly looking for some form of serious contraband, given the close attention they paid to it. I had pulled over ahead on the road to wait until the police were finished. The police questioned the three men, which they appeared to handle coolly while sipping illegally on ciders. Apparently satisfied with the men's responses, the cops let them go and entered the highway in the direction of Inanda. It appeared from the direction they were headed that the police were also going to the funeral, so I followed the Golf as best as I could, which in turn was following the speeding cop car in the hope it would lead us to Juba's gravesite.

We zoomed up to Ekuphakameni, the amaNazaretha holy site, before turning onto a worn side road, by now having lost the police car. We found ourselves in a cul-de-sac, leaving us with no clue where the funeral was. After several rounds of calls, several false starts, and several attempts to follow other speeding police cars, we found ourselves in a caravan to the funeral, assured that the driver in the lead knew the location.

Our initial intuition that the police would be monitoring the funeral turned out to be correct, even though none of the cars we were following ended up there. The police's interest in the funeral became clear as our caravan blazed down the road toward the funeral and the lead car suddenly hit the brakes: three police cars were sitting at the top of the road leading to the burial site. Our caravan gingerly pulled by them and we parked our cars off to the side of the road. The police then told us to park again so that we would be further out of the way. We respectfully complied. In addition to the three police cars sitting at our end of the road, there were three cars on the other end of the road, presumably ready to act should any problems arise. No need would arise, as it turned out. Their presence ensured a circumscribed peace.

The cemetery was precariously perched on the side of a hill abutting a long, straight dirt road. The scenery was unremarkable other than its being one of Inanda's more rural areas, which, if I hadn't known where I was, would have seemed like the deep country. Small houses and *rondavels* were scattered across the surrounding hills. The cemetery itself overlooked a backyard mechanic business with wrecked cars and spare parts littering the yard. There were no trees in the area that were any bigger than shrubs and the grave sites were overgrown with tall grass. Only a few of the dozen or so graves had permanent headstones. Most were marked by crosses made from scrap wood with the person's name and dates inscribed on them. The graves themselves were little more than mounds of soil.

As I took in the surroundings, the funeral proceeded apace, or, more accurately, the two funerals proceeded apace. The official amaNazaretha funeral was starting slightly down the hill from the road where I stood observing. About thirty mourners dressed in either worn dress clothes or the pristine white robes typically donned by adherents of the amaNazaretha church had assembled on a narrow path. The mourners carried the body, wrapped only in blankets, up a faint trail that headed up the other side of the mountain, around a bend out of view, and then back down the hill to the gravesite. Before setting off, mourners blew long horns reminiscent of the vuvuzelas played at South African soccer matches in an arrhythmic manner. As they marched barefooted down to the gravesite, they sang hymns in the isiZulu language. When they reached the gravesite, the men started to dig a hole in the side of the mountain in which to lay the body. As they dug, mourners sang and a preacher prayed. It was a solemn, dignified ceremony, despite the simple resting place.

The second funeral happening on the roadside up the hill was of an entirely different character. In contrast to the solemn amaNazaretha ceremony, the alternative funeral was a big party. House music blasted out of the back of several cars. People drank heavily, despite it still being morning. Young men and women danced. Some gawked at the funeral, but for the most part people chatted loudly, greeting friends among the new arrivals.

Aside from the dual ceremonies, perhaps the most striking thing was how many funerals were taking place at the tiny cemetery that day. AmaNazaretha tradition, Bhuti told me, dictates that people who have died violently are buried separately from those who have died from natural causes, and the cemetery where Juba was being buried was apparently reserved for people who died violent deaths.[10] Juba's funeral was the first that took place while we were there, but about halfway through his burial a second funeral procession blew their ceremonial horns and started moving up the path around the mountain. As Juba's funeral was ending, a third body was being carried up to the start of the path. Later, as Bhuti and I made our way up the road to where I had parked my car, three more rented buses, indicating up to three more funerals, were waiting to offload passengers, suggesting the possibility of six funerals for amaNazaretha who had died violently in the previous week.

As we made our way back to KwaMashu, our conversation turned to the police who sat at both ends of the road. Bhuti expressed disappointment that there wasn't more in terms of car spinning and shooting at the funeral, as would normally be expected, saying that it was due to a fear of the police.[11] As we drove back home to KwaMashu, we decided to pass by Juba's house to see if there was anything happening there. The scene was quiet, except for police patrols driving through the area, suggesting that there was indeed reason for the guys to be wary.

The Leviathan versus the Golem

I never conclusively learned how Juba died. It was known that he had ongoing disputes with other young men, but there was also talk that he had been killed by police while "on the round" (stealing) in a nearby neighborhood—rumors that were still alive several years later (Smith 2019, 210). That it was difficult to determine how he died was common, as the deaths of young KwaMashu men (and particularly young men involved in crime) were subject to any variety of rumors, stories, and speculation.[12]

That some of the rumors were about police violence was common and perhaps inevitable when a young man involved in crime died. Indeed, the idea that the state can be deadly isn't merely a product of rumor; it is borne out in police statistics. In the statistical year prior to Juba's death, 912 people died in police custody or as a result of police action—nearly three people per day (Burger 2010). Rates of police violence were particularly high in KwaZulu-Natal province, where KwaMashu is located. More than a quarter of the country's police-related deaths (258) occurred in the province, an increase of 47 percent over the previous year, when police commanders began to encourage police to "shoot to kill" when confronting criminals (ibid.). Not only the high death rate but the nature of the killings was of concern, as many appeared to be of dubious legality. Indeed, a former police officer turned scholar with the country's leading security think tank wondered during this period whether South Africa was witnessing "the beginning of police vigilantism in KwaZulu-Natal," given the suspicious nature of several of the deaths (ibid.).

Yet even as the rate of state violence was increasing and its legality was seemingly dubious, this violence, rather than indicating the police's ability to control crime, may reveal its limits. Indeed, such violence may reveal how the state's capacity to police effectively is episodic at best and therefore relies on exceptional means when regular policing fails.

We see this in a few ways at Juba's night vigil and funeral. For example, while the police did control the sometimes violent and often illegal rituals that normally accompany such funerals, they did so in an incomplete way. At the night vigil, young men still shot guns and spun cars when police were not present, even if not at the rate that they normally might at such an event. At the funeral, people still drank heavily in public and drove away drunkenly with no police interference. That the police could create some form of order is suggested by the nature of the scenes they encountered: large crowds in a relatively circumscribed space. The stationing of officers at each end of the road at Juba's funeral and the occasional patrols at his night vigil could keep the scenes comparatively, if imperfectly, tamed. But they were only able to create a semblance of order, and only able to do that much (or little) by looking past certain illegal activities. In this sense, the police were far from being a Leviathan.

Outside of these situations, their capacity seemed even more limited—as is suggested by the extraordinary volume of murders that occur in KwaMashu every year. As noted above, by the time of Juba's funeral, the country's overall murder rate had roughly halved since the transition period (Kriegler and Shaw 2016, 185). However, this decline was highly uneven across the country and was much less pronounced in KwaMashu than in South Africa as a whole. A year prior to Juba's funeral, for example, police recorded three hundred murders in the township, earning it the title of South Africa's "murder capital" (Dolley 2009). This concentration of violence was apparent at the cemetery where Juba was buried, where, if the usual burial customs were being followed, there may have been up to six funerals for young men who had died violently in the previous week. This incredible volume of violence suggests that the police have great difficulty penetrating society to reduce crime. Of course, prevention of murders is a problem for police everywhere, as most happen in private spaces, are unplanned, and are interpersonal in nature, making their prior policing very difficult (Manning 1977). Even the most overwhelming Leviathan would have difficulty stopping violence in these circumstances, as it is difficult to pacify private relations with force alone, despite Hobbesian fantasies to the contrary.

Yet even as the police have little ability to regulate violence, they are blamed when it occurs. To compensate, the police often perform *as if* they are capable of policing, dramatizing their capacity for force as a substitute for their effective capacity to maintain order (Comaroff and Comaroff 2004). Often, as Steinberg (2008) has shown, this has involved the police descending upon crowds at places like illegal shebeens and making mass arrests for petty illegalities—crimes that may not ultimately be prosecuted. Such tactics are reminiscent of the policing of the night vigil for Juba, where stories of police searches earlier in the evening greeted us shortly after we arrived.

More troublingly, acting as if they are capable of controlling crime frequently entails the police dramatizing their capacity for violence (Comaroff and Comaroff 2004; Comaroff and Comaroff 2016). As scholars have argued elsewhere (e.g., Taussig 2006), if the police see their regular means for controlling crime as limiting, they may turn to irregular and illegal means to bring crime down.

For example, at an after tears gathering (typically, a meal and drinking session held at the deceased's family home) following a funeral for another young man on the same day as Juba's night vigil, I found myself in conversation with an off-duty police officer. As part of a wide-ranging conversation about his experiences policing KwaMashu, he told me about his tendency to use a *sjambok* (a short, heavy whip typically used as a cattle prod) on suspected criminals until they confess their crimes. He related this through a specific story about confronting two young men he caught walking down the road with a suspicious set of articles in the middle of the night. After confronting them and demanding to know where they got the goods, he told me he *sjamboked* them to get their confession that the goods were indeed stolen. The officer then forced them to take him to the house where the goods came from, tracked down the home's owner, and had him come to the scene to reclaim his stolen possessions. The effectiveness of the tactic seemed to justify its practice to the officer, despite its illegality. The implication of the story was that the state sometimes needed to use violence in ways that exceeded its own bounds in order to achieve its ends of maintaining public order—an implication reflected in increasing rates of police violence and mounting suspicions of police vigilantism during this period (Burger 2010).

The Golem Slips Its Masters

What does such violence reveal about the nature of the South African state, though? If the state is a man-made monster, such quotidian police violence may suggest the postapartheid state is a monster that has slipped beyond the control of its master. In this sense, the state is much closer to a Golem than a Leviathan. That is, it may be that the means to control the monster—in this case, massive police reform efforts—have proven to be temporarily effective at best. Much as in the parable of the Golem, in which human's attempts to play God ultimately falter because of human's inherent fallibility, it seems that human's attempts to create a state like a "mortal god" (in Hobbes's words) have proven fallible too. Applied to this case, even as it is imagined as protective, the South African state—like the Golem—ultimately threatens to become erratic and therefore dangerous to the citizens who are its supposed beneficiaries. The prideful, illegal violence of the *sjamboking* police officer, the dubious search of the young men in the caravan to Juba's funeral, and the proclamations by the national police that in militarizing their ranks they are adopting an "approach of being fierce towards criminals, while lenient to citizens' safety" (South African Police Service 2010), all suggest this may be the case.

But if police claim their goal is to be "fierce towards criminals, while lenient to citizens' safety," why should we think of the police as having become a threat to their beneficiaries? There are at least two reasons. First, alleged criminals *are* citizens, not a separate class of people deserving differential treatment by the state. As citizens (or even for those who may be noncitizens, for that matter), they are entitled to the constitutional protections of due process and, at a deeper level, the constitutionally protected right to life, which should shield them from state violence. To be "fierce towards criminals" is inherently to be fierce towards citizens.

Second, even if one thinks of "criminals" as having forfeited rights because of their acts, divining who is a "criminal" and who is a separately classed "citizen" will inevitably lead to mistakes, with the consequence that other South Africans will be harmed. As one expert on policing wrote at the time of the remilitarization of the police, "If police ranks are to be militarised, commissioners becoming generals, superintendents becoming colonels, with whom are the police at war? . . . I can tell you that the answer isn't criminals; it is ordinary South Africans, especially young township men. In calling himself 'General,' police chief Bheki Cele has thrown in the towel. He has acknowledged that normality is too hard an ideal to achieve, that the police service will never be at peace with the people it serves" (Steinberg 2010). That is, despite more than a decade of reform efforts, the postapartheid state—much like its apartheid predecessor—is at war with the majority of South Africa's population, Steinberg's "ordinary South Africans," except now, with the end of apartheid, the state is tasked with protecting this majority. And to the extent that and as long as the police are not at peace with the people they serve, then its creators have lost control of this Golem-like state and it is a danger to those it is meant to serve: its citizens.

The Golem Terrorizes the Population

As the Golem slips away from control by its creators, its own ends are morphing and it is pursuing goals not envisioned by them. One particularly insidious way that officers have pursued unintended ends is extorting South Africans for personal gain under the guise of performing anti-crime work.[13]

A few days after Juba's funeral, for instance, Bhuti had gone into town for a dentist appointment, using Life's BMW. While driving through an inner suburb, he told me, he was stopped by police, taken to the police station, and detained on suspicion of driving a stolen vehicle. That he was profiled seemed clear. Although Life's BMW was supposedly of dubious provenance, the police wouldn't have been able to tell that just seeing it driving down the road and likely stopped Bhuti because of his age and race. Indeed, Bhuti claimed, the detention was a moneymaking venture for the officers, telling me, "They just want money. But there is no money, so fuck them." Suggesting the validity of his suspicions, he was eventually released from custody without charge, only to be detained again on the way out of town by different officers in a repeat of the same scheme.

While it seems Bhuti was targeted in a broad way because of his youth and race, young men can also be targets of extortion because of specific information about them. A couple of weeks after Bhuti was detained, for instance, Life disposed of the BMW, trading it to someone for a much less conspicuous *bakkie* (light truck). Life decided to do this after he and a group of guys he had been drinking with one day had apparently been arrested for possession of stolen property related to the car. The officers who arrested them then demanded they pay a substantial bribe to get themselves and the car out of police custody. They had supposedly been targeted because of a tip from a neighbor who was also mixed up in the criminal world and had become a police informer (*impimpi*). A close friend of Life's, Foresight, relayed the story to me, explaining that a police officer with whom Life was friendly had warned him that there was "a James Bond, a 'Spy Who Loves Me'" [*sic*] (that is, an informer) in the neighborhood who had told police his car was stolen. When I asked Foresight why the police officer would pass along this information to Life, he replied, "You know these police officers. They are all *izigebengu* [criminals]. They tell us everything."

Of course, Foresight's claim that police officers are "all *izigebengu*" is overstated. Nonetheless, officers' official capacity to use state violence with high levels of discretion easily leads to excess. Even more, such excess can blend into violence against South Africa's "civilian" population, citizens who are not involved in crime at all. Almost a decade after Juba's funeral, for example, as I was closing out my research in KwaMashu, I was still hearing stories of police violence. While driving with Bhuti one afternoon to visit a friend of his, for instance, he told me a story about an officer who was particularly feared for his supposed propensity to kill. "He had six bodies on him last year alone," Bhuti claimed. He went on to tell me of a case where the officer had supposedly killed a medical student, thinking the student was driving a stolen car because it was a model particularly prized by hijackers and it lacked license plates, as it was new. Upon looking in the car after shooting the student, the officer supposedly saw the student's school supplies and, realizing his mistake, planted a gun on the student to make it look like a legitimate shooting.

As with many stories of police violence I had heard over the years, the story seemed simultaneously unlikely and yet not implausible. I had heard numerous stories of illegal police violence over the years that were difficult to verify and had come to realize that, even if challenging to establish as fact, they nonetheless revealed truths about how young men experienced the world and particularly how they experienced policing (Smith 2019, chap. 9). In this case, the story suggested the ways in which the police's ability to distinguish between "criminals" and "citizens" is faulty and that the excessive violence often reserved for "criminals" inherently finds its ways to "citizens."

When the violent capacity of the police is combined with police criminality, the threat to "citizens" becomes even more severe. For example, later that evening, while writing up my day's fieldnotes, the story about the medical student roiled in my mind. I decided to see if anything had been reported in the media on the incident. (Bhuti told me the story had been reported, "but not the exact right story about what happened.") Although I didn't find an account that matched its details, in my search I stumbled across a series of news articles from two years prior about alleged police extortion and murder that were just as discomforting (Rall 2017a; Rall 2017b; Rall 2017c).

The articles recounted how two young men were sitting in a parked car when police officers from a specialized unit approached them, ordered them out of the car, and then accused one of them of having hijacked a car that belonged to one of the officer's sisters. After the young men denied knowledge of the incident, the officers reportedly took them to a vacant lot where the officers set dogs on them before demanding a sizable payment for their release. After the police threatened to kill the men, one of them called a female associate who provided the payment by draining her bank account and borrowing additional money from a loan shark (*mashonisa*).[14] The officers then allegedly forced the young men to hold a gun, so that the officers could charge them with possession of an illegal firearm to justify their detention. After the men were arrested and released, they pressed charges against the officers and filed a complaint with South Africa's police oversight agency. The woman was due to serve as a witness in the court proceedings, but before she could testify, she and her teenage daughter were shot to death in her bed. One of the young men was also killed, forcing the surviving man into hiding.

The Golem's Long Life

Such stories of extrajudicial violence and alleged extortion by specific officers may make it seem as if it is a few select "bad apples" who threaten South Africa's population. It is important to keep in mind, though, that such individuals are empowered by a policing system that is inherently antagonistic to South Africa's young Black men, given South Africa's racist history. However, one of the lessons of the Golem parable is that the inherently limited and partial nature of the Golem's agency underpins its threatening nature. The Golem is a creature with life but not self-control. As a consequence, to give it life in the first place is to create a threatening entity whose actions will take an unintended direction. Moreover, in the decade that followed Juba's funeral, this threat became apparent well outside the actions of "bad apple" officers like those engaging in these alleged incidents of extortion. Indeed, such threats were on display in some of the largest and most high-profile operations the police conduct: crowd control.

The most globally visible example of the police's threatening nature occurred during a wildcat strike at the Marikana platinum mine, when police killed thirty-four workers and injured dozens more. But even as police tried to excuse this particular onslaught of violence as a necessary response to an imminent threat the miners posed to officer safety, a series of other deadly incidents suggested that the use of deadly force to control crowds was far from an aberration. Indeed, police had increasingly unleashed deadly or injurious violence against crowds of South Africans protesting for better service delivery—protests that one scholar has aptly called a "rebellion of the poor" (Alexander 2010). Such protests mushroomed in numbers and frequency in the years just prior to police militarization and may provide a clue to the timing of the policy change. While citizen demands for more policing were cited by SAPS officials as the reason they needed to change the force's operation, the fact that they were confronting, with increased frequency, crowds of citizens who had not been given the better lives they had been promised with democratization presents a proximate reason why the police remilitarized and what one consequence of that militarization might be: the suppression of citizens' ability to demand the egalitarian social and political relations promised by democracy (Comaroff and Comaroff 2016, 62–67).

Although in its beginnings this violence was largely confined to South Africa's informal settlements and townships, where the largest concentrations of poor South Africans live, it, too, eventually escaped these confines. In 2015 and 2016, for example, the country reeled when shotgun-wielding police fired on students at South African universities as they demonstrated for a decolonized curriculum and an end to tuition as part of the Rhodes Must Fall and Fees Must Fall movements. In 2021, just as I was completing a draft of this chapter, a father of four was killed when he was hit at close range by four rubber bullets on the sidelines of a similar student protest after leaving a doctor's appointment in Johannesburg.

One might have hoped that in the wake of such incidents—and particularly in the wake of the Marikana massacre, which led to international demands for an end to police violence—the state would have begun anew on its police reform efforts, reengaging in order to build a respect for rights, or, perhaps even more radically, to dismantle the Golem police force altogether (however unlikely that outcome might be). None of this occurred. Instead, in 2018, after a period away from government, former police commissioner/general Bheki Cele—among the officials most closely associated with the remilitarization of the police—was elevated to become minister of police. Shortly after his installation in office he told police at an officer's funeral to effectively ignore alleged criminals' rights when engaging them (ENCA 2018). Cele's return—along with his celebration of police violence—might seem like a drop of water in the populist wave that swept the world's democracies in the late 2010s. He was elevated to the ministerial position, though, by the country's newly elected technocratic president, Cyril Ramaphosa. Rather than being a simple manifestation of populist politics, then, police violence works for many styles of democratic politics, including their most technocratic and institutional. This all suggests that such unpredictable violence may be a feature of democratic statehood, not a flaw in its operation.

I have suggested that considering the erratic violence of policing as central to the operation of modern democratic states should make us think differently about what the police *are* and the extent to which policing can be remade. Instead of fantasizing that the police can be sufficiently constrained to become solely protective Leviathans, I argue that states may be better thought of as unpredictable Golems—potentially protective but always threatening to become dangers to their ostensible citizen-masters. To think through the Golem metaphor is to be aware of the unintended consequences of humanity's creative endeavors, and to urge caution when we fashion creatures capable of force, because that force may slip its creator's control and take on a threatening life of its own. Put starkly, it may be that, when we seek to create a Leviathan, we may create a Golem instead.

Notes

Early drafts of the ideas presented in this paper were presented at the 2019 New England Workshop on Southern Africa, Southern Methodist University's 2019 Violence and the End(s) of Colonialism conference, and the 2020 Annual Meetings of the American Political Science Association and African Studies Association. Many thanks are due to Wale Adebanwi for the invitation to contribute this chapter and for comments on early drafts of it. Thanks are also due to Victoria Bernal, Casey Golomski, Diana Greenwald, Ke Li, Robyn Marasco, and these conferences' participants for questions and comments that helped to sharpen the ideas presented here. Thank you also to Lauren Jarvis and Nkosinathi Sithole for answering questions related to amaNazaretha burial practices and Ed Vesneske, Jr., for very careful copyediting. Kwazi Manzi, Mxolisi Motsepe, and Ayanda Sithole provided research assistance during the project from which this paper emerged.

1. According to police data, when South Africa democratized in 1994, the murder rate (widely accepted by criminologists as the most reliable violent-crime statistic) was 69 per 100,000 people. By 2010, the year police announced their remilitarization, the rate had more than halved to 33 per 100,000 (Kriegler and Shaw 2016, 185). Even as the murder rate had steadily declined over the first fifteen years of democracy, this rate was still considered very high by international standards (typically considered at a rate above 30 per 100,000) (ibid., 82).

2. To protect the anonymity of the individuals involved in these events, all names have been changed.

3. A note on capitalization is important here. In the original SAPS notification announcing these changes, "Force" was repeatedly capitalized, including in the quoted sentence (the original announcement is on file with the author). The capitalization has since been changed in the announcement currently available on the SAPS website (https://www.gov.za/police-ministry-announces-new -police-ranks, accessed 12 January 2022). The discrepancy is important to note, as there was ambiguiuty at the time of the announcement about whether the SAPS was changing its organizational name, alongside the militarization of its rank structure—something the capitalization of "Force" seemed to indicate. Changing the name from "Service" to "Force" would have potentially created legal challenges, as the 1995 act establishing the SAPS was specific in naming

the police a service, in line with the broader shift in how the early postapartheid government imagined the service would engage citizens. A name change from "Service" to "Force" was never adopted.

4. Over time, the nature of this battle and how its combatants were interpreted changed, depending on the era and who deployed the symbol. Variously, the Leviathan symbolized the devil, religious outsiders, an overwhelming threatening force, or an overwhelming protective force. This symbolic multiplicity remained in Hobbes's theory even as Hobbes utilized human forms to depict the Leviathan, rather than monstrous ones (Schmitt 2008, chap. 2). For a perceptive discussion of the role monstrous metaphors play in Hobbes's thought, see Robbins (2020).

5. It must be noted that Schmitt's account of the religious symbolism of the Leviathan and its impact as a political symbol was shadowed by his anti-Semitism (see Strong 2008, xiv–xviii).

6. Elsewhere, I have written that those on the receiving end of this violence experience the state as something akin to a large-scale vigilante group because they fear that any encounter with the police could result in illegal violence (Smith 2019, chap. 9). This is not the only way to read irregular state violence, though. Taking into account the words and actions of state leaders who trumpeted the state's capacity to kill, along with young men's experience of that violence, suggests multiple ways in which we may apprehend the state—including, as I argue in this chapter, as a Golem.

7. This is not to suggest that mythological creatures are the only useful way to complicate Hobbes's imagery. As I noted above, he transformed the Leviathan using both mythological and mechanical images—his depiction of the Leviathan as an "artificial man," for instance. To think through Hobbes's mechanical depiction of the state might be to think of the state, rather than as a Golem, as Frankenstein's monster—an image that carries a similar notion of hubristic human creation that escapes human control and wreaks havoc. I thank Robyn Marasco for pushing me on this point.

8. One exception of which I am aware are a few brief mentions by Carl Schmitt (2008, 71, 95–96) in his study of the figure of the Leviathan in Hobbes's thought. A second is Lee's (2012) analogy of the American administrative state as a lumbering Golem, although he uses it in a different sense than I do, to mean a cloddish, oafish actor, rather than a force that is dangerous because it has slipped out of the control of its creators.

9. Usually, larger cars with long tails, like certain older model BMWs, are preferred for spinning, as they provide more force to bring the back section around in an arc than a small car like a Citi Golf. At the time, though, Citi Golfs were popular cars to own, partly because they were cheap, partly because they were light on petrol, and partly because repairing them was comparatively easy. As a result, they were among the most frequently (and most easily) stolen cars in South Africa—as very well may have been the case with many of those spun at this memorial, given that spinning a car can damage any number of parts, and one would not want to risk damaging one's own car.

10. Bhuti's claim was only partially correct. Segregating the bodies of those who have died violently is a general Nguni (speakers of Bantu languages like

isiZulu and isiXhosa) practice and not limited to amaNazaretha. However, amaNazaretha practice is distinct in that church members slaughter a goat in order to cleanse the body and soul of a person who has died violently. My deep thanks Nkosinathi Sithole for clarifying these details about Nguni and amaNazaretha burial practice.

11. About five months later, at a funeral for an alleged gangster that I attended at Soweto's Avalon Cemetery, a heavy Metro Police presence and the young man's apparently antagonistic relationship with other young men produced a similarly subdued scene to the one at Juba's funeral, suggesting that these dynamics carry to other parts of South Africa.

12. The sad statistical reality is that young men of color in South Africa are by far the most likely victims of violence. Although the data are not representative of the entire country, according to a review of murder dockets in high-crime areas (one of which was KwaMashu) from a few years before Juba died, Black South Africans make up 89 percent of murder victims, 70 percent are between the ages of twenty and thirty-nine, and 89 percent are male (CSVR 2008, 24–26).

13. In this slippage, there are similarities to abuses carried out by other militarized police forces, with those perpetrated by Nigeria's Special Anti-Robbery Squad (SARS)—both leading to and following the rise of the End SARS movement—having particular resonance (see Maclean 2020).

14. The relationship between the man and woman is unclear in the reporting. In one story she is identified as his sister, while in another she is identified as a friend. It's possible the confusion comes from the common practice of calling a close friend "sister" or "brother," even in the absence of a familial tie.

References

Alexander, Peter. 2010. "Rebellion of the Poor: South Africa's Service Delivery Protests—a Preliminary Analysis." *Review of African Political Economy* 37 (123): 25–40.

Altbeker, Antony. 2001. "Who Are We Burying? The Death of a Soweto Gangster." In *Crime Wave: The South African Underworld and Its Foes,* edited by Jonny Steinberg, 88–94. Johannesburg: Witwatersrand University Press.

———. 2005. *The Dirty Work of Democracy: A Year on the Streets with the SAPS.* Johannesburg: Jonathan Ball.

Ashforth, Adam. 2005. *Witchcraft, Violence, and Democracy in South Africa.* Chicago: University of Chicago Press.

Brooks, Heidi. 2020. "'This Democracy Is Killing Us': Perceptions of Rights and Democracy in the South African Police Service." *Journal of Modern African Studies* 58 (2): 165–87. https://doi.org/10.1017/S0022278X20000191.

Bruce, David. 2012. *Marikana and the Doctrine of Maximum Force.* Johannesburg: Parktown.

Burger, Johan. 2010. "Are We Seeing the Beginnings of Police Vigilantism in KwaZulu-Natal?" ISS Africa, 1 March. https://issafrica.org/amp/iss-today/are-we-seeing-the-beginnings-of-police-vigilantism-in-kwazulu-natal.

Cohen, Simchi. 2015. "A Living Man, a Clay Man: Violence, the Zombie, and the Messianic in H. Leivick's *The Golem.*" *Cultural Critique* 90:1–21.

Comaroff, Jean, and John L. Comaroff. 2002. "Alien-Nation: Zombies, Immigrants, and Millennial Capitalism." *South Atlantic Quarterly* 101 (4): 779–805. https://doi.org/10.1215/00382876-101-4-779.

———. 2004. "Criminal Obsessions, after Foucault: Postcoloniality, Policing, and the Metaphysics of Disorder." *Critical Inquiry* 30 (4): 800–824. https://doi-org.brkproxy.minlib.net/10.1086/423773.

———. 2015. *Theory from the South: Or, How Euro-America Is Evolving toward Africa.* New York: Routledge.

———. 2016. *The Truth about Crime: Sovereignty, Knowledge, Social Order.* Chicago: University of Chicago Press.

CSVR. 2008. *Streets of Pain, Streets of Sorrow: The Circumstances of the Occurrence of Murder in Six Areas with High Murder Rates.* Johannesburg: Centre for the Study of Violence and Reconciliation.

de Lange, Deon. 2008. "New Crime Policy a Damp Squib." IOL News, 13 November. https://www.iol.co.za/news/politics/new-crime-policy-a-damp-squib-1.424194.

de Vos, Pierre. 2013. "Police Brutality Comes as a Surprise? Really?" Daily Maverick, 1 March. https://www.dailymaverick.co.za/opinionista/2013-03-01-police-brutality-comes-as-a-surprise-really/.

Dolley, Caryn. 2009. "Kwamashu Takes Over Nyanga's Title." IOL News, 22 September. https://www.iol.co.za/news/south-africa/kwamashu-takes-over-nyanga-s-title-1.459380.

ENCA. 2018. "Ignore the Human Rights of Criminals, Cele Tells Police." ENCA, 4 March. https://www.enca.com/south-africa/ignore-the-human-rights-of-criminals-cele-tells-his-charges.

Hornberger, Julia. 2011. *Policing and Human Rights: The Meaning of Violence and Justice in the Everyday Policing of Johannesburg.* New York: Routledge.

———. 2013. "From General to Commissioner to General—on the Popular State of Policing in South Africa." *Law & Social Inquiry* 38 (3): 598–614. https://doi.org/10.1111/lsi.12023.

Kriegler, Anine, and Mark Shaw. 2016. *A Citizen's Guide to Crime Trends in South Africa.* Johannesburg: Jonathan Ball.

Lee, Mordecai. 2012. "US Administrative History: Golem Government." In *The SAGE Handbook of Public Administration,* edited by B. Guy Peters and Jon Pierre, 215–27. Thousand Oaks, CA: Sage.

Maclean, Ruth. 2020. "Nigeria Goes on Offensive against Youth Protesting Police Brutality." *New York Times,* 13 November. https://www.nytimes.com/2020/11/13/world/africa/Nigeria-EndSARS-protests.html.

Manning, Peter K. 1977. *Police Work: The Social Organization of Policing.* Cambridge, MA: MIT Press.

Marks, Monique, Clifford Shearing, and Jennifer Wood. 2009. "Who Should the Police Be? Finding a New Narrative for Community Policing in South Africa." *Police Practice and Research* 10 (2): 145–55. https://doi.org/10.1080/15614260802264560.

Newham, Gareth, Themba Masuku, and Jabu Dlamini. 2006. *Diversity and Transformation in the South African Police Service.* Johannesburg: Centre for the Study of Violence and Reconciliation.

Nozick, Robert. 1974. *Anarchy, State, and Utopia.* New York: Basic Books.

Rall, Se-Anne. 2017a. "Ipid Probes Durban Police K9 Unit." IOL News, 19 May. https://www.iol.co.za/dailynews/news/ipid-probes-durban-police-k9-unit -9208959.

———. 2017b. "Woman Due to Testify against Cops Killed." IOL News, 29 May. https://www.iol.co.za/dailynews/news/south-africa/woman-due-to-testify -against-cops-killed-9430722.

———. 2017c. "K9 Cops Accused of Extortion Denied Bail." IOL News, 23 August. https://www.iol.co.za/dailynews/k9-cops-accused-of-accused-of-extortion -denied-bail-10905542.

Rauch, Janine. 2009. "Whose Idea Was This Anyway? Initiating Police Reform in the DRC." *South African Journal of Criminal Justice* 22 (2): 213–28.

Robbins, Nicholas W. 2020. "Hobbes's Social Contract as Monster Narrative: The Wolf-Man, Leviathan, and the Politics of Monstrosity." *Polity* 52 (4): 466–95. https://doi.org/10.1086/710686.

Schaffer, Frederic Charles. 2018. "Two Ways to Compare." *Qualitative and Multi-method Research* 16 (1): 15–20.

Schmitt, Carl. 2008. *The Leviathan in the State Theory of Thomas Hobbes: Meaning and Failure of a Political Symbol.* Chicago: University of Chicago Press.

Scholem, Gershom. 1965. *On the Kabbalah and Its Symbolism.* New York: Schocken Books.

———. 1966. "The Golem of Prague and the Golem of Rehovoth." *Commentary,* January, 62–65.

Smith, Nicholas Rush. 2019. *Contradictions of Democracy: Vigilantism and Rights in Post-apartheid South Africa.* New York: Oxford University Press.

South African Police Service. 2010. "Police Ministry Announces New Police Ranks." Press release, 11 March. On file with author.

Steinberg, Jonny. 2008. *Thin Blue: The Unwritten Rules of Policing South Africa.* Johannesburg: Jonathan Ball.

———. 2010. "Military Ranks for Police at War with Young Black Men." *Sunday Times* (Johannesburg), 28 March. https://www.timeslive.co.za/ideas/2010-03 -28-military-ranks-for--police-at-war-with-young-black-men/.

Strong, Tracy B. 2008. "Carl Schmitt and Thomas Hobbes: Myth and Politics." In *The Leviathan in the State Theory of Thomas Hobbes,* by Carl Schmitt, vii–xxviii. Chicago: University of Chicago Press.

Taussig, Michael. 2006. "NYPD Blues." In *Walter Benjamin's Grave,* 175–88. Chicago: University of Chicago Press.

White, Luise. 2000. *Speaking with Vampires: Rumor and History in Colonial Africa.* Berkeley: University of California Press.

Wiener, Norbert. 1964. *God and Golem, Inc.: A Comment on Certain Points Where Cybernetics Impinges on Religion.* Cambridge, MA: MIT Press.

NINE

Encountering the State in Times of Terror

The Case of the Civilian Joint Task Force

DANIEL E. AGBIBOA

THE DOMINANT TREND IN STUDIES OF THE BOKO HARAM insurgency in northeast Nigeria assumes a world cut in two, that is, the state and its security forces on one side versus armed insurgents on the opposite side. Such a bifurcated approach continues a dominant trope that focuses on nonstate armed groups motivated by antistate ideals (e.g., insurgents and terrorists) while marginalizing the agency of community-based armed groups (e.g., vigilantes, pro-government militias, and gangs) that emerge to protect their communities, either alongside or independent of the state (Bellagamba and Klute 2008; Jentzsch, Kalyvas, and Schubiger 2015; Schuberth 2015; Agbiboa 2019). Examples of such community-based armed groups include the Concerned Local Citizens ("Sons of Iraq") that supported the Coalition and Iraqi Security Forces by setting up security checkpoints and providing tips on suspected insurgents; the Arrow Boys that mobilized in southern Sudan to protect their villages against Joseph Kony's Lord's Resistance Army; the Kamajors in Sierra Leone that became the epicenter of community defense mobilizations against the rebel forces of the Revolutionary United Front (Hoffman 2007, 642; see also Jones 2008); and the Civilian Volunteer Organizations mobilized by the Aquino administration in the Philippines as a form of "people power" to defeat the communist rebels (Kowalewski 1991).

Studies have shown that civilian populations are often intentionally targeted during armed conflicts and that civilian-protection efforts launched by the international community have been largely ineffective, if they exist at all (Wood, Kathman, and Gent 2012; Jose and Medie 2016). Absent an effective state in the face of these so-called new wars (Kaldor 1999), local communities often must rely on themselves for protection, deploying their very insecurity and marginality as a social resource for communal organizing and collective action.

Foregrounding everyday life in conflict zones as a primary site of inventive responses to crises and contingencies, this chapter explores how civilian communities encounter and negotiate the state in times of terror. My overriding aim is to interrogate how these communities create a sense of order and predictability within an otherwise insecure and uncertain environment.

The above aim is addressed through a case study of the Civilian Joint Task Force (CJTF), a loosely knit vigilante group of "men with sticks" (in Hausa, *yan gora,* or *kato da gora,* youth with sticks) that emerged in Maiduguri, the capital of Borno State, in 2013 with the aim of protecting their communities from insurgent violence and indiscriminate state attacks. The CJTF is best imagined as an example of "complex hybrid structures of actors, knowledge, technologies, norms, and values" (Abrahamsen and Williams 2011, 171). The chapter sheds new light on why the CJTF *chose* to mobilize, the nature of their interactions with the state and military forces, their impact on Boko Haram's tactics and choice of targets, and their ramifications for sustainable peace. Unlike other vigilante groups in Nigeria, mobilization into the CJTF was not defined by essentialist identities such as ethnicity, religion, or region (as in Higazi 2008; Nolte 2008) but by comradeship and social bond, as evidenced by the willingness of CJTF members to die for their community. This comradeship has effects in terms of the display of what Sara Ahmed calls "withness," "whereby one is 'with others' and 'against other others'" (2004, 130). As one CJTF member in Maiduguri noted, "In our Civilian JTF we have Muslims and Christians. . . . Our mission is to see peace return to Maiduguri and the entire nation" (Ogene 2014). In exploring the role and impact of the CJTF, this chapter builds on existent literature that links vigilante groups to crime and/or social control (David M. Anderson 2002; Gore and Pratten 2003). It extends this literature by shifting the emphasis to vigilance against the more consequential threats posed by armed insurgents and brutal military forces.

Throughout this chapter, two basic assumptions are challenged: (1) that civilian communities are passive victims of war rather than active participants, and (2) that security provision is an arena of state monopoly rather than a pluralized field of delivery. Following the trails of studies that have problematized these assumptions (as in Bellagamba and Klute 2008; Jentzsch, Kalyvas, and Schubiger 2015; Young and Turner 1984), this chapter extends the notion that "local communities are not passive in the face of state failure and insecurity, but instead adapt in a variety of ways to minimize risk and increase predictability in their dangerous environments" (Menkhaus 2006, 75). At the same time, the chapter reinforces studies that have shown that community vigilante groups tend to go rogue (Rodgers 2007; Meagher 2012).

The research on which this chapter is based spans a period of six months (2017–18) during which I followed members of the CJTF as they socially navigated the ruptures and fractures of their dangerous environment. In total, I carried out sixty in-depth, semistructured interviews in Borno and Adamawa states. In Borno, the birthplace of both Boko Haram and the CJTF, interviews took place in Maiduguri and Abadam local government areas (LGAs). In Adamawa, I traveled on dangerous roads from Gombi to Madagali and from Mararraban Pella through Maiha and Mubi, interviewing hunters and vigilantes who joined forces with the CJTF and Nigerian security forces in 2014 to repel Boko Haram. Other key informants included motorists, traders, residents, and officers of Operation *Lafiya Dole* (peace by all means). A further analysis of media reports and public discourse contributed to fact-checking.

A Zone of Indistinction

In June 2011, the Nigerian government deployed a joint task force (JTF) called Operation Restore Order (ORO) to Borno State and other affected parts of the northeast zone to engage a resurgent Boko Haram. But soldiers of JTF ORO were unfamiliar with the geography, main languages, and locally known members of Boko Haram, making it difficult for them to build the networks of trust and reciprocity that are crucial for overcoming an enemy within. As Bukar, the secretary of the Borno State's Hunters Association, told me, "You cannot be brought from another part of Nigeria to Borno to fight insurgents without knowledge of the local terrain." Far from improvising clever ways of bonding with local communities that would have allowed them to "see things" (Göpfert 2016); that is, to overcome the problem of knowledge, JTF ORO lumped all locals into a suspect community, reducing chances of local cooperation. Thus, under JTF ORO, notions of civilians and insurgents became difficult to tell apart. "The military came with the mindset that everybody in Maiduguri was a Boko Haram member," said a local resident. Absent an effective system that makes society legible, "risk assessment becomes a matter of belief, and suspicion itself becomes the grounds for detention" (Ahmed 2004, 131), along with random killings and enforced disappearances. As Abdul Raufu Mustapha explains, "Facing unidentified enemies in the northeast, initially getting little cooperation from a population terrorized by the insurgents, and poorly provisioned, the tendency for some in the military was to shoot first and ask questions later" (2014, 14). A senior army official puts it even more bluntly: "When we can't *see* the enemy, civilians become the enemy" (Dietrich 2015, 6, emphasis added). The conflation of civilians and insurgents reflects what the cultural anthropologist Joseba Zulaika (2012) regards as a persistent "crisis of knowledge" in counterinsurgency caused by an organizing logic that is at once faulty and passionately ignorant.

As Ray Abrahams (2000) argues, "labels often have a lethal quality." With the label of suspect stamped on them by the JTF ORO that had been sent to restore order, civilian lives were rendered injurable and disposable and their spaces of maneuver transmogrified into a "happy hunting ground" (Breen-Smyth 2014, 233). In May 2012, the Usman Galtimari Presidential Committee on Security Challenges in the northeast zone concluded that JTF ORO could not win "the hearts and minds of the people" under the "present poisonous atmosphere." More importantly, the committee called for the immediate replacement of JTF ORO with a new set of troops that were familiar with the local terrain, spoke the main languages, and, crucially, had a "human touch" (Abbah 2012). Despite the expectations that greeted the disbandment of JTF ORO in August 2013 and its replacement with the Seventh Infantry Division, codenamed Operation *Lafiya Dole*, as the umbrella command for the war against Boko Haram, indiscriminate state violence against civilians continued unabated. "Sometimes, we don't even know who the real enemy is, whether Boko Haram or soldiers," said Hafsa, whose husband had been killed by Boko Haram insurgents.

The indiscriminate violence of the Nigerian military proved counterproductive and incendiary, further alienating local inhabitants from the state. An officer in Mubi recalled how a group of policemen burned a market in Bama town to the ground after their colleague was killed in a Boko Haram attack. In anger, a set of Bama traders pooled money and donated it to known insurgents to "teach the policemen a lesson." This example supports Marie Breen-Smyth's point that abuses by state security forces may lead to perceptions among the suspect group that the state, rather than terrorist groups, is the main source of worry (2014, 234). Consequently, bonds of "affective citizenship" (Casey 2008, 69) may develop based on shared experiences of victimization and a collective desire to avoid being targeted. What is less studied, however, is how indiscriminate state violence has also provoked loyalty, or at least non-betrayal, among victimized and targeted youth, reinforcing what Stathis Kalyvas calls "control by compliance" (2004, 98).

Youth with Sticks

On the origins of the CJTF, some commentators have argued that the vigilante group represents less a rising of the masses than a calculated

FIGURE 1. A car drives toward a Civilian Joint Task Force sector 5 sign in Maiduguri. Photo by Afolabi Sotunde/Reuters.

manipulation by state security forces. Most prominently, Kyari Mohammed argues that the CJTF "were not a spontaneous reaction to Boko Haram but part of a military counterinsurgency, because the CJTF was formed out of repentant members of Boko Haram who were recruited by the military and unleashed on society." He further claims that "soldiers order villagers to form CJTF and kill them if they refuse, accusing them of being Boko Haram—and if they do, they face Boko Haram reprisals" (New Humanitarian 2013). In a similar vein, Marc-Antoine Pérouse de Montclos contends that "the Nigerian military eventually realized that they needed to win the 'hearts and minds' of the people. So, they set up local militias, called *Kato da Gora* ('the men with clubs'), who knew the terrain better and were able to root out insurgents hidden among the population" (2016, 882). This reading makes light of the role of local agency in the formation of the CJTF. In fact, it reproduces reductionist images of Africa's young fighters "as victims—as tools of undemocratic military regimes or brutally unscrupulous 'warlords'" (Peters and Richards 1998, 183). In what follows, I argue that the mobilization of the CJTF was, ab initio, community-driven rather than state-imposed. Furthermore, I suggest that most youth in Maiduguri took up sticks *voluntarily* rather than coercively. Like the young combatants of Sierra Leone or the Aguentas of Guinea-Bissau, CJTF youths "[chose] to fight with their eyes open, and defend[ed] their choice, sometimes proudly" (ibid.).

The CJTF was first formed in Maiduguri's Hausari ward (neighborhood) in May 2013. Its early members, mostly young men and boys, gained the upper hand over gun-wielding insurgents while armed only with sticks [*goras*]. "It is unheard of for someone wielding a stick to arrest someone in possession of an AK-47," said Abdullahi, the chairman of the Mobile Phone Dealers Association in Borno State, who also lives in Hausari ward. "In front of my house, an insurgent firing a gun was arrested by a group of young men carrying only bamboo sticks and the insurgent did not succeed in killing a single person." The audacity of the yan gora took Boko Haram by surprise, said Yamani, a sector leader of the CJTF in Maiduguri. "When they shoot at us, we still pursue them . . . and that is why they fear us. God is always with us. How else do you imagine an insurgent with a sophisticated rifle running away when he sees a youth with a stick?" As the quasi-official story goes, Baba Lawan Jafar (alias Ba'alawan), a Kanuri trader from Hausari ward, was the first person to go after an insurgent with only a bamboo stick, capturing and delivering him to the authorities. Jafar's courage inspired several youths in Maiduguri to follow suit, including his close friend Modu Milo. By June 2013, some five hundred yan gora were patrolling the dusty streets of Maiduguri, conducting stop-and-search activities at local residences, market spaces, sacred grounds, and transit routes (ICG 2017, 4). Jafar would later become the overall chairman of the CJTF in Borno State, with Milo serving as his vice chairman.

Given its effectiveness, the vigilantism of the CJTF was soon replicated in various LGAs in Borno State, spreading further into Adamawa and Yobe states before making its way to neighboring Cameroon in 2014 and Chad in 2015 (ICG 2017), where the groups are known as *comités de vigilance*. Today, the CJTF has an estimated membership of between twenty-six and thirty thousand. A small portion of the yan gora are women (the bulk of whom are wives of the CJTF men) who help in screening other women in a culturally respectful manner as well as in the collection of local intelligence. The rise of female counterinsurgents became important considering Boko Haram's alarming use of females as spies and suicide bombers. Zainab Tijjani, a thirty-five-year-old mother of five, said she joined the CJTF after her brother, Ibrahim, was killed by insurgents in the Dala area of Maiduguri: "The loss made me vow to expose them so that peace can be restored" (BBC 2017). "Through their everyday work as household organizers, traders, mothers, stepmothers and co-wives," argues Insa Nolte, "women are often the holders of intimate knowledge about changes and news in their compounds as well as in markets, shops and schools" (2008, 96). A CJTF leader in Yola commented that "women play a vital role in this vigilante work because Islamic religion doesn't allow men to enter houses and we make use of the women to go into these houses for either surveillance or arrests." This role of CJTF women illustrates how "counterinsurgency practice makes men and women legible and assigns them to different categories of various utility for combat and pacification" (Khalili 2011, 1479).

Weapons of the Weak

The yan gora were originally armed with rudimentary weapons like sticks, machetes, and bows and arrows; "guns are too expensive," said a CJTF leader, "costing between six hundred naira and seven hundred naira. We cannot afford that." CJTF weapons were often fortified with "charms of invisibility and immunity" (Pratten 2008a, 10). "Some of them, if you shoot them, the bullet will not enter their bodies because they have taken bullet-proof medicine. So they fear nobody," said a security officer at Maiduguri International Airport. "We have personal protection from our parents that protects us from gunshots like this one you are seeing on my head. Some charms have been embedded in my skull to protect me from harm," said Bitrus, a bricklayer and CJTF member from Gombi in Adamawa State. The belief in magic as a tool of warfare is rooted in tradition in West Africa (Wlodarczyk 2009), where "the re-making of selves out of the secrets of the supernatural [is a] familiar and effective [framework] in the quest for order and certainty" (Pratten 2008b, 46). The use of magic by the yan gora reclaims the ways in which traditional Muslim youth groups in northern Nigeria (e.g., the *yan faratua*, "hunters," and *yan tauri*, those protected from weapons by medicine) "[emphasize] bravery and skill with weaponry and forms of magical protection" (Casey 2008, 73).

The CJTF's status as "sons of the soil" conferred local legitimacy, leading to trust and access, which proved key to weeding out insurgents living in their midst. Residents see the yan gora as more effective than the army because they are locals and thus "know the bad eggs in our midst." The vigilance and bravery of the yan gora also endeared them to local inhabitants, setting them apart from military forces, who many see as deserters and strangers. As one yan gora told me, "Our success hinges on two things: patriotism and bravery. The soldiers were not patriotic initially, as they were urging their colleagues to abandon the war since it's not their homeland that was at stake, and many of them either deserted or withdrew. For us, there is no going back." Thus, with the rise of the CJTF, communities "come to experience the state in the ways in which it does not exist for them and not just in the ways that it does" (Ismail 2006, 138). Said a sixty-eight-year-old man in Maiduguri, "Without the yan gora, the army and police will not go anywhere. Because where these boys will enter, a policeman or army officer will be afraid to enter. They have courage and want to give everything in protection of their land and people. That is why we proudly refer to them as 'our boys.'" For Usman, a resident of Maiduguri, the difference between the CJTF and the military boils down to one thing—trust: "We are with the army, but we know not to trust them to defend us. We have already had two situations [of Boko Haram attacks] in Gwoza and in Bama where soldiers ran away from their security posts. So how can you depend on them to protect you? In Bama town, I was an eyewitness. I saw them mingle with civilians to escape to Maiduguri. So how can you imagine they would protect you?" (TAP 2014). Usman's charge is not unsubstantiated. In a country where bribery and corruption are endemic (Agbiboa 2012, 2022), funds budgeted for military hardware and equipment are regularly stolen (BBC 2015).

Why They Fight

The CJTF was "a product of harassment by Boko Haram and the Nigerian military," said Ganiyu, the super overall chairman of the CJTF in Maiduguri. "Because security men did not know who the real Boko Haram was, they will just come and cordon off any area and take every male youth away for 'screening.' Then later on, we, the youth of Maiduguri, we decided that enough is enough. That's why we chose to cooperate with the military, that we are going to fish out those bad apples in our society. That's how we started this vigilante group." Ganiyu's account was reinforced by Sanusi, a taxi driver from the Wulari area in Maiduguri. "Let me tell you," said Sanusi, "we have three types of Boko Haram. We have a real Boko Haram. We have a military Boko Haram. And we have a political Boko Haram. You don't know who will save you. Only God. If Boko Haram doesn't kill you, soldiers will kill you. Therefore, those CJTF boys took up sticks. Because they say, if the state cannot protect us, let us protect ourselves." Statements such as this suggest that the Nigerian state is not only failing in its responsibility to protect—to secure life and property—but constitutes its own threat to the survival of its citizens. In times of terror, civilians routinely encounter the omnivorous potentialities of the postcolonial state in Africa (Mbembe 1992; Comaroff and Comaroff 1999); that is, with "its seemingly boundless capacity to prey upon its citizens" (Masquelier 2001, 268).

Although most Boko Haram members were known to locals in the neighborhoods where they grew up, "no one could identify them, because if you do they will sneak back and warn you and eventually kill you in public," said Bomboy, the super overall chairman of the CJTF in Hausari ward. The situation was complicated by the state's brutal counterinsurgency campaign, which indiscriminately targeted civilians. As Abba Ali, a sector commander of the CJTF in Maiduguri, told me, "When we first thought of joining the CJTF, there was still the fear that if we tell the military who Boko Haram really are, they will come around and eliminate us." In joining the CJTF, therefore, local youths risked exposing themselves and their relatives to the wrath of Boko Haram and/or the military (see the case of Bukar

FIGURE 2. Members of a civilian joint task force patrol in Maiduguri. Photo by Joe Penney/Reuters.

Bama Sheriff below). According to Bomboy, the initial mission of the yan gora was to prevent the violent extortion of traders by Boko Haram insurgents, especially Christian Igbo traders at the busy Monday Market, the commercial epicenter of Borno State. "Boko Haram had their informers everywhere," said Bomboy. "If you make big sales as a shop owner, they will come to you and request money. If you don't give them, they will kill you there and then and cart away the money. They killed hundreds of traders."

Many youths joined the CJTF out of a feeling of personal loss, which was then channeled toward extirpating Boko Haram from their community. As Ahmed (2015, 7) argues, emotions are intentional in the sense that they are "about" something: they involve an orientation toward an object. A survey by Umar Yusuf in Maiduguri and the Jere LGA of Borno State found that 70 percent of yan gora had lost a friend or relative to Boko Haram and were driven by this sense of loss (2014, 69). This was the case with Ganiyu, who joined the group in 2013 after his close friends were killed in a Boko Haram attack on their town. Prior to joining, Ganiyu spent sixteen years as a secretary in the People's Democratic Party (PDP). In 2013, as the insurgency intensified and his friends were violently killed by Boko Haram insurgents, Ganiyu "resigned voluntarily" from the PDP to join the fight against Boko Haram. "I feel very happy doing this work because I am protecting the lives and properties of my community," said Ganiyu. "I am a respected person in my community. When I talk, people listen. Just the respect we get compels us." The emotion of personal loss is also palpable in Bakura Wanzam's journey into the CJTF from the Gubja area of Yobe State. "I joined this fight to save our religion, our village, and our people. I want to inform you that my father was slaughtered like a goat in Yadi Buni, and you can see why I had to join this fight. We saw these insurgents killing our parents and relations, so we sacrificed our lives and said these are people like us and we must fight them to a standstill."

The Story of Bukar Bama Sheriff

Bukar Bama Sheriff is the overall chairman of the CJTF in Abadam LGA of Borno State. I first met Sheriff at an internally displaced persons camp in Abadam town, where his CJTF sector was manning the camp gates and providing security in the absence of the state. With its headquarters located in Malumfatori, Abadam town has an estimated population of one hundred thousand people and is one of the sixteen LGAs that constitute the Borno Emirate. In October 2014, Boko Haram captured Abadam, killing up to forty people and forcing residents to flee to border areas in Niger. In February 2015, a cross-border operation involving Nigerian and Cameroonian forces recaptured Abadam—but as early as August 2016, Abadam was once again a stronghold of Boko Haram (United Nations 2017, 3). Sheriff, who also holds a political position in Abadam LGA, said he first became involved in security surveillance work for the state in 2011, when soldiers of JTF ORO posted to Abadam sought his help in finding a suitable location to set up camp. Sheriff's cooperation with the troops exposed him to the wrath of the insurgents. "You know," he said, "Boko Haram has very strong local intelligence and network. So, if there is any cooperation between you and the Nigerian security forces, they will know and they will try to eliminate you."

Initially, Sheriff served as the vice chairman of the CJTF in Abadam, reporting to Adamu Buba, the overall chairman. Both Sheriff and Buba received death threats from the insurgents warning them to cease their support for the military or "prepare to die." Boko Haram made real its threat when it brutally attacked and killed Buba in his house, leaving a note of warning for Sheriff. Following Buba's death, Sheriff assumed the role of overall chairman and vowed to continue working for the military. With Sheriff on Boko Haram's most-wanted list in Abadam, his friends and relatives invariably became endangered and distanced themselves from him in public gatherings. "People around me reacted in two ways," said Sheriff. "People in Abadam community started hating me and isolating themselves from me. They don't want to talk or seat next to me in public gatherings out of fear of been associated with me. People always tried to convince me to abandon my support and intelligence work for the Nigerian military to save my head and that of my family. But I tell them that if you join the yan gora, Boko Haram will not rest until they finish you. They will target you until the very end." Hence, for Sheriff, there was no easy way out of his precarious existence. "Immediately you identify yourself with the CJTF, even when you leave your work, even when you resign publicly, you have only resigned for yourself in the eyes of Boko Haram insurgents. They will still hunt you down and kill you." There was also the small matter of dealing with an abusive Nigerian military. As Sheriff explains, "If you begin like me, by giving them information about the insurgents hiding in the neighborhoods, and then you later decide to stop, they, too, will start suspecting and targeting you. They will say you have changed your mind and started to work for the insurgents. This is why my situation is extremely difficult." Sheriff's sense of being caught between violent jihadists and brutal state forces characterizes the everyday life of state informants in the context of terror. Following Mirco Göpfert's ethnographic study of security surveillance in Niger, I suggest that state informants like Sheriff can be thought of as "knowledge brokers" who help state security forces to "see things" in times of terror, but whose relationship with the state involves "a balancing act between suspicion and trust" (2012, 44–45). Despite this harsh reality, Sheriff insists that "nobody forced me to join this group. I do this work voluntarily, because if I don't, the impact of Boko Haram will still affect me and my family."

"New National Heroes"

The CJTF emerged in Maiduguri in May 2013 and by late 2013 its local knowledge, daily patrols, and combat support had succeeded in disrupting Boko Haram's operational networks, forcing the insurgents to decamp to remote parts of Borno State (including the Gwoza Hills and Mandara Mountains), where hunter militias have spearheaded the war on terror. Boko Haram's relocation to the countryside represents a throwback to the Kanama phase of its formative years (2003–4), when it withdrew from the city, formed a puritanical Islamic community in the village of that name, and attacked the state from there. This is not an uncommon move for rebel groups in Africa. As Thandika Mkandawire writes, "The roots of revolt in most African countries lie in the cities, and more specifically, the capital cities. Most guerrillas are merely 'passing through' the countryside on their way to capture power in the city" (2002, 207).

In dire need of local collaboration, an overburdened and ill-informed Nigerian military was quick to recognize the potential of the CJTF, as well as the hunter militias (yan faratua), as a "force multiplier" and, crucially, "a feasible and effective means of counterinsurgency, providing valuable local knowledge and efficient means to collect intelligence" (Jentzsch, Kalyvas, and Schubiger 2015, 759). "When we came out, the military welcomed us one hundred percent," said Kalli, a CJTF leader in Maiduguri. The military helped to organize the yan gora along its own lines of command. Maiduguri, for instance, was divided into ten sectors, each led by a chairman selected by senior army officials with whom the chairmen worked closely. The sectors were equipped with vehicles and charged with identifying Boko Haram suspects, manning checkpoints, and guiding soldiers on patrols. Highly mobile, vigilantes in each sector could be deployed easily wherever needed. A yan gora from Mubi in Adamawa State told me that, though the CJTF participated in "combat battle," their major role was "to ensure peace and stability in any recaptured towns or villages by doing house-to-house searching and patrolling around the captured areas."

In Borno State, about 850 members of the CJTF were selected for military training in firearms and intelligence gathering. Upon completion, this group became known as the CJTF Special Forces and was charged with providing combat support to the army. This fusing of a nonstate armed group—volunteering to shield its community from Boko Haram insurgents—into an institution of legitimate violence underscores the limitations of conventional state/society dichotomies in analyses of how civilians in extremis imagine and encounter the state (Masquelier 2001, 269). It breaks down our normative understanding of distinctions between the state and civil society, as well as collapsing the traditional understanding of the state as the Leviathan possessing exclusive right to legitimate violence. Instead, the CJTF-state alliance in the war against Boko Haram signals a "hybrid security governance," which suggests that, "far from possessing an effective monopoly of force, states and their security institutions operate alongside a diverse array of non-state bodies, some violently challenging state authority, others working alongside or co-operating with it" (Bagayoko, Hutchful, and Luckham 2016, 1).

Members of the CJTF Special Forces upgraded from using sticks and machetes to pump-action guns. Abba Ali, a member of the CJTF Special Forces, told me that the upgrade became necessary in the face of Boko Haram's superior weapons: "When you get to Boko Haram camps you find that they have artillery pieces, anti-aircraft guns, and AK-47, while all we have are Dane guns [usually made by local blacksmiths, with the generic name dating back to Danish traders who imported flintlock muskets in the early-mid nineteenth century] that you load and shoot once before you load and fire again. This sometimes takes five minutes. Whenever we are not many, like one hundred of us, we can't face them. So when we go for an operation that is not that hot, we just use our Dane guns. But if the military think the war is going to be very hot, they must give us pump-action guns because there is no way you can fight Boko Haram with Dane guns." After combat, soldiers frequently retrieved the pump-action guns from the CJTF Special Forces for fear of arming potentially unreliable youth. The suspicion surrounding the CJTF is hardly surprising if we consider Sally Merry's point that local intermediaries are "often distrusted, because their ultimate loyalties are ambiguous and they may be double agents. . . . They are vulnerable to charges of disloyalty or double-dealing" (2006, 40). This notwithstanding, the cooperation between the CJTF and the military played a vital role in reclaiming several territories previously under Boko Haram's brutal control. For example, from late 2014 to early 2015, Boko Haramn controlled large swaths of Nigerian territory, including twelve of twenty-seven LGAs in Borno State, five of twenty-one in Adamawa State, and two of seventeen in Yobe State. However, strengthened by the support of the CJTF and hunters, only two LGAs in Borno State—Abadam and Mobar—were still under Boko Haram's control by the end of 2015 (UN Security Council 2017, 3).

The sacrifices of the CJTF earned them high praise from locals and public officials alike, with former Nigerian president Goodluck Jonathan hailing them as "new national heroes" (Idris and Sawab 2013). "If not for the CJTF, Maiduguri would have long [ago] fallen into the hands of Boko Haram," said Saad Abubakar, a community leader in Maiduguri. "They are a fearless band of committed youth who know Boko Haram members and the terrain very well." For Bulama Gubio, a leader of the Borno State Elders Forum, "the Civilian JTF are the saving grace for us in Borno State, in fact in northeast Nigeria. Without their efforts, the Boko Haram insurgency wouldn't have been put down by now. . . . They organised themselves from each ward in the city and some of the major towns and started fighting their own friends, their own colleagues who were members of Boko Haram" (Oduah 2016). Following a deadly Boko Haram attack on the Dalwa and Mafa areas of Borno State in February 2015, the governor of Borno State, Kashim Shettima, praised the yan gora, who had "moved to front lines to support our gallant armed forces in a patriotic battle to defend the soul of Borno State and its people from being seized by determined insurgents" (Odunsi 2015). The CJTF's role as first responders on the front lines of terrorism points toward the growing significance of community-based armed groups, including vigilante groups and civil militias, as responses to state failure or inability to secure lives and properties (Jones 2008). The CJTF's partnering with soldiers to deny access to insurgents also challenges simplistic renderings of the state and civil society in postcolonial Africa as distinctly separate entities (Smith 2004; Agbiboa 2019). The effectiveness of the CJTF in providing protection and the popular legitimacy it seems to enjoy not only highlight the potential of "governance without government" (Menkhaus 2006), but also demonstrate that the state does not have a legitimate monopoly over the use of violence. This is particularly true in weak or failing states where the incapacity to deliver security has eroded trust in their power and authority.

At Daggers Drawn

Research suggests that civilian victimization remains a key conflict strategy deployed by state and nonstate armed groups in a bid to control a changing conflict landscape and shape the behavior of a local population (Wood, Kathman, and Gent 2012; Kalyvas 2004). Thandika Mkandawire (2002), for example, argues that much of the bloodletting observed in African insurgencies derives from the incapacity of urban guerrilla groups to garner support among rural populations. A prime example is Uganda, where the Lord's Resistance Army's failure to mobilize support among the Acholi people was key to Joseph Kony's turn toward violence against locals (Branch 2005). The case of the CJTF is particularly revealing. The group's rise has been read as a central factor in Boko Haram's transformation from an antistate insurgency to instigators of a full-blown terrorism, putting insurgents and local residents at daggers drawn. As Kyari Mohammed argues, "by pushing Boko Haram . . . into the countryside, the CJTF and soldiers made life precarious to villagers" (New Humanitarian 2013, ellipsis in original). These findings are further supported by the admission of a captured Boko Haram sect member: "Our original target was security operatives and politicians. But since the formation of Civilian JTF who now reveal our identities and even arrest us, we decided to kill anyone that is from Maiduguri, because we believe every person in Maiduguri and some other towns of Borno State are members of Civilian JTF" (Strochlic 2014).

In light of Boko Haram's rage against communities that formed a CJTF, many yan gora told me that local residents have become fearful of identifying with them. As Kurna, the CJTF chairman for Adamawa State, told me, "I was ejected from a house I rented by my landlord for fear of attacks by Boko Haram. A lawyer was asked to serve me a quit notice." In June 2013, Boko Haram released an audio clip in which its spokesperson, one Abu Zinnira, declared an "all-out war" on the youth of Maiduguri "because you have formed an alliance with the Nigerian military and police to fight our brethren. . . . We call on any parent that values the life of his son to stop him from exposing our members, otherwise he is dead" (New Humanitarian 2013, ellipsis in original). In September 2013, following a violent attack on Benisheik town, about seventy kilometers west of Maiduguri, Boko Haram's leader Abubakar Shekau labeled the yan gora "infidels" for cooperating with the Nigerian military and threatened to avenge the deaths of his members at their hands. "We warn the . . . Civilian JTF to back out," said Shekau. "If not, there will be no place for them to hide. We have evidences [*sic*] of how you killed some of our brethren. . . . We will get to you. . . . We will . . . smash your heads and kill you all" (Odunsi 2014).

Against this backdrop, members of the CJTF say that they have crossed the Rubicon in their pledge to fight terror and keep the peace. As one yan gora noted, "there is no going back. Boko Haram have declared war on us and even if we stop hunting them down, they will still come after us, so we have to fight to the finish" (New Humanitarian 2013). The CJTF's steadfastness in the face of imminent danger echoes the way in which the rallying slogan *kamajor baa woteh* (do not turn back) among the Kamajors served as "an injunction against retreat from the battlefield, but . . . also a moral command not to betray the community one had been initiated to defend" (Hoffman 2007, 647). The resilience of the CJTF has come at a huge personal cost. "We have created a lot of enemies in this work. There are people that are still after us," said Alhaji Bako Ali Kurna. In Borno State alone, the official death toll for the CJTF between 2013 and 2017 is estimated at seven hundred (Omonigho 2017). However, leaders of the CJTF believe that the fatalities are considerably higher, because there has hardly been a military operation against Boko Haram since 2013 without the loss of at least one of the yan gora who routinely guide the troops during their operations.

Turning Bad

Vigilante groups tend to turn bad (Rodgers 2007; Meagher 2012). The CJTF is no exception. Since 2014, the widespread praise for the CJTF has paled in the face of growing public concern that it may represent "Nigeria's next security threat" (IRIN News 2016). As one astute editorial noted, "An unregulated, untrained and crudely armed civilian force may prove to be the last thing [Maiduguri's] imperiled residents need. Civilian gangs have in the past served as political enforcers around the country" (*Vanguard* 2013b). Another editorial published the following day pointed out that, "apart from risking their lives unnecessarily, a greater danger of exposing civilians to battle situations includes the possibility of some of these civilians turning into warlords. In the North, such warlords inevitably put on the religious garb. Before we know it, civilians helping to fight terrorists may fall under the influence of politicians and other foreign sponsors to float their own terror outfits" (*Vanguard* 2013a). Such concerns have not only tempered early images of the CJTF as "new national heroes," but also thrown into sharp relief Kate Meagher's argument that the alliance between state and nonstate security forces can be a "Faustian bargain" that may ultimately result in "the embedding of violent or illegitimate forms of order in the machinery of the state, with disastrous rather than transformatory consequences" (2012, 1097).

From the outset, a litany of human rights abuses has haunted the CJTF. In 2013 alone, ninety-nine members of the group were arrested for unauthorized attacks on suspected Boko Haram members. In the earliest incident, which occurred on 12 May 2013, the mansion of one Alhaji Mala Othman, chairman of the All Nigeria People's Party in Borno State, was burned to the ground by a group of yan gora who accused him of sponsoring Boko Haram. Notably, the group acted after the police refused to arrest Othman, saying they had no such evidence (New Humanitarian 2013). The incident illustrates how "competing idioms of accountability simultaneously contradict and complement each other" (Smith 2004, 449). Some members of the CJTF have also been implicated in extrajudicial killings of Boko Haram suspects, often with the tacit approval of or in conjunction with the military. Between January and April 2014, twenty-one CJTF members were arrested for unlawfully executing suspected insurgents in their custody. In March 2014, some yan gora and the military rounded up and killed hundreds of unarmed suspects who had escaped from a military detention center in Giwa, near Maiduguri (ICG 2017, 19). In August 2014, Amnesty International released "horrific images of detainees having their throats slit one by one and dumped in mass graves" by stick-wielding youth and men of the Nigerian military (Amnesty International 2014). In another incident that took place in November 2014, members of the CJTF cordoned off streets in Biu, a town in southern Borno State, parading the heads of forty alleged Boko Haram insurgents on pikes (Maina 2014). The youth claimed that the graphic display was intended to dispel local myths about the insurgents being invincible, and to mobilize collectivities. As Umar Hassan, one of the participants, said, "We beheaded the insurgents after the shoot out [*sic*] which lasted for about two hours and took their heads to Biu to show the people that the Boko Haram insurgents are human and not beasts and so, people should not fear them but instead, join hands with us and security operatives to ensure that the sect members who are enemies of Islam and the people of [Nigeria] are defeated" (Marama 2014). Hassan's comment reveals the extent to which violence in northeast Nigeria has become normalized as "a form of public pedagogy" (Evans and Giroux 2015a) and as spectacle, "a social relationship between people that is mediated by images" (Debord 1995, 12).

Since 2015, the CJTF has come under criticism for using children in their counterinsurgency operations; mounting arbitrary security checkpoints at which they extorted money from commercial drivers; engaging in cattle rustling; and sexually harassing women and girls under their watch in various internally displaced persons (IDP) camps (UN Security Council, 2017).[1] During my fieldwork in an IDP camp in Abadam town, a displaced woman described how she, along with several other women, had acquiesced to the sexual demands of the CJTF in order to escape starvation: "In the camp, we barely get something to eat. Food is given to only the pregnant women, children, and elderly. I was forced to sell my body to the CJTF to get an *indomie* [instant noodle packet] or a cup of rice." Another concern is the manner in which "young men posing as Civilian JTF" increasingly moonlight as political thugs and are hired to carry out "religious revenge missions" (GCCA 2014), reinforcing popular images of African youth as "ready recruits to the barbarities of life" (Comaroff and Comaroff 2011, 273). These concerns considered, the CJTF still retains support among a significant segment of locals who maintain that the group is the lesser of two evils. As one resident justified, "The Civilian JTF may bark and hurl abusive language at people [but] Boko Haram shoot, bomb and slaughter their victims" (*Vanguard* 2013b, edit in original). "For now, we have to bear with them," said Hussein Bala, leader of Maiduguri's Lawyers Union, adding that, "compared to what Boko Haram are doing, their own [abuses] are insignificant" (South African Press Association and Agence France-Presse 2013). A leader of the CJTF explained away the abuses by the group, blaming them on "a few bad eggs trying to soil our name." While the now former governor of Borno State, Kashim Shettima, has never hidden his admiration for the CJTF, describing their rise as "a divine intervention," he admits that "one may not rule out some infractions from some overzealous members" (Okeowo 2014). He has also stated that "unless deliberate efforts are made towards addressing issues of unemployment, illiteracy, hunger and extreme poverty, the C.J.T.F. will be the Frankenstein monsters that might end up consuming us" (Okeowo 2015).

The Borno Youth Empowerment Scheme (BOYES)

According to Meagher, "the mechanisms through which non-state forces acquire formal recognition, and the shifts in power and accountability that take place in the process, are critical to determining in whose interest these new sources of order will operate" (2012, 1096). For many members of the CJTF in Borno State, that "formal recognition" was acquired through participation in BOYES. The statewide scheme was established in November 2013 by the Borno State government in light of public concerns about the CJTF and upon realization that simply isolating or marginalizing these youth with sticks would bring more problems than solutions. According to Governor Shettima, BOYES was established to "indoctrinate [members of the CJTF] into having a better Nigerian love for their fatherland, make them conscious of what goes [on] within and around them, train them to be conscious of the security of [the] wider civilian population without taking laws into their hands so that they can lawfully help in policing their own communities" (Nigerian Bulletin 2013). CJTF members selected for BOYES (the criteria of selection are unclear) underwent a vetting process, including background checks and medical screening. Upon completion, BOYES graduates were provided with blue uniforms, blue patrol vehicles, ID cards, and a monthly stipend of N15,000 ($50). Some BOYES graduates were integrated into the Nigerian Army, Department of State Service, and Air Force. The state's initial plan was to train five thousand yan gora. However, in 2015, after graduating two batches totaling eighteen hundred yan gora, BOYES was suddenly terminated. According to government officials, BOYES was terminated to convert the training site into a camp for over one million IDPs seeking refuge in Borno State. However, a CJTF sector leader in Maiduguri told me that BOYES was stopped because of the fear among soldiers that Boko Haram spies had infiltrated CJTF ranks: "Initially, the state trained first batch and second batch. And gave us forms to be distributed for the third batch. But at that time, the Boko Haram in the bush just used this BOYES color of uniforms to mix up among us and confuse people. So automatically we stopped wearing the uniforms."

With the end of BOYES, the hopes of many yan gora of earning government income was dashed. Some yan gora felt deceived by the state. As one CJTF member noted, "I remember we completed lots of forms from army and government while fighting the war, with the promise that we will be recruited into the army or police. We have not heard anything after all these years." CJTF leaders have repeatedly called on the government to do more to reduce among their members what has been called the "sense of entrapment, of having nowhere to go" (Hage 2003, 20), the fear being that "by their sheer numbers, their availability, and their eagerness to take up anything that may relieve them of conditions of poverty, idleness or *ennui*, youth are easily recruited by political parties, armed groups or criminal networks" (Abbink 2005, 3). As a leader of the CJTF told me, "Our boys were promised jobs. If these jobs do not materialize, I fear the day when these boys will turn against us and our leaders in frustration." Said another leader, "It is very sad that people like to benefit from our contributions but they are unwilling to contribute to our upkeep." In Maiduguri, a CJTF commander commented that "the state government has done its best to end the war but has forgotten one thing. Soldiers have salaries and allowances set aside to treat those injured, but not CJTF and hunters. We don't know what is happening. Is it that the soldiers do not say that we are helping them or what? If you go around our houses now you realize that we don't have food provision to last us for three days." A recurrent source of frustration among the yan gora that I spoke to concerns the lack of support by the federal government for families of fallen comrades, many of whom are reduced to "bare lives." As Abba Ali explained, "You know the life of a human being is a very huge thing. The last group of yan gora that we lost to Boko Haram just last month, thirteen of them, the state gave the family N500,000 each and one plot of land. But the support of the federal government was totally zero. Even now, we by ourselves want to establish a school for children of the CJTF whose fathers were killed in service of this country, because nobody takes them to school. On our own, we are trying to open a school that would be called 'CJTF Orphans.'" Another respondent complained that "no one deem it fit to even pay condolence visits to the families of CJTF killed fighting Boko Haram."

Some CJTF drew a contrast between their neglect at the hands of the federal government and the lucrative Presidential Amnesty Program in Nigeria's oil-rich Niger delta, under which oil rebels were granted official pardon, put on the government payroll, and given vocational training and overseas scholarships (ICG 2017, 17). As one yan gora asked, "These Niger delta oil rebels get something, so what should we get, we who fought for the state?" Another CJTF leader noted that "the federal government has created a Ministry of Niger Delta. It has given them amnesty, they were taken abroad, they were trained, they were given jobs, and they are taking good care of them. But in the CJTF, we are sworn to protect the integrity of this country. Between the militants and the CJTF, who is supposed to be taken care of by the government? . . . I feel that if the government is taking care of those destroying the land, what about the CJTF?" (Idowu 2016). Despite their frustration with the state over BOYES, the yan gora I interviewed still nurtured hopes of transitioning into state law enforcement as soldiers, police officers, or vehicle inspection officers. Clearly, these youth were not just fighting against an enemy but for a better life.

This chapter has shown that civilians in search of protection and support in armed conflict are increasingly turning to community-based armed groups that assume the functions and symbols of the state rather than to ineffective and distant state agencies. This troubles our continued reliance on a state-centric model of security governance in Nigeria and, more broadly, Africa. Such a statist approach cannot adequately explain the complex relations between state and civil society, particularly their overlapping roles in security provision and service delivery. The chapter notes that encounters with indiscriminate state violence against civilians in times of terror does not automatically result in the rise of violent antistate movements. On the contrary, it may trigger the emergence of pro-government vigilante groups—such as the CJTF—committed to protecting their communities by working *with* rather than *against* the state. In analyzing the rise of the

CJTF, this chapter deviates from the common victimizing narratives of civilians in violent insurgencies.

On the one hand, the CJTF represents a community-driven (rather than state-orchestrated) civilian defense group that emerged and thrived in a context of state and nonstate terror. On the other hand, membership in the CJTF has provided an opportunity for marginalized youth to "insert themselves within political and economic niches of the state apparatus" (Pratten 2008a, 7). Thus, a study of the CJTF is also a study of how marginal youth survive and forge a future for themselves in a dangerous environment. By *choosing* to fight alongside the state, the yan gora defy usual analyses of nonstate armed actors in terms of "exit," invisibility, and state evasion (Mkandawire 2002). As Stef Jansen argues, much scholarship focuses on "people's evasion of state grids" and does not sufficiently "conceptualise their affective and practical investments in ordering statecraft, i.e., their hope for the state" (2014, 238). In yearning for inclusion in the state grid, albeit on their terms, the CJTF shows how "the state can be both the author of . . . atrocities and [still] represent the hope for a better future" (Stevenson 2007, 142), for "normal lives" (Jansen 2014, 243). Although the emergence of vigilante groups may be thought of as a response to weak or failing states, it is important to note that these groups generally aim for "more state, not less state" (Rasmussen 2010, 445).

Considering the CJTF's growing atrocities, there are increasing calls for more government oversight of the group (Hassan and Pieri 2018), even its total ban. Those making these calls, however, must come to terms with the fact that "under the economic and political influence of powerful state officials," vigilante groups often become "increasingly known for involvement in political reprisals, extortion, unjustified killings and other kinds of criminal activity" (Meagher 2012, 1093). Recent history tells Nigerians that the boundary between vigilantes and criminals is terribly blurred and manipulable (Abrahams 1987, 180), that "the 'goodness' of any action is never absolute, regardless of the evident 'evil' of its target" (McCall 2004, 57). If the existent literature on community-based armed groups is anything to go by (e.g., Schuberth 2015; Meagher 2012; Jentzsch, Kalyvas, and Schubiger 2015; Agbiboa 2019), then groups like the CJTF are *more*, not *less*, likely to transmogrify from protectors to predators, leaving their communities worse off than they were before.

Note

1. A report by the UN secretary general on children and armed conflict in Nigeria found that between November 2015 and December 2016, the CJTF used 228 children in its operations, including for intelligence gathering, night patrols, crowd control, identifying suspects, and active combat (UN Security Council 2017, 7–8).

References

Abbah, Theophilus. 2012. "White Paper on Security: Report Links Boko Haram with London Scholar." Daily Trust (website), 23 May.

Abbink, Jon. 2005. "Being Young in Africa: The Politics of Despair and Renewal." In *Vanguard or Vandals: Youth, Politics and Conflict in Africa,* edited by Jon Abbink and Ineke van Kessel, 1–33. Leiden: Brill.

Abrahams, Ray. 1987. "Sungusungu: Village Vigilante Groups in Tanzania." *African Affairs* 86 (343): 179–96.

———. 2000. "Anthropology and the Inner Frontiers of the State." *Cambridge Journal of Anthropology* 22 (3): 1–13.

Abrahamsen, Rita, and Michael C. Williams. 2011. "Security Privatization and Global Security Assemblages." *Brown Journal of World Affairs* 18 (1): 171–80.

Adebanwi, Wale, and Ebenezer Obadare, eds. 2010. *Encountering the Nigerian State.* New York: Palgrave Macmillan.

Agamben, Giorgio. 1998. *Homo Sacer: Sovereign Power and Bare Life.* Stanford, CA: Stanford University Press.

Agbiboa, Daniel E. 2012. "Between Corruption and Development: The Political Economy of State Robbery in Nigeria." *Journal of Business Ethics* 108:325–45.

———. 2019. "Origins of Hybrid Governance and Armed Community Mobilization in Sub-Saharan Africa." Washington, DC: RESOLVE Network.

———. 2022. *They Eat Our Sweat: Transport Labor, Corruption and Everyday Survival in Urban Nigeria.* Oxford: Oxford University Press.

Ahmed, Sara. 2004. "Affective Economies." *Social Text* 22 (2): 117–39.

———. 2015. *The Cultural Politics of Emotion.* 2nd ed. New York: Routledge.

Amnesty International. 2014. "Nigeria: Gruesome Footage Implicates Military in War Crimes." Amnesty International (website), 5 August. https://www.amnesty.org/en/latest/news/2014/08/nigeria-gruesome-footage-implicates-military-war-crimes/.

———. 2018. *"They Betrayed Us": Women Who Survived Boko Haram Raped, Starved and Detained in Nigeria.* AFR 44/8415/2018. London: Amnesty International.

Anderson, Benedict. 1983. *Imagined Communities: Reflections on the Origins and Spread of Nationalism.* London: Verso.

Anderson, David M. 2002. "Vigilantes, Violence and the Politics of Public Order in Kenya." *African Affairs* 101 (405): 531–55.

Bagayoko, Niagale, Eboe Hutchful, and Robin Luckham. 2016. "Hybrid Security Governance in Africa: Rethinking the Foundations of Security, Justice and Legitimate Public Authority." *Conflict, Security and Development* 16 (1): 1–32.

Bauman, Zygmunt. 1992. *Mortality, Immortality and Other Life Strategies.* Cambridge: Polity.

Bayat, Asef. 1997. "Un-civil Society: The Politics of the 'Informal People.'" *Third World Quarterly* 18 (1): 53–72.

BBC. 2015. "Nigeria's Dasuki 'Stole $2bn' from Anti-Boko Haram Fight." 18 November. https://www.bbc.com/news/world-africa-34855695.

———. 2017. "The Nigerian Woman Standing Up to Boko Haram." *BBC News,* 14 April. https://www.bbc.com/news/av/world-africa-39591879.

Bellagamba, Alice, and Georg Klute, eds. 2008. *Beside the State: Emergent Powers in Contemporary Africa.* Cologne, Germany: Rüdiger Köppe Verlag.

Branch, Adam. 2005. "Neither Peace nor Justice: Political Violence and the Peasantry in Northern Uganda, 1986–1998." *African Studies Quarterly* 8 (2): 1–31.

Breen-Smyth, Marie. 2014. "Theorising the 'Suspect Community': Counterterrorism, Security Practices and the Public Imagination." *Critical Studies on Terrorism* 7 (2): 223–40.

Comaroff, Jean, and John Comaroff. 1999. "Occult Economies and the Violence of Abstraction: Notes from the South African Postcolony." *American Ethnologist* 26 (2): 279–303.

———. 2011. "Reflections on Youth, from the Past to the Postcolony." In *Frontiers of Capital: Ethnographic Reflections on the New Economy*, edited by Melissa S. Fisher and Greg Downey, 267–81. Durham, NC: Duke University Press.

Debord, Guy. 1995. *The Society of the Spectacle*. Translated by Donald Nicholson-Smith. New York: Zone Books.

Debos, Marielle. 2011. "Living by the Gun in Chad: Armed Violence as a Practical Occupation." *Journal of Modern African Studies* 49 (3): 409–28.

Dietrich, Kyle. 2015. *"When We Can't See the Enemy, Civilians Become the Enemy": Living through Nigeria's Six-Year Insurgency*. Washington, DC: Center for Civilians in Conflict (CIVIC).

Evans, Brad, and Henry A. Giroux. 2015a. "Challenging a 'Disposable Future,' Looking to a Politics of Possibility." Interview by Victoria Harper. Truthout, 10 May. https://truthout.org/articles/challenging-a-disposable-future-looking-to-a-politics-of-possibility.

———. 2015b. *Disposable Futures: The Seduction of Violence in the Age of Spectacle*. San Francisco: City Lights Books.

GCCA. 2014. "JTF: Where Are the Christian Men Abducted in Barawa, Gwoza Local Government Area of Borno State?" Gwoza Christian Community Association press release, n.d. http://gwozacca.org/PRESS3.php.

Göpfert, Mirco. 2016. "Surveillance in Niger: Gendarmes and the Problem of 'Seeing Things.'" *African Studies Review* 59 (2): 39–57.

Gore, Charles, and David Pratten. 2003. "The Politics of Plunder: The Rhetorics of Order and Disorder in Southern Nigeria." *African Affairs* 102 (407): 211–40.

Hage, Ghassan. 2003. *Against Paranoid Nationalism: Searching for Hope in a Shrinking Society*. Annandale, Australia: Pluto.

Hassan, Idayat, and Zacharias Pieri. 2018. "The Rise and Risks of Nigeria's Civilian Joint Task Force: Implications for Post-conflict Recovery in Northeastern Nigeria." In *Boko Haram beyond the Headlines: Analyses of Africa's Enduring Insurgency*, edited by Jacob Zenn, 74–86. West Point, NY: Combating Terrorism Center at West Point, United States Military Academy.

Higazi, Adam. 2008. "Social Mobilization and Collective Violence: Vigilantes and Militias in the Lowlands of Plateau State, Central Nigeria." *Africa: Journal of the International African Institute* 78 (1): 107–35.

Hoffman, Danny. 2007. "The Meaning of a Militia: Understanding the Civil Defense Forces of Sierra Leone." *African Affairs* 106 (425): 639–62.

Human Rights Watch. 2013. "Nigeria: Boko Haram Abducts Women, Recruits Children." Human Rights Watch website, 29 November. https://www.hrw.org/news/2013/11/29/nigeria-boko-haram-abducts-women-recruits-children.

————. 2019. "Nigeria." In *World Report 2019: Events of 2018*, 431–36. New York: Human Rights Watch. Available at https://www.hrw.org/world-report/2019 /country-chapters/nigeria.

ICG. 2017. *Double-Edged Sword: Vigilantes in African Counter-insurgencies.* African report no. 251. 7 September. Brussels: International Crisis Group.

Idowu, Kayode. 2016. "Our Ex-fighters Now Serving in Army, DS—Civilian JTF Boss." *Punch* (Magboro), 24 July.

Idris, Hamza, and Ibrahim Sawab. 2013. "Hopes Turn to Fears over 'Civilian JTF.'" Daily Trust (website), 29 June.

New Humanitarian. 2013. "Civilian Vigilante Groups Increase Dangers in Northeastern Nigeria." 12 December. https://www.thenewhumanitarian.org/ar/node /254238.

————. 2016. "They're Defeating Boko Haram but Are They Nigeria's Next Security Threat?" 22 August.

Ismail, Salwa. 2006. *Political Life in Cairo's New Quarters: Encountering the Everyday State.* Minneapolis: University of Minnesota Press.

Jansen, Stef. 2014. "Hope for/against the State: Gridding in a Besieged Sarajevo Suburb." *Ethnos: Journal of Anthropology* 79 (2): 238–60.

Jentzsch, Corinna, Stathis N. Kalyvas, and Livia Isabella Schubiger. 2015. "Militias in Civil Wars." *Journal of Conflict Resolution* 59 (5): 755–69.

Jones, Rebecca. 2008. "State Failure and Extra-legal Justice: Vigilante Groups, Civil Militias and the Rule of Law in West Africa." Research paper no. 166. Geneva, Switzerland: UNHCR.

Jose, Betcy, and Peace A. Medie. 2016. "Civilian Self-Protection and Civilian Targeting in Armed Conflicts: Who Protects Civilians?" In *Oxford Research Encyclopedia of Politics,* online edition, edited by William R. Thompson. https://doi .org/10.1093/acrefore/9780190228637.013.216.

Kalyvas, Stathis N. 2004. "The Paradox of Terrorism in Civil War." *Journal of Ethics* 8 (1): 97–138.

Khalili, Laleh. 2011. "Gendered Practices of Counterinsurgency." *Review of International Studies* 37 (4): 1471–91.

————. 2014. "The Uses of Happiness in Counterinsurgencies." *Social Text* 32 (1 [118]): 23–43.

Kilcullen, David. 2006. "Twenty-Eight Articles: Fundamentals of Company-Level Counterinsurgency." *Military Review* 86:103–8.

Kowalewski, David. 1991. "Counterinsurgent Vigilantism and Public Response: A Philippine Case Study." *Sociological Perspectives* 34 (2): 127–44.

Maina, M. 2014. "Insurgency: 41 Boko Haram Members Beheaded in Biu after Failed Attack." *Daily Post,* 31 October. http://dailypost.ng/2014/10/31 /insurgency-41-boko-haram-members-beheaded-biu-failed-attack/.

Marama, Ndahi. 2014. "41 Boko Haram Members Beheaded in Biu." *Vanguard* (Lagos), 1 November. https://www.vanguardngr.com/2014/11/41-boko-haram -members-beheaded-biu/.

Masquelier, Adeline. 2001. "Behind the Dispensary's Prosperous Façade: Imagining the State in Rural Niger." *Public Culture* 13 (2): 267–91.

Mbembe, Achille. 1992. "Provisional Notes on the Postcolony." *Africa: Journal of the International African Institute* 62 (1): 3–37.

Mbembe, Achille, and Janet Roitman. 1995. "Figures of the Subject in Times of Crisis." *Public Culture* 7 (2): 323–52.

McCall, John C. 2004. "Juju and Justice at the Movies: Vigilantes in Nigerian Popular Videos." *African Studies Review* 47 (3): 51–67.

Meagher, Kate. 2012. "The Strength of Weak States? Non-state Security Forces and Hybrid Governance in Africa." *Development and Change* 43 (5): 1073–1101.

Menkhaus, Ken. 2006. "Governance without Government in Somalia: Spoilers, State Building, and the Politics of Coping." *International Security* 31 (3): 74–106.

Merry, Sally Engle. 2006. "Transnational Human Rights and Local Activism: Mapping the Middle." *American Anthropologist* 108 (1): 38–51.

Mkandawire, Thandika. 2002. "The Terrible Toll of Post-colonial 'Rebel Movements' in Africa: Towards an Explanation of the Violence against the Peasantry." *Journal of Modern African Studies* 40 (2): 181–215.

Mustapha, Abdul Raufu. 2014. "Synthesis Paper on Lessons Learned from Responses to Violent Conflicts in Nigeria since 2009: With Special Reference to Northern Nigeria." Abuja, Nigeria: Nigeria Stability and Reconciliation Programme.

Ndimele, Manuel. 2016. "Civilian JTF Member Held for Borno IDP Camp Bomb Attack." Legit (website).

Nigerian Bulletin. 2013. "Boko Haram: Borno Empowers 800 Youths for Civilian JTF." https://www.nigerianbulletin.com/threads/boko-haram-borno -empowers-800-youths-for-civilian-jtf.8130/.

Nolte, Insa. 2008. "'Without Women, Nothing Can Succeed': Yoruba Women in the Oodua People's Congress (OPC), Nigeria." *Africa: Journal of the International African Institute* 78 (1): 84–106.

Odunsi, Wale. 2014. "'Boko Haram Will Continue to Kill'—Full Text of Shekau's Speech Declaring Caliphate in Northern Nigeria." Daily Post (website), 25 August. https://dailypost.ng/2014/08/25/boko-haram-will-continue-kill-full -text-shekaus-speech-declaring-caliphate-northern-nigeria/.

———. 2015. "Borno: Shettima Salutes Youth Volunteers for Repelling Boko Haram." Daily Post (website), 2 February. https://dailypost.ng/2015/02/02 /borno-shettima-salutes-youth-volunteers-repelling-boko-haram/.

Ogene, Ashionye. 2014. "Nigerian Vigilantes Aim to Rout Boko Haram." Al Jazeera (website), 31 May. https://www.aljazeera.com/features/2014/5/31/nigerian -vigilantes-aim-to-rout-boko-haram.

Okeowo, Alexis. 2014. "Inside the Vigilante Fight against Boko Haram." *New York Times Magazine,* 5 November.

———. 2015. "The Women Fighting Boko Haram." *New Yorker,* 22 December. https:// www.newyorker.com/news/news-desk/the-women-fighting-boko-haram.

Omonigho, Matthew. 2017. "Boko Haram: Over 700 Civilian JTF Members Died Defending Borno—Jubril Gunda." Daily Post (website), 30 June.

Omoniyi, Tosin. 2009. "Nigeria: The Nation's Poor Record Keeping Culture." Daily Trust (website), 18 November.

Pérouse de Montclos, Marc-Antoine. 2016. "A Sectarian Jihad in Nigeria: The Case of Boko Haram." *Small Wars and Insurgencies* 27 (5): 878–95.

Peters, Krijn, and Paul Richards. 1998. "'Why We Fight': Voices of Youth Combatants in Sierra Leone." *Africa: Journal of the International African Institute* 68 (2): 183–210.

Pratten, David. 2008a. "Introduction: The Politics of Protection; Perspectives on Vigilantism in Nigeria." *Africa: Journal of the International African Institute* 78 (1): 1–15.

———. 2008b. "Masking Youth: Transformation and Transgression in Annang Performance." *African Arts* 41 (4): 44–59.

Pratten, David, and Atreyee Sen, eds. 2007. *Global Vigilantes: Perspectives on Justice and Violence.* London: Hurst.

Rasmussen, Jacob. 2010. "Outwitting the Professor of Politics? Mungiki Narratives of Political Deception and Their Role in Kenyan Politics." *Journal of Eastern African Studies* 4 (3): 435–49.

Rodgers, Dennis. 2007. "When Vigilantes Turn Bad: Gangs, Violence, and Social Change in Urban Nicaragua." In Pratten and Sen 2007, 349–70.

Schuberth, Moritz. 2015. "The Challenge of Community-Based Armed Groups: Towards a Conceptualization of Militias, Gangs, and Vigilantes." *Contemporary Security Policy* 36 (2): 296–320.

Smith, Daniel Jordan. 2004. "The Bakassi Boys: Vigilantism, Violence, and Political Imagination in Nigeria." *Cultural Anthropology* 19 (3): 429–55.

South Africa Press Association and Agence France-Presse. 2013. "Vigilantes Raise Concern and Hope in Embattled Nigerian City." Sowetan Live (website), 30 July. https://www.sowetanlive.co.za/news/world/2013-07-30-vigilantes-raise-concern-and-hope-in-embattled-nigeria-city/.

Stevenson, Lisa. 2007. Review of *Anthropology in the Margins of the State,* edited by Veena Das and Deborah Poole. *Political and Legal Anthropology Review* 30 (1): 140–44.

Strochlic, Nina. 2014. "Nigeria's Do-It-Yourself Boko Haram Busters." Daily Beast (website), 16 May.

TAP (Testimonial Archive Project). 2014. "How Can You Depend on [the Military] to Protect You?" 15 September. http://testimonialarchiveproject.org/2014/09/15/how-can-you-depend-on-the-military-to-protect-you/.

Oduah, Chika. 2016. "Nigerian Vigilantes Ponder Future after Fighting Boko Haram." 5 July. https://www.voanews.com/a/what-next-for-the-nigeria-vigilantes-fighting-boko-haram/3405851.html.

United Nations. 2017. *Borno State LGA's: Baseline Information for Planners.*

UN Security Council. 2017. *Report of the Secretary-General on Children and Armed Conflict in Nigeria.* S/2017/304. 10 April. New York: UN Security Council.

Vanguard. 2013a. "'Civilian JTF' Should Not Fight." *Vanguard* (Lagos), 31 July. https://www.vanguardngr.com/2013/07/civilian-jtf-should-not-fight/.

———. 2013b. "Civilian JTF vs. Boko Haram: Concern, Hope in Embattled Restive City." *Vanguard* (Lagos), 30 July. https://www.vanguardngr.com/2013/07/vigilantes-vs-boko-haram-concern-hope-in-embattled-restive-city/.

Vigh, Henrik. 2006. *Navigating Terrains of War: Youth and Soldiering in Guinea-Bissau.* New York: Berghahn Books.

Wlodarczyk, Nathalie. 2009. *Magic and Warfare: Appearance and Reality in Contemporary African Conflict and Beyond.* New York: Palgrave Macmillan.

Wood, Reed M., Jacob D. Kathman, and Steven E. Gent. 2012. "Armed Intervention and Civilian Victimization in Intrastate Conflicts." *Journal of Peace Research* 49 (5): 647–60.

Young, Crawford, and Thomas Turner. 1985. *The Rise and Decline of the Zairian State.* Madison: University of Wisconsin Press.

Yusuf, Umar Lawal. 2014. "The Role of the Civilian JTF in Tackling Boko Haram Problems in Borno." *Al-Mahram International Journal of Centre for Trans-Saharan Studies* 6.

———. 2020. "Community Perception of the Role of Civilian Joint Task Force (CJTF) in Resisting Boko Haram Culture of Violence in Borno State, Nigeria." PhD diss., University of Maiduguri and University of Hildesheim.

Zulaika, Joseba. 2012. "Drones, Witches and Other Flying Objects: The Force of Fantasy in US Counterterrorism." *Critical Studies on Terrorism* 5 (1): 51–68.

PART FOUR

The Social Life of Democracy

TEN

Fishing Nets, Kabila's Eyes, and Voter's Cards

Citizen–State Mediations in the DRC

KATRIEN PYPE

THE EDITOR OF THIS VOLUME INVITES US TO CONSIDER the "everyday grammars of the state and democratic life in contemporary Africa, and how these grammars are determined by local, regional and global processes." In this chapter, I will provide an ethnographic account of state-citizen relations in Kinshasa during the final eight years of Joseph Kabila's regime, which started in 2001 when his father, Laurent-Désiré Kabila, was assassinated, and ended in January 2019 when Félix Tshisekedi was sworn in as the new president. My analysis is centered around two innovations that occurred during these final years of Kabila's regime: the introduction of the voter's card (*carte d'électeur*) and the installation of surveillance cameras all around the city. Both objects constituted building blocks of new relationships between Kabila and Kinois (inhabitants of Kinshasa), providing rulers and citizens new themes through which they could articulate their relationships with one another.

The following note from fieldwork introduces the particularities of these two political innovations through the experience of Fiston,[1] a bachelor in his midthirties who holds a degree in informatics obtained at one of the local higher institutions. Fiston is one of Kinshasa's young adults who make ends meet mainly with money they receive from relatives living in the diaspora and through small moneymaking schemes (*coop*) they set up with friends. In early 2012, Fiston switched from Catholicism to Islam, out of disappointment with the Catholic Church's leadership in the Democratic Republic of the Congo. He had hoped that Catholic leaders would be able to impose democratic rule on Joseph Kabila and reacted radically when they failed to do so after the 2011 elections.

In mid-September 2016, Fiston joined anti-Kabila protesters who had gathered all around Kinshasa, marching, singing, chanting, and provoking policemen, soldiers, and special forces. Their anti-Kabila sentiment had been clear, loud, and full of frustration. That day of protest had been one in a long history of repeated manifestations in the capital city, expressing anger and resentment against Joseph Kabila's leadership and demanding the organization of democratic elections.

After a tumultuous day, Fiston was relieved to arrive safely in the small studio he was renting with his cousin. The father of one of his friends, a major leader of the Union for Democracy and Social Progress, then the opposition party, never returned home that evening. Until this day, his body has never been found. Kabila governed through *a politics of disappearance and silencing* of opposition voices, as if he were applying Achille Mbembe's (2003) concept of "necropolitics": the use of social and political power to dictate how some people must live and some must die.

The whole day had been one of playing hide-and-seek with the police and the army. At certain points, protesters fled to compounds where other citizens had kept their doors open to welcome and encourage the militants, and also to protect them against the *gaz lacrymogène* that the security forces had thrown in the small alleys in the quartiers. Residents sympathetic to the protest had given Fiston and fellow protesters some water to clean their eyes and wash their faces of the tear gas that was inflaming their skin.

The day after, Fiston gave me an account of the protests. His narrative was rich in detail about how he and other dissidents had challenged the police and army. For the purpose of this chapter, two threads of his report are significant. First, it was with bemusement that Fiston told me he had changed clothes throughout the day. During the days running up to the protest, friends had advised him to dress differently in the morning and the afternoon. Although Fiston had been participating in protest marches well before I first met him in 2010, this strategy of dressing differently was new. He had been told that it would be best if he wore a buttoned shirt with a T-shirt underneath it, and a hat. After a while, he should dispose of the shirt and hat and continue the demonstration in the T-shirt. Such advice had been common in the city ever since surveillance cameras had been installed. Although most people did not believe that these cameras were actually operational, nor that the footage was being monitored, the activists were careful and protected themselves as well as they could against being recognized. A boy in Masina (one of many overcrowded municipalities in Kinshasa) was rumored to have been assassinated because he had been "too recognizable." After his first run away from the police, Fiston had gone home, changed shirts, and removed his baseball cap.

Second, Fiston mentioned that he had deliberately not taken along his voter's card, not wanting to be identified in case he was arrested. "There are too many *incrédules* [incredulous people] and *barbares* [savages]," he argued, assuming that I understood he was talking about the excessive violence that the Congolese security forces enact on protesting citizens.

Both actions (changing clothes during the protest and being undocumented on the street) show that Fiston clearly refused to be identifiable to Kabila's security orders. This speaks in surprising ways to political subjectivities: it was a deliberate choice by Fiston to become invisible and anonymous. In contrast to narratives about citizens' empowerment, in which citizens need to be seen, heard, and recognized as citizens, Fiston's political actions included deliberately stripping himself of his individual identity. He *chose* to become an anonymous protester—to avoid surveillance by the state and to deny the state its capacity to identify and isolate a potential target.

Both the voter's card and the surveillance cameras illuminate in different ways the entanglements of the Kabila state and Fiston, and they push us to rethink state-citizen relationships. In particular, these ethnographic data allow us to refine Mbembe's notion of "mutual entanglements" in postcolonial political society. In his widely acclaimed *On the Postcolony*, Mbembe demands "a shift in perspective" regarding the postcolonial relationship between those in power and the ruled. Instead of characterizing this relationship as one "of resistance or of collaboration," we should see it as "convivial, a relationship fraught by the fact of the *commandement* and its 'subjects' having to share the same living space." This logic has, Mbembe continues, "resulted in the mutual 'zombification' of both the dominant and those apparently dominated" (2001, 104). The concept of "zombification" has shown to be very appropriate in defining postcolonial identities in the late Mobutu days (1990s) and early 2000s (De Boeck and Plissart 2004). The *kindoki* discourse (witchcraft/sorcery) so loudly proclaimed by new religious movements describes citizens as "living dead," subjected to a leadership that cannot provide viable futures, and, even worse, that is extracting the mystical life force of its subjects in order to enrich itself (ibid.). Fiston's narrative suggests a different kind of entanglement, one of mutual entrapment, and technologies such as the surveillance cameras and the voter's card are part of this logic.

The concept of "entrapment" was already present in Mbembe's earliest writings on the colony and postcolony. In the article "Provisional Notes on the Postcolony," he wrote that "recent Africanist scholarship has not studied in detail the logic . . . of capture and narrow escape, nor the way the traps are so interconnected that they become a unitary system of ensnarement. Yet on making sense of this network depends any knowledge we might have of the logics of 'resistance,' 'disorder' and conviviality that are all inherent in the postcolonial form of authority" (Mbembe 1992, 25; cf. Mbembe 2001, 128, for slightly different wording). A decade later, in the monograph *On the Postcolony,* Mbembe draws on a colonial text containing an elaborate description of how a hunter tries to trap his prey and argues that "what holds for the animal holds for the colonized" (2001, 193). Following here the major argument of *On the Postcolony,* that postcolonial commandment is a continuation of colonial governance, we might rephrase this sentence as "what holds for the animal holds for the postcolonial subject."

Based on his analysis of political culture in the 1980s, Mbembe identifies rituals as a major technology of entrapment: "individuals are constantly being trapped in a net of rituals that reaffirm tyranny" (2001, 128). In this chapter, rather than studying political rituals during the Kabila regime, I will disentangle the ways in which the voter's card and the surveillance cameras constituted the technologies of capture and entrapment. My ethnographic data will show how these objects enable both parties, the state and citizens, to ensnare one another, to lure one another. The grammar of "mutual entrapment" rests on two building blocks: one of confusion and one of distrust. The surveillance cameras and the voter's cards are embedded in webs of trickery, provocation, and lies from both sides.

The material also pushes us to take seriously the dialectics between contemporary politics and technology in sub-Saharan Africa. In recent decades, various historians and anthropologists have begun to explore the political meanings of technological innovation in sub-Saharan African societies (Breckenridge 2016; Gagliardone 2016; Mavhunga 2014; Mitchell 2002; Nuttal and Mbembe 2015). Their exciting accounts document that technological infrastructures have mediated political relationships in the colony and postcolony. One of the most significant political decisions that Joseph Kabila made was the introduction of digital voting machines for the democratic elections in December 2018. These elections marked the end of Joseph Kabila's regime (January 2001–January 2019). Yet the technological equipment, the voting machines themselves, were the object of protest, derision, and violent attacks throughout 2018.[2] The voting machine was only the last of a series of technological innovations that the Kabila regime had introduced during his reign. These include the imposition of payment into bank accounts for state agents (the so-called *bancarisation*), the introduction of centralized software to render customs more operational and transparent (*guichet unique;* Cuvelier and Muamba Mimbunda 2013), and also the voting cards and surveillance cameras. It is through and with these technological innovations that contemporary

African leaders such as Joseph Kabila, but also his successor Félix Tshisekedi, perform leadership and *statecraft*. It is also through these innovations that citizens make claims on their leaders and the state. Through these technological innovations, political futures are expressed and new ways of holding leaders accountable emerge, as well as new forms of disciplining, monitoring, and contesting power. Rather than performance and spectacle (Bloom, Miescher, and Manuh 2014), technology has become the key rubric and modality through which postcolonial commandment in the twenty-first century, under J. Kabila, was enacted.

The voter's card and the surveillance cameras are embedded in practices of signification. Ultimately, ethnography illuminates the flexibility of the category of the "citizen." The material will show how Kinois decide to be citizens at certain times and perform as such, while at other times they take on other identities, and sometimes even refuse that of a citizen. This flexibility or "play" with citizenship is what I will call "frontier politics." The new technologies of voter's cards and surveillance cameras have enlarged the political playground of "frontier citizens."

In the first parts of the chapter, I describe citizens' engagements with the voter's cards and the surveillance cameras. This is followed by a discussion of citizens' understandings of the state as a trap, and how camouflage was an apt strategy to engage with the Kabila state.

The analysis draws on field research in Kinshasa during the Kabila years. I first visited Kinshasa in February 2003, two years after Joseph Kabila took power. Since then, I have been going back regularly to Kinshasa, carrying out ethnographic research on media and society. The data for this chapter were mainly obtained during field research on "technology and the city" between 2014 and 2019, but I also rely on data and experiences collected during previous research visits, especially in 2009–11, when I followed television news journalists. My argument is limited to the Kabila period. Since January 2019, when Félix Tshisekedi was sworn in as president, Kinshasa's political society has been undergoing some changes. It is yet too soon to assess the continuities and ruptures in political culture under Kabila's command and after him.

The Voter's Card

Since 2005, when the Congolese were headed toward choosing a president for the first time, they have been invited to collect a voter's card (carte d'électeur) issued by the CENI (Commission Électorale Nationale Indépendante, or National Independent Elections Committee), a government parastatal that coordinates national elections. The paper document gave them the opportunity to vote during the elections in November 2011. With each election held after 2005 (November 2011 and November 2018), citizens have had to register again and collect a new voter's card.

Strictly speaking, the voter's card in itself was not a citizenship card. Formally, the document said only that the holder had the right to vote. In its campaign, the CENI officers talked about "becoming a voter" (*devenir un électeur*). The card communicated personal information about the card holder: first name (*prénom*), family name or surname (*nom*), and post-surname (*postnom*); the names of the holder's father and mother; date and place of birth; address; and "origin," meaning the name of home territory (*secteur ou chefferie ou commune/territoire ou ville/province*, translated as "zone or chieftaincy or municipality/territory or city/province"). It also showed a passport photograph; a signature; and, in certain areas of DRC since 2018, a digital fingerprint. In addition, the document contained codes of the voting office and the center of registration, as well as an individual number corresponding to the holder's place in the election list.

Applying for a carte d'électeur meant subjecting oneself to a lengthy process. It began with getting enrolled (*se faire enrôler*) on a list in one of the CENI administrative centers in Kinshasa, which depended on proving one had been born in the DRC and had Congolese parents. Aspirant voters were required to bring a national passport, birth certificate, driver's license, student's card, identification card from a company where one was employed, or document from the national pension service (Institut National de Sécurité Sociale). If one could not produce any of these documents (which was fairly common), there was an alternative procedure. Officially, one was required to bring along five people who were already registered at the same center of registration and who had been living for at least five years in that area. They could serve as witnesses to establish one's Congolese identity. In practice, that was pretty difficult to organize, and, from time to time, CENI agents would accept letters from three different individuals confirming that the applicant had been born on Congolese soil. However, these formalities were often waived for a small fee for the agent—who on the spot made some extra money.[3]

Once citizenship was verified, or a small fee paid in lieu of verification, one could get a card rolling out of one of the printers. If a card was lost, one needed to request a document from the police that allowed one to obtain a duplicate. However, cards (and duplicates) were only produced in particular windows of time: from a few months before the elections until three months afterward. After that, citizens who wanted to get a new voter's card (for example, because they had lost theirs, or it had become unusable due to rain, fire, or some other mishap) had no other recourse than to obtain a fake card, usually created in homes or cybercafes (see Adebanwi and Obadare in this volume).

Because of these laws and practices, within a few months after national elections—which have only been held three times since Joseph Kabila took power—it was impossible to either sign up for a new card or request a duplicate. This has had serious repercussions for people's social and economic lives, because the document became, first and foremost, an alternative identity card, thus filling a void in public administration. Very quickly, the card was taken on by public institutions, private companies, and international organizations as a way to identify employees and visitors. When visiting an office or a hospital, visitors were (and still are) requested to hand over their carte d'électeur in exchange for a token authorizing access. When withdrawing or sending money via a transfer agency, registering a SIM card, donating or purchasing blood at a blood bank, or visiting a bank or depositing money into an account, one was, and still is, asked to present the carte d'électeur. Students used and use this document to prove their identity during exams. Many people got a voting card specifically because there is a lack of other national ID, often without having any intention to vote. People took care of these cartes d'électeur because they bore so much effect, affect, and promise. This card offered security and opened up healthier and economically more livable futures. The political significance of the carte d'électeur thus transcended the initially intended meaning of the object.

The value of the carte d'électeur was especially significant in the protective role it played for nighttime wanderers encountering policemen or soldiers. If one could not prove one's alliance to Kabila (at least by carrying a voter's card) when encountering military men or police during the night, then often one could be arrested or become a victim of physical abuse. Carrying the voter's card suggested that one was subjecting oneself to the power of the CENI and the Kabila state. Not being able to procure this card defined one as a potential enemy of the Kabila state.[4] Here, the voter's card became a security device against state violence; thus, the state's documents were used as a shield against potential harm by the state and its agents.

The use of fake voting cards was an acknowledgment of the fact that the carte finds meaning in other spheres and usages in other networks, and that the state could not control these. However, the production and circulation of these fake voter's cards should not be seen as resistance toward the Kabila state. With fake cards, Kinois could stage other identities and take other people's places, just like anonymous phone calls allowed them to (Pype 2016). The economy of fake voting cards was embedded within a larger informal economy, resorted to by Kinois because of the country's ongoing economic crisis (*la crise*), which related economic instability to risk-taking and illegality (see Petit and Mulumbwa Mutambwa 2005).

Such ethnographic observations illustrate that the carte mediated in particular ways between the voter and the Congolese state. First and foremost, the stories about nocturnal wanderers illuminate the ways in which the carte was used within the context of the necropolitical quality of Kabila's regime. Practices of carrying the carte and displaying it to soldiers signal the intricate ways in which state and citizens negotiated life and death. The carte became a document that identified the individual as a political subject with the right to life and freedom of mobility, very much in the same way as a colonial travel permit (*laissez-passer*). Someone who could show evidence that she intended to participate in the elections of the Kabila state was not supposed to be beaten up or arrested. Losing the document introduced the risk that police, soldiers, or agents of Kabila's secret services could revert to a governmentality that treated people as animals, without any political rights.

Second, the continuous and deliberate displacement of the meanings of this political document testifies to mutual attempts at trapping in citizen-state relationships. The Kabila regime invested in the production of voter's cards rather than citizenship cards. Given the fact that elections are very often rigged (Cheeseman and Klaas 2018), this strategy could be perceived as part of Kabila's politics of trapping the Congolese in his own machinations. The document did not grant any rights or privileges beyond that of being allowed to vote. Still, despite the fact that the Kabila state firmly invested in the production of "voters," the usage of the cartes d'électeurs in other contexts illustrates that the Kinois refused to be caught in the position of "the voter." Rather, they added new meanings and significance to the document in their everyday lives that escaped the Kabila state. By deploying the voter's card in the hospital, in the exam room, and at the money transfer agency, Kinois displayed multiple identities and created multiple realms of sense-making and future-making with the card.

The document itself could also become part of another, more incisive way for the Kabila state to trap people. As mentioned at the beginning of this chapter, Fiston had decided to leave the voter's card at home during a day of protest. This calculation speaks to the logic of entrapment as well. Fiston's choice illuminates the possibility of the voter's card as technology of betrayal. The document literally could become a giveaway, as it contained Fiston's personal details, which could archive him as a rebel. Insofar as the mid-September 2016 protest itself was an expression of anti-Kabila sentiment, the voter's card could actually become a document that would endanger Fiston rather than protect him. For political subjects such as Fiston, the Kabila state was known to enact a politics of death and disappearance. Fiston knew very well that the voter's card could have been a trap for him during the day of protest.

The awareness of the kinds of relationships and political subjunctivity (full of possibility) that documents such as the voter's card exhibited and produced was part of a wider postcolonial history, in which both the state and citizens were playing with documents. During the Mobutu years, citizens would get a *carte d'identité pour citoyen* (identity card for citizen), showing a torch with red flame against a grass-green background. Yet in the early 1990s, the Zairian state suspended the validity of this card due to inefficient administration and the rampant use of fake cartes. Some elderly Kinois preserve the (real or fake) document with great caution until this very day. The carte d'identité pour citoyen remained for a very long time a rare material piece of evidence of their relationship to Zairian rule. During the Kabila years, however, this carte d'identité pour citoyen was stuck in tin trunks or plastic bags hidden away under mattresses. It certainly would never be in one's *trousse* (bag) when visiting relatives or just when going out on the streets. People did not dare to show their Mobutu documents to the Kabila police and soldiers. I was told that if the police or soldiers found this card on anyone, such a person would certainly be arrested, because holding on to that document would be interpreted as disloyalty to the Kabila state. It was assumed that it would be almost impossible to bribe one's way out.

Kabila's Eyes

In 2010, while the DRC celebrated the fiftieth anniversary of Congolese independence, Joseph Kabila was experimenting with surveillance cameras. In order to protect him against snipers, an Israeli company was hired whose cameras could peer through walls. In the week preceding the festivities on Independence Day (30 June 2010), several cameras were installed around the esplanade reserved for the military parade and the presidential speech and used to peer through the walls of compounds around the grounds to detect any weapons in these buildings. Very quickly, the Israeli technology proved too expensive for the Kabila state, so after the festivities the cameras were removed. However, by 2015, Kinois observed a gradual increase of surveillance cameras in their streets. These objects had a particular materiality and presence with a political goal: to intimidate potential enemies of the state.

These cameras were part of an aesthetics of vulgarity from above. In his seminal article, "Provisional Notes on the Postcolony" (1992), Mbembe discerned display, ceremonialism, grandeur, and impression management as major techniques of the postcolonial commandment's governance strategies. In the early twenty-first century, with electronic technologies increasingly being embedded in postcolonial politics, surveillance cameras should be added to that list of techniques.

Kinois nicknamed these cameras *misu ya Kabila* (Kabila's eyes), which expressed a transformation of governance practices in the Kabila era. The emphasis of Kabila's governance rested on the visual (see Pype 2012), while the Mobutu regime had relied on aural surveillance practices in which hearing and listening were central. During that time, the key technology had been the walkie-talkie, and later the mobile phone (Pype 2016), both materializing "the state's ear" (Schatzberg 1988, 30–31).

While most discussions of CCTV and other public cameras in the global north point to a loss of privacy, the core discourse in Kinshasa is about how the *caméras de surveillance* are embedded in *a relationship of mutual entrapment*. A first set of camera stories identified the state as the main "trapper." In these accounts, the cameras were considered to be just a continuation of other, more familiar surveillance practices such as the monitoring and control performed by the secret services of the ANR (Agence Nationale de Renseignement, or National Intelligence Agency) and Bureaux 2 (a section of the police, with agents patrolling without uniform) and the numerous spies in the city. Another set of stories pointed at the president himself being at risk. Some talked about the Kabila state being afraid of Kinois' mobility and their power as masses. The assumed goal of the cameras was to intercept any kind of mass gathering from its onset and thus aid in dispersing groups before they became too difficult for the police and the army to control. Other camera stories located the risk within the state apparatus itself. It was argued that only a few surveillance cameras were actually operational, and that these were installed at the entries of the military camps around the city. Rumors also emerged about more intricate, invisible, high-tech infrastructures of surveillance. Cracks in the tarmac near army camps and the international airport suddenly appeared to be politically significant: not to be confused with regular cracks in the roads, these supposedly hid detection mechanisms with infrared cameras and digital scales enabling the Kabila state to track whether passing cars and trucks were carrying guns and other weaponry.

The geography of these caméras de surveillance was part of the cameras' stories. It was mentioned time and again that they were placed at strategically important spaces: for example, at the entrances to the city and at various roundabouts or other spaces where protest could erupt (on campuses, at military camps, etc.). Many Kinois interpreted these locations as meaningful. In particular, they signaled that for the Kabila state danger was situated both outside and inside the state and its apparatuses (e.g., the military camps). The cameras suggested that the only way the state could respond to these hidden, unknown dangers was by setting up traps using the latest technologies.

These and similar narratives were difficult to verify, but all bore some truth, as they stood in a long history of armed violence and threats thereof. Probably one of the most recurring rumors I heard throughout the years of fieldwork in Kinshasa was that, at times of increased political insecurity, night wanderers observed tanks and heavy trucks with armed soldiers coming into the city from the airport (located on the outskirts of the city) or even further afield. These were supposedly being brought in by opposition leaders with the intention of starting a civil war. In addition, ever since the beginning of my fieldwork in Kinshasa in 2003, stories had been circulating about mutiny in one of the military camps. During times of political uncertainty, gunshots were part of the nighttime sounds, just like the gospel music coming from funeral wakes.

All of these stories and observations indicate how the *caméras de surveillance* became complicated objects through which people articulated their relationships with power and opened up a complex world of emotions centered around mutual distrust.[5] The camera became a focal point for these relationships and transformed the urban space into a zone filled with mutual anxieties, suspicion, and risk. In their camera stories, Kinois connected centers of everyday urban mobility with invisible loci of political control and supported the imagination of an occult, hidden world, close by and following their movements. Yet both the cameras and the assumed invisible digital technologies were embedded in a logic of mutual entrapment. The camera stories showed that citizens expected the state to try to trap its opponents, while Fiston's story at the beginning of this chapter describes how citizens themselves also fooled state agents through evasion.

However, for most Kinois, these cameras were fake, shallow signs, even though they were part and parcel of Kabila's apparatus of coercion and

FIGURE 1. Torn-down surveillance camera in Lemba, Kinshasa, 8 October 2016. Photo by Katrien Pype.

domination. Therefore, these objects quickly became the target of mockery and citizens' violence. In mid-September 2015, not even half a year after these new cameras had been introduced, Kinois took to the streets. The opposition parties, led by Étienne Tshisekedi (father of the current president) and Moïse Katumbi, a presidential candidate and one of Congo's most popular politicians, had called for the Congolese to march in order to strengthen their demand for Kabila's abdication. The day after, Kinshasa's streets were littered with torn-down, sometimes even burnt-down cameras, which the Kabila government never cleared. Residents in the vicinity would move them from the streets to the pavement so that traffic could flow.

The choice of the Kabila state not to remove these carcasses turned them into politically significant objects for two reasons. First, the Congolese state apparatus usually silenced and hid any signs of contestation. For example, during the national Independence Day festivities in 2010, the state television channel interrupted its broadcast of the military parade when the march turned into chaos and street children, citizens, and members of political parties invaded the parade space (Pype 2013). Second, Kabila himself had ordered the destruction of abandoned cars, and crumbling buildings when he introduced the "revolution of modernity" program (Révolution de la Modernité) in 2012 (Pype 2018). While at that time the ruins were evidence of Mobutu's failing program and had to disappear in order to make a clean slate, in the final years of Kabila's regime, the wrecks of the surveillance cameras seemed good to stay.

This inaction was interpreted as meaningful by many Kinois. Most would argue that the damaged objects laying on the pavements symbolized the state's lack of care for the citizens' well-being. Even if this was mainly a question of no state agent taking responsibility for cleaning up the streets, the cameras communicated that the commander was still in power and would decide himself if and how he would leave his post. Another narrative, mainly heard from pro-Kabila Kinois, understood the ongoing visibility of the damaged cameras as part of a "blaming the victim" policy. In such an interpretation, this ruined equipment signaled the investment of the leadership in high-tech devices and Kabila's efforts to bring the population into a new technological era. But, so the story went, sadly enough, the population did not agree with the new technological era, and blocked the way to a new future by actively destroying the high-tech equipment. In other, post-Kabila stories, the citizens were the heroes. During a visit in August 2019, the carcasses of "Kabila's eyes" had turned into objects of pride and souvenirs of the citizens' disruption of Kabila's efforts to surveil and intimidate them. Post-Kabila, the damaged cameras took on a similar role as the now obsolete phrase "talking like a Motorola" (*koloba lokola Motorola*). The latter evoked the dangerous outcomes from information that circulated over walkie-talkies and mobile phones during the Mobutu regime, because state agents and spies were at the time the only ones who used Motorolas (Pype 2016). It reminded people of how the circulation of information could harm one's safety in a regime where the state had numerous ears.

The State as Fishing Net

The logics of entrapment pervade in Kinois discourse and are not at all limited to an assessment of citizen-state relationships, but dominate people's perceptions of their social environment (Pype 2011), political developments on local and national levels, and economic opportunities (or lack thereof) and backlashes. In his ethnography of healing cults among Yaka communities southeast of Kinshasa, René Devisch writes about how "in village talks among men, Kinshasa represents the male realm of individual freedom and abundance, achieved through ingenuity or good fortune, comparable to that of the forest of which the hunter and trapper is so immensely fond" (1993, 16). In this imagination, the city emerges as a forest, a hunting ground; social mobility, opportunities, and money are an urban game.

While trapping can occur via various technologies (artisanal traps like using pitfalls, nooses, dressing up, and lying; and more sophisticated ones such as booby traps and using modern guns), in the political imagination under the Kabila state, the image of the fishing net, the *filet*, was more widely used.[6] Let me briefly describe one of the many occasions on which I heard a reference to the net as one of the state's trapping technologies.

August 2018. I had asked Papa Jeannot, a taxi driver, for an *express*, meaning he would drop me exactly at my destination, even if this was outside his regular driving territory. As we encountered a huge traffic jam, he got nervous, and did not feel like entering the enormous body of cars. He quickly played a clever trick and joined a number of other cars that were driving on the sandy area next to the tarmac road. He thus had to find his way among food stalls, displays spread on the ground of kitchen utensils and other goods for sale, and wooden sign boards for public phone booths. After having meandered for a while between these semi-fixed open shops, we suddenly got blocked by traffic at a crossroad, where three policemen were creating more chaos. We were on the sandy space next to the road, but the policemen did not pay any attention to us, as they were too busy trying to arrest the driver of a large van serving as a taxi, which was filled with passengers. As we were watching this scene, Papa Jeannot clapped both hands on the steering wheel and said, in Lingala, "Tchahaaa, *bazwami ye na filet!* Here in Kinshasa, you need to *tia mutu bakata*." Papa Jeannot added that "sometimes the police wins, and sometimes they lose." Papa Jeannot's exclamation was thick with political meaning: *bazwami ye na filet* translates as "they caught him in their net"; *tia mutu bakata* can be translated as "stick your head out." I will develop this thought further below.

The fishing metaphor aptly describes the relationship of catching and being caught. While citizens are fish, the policemen are the fishermen who cast out their nets and entrap citizens. There is an interesting analogy between fishermen and state agents. Just like fishermen, ANR and Bureaux 2 agents and the state's spies (see above) operate in hiding and are silent. They do not announce their arrival, nor do they present themselves, very much like fishermen who need to remain in the background and do not announce their presence to their prey while letting the bait and the net do the work, even if this requires waiting for hours. In the same vein, the ANR and Bureaux 2 agents follow their suspects for weeks and months before arresting or kidnapping them.

The image of the "state as net" illuminates an additional aspect of the relationship between the Kabila state and its subjects. As Devisch (1993) has described in his ethnography on the Yaka community, the image of relationships between people or of a community is articulated through the metaphor of weaving, of linking people to one another through (metaphoric) fibers. In this imagination, the Kabila state is situated *outside* the net. This expresses the lack of connection between the Kinois and the rulers. Even worse, Kabila has woven his own net, and the Kinois can only fall prey to it.[7] This is not surprising, as in Kinshasa there was a strong sense of fissure between residents and Joseph Kabila (Pype 2011, 638–39). One would often hear that Joseph Kabila was a foreigner. According to some, he was born to a Tanzanian mother, while others held that he had Rwandese roots. Kabila's lack of proficiency in Lingala, Kinshasa's lingua franca, also confirmed him as an outsider. This distance between the Kinois and the Kabila state engendered danger and even death.

Camouflage, a Tactic of Evasion

Mbembe writes that postcolonial subjects exist in several modes, "several beings, which, although sometimes mutually exclusive, are nevertheless inside one another." Thus, postcolonial subjects need "to know how to forget one's surname and how to remember it" (Mbembe 2001, 202). In the anecdote above, Fiston clearly existed in several modes during the day of protest: he became invisible by disguising himself and temporarily lost his official identity, but he also became multiple when he changed clothes. Fiston navigated perfectly the postcolonial commandment.

Nyamnjoh (2015) introduced the notion of "frontier Africans," which speaks poignantly to the above-mentioned uses of the voter's card and engagements with surveillance cameras as multiple ways of being political subjects. Nyamnjoh emphasizes incompleteness and conviviality in sub-Saharan African socialities. African societies, he argues, are "not steeped in dualisms, binaries, dichotomies and essences"; rather, they enjoy, applaud, and thrive on multiplicity. In similar vein, then, African identities are composites, full of possibilities, "amenable to being melted by possibilities" (2015, 258). In this reading of sub-Saharan African lifeworlds, the emphasis is on the "becoming" of people, realities, and universes. Nyamnjoh is careful not to oppose "African" versus "Western" lifeworlds and argues that not "all Africans" are living according to this adagio of becoming. Rather, it is only "when not pretending, claiming identities in abstraction or being defined and confined by others" that Africans "are frontier beings" (ibid.). According to Nyamnjoh, frontier Africans understand the world as always incomplete, unfinished, and ever-changing; this understanding of the world, self, and others pushes frontier Africans to form alliances with others and to multiply entanglements in order to enlarge possibilities and opportunities.

This has political meanings as well. According to Nyamnjoh, this experience of "the messy reality of entanglements" is an indicator "for the future direction of citizenship and what it means to belong in African and the world" (ibid., 266). We could call this an "and-and" condition rather than an "or-or" positionality. It helps us to make sense of the ever-switching alliances in Congo's macro-political field: throughout postcolonial Congolese history, members of apparently opposed political parties have regularly made sudden moves to the other side, thus baffling observers. But the concept is also enlightening for making sense of the above-mentioned micro-politics. On a mundane, everyday level, ordinary citizens easily change camps; or, perhaps better, they belong to several camps. This "frontier" concept puts in perspective the taken-for-granted notions of "confusion," "chaos," and "instability" that have been dominating political analysis of Zaire/the DRC for decades now, and that are used to diagnose the "failed" or "dead" character of the Congolese state (de Villers 1999; Willame 1999; Karlon 2010). Taking Nyamnjoh's cue, then, confusion, chaos, and instability are productive, sought after, and cultivated. We could call this frontier politics.

"Frontier citizenship" then involves a skillful navigation of multiple political subjectivities within institutional and social environments. Being a frontier citizen consequently entails knowing which rights, obligations, and opportunities to claim, enact, and display, depending on various assessments of outcomes. It should not be confused with "flexible citizenship" (Ong 1999). In her analysis of Chinese migrants in the United States, Aihwa Ong redefined the traditional approach to citizenship as an identity based on political rights and participation within a nation-state. Ong's interlocutors choose their citizenship based on economic and political calculations. The flexibility in Ong's analysis relates to migrants' economic opportunities obtained through documents such as guest worker permits (Germany) or residence permits (United States). These migrants do not get the same political rights in their country of residence as in their country of citizenship. Frontier citizenship, by contrast, references a multiplicity of identities. In the necropolitical regime of Kabila, people like Fiston did not switch between various kinds of citizenship. Rather, they considered the risks and benefits of identifying themselves as Kabila's citizens or not. Frontier citizens sometimes use their formal name, while in other instances they are anonymous or use pseudonyms; in another mode, they contribute to the same political violence and injustice that they may be enduring themselves.

This label of "frontier citizens" helps us to understand the eager adoption by Kinois and other Congolese of the voter's card. Rather than signaling that they agreed with Kabila as a ruler, Kinois understood very well that this document opened up various possibilities and opportunities, both on a collective and on an individual level. Insofar as the carte d'électeur is a promise of elections, holding on to this personal document means for some citizens that they can actively participate in the determination of political futures. Yet, as mentioned above, the carte also gains value in other environments and circumstances that have nothing to do with elections or the practice of voting. This card itself thus gains various other possible values, and becomes something else. The document is given a new kind of agency by the citizens, who thus also create performative political identities beyond that of voter. The carte is as incomplete and full of possibility as the citizen herself.

Frontier citizens in Kinshasa play with the police in the same fashion that Fiston changed his clothes so as not to be identifiable on the surveillance cameras in the city. Fiston was trying to blend into his surroundings and thus erase connections with his monitored persona. This kind of blending is not only a practice during days of protest; it is a long-standing tactic in Kinshasa's political history. When children of judges put a judge's robe in their car, they are not pretending to be judges themselves but showing they are associated with the profession and status. The robe in the car serves as a kind of mask, because people from the magistracy will not be detained by policemen. Others put fake or expired *laissez-passer* plates, often with the designation of a particular ministry or state media house, behind the windshield.

This taking on of others' identities (*kolata forme*) happens in other, more sophisticated ways.[8] Patience, a television journalist who used to work for the opposition movement during the Kabila years, painted his own car in the yellow and blue colors required by the Congolese state since June 2018 for all vehicles that serve as taxis. The journalist explained this investment in paint and the painter's work as a way of camouflage: "*Je me camoufle.*" He hoped to blend in with the taxis because drivers of private cars are harassed even more than taxi drivers by policemen. The reasoning is that policemen often feel sympathy for taxi drivers, who are employees of the car owners. As they know that private cars are mostly driven by the car's owner, they assume that the owner must have means because of the sheer fact that he owns a car. Therefore, some policemen prefer not to bother the taxi drivers. So, in order to minimize *des tracasseries* from the police, Patience *se camoufle*.

Camouflage is part of bluffing, of suggesting that one has power. Louisa Lombard's notion of blending as camouflage, developed in her analysis of armed conservation in the northeastern borderlands of the Central African Republic, is insightful here. She writes that camouflage is "a mode of agency and collaboration, . . . a skill, used as a means of positioning oneself and one's projects so that certain facets show but not others, in relation to the multi-faceted surroundings one seeks to inhabit, and through which one obtains an income and/or other sources of support and connection beyond one's place of location" (2016, 2). Kinois engage in similar blending practices when using fake voter's cards, or in changing clothes when participating in mass protest.

In line with Kabila's regime as characterized by "the state's eyes," other forms of surveillance, and capture, postcolonial subjects feel the need to play with their appearance. Vanishing is a tactic to avoid capture. Citizens can disappear by putting away their identification card, by vanishing in the crowd, and by literally taking on another appearance. This is exactly one of the qualities of "the postcolonial subject," according to Mbembe: "a 'postcolonial subject' . . . is publicly visible only at the point where the two activities overlap—on one hand, in the common daily rituals that ratify the *commandement's* own institutionalisation . . . in its capacity as a fetish to which the subject is bound; and, on the other, the subject's deployment of a talent for play and a sense of fun which makes him *homo ludens par excellence*" (1992, 5). The "postcolonial subject" moves in and out of the citizen modality, is multiple, is citizen at one moment and not a citizen at another.

These ethnographic data also need to be understood against the background of one of the basic premises of Kinois livelihood, *tia mutu, bakata*. Literally translated, *tia mutu, bakata* means "you have to put your head down, they might cut it." The implication of the phrase is actually "but if they don't cut your head, then you have won." It can thus aptly be formulated as "you need to stick your neck out." *Tia mutu* speaks to the idea that you have to go all the way, take all risks possible, because that is what life is. This is the most extreme form of courage. Life is for the *courageux*—being courageous is a requirement. A *tia mutu* is a person who is not afraid: "*il ne craigne pas l'affrontement*" (he doesn't fear a fight).[9]

Taxi drivers use the idiom when explaining that they are overtaking other cars while driving through parking lots of supermarkets, across food stalls on the pavement, or even driving in the opposite direction. Youth also referred to *tia mutu* when joking about their provocations of local police. Jisé, a young man in his early twenties, told me how he and his friends would from time to time steal the Congolese flag at the *sociat,* a police sub-office in their neighborhood. They would chant songs insulting and mocking the police. All of these performances of *tia mutu,* of putting their head out, spoke to a particular stance in life: you need to take risks, you need to be an "I don't give a damn" kind of guy, "whatever comes." In a political context, *tia mutu, bakata* is a response to the politics of intimidation. Opposition politicians said they had to *tia mutu* when explaining that they protested against the Kabila government despite the risk of being captured, either in the form of being arrested or, worse, kidnapped and killed.

All in all, frontier behavior is always risky: it is living on the edge, pushing the boundaries. Not everybody can be a frontier citizen, and not everybody felt secure enough to accompany Fiston and others during the protests, as they were not sure they were equipped to play the game with Kabila's police and army forces. Frontier citizenship, then, is based on a set of ever-accumulating formal and informal knowledges. Obviously, "sticking your head out" requires some skill and protective measures. While putting one's head out, one also tries to minimize the risk of being caught. Private car and taxi drivers avoid particular roundabouts or streets in Kinshasa when they do not possess the required documents (driver's permit, vehicle registration certificate, etc.) and thus could not defend themselves during police stops, or fear they would not be able to bluff their way out. In certain instances they take on other identities. They are Mbembe's ludic subjects, subjugating themselves to the state power when and how they want.[10]

Concluding Thoughts

In this chapter, I wanted to think through what kind of political subjectivities emerge in a Central African city in and through political objects such as the voter's card and the surveillance camera. Based on stories told about these objects, I have explored innovations in postcolonial commandment and citizenship during the Kabila regime. In general, the card is one of the most applauded innovations of the Kabila regime, while the *caméras* were heavily contested. People assumed these cameras would be operational on a day of protest. Burning or ruining them was a deliberate act to avoid being followed by those hidden behind the monitors.

The voter's cards gave the citizens some sense of control: they could make fake cards, they could use another's card, or they could refuse to show the document. With the cameras, citizens felt less in control—even if they doubted the operationality of the equipment. Maybe it is exactly this lack of self-governance and oversight with regard to the surveillance cameras that explains, to an extent, citizens' violent engagements with the cameras.

In the various sets of camera narratives that I presented, the president was not only pitched against the citizen, but the military apparatus was also identified as unruled and unruly. As such, these surveillance cameras were inherently embedded in a politics of confusion, suspicion, and anxiety. This was not new for Kinois citizens, as it had also marked Mobutu's regime. Going back further in time, nervousness and anxiety drove colonial history in the Congo (Hunt 2016). Michael Taussig (1992) has pointed to the fact that this nervousness is inherent in any governance context. We can assume that every era and regime have their own nervousness and technologies to deal with it.

Kabila's nervousness obviously drew on instability within his own state apparatus. During a famous interview with the American press in 2009, Kabila complained that there was no one in his entourage that he could trust. He also could not trust the Kinois population, which keenly repeated stories about Joseph Kabila being an impostor, being Rwandan, and being a puppet of Rwanda's Paul Kagame. The Kinois population had voted for Kabila's main opponent, Jean-Pierre Bemba, during the 2006 elections. At regular intervals, Kabila would receive death threats, and the population would ask him via various protest marches to leave his post.

As this chapter showed, Kinois' engagements with the surveillance cameras and voter's cards allow us to open up a reflection on citizenship during the Kabila years. In particular, the material has shown that we cannot assume that "citizenship" always means the same thing. Rather, citizens' actions need to be interpreted in light of vernacular imaginations of the state. Furthermore, citizenship is not only a malleable modality; sometimes it is an option from which citizens decide to opt out, in order to engage with the state. Both arguments are undergirded by my elaboration of the notion of frontier citizenship.

The material has shown a continuation of necropolitics during Kabila's regime. It is clear that citizens entered from time to time into the "animal" mode. This happened first and foremost when they walked around the city without the voter's card, but it was also poignantly clear in the discursive interpretation of the entrapments performed by state agents such as policemen and spies. In this imagination, citizens were reduced to being fish whose lives were seriously curtailed once these state agents randomly, or less randomly, decided to cast their net. Frontier citizens provoke the state and its "fishermen" because they have the skills to maneuver between the citizen and "fish" modalities. Some of these skills include camouflage, acts of appearance, and of disappearance.

Finally, this chapter opens up some more fundamental reflections about the interaction between politics and technology—in particular, it highlights the instability of the category of the "citizen" when new technological infrastructures mediate state-citizen relationships. This is not unique to the Kinois, Congolese, or even African context. In a fascinating account of the US government's engagements with tech companies for surveillance and strategies against cyberterrorism, Victoria Bernal (2016) describes how discourse about digital media and politics increasingly ignores the interests of "citizens" in favor of those of "consumers" and "users." Here, corporate logics enable the "disappearance of the citizen," though in a different way than happened during the Kabila regime. When technologies are embedded in state-citizen relationships, new grammars of the state and political life emerge that can only be uncovered through long-term ethnographic research.

Notes

1. I use pseudonyms for all interviewees.
2. See Odote and Kanyinga (2020) for a discussion of similar distrust in voting machines in Kenya.
3. These requirements seem to have been negotiated in various parts of the national territory. In Tshuapa province, for example, where a driver's license, student's card, and other documents were not easily available, the need of documented evidence was waived, along with the alternative ways of providing proof of citizenship called for elsewhere; nor was any payment required. This was probably due to an urge to get people in the interior registered, since voter registration functioned as an informal means of updating the census statistics (Lys Alcayna-Stevens, email to author, 21 January 2020).
4. Elsewhere, for example in Tshuapa province, which contains a dense network of waterways, police and agents of the Agence Nationale de Renseignement (National Intelligence Agency) require people traveling by boat to procure the voter's card. The document is thus also embedded in surveillance practices beyond the capital (Lys Alcayna-Stevens, email to author, 21 January 2020).
5. In neighboring Rwanda, similar politics of distrust are part and parcel of state governance. As Andrea Purdeková puts it, "Suspicion, distrust (strongly compounded by genocide), fear and the resultant decreased dissent all assure that the state is better able to gather and disperse, to stage and broadcast, to extract resources and attempt its desired transformations" (2011, 494).
6. This imagery may have roots in the Mobutu era, when many state agents came from Équateur, a place with many rivers and a strong fishing culture. Conversely, it may speak to the location of the seat of government in the Gombe area of Kinshasa, which is close to the Congo River.
7. I am grateful to Lys Alcayna-Stevens for this suggestion.
8. This *kolata forme* is also a strategy of *kindoki* (occult machinations involving witchcraft or sorcery): *bandoki* (witches/sorcerers) are in the vicinity but they are unrecognizable. It requires sophisticated, almost supernatural means of detection in order to unveil a *ndoki*. Yet the new *forme* protects the *ndoki* in

his/her surroundings. Camouflage and hiding thus are familiar practices that extend beyond the political sphere and are not exclusively used by people in their role as citizens. Sometimes, there is even overlap, in the sense that people assume that *bandoki* also operate among state agents.

9. It is considered to be "bad luck" (*makila mabe*) if you are caught by the police. It speaks to the game aspect of being a citizen: rules are there to be bent. It is a frontier area.

10. See Büscher and Mathys (2013) for an analysis of ludic subjects in Goma. The *enfants de Birere* (children of Birere, a neighborhood in Goma known for its commerce) strategically play with identities by manipulating and mobilizing discourse on autochthony, and thus could be called "frontier actors."

References

Bernal, Victoria. 2016. "Cybersecurity, America's 'War on Terror,' and the Disappearing Citizen." Paper presented at the Joint 4S (Society for Social Studies of Science) and EASST (European Association for the Study of Science and Technology) Conference, Barcelona, 31 August–3 September.

Bloom, Peter J., Stephan F. Miescher, and Takyiwaa Manuh, eds. 2014. *Modernization as Spectacle in Africa*. Bloomington: Indiana University Press.

Breckenridge, Keith. 2016. *Biometric State: The Global Politics of Identification and Surveillance in South Africa, 1850 to the Present*. Cambridge: Cambridge University Press.

Büscher, Karen, and Gillian Mathys. 2013. "Navigating the Urban 'In-between Space': Local Livelihood and Identity Strategies in Exploiting the Goma/Gisenyi Border." In *Violence on the Margins: States, Conflict, and Borderlands*, edited by Benedikt Korf and Timothy Raeymaekers, 119–42. Basingstoke, England: Palgrave Macmillan.

Cheeseman, Nic, and Brian Klaas. 2018. *How to Rig an Election: Tricks Despots Play*. New Haven, CT: Yale University Press.

Cuvelier, Jeroen, and Philémon Muamba Mimbunda. 2013. "Réforme douanière néolibérale, fragilité étatique et pluralisme normatif: Le cas du guichet unique à Kasumbalesa." *Politique africaine*, no. 129, 93–112.

De Boeck, Filip, and Marie-Françoise Plissart. 2004. *Kinshasa: Tales of the Invisible City*. Ghent: Ludion.

de Villers, Gauthier. 1999. "Confusion politique au Congo-Kinshasa." *Canadian Journal of African Studies/Revue canadienne des études africaines* 33 (2/3): 432–47.

Devisch, René. 1993. *Weaving the Threads of Life: The "Khita" Gyn-eco-logical Healing Cult among the Yaka*. Chicago: Chicago University Press.

Gagliardone, Iginio. 2016. *The Politics of Technology in Africa: Communication, Development, and Nation Building in Ethiopia*. Cambridge: Cambridge University Press.

Hunt, Nancy Rose. 2016. *A Nervous State: Violence, Remedies, and Reverie in Colonial Congo*. Durham, NC: Duke University Press.

Karlon, Nir. 2010. "The Great Lakes of Confusion." *African Security Review* 19 (2): 25–37.

Lombard, Louisa. 2016. "Camouflage: The Hunting Origins of Worlding in Africa." *Journal of Contemporary African Studies* 34 (1): 147–64.

Mavhunga, Clapperton Chakanetsa. 2014. *Transient Workspaces: Technologies of Everyday Innovation in Zimbabwe.* Cambridge, MA: MIT Press.

Mbembe, Achille. 1992. "Provisional Notes on the Postcolony." *Africa: Journal of the International African Institute* 62 (1): 3–37.

———. 2000. *De la postcolonie: Essai sur l'imagination politique dans l'Afrique contemporaine.* Paris: Karthala.

———. 2001. *On the Postcolony.* Berkeley: University of California Press.

———. 2003. "Necropolitics." *Public Culture* 15 (1): 11–40.

Mitchell, Timothy. 2002. *Rule of Experts: Egypt, Techno-politics, Modernity.* Berkeley: University of California Press.

Nuttal, Sarah, and Achille Mbembe. 2015. "Secrecy's Softwares." In "The Life and Death of the Secret," edited by Leslie C. Aiello. Supplement, *Current Anthropology* 56, no. S12:S317–24.

Nyamnjoh, Francis B. 2015. "Incompleteness: Frontier Africa and the Currency of Conviviality." *Journal of Asian and African Studies* 52 (3): 253–70.

Odote, Collins, and Karuti Kanyinga. 2020. "Election Technology, Disputes, and Political Violence in Kenya." *Journal of Asian and African Studies* 56 (3): 558–71.

Ong, Aihwa. 1999. *Flexible Citizenship: The Cultural Logics of Transnationality.* Durham, NC: Duke University Press.

Petit, Pierre, and Georges Mulumbwa Mutambwa. 2005. "'La crise': Lexicon and Ethos of the Second Economy in Lubumbashi." *Africa: Journal of the International African Institute* 75 (4): 467–87.

Purdeková, Andrea. 2011. "'Even If I Am Not Here, There Are So Many Eyes': Surveillance and State Reach in Rwanda." *Journal of Modern African Studies* 49 (3): 475–97.

Pype, Katrien. 2011. "Visual Media and Political Communication: Reporting about Suffering in Kinshasa." *Journal of Modern African Studies* 49 (4): 625–45.

———. 2012. "Political Billboards as Contact Zones: Reflections on Urban Space, the Visual and Political Affect in Kabila's Kinshasa." In *Photography in Africa: Ethnographic Perspectives,* edited by Richard Vokes, 187–204. Woodbridge, UK: James Currey.

———. 2013. "The Drama(s) of Independence Day: Reflections on Political Affect and Aesthetics in Kinshasa (2010)." In "National Days in Southern Africa," edited by Heike Becker and Carola Lentz. Special issue, *Die suid-afrikaanse tydskrif vir sosiologie/South African Journal of Sociology* 36 (1): 58–67.

———. 2016. "(Not) Talking Like a Motorola: Politics of Masking and Unmasking in Kinshasa's Mobile Phone Culture." *Journal of the Royal Anthropological Institute* 22 (3): 633–52.

Schatzberg, Michael G. 1988. *The Dialectics of Oppression in Zaire.* Bloomington: Indiana University Press.

Taussig, Michael. 1992. *The Nervous System.* New York: Routledge.

Willame, Jean-Claude. 1999. *L'Odyssée Kabila: Trajectoire pour un Congo nouveau?* Paris: Karthala.

ELEVEN

Encountering Cameroon's Garrison State

Checkpoints, Expectations of Democracy, and the Anglophone Revolt

ROGERS OROCK

IT IS THE EARLY HOURS OF THE MORNING OF 6 MAY 2018. I am traveling to Nigeria by road, with about seven more hours before I will arrive at the border town of Ekok. Right now, I am at a checkpoint established by police, gendarmes, and regular soldiers. "I just arrived in Cameroon because of a family emergency concerning my mother and brother, so I do not have money," I tell the police inspector. He is growing angry at my insistence that I do not have money to give him. "Do not annoy me this early morning. We are here breaking our sweat for your safety and comfort while you guys are enjoying yourselves abroad. Give me five thousand francs, I say!" The police inspector is yelling at me at the top of his voice. He seems unconcerned that other people around, including passengers in other vehicles at the checkpoint as well as his own colleagues, can hear him screaming at me in anger. We are at the Mbonge checkpoint, about eight or so kilometers from the city of Kumba. This is the last main checkpoint before admittance into this bustling city in Anglophone Cameroon. In the midst of all the confusing movements around this checkpoint, one thing is unmistakably clear: travelers are terrified of the gun-clutching and trigger-happy men and women in uniform.

This is a scene, one among many, of my encounters with state security forces at roadblocks, or checkpoints, in the war-ravaged parts of Anglophone Cameroon. At these checkpoints, every instant marks uncertainty and vulnerability for travelers who must negotiate these sorts of violent intimidation and extortion. Even over short distances, travelers on the roads in these parts of Cameroon negotiate checkpoints with anxiety, even terror. At these sites, travelers are faced with the violence of the security forces, or militants, and the power of their guns. Aside from a sense of humiliation that one may have after experiencing degrading and sometimes inhumane cruelty at the hands of some security agents, in these spaces of vulnerability anything can happen to upend the lives of travelers, including disappearing into one of the many despicable holding cells and prisons or meeting a violent end.

My encounters with state security actors at checkpoints in the context of the civil war between the two Anglophone provinces in Cameroon, the North West and South West regions, provide the basis for this chapter. Focusing on my experiences of military checkpoints and identification documents, such as the national identity cards (hereafter ID cards), as crucial material objects that mediate everyday life in these settings, I recount and discuss my encounters with this Cameroonian state during my travels there in 2018 and 2019. Since 2017, the two English-speaking regions have been engaged in war over separatist claims by a marginalized and resentful Anglophone minority whose youthful militants seek to establish an Anglophone "Federal Republic of Ambazonia" separate from the Francophone-dominated country of Cameroon (Konings and Nyamnjoh 1997, 2003; Ngoh 1999, 2001; Pommerolle and Heungoup 2017).[1] My experiences are embedded in this context of political violence and predation.

Mobility, Checkpoints, and the Everyday Violence of a Separatist Conflict

This volume invites us to think about people's everyday encounters with the state in Africa and to examine how these encounters affect their imagination and their relationship with the state. Despite the nominal claims of democratization in several parts of Africa, state power is still wielded in nakedly violent forms even as it is also negotiated along multiple registers of dissimulation (Roitman 2005). Under these conditions, the everyday state is lived as an aporia, simultaneously as arbitrariness, excess, and abjection (Mbembe 2001; Obadare and Adebanwi 2010). This chapter suggests that though still neglected as ethnographic objects in anthropological studies of the state in Africa, mundane sites of encounter, such as roads and checkpoints, are important to the ways that people experience and relate to the everyday state, especially in contexts of political violence and wars.

This chapter contributes to the literature on mobility, political violence, and the state in Africa. Since at least the 1990s, a vigorous and rich anthropological literature has developed on the state. Several studies in this area examine the state in its bureaucratic, colonial, and postcolonial character as well as its aesthetic forms (Geertz 1980; Herzfeld 1992, 1997; Young 1994; Coronil 1997; Hansen and Stepputat 2001, 2005; Navaro-Yashin 2002;

Apter 2005; Yurchak 2005; Gupta 2012). In recent years, a focus on mobility as well as on roads and government identification documents like passports have also been important to the discussions on the materiality of the state, sovereignty, and biopower. As Dimitris Dalakoglou writes in his ethnographic observations on the road along the Albanian-Greek border, an anthropological attention to people's "daily road-related practices and discourses" offers a valuable vantage for social and political analyses. Precisely by attending to people's subjective experiences of the road, the anthropologist can understand how they "reconstruct the road as a common subject of their narratives, of their intercommunity conflicts, and of their nationalisms" (Dalakoglou 2010, 133). Roads and the policing, or control, of circulation via the verification of government papers can be viewed as part of a broader assemblage of critical infrastructure for people's everyday mobility (West 2003; Allard 2012; Cooper-Knock and Owen 2018; Sheridan 2019). These are integral to people's encounters and relations with states (Pedersen and Bunkenborg 2012; Pedersen and Nielsen 2013; Agbiboa 2017).

Security checkpoints, or roadblocks, are increasingly recognized as central sites of state power. Checkpoints are concrete and intense sites of citizens' everyday encounters with the state. In situations of violent conflict such as I experienced in the areas of Anglophone Cameroon affected by the separatist conflict, these presumably marginal sites of the state amplify the general sense of vulnerability associated with conflict. As Veena Das and Deborah Poole remark in the introduction to their volume *Anthropology in the Margins of the State*, "contexts of civil war, general political violence, authoritarian rule, and emergency powers shape people's sense of community, self, and political future" (2004b, 11). Das and Poole are inspired by Agamben's conceptualizations of sovereignty in terms of notions of law, exception, and bare life to advance their own argument about the productivity of margins as "rivers" that "run through the body" of the state (2004b, 13).

Situations of war and violent conflict are, in their view, the extreme expressions of state(s) of exception or emergency. In such situations, the force of the law is simultaneously strengthened in some areas of life while it ebbs, is suspended, or retreats entirely in other areas to leave room for other forms of regulatory forces. As Das and Poole contend, in these situations of exception or emergency, "the policeman challenges, not this or that law, but the very possibility of law itself" (2004b, 15). Mobility, or the control of mobility, in situations of conflict is an example of an area in which the law is simultaneously more visible and arbitrary. More precisely, in *Anthropology and the Margins of the State*, checkpoints provide a focal point for examining the complexities and ambiguities of law, identification documents, and the vulnerability of some categories of citizens to the violence of the state. For example, in her chapter in the same volume, Poole describes how the fears of violence and the uncertainty and vulnerabilities of both government soldiers and civilian populations were mediated and lived through the control of identification in the names on travelers' lists at physical checkpoints in Peru during the civil war. Peruvian soldiers saw the control of passenger lists at these checkpoints as the "only material sites" from which to operationalize "instinctual mechanisms of fear" in order to "conjure identity"; civilian passengers viewed these controls in terms of "the ominous uncertainty of the war" as well as the arbitrariness of the state (Poole 2004b, 36; see also Jeganathan 2004 in the same volume).

I situate my chapter within this line of anthropological discussion on roads, government identification documents, and mobility. In my analysis of the situation in Cameroon, I focus primarily on my own encounters with and experiences at checkpoints established by the security forces of the Cameroonian government within the Anglophone war zone. I examine the dynamics of what I describe generically as a garrison state mentality that defines the everyday state in Cameroon. When Harold D. Lasswell (1941) first proposed the concept of the garrison state, he deployed it as a "developmental construct" to discuss the ways that the global Cold War environment and the struggle for supremacy among the world's superpowers were giving rise to new national security states. Under those conditions, Lasswell argued that in the United States, there was a discernible shift away "from the dominance of the specialist on bargaining, who is the businessman, and toward the supremacy of the soldier" (1941, 455). It is this supremacy of soldiers, especially within a state of war, that I situate and contextualize as an important facet for everyday encounters with the state in Cameroon.

Unlike Lasswell, however, I do not define the emergence and contours of this Cameroonian garrison state as the result of mainly international processes impinging upon its national security considerations. Rather, I describe this garrison state as the internal material arrangements of terror and violence that underpin a predatory economy of seizure and analyze it in a broader context of social, political, physical, and mental vulnerabilities (Joseph 1977; Mbembe 1996; Deltombe, Domergue, and Tatsitsa 2011, 2016). While applicable to the entire country of Cameroon, the power of the soldier, gendarme, or police (in that order) to intimidate, seize, or let go within this economy of terror and seizure is most inscribed in the everyday life of people living in the Anglophone war zone. In the context of the Cameroonian state more broadly and the parts currently experiencing the separatist civil war in particular, roads and the checkpoints established by police, gendarmes, military, or even secessionist militants are especially salient and terrifying sites of encounter between citizens and the state (whether of the established government or that clamored by rebels). The repressive, predatory, and frightening nature of such encounters have significant implications for how people understand their everyday situation and imagine their prospects for participating in the public deliberation of power and rule in Cameroon.

I have been largely absent from Cameroon since 2006. However, I have consistently returned to the country for fieldwork for a total of more than eighteen months now, excluding periodic returns for brief stays on family visits.[2] My choice to develop my analysis primarily from my own personal experiences and observations from traveling on the roads in Anglophone Cameroon is grounded in a view that "the fundamental requirement in anthropology is that it begins with a personal relation and ends with personal experiences."[3] Thus, I recount my personal encounters with soldiers at checkpoints during my travel in 2018 and then situate and contextualize these within the broader conditions of state repression and the dynamics of the civil war in Anglophone Cameroon since the onset of the popular revolt there in 2016.

After almost three years from my last visit here, I arrived in Cameroon on 2 May 2018 through the Douala International Airport. I made sure to go through all immigration procedures (though there is normally no other way) and have my passport stamped for "Entry," for reasons that will become clear below. I returned to Johannesburg on 13 May 2018. During this visit, I traveled across some of the main towns and cities in Anglophone Cameroon, including Buea, Kumba, and Bamenda and also drove through Douala, the economic hub of the country located in Francophone Cameroon. As my mother and siblings live right across the border with Nigeria, I also had to travel through Mamfe to the dusty border outpost of Ekok (on the Cameroonian side) and then across the bridge on the Cross River to Mfum, Ajasso, and Ikom (on the Nigerian side). The bulk of the observations discussed here result from this visit and are restricted to my experiences with the Cameroonian security authorities.

Additionally, I evoke aspects of these earlier observations in relation to the most current situation in the country, following my recent visit to Cameroon between 7 and 30 of November 2019. Again, this visit allowed me to travel to Buea, Kumba, Mamfe (on the Anglophone side), and onward to the Nigerian side, as well as to Douala and Yaoundé (on the Francophone side), where I stayed for almost two weeks. These observations are embedded in a variety of other ethnographic materials collected prior to, during, and after my visits to Cameroon. These include news reporting from local and international agencies as well as official statements or reports issued by local and international actors in relation to the political conflict in Anglophone Cameroon since 2016. Using these observations and materials, I discuss the broader context of the state in Cameroon and its ramifications for everyday life beyond the expectations of democracy that Cameroonians harbor.

Stories from the Road: Checkpoints in the Anglophone War Zone

Let me return, then, to my encounter with the police inspector at the checkpoint in Mbonge on the morning of 6 May 2018. Before arriving at that checkpoint we had passed a few other major checkpoints. About ten or so minutes after our departure from the Mile 17 Motor Park in Buea earlier that morning, we had sailed through the checkpoint in Muea without too much hassle. The driver had duly "settled" the mixture of police and gendarme officers who did not make much fuss about us in the vehicle. (To "see," or "settle," is a euphemism or code for bribing the security officers on the road.) Some twenty minutes later, we arrived at the checkpoint at the entrance of Ekona, another small town on the road between Buea and Kumba. Here, while seated in the van we heard bits and pieces of a discussion in French between the police and gendarme officers about a deadly gun battle that occurred the previous night around their checkpoint. From what we could hear, the government troops had successfully repelled the Anglophone separatist forces of the new Ambazonia ("Amba") Boys, with no casualties for the government troops. We could see bullet shells and traces of blood on the sidewalk by the tar. Understandably, for troops whose side just repelled an attack by the rebels, the officers seemed tired and angry. But they were careful not to cause any further incidents with the population that could spell some new trouble.

After the driver "saw" the commanding officer of the unit, a lieutenant of the gendarmerie, three officers proceeded to inspect our vehicle. They asked that everyone simply hold out national identity cards (hereafter IDs). They went by the vehicle and verified these cards against the faces in the vehicle. I duly held out my passport. The young officer, whose name I could only partly see as "Bekolo," took a look at my passport. He reluctantly returned it to me, asking, "Where is your ID Card?" I told him that I had arrived in the country just two days prior and was on my way that morning to attend to a very sick mother and a younger brother in the village. He let go pretty easily, saying, "Welcome back into the country. But try to establish a new ID card soon. These are dangerous times. I hope your mother recovers quickly." I smiled, thanked him politely, and leaned back comfortably into my seat as we drove off.

Long after we left that checkpoint, as we approached the villages around Muyuka, we passed two lifeless bodies by the side of the road. This was not the last I would see or hear of the dead bodies of young people. For example, between Banga Bakundu and Kumba, I saw two other bodies left to decompose under the scorching sun. The drivers who in ordinary time would have a story or two to share about the deaths (in cases of motor accidents, for example) simply sped past these without comment. Like the driver, passengers remained silent during much of the journey—and especially so after seeing the lifeless bodies. We simply rode along in the silent atmosphere of fear and tension. It was as if not talking about these corpses would mean we saw nothing. Nothingness, it seems, had become the defining characteristic for people in these parts of Cameroon. This stood quite in contrast to the bombastic discussions going in Douala, Yaoundé, and other centers of life in the French-speaking parts of Cameroon, where people talked prominently about the separatist war in the "NOSO" (short for northwest and southwest regions). And so we drove in almost absolute silence and almost sleepy numbness, only occasionally jerked back into consciousness when we were close to a checkpoint. The driver would simply announce "All man move yi ID" (Everyone should hold out his or her IDs).

Then we got to Mbonge, a small village situated about five or so kilometers from Kumba. This was the last checkpoint before entering the city. Ahead, around the checkpoint, there was quite a commotion. Movement and noise came partly from hooting from the vehicles and partly from soldiers, policemen, and gendarmes screaming orders. The confusing combination of movement and sound was jarring. Passengers in our vehicle came to life, peering outside the windows to look at several vehicles stationed by the roadside and people coming out or getting into them. "Why are these people walking?" I said to myself and then quickly got my answer. As we inched closer to the checkpoint, the driver came to a complete stop and announced: "All man must go down with yiown kako them. Dem go ckeckwunna bags. Then wunna show wunna ID card demand waka past checkpoint by wunnasef. I go di wait wunna for front, after checkpoint." (Everyone must get out of the vehicle, with your luggage. They will search your bags. Then you will present your ID cards and walk through the checkpoint. I will be waiting for you ahead, right after the checkpoint.)

Panic and confusion quickly took hold of some among the passengers in the vehicle. A few people asked why the driver was not going to "see" the military officers at the checkpoint. He replied that he intended to go and see them but that this was a required, non-negotiable practice at this specific checkpoint. Duly, we obeyed. I had only a small hand luggage filled with my clothing, a couple of books, and a few toiletry items—"nothing complicated that could be a cause for alarm," I reassured myself. I walked gently and calmly to the checkpoint. I was greeted by a police officer in black military fatigue holding tightly to his rifle. "Hello, put down your bag. Open it!" he screamed with an accent that showed me he was an English-speaking Cameroonian. "Hello, officer," I said in return, looking at the name tag on the right side of his chest as I placed my bag down. "Aminkeng, so Lebialem," I said to myself as I mentally situated the ethnic/territorial affinity of that name. "He is an Anglophone," I repeated to myself. I opened the bag.

The officer, a police inspector, looked into the bag as I took out the items to show him, including my underwear. Satisfied, he screamed "ID card!" I took out my passport and handed it to him. He took it and looked at it keenly, flipping through a number of pages. "Where are you coming from?" He shouted? "Buea," I said gently. "No, I mean which country are you coming from that you present me with your passport? And where is your ID card? A passport is not an ID card," he said in a tone that was growing slightly impatient. "Oh, I am coming from South Africa. I live and work there," I ventured, fully aware that this only answers the first part of his interrogation. He looked pensive for a short moment then blurted, "And so? Where is your ID card?"

In a calm manner, I explained that during my last visit to Cameroon in August 2015 I had applied for a new ID card in Yaoundé but that, unfortunately, I left before the ID was issued. However, I presented him with the receipt (popularly referred to by its French designation as a *récépissé*) of application that normally functions as an ID document until the holder collects the actual ID card. The receipt for the ID card application is usually valid for three months, but a superintendent of police can grant periodic "extensions" of validity of the card for three months at a time, though in principle no more than two extensions should be possible. In this instance, of course, my receipt was long expired (almost three years had passed). So he demanded simply: "Give me five thousand francs!"

At this point, my delay in making the payment led the officer to shout out at the top of his voice. The driver nodded at me, a signal that I should "settle" promptly and enable us to leave this rather tense checkpoint. I decided I would comply. As I took out a five-thousand-franc banknote, I saw the police officer relax and turn to his colleagues smiling. He then returned his gaze on me, saying, "This is how it should be. Welcome to your country. Please feel free. This is your country. By the way, as you are only coming into the country you have up to ninety days to use your passport as a valid form of identification. So, if anyone disturbs you on your way by asking for a bribe, do not give them. Tell them you have just arrived and your passport is a valid alternative to your national ID. Enjoy the rest of your journey, my brother." I froze for a moment, my body shifting in an emotionally confused state between anger and bemusement as I nearly burst out in laughter. I must have had my mouth open for a moment as I considered saying something very insulting and callous to him until the gun in his hands helped me to decide against that. In the end, I only managed to collect my passport and walk past him without saying a word. As all the other passengers in our vehicle had already walked to the van, only our driver had seen and heard everything in the last moments of our transaction. As I approached him, he smiled and told me, "Do not worry. This will all end someday soon enough." As I climbed back into the van, I burst out in laughter.

My experience at this checkpoint in Mbonge was painful. I felt humiliated and angry at having to open my bag of personal items and hold out my underwear for inspection by the police officer. I was especially enraged by the inspector's sense of entitlement to demand that I pay him five thousand francs CFA. I felt that my money was being seized from me at gunpoint. But I found the officer's decision to advise me on my rights, and especially his suggestion that I not pay other security officers who may try the same extortionist trick, to be utterly ridiculous.

My experience of this encounter illustrates, in part, the characterization of African lives under the repression of military dictatorships by the famous Nigerian Afrobeat singer Fela Anikulapo Kuti, who described the African condition as "suffering and smiling." Fela understood the African condition in which laughter and other comedic forms are the means of sublimation by which Africans make sense of their brutal abuse by colonial and postcolonial authoritarianisms (see also Mbembe 1997; Chabal 2009; Obadare 2010; Obadare 2016). However, this sense of humiliation and terror underwrites a broader and much deeper economy of predation through seizures (including by the widespread use of kidnappings) perpetrated by the security forces and the Ambazonia militants alike. As I discuss in the next section, another encounter with the security forces illustrates how the anger over the violence of seizure and extortion is one of the very important currents animating the Anglophone revolt and the ongoing civil war in Cameroon.

Checkpoints as Shakedowns

The afternoon of Wednesday, 9 May 2018, I traveled from Nigeria to Bamenda, the main city of the Northwest Region in Cameroon. I made the regular settlements at some of the checkpoints, I experienced an interesting moment of intense scrutiny from security officers at a checkpoint between Eyumojock and Mamfe. This was a unit of soldiers from Paul Biya's special military unit, the Battalion for Rapid Intervention, known most popularly as BIR. There, after checking my passport and professional ID card, a soldier asked that I bring my phone to him. I handed it to him and he asked that I unlock it for him so he couldlook through my *WhatsApp* and *Facebook* accounts. I asked him why that was necessary, and he replied that he had no explanation to give me, insisting I should comply with his instructions. Feeling powerless and angry, I opened my phone for him. After scrolling both of my social media accounts to his satisfaction he returned the phone to me and wished me a safe journey. Again, much like the incident at the checkpoint in Mbonge, I felt humiliated.

As we approached Bamenda, there was only one other remarkable episode. Our vehicle was stopped at the checkpoint in Batibo, a village some thirty or so kilometers from Bamenda. This checkpoint was situated right outside the local post of the National Gendarmerie in the village. Although the area seemed relatively quiet and deserted, the atmosphere around the checkpoint seemed rather tense. We found a small group of about six or seven soldiers, all young men who looked exhausted. The two soldiers who stopped us were Francophone. As usual, they asked for my ID documents and I offered my passport. Like the police inspector at the checkpoint in Mbonge, they demanded that I pay five thousand francs CFA. Explaining to them that I came into the country to assist my sick mother and brother, I told them I had no money left. The two soldiers immediately got angry, much like the policeman at the Mbonge checkpoint near Kumba. They called their leader, an Anglophone whose rank I determined to be warrant officer class 2 (*adjudant*). He asked why I did not have my ID card and I explained that I only arrived back in the country recently to assist an ailing mother and brother. He flipped through my passport, looking carefully at the visas and stamps.

Convinced that I truly live and work abroad on a permanent basis, he appeared to want to let me go. But before he spoke to me, he turned to look at the other soldiers. The angry looks on their faces and a comment from one of the Francophone soldiers, who asked, "Qu'est qu'il raconte la-bas?" (What story is he telling you there?), prompted the young Anglophone soldier to be more cautious. Apparently, in order to appease his colleagues, he turned and asked me if I had my vaccination card. I was rather surprised at this. But I quickly understood that this was his way of giving me a way out of a rather tense situation. I told him that my "yellow card" was in the vehicle with me and he asked that I fetch it and bring it to him. I brought it to him, and he told his colleagues that "this is a permanent resident of the United States" (probably because he saw a ten-year US visa in my passport) and then he ordered us to move on. This would not be my only and most worrisome encounter with the soldiers at Batibo checkpoint.

In Bamenda, I stayed with my in-laws for two days and the atmosphere in the city was tense throughout. There was a 6 p.m. curfew imposed by the military that appeared to be obeyed religiously. Some of my friends hurried me out of their homes to return to my sister-in-law's house in time, for my own safety. I heard harrowing stories of rape, disappearances of young men, and gruesome killings at night that left mutilated bodies on the streets by the morning. All of these were blamed on government troops. Indeed, during my two nights in the city, I would hear gun shots fired during violent clashes between the Ambazonian militants and the army.

Early morning on Friday, 11 May, I was back on the road, returning to Buea in the Southwest Region. From the hospital roundabout area, I boarded a Toyota sedan with five other passengers heading to Kumba. All were Anglophone from the Northwest Region, including the driver who was a middle-aged man from Nso. I sat in the back with three other passengers. A man of about seventy sat in the front passenger seat. As we set out, we went through three checkpoints just within the immediate vicinity of Bamenda. At each of these, we would get an easy pass once the older man in the front seat showed his ID card. The man explained that he was a retired superintendent (*commissaire*) of police, and at one of these early checkpoints some Anglophone police officers chatted happily with him.

Then we got to that checkpoint outside the gendarmerie post in Batibo. The atmosphere around the checkpoint seemed more relaxed this time, and there were more than ten soldiers out on the road. Three or so vehicles had been stopped for inspection when we got there. Several passengers had been pulled from those vehicles. I recognized one of the young soldiers from my previous encounter two days prior heading toward our vehicle. Everyone in our vehicle greeted him courteously. He asked for our ID cards. Everyone else in our car held out the ID cards, and I brandished my passport. After looking at the ID cards, the soldier took a quick look at my passport and demanded, "Give us two thousand francs." When I told him I had no money, he asked that I come out of the vehicle and walk with him to meet their leader, a Francophone with the rank of warrant officer class 1 (*adjudant-chef*). As I went down, my fellow passengers and the driver of our vehicle asked what the problem was, and I explained it to them. Then they all came out of the vehicle. The old, retired superintendent of police decided to walk with me to meet the leader of the checkpoint, who was sitting in a small spot of shade on the other side of the road with three other soldiers.

Quite a group of people had assembled around the leader and the other young soldiers around him, making payments to and collecting documents from them. The junior soldier explained to his leader that I had refused to pay even though I have no ID card. I repeated the same explanation I had offered several times before, emphasizing that it was simply that I had no money left after attending to my sick mother and brother. Visibly angered, their boss screamed that I should pay the money requested or discontinue my journey and be held there at the checkpoint. At this point, the retired superintendent approached the leader of the checkpoint and greeted him even though the latter was still visibly angry. He tried to explain to this leading soldier that he is a retired policeman and he showed his ID card to the warrant officer class 1, who looked at it and asked, "Et puis quoi?" (And so what?).

The older man explained that he was traveling in the same car as I was and begged that they consider this and let us pass. He told the soldier that it was not an ideal situation that I did not have a national ID card, but he emphasized that I did have a valid passport. Turning to another

young civilian man standing not too far from him, the warrant officer class
I said, "You see him there? He also has only a passport and we have taken
him out of their vehicle and asked him to pay. Why do you think your
boy's situation is different?" My defender replied that he did not know the
exact details of the other young man's situation but he knew the following
in my case: "He lives and works abroad, and, as you know, the law allows
for up to ninety days for citizens living abroad to use their passports as a
valid form of identification when they return into the country." This made
the soldier even angrier. Clutching his rifle and pointing it at the retired
policeman, the soldier screamed: "Dégage d'ici, sinon je t'abat et on ne
me fera rien. Vous ne viendrez pas m'enseigner comment je dois faire mon
travail. Je ne le laisse pas partir. Je dis que je peux te tuer maintenant et
sans conséquences. Nous sommes en guerre." (Leave this place or I shoot
you down. No action will be taken against me. You will not come here to
give me lessons on how to do my job. I will not let him go. I tell you that
I can kill you here without any consequences for me. We are at war.) The
old policeman responded by telling the soldier that he was being "arrogant
and a terrorist" by brandishing a weapon to intimidate civilians even when
he clearly had no basis for doing so. He told the soldier: "This is extortion.
And it is this arrogance, extortion, and terrorism that is inciting people
to revolt against the government. People like you are causing trouble for
the Anglophone population." At this point, I feared that the soldier could
actually shoot the superintendent, given how crazy the soldier sounded.
Other people around us were also scared at the way the situation had escalated. They pleaded with and convinced the retired policeman to return
to our vehicle. But many people around the checkpoint, including some of
the villagers and some of the drivers whose cars had been stopped, openly
denounced the brazen provocation from the soldier and his utter disregard
for the older man.

Unconcerned, the angry soldier shouted, "I am in charge here. I decide
what happens at this checkpoint." Our driver approached the soldier and
offered to pay the two thousand francs CFA they had first requested, but
the soldier refused. Instead, he now requested that our driver bring one
hundred thousand francs CFA! The driver said he did not have that kind
of money, further questioning the attitude put on display by this leader in
front of his junior colleagues at the checkpoint. Looking at me, the soldier
ordered: "Take him up to the post and lock him up. We no longer need his
money. Let us teach these people a lesson they are not soon to forget. In
fact, take that other young man with his passport too. Lock them both."

Alongside the other young man, a Francophone Cameroonian, I was
escorted up to the small post, a gendarmerie brigade. The small building
was clearly someone's personal house that had been converted into a village

security post. The living room, which was the largest room, served as the secretariat and had two desks adjacent to each other. One of the rooms, accessed directly from the living room, served as the office of the lieutenant who was the commanding officer of the brigade. Accessed through a narrow corridor, two other rooms served as holding cells where suspects were locked up and kept in total darkness. Between the living room and the corridor, the house had been adapted with a metal door with bars, and only a small window at the end of the corridor provided light.

As we climbed to the post, we met the young Anglophone soldier who had helped me two days earlier. Immediately, he asked his two junior colleagues escorting us why they were taking us to the station. They explained to him that we do not have our ID cards. "They have only their passports," one of the two said. The Anglophone warrant officer of class 2 tried to come to my rescue once again: "This guy has all his papers. It is not right to detain him." One of the two junior colleagues replied that they were just following orders and only a discussion with their leader at the checkpoint could change things at this point. The young Anglophone soldier followed us and sat at one of the desks in the secretariat, where a number of ledgers and papers were piled up. Another warrant officer of class 2, a Francophone, was sitting at the other desk, with only a ledger for recording the names of people brought to the station.

The two officers who escorted us explained to this warrant officer why we were there and they left. In turn, the warrant officer asked us to wait, and while he went to speak to the lieutenant, I took advantage of the time and made a call to some of my family members and friends in Bamenda, Douala, and Yaoundé. Not long afterward, the staff sergeant in charge of registration returned and asked us to submit all our identification documents and phones. We were then pushed into the narrow corridor and the metal door slammed shut. We could only see and speak to the soldiers through the iron bars. Standing in that corridor, we stood very close to two bedrooms that served as holding cells. Each of these was also locked and kept in darkness, with only small spaces left on the metal doors to talk with detainees. We could not see the people held in those cells. We occasionally heard loud cries coming from both cells. One detainee sobbed that he had been there for so long that he was wondering which day it was and whether his parents had any idea he was held there. He was scolded by another detainee who asked him to "shut up" since it was futile cry.

I asked my fellow detainee, a young trader of Bamiléké origin living in Douala, what his own situation was. He explained that he was heading to Nigeria to buy goods and, like me, only had a valid passport. When his last ID card expired in mid-2017, he made an application for a new one and was given a receipt that was valid for three months. As his new ID card had still not arrived at the police post in Douala where he applied for it, on two additional occasions the superintendent of police there had reauthorized his using that receipt. However, when the ID card had still not been delivered by April 2018, the same superintendent had turned down his request for a third extension of the validity of the receipt. Under these circumstances, he said, he resorted to presenting his passport as a national identification document during his travels. He said the soldiers at the checkpoint had asked him to pay thirty thousand francs CFA, which he judged to be too much for him to pay.

In the end, we spent several hours in that corridor. Throughout the time we were held there, the drivers transporting the young trader and me, as well as some of the passengers in our respective vehicles, struggled to secure our release. When the drivers were first allowed to speak to us, they informed us that the lieutenant had demanded that we pay 500,000 francs CFA (approximately US$900) each. They assured us that this was a ridiculous request even for these "greedy" soldiers. By 11 a.m., the drivers secured another meeting with the lieutenant. This time the discussion was heated, and we could hear all that was said in the lieutenant's office. Much like his warrant officer class 1 (*adjudant-chef*) who had ordered our detention in the first place, the lieutenant grew angry and at one moment he shouted: "This is a serious case. We are at war and we do not know the kinds of characters we stop on the road. In this instance, one of them has a very suspicious record of travel with visas and stamps showing him to be in several zones where the Ambazonian militants abroad reside. What if he has been going around collecting funds to support the terrorists? The least we can accept for these people to be released is one hundred thousand francs CFA."

Between the many attempts that our "team of negotiators" made at the lieutenant's office, I heard him answer two phone calls on my account that I later found out came from people in high places acting at the behest of one of my friends in Yaoundé. To the one, he claimed that we had just been brought in and he hardly knew the details of the case. He promised to look into the case and make a determination before 3 p.m., when temporary detainees would have to be moved to the Bamenda Central Prison, where getting our release would become more complicated. To the other caller, he admitted being aware of the case but claimed that this was sensitive given allegations that I was a potential suspect, a person of interest in their fight against Ambazonia militants and their supporters abroad. He, however, said he would examine the case carefully to determine if the allegations were founded. He could not promise more than that, he said in the end.

After he returned from his lunch break at 1:30 p.m., negotiations with our drivers were resumed and we were finally let out by 3 p.m. Once outside, our drivers told us they each paid ten thousand francs for our release, much to their own credit and surprise. When we got to the road the team of soldiers at the checkpoint had changed. Our oppressors had left. Other passengers in our respective vehicles were very relieved to see us released, and this allowed us to continue our respective journeys. In my vehicle we talked about the incident until we arrived in Kumba, where we parted ways. Everyone concluded that the war of liberation by Anglophone separatists was a just cause and must continue. That morning some of us might have still been unsure about this conflict. Maybe some of us still harbored a sense that moderation was important for peace. But we had just been pushed to the brink of radicalization by our experience at this checkpoint.

So how are my own personal experiences inscribed within a wider social reality of the everyday state in Cameroon, especially in the context of the current civil war in Anglophone Cameroon? To what extent does my sense of humiliation and violation at security checkpoints mirror some of the critical concerns driving the Anglophone separatist efforts? I suggest that my experiences of abuse and seizure at security roadblocks illustrate how the popular expectations for democracy in Cameroon, especially within the Anglophone political struggles, define both the separatists' vulnerabilities and determination to fight for a society of law and order in the face of increasing militarization.

After all, as my fellow travelers said during the conversations that animated our journey to Kumba, this was a war that Paul Biya had declared on Anglophone protesters. When they initiated their protests in September 2016, their community had only sought to denounce their humiliation at the hands of a Francophone majority and its oppressive security forces. They recounted (though I was also well aware of these) some of the grueling abuses suffered by Anglophone teachers and lawyers at the hands of the state security forces from the onset of their protests in late 2016, including those suffered by students at the University of Buea. Members of all three groups were beaten, arrested, and arbitrarily detained for long periods and, university students especially, were tortured, made to roll in the mud and puddles on the road, raped, and murdered by the security forces. These graphic scenes of abuse were filmed (sometimes by the security forces themselves) and circulated widely on social media. These images and videos helped to galvanize and mobilize Anglophone elites in Cameroon's national assembly, including the Honourable Joseph Wirba and the Anglophone diaspora, to support the claims of Anglophone separatists about the abjection of Anglophone life in Cameroon.

All of the current harsh realities reflected their historical fears about French Cameroon security forces and stood in stark contrast to the expectations for a society of democratic freedoms (Nkwi, Kah, and Ndeh 2016). Their leader John Ngu Foncha promised an inclusive society based on law and order and the respect for civil liberties in order to convince Anglophone Cameroonians in the former British Southern Cameroon to vote to join a "brotherly" French Cameroon rather than joining Nigeria in October 1961. Instead, as Foncha's leading opponent Dr. Emmanuel M. L. Endeley had predicted, Anglophone Cameroonians have lived with tyranny and the ruthlessness of the police, gendarmerie, and the armed forces, which has only become more pervasive. The current conflict in Anglophone Cameroon has escalated the role of the security forces in the country more generally. Roadblocks, or checkpoints, and identification documents, are critical material objects that ground an everyday economy of violent predation by the armed forces. To understand people's everyday encounters with the state in Anglophone Cameroon today is therefore to be aware of their historical aspiration for a democratic state in the face of an authoritarian and repressive order.

Beyond Democracy: Encountering Cameroon's Garrison State

A substantial part of postcolonial Cameroon (the Francophone part) was born as the extension of a violent colonial order. Between 1955 and 1960, the French army (alongside local foot soldiers) imposed a state of emergency and used violent repression against demands for independence and emancipation from the Cameroun nationalist movement, the Union des Populations du Cameroun. Led by Ruben Um Nyobe, these nationalists were hunted down in the forests during a guerrilla war that left tens of thousands of French Cameroonian militants dead. Under Ahmadou Ahidjo (1960–82), the repression and persecution of nationalists was pursued in earnest, as was the continued use of executive orders to perpetuate a state of emergency that lasted between 1958 and the 1970s (Fombad 2004; Kamga 2015). Today, Cameroon is nominally a multiparty democracy, with periodic elections that are repeatedly marred by allegations of fraud and voter intimidation by the ruling party, the Cameroon People's Democratic Movement (CPDM), and its leader, Paul Biya. These democratic gains were attained at least on paper in the 1990s and included constitutional guarantees for the safety and equal protection of citizens under the law as well as freedoms for the press and the rights of associations, protest, and strike.

At the end of a chaotic process of democratization, Biya ironically styled the country as an "advanced democracy" (Geschiere 2009; Nyamnjoh 2002; Takougang and Krieger 1998). In reality, despite the constitutional reforms and promises for redirecting the state toward greater enforcement of human rights, the state in Cameroon remained highly authoritarian and repressive. The democratic promises enshrined in the constitutional reforms of the 1990s were swiftly ignored once the fervor of popular mobilizations had died down by 1997. Mass uprisings and popular demands for political liberalization were met with violent crackdowns by Biya's government and security agencies, often resulting in deaths (Mbembe and Roitman 1995; Mbu 1993). Like its colonial progenitor, the postcolonial regimes of Ahidjo and Biya (since 1982) the state has crushed all forms of internal opposition. More particularly, to contain the popular demands for democracy, human rights, and the rule of law in the 1990s, Biya's regime "extended the role of the army to the tasks of the maintenance of law and order," including placing some parts of the country (some regions and cities) under special military commands called operational commands (see Mbembe 2005, 155). This scheme was revived again by the administration in order to deal with protests against a perceived rise in urban crime in Douala in the early 2000s (Orock 2014). In both instances, the security forces were widely accused of perpetrating extensive abuses of human rights, including torture, enforced disappearances and extrajudicial killings (see Amnesty International 2009; US Department of State 2004; Tumi 2006). In other words, neither the bribery and corruption of the elite through state patronage nor the party support of the ruling CPDM would have sufficed to maintain Biya in power for so long were it not for the visible threat of abuse that the army, gendarmerie, and the police (and the judicial system they underwrite) all pose for the forces of the opposition in the country since the late 1980s.

So, if clearly not a democracy, what kind of state is Cameroon? I have suggested that Cameroon is lived and largely experienced as a highly authoritarian and repressive state, one that I believe is beset by a garrison state mentality. A feature of the garrison state is its violent and militaristic character. Authorities pay lip service to discourses of freedoms and human rights to underwrite their political projects but hardly take these seriously. Instead, as Lasswell (1941, 459–61) outlines it, the political leadership in a garrison state considers its primary concern to be about how to maintain the populations under its rule in a state of "universal fear." Though "the use of coercion" is central in this, the leadership also depends on propaganda campaigns that effectively manipulate the symbols of violence in order to popularize terror as the defining logic and affect of power (Lasswell 1941, 461; see also Lasswell 1951; Sylvan et al. 2019). As part of this process of propaganda, also, a chief mode of political action that arises in the absence of deliberative spaces is the "practice of petition" writing in order to maintain the semblance or "mystic" of democracy (Lasswell 1941, 462).

Additionally, another important feature of the garrison state is the role of violence in the control over and distribution of the means of life, which are highly unequal. And while Lasswell recognized this, he did not explain how the violence and terror of the garrison state work to operate such inequalities. Instead, it is anthropologist Janet Roitman who offers a helpful insight on this point in her discussion of the emergence of a "garrison-entrepot" within the regional economy in the Chad Basin, an area of the Sahel region that includes Northern Cameroon, Chad, Niger, Nigeria, South Sudan, and others. She situates it as a constellation of actors and institutional forms that align "financial, commercial and even military relationships" so as to operate dispossession and create new forms of wealth. Roitman (1998, 2005) argues that the dominant practices of accumulation in the garrison-entrepot are "seizure and razzia," modes of economic predation that recognize "licit wealth" (spoils) and "banditry" (outright violent theft). With long and complex histories that traverse and link precolonial, colonial, and postcolonial modes of extraction, the ultimate outcome, however, is that social and economic regulation of everyday life here is emergent and constantly underwritten by the use or threat of violence to extort, confiscate, or expropriate value. In the wider context of Cameroon and elsewhere in Africa, particularly in zones where political conflicts exist, Achille Mbembe has also commented on how the military and associated armed forces (gendarmerie and police) have often been granted a broad political license to operate such a violent economy of seizure in exchange for the protection of the regime against popular mobilizations, protests, and resistance movements. As he remarks, "At the same time violent forms of the appropriation of resources have increased in complexity and links have appeared between the armed forces, the police, the justice system, and criminal milieus. Loci of enduring conflict make it possible to occupy part of the military permanently with tasks of internal repression (notably in frontier towns), or in wars on the frontiers, or on tasks of pacification in rebellious regions situated within the confines of the national territory" (Mbembe 2005, 155–56).

Mbembe's descriptions fit a situation that has prevailed in Cameroon since at least the early 1990s and even more so now that several parts of the country undergo one kind of violent conflict or another. Beside this backdrop of generalized authoritarian repression over the last three decades or so, since 2014 Cameroon is also a state at war. This situation exacerbates citizens' vulnerability to violence and brutality in their everyday lives. The country is currently fighting wars on at least three fronts. In addition to the civil war with Anglophone separatists, there is a long, evolving situation of civil wars and political instability along its southeastern border with the Central African Republic that has the government scrambling to contain the possibilities of Seleka and Anti-Balaka rebels spilling over into the Cameroonian territory.

Also, since 2014, in the northern regions the government's army is locked in an outright war against militants of the Islamist jihadist movement Boko Haram. Years later, it is unclear that the government troops are winning this war despite the establishment of a joint force with Nigeria,

Chad, and other countries affected by this jihadist movement in the Chad Basin. Added to this are the recurrent incidents of urban unrests related to political disputes over the outcome of the October 2018 presidential elections and the municipal and legislative elections in mid-2020. All of these conflicts keep the armed forces in a permanent state of mobilization, growth in numbers, and ballooning costs. The main goal is to ensure Biya's stay in power.

The Violence of Seizures

But what does the authoritarian and repressive posture of the state really mean in the current conditions of everyday life in Cameroon? First, in its official institutional arrangements Cameroon is a highly centralized state. This is a system with a very powerful president who is simultaneously the head of state, head of the judiciary, and head of the armed forces. Moreover, with an overwhelming majority of the elected representatives from Biya's ruling CPDM, the president has also traditionally exercised considerable dominance over the legislative branch of government that has remained subservient to him partly because the president is constitutionally empowered to dissolve Parliament according to Section 8 of the Constitution. Transformed from a unicameral house of representation during the previous era of the one-party state (1960 to 1990), the constitutional reforms adopted in 1996 provide that the Parliament should be constituted as a bicameral house of assembly of 180 and a senate of 100, among whom the president gets to appoint up to thirty senators.

In power since November 1982, Biya is also the head of the country's judiciary system. He has the sole power to appoint and remove judges and prosecutors that are all career civil servants. Since 2003 at least, Biya has used these powers in an anticorruption crusade dubbed Opération Épervier (Operation Sparrow Hawk) that in reality has served as a way for Biya to purge his rivals with imprisonment and judicial harassments. Several of his former members of cabinet, including a former prime minister, three former secretary-generals at the presidency, a former minister of finance, a former minister of public health, and a host of directors of public corporations have all been sentenced to long jail terms. Usually, after pleas and entreating from family and ethnic communities loyal to the detainees, only presidential pardons or special dispositions from the president have allowed these detained political figures to access freedom, whether permanently or temporarily for medical treatment.[4]

Lastly, there is also an executive branch of government headed by the president. This includes all government agencies as well as the national security agencies (police, prisons, gendarmerie, and the army, navy, air force, and intelligence services). Alongside the courts, government ministerial agencies (and their lower-level offices within the provincial governments and local government areas) are the primary material institutions that drive the everyday encounters between people and the state. And this centralization of state power creates several problems for how people negotiate their everyday bureaucratic interactions.

This centralization of state power lies at the heart of an institutional malaise that cripples governance and development initiatives in the country. Protests and mobilizations for political change are, in turn, repressed with deadly violence from the government. As the Central African project director for the International Crisis Group, Richard Moncrieff, remarks, "In Cameroon the problems can be broken down into three categories: governance, legality and the army." Especially in regard to governance, he writes, "Cameroon is one of the most centralised states in the world. All state resources, whether cash or jobs, flow from the centre, and mostly from President Paul Biya's office" (Moncrieff 2019). This assessment echoes the reflections of Titus Edzoa, Biya's former minister of public health and former secretary-general of the presidency between 1992 and 1997. Jailed by Biya because he had announced a presidential run against Biya in 1997, Edzoa diagnosed that "the system is built on a single individual and this individual is identified with the job. . . . If you try to go against Biya, you'll be crushed" (quoted in Kaze and Hauchard 2018).

The high degree of centralization lies in part at the root of the current Anglophone conflict. Pressure from the international community (mainly from the European Union and the United States; see, e.g., Reuters 2019b) has compelled the government to stage some semblance of efforts at decentralization as a step toward the peaceful resolution of the ongoing political conflict in the Anglophone regions. Since December 2019, the regime in Yaoundé has responded to this pressure with a proposal to implement laws on decentralization that had been adopted already since the 1996 constitutional reforms, including granting special status to each of the two English-speaking regions in the management of their local affairs.[5] The implementation of these reforms have remained rather perfunctory.

In these zones of war and conflict, and with a reinforced presence of government security forces, the vulnerabilities of the local populations to the exactions, abuses, and predation of soldiers, gendarmes, and police is significantly heightened in comparison to the generalized repression that marks everyday life elsewhere across the country. Checkpoints on the roads and verification of ID cards in the Anglophone war zone are important sites for everyday encounters with the state and enable their continued abuse of poor and rich Anglophones alike, though more so for the former. Yet complaints about roadblocks or checkpoints and the fear of these as sites of arbitrariness and abuse by the security forces in Cameroon have a longer history in Anglophone Cameroon, one that partly lies at the core of the current revolt and violent struggles.

For example, checkpoints featured prominently as an object of contestation during an earlier phase of Anglophone nationalism and demands for a return to the Federal Republic, including at the end of the first All Anglophone Conference (AAC I) that was held in Buea on 2 and 3 April 1993. This conference had been called by leading Anglophone voices to craft a "common purpose" Anglophone position in view of the calls for reforms toward a new, democratic constitution for Cameroon that was finally adopted in 1996. In their resolutions, the AAC I listed "road checkpoints" as a serious concern. The Anglophone elite deplored how "the hundreds of police, gendarmes, and customs checkpoints on our roads today seem normal and acceptable to Francophones." In their view, these checkpoints "really make this country strange to Anglophones" because they "restrict the free movement of people, goods, and services." For these early Anglophone nationalists, "what may originally have been an exercise with a noble objective has been reduced to a system of road tolls instituted by the forces of law and order with the tacit approval of the government" (see *Cameroon Panorama* 2018, 14).

This Anglophone resentment of the state security forces as perpetrators of violence and theft is echoed in a short piece written by Ndoh Emmanuel for *Bareta News*. The online opinion platform has been a leading site where supporters of the Anglophone revolt have expressed themselves and reported on the exactions of the state security forces since the war began. Facilitated by other social media platforms such as Facebook and WhatsApp, the content and graphics come mainly from people on the ground affected by the violent attacks, popularly referred to as those living in "Ground Zero," the place where the conditions of life for the population are rendered abject by the everyday violence. The online platform was established by Mark Bareta, one of the leaders of the Anglophone liberation movement in the diaspora. In his reflection of widely reported developments on the war front (e.g., BBC 2018; *Economist* 2019) only a couple of months after Biya issued the declaration of war, Emmanuel Ndoh (2018) tried to explain why government troops were "resorting to arson and looting" in the Anglophone zone. He argued that these must be recognized, unfortunately, as the "new war strategies of professionally trained soldiers of La Republique du Cameroun" (that is, the government). However, as many other observers also report, Ndoh remarked that once soldiers of La Republique opted for arson as a technique of combat in their war, "massive looting followed. Valuable items like household appliances, machinery, farming materials, farm produce, livestock and money were all taken away when found and what could not be taken away was burnt down. Large quantities of fuel in stock—a popular commodity for local traders—were confiscated and used to facilitate the burning down of property" (Ndoh 2018).

The editorial of the *Cameroon Panorama*, the monthly Roman Catholic newsmagazine of the Bishops of the Bamenda Ecclesiastical province (the whole of Anglophone Cameroon) described these recurrent instances of looting and pillaging as "tragic." By deploying "combat ready troops to the towns and villages of the North West and South West Regions of Cameroon," the editors argued, the outcome is not just that people have been killed, maimed, and abducted but also that these troops have "looted and destroyed their property at the slightest or no provocation." In the end, the areas affected by the separatist conflict have become "worse than a state of emergency," and everyday life in these areas is defined by an "abysmal contempt for the dignity of human life" (*Cameroon Panorama* 2017, 3).

We live in a time of "exit from democracy" and the proliferation and acceleration of states of "brutality and physical violence" around the world so that in the end we are left only with the "nocturnal body of democracy" (Mbembe 2019, 9–17). These states of violence assume and manifest themselves to us in different forms and guises, depending on our individual and collective circumstances. One such form is state terror (Aretxaga 2008; Sluka 2000), that is, states of fear. In this chapter I have offered an ethnographically grounded account of my encounters in Cameroon as one example of such contemporary states of terror in Africa that people have to negotiate in their everyday lives. I have characterized the current state of affairs in Cameroon as the result of a garrison state mentality that has long been the bane of public power, even though operating in markedly escalated forms these days. A main feature of the lived conditions of Anglophone Cameroonians in the areas of separatist conflict is the violence of their encounters with state security agents. I have situated both my experiences and the broader social conditions of such encounters within the specific register of everyday mobility. By situating and contextualizing my experiences of the security checkpoints as material sites where identification documents issued by the state are critical currencies for negotiating state power, I have discussed how fear, abuse, and humiliation are important features of everyday life in Cameroon.

Yet fear, abuse, and humiliation—the psychological conditions of abjection—are the very opposites of the freedom, rule of law, and equality that Cameroonians have aspired for since the transition to the formal trappings of democracy in 1990. Instead, security checkpoints by military, gendarmes, and police forces embody the wider political order of the commandment, where the everyday state seeks to impose itself by means of administrative orders, including arbitrary orders for arrests issued by district officers and regional governors, as well as the violent abuses and beatings by the military squadrons and brigades. In the end, Anglophone Cameroonians are revolting against this state of abuse.[6]

Notes

1. For recent reports of this civil war since October 2017, see *Cameroon Panorama* (2018), Reuters (2019a), Kindzeka (2019), *VOA* (2019) and Human Rights Watch (2019).

2. By contemporary standards of everyday life in Cameroon, I would be considered a moderately "successful" youth, with a university education up to doctoral level and a job abroad. In some sense, this situates some of my experiences of life during such periodic returns to Cameroon beyond the everyday hardships and struggles that "ordinary" young Cameroonians endure in the country. On youths and everyday struggles in Cameroon, see, e.g., Jua (2003), Fuh (2012), Orock (2013), and Fokwang (2016).

3. According to Mike Fortun, Kim Fortun, and George E. Marcus, these words are attributed to Claude Levi Strauss by Dell Hymes in an edited volume titled *The Uses of Computers in Anthropology* (London: Mouton, 1965), 5. Of course, this anthropological view has long been widely shared given the preeminent role of fieldwork of one kind or another in the discipline, including direct experiences by means of participant observation. For example, in the specific focus on the state, anthropologist Didier Fassin (2015: ix) writes that an ethnographically grounded approach to the study of the state is most fruitful when it is "inductive, micropolitical, and from below."

4. For example, in 2014 Biya granted a presidential "pardon" for the release of his former collaborator and political rival Titus Edzoa, who had been jailed since 1997. During the recent years the family and friends of some other high-profile detainees have been lobbying to secure a reprieve for them, mostly on medical grounds. This includes the former prime minister, Ephraim Inoni, who has been jailed since 2015 for his alleged financial misconduct in an affair related to the acquisition of a presidential jet as well as Yves-Michel Fotso (a former banking executive and the son of Fotso Victor, a wealthy businessman who is also a major donor to the ruling party). See, e.g., *Sun* 2019; *Cameroon Intelligence Report* 2019.

5. *Cameroon Radio and Television*, "National Assembly: Ground-Breaking Bill on Decentralization Adopted," 1 April 2019, http://www.crtv.cm/2019/04 /national-assembly-the-ground-breaking-bill-on-decentralization-adopted/; Africa News "Cameroon's Anglophone Regions Granted Special Status," 19 December 2019, https://www.africanews.com/2019/12/19/cameroon-s -anglophone-regions-granted-special-status/.

6. I am grateful to a number of friends and colleagues at the University of the Witwatersrand for discussions about my experiences in Cameroon that encouraged me to write this chapter. This includes Achille Mbembe, Sarah Nuttall, and Joshua D. Walker (at the Wits Institute for Social and Economic Research, WiSER) and Hylton White, Julia Hornberger, Nosipho Mngomezulu, and George Mahashe (at the Department of Anthropology). Peter Geschiere at the University of Amsterdam has been a formidable force for support in this and other writing projects that I struggled to put together following very

difficult moments I spent in Cameroon. I am also grateful to the Faculty of Humanities at the University of the Witwatersrand for awarding me a Mellon Staff Development Grant in 2017 to enable me travel to Cameroon to understand some of the violent events unfolding there.

References

Agbiboa, Daniel E. 2017. "Mobile Bodies of Meaning: City Life and the Horizons of Possibility." *Journal of Modern African Studies* 55 (3): 371–93.

Allard, Olivier. 2012. "Bureaucratic Anxiety: Assymetrical Interactions and the Role of Documents in the Orinoco Delta, Venezuela." *Hau: Journal of Ethnographic Theory* 2 (3): 234–56.

Apter, Andrew. 2005. *The Pan-African Nation: Oil and the Spectacle of Culture in Nigeria.* Chicago: University of Chicago Press.

Aretxaga, Begoña. 2008. "Madness and the Politically Real: Reflections on Violence in Postdictatorial Spain." In *Postcolonial Disorders,* edited by Mary-Jo DelVecchio Good, Sandra Teresa Hyde, Sarah Pinto, and Byron J. Good, 43–61. Berkeley: University of California Press.

Chabal, Patrick. 2009. *Africa: The Politics of Suffering and Smiling.* London: Zed Books.

Cooper-Knock, Sarah-Jane, and Olly Owen. 2018. "Government Paper: The Negotiated Production and Life of State Documents." *Canadian Journal of African Studies/Revue canadienne des études africaines* 52 (3): 269–87.

Coronil, Fernando. 1997. *The Magical State: Nature, Money, and Modernity in Venezuela.* Chicago: University of Chicago Press.

Dalakoglou, Dimitris. 2010. "The Road: An Ethnography of the Albanian-Greek Cross-Border Motorway." *American Ethnologist* 37 (1): 132–49.

Das, Veena, and Deborah Poole, eds. 2004a. *Anthropology in the Margins of the State.* New Delhi: Oxford University Press.

Das, Veena, and Deborah Poole. 2004b. "State and Its Margins: Comparative Ethnographies." In Das and Poole 2004a, 3–33.

Deltombe, Thomas, Manuel Domergue, and Jacob Tatsitsa. 2011. *Kamerun! Une guerre cachée aux origines de la Françafrique, 1948–1971.* Paris: La Découverte.

———. 2016. *La guerre du Cameroun: L'invention de la Françafrique, 1948–1971.* Paris: La Découverte.

Fassin, Didier. 2015. *At the Heart of the State: The Moral World of Institutions.* London: Pluto.

Fombad, Charles M. 2004. "Cameroon's Emergency Powers: A Recipe for (Un) constitutional Dictatorship?" *Journal of African Law* 48 (1): 62–81.

Fokwang, Jude. 2016. "Politics at the Margins: Alternative Sites of Political Involvement among Young People in Cameroon." *Canadian Journal of African Studies/Revue canadienne des études africaines* 50 (2): 211–28.

Fortun, Mike, Kim Fortun, and George E. Marcus. 2017. "Computers in/and Anthropology: The Poetics and Politics of Digitization." In *The Routledge Companion to Digital Ethnography,* edited by Larissa Hjorth, Heather Horst, Anne Galloway, and Genevieve Bell, 11–20. New York: Routledge.

Fuh, Divine. 2012. "The Prestige Economy: Veteran Clubs and Youngmen's Competition in Bamenda, Cameroon." *Urban Forum* 23 (4): 501–26. https://doi.org/10.1007/s12132-012-9157-x.

Geertz, Clifford. 1980. *Negara: The Theatre State in Nineteenth-Century Bali*. Princeton, NJ: Princeton University Press.

Geschiere, Peter. 2009. *The Perils of Belonging: Autochthony, Citizenship, and Exclusion in Africa and Europe*. Chicago: University of Chicago Press.

Gupta, Akhil. 2012. *Red Tape: Bureaucracy, Structural Violence, and Poverty in India*. Durham, NC: Duke University Press.

Gupta, Akhil, and Aradhana Sharma, eds. 2006. *The Anthropology of the State: A Reader*. Malden, MA: Blackwell.

Hansen, Thomas B., and Finn Stepputat, eds. 2001. *States of Imagination: Ethnographic Explorations of the Postcolonial State*. Durham, NC: Duke University Press.

————, eds. 2005. *Sovereign Bodies: Citizens, Migrants, and States in the Postcolonial World*. Princeton, NJ: Princeton University Press.

Harvey, Penny, Casper B. Jensen, and Atsuro Morita, eds. 2016. *Infrastructures and Social Complexity: A Companion*. London: Routledge.

Herzfeld, Michael. 1992. *The Social Production of Indifference: Exploring the Symbolic Roots of Western Bureaucracy*. Oxford: Berg.

————. 1997. *Cultural Intimacy: Social Poetics in the Nation-State*. New York: Routledge.

Jeganathan, Pradeep. 2004. "Checkpoint: Anthropology, Identity, and the State." In Das and Poole 2004a, 67–80.

Joseph, Richard. 1977. *Radical Nationalism in Cameroon: Social Origins of the UPC Rebellion*. Oxford: Clarendon.

Jua, Nantang. 2003. "Differential Responses to Disappearing Transitional Pathways: Redefining Possibility among Cameroonian Youths." *African Studies Review* 46 (2): 13–36.

Kamga, Gerard E. K. 2015. "The Origin and Development of Emergency Regimes in Cameroon." *Fundamina* 21 (2): 289–312.

Konings, Piet, and Francis B. Nyamnjoh. 1997. "The Anglophone Problem in Cameroon." *Journal of Modern African Studies* 35 (2): 207–29.

————. 2003. *Negotiating an Anglophone Identity: A Study of the Politics of Recognition and Representation in Cameroon*. Boston: Brill.

Lasswell, Harold D. 1941. "The Garrison State." *American Journal of Sociology* 46 (4): 455–68.

————. "Does the Garrison State Threaten Civil Rights?" *Annals of the American Academy of Political and Social Science* 275 (1951): 111–16.

Mbembe, Achille. 1996. *La naissance du maquis dans le Sud-Cameroun (1920–1960): Histoire des usages de la raison en colonie*. Paris: Karthala.

————. 1997. "The 'Thing' and Its Doubles in Cameroonian Cartoons." In *Readings in African Popular Culture*, edited by Karin Barber, 151–63. Bloomington: Indiana University Press.

————. 2001. *On the Postcolony*. Berkeley: University of California Press.

————. 2005. "Sovereignty as a Form of Expenditure." In Hansen and Stepputat 2005, 148–66.

————. 2019. *Necropolitics*. Durham, NC: Duke University Press.

Mbembe, Achille, and Janet Roitman. 1995. "Figures of the Subject in Times of Crisis." *Public Culture* 7 (2): 323–52.

Mbu, Aloysius N. T. 1993. *Civil Disobedience in Cameroon.* Douala, Cameroon: Imprimerie Georges Frères.

Navaro-Yashin, Yael. 2002. *Faces of the State: Secularism and Public Life in Turkey.* Princeton, NJ: Princeton University Press.

Ngoh, Victor J. 1999. "The Origin of the Marginalization of Former Southern Cameroonians (Anglophones), 1961–1966: An Historical Analysis." *Journal of Third World Studies* 16 (1): 165–85.

———. 2001. *Southern Cameroons, 1922–1961: A Constitutional History.* Rev. ed. Aldershot, England: Ashgate.

Nkwi, Walter G., Henry K. Kah, and Martin S. Ndeh. 2016. "The Gendarmerie, (In-)Security and Popular Reaction in West Cameroon, Federal Republic of Cameroon 1961–1964." *Modern Africa: Politics, History and Society* 4 (2): 117–39.

Nyamnjoh, Francis B. 2002. "Cameroon: Over Twelve Years of Cosmetic Democracy." *News from the Nordic African Institute* 3:5–8.

Obadare, Ebenezer. 2010. "State of Travesty: Jokes and the Logics of Socio-cultural Improvisation in Africa." *Critical African Studies* 2 (4): 92–112.

———. 2016. *Humor, Silence, and Civil Society in Nigeria.* Rochester, NY: University of Rochester Press.

Obadare, Ebenezer, and Wale Adebanwi. 2010. "Introduction: Excess and Abjection in the Study of the African State." In *Encountering the Nigerian State,* edited by Wale Adebanwi and Ebenezer Obadare, 1–28. New York: Palgrave Macmillan.

Orock, Rogers T. E. 2013. "Manyu Youths, Belonging and the Antinomies of Patrimonial Elite Politics in Contemporary Cameroon." *Cultural Dynamics* 25 (3): 269–90.

———. 2014. "Crime, In/security and Mob Justice: The Micropolitics of Sovereignty in Cameroon." *Social Dynamics: A Journal of African Studies* 40 (2): 408–28.

Pedersen, Morten A., and Mikkel Bunkenborg. 2012. "Roads That Separate: Sino-Mongolian Relations in the Inner Asian Desert." *Mobilities* 7 (4): 555–69.

Pedersen, Morten A., and Morten Nielsen. 2013. "Trans-temporal Hinges: Reflections on an Ethnographic Study of Chinese Infrastructural Projects in Mozambique and Mongolia." *Social Analysis* 57 (1): 122–42.

Pommerolle, Marie-Emmanuelle, and Hans de Marie Heungoup. 2017. "'The Anglophone Crisis': A Tale of the Cameroonian Postcolony." *African Affairs* 116 (464): 526–38.

Poole, Deborah. 2004. "Between Threat and Guarantee: Justice and Community in the Margins of the Peruvian State." In Das and Poole 2004a, 35–65.

Roitman, Janet. 1998. "The Garrison-Entrepôt." *Cahiers d'études africaines* 38 (150/152): 297–329.

———. 2005. *Fiscal Disobedience: An Anthropology of Economic Regulation in Central Africa.* Princeton, NJ: Princeton University Press.

Sheridan, Derek. 2019. "Weak Passports and Bad Behavior: Chinese Migrants and the Moral Politics of Petty Corruption." *American Ethnologist* 46 (2): 137–49.

Slukka, Jeffrey A., ed. 2000. *Death Squad: The Anthropology of State Terror.* Philadelphia: University of Pennsylvania Press.

Sylvan, David, Ashley Thornton, Juliette Ganne, and Laura Schenker. 2019. "From the Outside In: Fear, Security Agencies, and the Corrosion of Parliamentary

Democracy: Findings from the Garrison State Project." Unpublished manuscript. June. PDF file. https://a44c929e-df43-40ed-93eb-bc83c6ae20b2.filesusr .com/ugd/b437d0_90bd53800ac54028adc86b016f5c6ade.pdf.

Takougang, Joseph, and Milton Krieger. 1998. *African State and Society in the 1990s: Cameroon's Political Crossroads.* Oxford: Westview.

Tumi, Christian W. 2006. *The Political Regimes of Ahmadou Ahidjo, and Paul Biya, and Christian Tumi, Priest.* Douala, Cameroon: MACACOS.

Vohnsen, Nina H. 2017. *The Absurdity of Bureaucracy: How Implementation Works.* Manchester, England: Manchester University Press.

West, Harry G. 2003. "Tax Receipts, Virgin Mary Medallions, and Party Membership Cards: (In)visible Tokens of Power on the Mueda Plateau." In *Transparency and Conspiracy: Ethnographies of Suspicion in the New World Order,* edited by Harry G. West and Todd Sanders, 92–124. Durham, NC: Duke University Press.

Young, Crawford. 1994. *The African Colonial State in Comparative Perspective.* New Haven, CT: Yale University Press.

Yurchak, Alexei. 2005. *Everything Was Forever, Until It Was No More: The Last Soviet Generation.* Princeton, NJ: Princeton University Press.

Newspapers and Reports

Amnesty International. 2009. *Cameroon: Impunity Underpins Persistent Abuse.* AFR 17/001/2009. 29 June. London: Amnesty International Publications. https:// www.amnesty.org/en/documents/afr17/001/2009/en/.

BBC. 2018. "Burning Cameroon: Images You're Not Meant to See." 25 June. https:// www.bbc.com/news/world-africa-44561929.

Cameroon Intelligence Report. 2019. "Medical Tourism: Biya Regime Sending Jailed CPDM Barons Abroad, Inoni Is Next on the List." 29 August. https://www .cameroonintelligencereport.com/medical-tourism-biya-regime-sending -jailed-cpdm-barons-abroad-inoni-is-next-on-the-list/.

Cameroon Panorama. 2017. "Editor's Note: Remaining Silent in the Face of Evil is Sinful." October (no. 711), 3.

———. 2018. "Anglophone Crisis: Revisiting the Buea Declaration." April/May (no. 719), 10–17.

Economist. 2019. "English-Speaking Villages Are Burning in Cameroon." 7 November. https://www.economist.com/middle-east-and-africa/2019/11/07/english -speaking-villages-are-burning-in-cameroon.

European Union. 2019. "European Parliament Resolution on Cameroon." 16 April. http://www.europarl.europa.eu/doceo/document/B-8-2019-0249_EN.html.

Executive Office of the President. 2019. "Presidential Proclamation to Take Certain Actions under the African Growth and Opportunity Act and for Other Purposes." Proclamation No. 9974 of 26 December 2019, 84 Fed. Reg. 72187. https://www.federalregister.gov/documents/2019/12/30/2019-28285/to-take -certain-actions-under-the-african-growth-and-opportunity-act-and-for -other-purposes.

Human Rights Watch. 2019. "World Report: Cameroon." https://www.hrw.org /world-report/2019/country-chapters/cameroon.

Kaze, Reinnier, and Amaury Hauchard. 2018. "Cameroon's Biya at Helm of Six-Time Election Winning Machine." *Mail & Guardian* (Johannesburg), 7

October. https://mg.co.za/article/2018-10-07-cameroons-biya-at-helm-of-six
-time-election-winning-machine.

Kindzeka, Moki E. "Thousands Flee Violence in Cameroon's English-Speaking
Regions." *VOA: Voice of America,* 26 August. https://www.voanews.com/africa
/thousands-flee-violence-cameroons-english-speaking-regions.

Moncrieff, Richard. 2019. "Cameroon: Impasse in Democratic Politics Threatens
Nation's Future." International Crisis Group, 5 July. https://www.crisisgroup
.org/africa/central-africa/cameroon/cameroon-impasse-democratic-politics
-threatens-nations-future.

Ndoh, Emmanuel. "Why La Republique Soldiers Resort to Looting and
Arson." *Bareta News,* 19 January. https://www.bareta.news/la-republique
-soldiers-resort-looting-arson/?fbclid=IwAR1zJ1V6H4OCvTxylZ89qq
_moU9jE1Pc2GZHolQYKS-5d2DlVMkooHFFr-Q.

Reuters. 2019a. "Thousands Flee Deadly Violence in Cameroon's Separatist Regions:
Sources." 27 August. https://www.reuters.com/article/us-cameroon-separatists
-violence/thousands-flee-deadly-violence-in-cameroons-separatist-regions
-sources-idUSKCN1VH1UO.

———. 2019b. "Trump Scraps Trade Benefits for Cameroon over Rights Abuses."
1 November. https://www.reuters.com/article/us-usa-trade-cameroon/trump
-scraps-trade-benefits-for-cameroon-over-rights-abuses-idUSKBN1XA2TB.

Sun. 2019. "South West Chiefs Make One More Plea for Inoni's Evacuation." 25
October. http://thesuncameroon.cm/index.php/2019/10/25/south-west-chiefs
-make-one-plea-inonis-evacuation.

United States Department of State. 2004. *Country Reports on Human Rights Practices 2003.* Washington, DC: Bureau of Democracy, Human Rights, and Labor.
https://2009-2017.state.gov/j/drl/rls/hrrpt/2003/index.htm.

CHAPTER 12

Disputing Democracy and Challenging the State in Mozambique

JUSTIN PEARCE

THE SMALL SHOPS AND MARKETS OF MUXÚNGUÈ SPRAWL along both sides of the Estrada Nacional (EN) 1, the only main route connecting northern and southern Mozambique. Behind these strips of commercial activity, low-density and semirural residential neighborhoods dissipate quickly into the dispersed homesteads and landholdings typical of this region, the southern part of Sofala province. The infrastructure of the state in Muxúnguè is concentrated south of the commercial area, with a hospital, an administrative post, and a police station on the west side of the EN1. On the east side of the main road is a school. Further south on the east side of the road is the branch headquarters of Resistência Nacional de Moçambique (Renamo): a handful of small, thatched adobe huts alongside an outdoor meeting area under a tree, a humble local home for Mozambique's largest parliamentary opposition party in a region where it enjoys firm support. In its previous incarnation, before a peace agreement and adoption of multiparty democracy brought Renamo into formal politics, the movement fought a war, supported by white Rhodesia and later by apartheid South Africa, against the newly independent government controlled by Frente da Libertação de Moçambique (Frelimo) between 1976 and 1992.

Renamo's modest headquarters adjoins the EN1, and anything that happens there is plainly visible to passersby. In March 2013, according to the accounts of local residents, former Renamo combatants began gathering in this space until several hundred were present. All of these men were in their late thirties or older, with some apparently over seventy, all of them able-bodied adults when the war ended in 1992. None of them wore uniforms and no weapons were visible, people recalled. During the time the

FIGURE 1. Supporters of Renamo at a rally in Beira, 2014. Photo by Justin Pearce.

FIGURE 2. A Renamo supporter waving a flag at a rally in Beira, 2014. Photo by Justin Pearce.

men were there, they did fitness training exercises, cleared the long grass to increase the area of the Renamo compound, and used some of the grass to build "bathrooms," grass structures to provide privacy during ablutions.

On the morning of 3 April 2013, police from the riot unit named Força de Intervenção Rápida (FIR) fired teargas to disperse the men gathered at the Renamo compound and arrested a very few who had not managed to flee. Around 3:30 the following morning, local residents awoke to gunfire. Renamo members were attacking the police post, and several members of the force were killed before the attackers fled. In the months that followed, Renamo's men ambushed vehicles on the EN1 south of Muxúnguè. Similar ambushes later spread to other parts of Mozambique, suggesting that the clandestine remobilization of groups of Renamo men had not only been happening in Muxúnguè. The state's response came in the form of counterinsurgency measures that took a disproportionate toll on the civilian population while doing little to quell the insurgency. Successive rounds of peace talks first with local and then with international mediators achieved no more than a temporary truce. Direct talks between President Filipe Nyusi and Renamo leader Afonso Dhlakama, and, following the latter's death in 2018, with his successor Ossufu Momade, led to the signing of a political accord. The accord included the incorporation of Renamo men into the national police and addressed Renamo's demand for the devolution of democracy to the provincial level, ending the practice whereby the Frelimo-controlled central government had the power to appoint provincial governors. A faction led by Major-General Mariano Nhongo, who rejected the accord, continued with occasional attacks until Nhongo was killed in October 2021.

Sofala, like much of central and northern Mozambique, had registered strong support for Renamo in the first two postwar general elections, in 1994 and 1999. In subsequent elections, support for Renamo dropped sharply, as did overall voter turnout. The pattern suggested that former Renamo voters were not defecting to Frelimo but that, disillusioned with the apparent inertia in the system, they had either ceased voting altogether or were drifting toward the new parties founded by Renamo defectors: the Partido para a Paz, Democracia e Desenvolvimento (PDD) and later the Movimento Democrático de Moçambique (MDM). However, the 2014 election, which followed a year of violence, saw a resurgence in votes for Renamo countrywide but especially in pre-1999 Renamo electoral strongholds such as Sofala province. A central question in the research that I conducted between 2014 and 2017 was to understand the terms in which support for Renamo was constituted in a part of the country where twenty years of peace had been brought to an end by Renamo's return to arms. A peculiarity of the situation that prevailed in Mozambique from April

2013 onward was that while Renamo guerrillas were ambushing vehicles and engaging government forces, Renamo's deputies were participating in debates in the National Assembly. How, then, did people understand a Renamo that simultaneously played a constitutional role in formal politics and violently challenged the state?

Immediately striking in people's accounts of the events of 2013 was how untroubled they had been about having armed insurgents in their midst. While all expressed concern over the violent incidents and the disruptive effects that these had on their lives, no one ascribed blame specifically to Renamo. Violence used by Renamo was proportionate and politically motivated, they suggested, while violence used by the state was excessive and repressive. When interviewees—whether or not they explicitly identified with Renamo as a party—spoke about Renamo's motives and the government's shortcomings, a word that appeared repeatedly was "democracy." Democracy, in this view, was a desirable norm upheld by Renamo and betrayed by the government. This chapter seeks to understand the meaning of "democracy" as understood by critics of the Frelimo government in central Mozambique and how and why appeals to this democracy became central to opposition political claims, even to the point where it was offered as a justification for antistate violence. As Paley (2002) observes, "The use of the word 'democracy' occurs neither alone, nor steadily, nor completely; it is, rather, ethnographically emergent. Therefore we must ask: Whose term is it? What does its usage in any particular case signify? Where does the term arise and where not?" (486).

Various ethnographic studies of democracy in post-1990 Africa have observed how "democracy," or indigenous terms that are assumed to be equivalent to "democracy," often carry connotations quite different from those associated with Western-style liberal multiparty democracy. Typically, these connotations are of a consensual and/or deliberative style of political participation grounded in particular local political histories in which a mutuality of rights and obligations between the rulers and the ruled is essential (Karlström 1996; Comaroff and Comaroff 1997; Schaffer 1997). Just as Schaffer notes in the case of Senegal, the term "democracy" has also been appropriated in Mozambique as a way of making sense of everyday realities, and the interviews quoted later in this chapter indeed make a distinction between procedural and substantive democracy. However, my findings contrast with many earlier ethnographic studies in that there is little sense of a distinctly Mozambican meaning of the word "democracy" that adapts earlier local ideologies. Of interest to this chapter is how "democracy," in a conventional and globalized understanding of the word only slightly adapted to Mozambican reference points, is claimed as a legitimating discourse by critics of the state. This process necessitates making particular claims about the genealogy and ownership of democracy in Mozambique and framing local points of grievance and sites of struggle as part of a wider narrative about democracy and the suppression of democracy, which is less a matter of asserting a distinctive local meaning for democracy and more about what Hansen and Sepputat (2001) call the "invocation"—in this case with reference to particular Mozambican political problems—"of a bundle of widespread and globalized registers of governance and authority" (5).

My focus on how "democracy" is claimed by critics of the state also stands in contrast with much of the existing ethnographic literature on democracy and the state, which typically regards "democracy" or linguistic variants thereof as a part of a discourse that legitimates state power. Almost invariably, the chosen cases are of states where a ruling party appears entrenched in power and where the state is all but indistinguishable from the party, and the implicit burden of the argument is to explain how the party-state legitimates its rule and remains immune to pressures for a more plural party system in which the alternation of power between parties might be a possibility. This focus within the ethnographically based literature is symptomatic of a more general trend in historical or comparative studies of African politics to concentrate on states and on ruling parties, with the principal exception being some recent and valuable forays into the study of popular protest (Zeilig 2009; Branch and Mampilly 2015; Brown 2015; Ngwane, Sinwell, and Ness 2017). Yet across the disciplines, dissent in the form of organized party-political opposition has received less attention. This chapter examines the meanings and histories attached to "democracy" by critics of the government in central Mozambique and how these are used in the articulation of a critique of current politics.

As will become clear later in this chapter, popular understandings of the nominally democratic present in Mozambique are shaped by references to a supposedly socialist past. Postsocialism and postsocialist transformations have been the focus of a rich ethnographic literature, most of it based on European and Asian case studies (Buraway and Verdery 1999; Hann 2002; Scribner 2005; Svašek 2006; West and Raman 2009). The central concern in this literature is with people's responses to social, political, and economic changes. Although these studies emphasize that the lived realities of postsocialist transformations were anything but linear or predetermined, most of them take for granted that the implementation of socialism after World War II had profoundly transformed the societies that are being studied and that in the 1990s the change from socialism to market economies again had transformative effects. Therefore, while the idea of postsocialism may have some utility in understanding the transition in Mozambique, comparisons with the European and Asian experience run the risk of presupposing a more fully realized socialist project than ever actually existed in Mozambique.

In Mozambique, rather, whatever the rhetorical commitments to socialism made by Frelimo after independence, histories emphasize that the limited reach and capacity of the state ensured that the implementation of a transformative agenda was at best inconsistent (Cahen 1993) and at worst repressive (Machava 2011, 2019; Meneses 2015). Studies of contemporary Mozambique have emphasized continuity in how the country was governed from the colonial era to the "socialist" postindependence era and from that era to the present (Cramer 2006; West 2009; Sabaratnam 2013; Borges Coelho 2015; Bertelsen 2016). Among the people I interviewed in central Mozambique, there was no nostalgia for a socialist past. On the contrary, insofar as some of the older people I spoke to had been aware of Frelimo's efforts at social transformation, they regarded these as an alien imposition. Yet no less significant was Frelimo's *inability* to fulfill its intentions after independence. Some of those I spoke to had been relocated to collective villages at some point, but no one had been compelled to stay there. In rural southern Sofala, those who had felt Frelimo policy to be oppressive were able to move outside of the limited reach of the state. "Socialism" and "communism" were used as signifiers for policies, statements of political intent rather than for a lived system of social relations that people could remember. Similarly, while life in the region has changed in the past twenty years, these changes are not popularly attributed to shifts away from socialism. Rather, the dissatisfactions of the present are spoken about in terms of a continuation of practices associated with socialism rather than as a break from them. Most importantly, the terms "socialism" and "communism" provide a way of thinking about the past and about continuities between past and present that provide a point of negative definition for a desirable counterfactual that is termed "democracy."

Over the last three decades, these opposition claims on "democracy" have existed in tension with the incorporation of multiparty democracy into the Mozambican constitution and its formal endorsement by Frelimo. In formal legal terms, Renamo is one of various actors that contest for power within the state system. In looking at opposition politics, my focus here is not on contestation within the democratic system but rather on the contestation of the idea of democracy in public and political discourse. In the communities where I conducted research, most of the people I spoke to were critical of the Frelimo government, whether or not they actively supported an opposition party. Nevertheless, the recognition in the post-1990 literature on democratization that the idea of democracy during that period was the result of international trends as much as internal events—the "selective appropriation of aspects of foreign discourse" (Paley 2000, 485)—is highly relevant to a Mozambique in which Frelimo prior to the late 1980s had an explicit ideological commitment to rule by a single vanguardist party (Cabrita 2000, 263–95). A normative consensus on multiparty democracy in contemporary Mozambique has obliged the Frelimo government since the early 1990s to distance itself from its socialist past (Igreja 2008; Pitcher 2006). Much of my argument in this chapter is about how Frelimo's opponents, whether they are Renamo ideologues or simply critics of Frelimo without a firm party-political affiliation, question the authenticity of Frelimo's commitment to democracy, while Renamo devotees claim as their own a teleological narrative about the development of democracy in Mozambique, a narrative in which Frelimo plays a role as the suppressor of democracy in both the past and the present.

The particular way the word "democracy" makes itself available for appropriation both by state and by opposition discourses is the product of a particularly Mozambican history, one distinct even from other post-liberation regimes in late-decolonizing states in Southern Africa. Some comparison with other states in the region will illustrate this. While it is only since the 1990s that Frelimo has emphasized its own democratic legitimacy, this contrasts with South Africa, where "democracy" has a longer and more positive history from the point of view of the ruling party. Before the international trend of the 1990s, the African National Congress (ANC) and its allies were mobilizing a discourse around democracy, as evidenced by terms like "national democratic struggle" and organizational names like the United Democratic Front and Mass Democratic Movement. The ANC is therefore able to draw upon a discourse of democracy that is of its own making rather than one that it has strategically and reluctantly adopted. Hence, in postapartheid South Africa, a discourse that positions the ANC at the helm of a democratic transformation of the state is an important appeal to legitimation by the ruling party, even if this serves to conceal the often-messy realities of the party's relationship both with state and society (Jensen 2005).

While the ANC provides an example of a liberation movement that is comfortable speaking a language of democracy, ideas about democracy play a minimal role in the legitimating discourses of Angola's ruling MPLA (People's Movement for the Liberation of Angola). Recent studies of how the MPLA has legitimated its rule have emphasized politicized processes of reconstruction and development alongside a selective memorialization and/or forgetting of the war (Schubert 2010, 2017; Pearce 2015a, 2015b; Soares de Oliveira 2015) in which "democracy" barely features except insofar as the MPLA retains an ability to "'act out' democracy to gain international legitimacy (and rein in internal factions)" (Schubert 2010, 670). While the MPLA, like Frelimo, may have been a reluctant recipient of globally prescribed democracy in the early 1990s, the return to war soon after the 1992 elections made talk of democratization out of the question. By the time the MPLA state decisively defeated UNITA in 2002, the West was no longer so firmly committed to the democratization agenda (particularly in the case of a fast-emerging oil producer like Angola), and an emergent China offered an opening for international engagement without normative political prescriptions.

The term "democracy" has been claimed at different times by a variety of actors in Mozambique. Opposition to colonial rule emerged among communities of Mozambicans in exile. Of the various proto-nationalist movements that emerged and reemerged through the 1960s, only União Nacional Democrática de Moçambique (Udenamo) had the word "democratic" as part of its name. After the formation of Frelimo in 1962, Eduardo Mondlane, the leader who confronted the task of holding together a movement containing vast differences in political and strategic thinking, made frequent reference to "democracy" as a principle of anticolonial struggle. He explained that part of the problem faced by the anticolonial movements was the undemocratic nature of the Estado Novo in Portugal and described the governance of Frelimo's liberated zones as being democratic, albeit along the lines of a one-party democracy. Frelimo's Second Congress in July 1968 affirmed Frelimo's commitment to "the establishment of a social, democratic order in Mozambique" (Mondlane 1969). Duarte de Jesus (2010) goes so far as to describe Mondlane as a "social democrat" in the Western understanding of the term. The meaning of "democracy" was contested during the crisis that resulted from Mondlane's assassination in 1969 and the subsequent efforts by Samora Machel and Marcelino dos Santos to prevent Uria Simango from taking over the leadership of Frelimo. During this period, Simango released "Gloomy Situation in Frelimo" (1969), his critique of the direction taken by Frelimo after Mondlane's death that recalled in particular the murder of Silvério Nungu, who according to Simango was "killed because of his stand in defence of freedom, democracy and equality." The publication of "Gloomy Situation" led ultimately to the expulsion of Simango and to the consolidation of what has been called the radical line within Frelimo. This established the character of the postindependence Frelimo as a vanguardist party committed to social and political transformation and opposed to any form of political mobilization outside of the one-party system.[1] Histories of Mozambique sympathetic to the socialist agenda espoused by the post-1969 Frelimo, in contrast to the more recent interpretation by Duarte de Jesus, tended to emphasize the continuity between the Frelimo of Mondlane and the Frelimo of Samora Machel (Munslow 1983; Saul 1983).[2]

If a language of democracy had faded within official Frelimo discourse by the time of independence, Frelimo's opponents claim a consistent democratic legacy as long as Frelimo has been in power, even if the plausibility of the claim is debatable. João Cabrita's (2000) account of Mozambican political history from the 1960s to the 1990s identifies a consistent history of resistance to Frelimo, with democracy as its ultimate goal, that began not long after Frelimo took power in 1975 and which has its roots in anti-colonial mobilization that was regionally diverse and ideologically plural but which was supplanted by the authoritarian and centralizing tendencies represented by a southern elite personified by Samora Machel. The interviews that I will discuss later in this chapter demonstrate that Renamo has succeeded in taking much of the credit for upholding this democratic legacy through the decades.

The veracity of the claim about Renamo's particular role is a point of contention not only in Mozambican politics but in the historiography of the country. Cabrita (2000) finds that in the early years of the civil war, Renamo never aspired to be a political party (167–69), opting instead to wage a military struggle to the point where Mozambicans could "freely and contentiously choose their political future through parties to be organized after the liberation of the people of Mozambique" (see also Hultman 2009). Dhlakama in a 2007 interview with Domingos do Rosário (2018, 61) confirmed that such a reading of history was consistent with how Renamo itself liked to see its own past: "My assessor [adviser] told me to take power by force . . . but I gave up because my intention was not to take power by force . . . because I am the father of democracy." The Renamo statutes, drafted in 1979, promised the establishment of a multiparty democracy that would respect religious and traditional rights and establish a free enterprise economy. Cabrita interprets this adoption of a political program as a response to the dissipation of alternative anti-Frelimo groups; as Renamo "became aware of what it was capable of achieving with its own resources, it developed its own political structure and set out a more comprehensive political agenda" (2000, 170). Scholars critical of Renamo, conversely, interpret this relatively late adoption of a political program as evidence that Renamo's agenda was determined primarily by its Rhodesian and apartheid South African sponsors who sought only to destabilize a Frelimo that was committed to the support of liberation movements in the then white-ruled territories (Hall 1990). Either way, a plausible interpretation is that in the context of the Cold War the language of rights and free markets in the statutes was oriented at least as much toward potential foreign backers as it was toward Mozambicans.

Insofar as Frelimo from the late 1980s did move toward an acceptance of democracy, it accepted a form of procedural multipartyism designed to ensure its own survival rather than allowing a more participatory form of politics: "FRELIMO realised that pluralism might very well serve to destroy its opponent by offering certain RENAMO leaders the opportunity to give up the military struggle to form a political party" (Cahen 1998, 6). Interviews quoted in the following sections of this chapter reveal that people are aware of the ambiguities in how we are to understand "democracy," whether as a formal procedural system or as a more substantive kind of political participation with concomitant positive obligations on the state. Interviewees were also aware of how this ambiguity is politically functional, and they voiced their claims against Frelimo in terms of what they saw as Frelimo's strategic adoption of democratic discourse rather than a commitment to democratic practice.

Narratives of Democracy and Conflict

Interviews conducted in the southern part of Sofala province in central Mozambique over a period of six months during 2015 make up the primary material on which this chapter is based. These conversations took place in Muxúnguè in Chibabava district, where people had directly witnessed the violence that began in 2013, as well as at other locations in Chibabava district and in the neighboring district of Machanga. My initial point of contact was the Justice and Peace Commission of the Catholic Church, through which I made contact with farmers in the rural areas and traders, teachers, and students in the small towns. Conversations with people whose differing experiences of and perspectives on the past and present conflicts together illustrate the commonalities and variations in how "democracy" and its relationship with state power are understood.

Born in the mid-1950s, Catarina[3] was of a generation who could recall the uncertainties that accompanied independence and the privations of the civil war that followed. She lived in a part of Machanga district where people remembered attacks and abductions by Renamo during the civil war, as the government maintained a garrison but did not secure the wider area. With little trust for either of the warring parties, Catarina recalls alienation from the debates in the lead-up to independence but also indicates a preference for the side that, in her words, wanted democracy.

> Some said if we become independent we will go for socialism, others democracy. We didn't know, we just saw guns. The others talked about liberation for the colonies. We wanted democracy. Today it [war] is going on again. I don't know if democracy has been well implemented. The one who went to the bush, André Matsangaisse [the first leader of Renamo], wanted democracy. Today they [Renamo] are complaining that there is no transparency—that things went astray. There is always confusion between movements that are strong. But the people from here are more for the party that is not in power. Here the majority are not in power.

Asked whether Mozambique could be considered a united nation, Catarina's response is informed by a widely held belief that central and northern Mozambique are systematically discriminated against by a government based in the south and which has only southern interests at heart. Her reference to Mambone and Machanga is particularly poignant. These two small settlements lie on either side of the mouth of the Save River, the border between the provinces of Inhambane and Sofala and the conventional dividing line between southern and central Mozambique.

> To be Mozambican is to be a citizen of Mozambique. But we are divided by provinces. For the Mozambican people, goods and rights are more for the south. Cashew nuts are from Muxúnguè. The factory [for processing cashews] is in Maputo. The ones who go to work there are only from Maputo. If there were a factory in Muxúnguè, unemployment would be less. The refrigeration store is in Mambone but the fish come from Machanga. Who then benefits? Grain is from here, many things—but the factories are there. We are in a democracy, but the opposition is complaining that it isn't being implemented well.

Isaías and Marta, both born in the 1940s, are farmers who have spent their lives in a rural area of Chibabava district that was dominated by Renamo during the war. In the years after the war, the state established an administrative presence that remained concentrated in Muxúnguè, about a two-hour walk away along dusty paths. Renamo veterans living in the area were among those who took up arms in 2013. Renamo's political message from the war years, reinforced by Renamo activists working in the area, still colored people's understandings of the present. Isaías also implicitly drew links between the corrupt practices of policemen and state officials and the critique of the socialist state, disseminated by Renamo but widely shared in the region, as overly interfering with people's lives and livelihoods. Leaving the homestead and walking to the market involved passing into the area where representatives of the state were present and exercised an authority that was experienced as arbitrary and sometimes violent:

> If you buy something in South Africa and bring it home, from the border to Muxúnguè, at every checkpoint you have to pay, to the point where you have paid more than you paid to buy the thing. Or [when selling produce] when you arrive at the market, they take some of it—that's another tax. . . . I remember [Renamo's] "traditional" explanation: "fight for democracy, fight to feel free." [Those words] are worth more in the moment we are living in now.

FIGURE 3. A Renamo supporter distributes a campaign leaflet at a rally in Beira, 2014. Photo by Justin Pearce.

Marta added: "I heard what they [Renamo] said: 'We were fighting against Frelimo, war is bad, but we are fighting for people to feel free, to do as they wish, for us to live with democracy and to work.' We fought against the Portuguese in order to live in freedom, but Frelimo threw this away and is doing things we don't understand."

Isaías continued: "Since the General Peace Accord [1992] they say things have changed and we are living in democracy, but for me and for [this rural area] things have not changed. We go on making charcoal that no one buys, and we sell pineapples, but the other one [the buyer] sets the price."

David had been forced to join Renamo in 1986 as a boy of ten. In his words, "the suffering obliged me to be a soldier." At the time of the interview, he was running a small business as a mechanic in Muxúnguè. Having been only a child during the civil war, he had not internalized Renamo's wartime message in the way that older people like Isaías and Marta had done, but his understanding of Mozambican politics made him inclined to sympathize with Renamo during the more recent insurrection. When I explained that I was trying to understand the reason for the recent conflict, he replied:

> Mozambique is a democratic country but democracy is full of cor-
> ruption. There is a group defending all of our rights and another
> group saying, "All this is ours." We are equal in rights and law, but
> not in that which exists [i.e., in reality we don't have the rights
> that the law supposedly guarantees us]. Because of this, conflicts
> are not going to end because each year children are born with a
> different way of thinking. We are not using democratic law in a
> prudent manner.
>
> The conflict started when government forces went to interfere
> with a Renamo group. A party that defends democracy must not
> kill. We had an armed peace—because in the democracy there
> existed two armed parties. The government failed to comply with
> Rome accord. There should not be a force defending one party.
> When the [civil] war ended, they formed armed groups to defend
> their parties. When the war ended, they should have formed one
> group to defend the country. They should have demobilized every-
> body from Frelimo and Renamo.

I asked David if he knew any Renamo soldiers, and he said: "I can't say who is a soldier. There are soldiers but we don't know who they are. You have Renamo, they are organized. Where they are organized, we don't know. What is important is that the parties be united by ties of peace." When I asked whether there were soldiers in the town, he replied "government soldiers." What he went on to say about Renamo soldiers suggested that while he knew there were Renamo soldiers in the midst of the town, he was not prepared to identify individuals:

> Renamo defends democracy but is out there in the bush. Renamo
> men are our brothers. Always eating and drinking with us. We
> don't know who they are, only they know. They say the Renamo

men are all old but they aren't. In each place there are young men
and old men. I heard that when Renamo intended to rise up, they
formed a group of young men to fight for democracy. So there is
one party in the bush, one in the city. The opposition party isn't
able to come into the city. The attack on police was to free those
imprisoned. People don't want the state. Don't want those in the
bush. But we prefer the opposition.

One of David's friends who had been listening to the conversation
added, "The people who are considered Mozambican are from the south.
Here we want the opposition to govern us."

André was born in Renamo-controlled territory in 1990, toward the
end of the war, and as a very young child went with his parents to Zimbabwe to seek work, part of a long-established pattern of labor migration
across the border. They returned to Mozambique in 2004, after the confiscation of land from white commercial farmers diminished the demand for
Mozambican labor in Zimbabwe. André referred to this experience when
he spoke of the importance of jobs in a well-functioning government. He
spoke repeatedly of the lack of jobs today and of Frelimo's preferential treatment of its own members in government employment, which he suggested
was one of the reasons for the discontentment of Renamo veterans. When
interviewed in 2017, he was employed at a church mission in a rural part
of Chibabava, where many Renamo veterans lived and had taken up arms
in 2013. His recollections of the events in Muxúnguè emphasized how the
climate of fear in the surrounding rural areas was the result of government
counterinsurgency more than of the presence of Renamo fighters:

> When the conflict began in Muxúnguè everyone was unhappy.
> The people weren't used to being faced with troops or police. They
> were frightened. They fled to sleep in the bush. They would come
> back during the day, but they slept in the bush. They were left ill,
> coughing. Even the chief [régulo] abandoned his house—left his
> goats and everything behind. People from the different parties
> were fearful but mostly the Renamo members were frightened of
> being attacked. It was a very tough time. Some people disappeared
> and never appeared again. Some were killed and we don't know
> where they are, and others were found left dead in the bush. Now
> the situation is a bit calmer. . . . But the other problem is there is
> no employment here.

Asked about what he thought the reasons were for the recent conflict,
he replied:

The two parties don't have a good understanding. [Frelimo says,] "I alone am the government and I am going to govern alone." What the opposition wants to say is "This is what we need to do." The priority is work. Whoever is not a member of Frelimo doesn't get a job, whoever has a Renamo card isn't employed. This is what started the conflict. In Muxúnguè, Renamo went to make a demonstration, join people together to tell their story. The ruling party attacked them with flares—that thing that makes a person like they are drunk [teargas grenades]. The government was frightened so they sent the people away. That's how the conflict started. There was an agreement when Dhlakama came out to vote. Then Renamo said we won six provinces. How can the person who has only three provinces win?

This last reference to the provincial election results suggests he had uncritically accepted Renamo's claim to have gained a majority of votes in six provinces. André continued: "In Mozambique since 1975 freedom hasn't been well. There are young people who study but don't get jobs. . . . Every five years there's the possibility of changing. We see who is governing well and who isn't. . . . In the United States, Bush gave way to Obama who had his own party with its own way of governing."

These last remarks suggest that he saw an inherent value in an alternation of parties. He took up this theme again when I asked him whether he thought Mozambique enjoyed national unity:

I hope so. If there were a change [of government], it would be united. If one stays eating and the other hungry, that is not unity. Afonso Dhlakama spent twenty years in the bush while the other one had a house. Frelimo, while it is the father that governs Mozambique, if it agrees to make war that's not good for the country. [Renamo] soldiers were asking for money. They should have resolved this by talking to them and not by shooting. That's the kind of government we need. . . . Democracy must be more than just something that is talked about.

Using these examples as representative of the popular discourse on politics and history, one may identify the elements that make up the common idea of "democracy" as it is spoken of by opposition supporters in central Mozambique and see how these elements are articulated in a way that supports regional claims against the incumbent government. First, the way people talk about democracy makes a vigorous claim to inclusivity and equal rights of citizenship for all, regardless of their regional or ethnic origin, their political affiliation, or whether they are from the cities or the countryside or from any of the regions that make up Mozambique. Of course, a principle of nondiscrimination is not the same thing as democracy. But by making regional and ethnic equality preconditions for democracy, critics of the government allude to a long-standing criticism of Frelimo that the ascendancy of Samora Machel after 1969 marked not only the consolidation of Frelimo as a vanguard socialist party but also the triumph of a cabal of privileged urban southerners who neither understand nor care about the needs of rural people or anyone from north of the Save River. Names such as André Matsangaisse, Uria Simango, and Silvério Nungu are invoked not just because they are local but because they are believed to be early defenders of a politically plural Mozambique. While people also make claims of regional authenticity on behalf of a Renamo leadership that is overwhelmingly from the center and north of the country—Dhlakama himself was from Sofala—these claims are made to cohere with a nationalist vision of a unified Mozambique by presenting Renamo as the champions of the historic victims of discrimination who are seeking inclusion in a more comprehensively imagined Mozambican nation. In addition to the political meanings that are assigned to different regions of Mozambique, accounts of everyday grievance in a small town like Muxúnguè suggest that such towns are outposts of a state that is alien to that part of Mozambique, while the remoter rural homesteads are the unchallenged domain of a more locally rooted opposition.

Second, democracy is associated with freedom of expression and the freedom to trade, but again these civil liberties are spoken of not in the abstract but as part of an explicit critique of what the speakers say is a present reality. Free speech is invoked against what people say is the suppression of opposition ideas by Frelimo. This, incidentally, is a manifestation of a consistent tautology in the opposition discourse: the urgency to express dissent against Frelimo is to a large extent rationalized by the belief that Frelimo is intolerant of dissent. The demands for free trade are a call to stop corrupt police from harassing honest farmers and merchants. Even if Renamo's foreign enthusiasts (Wheeler 1985) and its critics (Askin 1990) have explained Renamo's motives in terms of a globalized right-wing politics, these calls for free trade by Mozambicans broadly sympathetic to Renamo are motivated by immediate local needs and not by an ideological commitment to a minimal state, as will become evident in the next paragraph.

The third characteristic of democracy as understood in central Mozambique is the right to work in salaried employment, or the right to receive a fair reward for one's labor in the fields. The appeal to such rights implies a positive obligation on the state that extends beyond minimal definitions of liberal democracy. The state, in this understanding, is expected to provide jobs or guarantee the income of market traders. In reality, of course, the price of pineapples in Muxúnguè is determined by the logic of the market and not by any machinations on the part of the government to suppress producer prices. The complaint here is not about the practices of the supposedly socialist past but of a free-market present. The liberalization of the Mozambican economy in the 1990s was the result of the imposition of structural adjustment by the Bretton Woods institutions as a condition for loan finance, a demand that Frelimo, initially at least, had no choice but to accept. Even if more recent studies have observed that the Frelimo government enjoys more autonomy from donors' prescripts than was initially supposed, intervention in agricultural marketing has never been on the post-1994 party's agenda. In the understanding of "democracy" put forward here, then, the desired "democratic" state appears to have a more interventionist, developmental role than that currently realized by Frelimo.

Fourth, interviewees expressed a preoccupation with procedural democracy and a respect both for the legal obligations of the General Peace Accord and for the Mozambican constitution. Although the observations so far indicate that people understand true democracy to be something more substantive than allowing the opportunity to vote once in five years, they also accept that the conduct of free and fair elections is nevertheless a minimal precondition for democracy. The frequent references to electoral fraud are presented as evidence that Mozambique is not a properly functioning democracy and that this is the fault of a Frelimo whose commitment to democracy is no more than strategic. Some, like André, expanded on this point by opining that the true test of democracy was an alternation of power between parties. While there is, plainly, no constitutional requirement for power to pass from party to party, the demand for a change of leadership as a gauge of democracy seems a logical corollary of a belief that the long incumbency of Frelimo demonstrates the party's lack of commitment to democracy. Democracy is thus both a necessary process and a desirable end goal.

Frequent references to "socialism" and "communism" by interviewees serve as a point of negative comparison that helps to shape the imagined ideal of "democracy." These terms are used to refer to the past practices of the Frelimo state and to account for Frelimo's more recent practices, which are seen as predictable behavior by a party that remains "socialist" or "communist" at heart. This discourse positions "socialism"/"communism" and "democracy" as polar opposites. Since it was a "socialist" Frelimo leadership that sought to erase cultural and regional difference in a way that amounted to the domination of the southern urban elite over the whole of Mozambique, it then follows that "democracy" means ensuring an equitable distribution of public goods through the whole of Mozambique and imagining a diverse and polycentric nation. If "socialism" is authoritarian, controls the flow of trade, and restricts dissent, then "democracy" is about the enjoyment of free expression and the opportunity to earn a decent living. The communities in question did not enjoy state employment or social security during the socialist era, so the nostalgia for jobs and stability noted in other postcommunist situations was absent.

By defining "socialism" and "democracy" as polar opposites, people are able to present the civil war, in which Renamo fought against an avowedly socialist Frelimo, as the beginning of a struggle for democracy that continues until this day. According to this telling, the transition to constitutional democracy in the early 1990s was due entirely to Renamo and was accepted only reluctantly by a Frelimo that has tried repeatedly to thwart the implementation of a more substantive democracy. If this demonizing of "communism" and "socialism" in current opposition discourse recalls the international right-wing agenda that was attributed to Renamo during the Cold War both by its left-wing detractors and by its conservative cheerleaders, the way the terms are used and applied to a contemporary Frelimo that is anything but socialist demonstrates that today's government critics have taken ownership of an old discourse for contemporary purposes in a way that asserts a historical antecedence for their calls for democracy.

As with other postliberation regimes in Southern Africa and elsewhere, Frelimo's domination of the state since independence has made state and party conceptually indistinct. This creates at least two areas of ambiguity in how people talk about opposition and political alternatives. The first question is whether Renamo poses a challenge to the state or to the party within the state; and the second is whether democracy necessarily means the defeat of Frelimo. There is a long-running debate in scholarly literature on Mozambique about whether Renamo represented an alternative vision of stateness (Geffray 1991), or whether its appeal was essentially a negative one based on a rejection of centralization (Lubkemann 2008), or whether in the post-1992 dispensation, Renamo provides a sense of citizenship for those who feel excluded by a state that offers benefits only to those associated with Frelimo (Schafer 2007; Wiegink 2015, 2020). Echoing these latter studies of Renamo since the civil war, the interviews that I have presented in this chapter suggest that contemporary popular understandings rest upon an acceptance of Renamo's position as an actor in what is at least in legal terms a constitutional democracy. If "Frelimo" and "the state" are sometimes conflated in popular discourse, this is hardly surprising in a situation where partisan loyalty is demanded of civil servants, and party officials see their role as one of "ordering society" and promoting development. Opposition supporters today present Renamo as an institution that is a potential contender for power within the current state system and whose accession to state power would both represent and guarantee a democratization of state power but which is currently barred from state power by a Frelimo whose monopolization of the state is precisely the problem that Renamo seeks to rectify. The peculiarity of a parliamentary opposition party taking up arms against the same state in which, legally, it plays a functional role, is accounted for by reminders that Frelimo, too, has neglected its constitutional obligations as it continues to behave like the one-party state of earlier decades.

As noted at the beginning, previous scholarship that has investigated the locally specific meanings and practices of democracy has done so on the assumption that appeals to democracy serve to legitimate a state that is indistinct from the prolonged rule of particular party. This chapter has demonstrated how the claims on the idea of democracy have become central to the contestation of the authority of the state in Mozambique, a contestation that was evident in the way people believed that Renamo's return to violence since 2013 was a legitimate challenge to a state whose own legitimacy was dubious. Understanding how the meaning of democracy has become politically charged has necessitated examining the history of the term in Mozambique and how that history has been selectively interpreted and appropriated as a way of weaving everyday grievance into a broader narrative of exclusion and resistance. An emphasis on the supposedly democratic character of the tendency within Frelimo that was suppressed after 1969, plus the fact that Frelimo through the 1970s and 1980s professed to be socialist, has allowed the creation of a binary opposition between "democracy" and "socialism"/"communism." The regional character of the pre-1969 tensions within the nationalist movement has allowed appeals to "democracy" to also be an appeal to redress what is seen as a regional imbalance of power within Mozambique. This has been used to bolster the claims of Frelimo's contemporary critics that they are working within a long tradition of democratic resistance against a Frelimo that endorsed democracy only recently and as a matter of strategy rather than conviction.

Notes

This chapter is based on research that was funded by a Leverhulme Early Career Fellowship (grant number 74978), held in the Department of Politics and International Studies, University of Cambridge, and supported by a research associateship at St John's College, Cambridge. My thanks are due to all those who gave of their time to be interviewed. For their help and hospitality, I am indebted to Dionísio Camacho, Fidel Salazar, José Luís, Andrzej Filip, Tom Bowker, Leigh Elston, Conceição Osório, and, especially, to Alberto Mudando.

1. A political claim in the name of "democracy" appeared again in the name of the Democratas de Moçambique (Mozambique Democrats), a group of liberal white professionals, mostly lawyers, who were critical of the colonial

regime but who soon lost patience with some of Frelimo's more heavy-handed measures following independence (Cabrita 2000, 79, 109).

2. I am grateful to Rahul Dev for pointing this out.

3. I use pseudonyms for all interviewees.

References

Askin, Steve. 1990. "Mission to Renamo: The Militarization of the Religious Right." *African Issues* 18 (2): 29–38.

Bertelsen, Bjørn. 2016. *Violent Becomings: State Formation, Sociality and Power in Mozambique.* New York: Berghahn Books.

Borges Coelho, João Paulo. 2015. "Abrir a Fábula: Questões da Política do Passado em Moçambique." *Revista Crítica de Ciências Sociais* 106:153–66.

Branch, Adam, and Zachariah Mampilly. 2015. *Africa Uprising: Popular Protest and Political Change.* London: Zed Books.

Brown, Julian. 2015. *South Africa's Insurgent Citizens.* London: Zed Books.

Buraway, Michael, and Katherine Verdery, eds. 1999. *Uncertain Transition: Ethnographies of Change in the Postsocialist World.* Lanham, MD: Rowman and Littlefield.

Cabrita, João. 2000. *Mozambique: The Tortuous Road to Democracy.* Basingstoke, UK: Palgrave.

Cahen, Michel. 1993. "Check on Socialism in Mozambique: What Check? What Socialism?" *Review of African Political Economy* 57 (July): 46–59.

Comaroff, John L., and Jean Comaroff. 1990. "Postcolonial Politics and Discourses of Democracy in Southern Africa: An Anthropological Reflection on African Political Modernities." *Journal of Anthropological Research* 53 (2): 123–46.

Cramer, Christopher. 2006. *Civil War Is Not a Stupid Thing: Accounting for Violence in Developing Countries.* London: Hurst.

Duarte de Jesus, José Manuel. 2010. *Eduardo Mondlane: Um Homem a Abater.* Coimbra, Portugal: Almedina.

Geffray, Christian. 1990. *La Cause des Armes au Mozambique: L'Anthropologie d'une Guerre Civile.* Paris: Karthala.

Hall, Margaret. 1990. "The Mozambican National Resistance Movement (Renamo): A Study in the Destruction of an African Country." *Africa: Journal of the International African Institute* 60 (1): 39–68.

Hann, C. M., ed. 2002. *Postsocialism: Ideals, Ideologies and Practices in Eurasia.* London: Routledge.

Hansen, Thomas Blom, and Finn Stepputat. 2001. *States of Imagination: Ethnographic Explorations of the Postcolonial State.* Durham, NC: Duke University Press.

Hultman, Lisa. 2009. "The Power to Hurt in Civil War: The Strategic Aim of RENAMO Violence." *Journal of Southern African Studies* 35 (4): 821–34.

Igreja, Victor. 2008. "Memories as Weapons: The Politics of Peace and Silence in Post–Civil War Mozambique." *Journal of Southern African Studies* 34 (3): 539–56.

Jensen, Steffen. 2001. "The Battlefield and the Prize: ANC's Bid to Reform the South African State." In Hansen and Stepputat 2001, 97–122.

Karlström Mikael. 1996. "Imagining Democracy: Political Culture and Democratisation in Buganda." *Africa: Journal of the International African Institute* 66 (4): 485–505.

Lubkemann, Stephen C. 2008. *Culture in Chaos: An Anthropology of the Social Condition in War.* Chicago: University of Chicago Press.

Machava, Benedito Luís. 2011. "State Discourse on Internal Security and the Politics of Punishment in Post-independence Mozambique (1975–1983)." *Journal of Southern African Studies* 37 (3): 593–609.

Machava, Benedito. 2019. "Reeducation Camps, Austerity, and the Carceral Regime in Socialist Mozambique (1974–79)." *Journal of African History* 60 (3): 429–55.

Meneses, Maria Paula. 2015. "Xiconhoca, o Inimigo—Narrativas de Violência Sobre a Construção da Nação em Moçambique." *Revista Crítica de Ciências Sociais* 106:9–52.

Mondlane, Eduardo. 1969. *The Struggle for Mozambique.* Harmondsworth, UK: Penguin.

Munslow, Barry. 1983. *Mozambique: The Revolution and Its Origins.* London: Longman.

Ngwane, Trevor, Luke Sinwell, and Immanuel Ness, eds. 2017. *Urban Revolt: State Power and the Rise of People's Movements in the Global South.* Johannesburg: Wits University Press.

Paley, Julia. 2002. "Toward an Anthropology of Democracy." *Annual Review of Anthropology* 31 (2002): 469–96.

Pearce, Justin. 2015a. *Political Identity and Conflict in Central Angola, 1975–2002.* Cambridge: Cambridge University Press.

Pearce, Justin. 2015b. "Contesting the Past in Angolan Politics." *Journal of Southern African Studies* 41 (1): 103–19.

Pitcher, M. Anne. 2006. "Forgetting from Above and Memory from Below: Strategies of Legitimation and Struggle in Postsocialist Mozambique." *Africa: Journal of the International African Institute* 76 (1): 88–112.

do Rosário, Domingos Manuel. 2018. "War to Enforce a Political Project? Renamo in Nampula Province, 1983–1992." In *The War Within: New Perspectives on the Civil War in Mozambique,* edited by Eric Morier-Genoud, Michel Cahen, and Domingos Manuel do Rosário, 46–74. Oxford: James Currey.

Sabaratnam, Meera. 2013. "History Repeating? Colonial, Socialist and Liberal Statebuilding in Mozambique." In *The Routledge Handbook of International Statebuilding,* edited by David Shandler and Timothy Sisk, 106–17. London: Routledge.

Saul, John. 1983. "Foreword." In *The Struggle for Mozambique,* by Eduardo Mondlane. London: Zed Books.

Schafer, Jessica. 2007. *Soldiers at Peace: Veterans of the Civil War in Mozambique.* New York: Palgrave Macmillan.

Schubert, Jon. 2010. "'Democratisation' and the Consolidation of Political Authority in Post-war Angola." *Journal of Southern African Studies* 36 (3): 657–72.

Schubert, Jon. 2017. *Working the System: A Political Ethnography of the New Angola.* Ithaca, NY: Cornell University Press.

Scribner, Charity. 2005. *Requiem for Communism.* Cambridge, MA: MIT Press.

Simango, Uria. 1969. "Gloomy Situation in Frelimo." Accessed 23 August 2019, https://macua.blogs.com/moambique_para_todos/2010/01/suponho-nunca-ter-sido-tornado-publico-na-sua-totalidade-o-documento-apresentado-por-uria-simango-em-novembro-de-1969-e.html.

Soares de Oliveira, Ricardo. 2015. *Magnificent and Beggar Land: Angola Since the Civil War.* London: Hurst.

Svašek, Maruška, ed. 2005. *Postsocialism: Politics and Emotions in Central and Eastern Europe.* New York: Berghahn Books.

West, Harry G., and Parvathi Raman, eds. 2009. *Enduring Socialism: Explorations of Revolution and Transformation, Restoration, and Continuation.* New York: Berghahn Books.

West, Harry G. 2009. "From Socialist Chiefs to Postsocialist Cadres: Neotraditional Authority in Neoliberal Mozambique." In *Enduring Socialism: Explorations of Revolution & Transformation, Restoration and Continuation,* edited by Harry G. West and Parvathi Raman, 29–43. New York: Berghahn Books.

Wheeler, Jack. 1985. "From Rovuma to Maputo: Mozambique's Guerrilla War." *Reason* (December). https://reason.com/1985/12/01/from-rovuma-to-maputo.

Wiegink, Nikkie. 2015. "'It Will Be Our Time to Eat': Former Renamo Combatants and Big-Man Dynamics in Central Mozambique." *Journal of Southern African Studies* 414:869–85.

Wiegink, Nikkie. 2020. *Former Guerrillas in Mozambique.* Philadelphia: University of Pennsylvania Press.

Zeilig, Leo, ed. 2009. *Class Struggle and Resistance in Africa.* London: Haymarket.

PART FIVE

Everyday Politics of
Rights and Responsibility

Education, Welfare, and Health

THIRTEEN

The Intimate State

Ethiopian Civics Teachers as the Fault Line between Repression and Revolution

JENNIFER RIGGAN

IN APRIL 2017, I OBSERVED A YOUNG, DYNAMIC SECONDARY school teacher, whom I will call Elsa, as part of an ethnographic study of Civic and Ethical Education (CEE) teachers in five Addis Ababa schools.[1] Elsa was energetic. The students were engaged, listening attentively, responding eagerly to her questions. They laughed and seemed at ease in her presence. As we walked back to the staff room after class, she apologized for being behind in the curriculum and explained that she had been in jail for four months.

A nationwide state of emergency, put in place to quell violent protests, had been in effect since October 2016. Shortly after the state of emergency was declared, one of her students asked her why the government was arresting protesters, given that, as they had learned in their civics class, it was their right to protest. Elsa answered the student by distinguishing between nonviolent protests, which are allowed, and violent protests, which are not. Shortly after that, two police officers came to the school and told her they wanted to ask some questions. She was subsequently arrested without trial and was not released until four months later. She suspected that some of her students reported the classroom exchange, resulting in her arrest.

Elsa's arrest gives us a chance to explore the complex, everyday nature of state repression. Going deeper into the nuances of this event, in particular, and debates over the teaching of civics during a time of turbulence in Ethiopia, more broadly, allows us to look closely at the how the state comes to *be* and *be thought of* as a particular kind of *thing*. In other words, looking closely at CEE teachers allows us to understand how the state comes to be both imagined and experienced through everyday encounters (Gupta 2012). Intimate, everyday experiences with state violence and repression undermine the state's ability to legitimate its use of force, but they also produce a complex, antipolitical counterimaginary of the state, resulting in what Mbembe calls "impotence" (2001).

Teachers give us a particular insight into the everyday state because they are not only charged with navigating the shifting fault line between state repression and revolutionary change but also *constitute* that fault line. Every time students walk into the classroom they are having an encounter with the state. Teachers are state employees, teach state curriculum, and uphold state policies. By disseminating the state curriculum, teachers are charged with producing a particular *idea* of the state (Abrams 1988), but teachers also operate with a good deal of professional autonomy, meaning that this state idea will be mediated by teachers' beliefs, values, memories, and experiences (Riggan 2016). Teachers may also be subjects of state discipline and, at times, violence. They and their students often experience political ruptures long before others. Teachers thus reveal and bring into being the fault lines between the idea of the state (Abrams 1988) and the enactment, or lack thereof, of that idea. In doing so, they produce complex and multifaceted state effects (Mitchell 1991, 2006).

The 2017 state of emergency in Ethiopia was arguably a manifestation of a long pattern of dissent sparked by peripheralized groups demanding greater rights, recognition, and political power on the one hand, and repression of dissent by the security apparatus in order to stabilize and retain the power of a centralized state on the other. I theorize the state of emergency as not only an intimate encounter with the security apparatus but also an instance of "pedagogical violence" (Ismael 2018) that evoked historical memories of earlier instances of state violence. However, pedagogical violence was juxtaposed with longings for stability, normalcy, and a benevolent state, creating a confusing, paradoxical condition that Aretxaga refers to as the "maddening state" (2003). Drawing on these longings for a stable normal, the state of emergency attempted to reify the state as a coherent entity that deployed violence rationally and legitimately, but for many Ethiopians the everyday experience of repression had the opposite effect.

The paradoxes of the maddening state emerged as the pedagogies of violence collided with longings for stability. These paradoxes framed debates over the teaching of CEE. I begin this chapter by providing background on the CEE program to explore its development against the backdrop of the political history that gave rise to the maddening state. The Ethiopian People's Democratic Revolutionary Party (EPRDF), the party that took power following the overthrow of the communist regime in 1991, initially looked as if it would usher in an era of democracy, human rights, and prosperity for Ethiopia. CEE was thought of as a way to produce a new kind of Ethiopian citizen who would understand citizens' democratic rights and duties, acquire the dispositions to enable national development to thrive, and adhere to the 1995 constitution. The CEE program was not only central to the EPRDF's vision for this country; it held that vision in place even after it became clear that the EPRDF had, arguably, abandoned it by failing to create the democratic Ethiopia that was promised. My discussion of debates about CEE during the state of emergency tells a complex story about how the content of the CEE text was alternately held up as an ideal, used to undermine the legitimacy of the government, and used as a critique of unruly young people who did not understand their responsibilities as citizens. CEE teachers remained on the fault line as they navigated increasingly complex paradoxes and found their work politicized even as they sought to depoliticize it.

Producing a Desire for Democracy: Ethiopia's CEE Curriculum

Ethiopia's Civic and Ethical Education program was designed to educate Ethiopians about liberal, democratic governance according to the 1995 constitution. This was no small task given that Ethiopia has never had a successful democracy. Since Ethiopia began a process of modern state consolidation in the mid to late 1800s, arguably there has always been a tension between a powerful central state vying to hold its power in the face of an array of marginalized groups throughout the rest of the country trying to find a foothold for themselves. A pre-national set of kingdoms and fiefdoms fought for the power to consolidate ever larger territories into what eventually became a modern state. At the turn of the century, Emperor Menelik transitioned the feudal empire into a modern one by consolidating control over an extended territory and exerted sovereignty over populations within more or less fixed boundaries that would eventually become a nation-state. Haile Selassie continued the process of modern state consolidation until leftist student movements in the late 1960s eventually led to his overthrow in the mid-1970s (Kebede 2006; Milkias 2006). The revolution was overtaken by a military dictatorship that very quickly consolidated control, once again, under the central government, this time under the auspices of a communist government referred to as the Derg.

In 1991, a coalition led by the Tigrayan People's Liberation Front overthrew the Derg and consolidated rule under the control of a single party, the Ethiopian People's Democratic Revolutionary Party. The 1995 constitution that the EPRDF set up reconfigured Ethiopia as a federation in which ethnically based states were supposed to have autonomy up to and including the right to secession. The reorganization of the country into ethnic "nations"was a radical deviation for a country long noted for its centralized, hegemonic, Amhara- and Christian-dominated national narrative (James et al. 2002; Smith 2013). Although the central state has retained a great deal of power, the redesigning of the country ostensibly allowed for a great deal of autonomy in several ethnic regions (Bariagaber 1998; Mains 2004; Keller and Smith 2005; Smith 2008).

When the EPRDF took over in 1991, it placed a high value on civics education beginning discussion about the curriculum immediately and implementing the curriculum in 1993 even before the development of the 1995 constitution, which it is often said to be based on (Yamada 2011). The CEE curriculum is a blueprint for the particular notion of citizenship developed under the post-1991 political dispensation.

Although this is the first Ethiopian Civics curriculum, it had predecessors in the curricula promoted by the previous two regimes. Under Haile Selassie, a course called "moral education" was taught that drew on Orthodox Christian morality, placing obedience at its center. Following the communist, military overthrow of Haile Selassie and the imperial regime, socialist "political education" replaced Orthodox Christian "moral education" (Bayeh 2016; Tesfaye et al. 2013). Both of these earlier forms of "civics" education had very specific ideological inclinations.

The CEE curriculum lays out a blueprint for how citizens should participate in a constitutional, multicultural democracy by fusing an overarching narrative of national belonging with understandings of rights-based citizenship and lessons on government and rule of law (Yamada 2012; Smith 2013). In doing so, it outlines a particular notion of personhood oriented around democratic citizenship, patriotism, tolerance, and economic productivity. There are eleven units in the secondary school curriculum that are repeated each year: Building a Democratic System, Rule of Law, Equality, Justice, Patriotism, Responsibility, Industriousness, Self-Reliance, Saving [Money], Active Community Participation, and Pursuit of Wisdom. Woven throughout the curriculum are lessons about human rights and equality (Wondimu 2008; Smith 2013) as well as the importance of hard work, industriousness, peace-building, and loyalty to the state. It encourages students to take personal responsibility for engaging in peaceful coexistence with other Ethiopians from diverse backgrounds (Tafese and Desta 2014). The emphasis on coexistence and collective effort toward development collectively mobilizes the population around collaboration and cooperation rather than threat and conflict.

The CEE curriculum has been revised three times since 1991 and is taught at the primary, secondary, and tertiary levels. The curriculum was developed and revised by a panel of academics at Addis Ababa University and Ministry of Education staff. CEE is not only a required subject from elementary school through university but a mandatory subject on the university entrance exams, meaning students have to not only take the civics course but must master the material if they wish to go to university. University students can also study CEE at the tertiary level.

Despite the government's emphasis on the CEE curriculum, there were a good deal of public complaints about the curriculum. Indeed, we might say that critique of the curriculum functioned as something of a repository for critiques of the country as a whole. A survey done by the Ministry of Education about the CEE curriculum in 2006 found that the curriculum was thought to be "too political." When I interviewed a Ministry of Education official about this, I was told that this critique was confusing and misguided because the curriculum was not political; it was based on the constitution (personal communication with Ministry of Education official). Missing in these comments is the fact that the 1995 constitution itself is tremendously political (Smith 2013). Not only does allocating rights to ethnically based states work against a history of centralized political control and cultural hegemony, but ethnic federalism is extremely contentious.

At the time of my fieldwork in 2016–17, the CEE curriculum was centrally situated in debates about the plight of youth, economic and political marginalization, the nature of citizenship and inclusive belonging for different groups, and the appropriateness of forms of civic participation, such as protests. There were also complaints that the curriculum was trying to undermine "Ethiopian culture." I heard comments that the curriculum reflected EPRDF propaganda by portraying Ethiopia's previous leaders—Haile Selassie and Mengistu Haile Mariam—in an overly negative and biased manner.

One of the main reasons why the CEE curriculum was politically contentious is that the messages it teaches about liberal democracy were belied by authoritarian practice. As one teacher noted, there was a big difference between what was taught in the civics curriculum and how it was being applied: "The book is good. The written part is good. The curriculum is good. The challenge is with the practical application." However, not everyone agreed that "the written part is good." Indeed, many came to regard the CEE curriculum as propaganda of the leadership.

Despite hopes, promises, and indications that Ethiopia would move toward multiparty democracy and devolve power away from the center under the EPRDF, the party managed to consolidate power and crack down on any viable political opposition. An increasingly widespread discourse was that the EPRDF had become as repressive as the Derg regime that preceded it. The 2005 parliamentary elections (1997 in the Ethiopian calendar) were particularly pivotal, as summarized by Abbink (2017). Opposition parties enjoyed unprecedented support, threatening the absolute control of the ruling EPRDF. Amid accusations of election fraud, there was widespread postelection violence that the party responded to by limiting the free press and violently cracking down on the opposition. Many members of the opposition refused to take their seats in Parliament, instead calling for more street protests, which were also violently repressed. Measures were put in place that inhibited future challenges to the EPRDF by opposition groups. The year 2005 is typically regarded as the time when the ruling party consolidated its rule and began the country's progress toward authoritarianism. We also might think of 2005 as the year many Ethiopians began to regard the party as abandoning democracy and using force illegitimately.

Currently, the regime can be categorized as a neoliberal, competitive, or hybrid authoritarian regime (Brownlee 2007; Levitsky and Way 2010). However, Ethiopia's leaders and many civil servants and even citizens still believe that the country is still a democracy-in-progress, despite often-violent centralizing tendencies and strategies used by the ruling party to maintain single-party control, which it has done effectively since 1991.

While the EPRDF has failed to practice democracy, the party has done a very good job of educating the population about liberal, constitutional, democratic ideas through the CEE curriculum. Promoting the idea of Ethiopia as a liberal democracy arguably has played a key role in the global perception of Ethiopia as a sort of stable island of civility in a volatile sea of unstable neighbors. But I would also argue that the promotion of the idea of Ethiopia as a liberal democracy has created a desire for democracy that is incongruent with everyday encounters and experiences with the authoritarian state and therefore creates complex state effects.

Alongside the desire for democracy, there is also a strong desire for stability. The state's ability to maintain stability at the center, in Addis Ababa, is central to popular imaginings of whether or not the state itself is stable. During my conversations with Ethiopian colleagues at Addis Ababa University and middle-class neighbors and friends, the desire for return to some version of normal, even if that normal was decidedly nondemocratic and authoritarian, was palpable. Normal meant stable, predictable—a world in which one could go about one's ordinary duties. While there was concern about corruption, youth unemployment, and the increasingly strong-armed tactics the government used to quash dissent, there was also an expectation that the state would return things to normal. This critique of the state as overly repressive, authoritarian, and corrupt coexisted with the desire for a stable, if authoritarian, normal and set the stage for the declaration of the state of emergency in 2016.

Intimate Encounters with the Maddening State of Emergency

Elsa was arrested at a particular moment of political crisis in an ongoing series of crises as the need to stabilize, secure, and expand the reach of central state and ruling party clashed with demands from the periphery for greater rights. Beginning in 2014, the areas bordering Addis Ababa in Oromia (the Oromo Ethnic State) had been embroiled in recurrent protests initially due to anger over a plan for the central government to expand Addis Ababa into Oromia (Fasil and Lemma 2015). Protests gathered momentum and support throughout 2015. Despite the government canceling the controversial Addis Ababa Master Plan, which was the initial focus of protests, unrest continued, often targeting businesses (particularly foreign-owned businesses) throughout the state.

At this tense and uncertain moment, I arrived in Addis Ababa for a yearlong fellowship with two small children and my husband, an Eritrean who had grown up in Addis but had not been back since his family was deported during the border war with Eritrea that began in 1998. Vague state department warnings told us to exercise caution, avoid large gatherings, and not travel outside of Addis Ababa by road, which would require crossing into Oromia. September 2016 later proved to be a moment of calm amid a several-years-long period of turbulence that continues at the time of writing. Addis Ababa in 2016 came to feel like an island under siege. Protests and unrest surrounded the city. Everyone worried that they would pose a danger.

On 2 October 2016, tensions came to a head at the annual Oromo Ireecha celebration in Bishoftu, forty kilometers outside of Addis. The Ireecha, a political, spiritual, and cultural gathering, is the most important annual celebration of the Oromo, Ethiopia's largest ethnic group. Tensions at the 2016 Ireecha steadily rose over the course of the celebration, in no small part because, according to attendees, the government was trying to co-opt and control events that should have been organized by Oromo leadership (Begna 2017; Human Rights Watch 2017). The military and police presence was excessive. Accounts of the events vary somewhat, but it seems clear that one of the speakers, sparked by frustration over the government co-optation of the event, began chanting antigovernment slogans. Some combination of tear gas, rubber bullets, and live rounds were fired in the air or at the crowd. This set off a panic and led to a stampede in which large numbers of people were crushed to death. Estimates of the numbers of fatalities immediately after the incident ranged from the government's official count of fifty-five to opposition groups estimate of seven hundred deceased, revealing the lack of accurate reporting on the incident and the government's unwillingness to investigate (Human Rights Watch 2017).

Back in Addis, the story trickled to us in alarming bits and pieces. One rumor floated around that the government had had a military helicopter on site and had fired on people. A friend visiting us who had lived through the Red Terror—an extremely violent period of infighting that occurred as the Mengistu Haile Mariam's Derg solidified its power—panicked upon hearing this. He broke down as he recalled a time when students were sent home from the technical school he attended and a military helicopter trained its guns on the school. It later turned out that there had been an attempted coup. He was distressed, saying, "I don't know where this is heading. Will we be safe?" We later learned that there was a military helicopter present at the Ireecha but that it was dropping leaflets that read "Happy Ireecha," not firing on the crowd. Nonetheless, the presence of the helicopter was a powerful material and symbolic signifier of state repression that viscerally evoked feelings—and embodied memories—of fear, violence, and uncertainty.

On 8 October, the six-month state of emergency that led to Elsa's arrest was declared (Al Jazeera 2017). Although the state of emergency temporarily restored calm and normalcy, it also resulted in mass arrests, significant repression, and the banning of terminology, symbols, TV stations, and publications associated with opposition groups. During the state of emergency, mobile internet and access to social media was blocked throughout most of the country, and in some cases access to the internet as a whole. Outside of Addis, particularly in Oromia, the effects of increased state repression were felt strongly, but in Addis Ababa we quickly adapted to our lack of connectivity and almost immediately forgot the turbulence that was so pervasive just a few months before.

In Addis Ababa, the ease with which the tension was forgotten and the pervasive desire for a return to normal is encapsulated by Begoña Aretxaga's (2003) notion of the "maddening state" and Michael Taussig's (1992) notion of the "nervous system." Both concepts refer to a powerful desire for normalcy that erases and hides state violence. The maddening state refers to the maddening condition as our desires for a paternalistic state, a state that is thought to care for its subjects even in the face of evidence of egregious state violence, coexists with the awareness of state violence, an awareness that is often quashed in short-term memory once some semblance of normal returns (Aretxaga 2003). But the memories and experiences of violence don't go away; they are integrated into our individual nervous systems and into the collective social nervous system, as Taussig notes (1992). Violence, fear, and the normalization of both are infused throughout the system, putting us constantly on edge, leaving us to oscillate between the specter of possible violence and the necessity that we get through our everyday lives acting as if everything is normal.

We might argue that the maddening state and the nervous system are a manifestation of the discrepancy between what Phillip Abrams refers to as the state idea and the "palpable nexus of practice" (1988). Under conditions of state violence and authoritarianism, state ideas, and particularly ideas that the state produces about itself, clash with state practice. In Ethiopia, authoritarian practice and state violence that revealed fissures in state stability coexisted with claims that (and desires for) the state was democratic, benevolent, stable.

Violence presents a challenge for thinking through everyday perspectives on the state. In the face of state violence it is tempting to reify the state, something that Timothy Mitchell cautions against doing even as we work to "bring the state back in" (1991, 2006). The commonplace assertion that states are defined by the legitimate use of force both reifies the state and normalizes violence as part of its functions. All states have power over the bodies of their subjects, including the capacity to relocate, detain, hurt, and kill them. Many states, including stable democracies, are adept at legitimating this violence, but while authoritarian regimes tend to be more reliant on violence as a technology of governance, they are less adept at legitimating this violence. Achille Mbembe refers to this condition as the "impotence" and "mutual zombification" that emerges when rulers rely on their absolute capacity to command the bodies of the ruled (2001). He demonstrates that while violence may result in compliance, the rulers' inability to legitimate the use of force results in transgression, ridicule, and undermining the legitimacy of the state. In a similar vein, Lisa Wedeen (2015) shows the multiple ways that subjects perform "as if" they are complying with commands, while often undermining them. The ruled may have no choice but to comply, but rulers lose their buy-in, their trust. Securing legitimacy is difficult, resulting in an impotent situation where neither reform nor control is fully possible. It is a stalemate that we see Ethiopia and other places falling into repeatedly.

Meanwhile, recurrent state violence produces and shapes a particular state-subject relationship, drawing on memories of previous encounters with the violent state, evoking fears of future waves of violence. Salwa Ismail's work on Syria argues powerfully that violence is a technology of the state. Ismail coins the term "pedagogical violence" to talk about what extreme violence teaches state subjects about how to live amid violence. My friend's reactions to the show of force at the Ireecha and the manner in which the rumors of a helicopter's presence evoked traumatic memories is illustrative of the pedagogies of violence. Building from Ismail's thinking about the pedagogical functions of violence I argue that violent forms of state coercion lay the groundwork for the discursive production of the state itself. In my work on Eritrea, the notion of state punishment and the idea that the governing apparatus was inherently bent on punishing its people circulated widely in common talk about the government and was routinely experienced in everyday encounters with the state. Similar to "pedagogical violence," the arbitrariness of punishment produces what we might think of as pedagogical coercion (Riggan 2013, 2016; Ismail 2018).

Understanding the pedagogical effects of state violence is particularly important when state subjects hold two "maddeningly" contradictory imaginaries of the state in their minds at the same time: the idea of a benevolent, stabilizing state, and the idea of a violent, repressive state (Aretxaga 2003). Teachers certainly existed in this maddening condition. In addition to working through their own desires for stability and normalcy, their fears of repression, and their critique of the state, teachers were charged with discursively producing a particular idea of the state in their everyday encounters with students. Teachers' responsibility for intimately producing and reproducing the state locates them in the gap between the discursive production of the state and the encounters between state and people in the everyday realm (Gupta 2012). But through their close relationships with students, they were also poised to engage on a daily basis with what Michael Herzfeld (1992, 1997) calls "cultural intimacy," or a discursive, interactive process in which the less savory elements of national belonging are circulated, ascribed with meaning, and made collective. Because the state of emergency in Ethiopia was a time in which a sense of fear and repression got close to the skin of state subjects, teachers faced a particular challenge. How could they continue to promote the idea of the democratic state, an idea that was written into the curriculum, without placing themselves at risk, as Elsa did? Should they continue to promote with the idea of the democratic state? Or should they engage with students who were having "culturally intimate" conversations by highlighting the realities of the repressive state? In response to the pressures they felt, teachers tried to depoliticize their work and emphasize its "secular" nature, but their role was constantly re-politicized.

"They Think We Are Political Missionaries, but We Are Citizenship Missionaries"

CEE teachers were initially attracted to teaching civics because they genuinely liked the subject matter and believed in its importance. When I asked whether they thought the CEE curriculum was successful, many teachers expressed a belief in the value of the subject. One told me: "CEE is a multidisciplinary subject. There is nothing that it doesn't touch. It is important to make students interactive in their society and its political aspects. It is a laboratory to enhance their education level and participation in their country." In conversations with civics teachers, what came across was that they

believed in the curriculum, the ideal of citizenship, and the national constitution it was based on. Teachers consistently said that they liked teaching
civics for many reasons, including that "it enables you to speak about rights
and obligations," "it enables you to know about democracy," "it teaches people to be citizens and have awareness of good government," and "it widens
their [students'] minds to be rational instead of emotional."

Teachers thought of themselves and CEE itself as apolitical. Teaching
CEE was a technical process, not a political one. One teacher even said
repeatedly that their work and the curriculum should be "secular." Secular
to him meant that they should not be seen as attached to any particular
party or political group; rather the work of civics was to be neutral and to
transcend partisan politics and teach concepts and ideas that would make
a democracy work.

At the same time, CEE teachers knew they were commonly labeled
"political teachers" by students and other teachers. One teacher stated,
"Other teachers perceive us as instruments of the government. We are perceived as political missionaries. But we are citizenship missionaries." One
teacher thought that the reason they were labeled as political teachers was
because the curriculum was, in fact, propaganda: "Another problem is that
the subject has not been changing the attitude and behavior of the students.
They consider students as political subjects. The government has been using
the curriculum as an instrument of propaganda." In other words, while
teachers thought of their work as "secular," the government treated the
students and the curriculum as political, a term that refers here to supporting the party's political agenda. Because the curriculum was propaganda, it
could not effectively do its work—it did not change the attitude or behavior
of the students.

Another teacher elaborated the difference between how they were perceived and how they saw their own work, and the challenges this created
for teachers:

> Most of the time civics is considered a political subject, but it is
> about social and moral issues. There are different ideas that side
> to the ruling party. People think that they [the party] just give
> different ideas to us that they want. The first challenge of civics for
> the teacher is that mostly people consider us as political teachers.
> Society thinks teachers are spreading propaganda for the ruling
> party. But we are trying to make change in the society. Most of the
> time the society's attitude is that the curriculum is biased.

The quotation explains the paradox teachers experienced. Due to
the widespread public perception that the CEE curriculum was party

propaganda and teachers were merely disseminating it, CEE teachers were inhibited in what they thought their real work was: teaching about moral and social issues that transcended the party and were essential for building democracy.

Teachers noted that people had not always thought of civics as political propaganda and civics teachers as party pawns. This critique of CEE paralleled a loss of faith in the ruling party. One teacher explained that perceptions about the CEE curriculum began to change in 2005, the year many Ethiopians lost hope that the EPRDF intended to support the development of democracy in Ethiopia: "Students do not have a good outlook toward CEE teachers because they think they are political. Students think the country has not been building democracy and peace. Since 1997 in the Ethiopian calendar [2005], the attitude of students toward building a democracy has declined so we can say [the] subject has no contribution." After 2005 it became difficult for CEE teachers to convince anyone that they were doing anything other than spreading party propaganda. The curriculum no longer reflected the realities outside the classroom. Meanwhile, CEE teachers were left promoting the *idea* of the democratic state in a place where students and others routinely felt the *effects* of an authoritarian state that belied that idea. Not surprisingly, it was difficult to convince students of the value of the *idea*. Teachers witnessed firsthand the ways in which everyday experiences outside the classroom clashed with what they were teaching and delegitimized the idea of liberal, constitutional democracy promoted in the curriculum and the leadership that promoted it.

As a result, teachers found themselves stretched between their belief in the idea of the democratic state and their awareness of the effects of state coercion, authoritarianism, corruption, and other nondemocratic practices. They described this discrepancy between the written curriculum and what was happening in reality as fundamentally challenging their teaching and undermining their authority. One teacher said: "I have a mission to transmit civics values. When students understand their rights, some use them, some abuse them. Some have no understanding of them. You have to model character. But they laugh at you because they observe corruption. Honesty is the best policy, but they don't see this in society, so they laugh at you. There are contradictions." Another teacher explained how this contradiction resulted in the loss of credibility for both the curriculum and the government. "Initially it was successful, but it has lost its credibility. People see corruption. And the government is deceiving people through media. Through time it has lost its honesty. But initially we were very interested but through time it deteriorated. Now there is rampant corruption."

Or as another teacher echoed, the critique of civics teachers and the critique of the government mirrored each other: "Things are changing. In

1991 and now things are not the same. Problems mounted and created great volcanoes of dissent. The government became alert. Tomorrow the new generation will change the situation." In the process of trying to convey the importance and legitimacy of the idea of the democratic, constitutional state, teachers became the fault line—labeled by students as "political," which in this case meant co-opted by party propaganda, but also in danger if they did not correctly toe the party line. And yet, ironically, despite their belief in the teaching of civics and their belief in the next generation, teachers also worried about the next generation being too political.

"Patriotism Means Being Loyal, Peaceful, and a Good Student"

A second paradox teachers experienced was that, although they believed deeply in teaching students about their democratic, constitutional, and human rights, they worried that students were overly fixated on their rights and were not considering their responsibilities. Teachers worried about young people's approach toward their future. A common theme I heard from both teachers and other adults in Ethiopia at this time was that the civics curriculum clearly had not worked and that the presence of protests in Ethiopia was evidence of this. When I asked why the protests showed that the curriculum had not worked, a common response was that students were overly focused on their rights because they had not been taught enough about their responsibilities.

When I asked teachers what they meant by student responsibilities, their answer noted that students should be disciplined, respectful, and rule abiding. The following notes from a focus group conversation are indicative of the way many teachers thought of student responsibilities:

> The teachers were saying that students were not taught about their obligations. I asked what the obligations of students were, one teacher answered, "Wearing the uniform, respecting the teacher and their friends."
>
> I then asked what the rights and duties of a citizen were and he said, "Paying taxes, protecting the constitution, and performing according to the constitution."
>
> Another teacher chimed in, saying, "The students know about their rights and responsibilities, but there is a problem with implementation."
>
> Another commented that the problem was a lack of control: "When they miss their responsibilities, they should be punished by the school. The most known responsibility is wearing their uniform and attending class. But there is no correct measurement. They are not committed to obey their duties."

I then asked how wearing a school uniform taught students about their duties as citizens, and the same teacher answered: "If they wear the school uniform, they follow the school regulation. Being a good citizen is about obeying the law."

And another teacher added that other disciplined behaviors would also reflect on their citizenship: "If they cover their exercise book it creates a good environment to promote teaching and learning. And cultivating the school means cultivating themselves and cultivating the country. The school is like the country."

Teachers had the sense that, in addition to teaching about democracy, the constitution, and other topics in the curriculum, which conveyed a sense of rights to students, they also needed to teach students responsibilities, which was done through discipline and, at times, punishment. If rights were taught through the curriculum, responsibilities, it would seem, were taught through the not-so-hidden, embodied curriculum of school discipline.

Alongside this sense that students were not learning responsibilities, many teachers said that students' patriotic duty was to study and not to get involved in politics. The reduction of the student role to that of studying and learning effectively functions as a sort of anti-politics machine (Ferguson 1994) whereby the role of students is limited one: study and get As. Teaching, thus, becomes a technical process of disseminating information and testing students on it. In my observations of civics classes and interviews with civics teachers, I repeatedly heard teachers tell students that their patriotic duty was to "study hard." They cautioned that the time to become involved in politics would be later in life when they had matured. For example, in a ninth-grade civics class, the teacher defined patriotism as follows: "If you work for democracy and human rights you are a patriot. If you are a student, you should study. If you get an 'A' you are a patriot. Patriotism is working hard. Patriots work for the community." The lesson went on to further detail the attributes of a patriot as defined by the textbook as including:

Maintaining internal peace and security
Tolerating diversity
Fighting against terrorism, poverty and corruption.
Keeping state secrets.
Working hard.
Promoting the common good.
Respecting the rights of others.
Respecting the laws of the country

After going through the entire lesson and detailing each of these points, the teacher differentiated between patriotism and chauvinism. "Chauvinism is blind love," he told them. "Patriotism is a quality of loyalty and being peaceful." A few minutes later, in the class, the teacher again encouraged students toward peace and cautioned against "selfish groups," saying, "A community can be disturbed because of many things, because of selfish groups. We are patriots if we restore peace to the community." Patriotism, thus, was characterized as cool, rational, and peaceful in contrast to the "selfish" desires of some communities.

After observing the entire lesson, I probed the teacher to tell me more about the patriotic work of students particularly with regard to human rights and democracy. He clarified and expanded on what he had said to the students earlier, repeating again that students' patriotic duty was only to study; then he noted, "At the grassroots level if they work hard they are patriots. When they grow up, their roles will be diverse. But right now we don't expect them to do other roles." The idea that students' duty was to study, nothing more, was a common theme that I heard among CEE teachers. Despite the fact that teachers and students seemed to be in agreement that there were widespread problems in the country, many teachers seemed to think that students should not engage in politics until they had fully matured.

Why, given the widespread frustrations with the "practical application" of the curriculum and the anger at a ruling party that had clearly privileged maintaining its own power over building a democracy, were teachers critical of student participation in politics and intent on depoliticizing the appropriate way for young people to enact their citizenship? The answer is complex. At one level, authority structures in households and society at large maintain expectations that young people should be docile, subservient, and *wait* to take leadership (Poluha 2004; Smith 2013). We see resonances of these cultural expectations in the assertion that a student's role is to study, not to be involved in politics; the broader discomfort with youth activism; and the characterization of youth unrest as an emphasis on rights, rather than obligations. One teacher explained, "Students practice rights, not duties. The community wants democracy to be perfect and don't understand it is a process." Students were categorized as impatient and unwilling to wait for democracy.

The concern about youth unrest is also contextualized by the characterization of youth in general, and their involvement in street protest in particular, as unruly and irrational, on one hand, and on the other hand a desire for a return to a stable, if undemocratic, normal, which I discussed in the first section of this chapter. Teachers, effectively, were caught up by the "maddening state" (Aretxaga 2003). They knew that state authoritarianism was problematic, but somehow they desired the paternalistic role it played through enabling stability and a sense of normalcy. Teachers and other professional adults were thus wary about the restiveness of youth and concerned about the instability it would bring. Teachers also were positioned as a key technology in the anti-politics machinery. Despite the fact that teachers resisted having their work politicized, perhaps their most important political task to ensure that students would not understand the teachings of civics as political teachings but rather as social and moral ones. When viewed in this light, Elsa's arrest starts to make a great deal of sense. By even addressing and engaging in discussions with students about protests, she is stepping away from a technocratic role as disseminator of information about civics and acknowledging that students are political. She inevitably faces an almost impossible dilemma: to politicize or to depoliticize?

"The Students Are Not Afraid, but the Teachers Are Afraid"

In her analysis of the governmentality of violence in Syria, Salwa Ismail (2018) discusses practices of pedagogical violence inherent in forms of torture, imprisonment, and humiliation, particularly the practice of marking an individual in a way that is referenced by others and constrains or produces particular kinds of behavior. According to Ismail, pedagogical violence not only breaks down people's sense of personhood but produces certain forms of political subjectivity.

It is interesting to think through violence, specifically, and repression, more broadly, as pedagogical. Arguably, teachers' fear, or caution, about what and how to teach is the manifestation of what we might think of as pedagogical repression. Teachers circulate stories of what has happened to other teachers, and it makes them fearful of teaching the very subject they have been charged to teach and have chosen to teach. Furthermore, teachers and other Ethiopians circulate stories that suggest that they have also been instructed by the violent pedagogies of previous regimes.

Even though CEE teachers saw themselves as doing "secular" mission-driven work, they were scared that if they did that work well, bad things might happen to them at the hands of other state actors, particularly party representatives or the police. CEE teachers were under political pressure from the party and sometimes the police to represent a particular political stance. One teacher said:

> The perception of people in Ethiopia is that CEE is a means to propagate the political agenda of the government. In some cases it may be true. The government interferes in schools. When I was teaching in rural areas, the *woreda* [local government] leader

tried to ask me to join the party, saying, "How can you teach CEE without belonging to the party?" People think that we are members of the party. The government should not intervene in school affairs. But the government is blaming some teachers and can fire teachers.

Many teachers had stories about being coerced into joining the party, being threatened, having their pay docked, or even being stopped from working simply for doing their job. As one teacher told me: "A teacher was teaching civics. And he raised students' political consciousness to the highest level and they removed the person. They denied him to teach CEE because he raised the consciousness of the students. They stopped him from teaching." The politics of teaching civics revolved around the discrepancies between what was in the curriculum and what was happening outside school walls, which I discussed above. But what made teachers particularly vulnerable to being disciplined or punished was the fact that students were asking challenging questions. This was perhaps the greatest pitfall and paradox for CEE teachers. As one teacher noted: "What they [the students] are learning in the school and what they observe is not the same, so they ask us, what you are teaching us is not what they [government] are doing. This is a challenge for the teacher. To say this is very hard." Another teacher explained that students specifically ask about the status of multiparty democracy in Ethiopia, noting that the failure to implement multiparty democracy is illuminated by the curriculum:

We teach [about] the multiparty system and party competition. These are the principles. The constitution talks about these things. But how are these principles carried out? But are they there? The governing party undermines the existence of other parties. So weak parties exist. Who cannot challenge the system. *Students ask us, Where are the parties?* They say, "These are fake parties." Also we teach them about accountability and what abuse of power is. When someone abuses his power, no one questions it. Students want to see these things in reality. Also the problem of blaming the past. This is not a solution. When you make a mistake, you have to take responsibility. How can students learn from this? When I am incapable, I have to resign. Politics is a challenge. When the leader is unable to cope with a challenge, they have to resign, but they are deeply rooted. If you question harshly, you will be put in prison. If you say, you have to resign, you will be hunted down and go to prison. The students know these problems. (emphasis added)

Another teacher talked about teaching students that they have the constitutional right to protest and critique but how that can also become a danger:

> Constitutionally, it is written that you can oppose the government, but if you criticize seriously you will be questioned. Critical opposition is not allowed. We teach critical thinking and expression. We teach students to criticize, but they observe that practically when someone criticizes they will be hunted and questioned and may disappear. In each topic, there are twelve contents. In each question, how you practice it is a question. For example, tolerance, if you enact this, you may be hunted as a fundamentalist. Your family may be disparaged for being different.

Given the political pressures teachers were under, they often recounted feeling afraid of students' challenging questions. One teacher noted, "The students are not afraid, but the teachers are afraid." There could be very real repercussions for teachers who identified too strongly with students. The anecdote of Elsa's arrest that I began with is one example of this, but there are others as well. When I asked a group of teachers in a focus group whether students openly debated the curriculum and issues facing the country, a teacher replied:

> Teachers allow them to debate anything. It may be determined by the topic. They talk about building a democratic system. In relation to justice, they discuss the justice system freely. Students don't have fear of speaking openly. In fact, teachers don't fear their principal, but we fear the government. Students don't fear the teachers or the government.
>
> The government is not good to teachers in general. They fear that teachers will challenge the system. Teachers raise different questions to the society in general regarding the living condition of Ethiopian people. Because of this the government fears the teachers and the teachers fear the government. And the government doesn't allow teachers to participate in different things.

The comment "the government fears the teachers and the teachers fear the government" epitomizes Mbembe's notion of "impotence," whereby the ruler is trying to control subjects whose unruliness the ruler is afraid of and the ruled are behaving either aggressively or evasively to avoid violence, repression, and punishment. Despite their education in civics, neither students nor teachers have any mechanism to use their critical-thinking skills to improve the country or put it on back on a democratic track. All they can do is respond to fear and disillusion.

When I asked why students are not afraid, one teacher explained:

> They have their own information from home. In school students talk about what is happening in reality. When people are talking about these things, they are arrested. When we teach these things, they get confused. Most civics teachers are afraid to answer questions. They compare and contrast different ideas. When they see the differences between the principles in text and the real world, I am happy to answer and debate, but it may cause different problems. Mostly this is our challenge. When I started teaching it was good. We would freely talk about these issues. [Now] when I get a question from these students I'm afraid. The students speak freely. Teachers have been in prison during the previous regime. When I was teaching about the democratic system, the students said, "You taught us that opposition is a democratic right but now people are arrested." I answered that the opposition is not going right. Now I've learned to just tell them about the principles—stick to the text and not talk about the real world.
>
> Education should be secular. You should give them explanations as you teach. You should update yourself and give them examples, but when I do this in the classroom, someone doesn't like this. Students may deliberately ask questions like "Is Ethiopia a democratic state?"

The teacher begins with a brief explanation of why students are not afraid—they have information from home. He spends most of his time articulating the pedagogies of state violence and repression, which affects students and teachers in very different ways, making teachers cautious and students bold. As the teacher above notes, this was in no small part due to teachers' memories of the Derg regime and the capacity of the state to do violence. Students, in contrast, who not only did not have visceral embodied memories of the Derg, but had been inculcated by the idea of democracy through the auspices of the CEE curriculum, in contrast, "spoke freely." During these tense times, particularly after the state of emergency was declared, this put teachers in a tough spot as state idea and repressive practices of the government deviated from each other. As the teacher quoted above said, most teachers responded by sticking close to the text and falling back on teaching in theoretical rather than practical ways. As one teacher noted, "In general, what we teach theoretically is different in practice. In the living standard, there is a difference between theory and practice." Another teacher expanded on these thoughts, noting the importance of teaching theoretically in order to stay safe. When asked how he addressed challenging questions, he responded:

> You go back to what you are taught. Look at yourself by these instruments. They know it very well. Teachers don't react to the students. The teacher fears that if they answer that question there will be a problem. So the teacher refers back to what is written. The teacher does not judge. They never say that is wrong. In order for the students to accept them, they have observed what is wrong. The instrument is what is written here.

At the same time, amid fear of repercussions, teachers remained "strong" and retained a deep belief in the subject matter they were charged to teach. They remained committed to "the struggle": If you don't struggle the future won't be better. A lot of teachers are struggling. As civics teachers, the government has prepared this topic. Most civics teachers have criticized the government. Keeping silent cannot be a solution.

Similarly, Elsa noted that she remained strong. Even in the face of what had happened to her, she was determined to stay strong and offered a critique of what should have happened, which is perhaps both mundane and revolutionary. She noted that there were many gaps that made teaching civics difficult. When I asked what the gaps were, she answered:

> What are the gaps? Unnecessary interference by the sub-city administrators. Like in my situation, it could have been addressed in the school. No other interference was necessary. The solution has to be here. When I fail in [teaching] this subject, when I am not correct in trusting the lesson, the school could handle that. Police and academicians are not working for a common purpose. Even if there is a complaint from the students, they can talk to me clearly. I am strong now. Even stronger than before. I am a civics teacher, and it is my responsibility to talk about democracy, but when we talk about the reality it is horrible.

The disconnect here is between a belief that schools and teachers should be independent of the central state, which teachers believed, and that they were a central component of it, which seemed to be the stance of the central government. In many ways we might see Elsa as advocating for the sovereignty of the school and teachers, for autonomy from the state as a whole. Civics teachers believed that they are the ones responsible for shaping the future and its citizens. They bought into a mission and a vision—not a political one, according to them, but one of building the nation's citizens.

Pedagogical Repression and the Politics of the Political in Times of Transition

Elsewhere I have argued that teachers are very much in the middle—in the middle of "state" and "society" but also in the middle of repressive mechanisms of governance and their future building work as teachers (Riggan 2020). However, teacher *middleness* should not assume two discrete objects that confine teachers. Rather, if we take seriously Foucault's notion of power as productive then we need to consider what happens when those in a key nodal role, who are positioned to sit at the nexus of that productive power, are faced with the paradoxes of an uncertain political transition. What effects do pedagogical repression and violence, on one hand, and the "maddening state," on the other, have on the ways that teachers produce state effects in the classroom? How do notions of legitimacy and politics shift in these moments? What is regarded as political in moments when the definition of politics is in flux? These questions are central to the ethnography of the state and democracy in Africa.

Debates over civics teaching and learning in Ethiopia during the state of emergency reflected a debate over what politics should be, where politics should take place, who should legitimately participate in it, and what the appropriate means of political participation is. During the state of emergency, and at the time of this writing, these debates continue.

What becomes clear through this exploration of CEE teaching in Addis Ababa during the 2016–17 state of emergency is that there was a direct tension between politics and anti-politics. Politics and being political, as associated with partisanship, was thought to have no place in schools. Regardless of whether teachers supported the ruling party, they were labeled "political" because they taught a subject that was believed to have a political bias, even though the party itself seemed to be threatened by the curriculum they designed. Meanwhile, teachers thought their subject matter transcended politics by teaching values and morals. Furthermore, teachers sent students explicit messages that their role was only to study and not to be "politically" engaged.

Where does teachers' antipolitical stance come from? It reflects the condition of living and working in the maddening state. On one hand, teachers experienced the effects of pedagogical violence; teachers cited the history of teacher repression and noted their fear of government repression. On the other hand, teachers longed for stability and had concerns that angry youth would create volatility. They worried that these youth had learned, through the civics curriculum, to demand rights but not to exercise responsibilities.

Much can be learned from a fine-grained unraveling of this politics of politics and anti-politics, especially if we understand Ethiopia's long history of authoritarianism, something which many have argued is infused in intimate and familial relationships and cultural patterns (Poluha 2004; Smith 2013). In many respects, what is at stake in Ethiopia right now is a manifestation of figuring out what politics is, where it happens, who gets to participate and how.

Cycles of unrest and government repression have continued since the 2016–17 state of emergency. One of these waves dislodged the EPRDF and placed Prime Minister Abiy Ahmed in power. The first leader of Ethiopia to hail from the majority Oromo ethnic group, Prime Minister Abiy, came to power amid poetic and effervescent statements and gestures about openness and love. But the country is still embroiled in political turbulence as the marginalized periphery challenges the central state and the central state responds with violence. Building on long-standing ethnic grievances, dissent *and* government repression have transformed, at times, into horrific instances of ethnic violence and cleansing. In the face of such violence, it is understandable that many argue that the civics curriculum has failed to create peaceful citizens of a multicultural, tolerant, ethnically plural state. But the presence of widespread violence also reflects the limits of curriculum and classroom pedagogy in the face of everyday pedagogies of a violent state that fails to uphold the mission stated in its curriculum.

In this situation, teachers are still on the fault line, with restive youth on one side and the CEE curriculum and state security apparatus on another. They are remarkably resistant to co-optation by the state, but they are also resistant to radicalization and revolutionary change. Their work is both political and antipolitical, ultimately revealing that anti-politics, like violence, is a form of politics that reveals political contests as they inhabit the everyday realm.

Note

1. All names have been changed in accordance with principles and ethics of human subjects' protection.

References

Abrams, Phillip. 1988. "Notes on the Difficulty of Studying the State (1977)." *Journal of Historical Sociology* 1 (1): 58–89.

Abbink, John. 2017. *A Decade of Ethiopia: Politics, Economy and Society, 2004–2016.* Boston: Brill.

Al Jazeera. 2017. "Ethiopia Lifts State of Emergency Imposed in October." 5 August 2017. https://www.aljazeera.com/news/2017/8/5/ethiopia-lifts-state-of-emergency-imposed-in-october.

Aretxaga, Begoña. 2003. "Maddening States." *Annual Review of Anthropology* 32:393–410.

Bariagaber, Assefaw. 1998. "The Politics of Cultural Pluralism in Eritrea: Trajectories of Ethnicity and Constitutional Experiments." *Ethnic and Racial Studies* 21 (6): 1057–73.

Bayeh, Endalcachew. 2016. "Role of Civics and Ethical Education for the Development of Democratic Governance in Ethiopia: Achievements and Challenges." *Pacific Science Review B: Humanities and Social Sciences* 2:31–36.

Begna, Lammi. 2017. "Irreecha 2016: An Eyewitness Account of What (Actually) Happened." Opride, 19 September 2017. https://www.opride.com/2017/09/19/irreecha-2016-went-wrong/.

Brownlee, Jason. 2007. *Authoritarianism in an Age of Democracy.* Cambridge: Cambridge University Press.

Donham, Donald. 2002. "Introduction." In *Remapping Ethiopia: Socialism and After,* edited by Wendy James, Donald Donham, Eisei Kurimoto and Alessandro Triulzi, 1–7. Oxford: James Currey.

Fasil, Mahlet, and Tsedale Lemma. 2015. "Oromo Protests: Defiance amidst Pain and Suffering." *Addis Standard,* 16 December 2015. https://addisstandard.com/oromo-protests-defiance-amidst-pain-and-suffering/.

Ferguson, James. 1994. *The Anti-Politics Machine: Development, Depoliticization and Bureaucratic Power in Lesotho.* Minneapolis: University of Minnesota Press.

Gupta, Akhil. 2012. *Red Tape: Bureaucracy, Structural Violence, and Poverty in India.* Durham, NC: Duke University Press.

Herzfeld, Michael. 1992. *The Social Production of Indifference: Exploring the Symbolic Roots of Western Bureaucracy.* Chicago: University of Chicago Press.

———. 1997. *Cultural Intimacy: Social Poetics in the Nation-State.* New York: Routledge.

Human Rights Watch. 2017. *Fuel on the Fire: Security Force Response to the 2016 Irreecha Cultural Festival.* N.p.: Human Rights Watch. https://www.hrw.org/sites/default/files/report_pdf/ethiopia0917_web.pdf.

Ismail, Salwa. 2018. *The Rule of Violence: Subjectivity, Memory and Government in Syria.* Cambridge: Cambridge University Press.

Kebede, Messay. 2006. "The Roots and Fallouts of Haile Selassie's Educational Policy." Philosophy Faculty Publications. Paper 113. http://ecommons.udayton.edu/phl_fac_pub/113.

Keller, Edmond, and Lahra Smith. 2005. "Obstacles to Implementing Territorial Decentralization: The First Decade of Ethiopian Federalism." In *Sustainable Peace: Democracy and Power-Dividing Institutions after Civil Wars,* edited by Philip Roeder and Donald Rothchild, 265–92. Ithaca, NY: Cornell University Press.

Levitsky, Steven, and Lucan Way. 2010. *Competitive Authoritarianism: Hybrid Regimes after the Cold War.* Cambridge: Cambridge University Press.

Mains, Daniel. 2004. "Drinking, Rumour, and Ethnicity in Jimma, Ethiopia." *Africa* 74 (3): 341–60.

Mbembe, Achille. 2001. *On the Postcolony.* Vol. 41. Berkeley: University of California Press.

Milkias, Paulos. 2006. *Haile Selassie, Western Education and Political Revolution in Ethiopia.* Amherst, MA: Cambria Press.

Mitchell, Timothy. 1991. "The Limits of the State: Beyond Statist Approaches and their Critics." *American Political Science Review* 85 (1): 77–96.

———. 2006. "Society, Economy, and the State Effect." In *The Anthropology of the State: A Reader,* edited by Aradhana Sharma and Akhil Gupta, 186–96. New York: Blackwell.

Poluha, Eva. 2004. *The Power of Continuity: Ethiopia through the Eyes of Its Children.* Uppsala, Sweden: Nordic Africa Institute.

Riggan, Jennifer. 2013. "'It Seemed like a Punishment': Teacher Transfers, Hollow Nationalism, and the Intimate State in Eritrea." *American Ethnologist* 40 (4): 749–63.

———. 2016. *The Struggling State: Nationalism, Mass Militarization, and the Education of Eritrea.* Philadelphia: Temple University Press.

———. 2020. "The Teacher State: Navigating the Fusion of Education and Militarization in Eritrea and Elsewhere." *Compare: A Journal of International and Comparative Education* 50 (5): 639–55.

Smith, Lahra. 2013. *Making Citizens in Africa: Ethnicity, Gender and National Identity in Ethiopia.* Cambridge: Cambridge University Press.

———. 2008. "The Politics of Contemporary Language Policy in Ethiopia." *Journal of Developing Societies* 24 (2): 207–43.

Tafese, Gosa Setu, and Desta Tamrat Desta. 2014. "The Roles of Civics and Ethical Education in Shaping Attitude of the Students in Higher Education: The Case of Mekelle University." *International Journal of Scientific and Research Publications* 4 (10): 1–4.

Taussig, Michale. 1992. *The Nervous System.* New York: Routledge.

Tesfaye, Semela, Thorsten Bohl, and Marc Kleinknecht, 2013. "Civic Education in Ethiopian Schools: Adopted Paradigms, Instructional Technology, and Democratic Citizenship in a Multicultural Context." *International Journal of Educational Development* 33 (2): 156–64.

Wedeen, Lisa. 2015. *Ambiguities of Domination: Politics, Rhetoric, and Symbols in Contemporary Syria.* Chicago: University of Chicago Press.

Wondimu, Habtamu. 2008. *Handbook of Peace and Human Rights Education in Ethiopia.* Addis Ababa: Organization for Social Science Research in Eastern and Southern Africa.

Yamada, Shoko. 2011. "Equilibrium on Diversity and Fragility: Civic and Ethical Education Textbooks in Democratizing Ethiopia." *Journal of International Cooperation in Education* 14 (2): 97–113.

———. 2012. "Domesticating Democracy? Civic and Ethical Education Textbooks in Secondary Schools in the Democratizing Ethiopia." In *(Re)Constructing Memory: School Textbooks and the Imagination of the Nation,* edited by James Williams, 35–59. Rotterdam: Sense Publishing.

FOURTEEN

The State and "Its Responsibilities"

School, Welfare State, and Community Building in Lubumbashi
(Haut-Katanga, Democratic Republic of Congo)

EDOARDO QUARETTA

> The important things are always
> non-negotiable.
>
> —Strauss (1978, 248)

1992. FOR MOST OF THE PEOPLE I MET DURING FIELDWORK in Lubumbashi,[1] this was the year that is fundamental for understanding the evolution of the education system in the Democratic Republic of Congo. The year is a sort of ground zero to which it was necessary to come back to every time I began to talk about education, school, and, above all, the state. What happened in 1992? Why is it so important to my informants? To put it briefly and to borrow from the refrain I constantly heard, "In 1992, the state abandoned its responsibilities" (En 1992, l'État a abandonné se résponsabilités).

This refrain was the inevitable beginning of any discussion on the subject. It expresses one end of the spectrum of perspectives Congolese have about their nation, or at least of many of Lubumbashi's inhabitants. This idea is mainly about what the state is not: the Congolese state is not a welfare state able to provide public services to its citizens. At the other end of the spectrum is the idea of what the postcolonial state actually is, according to the Lushois (Lubumbashi's inhabitants): a "sorcerer state" (*état sorcier*)—that is, an entity whose structure and functioning is often inscrutable and thought of in terms of an occult congregation operating behind the scenes. To fully grasp the meaning of this idea, as Filip De Boeck (2000, 34) noted

FIGURE 1. Moke Fils, *Parlement-Debout,* Kinshasa 2006. © Collection Horvath for Political Art.

about Kinshasa, "it is essential to recall that the legacy of colonial modernity, as embodied in the postcolonial state, is sometimes perceived in itself as a source of witchcraft and evil." Father Peter,[2] principal of a well-known Catholic high school in inner Lubumbashi, expressed this idea better than others. He was explicit in saying that his school has always educated the Congolese ruling class. The problem according to him, was that politicians, once in power, reject Catholic values in order to get into "occult circles" (*circles occultes*).

Focusing on two case studies, a high school in a Lubumbashi suburb and a Catholic school complex in the city center, this chapter shows that the educational sector—and precisely schools—are a "negotiated order" (Strauss 1978) through which ordinary people and institutional actors (state and non-state agents) enable its survival and shape ideas about the postcolonial state. In Congo, as elsewhere, schools are places that encourage discourses about the functions and the meaning of the state. Like in the well-known Moke Fils painting *Parlement-Debout* (standup parliament), every morning it is usual to see at the entrance of any school in Lubumbashi groups of parents talking over school fees, the quality of education, politics, and state institutions.

In this chapter, I explain some ideas discussed in these standup parliaments and, more specifically, those ideas about the state expressed when people talk about education. It is important to remember from the onset that it is not only a matter of "words" and "discourses": Lushois experience concretely the consequences of the presence/absence of the state in their everyday life. That is why I focus on a specific feature of the educational system upon which the whole sector is largely based: the so-called FIP system, or the *frais d'intervention ponctuelle* (occasional intervention fees). Informally instituted in 1992, this is a practice that involves parents paying the teachers' salary. The FIP system is an example of a negotiated order between the state, education-related actors, and ordinary people. Through this practice, the schools, which are confronted with state financial shortages, can keep functioning and formal education can be provided. The practice therefore shapes specific concepts of the state, education, citizenship, and democracy in the DRC.

The first section of the chapter presents a brief review of the literature on the studies of the Congolese state. Literature on the Congolese state is important for providing a theoretical framework for understanding the postcolonial situation, especially the legacy of the colonial state. It provides constructive criticism to the paradigm of the "failed state" that has dominated the study of the postcolonial state within the second half of the twentieth century. Literature on the Congolese state also suggests insights for how we can replace this paradigm with the concept of real governance that allows the production of a more informed knowledge about the functioning of the contemporary African state. The second section presents the education sector's evolution since the 1990s, when many economic and social sectors of the country were being liberalized. Officially, the education sector has not been liberalized, and the management of public schools has remained in the hands of the state or has been delegated to religious congregations. However, as already mentioned, the entire system is based on FIP, which makes it an example of "internal privatization" (Hibou 2004) or, according to others, of a process of commodification. The third section analyzes the case of a high school in Kasungami, a Lubumbashi suburb. The fourth and final section compares Kasungami's data with those of a renowned Catholic high school located in Lubumbashi's city center. In the final section, I provide a comparison between state representations in the suburbs and the city center of Lubumbashi.

Failed State and Real Governance in the Katanga Province

Most of the scholarly literature on the postcolonial state in Congo basically falls into two major paradigms: the "failed state" approach that claims the failure of the postcolonial state and the "practical statehood" approach that analyzes the process of negotiation between social actors beyond the formal structure and functioning of African institutions. Social negotiations are the cornerstone of the actual functioning of public services in the country.

The failed state approach (or "weak" or "collapsed" state) argues that the postcolonial state, especially in Africa, has retreated from providing any basic public services (Rotberg 2003), and is characterized by a lack of authority (Chabal and Daloz 1999). According to this view, the state is simply considered a formal framework (Trefon 2004), a sort of empty shell. The limitations of the failed state approach reside primarily in the attempt to compare an African state's performance with Western welfare state models. The analysis is focused on all the shortcomings of postcolonial states with respect to a utopian and ahistorical definition of statehood (Hill 2005).

The second approach seeks to overcome the failed state paradigm (Hameiri 2007). It attempts to describe how basic services continue to be provided in specific institutional contexts. A key concept of this approach is "real governance" (Olivier de Sardan 2008; Titeca and De Herdt 2011). Scholars working on real governance agree that, despite years of economic and political crisis, the Congolese state apparatus has survived as an administrative framework. While the formal functioning of the state machine may be apparently configured according to national policies, the logic behind it and the meanings attributed to it by its people are not the same in all services and in all social contexts. The actual, everyday functioning of state institutions are not guaranteed by well-developed infrastructures but rather through continuous negotiations between an array of social actors, including state, nonstate, religious institutions, and ordinary citizens. The importance of social negotiations over the material infrastructures of state institutions has led some scholars to talk about "invisible cities" (De Boeck and Plissart 2014) and "people as infrastructure" (Simone 2008). These analyses suggest the need for a realistic ethnography of African postcolonial institutions: observed from the correct angle what looks like a chaotic, incoherent, discontinuous organization turns out to be part of a wider, more solid organization than that present in material and formal infrastructures.

Real governance echoes the concept of "negotiated order." I borrow this concept from Anselm Strauss, who used it in the study of caregiver/patient relationships in hospitals. Strauss (1978) argued that all social order is negotiated order, which is to say that social structures are created, maintained, and transformed by an ongoing process of negotiation between an array of social actors. According to this definition, we may understand governance of state institutions as something not related to a rigid and generic idea of "state." Rather it is a practice emerging from an order negotiated between a complex interweaving of interests, social relations, economic exchanges, and cultural elements. In this process, state agents are only a social category of actors, among many others. Such an approach is valuable for an ethnographic inquiry, as it opens up possibilities for investigating the relationships between social actors within a constantly changing social structure and understanding people's points of view and their ways and means in creating alternative collective actions.

Returning to our case study, in the educational institutions in the DRC and in Katanga, no actor has enough political, symbolic, or economic strength to impose its organizational rule over others. The absence of a central authority that can successfully impose a formal order leaves room for local negotiations. While this keeps the system working, as in the case of education in DRC, it also produces a certain degree of inconsistency in the provision of the service and consequently of uncertainty among citizens. Uncertainty increases in times of crisis. It is useful to consider the "crisis" of the Congolese education system through the definition provided by Achille Mbembe (2000, 269) that there is a crisis when there is no longer a coincidence between the "everyday practice of life" and "the stock of signifiers or meanings available to explain and interpret what happens." According to him, crisis is also a time when the perspectives of short term, middle term, and long term are so deeply intricate that traditional ways of acting are no longer available. As an example, in the early 1990s there was an immediate need to guarantee the functioning of the school system; in the middle term, teachers and staff had to be paid for the current year, and in the long term was the need to make the education sector work. The postcolonial system in place until then was no longer practicable.

In order to reconstruct the logic behind the "maneuvers" and the solutions people employed to keep school running despite the crisis, Mbembe suggests paying attention to what and how they speak about it. He writes that they tell us a lot about how they perceive themselves as agents in what is happening or what they are trying to make happen (272). My informants reminded me that the national state and the regional divisions provide national guidelines[3] for the entire country but that these are not applied everywhere and not consistently. I inferred that we can talk about "multiple legitimate practices" (Titeca and De Herdt 2011) at work within the negotiating context of education. This means that a variety of actors operate within the education sector: national and regional state institutions, religious congregations, and private individuals who possess capital for building up and running a private school.

It is important to remember that concepts such as "real governance" and "negotiated order" are not exclusive to postcolonial states. Worldwide, the state is, to a certain extent, founded upon a negotiated order between formal institutions and society, a negotiation that takes place at different levels of the social structure and with a varying degree of flexibility.

However, in postcolonial contexts, these concepts allow us to question the validity of some ideas related to Western states that do not function appropriately when applied to Africa. I refer, for instance, to concepts such as "corruption" (Blundo et al. 2006), "public service" (Olivier de Sardan 2010), and "informal economy" (Guyer 2004, 2014; Adebanwi 2017).

In my fieldwork, people I met often spoke about the national state in terms of "absence." As mentioned in the introduction, people talk about the state both in terms of a lack of taking responsibility on the part of state representatives and in terms of "occultism." These representations of the state, as expressed by Lubumbashi's inhabitants, are expressed in very similar terms in other cities of Congo as well. In the capital city of Kinshasa, the Kinois talk about *mboka ekufi* (a dead country), meaning that death is the only element of democracy currently present in the DRC (De Boeck 2005, 17).

In Lubumbashi and Kinshasa, the meanings associated with the state are different from the ideas of a "failing," "weak," or "collapsed" state. I would say that they express quite the opposite. They reflect a moral discourse about "those in power." As I understand it, the moral concept of the state put forward by the Lushois, at least, is a legacy of the colonial era. More specifically, it is a sort of nostalgia for the *État providence* (welfare state) (Jewsiewicki 1976), a paternalistic regime imposed by the colonial administration, the mining industry, and by the religious missions involved in the educational sector (Dibwe 2001; Rubbers 2013).

The Evolution of the Education Sector since the 1990s

The origins of the Congolese school system date back to the colonial period. Since the time of King Leopold's Congo Free State and, above all, from 1908, when Leopold handed over the Congo to the Belgian administration, colonial administrations gave a near monopoly to the churches, especially the Catholic Church, to organize the education sector (Boyle 1995), and the 1906 convention between the Vatican and the Congo Free State established the basis for Catholic school development. In 1908, the few public schools founded under the colonial administration, run by lay staff, were transferred to Belgian teaching congregations (Tshimanga 2001).

A fundamental step in the evolution of the education sector occurred in the second half of the twentieth century. Mobutu's Mouvement Populaire de la Révolution imposed the complete nationalization of the education sector and school buildings in 1971. In 1977, Mobutu's regime acknowledged its inability to manage the school system and gave schools back to the church. While claiming that the only organizing power responsible for education was the state, the regime signed the Convention de gestion des écoles nationales (Poncelet, André, and De Herdt 2010). The education sector was thus divided into five networks: the official network (*écoles officielles*), where schools are directly managed by the state, and four "conventionized" networks in which schools are each managed by a different religious network, namely Catholic schools (*écoles conventionnées catholiques*) run by either a Catholic congregation or a parish and its priest; Kimbaguiste schools; Protestant schools; and Islamic schools. There also exist private schools that are not financed by public authorities. Each of these networks has its own administration, even though they are strongly linked to state institutions. For example, every Catholic diocese has a Catholic coordination office (*Coordination diocesaine des écoles conventionnées et privées catholiques*). While the Coordination responds to the Catholic bishop, it is subjected to control by regional state agents. Moreover, the agents who work in these offices are civil servants who receive state salaries (Titeca and De Herdt 2011). It is a rather complex administrative organization considering that three-quarters of primary schools are Catholic conventionized schools (De Herdt, Titeca, and Wagemakers 2011).

With the application of the adjustment programs in 1980, the hybrid system of the Congolese education sector was quickly unable to provide a salary to teachers.[4] In 1992, following the strike by unpaid teachers, the Zaïre Episcopal Conference (Conférence épiscopale du Zaïre) and the National Parents Association (Association nationale des parents d'élèves [ANAPE]) took over the payment of teachers' salaries within the Catholic network under the form of a "motivation bonus" (*prime de motivation*). This was meant to be a temporary solution; however, it has become an institutionalized practice. Today, in any school's administrative office in Katanga, and throughout the country, school staff and parents have to deal with the *frais d'intervention ponctuelle* (FIP), which have been popularly, and ironically, renamed *frais d' intervention permanente* (permanent intervention fees). Over time, the FIP system has become complex and now supports the entire school system, from the remotest school to the highest offices responsible for the public management of the education sector (Titeca and De Herdt 2011, 222). Scholars commenting on the education sector in the DRC emphasize that the FIP system is a de facto private system that proved particularly effective to the point of financing about 90 percent of all costs of the sector (ibid.). This explains why, when confronted with an ongoing process of deinstitutionalization, the school sector has not only survived but expanded, with the number of enrollments increasing exponentially over the last two decades (De Herdt, Tshipamba, and Musasal 2008; Poncelet, André, and De Herdt 2010; Titeca and De Herdt 2011).

What do school staff and parents think about the current situation of the Congolese education sector? These are some of the most recurrent ideas running throughout my interviews:

"Here, in the Congo, education is a competitive institution" (Ici chez nous l'enseignement est un pouvoir compétitif)—administrative officer;

"The state has liberalized education: it has become like a commercial business" (L'État a libéralisé l'enseignement: ça devient comme une affaire commerciale)—a pupil's father;

"The school has become like the market: there is competition" (L'école devient comme le marché: il y a une concurrence)—a teacher at the Kasungami's secondary school;

"The state must take up its responsibilities" (L'État doit prendre ses résponsabilités)—a secondary student's parent.

Broadly speaking, awareness of how the education sector functions leads staff and parents to express fierce criticism about the dramatic commodification of education. Despite the fact that the state plays a formal role in regulating the education sector, informants, almost without exception, address their criticisms toward two key school figures: the school promoters (*promoteurs des écoles*) and the school principals (*chefs d'établissement*)—and less frequently to teachers. Promoters and school principals are thought to be more interested in the economic return secured by the FIPs than in providing their schools with easy access to, and a good level of, education. A young father in Kasungami was clear in pointing out: "Most of the promoters are businessmen; they have a lot of money; they build it [school buildings], and what they are interested in is the monthly fees. . . . Formally the education system remains managed by the state. . . . But from an economic point of view, those who support schools are the parents."[5]

I don't think it's that relevant here whether all school promoters are businessmen (*commerçants*) or not. What I found interesting in this kind of argument is parents' awareness about the "indirect private government" (Mbembe 2001) of the Congolese education sector. As effectively explained by the father quoted above, despite the fact that free compulsory education is a state obligation,[6] education is either provided by private operators, as for private schools, or, for public schools, supported by parents. This system clearly contradicts the idea of education as a public service, and the Lushois see that. From this contrast derives a widespread narrative that depicts the state as an "irresponsible" institution. I have heard the following example of this narrative many times in Lubumbashi: "In the past, it was when *the state has resigned* and no longer paid teachers [and] students could not study anymore. So there were parents who realized that *children of politicians* were sent to study elsewhere because *they had means:* to Europe, to South Africa, to much more developed countries. Now, *children of the poor* remained uneducated since the state could not pay. So there has been an agreement between parents and teachers. Parents thought that, as the state had become negligent, they had to support themselves."[7]

The discourse on *l'État démissionnaire* is a widespread narrative in Lushois society. It expresses some local concepts about the evolution of the educational sector and of the contemporary state. Rather than an account of a failed state, the "state that resigns" expresses an open accusation to the ruling class ("the politicians") who divert the state's resources for personal benefit. As previously said, this is, above all, a moral discourse.[8] A second aspect that frames this discourse is the sharp contrast between two "social classes": politicians' children and the children of the poor. While most likely not all wealthy children are children of politicians, this account structures the narrative through which people feel and see social differentiation. Formal education is therefore a powerful instrument of social differentiation through which people define themselves as belonging to a more or less well-off social milieu, between those who have means and those who are "poor." In the memories of my informants, the event of 1992 remains alive: the agreement between the social parties that prevented a national strike of teachers (*l'année blanche*). Beyond the actual "contract" between the Catholic Church and the parents' associations, my informants insisted on the social value of this agreement that provided teachers a salary. For them, it was an agreement made out of the institutional space and between people who share the same problems (mainly economic) and who share the same desire of not excluding their children from formal education. In this regard, it is important to note that formal education in Katanga is not considered exclusively as a right to schooling. For Lushois, it is also a right to citizenship, to belonging to the city, a crucial element of the postcolonial identity associated with modernity. This concept is a colonial legacy. At least until the 1950s, the colonial state established a basic education with the aim to train natives as a workforce necessary for the modern economy (Masandi 1982). Colonial educational policy was designed to create a large literate base from which a cultural elite could be molded in some distant future (Vanthemsche 2012, 31). Only a minority of Congolese benefited from Western education and, consequently, to this modernity (a salary, the access to the city, an urban lifestyle, learning French, getting a Catholic education) (Yates 1981; Boyle 1995). This is the reason school education under Belgian administration was initially provided in regional languages rather than in French. Things changed on the edge of independence, and by late 1950 limited access to French-language education and to the metropolitan system was available (Jewsiewicki 1976, 102). From then, school became an effective interface providing people with an access to modernity. From the 1990s onward, despite the decline of the education sector, access to formal education remained a sort of filter between modern people and those considered "uncivilized"—that is, coming from the countryside.

The desire to belong to modern society is essential to grasping what my informants meant when they talked about the 1992 agreement between the Catholic Church and the parents' associations. In their discourses, the "social contract" that allowed their children to get access to formal education is not an agreement made with the national state but, rather, between men and women, fathers and mothers, who consider themselves members of the same society. This idea is well expressed by the phrase "support ourselves" (*nous nous prenons en charge*) used by one of my informants. "Support yourself/ourselves" is an idea slightly different from *se débrouiller* (fend for yourself), considered by many scholars the main feature of the ordinary ethics of the Congolese (Ayimpam 2014). As I understand it, in the Katangese context, which is different from Kinshasa,[9] "support yourself" shows an ethics of responsibility that is inherent in the history of the region.

Discourses on education and the state are shared within very different social contexts, from the Lubumbashi city center to its outskirts, including Kasungami. As we move from discourse to practice, from one social context to another, the differences between how people talk about the state and education become more evident. The variety of the practices used to manage schools on a daily basis depends on a particular negotiated order and on multiple legitimate practices within the same negotiating context. The discourses deriving from these practices may also be different from one context to another.

In order to get deeper into this question, I propose a comparison between a school complex in Kasungami and that of a well-known Catholic school of the city center.

"Beacoup de théorie et peu de pratique": Everyday School Interactions in Kasungami

The quotation in this section's title is taken from a conversation I had with the accountant of the Kasungami primary school where I based my research. "Much theory and little practice" reflects the nature of the relationship between people involved in the school and the state agents.

Kansungami is an unplanned and semirural district of the suburban belt south of Lubumbashi (*commune* Annexe).[10] Heavily populated, unofficial estimates report that Kasungami's population, in a little more than ten years, has increased from nineteen thousand to more than forty-six thousand inhabitants, of which 60 percent are children and young people of school age (zero to seventeen years).[11]

The most frequent subject when talking with Kasungami's dwellers is that of security. In this respect, the perception of the state is, at best, one of complete absence, and often of one that colludes with criminals and thieves. It does not seem to be simply a matter of "perception." As with other suburbs of Lubumbashi, Kasungami is a neighborhood that often makes headlines for murders, thefts, and attacks by armed men who are suspected of being complicit with policemen. This is why the new police station in the district has not really made people feel safer.

Concerning the education sector, according to unofficial estimates, there are seventy-five schools in Kasungami. Only two are Catholic conventionized schools and are therefore run conjointly by the state and the religious congregation. All the other schools have been promoted, and built, by private individuals. For the inhabitants of Kasungami, the state's inertia in school construction is the clearest sign of its absence and its lack of interest in the well-being of the population. Conversely, the Catholic Church has always played a role of a "parastate." The oldest school in Kasungami is a Catholic primary school founded in 1983 by an Italian missionary and managed by the regional division of the Department of Education.

During my fieldwork, I spent much of my time in this school, which is part of the largest school complex in Kasungami. It houses a primary school and a secondary school promoted by Kasungami's parish. This school has long been in an ambiguous situation in regard to its official status. For many years it has been *mécanisée,* or "mechanized," meaning owned by the state but managed by a Catholic congregation. Nonetheless, it turned into a private school in 2017. As we will see, this is not a minor detail.

This school complex is an example of the institutional fragmentation that characterizes the Congolese school system. The promoter of both schools, primary and secondary, is the Catholic parish, which had been managed for over thirty years by the same Catholic congregation. Recently, pointedly, it passed from one congregation to another with the new curate, who, in October 2017, had taken office just a week before my arrival in Kasungami. Both schools depend on the Catholic Bureau of Education (Coordination diocesaine des écoles conventionnées et privées catholiques). Nevertheless, the Coordination, despite being an administrative office of the Catholic diocese, works as an intermediary body between the state and the school. Like all the others, Catholic schools must be recognized by the state and have to respect the national program and legislation. They are subjected to controls made by the competent provincial subdivision. A small number of Kasungami school teachers are mechanized (mécanisée), which means they are officially employed by the state from which they receive a wage. My informants claimed to get between 60,000 to 100,000 FC ($50–$83) per month from the state, depending on their position. However, the functioning costs and the bulk of teachers' salaries are paid by the school itself through the FIP.

In a social context of poverty like in Kasungami, the FIP system requires a flexibility with the fixation and payment of school fees. "I think that 95 percent of parents in Kasungami are unemployed, in the sense that they do not have a fixed salary,"[12] said the director of the primary school. He continued, "That's why, when you ask for the parents' profession on the enrollment form, you will find 'liberal.'"[13] And in regard to flexibility, the director commented that "the decision about the fees is not the school's responsibility; the school can and must have arguments to defend why it is asking for that [amount]."[14]

A contradiction that arises in trying to reconcile the formal administrative needs with the flexibility of fees payment is beautifully summarized by the already quoted accountant of the primary school: "it's all about much theory and little practice." He referred to the disposition of the national government, which declares at the beginning of every school year that primary and secondary education is free of charge for parents.[15] In Katanga, for the year 2017–18, the provincial government announced free elementary school; however, the government directive referred opaquely only to the cost of annual enrollment fees of 100 FC. It did not refer to the administrative and teachers' salaries that the school is forced to bear, which it does by demanding a monthly contribution from parents. This means that families, despite the "free" enrollment for the year 2017–18, would still have to pay the usual long list of fees.

The distance between "theory" and "practice," to requote the primary school accountant, is found also in some examples taken from the ethnography of the Kasungami secondary school. The school is headed by a principal (*préfet*), an educational director (*responsable pédagogique*), and an administrator (*administrateur économique*). At the high school, Salomon and Innocent, the educational director and the administrator, respectively, have been my key informants. The school has approximately 350 students. School fees are divided in "payable fees" (*frais versable*) and "monthly fees" (*frais mensuelles*). In the 2017 school year, the FIP was fixed at 21,000 FC ($10.50) per student. The school's total income per month was thus 7,350,000 FC (ca. $3,700). Up to 80 percent of these fees were allocated to teachers' salaries. The daily functioning of the school and the quality of the teaching depend, above all, on the availability and regularity of the parents' FIP payment. However, the parents' monthly payment is not the only factor that permits the school's daily functioning. Another fundamental factor is the internal balance between three key figures: the promoter, the principal, and the administrator. Negotiations between these three figures depend on the official status of the school.

Let's take the case of the school principal in Kasungami. For many years the school had the status of a Catholic conventionized school: owned by the state but managed by a Catholic congregation. With this status, the principal was appointed by the provincial subdivision of the Department of Education. His role was that of *chef d'établissement,* and the school fees passed through his hands. As in many other schools in the city under these conditions, the principal's financial management responsibilities were unclear. Thus, the parish of Kasungami decided in 2016 to privatize the school, becoming the promoter and also the administrator. The role of the principal was consequently diminished in favor of the promoter and the administrator. The latter, in particular, took charge of the perception and redistribution of the FIP. The change of the school's status led eventually to a tough confrontation between the principal, the curate—who had become the promoter—and the administrator. Innocent recalled the conflict in these terms: "Now when they changed [status] and it became private, and I, a simple teacher, became an administrator, I had to manage the money. He [the principal] was in charge of the pedagogy. It's like he didn't accept it. So he was always out of school. He provoked a form of revolt. He pushed parents to revolt against the parish. He had become such a danger to the school that he sabotaged some of the school's practices so that it would not move forward."[16]

After the school changed from conventionized to private, the principal, who was still formally entitled to be the *chef d'établissement,* was no longer in charge of the school's management and lost any legitimacy he had in the eyes of school staff and parents. The principal was seen, by my informants, as being a state representative without any link to the Catholic community of Kasungami. He was accused of being interested only in "money," rather than in raising the quality of education (Il était venu pour l'argent [I was so often told]).

The real, day-to-day school managers were Innocent and Salomon. They ran the school and negotiated everything economic and organizational with teachers and parents. Innocent and Salomon roles were seen as legitimate because they were crucial figures within the Kasungami Catholic parish, which, beyond being the promoter of the school, makes up the core of the oldest Kasungami community. Moreover, Innocent and Salomon had extensive knowledge of Kasungami's families and community. Therefore, Innocent and Salomon were simultaneously school staff and important community representatives.

During the weeks I spent in the school office, I observed that, unlike the principal, Innocent and Salomon worked to constantly weave relationships in order to create a "negotiated order" between the school and its teachers, between the needs of the parents and pupils. There are many examples. Parents visited the school daily, especially in September and the first days of every month throughout the year. Each one came with a different problem:

a grandmother without a bulletin for the enrollment, a father who didn't have enough money for the monthly fees, a brother complaining that his younger brother stole the money for the FIP, and a young mother asking for a postponement of her three months' debt, just to give some examples. School administration was a point of reference for a variety of other issues as well. I have repeatedly heard of problems with electricity or with the district water supply brilliantly figured out by Innocent and Salomon. In some cases, private and family issues are at the heart of the negotiations taking place at school. For instance, on one of the first days of my stay in Kasungami, I found Cinzia, a sixteen-year-old girl, arguing with Salomon and Innocent because she wanted them to give her back the 21,000 FC her mother paid for enrollment, a sum that her father, a now-unemployed man, had provided after being accused by his own wife of "not being able to take on his daughter's debts." In Cinzia's case, school administrators played the role of mediators between the community's values and the conflict between Cinzia's parents. They said they "fought against anti-values" (Nous luttons pour l'harmonie au foyer, contre les anti-valeurs). By this, they meant that her father was expected to pay the school debt rather than her mother. School administrators "allowed time" for Cinzia's father to look for money and settle his debts, and they allowed that because of his reputation as a "responsible father." In cases like these, children stay enrolled, and parents can pay accumulated debts progressively. Administrators and parents thus create not only an economic agreement but also a social one based upon a common social order and a shared moral economy. In this way, the school becomes a "negotiated order": the community participates in the financial survival of the school, which is, at the same time, the context where social roles and cultural values are reaffirmed and allow a certain degree of unity within the community itself.

These examples should demonstrate the strong link between the community and its school. On the one hand, in Kasungami, state authority (in this case the principal) did not seem to have any kind of legitimacy. On the other, most negotiations were based not so much within an institutional framework but rather on a relational framework based on trust. "Trust" is an element that constantly returns in conversations with my informants in Kasungami, as it did with Innocent, who said: "Education is not a business. You must also aim at education. Insolvent cases normally exist in all schools. As you live together, you know the rhythm of payment; I know Kasungami's families, their economic and social conditions. In other cases you feel that the family has the money but there is bad will."[17]

In Kasungami, school seems to be a vector that creates unity in the community. The work that Innocent and Salomon did with parents was that of building relations based on reciprocity and trust. The core of

Kasungami's community revolves around the parish, and it does so in terms of spatial distribution, that is, the distance between the priest's house and the houses of other people. School administrators and parents know one another; to a large extent they belong to the same community, where shared social and cultural elements come into play. Much of the school staff is connected, in one way or another, with parents and community members. They may be linked by family, religious ties, or simply by friendship. Also, many members of the community work in the school (as teachers, administrators, and staff). Belonging to the same community allows them to overcome economic differences and social stigmatization, at least at school. The social and cultural closeness of the Kasungami community is what makes this school different from others in Lubumbashi's neighborhoods. Having the feeling of being part of the same community allows administrators and parents to negotiate a "social order" and to share the same "moral economy."

The management of a school that generates significant income, as in the case of Kasungami ($4,000 per month is enormous considering the economic conditions of the neighborhood), depends very concretely on the distance between the school staff, in particular those who manage the money on a daily basis, and the users of the service. In Kasungami, everyone has free access to the school administration office. It is nothing more than a large, dusty room with no functioning PCs inside.

There are no barriers, guards, or desks. There are no intermediate structures or technologies to mediate the face-to-face relationship between people. This has two main consequences. The first is that the relationship, spatial and relational, between staff and users is direct and mediated only by the social distance their roles may impose. It is a situation diametrically opposed to that in the Catholic high school in the city center. The second is that the school office becomes a main point of reference for any matter that concerns the community.

In the last part of this section, I give a brief example, taken from my ethnographic notes, that demonstrates the effect of the lack of intermediate formal structures. This absence allows, on the one hand, a "real governance" of the community and on the other hand gives room to less virtuous dynamics. The "negotiated order" performed at the high school does not exempt Innocent and Salomon from working within a context where the school is also perceived as a field of economic opportunities and personal interests. This is the case of the parents' committee of the school. In a meeting with five fathers recently appointed to the parents' committee (*comité de parents*), the men explicitly expressed to Innocent their personal interests in playing the role of parent in the committee. They asked when Innocent "was going to water their role" (il allait arroser leur rôle), which meant exempt them from the fees payment for their children and enable them to receive a *prime de motivation*. The young *papa* who led the delegation seemed to me a caricatured figure of a postcolonial subject: he was a man who showed off many "links" in Lushois society, expressed his fervent religious faith (he demanded to pray before starting the meeting, and, informally and in a funny way, claimed to "know how things work" in the school). When Innocent reminded them that the comité de parents is a voluntary service, the man replied, pretty irritated: "Think deeply [because] you have to learn to eat together" (Réfléchissez profondement [parce que] il faut apprendre à manger tous ensemble). After the meeting, while Innocent and Salomon were laughing at that, I grasped the parent's attitude and his phrase as the expression of what Jean-François Bayart (1993) called the "politic of the belly," that is, an ideology of rapacious exchange of power and a regime of opaque reciprocity.

"L'État doit prendre ses responsabilités": The "Gordian Knot" of Being a Teacher and a Parent in Lubumbashi

A huge sign, "IMARA," hangs over the entrance of the Catholic school where I conducted part of my fieldwork in 2018.

What is written upon it means, in Swahili, "strength/stability." From the very first steps into the school's courtyard, it is easy to see a big difference with respect to the precariousness of the "popular neighborhoods" (*milieux populaires*), as said by the Lushois, such as in Kasungami. Even though I had known this school for a long time, it was only in October 2017 that I came into contact with the priest who was the school's principal and the director of the religious community attached to the school complex. The school complex is a large compound in the city center of Lubumbashi. Inside the compound one finds colonial-era buildings housing secondary school classes, a primary school, a football yard, a church, and the houses of the religious community.

At our first meeting, I waited for the principal for about an hour at his office door. Another Italian priest, who had been a missionary in Congo for about sixty years, was to introduce me to him. It just so happened, while we were waiting for the principal, that the Italian priest talked to me about Kasungami, a district where he spent forty years as the parish priest and where he built the primary school.

When Father Peter arrived and I tried to introduce my research, he was keen to point out right from the start that "there are things that are not negotiable: punctuality, cleanliness, and discipline" (Il y a des choses qui ne sont pas négociables: la ponctualité, la propreté et la discipline).

The brief but powerful introduction of Father Peter was important in helping me to understand the context that I was in. Although the pride of the whole school is its claim that it educates the ruling class, the *père préfet*

FIGURE 2. Catholic High School in Lubumbashi's city center, 23 September 2018. © Edoardo Quaretta.

said, "The state? It doesn't exist" (L'État? Ça n'existe pas). This apparent contradiction in terms is a kind of fundamental postulate around which Father Peter builds his discourse on the state, which is based upon the opposition between "values" and "anti-values" (*valeurs* and *anti-valeurs*). The former are "non-negotiable" and, according to him, are learned in Catholic schools; the latter belong to the ruling classes and to the state's representatives, who should be purified from "anti-values" (il faut purifier l'État des anti-valeurs). Compared with other registers used by people to talk about their experience as citizens (the state's absence, the state that resigns) in this huge former colonial school, the Catholic Church, rather than a "substitute" of the state, as in the case of Kasungami, seemed to be a competitor.

The fundamental difference between the school in Kasungami and the large complex in the city center (2,200 students) is that, as evidenced by the short sentences of the principal, relations between the school staff, and among parents, are based on non-negotiable "values" ("punctuality, cleanliness, discipline"). The management of the school administration is in fact hierarchically structured and is characterized by a strict separation of roles and control of tasks.

The secretariat building was built in 2016, on the initiative of the dynamic Father Peter. Located in the center of the compound, it has a balcony along all its sides from which the principal could observe every corner of the compound, but no one could see him, since windows and doors were mirrored.

On the ground floor was the library, and on the first floor was the director's office, furnished with a large wooden desk and leather chairs and decorated with expensive tiles. The small, narrow secretariat was located next to the office of the father. A young *frère* (brother) who patrolled the courtyard was "responsible for the discipline." Enrollment at this school is permitted only for students from other schools run by the same congregation or that guarantee a similar level of education: "C'est plus facile" (It is easier), Father Peter told me. "Ils sont déjà disciplinés," (They are already disciplined), he explained further.

Mama Jeanne was in charge of the *perception* of school fees ("I have work here since I got my bachelor in commercials in 1982"). At the end of the workday, she gave all the money and "reports" to the young *frère*, who was in charge of the "maintaining of discipline." The *frère* delivered the school's daily income to the *père préfet*. The delivery of school fees from parents did not require any direct contact between administrators and parents. Instead, it was mediated through a *logiciel d'explotation* (computer software). Parents paid fees for the current month to Mama Jeanne, which allowed no room for negotiation on the amount and timing of payment. To parents approaching the desk, Mama Jeanne asked the name of the student for whom they were paying. From behind the glass, behind the computer screen of the logiciel d'explotation of which Mama Jeanne was proud of ("I learned to use it in two days"), she issued payment receipts. "It's the machine, my brother," said Mama Jeanne to anyone who tried to protest about the fees increase or the rise in the exchange rate from the Congolese franc to dollars.

The payment of teachers was also made through a procedure that excludes any form of negotiation. Their salaries are paid directly to their bank accounts. The teachers' salaries, just like in any other school, depended on

FIGURE 3. The secretariat building built in 2016 on the initiative of the dynamic Father Peter Lubumbashi, 23 September 2018. © Edoardo Quaretta.

the FIP and therefore on the number of students enrolled. In contrast with Kasungami, where the school's "social order" was negotiated essentially between parents and administrators, in Father Peter's school the negotiating space was dominated by the relationship between administrators and teachers. Thus, it was all about negotiation within the institution. That was because, as we have seen, the formal organization of the school did not leave the parents any room for negotiation with school staff.

In this context, my research focused on teachers. In the conversations I had with them, they often referred back to "1992," just like their colleagues in Kasungami. The year 1992 was crucial for them, because it changed the school sector. For instance, Mama Marie, a teacher mécanisée of the French language and culture who had been employed since 1986, had lucid memories of those years: "When I started, there was no FIPs. We survived with the government's pay. It was insignificant, but we survived with that. Now, following the strikes of 1992, we started with the FIPs. At first it was insignificant, but it was something more than what we received from the state. Today, because it is normal, there are FIPs in state schools."[18]

Although the FIP system allowed the teachers in this large Catholic school to receive a decent salary (approximately $700 per month), the sharpest criticisms were directed to the system imposed by the *reseau catholique* (the Catholic Coordination) of the *partage de l'enveloppe* (literarily "the envelope sharing"), as the "ventilation" mechanism of FIPs was usually called. This latter is a distribution mechanism (ventilation) in which money collected from parents is filtered up to the highest levels: the fees are collected from parents at the school level, and the money is passed on to the district level (for state schools this is the division, and for religious schools it is the Catholic network offices). In turn, these offices passed the money on to the various state institutions responsible for running the "public" education sector.

Most teachers considered the system of redistribution of FIP as something concealed, an occult mechanism imposed from above. In the 1990s, the money from the FIP was intended, as the teachers explained to me, to pay the so-called *enseignants débuts* (standup teachers). The FIP was not meant to "feed the system" of the *enseignants assis* (seated teachers), that is, the administrators, who were from the offices of the Coordination Catholique and the Ministry of Education, who "all benefit from FIPs" (tous en tirent profit de FIP). Like in Kasungami, and also in the context of this Catholic school, the opposition to the state, understood as an undefined social space with an obscure functioning, punctuates teachers' discourses. In these discourses, however, unlike the ones in Kasungami, there emerged more clearly the issue of social conflict between the ruling class and ordinary people: "Parents want that their children can study. Because the authorities can send their children to Europe, South Africa or elsewhere. Their children do not study here; they study in good conditions. But when there will be a change at the head of state, who will replace the ruling class? Their own children in whom their system of government has been instilled. So we'll always have the same problem. That's how the parents thought, we might as well let our children study . . . so they can also replace those in government positions."[19]

Here again, the conception of the state was, on the one hand, described as an entity whose representatives are greedy, think about their own interests, and are negligent toward those of their citizens. Thus we return to a moral discourse, according to which, concluded Mama Marie, "FIPs allow me to make ends meet, send my children to school, and pay the rent. But the state must take up again its responsibilities."[20] Many teachers, who still taught in this school, have been employed for more than twenty years, and in some cases thirty. Many shared a feeling of nostalgia for an *État providence,* that "foresaw a certain budget for education, in colonial times, and even a few years after independence, which is no longer the case now."[21]

The discourse of an "absent" and "occult" state is directly linked to the ambivalence of many toward occupying the double role of teacher and parent at the same time. "We parents, we have put the rope around our necks without knowing it" (Nous, les parents nous nous sommes mis la corde au cou sans le savoir) said Papa Jacques, the teacher of pedagogy. Jacques talked about a "Gordian knot" for those who were in the condition of being both parent and teacher. The system that allowed him to survive was also the one that put them in crisis: "We, teacher-parents, who pay the FIPs, we are between the hammer and the anvil" (Nous les enseignants-parents, qui payons le FIP, nous sommes entre le marteau et l'enclume). The main problem, according to Papa Jacques, was the ineffectiveness of the state in regulating access to primary and secondary education and the informal institutionalization of the FIP, which has transformed since the 1992 agreement, and which initially was stipulated between teachers and parents. Papa Jacques explained to me that "parents' will" to support the teachers' salary, who were themselves considered primarily as parents, has gradually become institutionalized into a *droit:* a right claimed by school staff and a social obligation for parents. The whole system was therefore conceptually based on the concept of parents' "responsibility," a responsibility toward children and family and one toward schools. The burden for teachers and parents to define themselves as "responsible" was such that it allowed the perpetuation of the system. This was particularly true for those parents who were also teachers: "So not to be accused of being irresponsible, so that my children do not come here to the workplace if chased from their school, I even go into debt" (Pour ne pas être taxé d'irresponsable, pour que mes enfants ne viennent pas ici sur le lieu de travail si chassés de leur école, je vais même à m'endetter), concluded Papa Jacques.

A final issue mobilized by teachers was about their retirement. Given that neither the state nor the Catholic Coordination guaranteed a pension to teachers, investing in their children's education was a means to secure one's future. When teachers talked about the future, they directed their discourse toward the younger generation: "We spend because it is a long-term investment. We have to send them to school [our children]. We must fulfill our duty as parents. In the meantime, we are getting older, and won't these children take care of us? It's the other way around. We must prepare for our old age. When you're old, you expect your children to take care of you too."[22]

This quote reminds us that in Lubumbashi, formal education constitutes a pillar of the social contract among generations. It defines the logic of reciprocity between parents and children (Alber, van der Geest, and Whyte 2008). Much more so than in Kasungami, in the city center Catholic school conversations with teachers reminded me that parents and elders (*ainés*) found their authority in their ability to meet their children's basic needs (food, clothes, a home) and, above all, to pay school fees. To define oneself as a responsible and reliable father or elder implies the ability to access the education system (*faire grandir à l'école*). In this sense, the FIP system, while ensuring the functioning of the education sector, unloaded the burden onto families and individualized school access. It thus generated the paradox that teachers and parents have tried to explain during my fieldwork in this school in the city center of Lubumbashi.

In the school year 2019–20, like every year, the debate about—and the government's declarations about—free schooling, made the headlines of Congolese newspapers.[23] As in the past, the announcements of the new government created expectations and uncertainty in regard to school access for millions of Congolese children.

I have tried to demonstrate that the resilience of the educational system and the resistance of its administrative configuration is an example of what Achille Mbembe calls "indirect private government" (2001). While giving an illusion of being state apparatus, this process of privatization has consequences on the functioning of the educational institutions, and, more widely, on the construction of the social reality within and beyond schools.

Indirect school privatization has created a market system where the desire of individual enrichment seems to be dominant. However, Kasungami's case study shows that, in a social reality dominated by a feeling of trust, there is room for community practices. In this context, the school plays the role of "social interface" in driving these practices, where a social order and a moral economy of a small community are reaffirmed in school public space against conflicts and contestations actually taking place in the private and domestic spaces of families.

In suburban areas such as Kasungami, the state is mostly perceived as absent. The absence of public school is, for people, the clearest sign of the state's absence and its lack of interest in the well-being of the population. Interpersonal relations of the community are thus fundamental, and the Catholic parish is the institutional agent that regulates the governance of the school and acts as the interface between the Church and Kasungami inhabitants.

In the school complex in the city center, "bureaucratization" consists of a process of depersonalization and mechanization of relationships and social practices. This leads to a decrease in social negotiation that, in turn, increases the school's effectiveness but, nevertheless, also in an individualization of school costs and a limitation to school access. In this context, teachers are subjects who allow the reproduction of the FIP system, but, at the same time suffer its adverse effects. Most teachers consider the system of redistribution of FIP, and the entire institutional apparatus, in terms of *occultism,* a word that echoes the concept of "sorcerer state." This narrative is particular significant. "Sorcerer state" expresses the same dangers as "witch" in popular speech. As an individual who increases his or her power and well-being to the detriment of others, a witch "eats others" and is antisocial—just like politicians.

Congolese narratives on the state (the state's absence, the sorcerer state, the resigning and irresponsible state) reveal daily anxieties not only about people's present but also about the future of their children. The absence, irresponsibility, and rapacity of the state gives citizens the sense of being deprived of what they need, be it vital force, luck, health, or offspring. This is why these narratives are so widespread in the discussions about school.

Notes

1. Data and analyses presented in this article are the result of ethnographic research I conducted in Lubumbashi October–November 2017 and September–October 2018.
2. In order to maintain confidentiality for my informants' personal data, I will use pseudonyms throughout the text and will not use the real names of schools and institutions concerned.
3. The national ministry in charge of education policies is Ministère de l'Éducation; at the regional level, it is the Division de l'enseignement.
4. "Real expenditure per pupil dropped from US\$159 in 1982 to \$23 in 1987 and finally to around \$4 in 2002. Teachers' salaries dropped from \$68 to \$27 per month between 1982 and 1987, reaching an absolute minimum of \$12.90 in 2002" (Titeca and De Herdt 2011, 221).
5. Interview with Christophe, Lubumbashi, 26 September 2018. My translation from the French: "La plupart des promoteurs ce sont des commerçants, ils ont beaucoup d'argent; ils construisent [des bâtiments scolaires] et ce qui leur intéresse ce sont les frais mensuelles. . . . Formellement le système éducatif reste géré par l'État. . . . Mais d'un point de vue économique, ce qui prennent en charge l'école sont les parents."
6. This right is guaranteed by the Congolese Constitution, article 46: "Education in primary public schools is free and compulsory."
7. Interview with Innocent, Lubumbashi, 10 October 2017. Emphasis added. My translation from the French: "Dans le temps, c'est quand *l'État a démissionné* qui ne payait plus les enseignants [et] les élèves ne pouvaient plus étudier. Alors il y a [eu] les parents qui ont constaté que *les enfants des politiciens* on les envoyait étudier ailleurs parce qu'*ils ont des moyens:* en Europe, en Afrique du Sud, dans les pays beaucoup plus développés. Maintenant *les enfants des pauvres* se trouvaient sans éducation, puisque l'État ne savait pas payer. Alors il y eu une convention entre les parents et les enseignants. Les parents se sont dit que comme l'État devient démissionnaire nous nous prenons en charge."
8. Such narratives are also expressed in contemporary popular music and the arts. The young generation of Katangese musicians, for example, denunciate corruption among politicians through their songs. See Mutombo (2019).

9. For a recent analysis of the education sector, with a focus on Kinshasa, see Pype (2015). In this article the author claims that the meaning of being a *diplômé* in the capital city has changed from describing a figure who possesses book knowledge to a person who possess street knowledge, which itself comes from experience with the informal and the illegal.

10. Cf. Bruneau and Pain (1990).

11. *Rapport annuel de la Commune Annexe 2015,* quoted in Ngonga Kasawa (2017, 34).

12. "Je pense que 95 percent de parents à Kasungami sont des chômeurs, dans le sens où n'ont pas de salaire fixe."

13. "C'est pourquoi quand on demande la profession des parents sur la fiche d'inscription vous trouverez 'libéral.'"

14. Interview with Oscar, Kasungami primary school, 30 September 2017. My translation from the French: "la fixation des frais, ce n'est pas l'école qui s'impose; l'école peut proposer et doit avoir des arguments pour défendre pourquoi elle demande ça [un tel montant]."

15. Similar claims were made as I wrote this: https://www.radiookapi.net/2019/08/22/actualite/education/rdc-le-gouvernement-supprime-les-frais-de-scolarite-de-lenseignement.

16. Interview with Innocent, Lubumbashi, 26 September 2018. My translation from the French: "Maintenant quand ils ont changé [de statut] et c'est devenu privée, et moi, un simple enseignant, suis devenu administrateur je devais gérer l'argent. Lui [the principal] devez s'occuper de la pédagogie. C'est comme s'il n'acceptait pas. Donc il s'absentait. Il a mis en oeuvre une forme de révolte. Il sensibilisait les parents afin que ils se révoltent contre la paroisse. Il était devenu un danger pour l'école au point de saboter certaines pratiques de l'école afin qu'elle n'avance pas."

17. Interview with Innocent, Lubumbashi, 26 September 2018. My translation from the French: "L'enseignement n'est pas un commerce. Vous devez viser aussi à l'éducation. Les cas insolvables existent normalement dans toutes les écoles. . . . Au fur et à mesure que vous vivez ensemble vous connaissez le rythme de payement; je connais les familles de Kasungami: leur condition économique, sociale. Dans d'autres cas vous ressentez que la famille a l'argent mais il y a mauvaise volonté."

18. Interview with Marie, Lubumbashi, 2 October 2018. My translation from the French: "Quand j'ai commencé, il n'y avait pas de FIP. On se contentait de la paye de l'État. C'était insignifiant mais on se contentais de ça. Maintenant, suite aux grèves de 1992 on a commencé avec le FIP. Au début c'était insignifiant mais c'était quelque chose de plus par rapport à ce que nous recevions de la part de l'État. Jusqu'aujourd'hui car on trouve normale qu'il y ait des FIP dans les écoles de l'État."

19. Interview with Marie, Lubumbashi, 2 October 2018. My translation from the French: "Les parents tiennent à ce que leurs enfants puissent étudier. Parce que les autorités envoient leurs enfants en Europe, en Afrique du Sud ou ailleurs. Leurs enfants n'étudient pas ici, ils étudient dans des bonnes conditions. Or, quand il y aura changement à la tête de l'État, qui va remplacer la classe dirigeante? Leurs propres enfants à qui ont inculqué leur système de

gouvernement. Donc on aura toujours le même problème. C'était ainsi que les parents se sont dit, autant faire étudier les nôtres . . . de sorte qu'ils peuvent aussi remplacer ceux qui sont aux postes de direction."

20. Interview with Marie, Lubumbashi, 2 October 2018. My translation from the French: "les FIP me permet de nouer les deux bouts du mois, de scolariser mes enfants, de payer un logement. Mais l'État doit reprendre ses responsabilités."

21. Interview with Jacques, Lubumbashi, 1 October 2018. My translation from the French: "[l'État] renfermait un certain budget pour l'éducation, à l'époque coloniale, et même quelques années après l'indépendance. Ce qui n'est plus le cas maintenant."

22. Interview with Jacques, Lubumbashi, 1 October 2018. My translation from the French: "Nous faisons des dépenses parce que c'est un investissement à long terme. On doit les scolariser [nos enfants]. Nous devons accomplir notre devoir de parents en tant que parent. Entretemps nous vieillissons, est-ce que ces enfants-là ne vont pas nous prendre en charge? C'est vice-versa. Nous devons préparer notre vieillesse. Quand on est vieux, on s'attend que nos enfants nous prennent aussi en charge."

23. See, for instance, Revue de Pressecongolaise, par Congo Forum, 12 September 2019, https://www.congoforum.be/fr/; "RDC: le gouvernement supprime les frais de scolarité de l'enseignement primairedans les écoles publiques," Radio Okapi, 21 August 2019, https://www.radiookapi.net/2019/08/22/actualite/education/rdc-le-gouvernement-supprime-les-frais-de-scolarite-de-lenseignement; "RDC: des experts de l'éducation réfléchissent sur la matérialisation de la gratuité de l'enseignement primaire Publié," Radio Okapi, 22 August 2019, https://www.radiookapi.net/2019/08/22/actualite/education/rdc-des-experts-de-leducation-reflechissent-sur-la-materialisation-de.

References

Adebanwi, Wale, ed. 2017. *The Political Economy of Everyday Life in Africa. Beyond the Margins.* Woodbridge, UK: James Currey.

Alber, Erdmute, Sjaak van der Geest, and Susan Reynolds Whyte, eds. 2008. *Generations in Africa: Connections and Conflict.* Berlin: Lit Verlag.

Ayimpam, Sylvie. 2014. *Économie de la débrouille à Kinshasa: Informalité, commerce et réseaux sociaux.* Paris: Karthala.

Bayart, Jean-François. 1993. *The State in Africa: The Politics of the Belly.* London: Longman.

Boyle, Patrick M. 1995. "School Wars: Church, State, and the Death of the Congo." *Journal of Modern African Studies* 33 (3): 451–68.

Blundo, Giorgio, Jean-Pierre Olivier de Sardan, N. Bako Arifari, and M. Tidjani Alou. 2006. *Everyday Corruption and the State: Citizens and Public Officials in Africa.* London: Zed Books.

Bruneau, Jean-Claude, and Marc Pain. 1990. *Atlas de Lubumbashi.* Université de Paris X Nanterre, Centre d'Étudesgéographiques sur l'Afrique Noire.

Chabal, Patrick, and Jean-Pascal Daloz. 1999. *Africa Works: Disorder as Political Instrument.* Oxford: James Currey.

De Boeck, Filip. 2000. "Le 'deuxième monde' et les 'enfants-sorciers' en République Démocratique du Congo." *Politique africaine* 80:32–57.

————. 2005. "The Apocalyptic Interlude: Revealing Death in Kinshasa." *African Studies Review* 48 (2): 11–32.

De Boeck, Filip, and Marie-Françoise Plissart. 2014. *Kinshasa: Tales of the Invisible City.* Leuven: Leuven University Press.

De Herdt, Tom, Kristof Titeca, and Inga Wagemakers. 2011. "Making Investment in Education Part of the Peace Dividend in the DRC." Unpublished paper written for UNESCO.

Dibwe dia Mwembu, Donatien. 2001. *Bana Shaba abandonnés par leur père: Structure de l'autorité et histoire sociale de la famille ouvrière au Katanga 1910–1997.* Paris: L'Harmattan.

Guyer, Jane I. 2004. *Marginal Gains: Monetary Transactions in Atlantic Africa.* Chicago: University of Chicago Press.

————. 2014. "Gains and Losses in the Margins of Time: From West and Equatorial History to Present Day South Africa." *Africa* 84 (1): 146–50.

Hameiri, Shahar. 2007. "Failed States or a Failed Paradigm? State Capacity and the Limits of Institutionalism." *Journal of International Relations and Development* 10 (2): 122–49.

Hibou, Béatrice. 2004. "From Privatizing the Economy to Privatising the State." In *Privatizing the State,* edited by Béatrice Hibou. New York: Columbia University Press.

Hill, Jonathan. 2005. "Beyond the Other? A Postcolonial Critique of the Failed State Thesis." *African Identities* 3 (2): 139–54.

Jewsiewicki, Bogumil. 1976. "L'expérience d'un État-Providence en Afrique noire." *Historical Reflections/Réflexions Historiques* 3 (2): 79–103.

Masandi, Kita Kyankenge. 1982. *Colonisation et enseignement: Le cas du Zaïre avant 1960.* Kisangani: Éditions du CERUKI.

Mbembe, Achille. 2000. "Everything Can be Negotiated: Ambiguities and Challenges in a Time of Uncertainty." In *Manoeuvring in an Environment of Uncertainty. Structural Change and Social Action in Sub-Saharan Africa,* edited by Boel Berner and Per Trulsson, 265–75. Aldershot, England: Ashgate.

————. 2001. *On the Postcolony.* Berkeley: University of California Press.

Mutombo, Marcel Ngandu. 2019. "Les députés nationaux perçus par les artistes musiciens de Lubumbashi." In *Dynamiques sociales et representations congolaises (RD Congo): "L'expérience fait la différence,"* edited by Rosario Giordano, Eduardo Quaretta, Donatien Dibwe dia Mwembu, 201–16. Paris: L'Harmattan.

Ngonga, Kasawa O. 2017. "Dynamique demo-spatiale de la ville de Lubumbashi, cas du quartier Kasungami." BA final diss., I.S.P. de Lubumbashi.

Olivier de Sardan, Jean-Pierre. 2008. "Researching the Practical Norms of Real Governance in Africa." APPP Discussion Paper 5. London: Overseas Development Institute.

————. 2010. "Local Governance and Public Goods in Niger." APPP Working Paper 10, London: Overseas Development Institute.

Poncelet, Marc, Géraldine André, and Tom De Herdt. 2010. "La survie de l'école primaire congolaise (RDC): héritage colonial, hybridité et resilience." *Autrepart* 2 (54): 23–41.

Pype, Katrien. 2015. "Becoming a Diplômé in Kinshasa: Education at the Intersection of Politics and Urban Livelihoods." *Diversité urbaine* 15 (1): 5–26.

Rotberg, Robert I. 2003. "Failed States, Collapsed States, Weak States: Causes and Indicators." In *State Failure and State Weakness in a Time of Terror,* edited by R. Rotberg, 5–26. Cambridge: World Peace Foundation.

Rubbers, Benjamin. 2013. *Le Paternalisme en question: Les anciens ouvriers de la Gécamines face à la libération du secteur minier katangais (RD Congo).* Paris: L'Harmattan.

Simone, Abdoumaliq. 2008. "People as Infrastructure." In *Johannesburg: The Elusive Metropolis,* edited by Sarah Nuttall and Achille Mbembe, 68–90. Durham, NC: Duke University Press.

Strauss, Anselm L. 1978. *Negotiations: Varieties, Contexts, Processes, and Social Order.* San Francisco: Jossey-Bass.

Titeca, Kristof, and Tom De Herdt. 2011. "Real Governance Beyond the 'Failed State': Negotiating Education in the Democratic Republic of the Congo." *African Affairs* 110 (439): 213–31.

Trefon, Theodore. 2004. *Reinventing Order in the Congo: How People Respond to State Failure in Kinshasa.* London: Zed Books.

Tshimanga, Charles. 2001. *Jeunesse, formation et société au Congo-Kinshasa, 1890–1960.* Paris, L'Harmattan.

Vanthemsche, Guy. 2012. *Belgium and the Congo, 1885–1980.* Cambridge: Cambridge University Press.

Yates, Barbara A. 1981. "Educating Congolese Abroad: An Historical Note on African Elites." *International Journal of African Historical Studies* 14 (1): 34–64.

FIFTEEN

Fragile Relationships

Elusive Encounters with Public Services in Rural Burkina Faso

HELLE SAMUELSEN

ON A HOT AFTERNOON IN JANUARY 2014, I VISITED
Thomas Kéré, my friend and key interlocutor, in the village of Keru,[1] located
in the east-central part of Burkina Faso. We were sitting inside Thomas's
compound, close to the wall separating his house from the house of his
wife, Beatrice. One of Thomas's children had arranged the two white, weary
metal chairs owned by the household in the shadow. The sun was baking
this afternoon as on most days of the year. At this time of the day, the
narrow spot between the two small houses is the most comfortable place in
the compound as it is the only place where shade can be found, except for
the benches under the thatched hangar where Beatrice runs her "cabaret," a
small tavern, where she sells her home-brewed millet beer. I had just arrived
at the village from Ouagadougou, the capital of Burkina Faso, and we were
sitting and exchanging news about our families since my last visit to the village. It was a good day for me to visit Thomas since many family members
were home. Beatrice was home, busy, preparing for the next cabaret, which
was to be held the following day. Pascal and Michel, Thomas's two adult
sons were there, as was Honorine, one of his five daughters, accompanied
by her little daughter. January is not a busy month in rural Burkina Faso, as
it is the dry season with no major agricultural tasks.

Many villagers use this part of the year to repair their houses and compound walls after the rainy season. Houses used to be constructed with
mud bricks with thatched roofs, and this is still quite common, though
houses are increasingly constructed with bricks made of cement and with

corrugated metal roofs. Thomas is a subsistence farmer, like most citizens living in the rural areas who have plots of land outside the village. He tends his fields with help from his children, but it is not an easy life. With seven children and a commitment to send them all to school—and a few even to high school—he struggles to make ends meet. At around sixty years old, Thomas is by local standards an elderly man. He is a devoted Christian who served for many years as a catechist in the local Catholic church. Being in the succession line of the founder of the village going at least six generations back, Thomas is a respected man in the village and is often consulted by community members for advice on various family matters. He is also a very serious and reflective man with a great interest in the world around him. I have known Thomas for more than twenty years, and we have had many conversations about family life, health, politics, and village life at various spots within the compound sitting in those two white metal chairs, where shade could best be provided at the time of the talk. However, I was taken by surprise this afternoon, when during our conversation about politics Thomas suddenly disappeared into his little bedroom house, where he keeps his few personal items, and came out a couple of minutes later with a copy of Burkina Faso's constitution in his hands. Agitated, he read from article 37, where it is explicitly stated that the president of the country can be elected for only one additional term. I was impressed, asking myself how many Danish, French, or American citizens would actually have a copy of their country's constitution at home? We had been talking about then-president Blaise Compaoré's move to change the constitution so he could run for a third term.

Compaoré had been president since 1987, and he wanted to continue for another five-year period. This proposed change of constitution was by most people seen as a strategic maneuver that should open the door for a presidency for life (Hagberg et al. 2018, 16). Obviously, he had already been reelected more than twice, but this proposed change to the constitution stirred a lot of protests and resistance toward Compaoré and his brother, who also had a prominent position in the government. It was clear from our afternoon conversation that Thomas also had strong opinions about the ruling president and his plan to stand for yet another election. As a member of the Catholic mission, Thomas had previously been involved in elections as an official at the village level. A few family members and friends passing by to say hello engaged themselves in the heated conversation and all agreed that it was unacceptable to change the constitution just to keep himself in power. Dissatisfaction and disappointment with the president and the ruling party was not new, but this new "trick" as they said, was the limit. Sitting in the shade discussing the referendum that day, Thomas and others talked positively about Sankara, the revolutionary figure who, after a coup in 1983 arranged with his friend Compaoré, served as president until 1987, when Compaoré initiated a coup against him and Sankara was killed. Sankara did positive things for the poor, they said, such as introducing an arrangement for some workers to receive part of their salary in rice and other foodstuffs to make sure that they did not drink up their whole salaries. Sankara continues to have a kind of hero status among citizens in both urban and rural Burkina Faso.

Discussions about the new presidential referendum were going on in the whole country during 2014, and a very intense period of transition took place in October and November during an "insurrection populaire"[2] (popular uprising), with a number of demonstrations in the major cities of Burkina Faso (Hagberg et al. 2018). The uprising was partly organized by the movement Balai Citoyen (the broom citizen), led by a famous Burkinabé musician. Trade unions and women groups played important roles in the protests. As a result of the uprising and strong political pressure from the international community, Compaoré finally resigned and apparently managed to escape to Côte d'Ivoire in exile with cars loaded with "state money." After a short-lived military coup in September 2015, elections were held in November 2015. The presidential election didn't go as Compaoré had wished, nor did it go as Thomas had wished.

I have carried out research in Keru and surrounding villages during different periods of fieldwork since mid-1996 (Samuelsen 1999, 2004a, 2004b; Østergaard, Bjertrup, and Samuelsen 2016). In this chapter I explore the critical relationship between rural citizens and the state from "below," taking a point of departure in the everyday formal and informal experiences of ordinary people with the state and its local representatives. While efforts to change the constitution, popular insurrections, military coups, and presidential elections are not everydayness, or part of everyday life, this recent dramatic period in Burkina Faso's history exposes the Bukinabé state as fragile. With a particular focus on the often shambolic relationship between rural citizens and the public health care system, I will discuss the consequences the "absent-present" Burkinabé state have for the everyday life of rural citizens and how it may affect the rural citizens trust in the democratic state.

Political and Social Distress

In the last decade or so, the West African region has been prone to a number of political, social, and religious conflicts. In Côte d'Ivoire, long-term political conflicts, particularly during the presidential elections in 2010, have revealed fundamental ethnic and regional tensions (Piccolino 2016). The borders to Burkina Faso were closed for a period, and when the economy of Côte d'Ivoire slowed down many Burkinabé migrants had to return to Burkina with little prospect of finding jobs. The political conflict in Mali, where jihadists have succeeded in controlling the northern part of the country has also revealed the democratic government of Mali as extremely fragile (Benjaminsen and Ba 2019). Terrorist attacks mainly by AQIM (Al-Qaeda in the Islamic Magreb) and Ansarul Islam have become more frequent, and the terrorists no longer restrict their activities to the northern part of the Sahel, where the security situation has been delicate for years. AQIM and other groups of jihadists have added new types of activities to their violent agenda through the inclusion of new spectacular actions inside the countries of Mali and Burkina Faso. In January 2016, two bomb blasts took place at a hotel and a café in Ouagadougou, the capital of Burkina Faso. AQIM claimed responsibility for the attacks. Both places were known as hubs for Western tourists, aid workers, and well-off Burkinabé citizens (all of whom have been targeted for kidnappings in recent years). New attacks followed both in different regions of the country as well as in Ouagadougou. Parallel to terrorist attacks, organized crime has also increased over the last few years, creating even more insecurity (Hagberg et al. 2018). The Ebola epidemic in Guinea, Sierra Leone, and Liberia in 2014–16 revealed how weak and vulnerable the health care systems of these countries actually were. The epidemic shattered the economies of three countries that were already among the poorest in the world. The West African region is, in other words, politically tense and economically fragile. While I agree with Mbembe (2016) that Africa as a continent has a huge future potential in business and art and in addressing the global environmental crisis, the West African region is experiencing an acceleration of insecurity and fragility.

While Burkina Faso's economy grew an average of more than 5 percent annually between 1991 and 2016, the notion of "Africa rising," a phrase used to characterize the impressive economic growth rates of many African countries, would not apply if we look at the living conditions in the rural areas of the country. The economy of Burkina Faso relies heavily on agriculture, where almost 80 percent of the population works in farming, most of them as subsistence farmers. Burkina Faso is a landlocked country with few natural resources. Cotton is the main cash crop, with gold exports playing an increasingly important role for the country's economy (Pieper, Mkandawire, and Van der Hoeven 2016). According to the World Bank, "Burkina Faso remains vulnerable to shocks related to changes in rainfall patterns and to fluctuations in the prices of its export commodities on world markets."[3]

The political history of Burkina Faso exposes the depressing facts that the government has not managed to improve the living conditions of the ordinary people significantly and that many, many people still live in absolute poverty. Burkina Faso is consistently ranked at the bottom end of the United Nations Development Programme's human development index. In 2016, the country was ranked no 185 out of 188 countries; 46 percent of the population lives below the poverty line (Zeilig 2017). Although statistics from Burkina Faso show progress over the last twenty years, the progress is considered below average for countries with a low human development index.[4] In 1996, when I started fieldwork in Burkina Faso, the total population was estimated at around 10.5 million; now it is more than 19 million, an increase that puts a lot of pressure on the land resources, the political system, and on individual families.[5] With high unemployment rates in the urban areas and a weak government that faces difficulties in delivering even the most basic services to its population, the majority of the population is to a large extent left to care for itself (Agamben 1998). Many families depend on remittances from the millions who, for shorter or longer periods, move to other countries in the region or abroad to work as unskilled laborers in the agricultural or the service sectors. It is estimated that between 1.5 and 2 million Burkinabé are migrant workers. The most popular destinations are neighboring West African countries and Gabon, Nigeria, Italy, France, and Germany. In the village of Keru, most families include one or more migrant workers, and many women and children are dependent on the remittances sent home inconsistently.

When observing everyday life and talking to the citizens of Keru, it is clear that far from all migrant stories are success stories. During my visit to Keru in 2014, when discussions about the proposed changes of the constitution were common, Thomas's family discussed the possibilities of sending Michel, the nineteen-year-old son of Thomas and Beatrice, to Côte d'Ivoire or another neighboring country to find work. They felt that he should, like many other young men, leave to make a living for himself and support the family economically, as the local options for finding work or making a living based on subsistence agriculture were very limited. He eventually went to Libya, since the borders to some of the other West African countries were closed due to the Ebola outbreak. Michel has been in Libya for more than six years but has not been able to save enough to send remittances home to the family in Keru. Pascal, Michel's older brother, had been in Côte d'Ivoire to work, but he had to return due to a serious wound in his leg that would not heal. Now, Pascal was helping in the fields and selling beer and soft drinks on market days.

The Absent-Present State

Within the social sciences we encounter a substantial amount of literature (and debate) about the definition and the role of the state, both in postmodern societies and in the postcolonial world—and, more recently, in the context of a globalized world (Bayart 1993; Blom Hansen 2001; Inda and Rosaldo 2002; Das and Poole 2004; Ferguson 2006; Sharma and Gupta 2006; Engberg-Pedersen and Andersen 2008; Adebanwi and Obadare 2010; OECD 2010; Bouchard 2011; Gupta 2012; Street 2012; Adebanwi 2017). Here, I will adopt the analysis of the state as a cultural constitution—that is, I will approach the state in terms of "how people perceive the state, how their understandings are shaped by their particular locations and intimate and embodied encounters with state process and officials and how the state manifests itself in their lives" (Sharma and Gupta 2006). This approach implies an investigation of the sphere of everyday practices, where rural citizens encounter representatives of the state, whether registering for upcoming elections at the municipality or visiting the health center. It is through such banal bureaucratic practices that the state—in the sense of it being a set of institutions—is substantiated (Sharma and Gupta 2006). How do the local bureaucrats perform their authority and how do the rural citizens relate and respond to this type of authority?

This question relates closely to Foucault's work on the history of the modern state, where the focus shifted from state sovereignty to the management of human life (Das and Poole 2004; Samuelsen and Steffen 2004; Foucault 2012). With the current political situation and the Burkinabé history in mind, I agree with Gupta (2012) that we have to look critically at both Foucault's and Agamben's theories of the state as they both position a strongly unified state apparatus as a point of departure for their respective arguments about biopolitics and sovereignty. Their analyses are mainly based on the history of state formation in the European region. The Burkinabé state has a completely different history (Savonnet-Guyot 1986) and has never been a strong unified state with a coherent bureaucracy.

Through a focus on the everyday encounters (and lack thereof) with state representatives in the village of Keru, I explore the *everyday grammar* of the state by looking at the state from "below," or from the "margins" (Das and Poole 2004). The state itself is an elusive object to study, both practically and conceptually (Bernstein and Mertz 2011), but analyzing everyday relations between citizens and state representatives will provide us with a better understanding of how the state can be (re)constituted or weakened.

Located about 250 kilometers from Ouagadougou, Keru is marginal in a simple geographical sense. In spatial terms, the village is far from the main government facilities and business locations. An infrastructural map would show how roads and facilities, such as electricity and water provision, diminish in terms of quantity and quality with distance from the capital. The citizens of Keru see themselves as marginal in many ways. Their sense of marginality is embedded in a strong hierarchical local culture, which is conscious of formal positions, age, education, and gender (Badini 1994).

The Burkinabé state takes on its role as order-maker and in a Foucauldian sense is working hard at controlling the population. On the other hand, it is a state that doesn't have the means, the capacity, or the will to secure the "bare" life of its citizens. The contemporary state of Burkina Faso is politically and institutionally fragile and incoherent; when seeing the state from below, from its margins, it could be characterized as absent-present (Law 2002; Street 2012, 2014). I understand the notion of an absent-present state in the sense that the institutions of the state are *present* (the president, the army, the schools, the health facilities, and so on), but at the same time, the state is *absent* in the sense that many of the state institutions do not manage to deliver basic services to the public (Prince 2014). Here, I draw on the definition of the absent-present in John Law's (2002) analysis of aircraft stories (and about modernity and postmodernity), where he asks: "How it is that whatever is not there is also there? How that which is there is also not there. Both/and rather than either/or. Or both/and either/or and both/and. Heterogeneity, then, is about the differences that reside in connection and disconnection. Or, more precisely, it is about the ambivalent distributions entailed in dis/connection" (96). The discourse on weak or absent-present states as discussed by Alice Street (2014) in her work on Madang Hospital in Papua New Guinea resonates very well with the situation in Burkina Faso. Street notes that in Papua New Guinea, "the state exists primarily as an absence. The state is not imagined as an abstract entity but as an urban elite of politicians and administrators who have little interest in bringing governance, and associated 'development,' to the nation's rural inhabitants" (Street 2012, 16).

Everyday Citizenship

As emphasized by Veena Das, most people encounter the state through documents such as ration cards, identity cards, criminal complaints, court papers, birth certificates, and death certificates. These documents bear the double sign of the state's distance from and its penetration into the life of the everyday. Several scholars have recently argued that it is through these documentary practices that the state makes the population legible to itself, creating what has been referred to as a "legibility effect" (Das et al. 2004, 15–16; Auyero 2012). This is also the case in Keru. The children's vaccination cards are very important documents, and mothers guard these cards carefully. Losing or misplacing a vaccination card can cause problems. Mothers are often scolded if they show up on vaccination days without the vaccination card or the antenatal care card they received when attending antenatal care services.

Documents are also required to become a voter in Burkina Faso, and this can make voting a challenging task. As Thomas explained during our long conversation about the upcoming elections that January afternoon, in order to vote one needs to bring the personal *carte d'identité* and an election card. An election card can be obtained by Burkinabé citizens over eighteen years of age; however, obtaining an election card requires bringing a birth certificate and identity card to the prefecture, where the election card then can be issued. Many people do not have a birth certificate, and some do not have identity cards either, since these are mainly used for traveling. Still, the eligibility of voters is secured through this bureaucratic and rational procedure.

In Keru, the state institutions are visible: the school and the dispensary are located at central spots in the village, and the prefecture and major's office are located in the neighboring village. The buildings are distinct from any other house or building in the village, as the architecture is unmistakably governmental. The buildings are large, square concrete constructions, usually painted red or smeared with ocher or clay and often in two colors. The glassless windows have metal blinds that are usually painted blue or white. The cement floors inside are often painted gray or brown. Generally, one finds very little furniture inside, except for a few metal benches for the public at the health centers and at the major's office and office table and chairs for the employees. At the school in Keru, which expanded from two classrooms in 1996, when I started fieldwork in the area, to six classrooms today, the classrooms are furnished with a fair number of wooden benches and tables for the children and a table and chair for the teachers and a blackboard in each classroom. However, there are no books, and the children have to bring their own pencils and notebooks. The harsh climate makes the buildings look dreary no matter the year of construction, and a fine layer of red dust mercilessly covers everything.

In everyday life, the relationship between the public school and the rural citizens is probably the most noticeable compared with other state-citizen relationships in the rural areas. Most children attend primary school, at least for a few years, though the dropout rate is fairly high. It is my impression, however, that this relationship does not involve other citizens than the children to any significant degree. During the twenty years that I have been in contact with the Kéré family, I have never heard Thomas talk about attending meetings at the school or being involved in any school activities, despite the fact that all of his seven children have attended the local primary school. Apart from the school, which most children in Keru attend, the local dispensary is the government representation that citizens in Keru have most contact with day to day. The nurses and auxiliary midwives are the representatives of the state many rural citizens have most contact with, especially mothers, who are the primary caregivers of small children.

Elusive Health Services

The first time I visited the dispensary (CSPS—Centre de Santé et de Promotion Sociale), I was struck by its emptiness. The dispensary is the primary level of the health care system. In 1996, it was located in Tenga, a neighboring village. At that time, the dispensary in Keru had not been built. Before coming to Tenga, I had studied the basic health statistics documenting the high morbidity and mortality rates among the rural population. Naively, perhaps, I had imagined that the line at the center would be long and that the small ward would be full of sick people receiving acute treatment. When I visited, I was surprised to find an almost empty building with only a few mothers and their small children waiting for the nurse. Entering the consultation room, I was also (again somewhat naively) struck by the lack of infrastructure and equipment. The dispensary did not have electricity or running water. Vaccines and medicines were kept in a gas refrigerator and water was fetched in the nearby well. The diagnostic equipment consisted of a weighing scale, a blood-pressure meter, and the wooden stethoscope for checking the heart rate of a fetus during pregnancy. They had needles and syringes for injections but no equipment to test for malaria or a microscope to test for parasitic diseases. During fieldwork in 2015, I was able to interview the responsible nurse at the dispensary in Keru. I had not made an appointment for the interview but hoped that he would be available.

Arriving at around 11 a.m., I encountered the nurse and the auxiliary midwife sitting outside in the shade. There were no patients around, and

FIGURE 1. Rural dispensary. Photo by Helle Samuelsen.

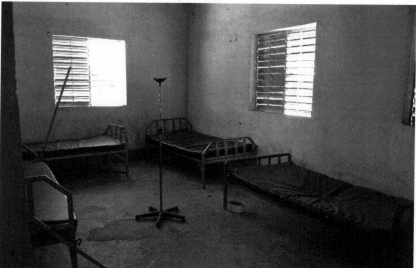

Amadou, the nurse, was sitting with his rucksack during the entire interview, as if he were ready to leave. Again, I was surprised to see a dispensary with no patients. Although they now have the rapid diagnostic test for malaria and solar panels that provide electricity at critical times, the dispensary was still remarkably quiet. Amadou told me that they typically see around twenty patients a day during the dry season. Later, when I was talking with the local chief outside his compound, I noticed Amadou on his motorbike driving in the direction of the nearby town, and a few minutes later I saw the auxiliary midwife driving out of the village in a different direction. This is not to say that Amadou and his colleagues are not doing their jobs, or that they are not performing well. They may have had very good reasons to leave the dispensary that morning. It is, however, a general observation that rural dispensaries lack diagnostic equipment, care facilities, and occasionally essential medicines and that, for various reasons, health care staff is often absent (see also Banerjee and Duflo 2006). In other words, emptiness and absenteeism seem to be common characteristics of the rural dispensaries in Burkina Faso. Amadou formulated it in the following way: "As we are not well equipped in terms of material equipment and staff, there are examinations we cannot do. Our examinations are essentially based on the clinical and physical signs."

The clinical encounter at the dispensaries follows a standard procedure: the patient (or mother with a sick child) enters the consultation room where the nurse in charge is sitting behind a desk. A few questions are asked about the condition and the specific symptoms, such as fever or coughing. In some cases, the nurse examines the patient (lifting the eyelids to look for anemia, for example) or checks for fever. The rapid diagnostic test for malaria is available, and due to a policy of presumptive treatment many cases of illness are categorized and treated as malaria (Samuelson 2020). After the short conversation and examination, the nurse writes a prescription and asks the patient to go to the medical depot to get the medicines (including needles and syringes if injections are needed); when patients need injections they are asked to return to the nurse for further instructions. The consultation process itself is routinized in the sense that the main component in the consultation is a short exchange between the patient, or the mother of a sick child, and the nurse, with the purpose of diagnosing the illness and deciding on the treatment. Morning hours are the busiest.

Policies regarding payment for medicines and services at the public health facilities in Burkina Faso have shifted over the years. The government elected in 2016 granted free health care for children five years old and younger (Hagberg et al. 2018, 67), but the reality is that care is not always free. If, for example, the prescribed medicine is not available at the medical depot, the patient or caregiver has to buy the medicine somewhere else.

Poor rural patients and caregivers in Keru worry about potential demands for payment, both direct payment for medicines and indirect payment in terms of transportation cost or loss of income while spending time at the health facility.

Alimata's Case

One morning, Alimata decided to consult the nurse at the dispensary. Her ten-month-old son had been ill with *corps chaud* (warm body) for a couple of days. She already treated the boy herself with some herbal plants she had bought at the local market. She had boiled the herbs and given it to her child to drink every morning for a few days. At the dispensary, the routine consultation took place, and the child was tested for malaria with the rapid diagnostic test. The test was negative, but the nurse handed Alimata a prescription for malaria medicine.

Alimata's case is typical in many ways. Alimata lives alone with her three children. The two other children are seven and five. Idrissa, Alimata's husband, migrated to Côte d'Ivoire, where he has worked for two years on a plantation. According to Alimata, he sends her money only once a year. She has to manage farmwork and childcare by herself. When a child falls sick, she does not necessarily go directly to the dispensary, though it is located close to her house. In each new case of sickness, she considers the various options, like many other mothers do: consulting the public health facility, consulting a traditional healer, or treating the child herself with herbal plants or medicines bought at the local market—or taking several parallel initiatives. Often, she tries various kinds of indigenous treatments at home to see whether she can manage the illness herself. If symptoms persist, she might eventually go to the dispensary, where she knows that the child, in case of fever, will get a prescription to treat malaria. As she explained, "I only go to the dispensary if the disease does not finish [with home treatment], if it is grave, because I don't have money. My husband is in Côte d'Ivoire, he only rarely sends me 5,000 CFA [US$8.50]."

As analyzed elsewhere (Samuelsen 2020), the activities of the rural dispensaries in Burkina Faso are mainly geared toward diagnosing and treating cases of malaria as well as managing some routine procedures concerning mother-child health care. The diagnostic and treatment repertoire is limited at these facilities, and the supply of medicines is irregular, which creates difficulty for parents who have to locate and purchase medicine themselves. Thomas explained: "If they don't have the products [at the dispensary], the parents have to pay. If they don't do that, the child will die. The parents complain saying that the treatment is supposed to be free. But you have to go and buy the products and return to get your child treated. Often, they don't have the medicines. They only give out Paracetamols, the rest you have to buy yourself."[6] Such situations place parents in an acute dilemma at the particular consultation and create uncertainties for them about whether they should include the public health facility in the therapeutic trajectory or whether it would make more sense to try out other treatments first. The uncertainty about whether the dispensary will have medicines available and the subsequent uncertainty about whether the patient should prepare to spend time and money to seek out the medicines complicates the treatment-seeking process. Rural citizens make careful considerations about their options in cases of illness. Many mothers of sick children express that they feel under constant pressure because they lack the means (or time) for transportation to a health facility. They are constantly anxious about costs (direct and indirect costs), so during each illness episode they take stock of the situation, in each case balancing the question of "What would be adequate to do?" against "What would be the best to do in this case of sickness at this moment in time?" Delphine, whose husband has been based in Equatorial Guinea for six years, said that she either used herbal medicine or consulted the dispensary when one of her five children fall sick: "For the last six years, I have taken care and paid for medications when they are sick. I also sell my animals to treat children in case of illness." Delphine is farming the family land, producing crops exclusively or mainly for subsistence, like so many other women who stay behind while their husbands are on migratory "adventure" (Bredeloup 2017). Decisions about what to do in cases of illness are not easy, and although Delphine was in regular contact with her husband it was difficult for her to make ends meet, saying "he used to send [money], but since he started building his house we don't get any money anymore except when Christmas is approaching. If he's sending money, it will be for next Christmas. If there are expenses in the family, I bear them." In other words, consulting the rural dispensary is an option, but due to concerns about cost it may not necessarily be the first choice (Østergaard, Bjertrup, and Samuelsen 2016).

Child sickness in this part of the world is characterized by infectious diseases and different types of comorbidities. Some children suffer from malnutrition, but most children under five years of age suffer recurrent bouts of illness, such as respiratory infections and diarrhea, as a result of infectious disease, including malaria. The chronic nature of their illness results in worry every time a child relapses, and each little deterioration generates new uncertainties. The chronic nature of the conditions is characterized by everyday emergencies (Vigh 2008; Millar 2014).

"Little Money—Little Work"

Amadou, the nurse, expresses his frustrations about the health-seeking practices of the villagers when responding to my question about the main challenges in his work, saying, "It is the fact that people do not come early for consultation. It is also about awareness, we don't know if people do not understand the importance, or if they refuse to understand."

The regional director of health stresses the lack of resources as the main challenge, saying:

> The actual problems are related to our finances. This includes different aspects: the demand for health care is increasing, but the number of health staff does not match the demand. Also, our budget for reparations and improvements of our equipment and infrastructure is limited and the logistics of our vehicles for supervision and motorcycles for vaccinations are part of our financial challenges. We are also in a phase of decentralization involving a transfer of resources and power to the municipalities, but the capacity of the ministry to advise the municipalities is very slow. . . . Over the years, you see a change in the new generation [of health staff]. There is an expression saying "little money—little work," you sense that more and more.

The limited availability of diagnostic equipment and the poor infrastructure was recognized by the health staff and by the regional management as central challenges. "Our diagnostics are mainly based on clinical signs, physical signs, and the simple examinations such as RDTs [rapid

FIGURE 2. An ambulance that had broken down parked in front of a dispensary. Photo by Helle Samuelsen.

diagnostic tests]," Amadou said. Nurses at the rural dispensaries expressed frustrations about their limited capacity to diagnose and treat their patients, and striking for better working conditions among health staff is a recurrent phenomenon (Østergaard 2016). Many hope to be transferred to an urban health facility or, like Amadou, dream of migrating to Canada or another place where the working and living conditions are better.

The relationship between citizens and the public health care system in rural Burkina Faso appears to be very fragile, both when seen from the point of view of citizens and health staff. Although the rural citizens know from experience that in cases of fever, a rapid diagnostic test for malaria will be provided and that they will probably be prescribed medicine for malaria, they are also aware of the diagnostic limitations at the dispensary and of the fluctuations in the supply of medicines. These realities are why self-treatment with herbs from the bush or medicines bought at the market are quite common; consultation with various types of traditional healers is widespread. Caregivers are therefore very pragmatic when taking decisions about treatment seeking.

It is a high priority for the government of Burkina Faso to increase the number of dispensaries to bring health care closer to the population and improve the quality of care at the peripheral level (Ministère de la Santé, 2011). At this point, however, the provision of public health care to the rural population remains elusive. The dispensaries are peripheral, not only in the geographical sense but also in terms of equipment and capacity. As sites of biomedicine and public health care, they often appear empty. With their empty rooms, limited diagnostic equipment, and sparse professional staffing, the dispensaries are instantiations of the absent-present state. In complicated cases of illness, the dispensaries may refer patients to higher levels of the health system, but ambulance services are scarce and in the majority of cases patients have to provide their own transportation.

As representatives of the state, the health staff at the dispensary level do have what Leclercq and Matagne (2020) call "input legitimacy" but due to weak infrastructure and the lack of medical equipment, their "output legitimacy," their effectiveness, is relatively low. A report from REN-LAC, the national anticorruption network, confirms the experience of the residents of Keru. The report finds that the payment structure at public health facilities is opaque and documents widespread corruption at all levels of the health care system in Burkina Faso, concluding: "The population in general, and the patients in particular, are abandoned and left to themselves in a complex operational health care system, where they bestow themselves to irrational solutions with disastrous consequences for their little income" (REN-LAC 2018, 75). The major part of the formal health care system in Burkina Faso is public with few faith-based or private health care facilities.

However, in addition to the services offered in the professional sector, traditional healers, including herbalists, marabouts, bonesetters, and diviners, offer health care as part of the folk sector (Kleinman 1980), and self-treatment, as in Alimata's case illustrates, is also widespread (Samuelsen 2004b; Gnawali et al. 2009; Østergaard, Bjertrup, and Samuelsen 2016). It is important to emphasize that the state-margin relationship is a two-way relationship, where the health staff (or other government employees), have the ability and legitimacy to command and manage the medical treatment of the patients. To ensure this, they are, however, dependent both on having the relevant technologies to execute their power and on being recognized by the patients as professional experts with the ability to act decisively. The capacity of the dispensaries (and the district hospitals) in rural Burkina Faso to enact medical sovereignty over biological bodies is limited. The health care professionals do not have the capacity nor the technology to accommodate the biomedical and bureaucratic agenda of governmental institutions. These institutions are the loci for biopower, but their institutional poverty weakens the efficacy of bureaucratic and biomedical technologies (see also Street 2012, 2014; Pare Toe and Samuelsen 2021). They become void spaces, where the staff has difficulties keeping up their motivation and their desire to nurture relationships with the rural population.

In this analysis of the everyday relationships (and lack hereof) between the citizens of Keru and the local state representatives, it becomes clear that these relationships are rather fragile. The transition period spurred by the insurrection, followed by a coup and new elections in 2015 instigated local discussions about the role of the president and the responsibility of the government. Many hopes were raised during this period. After twenty-seven years with a despotic president, many people in Burkina Faso had high hopes for real change, where basic needs such as health care, employment, and security would be provided. However, for the villagers in Keru, nothing much has changed. The state is for many villagers still both present and absent. It is present in the sense that everybody knows (and knew) who the president is. (During his rule, Compaoré was recognized as a very powerful man.) The state is also present in the sense that public institutions are physically located in the village and staffed with government representatives. However, they are absent in the sense described by Alice Street in her work on Madang Hospital in Papua New Guinea, where "the state exists primarily as an absence" (2012, 16). Furthermore, most local government institutions in Burkina Faso are characterized by forms of emptiness and absenteeism.

In Burkina Faso, we do not find a unified state apparatus but a state characterized as being absent-present. In one sense, the presidency of

Compaoré was regarded as having a strong central leadership, but it was also clear that the peripheral structures were weak, incoherent, and underfinanced, particularly at the district level. During Compaoré's many years of rule, he in some ways personalized the state with a well-armed presidential guard, while at the same time the governmental services at the rural level were characterized by low capacity and arbitrariness in terms of service provision. Recent terrorism by various jihadist groups in many parts of the country and the general escalation of security threats have not improved the situation. In addition, the government of Marc Roch Kaboré, who was elected in 2015 and reelected in 2020, seems not so different from Compaoré's. The everyday grammar of the state in rural Burkina Faso continues to be characterized by emptiness, absenteeism, and arbitrariness.

Analyzing the grammar of the state by taking a perspective from below or from the margin helps to understand the relatively low use of public health facilities in Burkina Faso. Furthermore, that perspective contributes to a larger debate about how we should analyze and understand the state and democracy in a fragile African country as Burkina Faso. As pointed out by Lauren MacLean (2011), Africans who had experiences with public social services (particularly public schools and clinics) also vote at higher rates and participate in community meetings and other joint activities more frequently. The fragile relationship between citizens and the public services in rural areas like the village of Keru may affect how citizens involve themselves in democratic processes. Thomas did not participate in demonstrations, but he followed the political process throughout and voted at the presidential elections in November 2015 and again in 2020. So far, the results of the new government are not impressive when seen from the perspective of Keru. There has not yet been any significant change or improvement in government services. Thomas is an engaged citizen, but he and many other citizens in Keru feel that they were let down by Compaoré during his twenty-seven years of presidency. If the present government also fails to deliver basic health care and security, it becomes relevant to ask how long the citizens of Burkina Faso will continue to see themselves as citizens of the nation-state.

The current situation in Burkina Faso is dangerous. When the services provided are so hollow and the relationship between citizens and the state in everyday life is so fragile, it may become increasingly difficult for people to identify with, or relate to, the nation-state. Burkina Faso seems to be moving toward a point where new popular uprisings or insurrections may emerge or where young men and women for whom the future looks dystopic start joining the militia groups, whether the local "koglweogo" groups or international jihadist groups like AQIM.

Notes

This chapter is mainly based on data collected in relation to the project titled "Fragile Futures: Rural Lives in Times of Conflict" funded by Danida (grant no: 11–04-KU).

1. I use synonyms in order to provide anonymity.
2. See Hagberg et al. (2015) for a detailed description of the uprising and a discussion of labeling it as "insurrection."
3. "The World Bank in Burkina Faso," http://www.worldbank.org/en/country /burkinafaso/overview.
4. United Nations Development Programme, http://hdr.undp.org/en/countries /profiles/BFA.
5. Trading Economics, Burkina Faso GDP Annual Growth Rate, https:// tradingeconomics.com/burkina-faso/gdp-growth-annual.
6. Interview with Thomas, February 2020.

References

Adebanwi, Wale. 2017. "Africa's 'Two Publics': Colonialism and Governmentality." *Theory, Culture & Society* 34 (4): 65–87.

Adebanwi, Wale, and Ebenezer Obadare. 2010. *Encountering the Nigerian State.* London: Palgrave Macmillan.

Agamben, Giorgio. 1998. *Homo Sacer: Sovereign Power and Bare Life.* Stanford, CA: Stanford University Press.

Auyero, Javier. 2012. *Patients of the State: The Politics of Waiting in Argentina.* Durham, NC: Duke University Press.

Badini, Amadé. 1994. *Naître et grandir chez les Moosé traditionnels: Découvertes du Burkina.* Paris: SÉPIA A.D.D.B.

Banerjee, Abhijit, and Esther Duflo. 2006. "Addressing Absence." *Journal of Economic Perspectives* 20 (1): 117–32.

Bayart, Jean-François. 1993. *The State in Africa: The Politics of the Belly.* London: Longman.

Benjaminsen, Tor A., and Boubacar Ba. 2019. "Why Do Pastoralists in Mali Join Jihadist Groups? A Political Ecological Explanation." *Journal of Peasant Studies* 46 (1): 1–20.

Bernstein, Anya, and Elizabeth Mertz. 2011. "Bureaucracy: Ethnography of the State in Everyday Life." *PoLAR: Political and Legal Anthropology Review* 34:6–10.

Blom Hansen, Thomas, and Finn Stepputat, eds. 2001. *States of Imagination: Ethnographic Explorations of the Postcolonial State.* Durham, NC: Duke University Press.

Bouchard, Michel 2011. "The State of the Study of the State in Anthropology." *Reviews in Anthropology* 40 (3): 183–209.

Bredeloup, Sylvie. 2017. "The Migratory Adventure as a Moral Experience." In *Hope and Uncertainty in Contemporary African Migration,* edited by Nauja Kleist and Dorte Thorsen, 134–53. New York: Routledge.

Das, Veena, and Deborah Poole. 2004. "Anthropology in the Margins of the State." *PoLAR: Political and Legal Anthropology Review* 30 (1): 140–44.

Engberg-Pedersen, Lars, Louise Andersen, and Finn Stepputat. 2008. "Fragile Situations. Current Debates and Central Dilemmas." DIIS Report 9. Copenhagen: Danish Institute for International Studies.

Ferguson, James. 2006. *Global Shadows. Africa in the Neoliberal World Order.* Durham, NC: Duke University Press.

Foucault, Michel. 2012. *The Birth of the Clinic.* New York: Routledge.

Gnawali, Devendra Prasad, Subhash Pokhrel, Ali Sié, Mamadou Sanon, Manuela De Allegri, Aurélia Souares, Hengjin Dong, and Rainer Sauerborn. 2009. "The Effect of Community-Based Health Insurance on the Utilization of Modern Health Care Services: Evidence from Burkina Faso." *Health Policy* 90 (2–3): 214–22. https://doi.org/10.1016/j.healthpol.2008.09.015.

Gupta, Akhil. 2012. *Red Tape: Bureaucracy, Structural Violence, and Poverty in India.* Durham, NC: Duke University Press.

Hagberg, Sten, Ludovic Kibora, Fatoumata Ouattara, and Adjara Konkobo. 2015. "Au cœur de la révolution burkinabè." *Anthropologie & Developpement* 42:199–224.

Hagberg, Sten, Ludovic Kibora, Sidi Barry, Siaka Gnessi, and Adjara Konkobo. 2018. *"Nothing Will Be as Before!": Anthropological Perspectives on Political Practice and Democratic Culture in a "New Burkina Faso."* Uppsala: Uppsala University.

Inda, Jonathan Xavier, and Renato Rosaldo. 2002. *The Anthropology of Globalization: A Reader.* Malden, MA: Blackwell.

Kleinman, Arthur. 1981. *Patients and Healers in the Context of Culture: An Exploration of the Borderland between Anthropology, Medicine, and Psychiatry.* Berkeley: University of California Press.

Law, John. 2002. *Aircraft Stories.* Durham, NC: Duke University Press.

Leclercq, Sidney, and Geoffroy Matagne. 2020. "'With or Without You': The Governance of (Local) Security and the Koglweogo Movement in Burkina Faso." *Stability: International Journal of Security and Development* 9 (1): 4. http://doi.org/10.5334/sta.716.

MacLean, Lauren M. 2011. "State Retrenchment and the Exercise of Citizenship in Africa." *Comparative Political Studies* 44 (9): 1238–66.

Mbembe, Achille J. 2016. "Africa in the New Century." *Massachusetts Review* 57 (1): 91.

Ministère de la Santé. 2011. *Politique Nationale de Santé, 2011–2020.* https://www.sante.gov.bf/fileadmin/user_upload/storages/fichiers/pns_version_adoptee_paraphee.pdf.

OECD. 2010. *The State's Legitimacy in Fragile Situations: Unpacking Complexity.* OECD.

Østergaard, Lise Rosendal. 2016. "Occupational Citizenship: Practice, Routine, and Bureaucracy among Nurses and Midwives in Rural Burkina Faso." *Medicine Anthropology Theory* 3 (2): 244–68.

Østergaard, Lise Rosendal, Pia Juul Bjertrup, and Helle Samuelsen. 2016. "'Children Get Sick All the Time': A Qualitative Study of Socio-cultural and Health System Factors Contributing to Recurrent Child Illnesses in Rural Burkina Faso." *BMC Public Health* 16 (1): 384.

Pare Toe, Lea, and Helle Samuelsen. 2021. "Balancing Professional Autonomy and Authority at the Margins of a Fragile State: Front-Line Health Workers' Experiences in Burkina Faso." *Global Public Health* 16 (7): 1099–110.

Piccolino, Giulia J. 2016. "Infrastructural State Capacity for Democratization? Voter Registration and Identification in Côte D'ivoire and Ghana Compared." *Democratization* 23 (3): 498–519.

Pieper, Henning, Thandika Mkandawire, and Rolph Van der Hoeven. 2016. *Africa's Recovery in the 1990s: From Stagnation and Adjustment to Human Development.* London: Palgrave Macmillan.

Prince, Ruth, and Rebecca Marsland. 2014. *Making and Unmaking Public Health in Africa: Ethnographic and Historical Perspectives.* Athens: Ohio University Press.

REN-LAC. 2018. *Etude sur les presomptions de corruption et pratiques assimilees dans le systeme et les services de santé au Burkina Faso.* Ouagadougou: Réseau National de Lutte Anti-corruption.

Samuelsen, Helle. 1999. "The Topology of Illness Transmission: Localizing Processes among Bissa in Burkina Faso." PhD diss., Department of Anthropology, University of Copenhagen.

Samuelsen, Helle. 2004a. "Illness Transmission and Proximity: Local Theories of Causation among the Bissa in Burkina Faso." *Medical Anthropologie* 23 (2): 89–112. https://doi.org/10.1080/01459740490448885.

———. 2004b. "Therapeutic Itineraries: The Medical Field in Rural Burkina Faso." *Anthropology & Medicine* 11 (1): 27–41.

———. 2020. "Accelerated Fragility: Exploring the Supply-Demand Nexus at Health Facilities in Rural Burkina Faso." *Africa* 90 (5): 934–51.

Samuelsen, Helle, and Vibeke Steffen. 2004. "The Relevance of Foucault and Bourdieu for Medical Anthropology: Exploring New Sites." *Anthropologie and Medicine* 11 (1): 3–10. https://doi.org/10.1080/1364847042000204951.

Savonnet-Guyot, Claudette. 1986. *État et sociétés au Burkina: essai sur le politique africain.* Paris: Karthala Editions.

Sharma, Aradhana, and Akhil Gupta. 2006. "Introduction: Rethinking Theories of the State in an Age of Globalization." In *The Anthropology of the State: A Reader,* edited by Aradhana Sharma and Akhil Gupta, 1–41. Malden, MA: Blackwell.

Street, Alice. 2012. "Seen by the State: Bureaucracy, Visibility and Governmentality in a Papua New Guinean Hospital." *Australian Journal of Anthropology* 23 (1): 1–21. https://doi.org/10.1111/j.1757-6547.2012.00164.x.

Street, Alice. 2014. *Biomedicine in an Unstable Place: Infrastructure and Personhood in a Papua New Guinean Hospital.* Durham, NC: Duke University Press.

Zeilig, Leo 2017. "Burkina Faso: From Thomas Sankara to Popular Resistance." *Review of African Political Economy* 44 (151): 155–64.

Afterword

Postcolonial Powerscapes

VICTORIA BERNAL

THIS VOLUME BRINGS TOGETHER A SET OF ENGAGING ethnographic essays that advance our understanding of state and citizenship in contemporary Africa. In what follows, I draw out some themes that connect across chapters and reflect on the visions of state and citizen relationships that emerge from the collection as a whole.

Pype's insightful analysis of the voter ID card and surveillance cameras in Kinshasa reveals the dynamics of state-citizen relations in a way that explodes crude notions of repression and resistance. She starts with a simple protest but uses it to open up a view of a complex, unstable powerscape mutually constructed by the state and citizens. This powerscape is tenuously balanced so that it is perpetually in motion animated by relations of distrust, deception, visibility, invisibility, illusion, and subterfuge that alternately express state control and are used to evade it. Ethnography reveals an intriguing tension between materialities—the physical surveillance cameras and the voter ID cards—and the intangibles, invisibilities, and imaginaries that give these cameras and cards greater capacities or, on the contrary, render their authority illusory. Kinois, for example, doubt the cameras are operational or that their feeds are monitored, while the presence of the camera in itself makes state power visible and goes further by suggesting the hidden powers of the state that lie somewhere behind the surveillance apparatus. And as Pype argues, the state plays a shrewd game in offering "voter IDs" rather than national IDs because voter IDs, while serving as official IDs in many transactions, legally accord citizens only the right to vote.

Adebanwi and Obadare's study of bureaucracy and the circulation of documents in Lagos's visa economy resonates with themes raised in Pype's chapter. Like the Kinshasa protesters described by Pype who change clothes in the middle of the day to be less recognizable to state surveillance, visa applicants in Nigeria negotiate the power of consular authorities by disguising themselves in fancy clothes and presenting fake documents. The chapter starts out with a critique of the inhumane, arbitrary bureaucracies of foreign consulates in Lagos and of Nigerians' own government. The analysis leads us from the exacting requests for documentation by visa authorities to the thriving informal economy in fake documents. In this process, would-be Nigerian migrants are confronting the limitations of citizenship and resisting state authority, while their desires for international mobility can be seen in part as longing for a different form of citizenship.

Citizens' longings, hopes, and imaginations of more positive engagements with the state is a theme running through most of the chapters. In contrast, the conditions on the ground ethnographically detailed here show citizens living with the constant potential for state violence and the routine experience of humiliation at the hands of state agents. Citizens' affective ties to the state and their desires for belonging and respect are powerful; their expectations of the state cannot be reduced to financial, material interests. Indeed, it is remarkable in Orock's harrowing description of being extorted, threatened, and jailed by gun-wielding soldiers who put his life in danger that he nonetheless emphasizes his feelings of humiliation. What emerges from his vivid account, also should caution us against simply seeing "the state" everywhere. Each Cameroonian checkpoint he encountered operated differently, with much being left to individual discretion rather law or policy. During Orock's most dangerous encounter, even those staffing the same checkpoint were not uniform in their approach.

One of the most generative themes in the collection is that of falsification, forgery, and fakery. Adebanwi and Obadare's research reveals that the very stringency of the requirements for documents in formal procedures creates the need for fakes. Officials and forgers are therefore not opposites but rather partners in the same system. Provocatively, the authors suggest that the question here is not about what is real and authentic versus what is made up and falsified, because the state itself is a massive forgery. Indeed, this argument reminds us that even the borders that visas are needed to cross are made up and that official documents too are made up by the state—Kabila's introduction of voter IDs being a case in point. Visa requirements also are made up, and the fact that they are applied arbitrarily adds to the sense that they are artificial and lack any real basis.

This artificiality is evident in Løvgren's analysis of Rwandan politics, where the state engenders fear and compliance through its disingenuousness and sudden reversals of rules. In Ethiopia, where the ruling party dominates despite the multiparty state outlined by the constitution, Riggan recounts students speaking of fake parties. Quaretta quotes Congolese talking of "the sorcerer state" operating secretly behind its facade through occult powers. The Trovallas describe the instability of public infrastructure in Nigeria engendering in citizens the sense that nothing can be counted on to be what it seems. The theme of fakery and deception also brings to mind the concepts of "alternative facts" and "fake news" that thrived under Trump's presidency in the United States, along with the constant stream of lies from the president and officials he appointed. Fakeness is often produced from the top down.

There are many contexts where the fake may be more convincing than the real or true. I have heard from Eritrean refugees, for example, that people repeat narratives that they believe have succeeded with authorities before, rather than risk telling their own true story that might not be believed or might not be compelling enough to gain asylum. Of course, that strategy can backfire when the sheer repetition of the same story by different individuals causes authorities to become skeptical. There is a ritualistic aspect of these processes for visas or asylum when everyone knows that deception and fakery are widespread, and that the bureaucratic demands and outcomes are often arbitrary, yet applicants and bureaucrats go through the motions and play their parts. The beggar outside the consulate in Lagos with his repeated incantation of "come-today, come-tomorrow" suggests a ritual of power relations, suffering that must be endured before a wish for a valued visa can be granted.

While bureaucracy is a standard feature of states, it is noteworthy that in so many of the chapters here what is at stake are official documents of citizenship—national ID cards, voter IDs, passports, and visas as well as embassies and assorted checkpoints. In Nigeria, documents might very well be fakes, while in South Sudan only the relatively elite possess such documents at all, and in Congo protesters hope to evade the state by leaving IDs at home, while Markó escapes unscathed from one situation in South Sudan by showing his ID. In Burkina Faso, Samuelsen observes that a birth certificate might be needed to obtain a voter ID card but that many people in rural areas lack such a document. Citizenship in postcolonial Africa seems to remain elusive and ambiguous, where IDs and other official documents are difficult to obtain and do not necessarily accord rights and privileges but may help the holder to evade abuse, extortion, and violence.

Leonard's chapter on energy policies in Chad and Trovolla's analysis of infrastructure in Nigeria present a complex picture of what happens when the state's ambitions and promises to citizens fail. In Chad, the failure to deliver the promised future of energy sovereignty is all the more disastrous because the state disrupted existing fuel practices. People became dependent on national supplies of gas for cooking. Then, when shortages hit people were desperate, and the state was compelled to turn a blind eye to charcoal-selling, which it had earlier outlawed. Here the state's goals of ending charcoal production and gaining energy sovereignty over gas are good ones, but the consequences of falling short are dire for the people. And to respond to citizens' needs, the state had to act hypocritically, accepting the practice of charcoal use. In Nigeria, unreliability is the only constant with regard to national infrastructures. Various workarounds, improvisations, and black-market distribution networks become the norm, while reliance on government services becomes the exception. Such examples give new meanings to the term *power failures*. Under such circumstances, which are not uncommon, how can citizens believe the state or trust it? In such cases, do citizens see the crisis as simply the result of technocratic mistakes, or do they suspect deeper motives and machinations at work? Does such a debacle alter state-citizen relations, or is it experienced as just one more in a series of a state's failures to deliver on its promises? The answers to these questions might determine whether or not crisis leads to transformation.

Smith's chapter follows nicely on Leonard's account of Chad in the way that South African police, like the Chadian state, must strategically look away sometimes in order to maintain the appearance of being in control. There is something of a ritualistic aspect here too as the police go through the motions of asserting their authority at the vigil and the funeral (which are both rituals in themselves) without really doing much. Similarly, local youth engage in ritual displays of lawlessness—spinning cars and shooting off guns—that are more symbolic expressions of power or freedom from authority than any actual challenge to the order.

Smith connects the spectacular violence of a massacre to the everyday police violence that South African township youth experience but that is largely ignored by society. He asks: How does police violence change our theory of the state? To theorize the state, he explores the metaphors of the Leviathan, a powerful behemoth, and the Golem, a creation that gets out of control. Seeing the state as a Golem, rather than a Leviathan alerts us to its dangerous potential. The question I have about the Golem metaphor is: Who is the master of the state in this scenario? If we see the state as belonging to the rulers then it may not be out of control in harming citizens but doing the master's bidding. Clearly, once we accept that police violence is not simply a malfunction of the system but an integral part of how the state operates, we need a critical theory of the state.

The metaphor of the Golem or a Frankenstein may be one way to think about the ambiguous potentials of power. This can also apply to nonstate actors, such as the community defense forces analyzed by Agbiboa, which occupy a precarious position between Boko Haram and the state. Once established, there is no going back; these nonstate security forces become a force to reckon with, and they may morph into the kind of insurgents they arose to combat. Ikanda's analysis of Somali refugees in Kenya also reveals the engagement of nonstate actors in policing and security. UNHCR exercizes state-like control over the camps, while order is maintained by "community peace and security teams" made up of Somalis themselves. Across the continent, we see how state indifference, intentional neglect, and/or incapacity fosters complex systems of power where local intermediaries arise, working sometimes in concert and sometimes against international and national institutions. In Pearce's account Renamo is both a political party inside the Mozambiquan state and a force of armed opposition to it. In rural Burkina Faso, Samuelsen suggests that the state's failure or incapacity to provide any hope for the future may lead youth to join insurgent militias operating in the region.

As the chapters in this volume make clear, the state does many things—creates ID cards, issues or denies visas, adopts technologies, makes energy investments and policies, and so forth, so security and policing are only one aspect of the state in relation to citizens. The historical shifts in policing in South Africa that Smith references are suggestive for deepening arguments about state violence and policing. The shifting relations of state/police and citizens under apartheid, after apartheid, and during the recent remilitarization of the police reveal different possibilities of states and police in relation to citizens. Smith's chapter calls to mind the ongoing crisis of police violence in the United States, the Black Lives Matter movement, and calls to defund the police and invest resources in community welfare and services. There is an ongoing global trend of the state's role in providing security becoming more central and a concomitant process of militarization of the police. Perhaps the shifts in South Africa are particularly illuminating or themselves become more legible when read against this larger context. Indeed, security and policing are themes that run through several chapters where state agents often engender feelings of insecurity rather than safety among the people. Quaretta found in the DRC, moreover, that people understood neighborhood criminals to be operating with the complicity of the local police.

What comes through all of the essays is what Smith calls a "partial and uneasy order." State agents are not completely in control and state procedures and policies are never fully enforceable or fully enforced. These failures, however, keep state authority in place, and order is sustainable in part because of the state's lapses, hypocrisies, and strategic retreats. These gaps are where citizens come into view as distrusting and fearful while also inventive and wily, exercising forms of agency and imagination from positions of less power. What the state excludes or denies sometimes creates not a lack but an excess in the form of local activities, whether supporting local schools, supplying black-market fuel and forged documents or taking shape as insurgencies, protests, and the production of alternate centers of power. Citizens imagine and enact forms of citizenship beyond what the state has defined or delivered.

Ethnographies of these everyday encounters unpack the state from a black box of central power and reveal it as a diffuse, complex assemblage. We see the state as surveillor and innovator, as killer and negotiator, as routinely violent and bureaucratically oppressive, as a builder and a performer, and as an illusionist that conjures imaginary realities and futures.

Adabanwi and Obadare pose a question about ethics and morals in relation to the production of forgeries. Forgery is more than simple deception since it involves intimate knowledge of official realms and documents in order to successfully imitate official forms. This mimicry might sustain the status quo or it could be transformative, creating parallels and alternatives that ultimately undermine official authority. Tactics of survival in the context of mutual deception may open up spaces for imagining things differently. The contours of these processes and techniques of subterfuge and forgery are changing as biometric identification technologies proliferate globally. Digitization, datafication, and the technologizing of the relations between citizens and states cannot resolve questions of rights, the nature of the social contract, or even the issue of transparency, however.

What comes across from this anthology is not the conventional social contract binding states and citizens but rather a cynical relationship in which states don't trust citizens and citizens don't trust the state. Citizens cannot rely on the state and are themselves unreliable state subjects. Rather than a social contract, it is an uneasy order where much is open to negotiation and manipulation, and citizens and states engage in symbolic performances. The resulting social reality is one where people live with uncertainty and instability, yet things usually bend rather than break so that the resiliency of people and institutions maintain the uneasy order.

Contributors

WALE ADEBANWI is the Presidential Penn Compact Professor of Africana Studies at the University of Pennsylvania, United States. He is also an Honorary Research Associate at the African Studies Centre, Oxford University, United Kingdom. Before he joined UPenn, he was the Rhodes Professor of Race Relations at Oxford. He is the author and (co)editor of many books, including *Yorùbá Elites and Ethnic Politics in Nigeria: Obáfémi Awólówò and Corporate Agency* (2014) and *The Political Economy of Everyday Life in Africa: Beyond the Margins* (2017).

DANIEL E. AGBIBOA is Assistant Professor of African and African American Studies at Harvard University, Member of the Institute for Advanced Study at Princeton, and Fellow at the Woodrow Wilson International Center for Scholars in Washington, DC. He holds a PhD from the University of Oxford and an MPhil from the University of Cambridge. His research focuses on the relationship between state and nonstate actors in urban Africa. He is the author of several books, including *They Eat Our Sweat: Transport Labor, Corruption, and Everyday Survival in Urban Nigeria* (2022) and *Mobility, Mobilization, and Counter/Insurgency: The Routes of Terror in an African Context* (2022).

VICTORIA BERNAL is Professor of Anthropology at the University of California, Irvine. Her scholarship in political anthropology contributes to media and IT studies, gender studies, and African studies. Bernal's research is particularly concerned with relations of power and inequality and the dynamic struggles of ordinary people as they confront the cruel and absurd contradictions arising from the concentration of wealth and political power locally and globally. She is the author of *Nation as Network: Diaspora, Cyberspace, and Citizenship* and *Cultivating Workers: Peasants and Capitalism in a Sudanese Village*. Bernal coedited the anthology *Theorizing NGOs: States, Feminisms, and Neoliberalism*. She has carried out ethnographic research in Sudan, Tanzania, Eritrea, Silicon Valley, and cyberspace.

JEAN COMAROFF is Alfred North Whitehead Professor of African and African American Studies and of Anthropology and Oppenheimer Fellow in African Studies at Harvard University. She was educated at the University of Cape Town and the London School of Economics. After a spell as a research fellow in medical anthropology at the University of Manchester, she moved to the University of Chicago, where she remained until 2012 as the Bernard E. and Ellen C. Sunny Distinguished Service Professor of Anthropology and Director of the Chicago Center for Contemporary Theory. She is also Honorary Professor at the University of Cape Town. Her writing has covered a range of topics, from religion, medicine, and body politics to state formation, crime, democracy, and difference. Her publications include *Body of Power, Spirit of Resistance: The Culture and History of a South African People* (1985); "Beyond the Politics of Bare Life: AIDS and the Global Order" (2007); and, with John L. Comaroff, *Of Revelation and Revolution*, vols. 1 (1991) and 2 (1997); *Ethnography and the Historical Imagination* (1992); *Millennial Capitalism and the Culture of Neoliberalism* (2000); *Law and Disorder in the Postcolony* (2006); *Ethnicity, Inc.* (2009); *Theory from the South: Or, How Euro-America Is Evolving toward Africa* (2011); *The Truth about Crime: Sovereignty, Knowledge, Social Order* (2016); and *The Politics of Custom: Chiefship, Capital, and the State in Contemporary Africa* (2018).

JOHN L. COMAROFF is Hugh K. Foster Professor of African and African American Studies and Anthropology and Oppenheimer Research Scholar at Harvard University. Before moving to Harvard, he was the Harold H. Swift Distinguished Professor of Anthropology at the University of Chicago, Honorary Professor of Anthropology at the University of Cape Town, and Research Professor at the American Bar Foundation. His writings have focused primarily on African politics and law, on colonialism and postcoloniality, on identity and ethnicity, and on crime and policing. His authored and edited books include, with Jean Comaroff, *Of Revelation and Revolution* (2 vols.; 1991, 1997); *Ethnography and the Historical Imagination* (1992); *Modernity and Its Malcontents* (1993); *Civil Society and the Political Imagination in Africa* (1999); *Millennial Capitalism and the Culture of Neoliberalism* (2000); *Law and Disorder in the Postcolony* (2006); *Ethnicity, Inc.* (2009); *Zombies et Frontières a l'Ère Néolibérale* (2010); *Theory from the South: Or, How Euro-America Is Evolving toward Africa* (2011); *The Truth about Crime: Sovereignty, Knowledge, Social Order* (2016); and *The Politics of Custom: Chiefship, Capital, and the State in Contemporary Africa* (2018).

E. FOUKSMAN is a Lecturer/Assistant Professor at the Centre for Public Policy Research at King's College London. She is also a Research Associate at the Society, Work and Politics Institute at the University of the Witwatersrand and at the University of Oxford's African Studies Centre. Fouksman's current research revolves around two projects: the first around perceptions of work, deservingness, and the redistribution of wealth, particularly in Southern Africa, and the second focused on the way networks of development organizations influence epistemic globalization, with multi-sited case studies spanning Kenya and Kyrgyzstan. Recent publications include, with Elise Klein, "Reparations as Rightful Shares," in *Development and Change* (2021); "The Moral Economy of Work," in *Economy and Society* (2020); and, with Hannah Dawson, "Labour, Laziness and Distribution," in *Africa* (2020).

FRED NYONGESA IKANDA is a social anthropologist and holds the position of Senior Lecturer and Chair in the Department of Sociology and Anthropology, Maseno University, Kenya. His research interests focus on refugee studies, kinship, legal anthropology, humanitarianism, anthropology of Islam and gender relations. He has published numerous journal articles and book chapters based on his research at the Dadaab refugee camps in Kenya.

LORI LEONARD is a Professor and chair in the Department of Global Development at Cornell University. Her most recent work centers on environmental themes, including extractivism and waste. Since 2000, she has studied the phenomenon of oil-as-development via a "model" pipeline project in Chad. Her manuscript, *Life in the Time of Oil: A Pipeline and Poverty in Chad* (Indiana University Press), is based on twelve years of fieldwork in the oilfields of southern Chad. She is also the coeditor of *Governance in the Extractive Industries: Power, Cultural Politics, and Regulation,* part of the Routledge Studies on Extractive Industries and Sustainable Development series. Her most recent projects include a study of used-car markets and the regulation and repair of "junkers" in West Africa and a project on waste, value, and risk in upstate New York in the wake of new environmental legislation that bans the landfilling of food scraps.

ROSE LØVGREN is a PhD graduate from University of Copenhagen. Her work has centered on the workings of sovereignty and the formation of political subjectivities in the context of Rwanda. Through ethnographic and philosophical discussions, her research concerns everyday post-conflict life with a focus on masculinities, war legacies, state and structural forms of political violence, ethnographic dilemmas and opportunities, and the cultural, ontological, and psychological idea of patience in Rwanda.

FERENC DÁVID MARKÓ is a Researcher at Small Arms Survey at the Graduate Institute, Geneva, and a recurring Visiting Lecturer at the Department of Cultural Anthropology, Eötvös Loránd Science University, Budapest. His PhD fieldwork was a yearlong ethnographic observation of the citizenship office of South Sudan in 2013. His publications have appeared in *African Studies Review, Journal of Eastern African Studies, African Arguments,* and *Acta Ethnographica.* His research interest is the everyday working of the South Sudanese state bureaucracy and the conflict dynamics of the civil war.

EBENEZER OBADARE is Douglas Dillon Senior Fellow for Africa Studies at the Council on Foreign Relations and Fellow at the Research Institute for Theology and Religion, University of South Africa. Author of numerous works on religion and politics and civil society and the state in Africa, he is the editor of *Journal of Modern African Studies* and contributing editor of *Current History.*

ROGERS OROCK is a Senior Lecturer in the Anthropology Department, University of the Witwatersrand, Johannesburg, South Africa. He is also affiliated with the Department of Sociology and Anthropology at the University of Buea, Cameroon. His essays on elites and related themes of governance and development have appeared in peer-reviewed journals such as *AFRICA, Cultural Dynamics, Critique of Anthropology,* and *Anthropological Quarterly.* He is the coeditor of *Elites and the Politics of Accountability in Africa* (2021).

JUSTIN PEARCE is a Senior Lecturer in History at the University of Stellenbosch. His work concentrates on histories of anticolonial struggles in Angola and Mozambique, particularly the exchange of political ideas within and between nations—and the legacies of these in contemporary politics. He is the author of *Political Identity and Conflict in Central Angola, 1975–2002* (2015) and has published articles in *Africa, African Affairs, Government and Opposition,* and *Journal of Southern African Studies,* of which he is an editor.

KATRIEN PYPE is Associate Professor in Anthropology at KU Leuven University. She researches Kinshasa's media and technology worlds. She is the author of *The Making of the Pentecostal Melodrama: Religion, Media, and Gender in Kinshasa* (2012) and coeditor (with Jaco Hoffman) of *Ageing in Sub-Saharan Africa: Practices and Spaces of Care* (2016). Her articles have appeared in, among others, *Journal of Modern African Studies, Africa, African Studies Review, Politique Africiane,* and *Journal of African Cultural Studies.* Her research has been funded by an Odysseus grant (FWO G.0.E65.14N) and an FWO-ERC-Runner Up Budget (FWO G.A005.14N). She co-initiated the Congo Research Network.

EDOARDO QUARETTA, PhD in Cultural Anthropology, is Associate Professor at Link Campus University, Rome, Italy. He has conducted fieldwork in the Democratic Republic of the Congo since 2006 on a range of research topics such as childhood, witchcraft, Pentecostal churches, education, international aid, and Catholic missionaries.

JENNIFER RIGGAN is Professor of International Studies at Arcadia University. She studies nationalism, the state, militarism, and education and is the author of *The Struggling State: Nationalism, Mass Militarization and the Education of Eritrea* (2016). Along with Amanda Poole, she is the author of *The Hosting State and Its Restless Guests: Time-Making, Mobility and Containment among Eritrean Refugees in Ethiopia* (forthcoming). She has held fellowships from the Georg Arnhold Program (2019), Fulbright (Addis Ababa University, 2016–17, and Asmara University, 2004–5), the Spencer Foundation/National Academy of Education (2012–14), and the Social Science Research Council (2004–5).

HELLE SAMUELSEN is Associate Professor at the Department of Anthropology, University of Copenhagen, Denmark. She served as Head of Department for thirteen years (2007–19). Her research focuses on medical anthropology and global health with a special focus on health systems and the relationship between citizens and the state. Her research is based on more than twenty years of engagement in Africa, particularly in Burkina Faso, and she is currently working on a project titled "Emerging Epidemics: Improving Preparedness in Burkina Faso."

NICHOLAS RUSH SMITH is Associate Professor of Political Science at the City University of New York–City College and Research Associate, Faculty of Humanities in the Department of Sociology, University of Johannesburg. His first book, *Contradictions of Democracy: Vigilantism and Rights in Post-apartheid South Africa,* was published by Oxford University Press in 2019.

ERIC TROVALLA holds a PhD in ethnology and is a Researcher at the Department of Cultural Anthropology and Ethnology at Uppsala University. His research has mainly considered urban everyday life, materiality, and infrastructure. He has been doing recurring fieldwork in Jos, Nigeria, since 2007, and is currently engaged in the research project "Suspicious Materialities: Egyptian and Nigerian Cityscapes."

ULRIKA TROVALLA holds a PhD in cultural anthropology and is a Researcher at the Department of Cultural Anthropology and Ethnology at

Uppsala University. Working on issues of urban life, conflicts, traditional medicine, materiality, and infrastructure, she has been doing recurring fieldwork in Jos, Nigeria, since 2000. She is currently working within the research project "Suspicious Materialities: Egyptian and Nigerian Cityscapes."

Index

The letter *f* following a page number indicates a figure.